METHODS AND TECHNIQUES
OF BUSINESS FORECASTING

METHODS AND TECHNIQUES OF BUSINESS FORECASTING

Edited by

WILLIAM F. BUTLER

Chase Manhattan Bank

ROBERT A. KAVESH

Graduate School of Business Administration
New York University

ROBERT B. PLATT

Delafield Childs, Inc.

PRENTICE-HALL, INC., Englewood Cliffs, New Jersey

Library of Congress Cataloging in Publication Data

Methods and techniques of business forecasting.

First ed. (1966) entered under: Butler, William
F., ed. How business economists forecast.
Includes bibliographies.

1. Business forecasting—Addresses, essays, lectures.
2. Economic forecasting—Addresses, essays, lectures. I.
Butler, William F., ed. II. Kavesh, Robert A., ed.
III. Platt, Robert B., ed. IV. Butler, William F., ed.
How business economists forecast.
HB3730.M42 1973   338.5'442   73–7564
ISBN 0-13-578914-1
       0-13-578930-3P

©1974 by Prentice-Hall, Inc., Englewood Cliffs, New Jersey

Printed in the United States of America.

10 9 8 7 6

PRENTICE-HALL INTERNATIONAL, INC., *London*
PRENTICE-HALL OF AUSTRALIA, PTY. LTD., *Sydney*
PRENTICE-HALL OF CANADA, LTD., *Toronto*
PRENTICE-HALL OF INDIA PRIVATE LIMITED, *New Delhi*
PRENTICE-HALL OF JAPAN, INC., *Tokyo*

CONTENTS

Part Two:

Part Three:

PROLOGUE

Readers of books, in contrast to those who write or edit them, often assume that the creative process is essentially a timeless one—that the ideas, words, organization, printing and distribution take place in a smooth, perhaps mechanical, fashion. Anyone who has ever had anything to do with putting out a book can put the lie to these beliefs.

This has been no exception. Thirty-nine people collaborated to produce thirty-two chapters. If nothing else the mere appearance of this volume is a triumph of logistics, a synthesis of "styles." Some contributors met deadlines religiously, much to the gratitude of the editors; others—and always for "good" reasons—held back.

Consequently, the date of publication has been postponed longer than anyone would have liked. And what an environment for delay! Phase I has progressed to Phase IV (not to mention Freezes I and II). Forecasters have been caught in a whirlwind of policy shifts, but—amazingly—the better forecasters have been able to operate effectively in this newer, more perplexing arena.

So, books take time. And time has a way of making all matters temporary, fleeting. The forecaster is always anxious to tinker with his results, to "fine-tune" his figures. A forecast by its nature is always transitional.

And what is true for forecasts is also true for each and every one of us. Bill Butler, senior editor of this volume, passed away suddenly and tragically while on a business trip overseas. He died with his boots on, and those of us who knew him were shocked beyond belief. Bill was one of the best-beloved people in the profession—a kindly person, a gentleman. And, importantly, he was a damn good forecaster.

We dedicate this book to our friend and colleague, Bill Butler.

August 1973

ROBERT A. KAVESH
ROBERT B. PLATT

PREFACE

This book is a guide to business forecasting as it is practiced by economists in industry, government and academic life. More than thirty experts in various phases of forecasting have focused their talents on the tools, techniques and problems involved in this rapidly growing, and important, part of economic activity.

Important is hardly the word. Almost every day newspapers carry reports forecasting the sales of a firm or an industry, the future of the balance of payments, or estimates of the gross national product. Weekly and monthly business magazines devote considerable space to "outlook" articles. Statistics of all sorts are continually being collected and released, calling attention to a new development here, a significant shift there.

We can see the relevance of business forecasting in many ways. Every year, in late December and early January (the peak forecasting season) key estimates are released by the Council of Economic Advisers, the Treasury Department, and the Office of Management and Budget as to the course of over-all business activity for the year ahead. These figures affect the role the federal government will play in taxing and spending, and in its stabilization and growth policies. Congressional hearings are held, controversies are aired—frequently in terms that are either puzzling or seemingly contradictory to the typical businessman or layman.

And in the world of the business firm itself, forecasting has its growing place. Most large corporations (and many smaller ones) are deeply involved in detailed studies of product prospects, sales, profit margins, opportunities for diversification and the like. Here, the corporate economist combines, improvises, selects and adapts information and material that will be useful in furnishing guidelines for managerial decision-making. Successful forecasting pays off in profits, and management is well aware of this.

Granted, then, that forecasting is important. Yet the fact remains that the techniques utilized by economists in preparing and evaluating various kinds of forecasts present a confusing pattern of science and art. The immeasurable debt to economic theory and analysis is evidenced by both the basic concepts with which a forecaster works and the impressive array of relationships he constantly uses. Theory, in the last analysis, is king—and no serious economist would deny this.

But forecasting, in its truer meaning and form, involves substantially more than merely the application of ratios, formulas and historical relationships. It is very much a venture into the unknown—a journey into the land of "if," "probably," and "perhaps." In short, the study of the future—whether it be of a company's sales prospects or the level of industrial production—requires the exercise of *judgment*. This is the key to realistic forecasting.

Judgment, however, is a much abused term. To many it is a substitute for analysis, a means to cover up gaps in personal knowledge. At its worst it is an invitation to whimsy and conjecture rather than an adjunct to sound, rigorous thinking. The true exercise of judgment in business forecasting is an art, but like most arts its practice can be improved by study and experience. Ultimately, then, much of what may pass for judgment is, in truth, a distillation of considerable hard work and a reliance upon a sound methodological framework. And, in this sense, it would be accurate to say that the productive forecaster relies heavily upon judgment in trying to narrow the range of uncertainty in which business decisions are made.

The purpose of this book is to bring together the combined wisdom, experience and insights of the various contributors, and to apply these skills to a broad range of business forecasting applications. This book is intended to be of practical value to many groups. *Business economists* (and their academic brethren) will be able to utilize many of the methods in preparing or understanding forecasts of general or specific business activity. *Businessmen* should be able to gain insight into the workings of the economy and be better able to supervise or evaluate forecasts. Finally, *students* in courses in forecasting should be able to blend their theoretical knowledge with the applications given here.

Since the publication of the our earlier book, *How Business Economists Forecast,* many important changes have taken place in the methodology and techniques of business forecasting. Following the format used in the preparation of the first edition, a conference was held at the Graduate School of Business Administration of New York University at which these developments were discussed by many of the leading business forecasters. The papers that were presented at that time provided the preliminary material on which this book was based. Later, they were extensively revised and edited; in addition many new papers were solicited to round out the book.

Forecasting is frequently a frustrating and vexing chore, yet the work must be done. All these economists fully realize this; and in their willingness to attempt to chart the future, they display the essential ingredient of the true forecaster—guts!

WILLIAM F. BUTLER
ROBERT A. KAVESH
ROBERT B. PLATT

BIOGRAPHICAL SKETCHES
OF THE AUTHORS

WILLIAM F. BUTLER (deceased) was Vice-President and Director of Economic Research for the Chase Manhattan Bank. He also served as President of the National Association of Business Economists. He was a member of several Governmental Commissions and was Chairman of the prestigious Business Economists Council.

ROBERT A. KAVESH is Professor of Economics and Finance at the Graduate School of Business Administration of New York University. He is also Executive Secretary and Treasurer of the American Finance Association. A former bank officer, he serves on the Board of Directors of several corporations and has been a member of the Economic Advisory Board of the U. S. Department of Commerce.

ROBERT B. PLATT is Senior Economist for the investment firm of Delafield Childs, Inc. He is also an Adjunct Professor of Economics at the Graduate School of Business Administration of New York University. Earlier he worked for the Federal Reserve Bank of New York where he became a specialist in monetary economics and forecasting.

JOHN G. MYERS is Economist for the Conference Board and is a frequent contributor on business conditions analysis to that organization's *Record*. In addition, he has taught economic theory and econometrics at New York University.

JULIUS SHISKIN is Chief Statistician of the Office of Management and Budget. His long and distinguished career in Government was highlighted by his development of *Business Conditions Digest* for the U. S. Department of Commerce.

LEONARD H. LEMPERT, Director of Statistical Indicator Associates of North Egremont, Mass., publishes a weekly report on the basic indicators developed by the National Bureau of Economic Research. He has spent many years utilizing economic indicators for forecasting.

MORRIS COHEN is a Consulting Economist and Director of the investment counselling firm of Schroder Naess and Thomas. He is also Professor of Economics and Finance at Long Island University and a Fellow of the American Statistical Association.

NANCY H. TEETERS is a Senior Fellow of the Brookings Institution and is a member of the Brookings Panel on Economic Activity. She has served as a staff economist with the Federal Reserve Board and the Council of Economic Advisers.

JUSTINE RODRIGUEZ is Deputy Director for Income Security of the U. S. Cabinet Committee on Human Resources. Formerly, she served in the Director's Office of the Office of Management and Budget and was an officer of the Chase Manhattan Bank.

MICHAEL K. EVANS is President of Chase Econometric Associates, Inc. He is the author of *Macroeconomic Activity* and has served as a consultant to major industrial, financial and government organizations in the U. S. and abroad.

ARTHUR GERSTENFELD is Professor at the College of Business Administration at Boston University. He serves as a Consultant to the Department of Health, Education and Welfare and other public and private agencies. He has published widely on the organization of research and development.

MURRAY L. WEIDENBAUM is the Mallinckrodt Distinguished University Professor at Washington University in St. Louis. He served as Assistant Secretary of the Treasury for Economic Policy and is the author of *The Modern Public Sector* and many journal articles.

HARVEY GALPER is a Senior Research Economist at the Urban Institute where he is currently working on problems of municipal finance. Previously, he did work on defense forecasting for the Federal Reserve System.

EDWARD GRAMLICH is a Senior Fellow of the Brookings Institution. His work centers upon Federal grants and their impact on state and local budgets. Earlier, he was on the staff of the Federal Reserve Board.

LAWRENCE P. HAWKINS is Economist for the Chase Manhattan Bank in charge of domestic business forecasting. He has written several articles on business and financial market forecasting.

ROBINSON NEWCOMB is a private consultant, specializing in construction industry research. He has worked for many Federal agencies and was Director of Construction Research for the War Production Board during W W II.

LOUIS J. PARADISO was formerly Associate Director of the Office of Business Economics of the U. S. Department of Commerce. Now retired, he is an economic consultant to the First National Bank of Boston and other companies.

JAMES BURTLE is a Vice President of W. R. Grace and Co. Previously, he was on the staff of the International Labour Office in Geneva. In addition, he has taught at New York University and Columbia University.

RICHARD H. KAUFMAN is a Vice President of the Chase Manhattan Bank, specializing in international economic and financial issues. He has served as a consultant to corporations around the world.

HERBERT BIENSTOCK is Regional Director of the Bureau of Labor Statistics, U. S. Department of Labor. He has lectured widely on subjects related to manpower and is the author of numerous articles in this field.

LAWRENCE A. MAYER, a member of the Board of Editors of *Fortune* Magazine, is a regular contributor of articles on economics to its pages. His fields focus upon domestic and international economic activity, as well as on U. S. population trends.

KAREN GERARD is Economic Consultant on Urban Affairs at the Chase Manhattan Bank. She specializes in the analysis of urban problems, generally, and the economy of New York, in particular. Ms. Gerard is also an Associate Editor of *Business Economics*.

ROBERT S. SCHULTZ, Assistant Executive Director of the New York State Council of Economic Advisers, was formerly Economist for Union Camp Corp. He is a Fellow of the American Statistical Association and served as President of the New York Association of Business Economists.

ROBERT J. EGGERT is Staff Vice President, Economic and Marketing Research, of RCA Corporation. He is President of the American Marketing Association and is recognized for his work in the application of economic and marketing research to management problems.

JANE R. LOCKSHIN is Manager of Economic Research for RCA Corporation. She currently serves as co-chairman of the Research Applications of Data Section of the New York Association of Business Economists.

WILLIAM HOPPE is Assistant Manager of Marketing Research at Bethlehem Steel Corporation. He has been involved in all phases of economic and market analysis work related to the steel industry.

DAVID M. BLANK is Vice President, Economics and Research, for the CBS Broadcast Group. He has conducted extensive research on the economics of advertising; his articles have appeared in many journals.

GEORGE W. McKINNEY, JR. is Senior Vice President of the Irving Trust Company, in charge of the bank's Investment Administration Division. He has been President of the National Association of Business Economists and is Chairman of the ABA's Bank Investments Division.

DAVID M. JONES is Vice President and Economist at Aubrey G. Lanston & Co., Inc. He previously served as financial economist at the Irving Trust Co. Prior to that, he was an economist with the Federal Reserve Bank of New York.

LEONALL C. ANDERSEN is Vice President of the Federal Reserve Bank of St. Louis. In charge of their research department, he has been a leader in the development of monetarist forecasting models.

EDMUND A. MENNIS, is Senior Vice President and Chairman of the Investment Policy Committee of the Security Pacific National Bank in Los Angeles. He is a past President of the Institute of Chartered Financial Analysts and a frequent contributor to professional journals.

PETER L. BERNSTEIN is President of the investment counselling firm bearing his name. Formerly a Senior Vice President with CBWL-Hayden Stone, Inc., he has written several books on economic issues and investment analysis.

DAVID BOSTIAN, JR. is Vice President and Director of Technical Research at Loeb, Rhoades & Co. He has taught at the New York Institute of Finance and frequently addresses groups on investment techniques.

VICTOR ZARNOWITZ is a Professor of Economics at the Graduate School of Business at the University of Chicago. He has written several monographs and articles dealing with the methodology and accuracy of economic forecasts.

WALTER E. HOADLEY is Executive Vice President and Chief Economist of the Bank of America. A former Treasurer of the Armstrong Cork Company, he has served as Chairman of the Federal Reserve Bank of Philadelphia and President of the American Finance Association.

HAROLD C. PASSER is an Assistant Treasurer of Eastman Kodak Company. Prior to this he was Assistant Secretary of Commerce for Economic Affairs. He has been active in the work of the National Association of Business Economists.

EDGAR R. FIEDLER is Assistant Secretary of the Treasury for Economic Policy, actively involved in economic forecasting and its policy implications. He has done extensive research in financial matters and formerly was with Bankers Trust Co.

ALAN GREENSPAN is President of Townsend-Greenspan & Co., Inc., economic consultants to many of the nation's largest corporations. He has served on numerous Government commissions and is a past President of the National Association of Business Economists.

M. KATHRYN EICKHOFF is Vice President and Treasurer of Townsend-Greenspan & Co., Inc., and editor of all their publications. She is active in the Business Economists Council and the American Finance Association.

METHODS AND TECHNIQUES OF BUSINESS FORECASTING

THE EDITORS

Economic Forecasting: Some Introductory Remarks

INTRODUCTION

This book is concerned with the tools and methods currently used by practicing business forecasters to prepare forecasts of a wide assortment of economic variables which are of particular relevance to the operations of large business organizations. Each of the chapters describes some particular aspect of economic forecasting and each is written by a leading expert on the subject covered.

In reading the various chapters it is easy to be overwhelmed by the diversity of approaches used by the business forecaster, and to be left with the clear impression that forecasting is little more than a confusing collection of ad hoc techniques tailored to special, often one-of-a-kind, situations. This is a common criticism made by those who are uninitiated in the mysteries of forecasting. Many forecasters themselves, feeling somewhat uncomfortable with this diversity, often reply to the criticism with the cliche: "After all, forecasting is an art and not a science." And indeed this is true. But art— at least good art—is not without structure. On the contrary, there are definite and systematic rules to be followed, and there are special tools and techniques which are used. This is certainly true of economic forecasting. No matter what economic variable is being forecast, no matter how diverse the special factors which may influence that vari-

able, all economic forecasters ultimately rely on a standard kit of tools and methods. It is this which gives economic forecasting its unity and makes it possible to treat it as an academic discipline.

This last statement is not meant to imply that we think it is possible to teach someone how to be a good forecaster. This cannot be done any more than it is possible to teach someone how to be a good artist or a good musician. The practical art of economic forecasting, like all of the fine arts, will always depend in large measure on the practitioner's feel for his subject, i.e., on his intuition and good judgment. However, in order for him to make the most effective use of his talent, the forecaster must also have a firm grasp of the technical aspects of his subject. It is these that are described and illustrated in this volume.

ECONOMIC FORECASTING AS APPLIED ECONOMIC THEORY

While much of this book is concerned with the tools of economic forecasting, there is hardly any specific mention of the most important tool of all—macroeconomic theory. This is not quite as serious an omission as it may at first appear, since even though it is rarely mentioned explicitly, the influence of theory is pervasive throughout the book. It is macroeconomic theory which provides the overall framework for each of the specific forecasting examples which are discussed. It does so by providing the core of hypotheses which explain economic behavior and on which the choice of causal variables used in deriving the forecasts, and our expectations of the direction and magnitude of their influence, ultimately rests.

To be sure, one does not need to make use of economic theory to forecast economic variables. There are numerous purely statistical approaches—some of which are mathematically very sophisticated[1]—which extrapolate the past systematic behavior of economic time series and which have been used with some success by business forecasters. These approaches, however, are rarely mentioned in this volume. This is not because we feel that they are unimportant, although they do have some technical limitations in forecasting economic variables. Rather, we feel that in most cases business managers who use forecasts are not merely interested in what is going to happen but also in why it is going to happen. They often ask very specific questions of forecasters; for example: What is the implication of an investment tax credit on business spending for plant equipment? How will aggregate demand be affected by an increase in the federal budget deficit or by an increase in the rate of growth of the money supply? Questions like these can only be answered if the forecasts are structured in some model (either formally or informally) which recognizes the effects and interactions of economic decisions. It is this type of forecasting, then, which is the concern of this volume. We call it *economic forecasting* to distinguish it from the purely statistical approaches, where the term economic forecasting is meant to imply that ultimately the forecast depends on some underlying model

of economic behavior. Economic forecasting, in short, is applied macroeconomic theory.

The key word in the preceding sentence is the word *applied.* Macroeconomic theory is no more than a highly stylized and simplified representation of how major classes of economic units—households, business firms, and governments—behave and interact in the market place. It is a model of reality, and like most models it most often lacks a considerable amount of sometimes important detail. In purely analytical applications the very simplified structure of macroeconomic theory is an advantage. It permits theoreticians to reach many important policy conclusions, and to discuss many important implications of the economic structure, by focusing only on a few key relationships, unencumbered by "messy" institutional considerations or by purely empirical problems such as the lack of data or the problem of operationally defining important but somewhat ambiguous concepts. But it is rare when these complicating factors can, or at least should be, ignored by the business forecaster. As a result, the tool of macroeconomic theory is seldom entirely adequate for his purpose.

All of the institutional complexities which are swept under the rug in purely analytical treatments of macroeconomics must be added back by the forecaster to the macroeconomic model in order to make it a practical business tool. It is this wealth of institutional detail which becomes such an important part of the practical problem of business forecasting—as is amply evidenced in the chapters of this book—that tends to obscure the ultimate reliance of economic forecasting on the basic core of macroeconomic theory.

SOME SPECIAL FORECASTING TOOLS

There are many complexities faced by the economic forecaster in attempting to put

---

[1] A very important recent addition to the literature of statistical forecasting is the work of George E. P. Box and Gwilym M. Jenkins, *Time Series Analysis, Forecasting and Control* (San Francisco: Holden-Day, Inc., 1970).

empirical meat on the skeleton of economic theory. It is not enough for a forecaster to say (for example, as the theory textbooks do) that increases in government expenditures, through the multiplier, cause income and employment to rise, or even to say that fixed business investment will drop with a rise in the cost of borrowed funds. A forecaster must measure these impacts with "reasonable" precision in order to make the statements meaningful. This need results in numerous problems and requires the use of special tools. Many of these tools are described in specific chapters of this book, and their use in the context of forecasting particular economic variables is illustrated throughout. While it is not our purpose here to give a detailed discussion of them, we can briefly outline some of these tools and point to the specific forecasting problem that they are designed to overcome.

For example, the essentially empirical nature of economic forecasting results in a number of purely statistical concerns. One of these is the very practical problem of finding reliable and up-to-date data which are needed inputs in the forecasting exercise. Another is the need to use statistical methodology to formulate and estimate dynamic economic relations from historical data. Some of the statistical techniques which are especially useful to the business forecaster, particularly various aspects of regression analysis and its associated statistical tests of hypotheses, are introduced in part one of this book, along with the questions of what data are available for use by the business forecaster, their source, and frequency of publication.

Another empirical problem often faced by a business forecaster is to define operationally and to measure variables which are not observable but which theory tells us are important factors in determining economic behavior. This problem arises most frequently for the forecaster in connection with determining how that rather ambiguous factor, expectations, influences the public's investment decisions. The most common tools used by the business forecaster for this purpose are the numerous surveys conducted by governmental and private research agencies which sample households and business firms to determine their future investment plans.

There are many such surveys, some of which have been of only limited use to the business forecaster. Others, however, have become essential implements in his kit of tools. Particularly useful have been the two surveys of businesses anticipated spending on plant and equipment conducted by the Office of Business Economics of the Department of Commerce and by the publishing firm of McGraw-Hill, Inc. For some forecasters, these surveys have become the primary, if not the sole, inputs in their forecasts of fixed business investment. These investment surveys—as well as many others which are available to the business forecaster—their content, where they can be found, and their prediction records are the topics of chapter 3 in part one.

Still another problem faced by the business forecaster is to determine preliminary estimates of autonomous, or so-called exogenous, variables. These are variables which cannot be explained by theories of economic behavior but which often have very significant influences on our forecasts and therefore cannot be ignored. The most important of these exogenous influences are government fiscal and monetary policy decisions. For fiscal policy, the task faced by the forecaster boils down to the need to determine estimates of receipt and expenditures of major governmental units which are then used as inputs into a mathematical or intuitive forecasting model which determines their impact on other economic variables.

Forecasts, at least of expenditures, of decisions at all levels of the government—federal, state, and local—are typically required. State and local expenditures, however, have been growing fairly smoothly over time as a result of the increasing demands for public services, and forecasting their trend typically has posed few problems for the business forecaster. At the federal level, however, the data have displayed substantially more variation, so that the forecasting problem is more difficult. The budget document furnishes the major source of information for the business forecaster. Its use for this purpose, and the special problems involved in forecasting the major and most volatile federal expenditures component, defense expenditures, are the topics treated in chapter 4 of part one and chapters 1 and 2 of part three.

Forecasting monetary policy poses special difficulties for the business forecaster, since there is still substantial disagreement among economists about which variables best measure Federal Reserve policy actions, and on the mechanism through which these actions exert their influence on economic activity. These difficulties as well as the techniques employed by business forecasters to forecast monetary policy are discussed at length in chapter 1 of part five.

Finally, major problems in business forecasting result from the inherently cyclical nature of the U.S. economy. It was fashionable in the financial press and even among some business economists in the early 1960's to talk of the demise of the business cycle. But recent economic history unfortunately has proven all too clearly that economic variables are still prone to move up and down over time in fairly rhythmical but not precisely periodic cycles of activity. These cycles are of particular concern to the forecaster since they are one of the principal causes of uncertainty in business planning.

The work of the National Bureau of Economic Research (NBER) in analyzing, dating, and measuring the business cycle has greatly increased the business forecaster's knowledge of the characteristics of this phenomenon in the U.S. economy. Also, the work of the NBER in isolating statistical data series with cyclical turning points which consistently lead cycles in aggregate economic activity has added important tools for the economist in his efforts at predicting the

business cycle. This work of the NBER and the use of statistical indicators for obtaining early warnings of turning points in economic activity are discussed in chapter 2 of part one.

METHODS OF ECONOMIC FORECASTING

The special tools mentioned above enable forecasters to accomplish some specific task or to overcome some particular forecasting problem. These tools, however, are rarely used directly as a means for generating forecasts, but rather as components of a larger and more comprehensive forecasting system.

What, then, are the methods of economic forecasting? In a strict sense, it is impossible to answer this question since forecasting is a most practical art, and generally anything that works will be used. As a result, it is rare when we find any forecaster relying on a single definable forecasting method. However, economists have an almost unlimited capacity to categorize, and it has become fashionable in the literature of forecasting to distinguish between what is often called *scientific* and *judgmental* (or *intuitive*) forecasting methods.

Scientific Forecasting

There are several ways that the term *scientific forecasting* can be defined, but in the end all of them lead to the same conclusion. The most distinguishing characteristic of scientific forecasting is replicability. For a forecasting method to be scientific it must use a clear, precise, logical, and explicitly laid out set of steps leading from the assumptions used in generating the forecast to the actual forecast itself. In other words, the method must be so explicit that *any* forecaster using the techniques with the same set of assumptions will produce the same forecast.

To obtain this degree of explicitness almost invariably requires the representation of the forecasting process in a precise set of formulae or mathematical expressions. Since we are concerned in this volume only with what we have called economic forecasting, i.e., forecasting which depends ultimately on economic theory, we can redefine scientific forecasting as the use of mathematical equations which represent some aspect or aspects of economic behavior. In this volume, scientific forecasting is represented by two methods: econometric models and input-output models.

An econometric model is sometimes defined as an explicit mathematical representation of the economy or some portion of it. Thus, in a sense virtually all forecasting which is both economic and scientific can be called econometric. However, the expression *econometric model* is most often used in a more restrictive way. It usually implies a mathematical representation of the process of aggregate income determination and the interaction between the product and financial sectors of the economy. It is, therefore, an explicit mathematical representation of those aspects of economic behavior usually described by macroeconomic theory.

The theoretical structure which underlies most econometric models is Keynesian macroeconomics with varying degrees of disaggregation and modification depending on the purposes for which the model was constructed. Some of the recent developments in "Keynesian" econometric model building, with a particular emphasis on their use for forecasting, are discussed in chapter 1 of part two. Recently, however, some non-Keynesian econometric models have been developed. These rely on a brand of macroeconomic theory which is often called the Modern Quantity Theory or more simply the Monetarist school. The theoretical framework for these models depends heavily for its inspiration on the work of Milton

Friedman, and its most distinguishing characteristic is its emphasis on the role played by the money supply in determining aggregate demand. A description of a Monetarist econometric model which has had an important impact on economic forecasting is the principal theme of chapter 2 in part five.

The second scientific forecasting method described in this book is the input-output model. This model can be defined as a system of simultaneous mathematical equations which link the output of specific industries (or companies) to the amount of inputs used in production. It is, in other words, a mathematical representation for a group of industries of the familiar economic concept, the production function.

The importance of the input-output model to economic forecasters is that it can be used to analyze and predict all of the production transactions by industry categories that go into the determination of the gross national product. Thus, it provides a means by which the economic forecaster can convert his estimates of aggregate final demand (GNP) into estimates of total industry output and resource use. An introductory description of input-output, its use for business forecasters, and some of its problems are all discussed in chapter 2 of part two.

Judgmental (or Intuitive) Forecasting

The use of the term *scientific forecasting*, although becoming increasingly common among economic forecasters, is somewhat unfortunate. Its use implies a value judgment: scientific forecasting is "good" and all other forecasting is "bad." This is not true at all. Indeed, the use of the terms *good* and *bad* to describe forecasting methods has very little meaning.

To be sure, we would expect a "good" forecasting method to produce relatively accurate forecasts as judged by usual statistical standards.[2] But there are other dimensions of "good" and "bad" in forecasting which depend crucially on the uses to be made of the forecasts. For example, the cost of deriving a forecast with a particular degree of precision is certainly a relevant factor. Other considerations which may be important in the decision include the degree of sectoral detail provided by the forecasting method or the ability or inability of the forecaster to interact with the forecasting system, i.e., to alter easily the assumptions underlying the forecast and thus to provide alternative forecasts. Finally, there is an element of the decision which is often ignored in discussions of the use of alternative forecasting methods, but one which is very important, specifically the human factor. Forecasts are not prepared as idle academic exercises, but as inputs into specific managerial decisions.[3] To be used by management, the forecasts must be trusted by them, and this often depends directly on their understanding and acceptance of the method used in generating the forecasts.

Scientific forecasting methods in general are particularly useful where considerable sectoral detail, all derived within a consistent framework, and a large degree of interaction with the forecasting system are required. However, these advantages are not always those which are of the most importance to business organizations. Moreover, the scientific methods are typically very costly to construct and to operate since they require a staff of high-priced experts in such fields as economics, statistics, and computer science. For these reasons, and also because in general there does not appear to be any clear advantage yet for the scientific methods

in terms of forecast accuracy,[4] the most commonly used methods of forecasting are the *judgmental* or, as they are sometimes called, the *intuitive* methods.

Judgmental methods differ widely from one another. At their best, they are fairly systematic and use the same underlying theoretical framework of macroeconomics that is used in the scientific approaches. The difference between the two approaches is that the theoretical model used by the judgmental forecaster is implicit, while the scientific methods use an explicit (usually mathematical) representation of the same basic theoretical model. As a result, the predictions of each judgmental forecaster are determined by his subjective and often changing evaluation of the weights to be given each of the causal factors. Thus, it is rare when the forecasts derived from a judgmental approach can be replicated by any other forecaster. Nevertheless, these methods have been very successful in practice. In large part this success has resulted from the great diversity of factors which influence economic activity. No cycle of business activity ever conforms precisely in structure and causal influences to any other. Therefore, any static set of mathematical relations with precise parameter values determined from historical data has an inherent disadvantage in forecasting future events. Judgmental forecasters using their intuition and feel for the numbers can adjust to these changing circumstances. And this flexibility has undoubtedly contributed much to the continued good success of judgmental forecasters.

But despite this, there has been a noticeable increase in the use of econometric methods by business forecasters since the publication of the first version of this volume in 1966. This can be seen by comparing

---

[2] Some of the statistical criteria useful for forecasters in measuring the accuracy of forecasts and which help in improving accuracy are described in chapter 2 of part six.

[3] The use of forecasts by business and government are topics which are treated in chapters 3, 4, and 5 of part six.

[4] Chapter 1 of part six discusses in detail some of the evidence that we have concerning the forecast accuracy of alternative methods.

the content of the many chapters on forecasting specific economic variables which are common to both editions. This trend will undoubtedly continue into the future. The reason for this is clear: the use of the mathematical approaches is the only way that economic forecasting can advance as a science. Only when we have made explicit the way our sectors interact and have defined precisely the causal variables and the magnitude and timing of their impact, can we systematically isolate the causes of forecast errors and improve our forecasting model. Judgmental forecasting is not truly a method at all. The model used exists only in the brain of the forecaster; there is no way that he can pass it on to others so that they can build upon his experiences.

This does not mean, however, that judgment and intuition will in the future no longer play an important role in business forecasting. In the actual application of the scientific approaches, judgment plays, and undoubtedly will always play, an important role. In the early days of econometric forecasting, it was possible to find forecasters who thought that their models could capture all of the relevant systematic economic influences. Econometric forecasting has matured since then, however, and increasingly the users of econometric models have come to realize that their models can only be relied upon to provide a first approximation—a set of consistent forecasts which then must be "massaged" with intuition and good judgment to take into account those influences on economic activity for which history is a poor guide.

FORECASTING IN PRACTICE

The bulk of this book is concerned with how practicing business forecasters actually go about forecasting specific economic variables. Each of the variables covered in these chapters was selected for one or more of the following reasons: (1) it is a major component of the gross national product; (2) it is of particular interest to a wide range of managerial decisions; or (3) it has important social implications. For the most part, the chapters cover topics treated in the first edition. However, each chapter has been completely redone or thoroughly revised to incorporate all of the latest advances in tools and techniques. A number of new chapters have been added. These cover topics which since the last edition have become of increasingly greater concern to the users of economic forecasts. These new chapters cover forecasting technological change (chapter 4, part one), urban and regional developments (chapter 10, part three), the environment for overseas investment and financial planning in overseas business (chapters 6 and 7, part three), and an introductory survey of the special problems and techniques of long-run economic forecasting (chapter 9, part three). To make room for the expanded content, a small number of chapters from the first edition which covered topics not of sufficiently general interest have been deleted.

Despite the many changes in the approaches to forecasting which can be found in these "how-to-do-it" chapters, a characteristic of the first edition is still very much in evidence in this revised edition. An overall observation which characterizes these chapters, and also the state of the forecasting art, is that in none of them can we find a total reliance on any one single approach or tool of forecasting. More often than not we find that use is made of surveys, indicators, and a variety of statistical data and techniques. Often we find use made of both econometric and judgmental methods. The approaches to economic forecasting are so eclectic because the needs are so practical, and forecasters will always use the tools or methods that work best for them.

Part One

THE FORECASTERS' KIT OF TOOLS

Business forecasting, in one form or another, has been practiced for literally thousands of years—if Joseph's Old Testament prophecy about the seven good years and the seven lean years is considered to be the first valid exercise of this function. Joseph's record on that occasion was perfect; accordingly, Pharaoh rewarded him handsomely.

It would be difficult to match that example, both in terms of the precision of the forecast and the rewards accruing to the practitioner. But the work goes on—some of it based upon the dreams and hunches that did so well for Joseph, but far more of it based upon increasingly sophisticated tools.

Prior to the Great Depression the analysis of the business cycle was mainly the province of the theorists. Dozens of books appeared advancing various causes for cyclical change. Most tended to emphasize a single factor or group of factors; few relied upon empirical evidence (statistics were largely unavailable).

But with the depression of the 1930s and the outbreak of World War II, much more attention was focused on the anatomy of economic change and the means for controlling business fluctuations. From these two developments the modern business economist derives his roots and techniques. Analytical frameworks were developed and tested in light of a mounting volume of data. Procedures were refined and perfected.

Today, the business forecaster is equipped with a whole set of tools, relationships, and data which he uses in his attempts to chart the course of economic activity. He is coming to rely more and more upon the concepts and methodology of statistics and econometrics in his approach to problem solving. The first chapter illustrates both the simple and complex uses of these aids in forecasting.

But forecasters are more interested in change than in structure. How can one determine when a cyclical turning point will occur, or how strong an advance or decline will be? The second chapter highlights the major methods used in arriving at a first approximation to these answers. The indicators are cited and appraised as techniques for measuring and anticipating change.

The use of surveys of all kinds is described in the third chapter. Here, the emphasis is upon the response to questionnaires (by businessmen and consumers) as a guide in determining the evolving forces that influence economic activity.

It would be a mistake to look upon these tools as competing with each other. Far from that, they frequently supplement each other in the elusive quest for a more accurate forecast.

Following these chapters is a section dealing with the use of the federal budget as an important tool in helping to frame aggregate forecasts. The final chapter in this part details the sources of the major statistical series which provide inputs for economic forecasting.

JOHN G. MYERS

Statistical and Econometric Methods Used in Business Forecasting

This chapter[1] is devoted to a survey of the statistical and econometric methods that are available for use as tools in preparing business forecasts. The emphasis in the discussion is on the word *tool*. The statistical and econometric techniques presented here are not alternatives to other, nonstatistical forecasting methods, but are helpful adjuncts in all forecasting. A survey of techniques is not a substitute for a thorough treatment of the topics. The reader who wishes to delve more deeply into specific problems will find references in the text and a bibliography at the end of the chapter.

The discussion is concentrated on the use of regression analysis to estimate models, and the use of the estimated models in preparing forecasts. A necessary first step, therefore, is to define what is meant by a model. A simple, working definition of a model is "a set of noncontradictory assumptions." The three senses in which the term *model* is encountered in the context of business forecasting can be confusing to the reader. These are: statistical model, economic model, and econometric model. All three fit well under the simple definition used here.

Statistical models are statements of assumptions about the probability distributions of variables and their mathematical interrelations. Economic models are state-

ments of assumptions about interrelations among economic variables, ordinarily in exact form (that is, nonprobabilistic); they include behavioral relationships, empirical regularities, definitions, and technological relationships. Econometric models are economic models stated in mathematical form with the probability distributions of the variables explicitly stated; they are, therefore, combinations of statistical and economic models, combining assumptions about economic relationships with assumptions about probability distributions. In another terminology, deterministic models may be distinguished from stochastic models; the former are exact while the latter are probabilistic. Economic models are ordinarily deterministic, while econometric models are stochastic. The distinguishing feature of a stochastic model is the presence of a disturbance, or error term, which has a probability distribution. Deterministic models do not have disturbance terms.

It is important in applying the methods described in this chapter that care be devoted to the choice of appropriate data for use in estimation of models. Thorough knowledge of the concepts, the collection and sampling methods employed in gathering the data, and the methods used to process the data (including such things as coverage adjustment, interpolation, and seasonal adjustment) is essential to estimation. Failure to ensure that the nature of the data used

[1] A glossary of technical terms is appended to this chapter.

corresponds closely with "operating definitions" of the variables in the model jeopardizes the outcome of the forecasting study. The question of appropriate data can only be touched on in this chapter in the course of presenting examples of empirical work, but it is of great importance in practical applications.

The bulk of the discussion of estimation is concerned with single equation techniques, specifically with ordinary least squares (OLS). OLS is the most widely used method in estimating models and a thorough knowledge of it is essential to understanding other estimating methods. It is used in estimating single equation models as well as in estimating the components of simultaneous equation models. (OLS is sometimes the first step in estimating simultaneous equation models, followed by the use of a simultaneous equation estimating method.) A single equation model is "wrong" if the underlying economic structure contains more than one equation. If some of the independent variables in a single equation model are themselves influenced by the dependent variable, additional equations are needed to describe the underlying economic structure. The pragmatic approach adopted here is that a choice between a single equation and a multiple equation model is based on whether or not the error made in using the former is serious enough to produce a bad forecast.

A frequent problem in forecasting is "structural change," when the relationships among the variables are not the same in the forecast period as in the historical period. The model is estimated using data from the historical period, but a change takes place (a new tax law, for example) which makes the estimated model obsolete. Structural change can be allowed for by ad hoc changes in the estimate of the model, or by including an equation in the model that explicitly shows the change in the relationship—such as a tax function. The latter course leads to a multiple equation model.

SIMPLE REGRESSION ANALYSIS

The simple linear equation (1) states that in period t the value of Y, the dependent variable, is determined by four factors:

$$(1) \qquad Y_t = A + BX_t + u_t$$

the population constant A; the population (constant valued) regression coefficient B; the level of X, the independent variable; and the level of u, the disturbance term. (u is the sum of all the other factors that influence Y, but which are assumed to be each of minor importance.) The equation is *simple* because only one important independent variable is specified; it is *linear* because the effect on Y of a one-unit change in the variable X is the same amount regardless of the value of X from which the change takes place (the size of the effect is shown by B). A and B are *parameters*, constant population values.

Simple least-squares regression analysis is a technique for estimating A and B from a set of sample values of X and Y. If we have, say, 40 pairs of values of X and Y (or 40 observations on X and Y) we can readily calculate the least-squares estimates of A and B. In (2), the dependent variable Y_t is shown to depend on the estimators a and b, the independent variable X_t, and the residual e_t.

$$(2) \qquad Y_t = a + bX_t + e_t$$

Here a and b are *statistics* which serve as estimators of A and B.[2] The least-squares technique yields estimates which have the property that the sum of squares of the residuals, for a sample, are minimized. A residual is the difference between an actual and a

---

[2] Formulas for deriving a and b are shown below. The derivation of these formulas may be found in many textbooks, for example Hoel (1954) and Johnston (1972).

TABLE 1.   PAPERBOARD PRODUCTION, 1960-71

Year	First Quarter	Second Quarter	Third Quarter	Fourth Quarter
	Thousands of Tons			
1960	4,107	4,068	3,851	3,857
1961	3,919	4,216	4,094	4,425
1962	4,364	4,559	4,328	4,453
1963	4,411	4,699	4,511	4,847
1964	4,651	5,086	5,295	4,908
1965	5,276	5,350	5,176	5,543
1966	5,728	5,990	5,611	5,812
1967	5,694	5,900	5,510	5,962
1968	5,967	6,314	6,050	6,627
1969	6,344	6,811	6,483	6,740
1970	6,353	6,658	6,072	6,346
1971	6,271			

Source: Compiled from weekly releases of the American Paper Institute.

fitted value of the dependent variable, where the fitted value for period t is given by $(a + bX_t)$.

This technique has great flexibility in application. It can be used to estimate a linear trend, for example, by defining X as time, measured from a value of 1 in the first period (the first observation on Y) to a value of n (or 40 in our example) in the last period. A linear trend can also, of course, be estimated by other methods. One such method is by drawing a line through a set of plotted points of the dependent variable. Another method is by computing the average of the first few values of the dependent variable, and the average of the last few values, and fitting the trend through these averages. The reason for calculating the trend by least-squares regression is that the trend fitted in

this way has the property that the sum of squares of the deviations for the entire period is minimized.

To illustrate most of the methods discussed in this chapter, the example of estimating the production of paperboard will be used. Quarterly values of paperboard production are shown in table 1 for the period from the first quarter of 1960 through the first quarter of 1971, or 45 observations in all. A linear trend fitted to the observations from first quarter 1960 through fourth quarter 1969 (40 observations)[3] by least-squares regression, yields the following results:

$$(3) \quad P_t = 3671.8 + 74.12t + e_t$$

Here P_t is paperboard production in thousands of tons, t is time, and e_t is the residual. The estimated equation states that paperboard production rises on the average by 74 thousand tons each quarter and that a trend value of Y can be estimated by the sum of a and bt. For example, the trend value in the

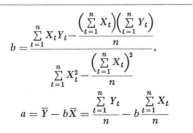

$$b = \frac{\sum\limits_{t=1}^{n} X_t Y_t - \frac{\left(\sum\limits_{t=1}^{n} X_t\right)\left(\sum\limits_{t=1}^{n} Y_t\right)}{n}}{\sum\limits_{t=1}^{n} X_t^2 - \frac{\left(\sum\limits_{t=1}^{n} X_t\right)^2}{n}},$$

$$a = \bar{Y} - b\bar{X} = \frac{\sum\limits_{t=1}^{n} Y_t}{n} - b\frac{\sum\limits_{t=1}^{n} X_t}{n}$$

[3] The shorter time period was used in order to save some observations for forecasting in a later section of this chapter.

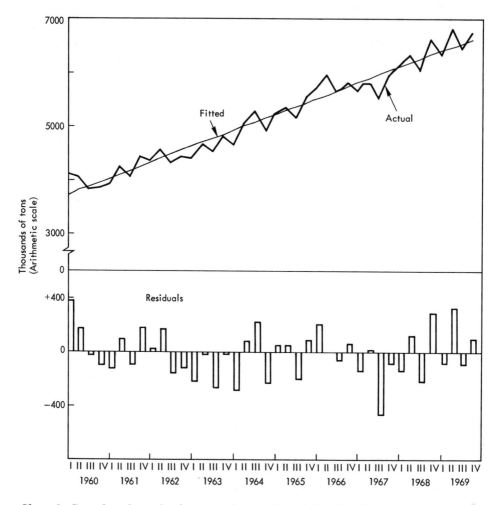

Chart 1 Paperboard production: trend, actual and fitted values from Model (3), quarterly, 1960–1969

first quarter of 1970 is 3,671.8 + 74.125 (41) = 6,711. This is an example of extrapolation, a simple forecasting technique. The values of paperboard production and the fitted linear trend are shown in chart 1, together with the residuals (deviations of the actual from the fitted, or trend values). The long-term movement in the series appears to be reasonably well explained by the fitted values; that is, no long-term systematic pattern is apparent in the deviations. A short-

term pattern seems to be present, however, in the form of seasonal variation. Apparently, the equation just fitted has a *specification error* insofar as it is purported to be a description of paperboard production; this specification error is the result of omitted variables.

Another possible specification error might be in the *functional form* of the equation. If the dependent variable grew at a constant *rate* rather than by a constant *amount,* a logarithmic transformation of the dependent variable would be appropriate. (The original series might be the variable Z_t, then regression analysis could be applied to equation (1), where $Y_t = \log Z_t$.)

It is helpful at this point to distinguish between *linearity in the parameters A* and *B,* and *linearity in the variables X and Y.* Economic applications of regression analysis are usually concerned with equations that are linear in the parameters, as in the case at hand. If the parameters are linear, linear regression analysis is applicable. The variables need not be linear, however, because variables that have been transformed (by taking logarithms, square roots, or reciprocals; by squaring; or by other transformations of the original values) can always be relabeled as ordinary variables (X, Y, etc.) and the standard methods described in this chapter applied.

Examples of equations with nonlinear parameters are:

$$(4) \qquad Y_t = A + BX_t^C + u$$

$$(5) \qquad Y_t = AB^{X_t} + u_t$$

Neither of these equations can be transformed into an equation of type (1). More complex, nonlinear estimating methods must be used to estimate their parameters.

Two approaches to the problem of seasonal variation are considered here. The first approach is to adjust the values of the dependent variable for seasonal variation and to use the adjusted, or deseasonalized, values in the regression. Again, if the dependent variable, in original values, is Z_t, and the series of adjusted values is Z_t', then $Y_t = Z_t'$ is the appropriate dependent variable for the fitting of a linear trend, and $Y_t = \log Z_t'$ is appropriate for a logarithmic (constant rate of growth) trend. Seasonal adjustment can be readily performed on a computer by means of a standard program such as the X-11 program, provided a sufficiently large number of observations are available.

The X-11 seasonal adjustment program was developed by the Bureau of the Census. (Less complex techniques than X-11 are also available; these require fewer observations and provide adequate seasonal adjustment for many series.)

A second approach to seasonal variation is to include in the equation additional independent variables that are meant to represent seasonal effects. This method has the advantage of showing the seasonal effects explicitly in the model.

MULTIPLE REGRESSION ANALYSIS

With the inclusion of more than one independent variable, an equation with several variables is needed. The general form is shown in (6):

$$(6) \qquad Y_t = B_1 + B_2 X_{2t} + B_3 X_{3t} \\ + \cdots + B_k X_{kt} + u_t$$

or

$$Y_t = B_1 + \sum_{j=2}^{k} B_j X_{jt} + u_t$$

Here j is a subscript ranging from 1 to k; the constant term is now B_1; and X_2 through X_k are the independent variables. (In principle, any number of independent variables can be used, provided a sufficiently large number of observations is available for estimation.) The meaning of (6) is that in period t, the value of Y is equal to the constant B_1 *plus* the sum of the values X_2 through X_k, each multiplied by its respective regression coefficient (B_2 through B_k), *plus* the value of the disturbance term u. Each of the regression coefficients shows the average change in the dependent variable resulting from a one-unit change in the respective independent variable, when the effects of the other independent variables are held constant.

In economic terminology, a regression

coefficient approximates the relation between the associated independent variable and the dependent variable, *ceteris paribus*. In mathematical terminology, a regression coefficient is an approximation of the partial derivative of the dependent variable with respect to the associated independent variable.

The technique for estimation of (6) that will be examined is multiple regression analysis. It is obvious that simple, or bivariate, regression analysis is a special case of multiple regression analysis.[4]

Returning to the paperboard analysis, the equation to be estimated with a linear trend and variables for seasonal effects takes the form:

$$(7) \qquad P_t = B_1 + B_2 t + B_3 Q_2 \\ + B_4 Q_3 + B_5 Q_4 + u_t$$

where P_t represents paperboard production; t is time; and Q_2, Q_3 and Q_4 are dummy variables representing seasonal influences in the second, third, and fourth quarters of each calendar year. A dummy variable assumes only two values, 0 and 1, according to whether the effect it represents is present or not. Q_2 is equal to 1 in the second quarter, and is equal to 0 in each of the first, third, and fourth quarters.

The values assumed by the dummy variables are illustrated in the following table:

Seasonal Dummy Variable	First Quarter	Second Quarter	Third Quarter	Fourth Quarter
Q_2	0	1	0	0
Q_3	0	0	1	0
Q_4	0	0	0	1

[4] Formulas in terms of summations for the estimation of B_1 through B_k become quite cumbersome when more than two independent variables are used, so matrix algebra is customarily employed. The interested reader may refer to Johnston (1972, chaps. 4 and 5) or to Goldberger (1964, chaps. 2 and 4).

All three seasonal variables have the value of zero in the first quarter of each year; in each of the other quarters, all but one are zero. The average seasonal effect of the first quarter is captured by the constant term B_1, while the coefficient of each of the other seasonal variables shows the average change in the dependent variable from the first quarter to the quarter in question. For example, B_3 shows the average change due to seasonal influences from the first quarter to the second. When the equation contains a constant term, a complete set of dummy variables must not be included, or the equation cannot be estimated. For example, if a dummy variable representing the first quarter were included in (7), estimates of the coefficients B_j could not be obtained by regression analysis. (The technical reason is that the matrix of values of the X_j, including unit values for B_1, would be singular and could not, therefore, be inverted for solution.)[5] This property of dummy variables—that one must be excluded when a constant term is present—applies to all uses of dummy variables, whatever they represent. Correct usage of dummy variables can be checked by preparing a table such as the one above, where the dummy variables are listed in the stub and the characteristics they represent are shown in the column headings; correct usage requires that the *sum* of the values in one column be zero. Discussions of dummy variables in regression analysis may be found in Suits (1957); Johnston (1972, pp. 176–92); and Goldberger (1964, pp. 218–27 and 229–31).

Regression estimates of the values of

[5] Alternatively, the constant term can be omitted and four seasonal dummy variables shown, provided the computer program used permits the omission of the constant term (many do not). For model (7), the assumption implicit in this procedure is that the dependent variable has the value of zero when $t = 0$, that is, in the period preceding the first observation. This assumption would clearly be contrary to the facts for paperboard production.

the B_j for paperboard production, based on the same observations (first quarter 1960 through fourth quarter 1969), were obtained with the use of a computer. The coefficient b_2 shows that the dependent variable, paperboard production, rises by an average value of 74 thousand tons each quarter, when seasonal effects are eliminated. The trend value of paperboard production in the fourth quarter of 1968 is equal to $b_1 + b_2(36) = 6,303$ thousand tons. Adding b_5, the average difference between the seasonal effect in the fourth quarter and that in the first quarter yields a trend-seasonal value of 6,378 thousand tons. Extrapolated values for periods after 1969 can easily be calculated in this way.

Coef-ficient	Estimated Value	Meaning
b_1	3632.2	Constant term
b_2	74.19	Quarterly trend
b_3	185.51	2nd quarter seasonal effect
b_4	−108.88	3rd quarter seasonal effect
b_5	75.33	4th quarter seasonal effect

The actual and calculated values are shown in chart 2, together with the residuals. No long-term or seasonal pattern is now evident in the residuals. However, there is much variation in paperboard production not accounted for by the mechanistic, trend-seasonal model just measured. A model with economic components will hopefully yield a better explanation of past paperboard production and provide the basis for a reasonably accurate forecasting method. First, however, the statistical basis for estimation and testing of hypotheses in regression will be discussed.

Some Statistical Underpinnings of Regression Analysis

A typical computer program for multiple regression analysis provides many measures that are helpful in evaluating the explanatory power of an estimated model and the accuracy of the estimates of the coefficients. It also provides clues to weaknesses in the specification of the model or in the data employed in the analysis. In order to understand and utilize these measures effectively, a brief review of the assumptions of linear regression analysis is necessary.

A key element in statistical estimation and testing is the nature of the disturbance term u. As noted earlier, this is the sum of all the neglected influences on the dependent variable—all those not shown explicitly in the equation. (There are always some influences that are too small to deal with or that cannot be isolated.) It is the presence of this term in a model that makes regression analysis a stochastic or probabilistic study rather than one of exact measurement. A disturbance term changes a deterministic, economic model into a stochastic, econometric model. The disturbance term is assumed to have certain properties in order to carry out statistical estimation and tests of significance (discussed in later sections of this chapter). Departures from these assumptions bring about some of the characteristic problems of econometrics.

ASSUMPTION A. For each observation used in estimation, the disturbance term is expected to have the value of zero. That is, the many influences that are combined in u are assumed to be unrelated to one another and to offset each other so as to sum to zero, in each time period.

ASSUMPTION B. A related assumption is that all pairs of values of u, whether adjacent in time or not, are not correlated. For example, it is assumed that u_t is not correlated with u_{t-1}. The seasonal pattern of the residuals in chart 1 indicates a departure from this assumption; the residuals for the second quarter of each year are generally larger than those for the third quarter, for example. A departure from assumption B gives rise to the problem of *autocorrelation*, a systematic time pattern in the residuals.

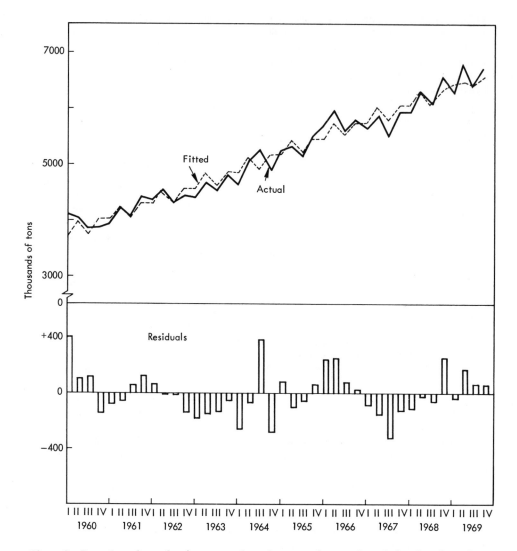

Chart 2 Paperboard production: trend and seasonal—actual and fitted values from Model (7), quarterly, 1960–1969

When autocorrelation is present, the usual tests of significance are not valid.

ASSUMPTION C. The third assumption is that the variability (strictly, the variance) of u is the same for all observations. A departure from this assumption might occur if the disturbance term were usually greater in absolute size (further from zero) when the dependent variable Y is large than when it is small. The converse, larger variance with small values of Y, would also be a departure. When the assumption does not hold, the result is called *heteroscedasticity*, or variation in dispersion of the disturbance term. Agreement with the assumption is called *homoscedasticity*. Heteroscedasticity results in less precise estimates of the regression coefficients; that is, the estimates are subject to greater variability and are thus less certain.

ASSUMPTION D. Another assumption is that u is not correlated with the independent variables in the equation. If the disturbance term is correlated with an independent variable, heteroscedasticity may result; as X becomes larger, so does u, for example. This assumption is also related to the problem of *simultaneity*, where an independent variable in the equation being estimated is influenced by the dependent variable at the same time. Another equation can be written which shows the dependence of the X_j in question on Y (and other variables). The result is a departure from the assumption that u is not correlated with the independent variables in the equation.

ASSUMPTION E. An assumption that causes much confusion is that no two independent variables, or no two groups (strictly, linear combinations) of independent variables, should be identical. If this assumption is violated, estimates of the coefficients of the equation cannot be obtained by least-squares regression analysis. (The requirement that one dummy variable be omitted is a consequence of this assumption; the reason given above holds true in general—when the assumption is violated, a singular matrix is obtained which cannot be inverted for estimation.) A departure from this assumption is an extreme case of *multicollinearity*, a more general problem in regression analysis.

When two or more independent variables are highly correlated in a set of sample data, they are said to be collinear, and in this case multiple regression analysis gives inaccurate estimates of regression coefficients. The presence of multicollinearity in a set of observations is often recognized by rules of thumb, such as coefficients with the "wrong" sign, or low t-ratios along with a high value of R^2 (t-ratios and R^2 are discussed later in this chapter). The basic reason for multicollinearity is that the data are not sufficiently rich or varied—the values of

the independent variables in the sample observations may move similarly over time, for example. Just what degree of correlation among two independent variables will make a set of data valueless for estimation is very difficult to determine. It should be emphasized, however, that nearly all economic variables observed over time are intercorrelated, positively or negatively, and it is only very high degrees of association that cause difficulty.

ASSUMPTION F. Finally, it is usually assumed that the disturbance term is normally distributed; that is, the frequency distribution of u is described by the normal curve of error. This assumption is not so strong as it might appear. If a variable is the sum of a large number of small factors that are not correlated with each other, as was specified for the disturbance term, the distribution of the variable will be approximately normal. This is a consequence of the central limit theorem of probability theory, the "law of large numbers."

A parameter is a constant value of the population, such as B_j, which relates variables in the model to one another, or characterizes such variables. The value of a parameter is unknown and must be estimated. A statistic, such as b_j, is calculated from sample data and is used as an estimator of a parameter. Examples of parameters and statistics, in the notation that is used in this chapter, are the following:

Name	Parameter	Statistic
Regression coefficient	B_j	b_j
Disturbance term u and		
residual e	u	e
Variance of u	σ_u^2	$\hat{\sigma}_u^2$
Standard error of u	σ_u	$\hat{\sigma}_u$
Simple correlation		
coefficient	$\rho(X_i, X_j)$	$r(X_i, X_j)$
Standard error of		
regression coefficient	σ_{b_j}	$\hat{\sigma}_{b_j}$

The variance of u, and its square root, the standard error of u, are measures of the variability of Y, the dependent variable, not explained by the independent variables. The simple correlation coefficient is a measure of strength of linear association between two variables; it takes values from -1 to $+1$, the former implying perfect negative, the latter perfect positive linear association. The standard error of the regression coefficient is a measure of the sampling variability of the *estimated* regression coefficient b_j.

The multiple correlation coefficient R and the square of that measure, R^2, are summary statistics of the "goodness of fit" or explanatory power of the estimated equation. They are computed from sample values.[6] Specifically, R^2 shows the proportion of the variance of Y in the sample that is accounted for by the estimating equation

$$(8) \qquad R^2 = \frac{\sum_{t=1}^{n} (\hat{Y}_t - \bar{Y})^2}{\sum_{t=1}^{n} (Y_t - \bar{Y})^2}$$

Here the numerator is the sum of the squares of the deviations of the fitted values of Y_t ($\hat{Y}_t$) from the sample average ($\bar{Y}$); this is the "explained" variation in Y_t. The denominator is the sum of squares of the deviations of the actual values of Y_t from the sample average; this is the total variation in Y_t. If $R^2 = 0.90$, then 90% of the variation of the sample values of Y are accounted for or "explained" by the regression equation. This measure increases in value, for a given set of sample data, as more variables are added to the equation, regardless of the relevance of these variables. It is fairly common, therefore, for computer programs to present an additional measure, "R^2 adjusted for degrees of freedom"[7] often shown as $\bar{R}^2$. This last-named measure does not automatically increase in value with additional indepen-

dent variables and is more useful, therefore, in comparing alternative specifications of a regression model. For a large number of observations, however, R^2 and $\bar{R}^2$ are nearly the same. [The formula for computation of $\bar{R}^2$ is given in Johnston (1972), pp. 129–30.]

Tests of Hypotheses About the Regression

The problem of estimating a regression model for paperboard production can now be returned to. It will be recalled that the purpose of studying this problem is to obtain a technique for forecasting paperboard production.

A leading characteristic of paperboard is the great generality of its use. All sectors of the economy employ this product in some form, the most common of which is packaging. It seems reasonable, therefore, to relate the effective demand for paperboard to an aggregate measure of economic activity, specifically to gross national product. GNP has the advantage that forecasts of its future values are available from a number of sources. It is obvious that a forecasting method will be of little value if it requires explanatory factors which cannot themselves be forecast with reasonable accuracy; this consideration is particularly important for periods characterized by cyclical fluctuations.

Paperboard production has a seasonal pattern, as noted above; the second and fourth quarters tend to be higher, and the third quarter lower, than the first quarter (when the trend is held constant). The quarterly values of GNP are seasonally adjusted, while the paperboard values are not. Therefore, the seasonal variation in paperboard production will not be explained by GNP, and dummy seasonal variables should be retained in the model. It is reasonable to assume that paperboard is linearly related to GNP; this assumption can be checked by use of a different functional form. The model

---

[6] There are also corresponding parameters, but these are not needed for the present discussion.

[7] See the definition of *degrees of freedom* in the glossary.

TABLE 2.   MULTIPLE REGRESSION ANALYSIS COMPUTER OUTPUT FOR MODEL (9)

Paperboard Production, 1960-69

```
INDEX              MEANS              STANDARD DEVIATIONS
  1               603.197                  83.7666
  2                 0.25                  0.438529
  3                 0.25                  0.438529
  4                 0.25                  0.438529
  5               5191.33                  889.538


CORRELATION COEFFICIENTS
  1.000E+CO   -2.002E-02   2.501E-02   6.095E-02   9.778E-01
 -2.002E-02    1.000E+00  -3.333E-01  -3.333E-01   7.308E-02
  2.501E-02   -3.333E-01   1.000E+00  -3.333E-01  -7.232E-02
  6.095E-02   -3.333E-01  -3.333E-01   1.000E+00   9.753E-02
  9.778E-01    7.308E-02  -7.232E-02   9.753E-02   1.000E+00


INDEX           B             STANDARD ERROR      T-RATIO       BETAS
0 -- CONSTANT  -1122.25          187.282         -5.99232        0
  1              10.3816         0.303924        34.1584         0.977617
  2             192.389         70.8875           2.71401        9.45451E-2

  3             -95.7717        70.9699          -1.34947       -4.72141E-2

  4             109.163         71.0744           1.5359         5.38158E-2


R-SQUARED=0.971527        R=0.985661
R-SQUARED ADJUSTED FOR DEGREE OF FREEDOM=    0.968273

STANDARD ERROR OF ESTIMATE= 153.446 D.F. = 35


DURBIN-WATSON STATISTIC= 1.7512
```

Source: Rapidata, Inc.

(9) is similar to (7) except that G_t (= GNP in constant, 1958 prices) replaces t, the time variable.

$$(9) \qquad P_t = B_1 + B_2 G_t + B_3 Q_2 \\ + B_4 Q_3 + B_5 Q_4 + u_t$$

A computer output representing regression analysis of (9) is reproduced in table 2. This output was produced by the multiple regression program of Rapidata, Inc., a time-sharing company. The meaning and use of each of the statistics shown in the table is described in the following paragraphs.

The variables are identified by the "index": 1 is GNP; 2, 3, and 4 are Q_2, Q_3, and Q_4; and 5 is P, the dependent variable.

The *means* and *standard deviations* are the familiar measures of the sample observations. The simple *correlation coefficients* show the association between pairs of variables; for example, the correlation between paperboard and GNP is 0.9778. It should be noted that the array (or matrix) of correlation coefficients is symmetric about the diagonal, because by definition the correlation of X_1 with X_2 is the same as the correlation of X_2 with X_1.

Several of the values in table 2 are expressed in floating point notation, such as 9.778 E-01. To properly place the decimal point, the number preceding E must be multiplied by 10 raised to the power following E. Thus, E-01 means that 9.778 must be multiplied by $(10)^{-1} = \frac{1}{10}$, which yields 0.9778. In practice, a negative value following E means that the decimal must be shifted to the left as many places as the value following the minus sign; a positive value means that the decimal must be shifted to the right as many places as shown in the value.

In the section following the correlation coefficients, the estimated regression coefficients are shown in the column headed "B" (these are the b_j's in the notation of this chapter). The constant term is -1122.25, the coefficient of GNP is 10.3816, etc. The meaning of the GNP coefficient is that if GNP changes by one billion dollars (in 1958 prices), paperboard production changes by 10.4 thousand tons, in the same direction.

The next column shows estimates of the *standard errors of the regression coefficients* (σ_{bj}). These are measures of the variability of the estimates of the regression coefficients. The *t-ratios* shown in the next column permit an evaluation of the precision or accuracy of the estimates of the regression coefficients. The *t*-ratios are computed by dividing each b_j by its corresponding standard error. The larger a given b_j is relative to the variability of its estimate, the more precise, and therefore reliable, is the estimate—the *t*-ratio shows this relation. On the next to bottom line of table 2 is the number of *degrees of freedom*, or D.F.; the sample of 40 observations, with five regression coefficients estimated, has 35 (40-5) degrees of freedom.

At this point, the meaning of a regression coefficient should be recalled: it is the effect of the corresponding independent variable on the dependent variable, when the effects of the other independent variables are held constant. The *t*-ratio permits a test of the hypothesis that a given independent variable has no effect, based on the set of sample observations used for the regression analysis. For the constant term B_1, the hypothesis to be tested is that the dependent variable is proportional to the independent variables; that is, when the independent

variables are zero, the dependent variable is zero. Another way of stating this is to say the regression plane goes through the origin.

A table of values of t shows that with 35 degrees of freedom, the upper 5% of the t-distribution lies beyond 1.69, while the upper $2\frac{1}{2}\%$ lies beyond 2.03. If it is known in advance that an independent variable should have a positive effect on the dependent variable, the upper 5% tabulated value should be used. An observed t-ratio less than this *critical value* means that a nonzero *estimate* of B_j could easily have been obtained by chance, even though the true value of the parameter B_j is in fact zero. The test indicates, with a probability of 0.05, or 5%, that the independent variable X_j has no effect on Y. In the case of paperboard production, it is assumed in advance that GNP has a positive effect; the observed t-ratio of 34.2 is well in excess of the critical value of 1.69, so the hypothesis that GNP has no effect is rejected—the effect is apparently quite strong.

This is an example of a *one-tail test* of the null hypothesis of no effect, in the sense that only one tail of the t-distribution is used in the test. When the direction of influence can be specified in advance, either positive or negative, as can often be done with the aid of economic theory or institutional knowledge, a one-tail test is appropriate. Since the t-distribution is symmetrical, the critical value for a negative effect is simply the negative of the positive value. In the example at hand, the critical value for the lower 5%, appropriate for a test of a negative effect, is -1.69.

If there are no *a priori* grounds for specifying the direction of influence, a two-tail test is appropriate. For example, it was not known in advance what the direction of the seasonal effect for the third quarter (in terms of average change from the first quarter) would be. An observed t-ratio either greater than $+2.03$ or less than -2.03 is required, therefore, to reject the hypothesis that the average seasonal influence in the third quarter is the same as in the first quarter. The observed t-ratio of -1.35 does not permit rejection of that hypothesis. The t-ratio for the second quarter does exceed the critical value, however. A more elaborate test of the set of three seasonal variables would be desirable. But, as a rule of thumb, it is customary to accept all the seasonal variables as useful if one of them is *significant* (that is, if the t-ratio for one of them exceeds the critical value).

It should be noted that the tests of hypotheses just discussed are valid only if the probability distribution of u, the disturbance term in the model, has a normal distribution. Use of a table of critical t-values is justified only if u is normally distributed; this underlines the importance of assumption F of the regression model, stated in the preceding section.

The *betas*, shown in the column of table 2 following the t-ratios, are values of the regression coefficients that have been adjusted for comparability with each other. A beta coefficient can be derived by multiplying the corresponding regression coefficient by the ratio of the standard deviation of the independent variable to the standard deviation of the dependent variable. For example, the beta for GNP is 10.3816 (83.7666/889.538) $=$ 0.97762. Beta measures are little-used in present-day economic statistics, because they are misleading if there is any correlation among the independent variables, which is almost always true in economic time series.

The *coefficient of multiple correlation* R and its square, the *coefficient of multiple determination*, show the degree of association of the dependent variable with the entire set of independent variables. R-squared adjusted for degrees of freedom equals 0.97 in table 2; this indicates that 97% of the variation in paperboard consumption is "explained" by GNP and the seasonal variables. The values of the coefficient of multiple determination for the three models (3), (7), and (9) can be compared to see if the apparent result of a progressively better fit to the data was in fact obtained. For this purpose, R-squared *adjusted for degrees of freedom* is appropriate, since the number of degrees of freedom for (3), (7), and (9) differ (38, 35, and 35 respectively). Model (3) yielded an adjusted value of R-squared of 0.948; model (7), 0.960; and model (9), 0.968. The fit does improve, though very slightly.

The *standard error of estimate* is the standard deviation of the residuals; it is an estimate of the standard deviation of the disturbance term, and is used in the computation of R-squared and of the standard errors of the regression coefficients.

The *Durbin-Watson statistic* is a measure of autocorrelation of the residuals. This measure (D-W) can assume values from zero to 4. If no autocorrelation is present in the residuals, the average value in repeated sampling (the expected value) of D-W is 2. Small values of D-W result when values of the residual adjacent in time are similar in size; that is, when successive values of the residual term are positively correlated, the D-W will be low.

In economic time-series data that have not been manipulated by taking differences between successive values of the variables [such as $(Y_t - Y_{t-1})$ and $(X_t - X_{t-1})$], positive *serial correlation* is to be expected, rather than negative serial correlation. Serial correlation in a variable means that successive values of the variable, over time, are correlated with one another. The reason that economic data are characterized by positive serial correlation is that the systematic time patterns present in economic data (trends, cycles, and seasonals) lead to similar values for adjacent observations. However, serial correlation in the variables in the model need not, and indeed should not, imply autocorrelation, or serial correlation of the disturbance term. To the extent that the model has been correctly specified, the serial correlation in the dependent variable will be explained by the serial correlation in the independent variables, and no remaining serial correlation will be present in the disturbance term.

If the model has not been correctly specified, some of the systematic variation in the dependent variable will not be explained by the independent variables, and will be present in the disturbances. An example of this is found in (3), where the dependent variable has seasonal variation but the (sole) independent variable, a linear trend term, does not. The result is a seasonal pattern in the disturbance term, suggested by the results illustrated in chart 1. Another example would be when the dependent variable has a seasonal (or trend, or cyclical) pattern but the independent variables do not because they have been previously adjusted (as for GNP). In all such cases, correct specification will entail accounting for the unexplained serial correlation in the dependent variable; this was attempted by the inclusion of seasonal dummy variables in (7) and (9).

If autocorrelation is present in the residuals from an equation estimated with economic time-series data, such autocorrelation should be positive, as explained above, unless the variables were expressed as changes, or differences. A one-tail test (the lower tail) for autocorrelation is therefore appropriate. The hypothesis is that no autocorrelation is present. Tables of critical values of the D-W statistic may be found in Johnston (1972), pp. 430-31, in the original article by Durbin and Watson (1950, 1951), in an article by Theil and Nagar (1961), or in Christ (1966). The critical value, for a sample size of 40 and 5 regression coefficients at 5% probability, is approximately 1.72 (taken from a table in Theil and Nagar). Since the observed value of 1.75 is greater than the critical value, the hypothesis of no autocorrelation is *not* rejected; that is, autocorrelation does not appear to be present.

When the variables in the model are expressed as changes, or differences between values in succeeding time periods, either positive or negative autocorrelation may be present in the residuals. In this case, a two-tail test of the Durbin-Watson statistic is appropriate. For example, if changes in paperboard production and in GNP were used instead of levels of these variables in model (9), either positive or negative autocorrelation might be suspected, and a two-tail test should be used.

An *F-test* is important because it is a significance test of the entire regression. *R*-squared provides a summary measure of the goodness of fit, but a significance test of the explanatory power of the set of independent variables is valuable, particularly in borderline cases where *R*-squared is low. The hypothesis to be tested is that there is no relation between the dependent variable and the set of independent variables, or that the population regression coefficients are equal to zero ($B_2 = B_3 = \cdots = B_k = 0$). The test statistic is included as part of the output of some computer programs. In other computer programs, summary statistics are given with which the test statistic can easily be compared. From the information given in table 2, the test statistic F can be computed by formula (10), where k is the number of regression coefficients in the model (including the constant term).

$$(10) \qquad F = \frac{R^2/(k-1)}{(1-R^2)/(n-k)}$$

The *R*-squared in (10) is the unadjusted measure, and n is the number of observations. For the statistics in table 2,

$$F = \frac{0.9715/4}{0.0285/35} = 298.3$$

A table of values of F gives a critical value of 2.65 at 5% probability, with 4 ($k - 1$) and 35 degrees of freedom. If there is no association between the dependent and the set of independent variables, a test statistic of F will exceed this critical value with less than 0.05 probability, or less than 5% of the time. For the results in table 2, the hypothesis of no association is clearly rejected. As in the case of the t-tests, the F-test also depends on assumption F, that the disturbance term is normally distributed; that is, use of the table of critical values of F is justified by that assumption.

Lagged Variables

Forecasting models often incorporate lagged values of independent or dependent variables. Inclusion of lagged values of independent variables presents no new problems, except insofar as the presence of both $X_{2,t}$ and $X_{2,t-1}$, for example, may lead to difficulty with multicollinearity. Economic time series are typically serially correlated, so the value of X_2 in time period t is likely to be very similar to the value of X_2 in time period $t-1$, thus leading to possible multicollinearity.

If a lagged value of the dependent variable is used as an independent variable (the equation is then termed autoregressive), the Durbin-Watson statistic is no longer a guide to the presence of a departure from assumption B of the linear regression model. This may not invalidate the use of the regression formula in forecasting, but it does make tests of significance using t-ratios and F-statistics of uncertain meaning.

A popular technique in regression analysis for forecasting is that of distributed lags. A distributed lag model seeks to explain delays in the effects of independent variables on the dependent variable. It might be realistically hypothesized that the effects of a change in a causal variable on the dependent variable are spread out over a large number of time periods. A direct way of expressing the delays in these effects would be to include the value of the causal variable as an independent variable for each relevant time period. For example, if the effects of a causal variable on the dependent variable were spread out over the current and the next 10 time periods, the equation would be as follows:

$$(11) \quad Y_t = B_1 + B_2 X_{2t} + B_3 X_{2,t-1} + \cdots + B_{12} X_{2,t-10} + u_t$$

If it were attempted to estimate this equation, it is highly unlikely that useful estimates of the regression coefficients would be obtained. The reason is that the values of the independent variables would be so highly correlated, or multicollinear, that the estimates of the B_j's would be highly imprecise. In other words, there would not be a sufficient amount of *independent variation* among the independent variables to permit accurate estimation of the B_j's.

Several methods of circumventing this difficulty have been developed. These methods involve the use of a mathematical function to represent the time pattern, or profile, of the weights (regression coefficients) to be attached to the lagged values, such as those shown in (11). One method in common use is the Almon lag estimating procedure developed by Shirley Almon (1965). The Almon lag is a highly flexible tool, the basic assumption of which is that all the coefficients of the lagged variables lie on a polynomial. The degree of the polynomial is specified by the model builder; by choosing different degrees of the polynomial (linear, quadratic, cubic, etc.), a wide range of time patterns can be fitted by the coefficients.

The technique was originally derived by Mrs. Almon to provide forecasts of capital appropriations, using data for the 1,000 largest manufacturing companies prepared by the Conference Board. A fourth-degree polynomial was used in the original study, and the current quarter plus the seven preceding quarters were found to give the best fit for all industries combined. The lag pattern was reestimated using seasonally adjusted quarterly data, for both expenditures and appropriations, for the period from first quarter 1960 through fourth quarter 1969. The model is given in (12); a computer output showing the empirical results is reproduced in table 3. The output was produced by the Almon program of Rapidata, Inc.

TABLE 3.   DISTRIBUTED LAG REGRESSION, COMPUTER OUTPUT FOR MODEL (12)

Capital Expenditures, 1960-69

```
R-SQUARE:   UNADJUSTED=               0.9946
            ADJUSTED  =               0.9940
STANDARD ERROR OF ESTIMATE=           112.7805
   TEST FOR ALL B'S=0:   F(3, 29) =   1772.754873
DURBIN-WATSON               0.7118


VARIABLE LAG              B          T-RATIO


CONSTANT           -135.3453        -1.9754


FCAPR      0         0.115775        5.126374
FCAPR      1         0.165864       10.965765
FCAPR      2         0.174012       13.549056
FCAPR      3         0.158632        6.920750
FCAPR      4         0.132805        5.881036
FCAPR      5         0.104279        8.506236
FCAPR      6         0.075470        4.679581
FCAPR      7         0.043460        1.843181
FCAPR    SUM         0.970297        6.555100
FCAPR AVERAGE LAG=       2.885138


MAXIMUM NUMBER OF LAGS=             7
```

Source: Rapidata, Inc.

$$(12) \quad E_t = B_1 + \sum_{L=0}^{7} B_{2+L} FCAPR_{t-L} + u_t$$

E_t is capital expenditures in period t, B_1 is the constant term, L is the lag, $FCAPR_t$-L is the value of capital appropriations in period $t - L$, B_{2+L} is the weight given to the capital appropriations value in period $t - L$, and u_t is the disturbance term in period t.

The results in table 3 indicate that the data provide a good fit to the model. Adjusted R-squared and the F-value are both very high, and the t-ratios are all large. The low value of the Durbin-Watson statistic indicates the presence of autocorrelation, however, which makes the values of R-squared, F, and the t-ratios of doubtful validity; they doubtless exaggerate the explanation given by the model. The estimated regression coefficients B_{2+L} show the effects of appropriations data with different lags on expenditures in period t. Appropriations lagged two quarters are seen to have the

greatest effect; from that point the effects diminish as the lag increases or diminishes. The sum of the weights, 0.97 in table 3, shows that on the average 3% of capital appropriations are not spent. The fourth-degree polynomial was fitted so as to force the weights for periods with lags greater than seven, or less than zero (periods before t), to be equal to zero. The actual and calculated values of capital expenditures, together with the residuals, are shown in chart 3.

The time pattern of the estimated regression coefficients shown in table 3 differs from that found by Mrs. Almon. Her estimates, based on data for 1953–61, gave greater weight to earlier appropriations values—the peak weight was for appropriations lagged four quarters, for example. In order to investigate this change, model (12) was reestimated for the period 1953–61 using revised, seasonally adjusted data (as was used to produce the results shown in table 3). Both sets of weights are shown in chart 4, where the shift in the time pattern from the fifties to the sixties is easily seen. There has

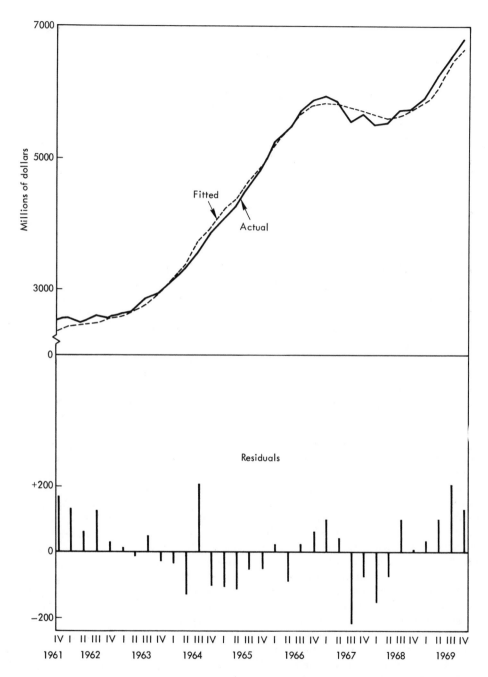

Chart 3   Capital expenditures, seasonally adjusted—actual and fitted values from Model
(12), quarterly, 1961 IV to 1969

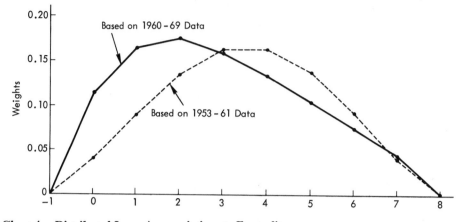

Chart 4   Distributed Lags, Appropriations to Expenditures

apparently been a structural change in the relation of appropriations to expenditures, not explicitly shown in model (11). Large manufacturing companies seem to have spent their appropriations more promptly, on the average, in the sixties than in the fifties.

FORECASTING WITH REGRESSION MODELS

The estimated regression coefficients can be applied directly to known or estimated future values of the independent variables to produce forecasts of the dependent variable. Those forecasts are *point estimates*, single values. Interval estimates can also be computed; here a range of values of the dependent variable is forecast, with an associated probability. In order to prepare an interval estimate, the standard error of the forecast must be computed. When the model contains more than one dependent variable, computation of the standard error of the forecast is rather complex and requires information not ordinarily given as part of the output of computer programs. For these reasons, the discussion will be restricted to point estimates, or point fore-

casts. The interested reader may consult Johnston (1972, pp. 38–43 and 152–55).

When the independent variables are simple trend, or trends plus dummy seasonal variables, as in (3) and (7), the future values of the independent variables are obviously known and forecasting is simply a matter of extrapolation. Forecasts of the gross national product, and of its components, are available from econometric models and other forecasting methods as discussed in subsequent chapters of this book; the estimated regression coefficients shown in table 2 can be used with a set of GNP forecasts to produce forecasts of paperboard production, for example. Ex post forecasts of paperboard, prepared with models (3), (7), and (9), for the four quarters of 1970 and the first quarter of 1971 are shown in table 4, together with actual values of paperboard production and of GNP. The forecasts are ex post because the values of the independent variables for 1970 are known. Ex ante forecasts are made with forecast values of the independent variables [such as forecasts of GNP for model (9)].

Errors in ex post forecasts result from inadequacies of the forecasting model, while errors in ex ante forecasts result from both inadequacy of the forecasting model and errors in the forecasts of the independent

TABLE 4.   EX POST FORECASTS OF PAPERBOARD PRODUCTION

Year and Quarter	GNP, Seasonally Adjusted Annual Rate (Billions of 1958 $)	Paperboard Production				Forecast Error (Forecast Minus Actual)		
		Actual	Ex Post Forecasts					
			Model (3)	Model (7)	Model (9)	Model (3)	Model (7)	Model (9)
		Thousands of Tons						
1969, Fourth	$729.2	6,740	...	...	...	...	...	...
1970, First	723.8	6,353	6,711	6,674	6,392	+358	+321	+39
1970, Second	724.9	6,658	6,785	6,935	6,596	+127	+277	−62
1970, Third	727.4	6,072	6,859	6,713	6,334	+787	+641	+262
1970, Fourth	720.3	6,346	6,933	6,972	6,465	+587	+626	+119
1971, First	732.7	6,271	7,007	6,971	6,484	+736	+700	+213

variables. Ex ante forecast errors are of course more relevant, since they are the kind that result in practical applications. If forecasting models are to be useful, they should forecast well with the incomplete, preliminary information available to the forecaster in a practical situation. Particularly when forecasting a period of cyclical fluctuation, however, analysis of ex post forecasts is a necessary step in refining and choosing among forecasting models.

The inadequacy of models (3) and (7) for forecasting is readily apparent. Paperboard production fell sharply in the first quarter of 1970 and again in the third quarter; these movements were undoubtedly the result of the recession which began in November 1969 and continued until November 1970. If the variable to forecast is responsive to cyclical fluctuations, as is the case with paperboard production, forecasting with a trend, or trend plus seasonal, will usually lead to inaccurate forecasts.

Forecasts prepared with model (9) are more satisfactory. The cyclical downturn in 1970 was reasonably well approximated and the forecast errors are of moderate size, each less than 5%. Cyclical patterns in paperboard production are apparently greater than those in total GNP, however. A model incorporating individually the cyclically sensitive components of GNP, such as *gross pri-* *vate domestic investment* and *consumption expenditures on durable goods*, as independent variables would probably yield better forecasts for paperboard production.

In discussing the coefficient of multiple correlation above, it was noted that the values of adjusted R-squared for the three paperboard models, (3), (7), and (9), were quite similar: 0.948, 0.960, and 0.968 respectively. Yet the forecasting performance of the three models differs widely. This illustrates a principle of general importance—the closeness of fit of a model to a set of historical data does not ensure that the model will provide good forecasts. Although obviously important, the value of R-squared is only one consideration in evaluating the potential of a model for forecasting. Another important consideration is the extent to which the model is based on economic theory or institutional knowledge. Model (9), based on economic considerations, performs much better than models (3) and (7), which are purely mechanical. The period 1960 to 1969 saw fairly steady growth in the economy, so a simple trend agreed closely with observed data. The onset of a cyclical downturn, beginning in November 1969, interrupted the growth trend in paperboard production. Only the model that included a cyclical component, (9), captured this movement.

TABLE 5.   FORECASTS OF CAPITAL EXPENDITURES BASED ON MODEL (11)

Year and Quarter	Capital Appropriations		Capital Expenditures			Ex Post Forecast Error	Adjustment in Ex Ante Forecast
	Actual	Forecast	Actual	Ex Post Forecast	Ex Ante Forecast		
	Millions of Current $ at Quarterly Rates						
1969, Fourth	$7,592	$ ...	$6,823	$ ...	$ ...	$ ...	$ ...
1970, First	6,578	...	6,631	6,784	...	+153	...
1970, Second	6,508	...	6,724	6,772	...	+48	...
1970, Third	6,615	...	6,713	6,694	...	−19	...
1970, Fourth	5,999	...	6,336	6,528	...	+192	...
1971, First	5,618	...	6,127	6,281	...	+154	...
1971, Second	...	6,000	...	...	5,872	...	−173
1971, Third	...	6,400	...	...	5,799	...	−115

Source: Actual appropriations and expenditures data from The Conference Board, Inc.

The ex post forecasts from all three models, shown in table 4, tend to overestimate paperboard production, particularly for the three quarters beginning with the third quarter of 1970. Allowance for this tendency should be made in preparing forecasts for future periods. One technique is to adjust the level of the forecast to account for recent errors; this is equivalent to adjusting the constant in the regression equation. For example, in preparing ex ante forecasts with model (9), an average of the errors in the last three quarters shown in table 4 might be subtracted from the forecast produced by the regression equation for the second quarter of 1971. The adjustments to the forecasts for subsequent quarters, made at the same time, should be of progressively smaller size, so that the calculated series produced by the regression equation is gradually approached. It is likely that the cyclical recovery in paperboard production will be more rapid than that in GNP since the cyclical downturn was greater in the former; adjustments of the type just suggested can aid in capturing that movement.

Capital expenditures forecasts for the 1,000 largest manufacturing companies, prepared with the estimates from table 3, are shown in table 5. The forecasts for the four quarters of 1970 and the first quarter of 1971 are ex post, prepared with published values of appropriations. Those for the second and third quarters of 1971 are ex ante, prepared with the forecasts of appropriations and the adjustments shown for those two quarters.

The ex post forecasts overestimate expenditures in four of the five quarters; the largest ex post error is +3%. Adjustments to correct for this tendency in preparing ex ante forecasts were computed as follows. For the second quarter of 1971, the average of the errors in the two preceding quarters was combined with the calculated value; for third quarter 1971, two-thirds of that average. Capital appropriations should turn upward as the economy recovers from the 1969–70 recession; the appropriations forecasts shown for the second and third quarters of 1971 incorporate arbitrarily chosen amounts to produce a gradual increase from the present depressed level. [Sophisticated techniques are available for forecasting appropriations; the interested reader may refer to Almon (1968).] The ex ante forecasts were computed with the weights given in table 3, applied to the actual and forecast values of appropriations shown in table 5, and then reduced by applying the adjustments of table 5; these forecast a decline in capital expenditures in the second and third quarters of 1971.

Glossary of Technical Terms

The reader of literature on statistical methods for forecasting is confronted with a bewildering profusion of technical terms. The following list of brief, nonrigorous definitions or descriptions is offered for reference. Terms with an asterisk (*) are discussed in the chapter.

Almon lag.* A distributed lag model which forces the values of the coefficients of lagged variables to lie on a polynomial. The degree of the polynomial is selected by the researcher.

Alternate hypothesis.* If the null hypothesis is rejected, the alternate hypothesis is accepted. The alternate hypothesis resembles the null hypothesis except that the equality is replaced by "greater than," "less than," or "not equal to," according to prior information. For example, if the null hypothesis is $B_2 - 0 = 0$ (X_2 has no effect on Y), the alternate hypothesis will be one of the following: (a) $B_2 - 0 > 0$ (X_2 has a positive effect on Y); (b) $B_2 - 0 < 0$ (X_2 has a negative effect on Y); or (c) $B_2 - 0 - 0$ (X_2 has either a positive or a negative effect on Y, there is no sound basis for specifying the direction of effect in advance). Economic theory or institutional knowledge often permit the direction of effect (positive or negative) to be specified in advance. It is desirable to adopt an alternate hypothesis of type a or b for two reasons: "nonsense" results are less likely to be accepted; and the associated test is more powerful, that is, wrong conclusions are less likely to be drawn from the outcome of the test.

Autocorrelation.* Interdependence among the disturbance terms of different observations; the value of the disturbance term in one time period is correlated with the value in another time period. Autocorrelation is serial correlation of the disturbance term.

Autoregressive model. A model in which a lagged value of the dependent variable appears as an independent variable.

Bias. The amount by which the expected value of a statistic differs from the parameter the statistic is used to estimate. If the expected value of a statistic is equal to the parameter, the statistic is *unbiased.*

Coefficient of multiple correlation.* The square root of the coefficient of multiple determination.

Coefficient of multiple determination, *R*-squared.* Shows the degree of association between the dependent variable and the set of independent variables in a regression equation. *R*-squared shows the proportion of the variation in the dependent variable that is accounted for or "explained" by the set of independent variables. *R*-squared may be adjusted for degrees of freedom, to take account of the number of independent variables in the equation.

Correlation matrix. Part of the computer output of most regression programs. An array of the simple correlation coefficients of all pairs of variables. The correlation matrix may refer to the variables in a specific equation, or to all the variables read into the computer, from which groups of variables are selected for specific equations. Because the correlation coefficient of X_2 with X_3 is the same as the correlation coefficient of X_3 with X_2, the correlation matrix is symmetrical about the diagonal.

Degrees of freedom. The number of observations not used up in the estimation process; that is, the number of independent observations. In linear regression analysis with a sample of n observations, the number of degrees of freedom equals n minus the number of regression coefficients (including the constant). The larger the number of regression coefficients estimated, the larger the number of constraints imposed on the sample, and the smaller the number of variations left to provide precise estimates of the regression statistics. A greater number of degrees of freedom provides more reliable estimates.

Distributed lag.* The effects of an independent variable on the dependent variable are often spread out over several time periods. This requires that the same variable be included several times in a forecasting equation, each time with a different lag. Direct estimation of such an equation would be unlikely to produce useful results because of multicollinearity (values of economic variables in successive periods are often highly correlated). Indirect methods of estimation of distributed lags impose constraints on the values of the coefficients of the lagged variables.

Disturbance term.* Represents the sum of all the factors that affect the dependent variables that are not explicitly shown in the equation. The disturbance term is the portion of the value of the dependent variable not accounted for by the corresponding values of the independent variables and the *population* regression coefficients.

Dummy variable.* A variable that assumes only two values, zero or one. May be used to represent seasonal influences, nonquantitative variables (such as a war period), and so forth. The coefficient of a dummy variable in a regression equation shows the average effect on the level of the dependent variable when the dummy variable assumes the value of one. For example, a dummy variable might represent a tax measure that was applied during only part of a time series. The variable would then take the value of one when the tax measure was in effect and the value of zero when the measure was not in effect. The regression coefficient would show the change in the level of the dependent variable during the period of application of the tax measure.

Durbin-Watson statistic.* A measure of the autocorrelation in the *residuals*. Values of the statistic range from zero to 4. If no autocorrelation is present in the *disturbances*, the expected value, or population mean of this statistic is 2. Small values of the statistic (less than 2, approaching zero) suggest positive autocorrelation; large values (greater than 2, approaching 4) suggest negative autocorrelation.

Endogenous variable. A variable that is determined by the model. In forecasting, a model produces forecasts of the endogenous variables.

Ex ante forecast.* True forecasting of the future. The values of the independent variables must often be forecast themselves and the actual value of the dependent variable is not known.

Exogenous variable. A variable in a simultaneous equation model that affects the model but is *not* determined by the model. In forecasting, the exogenous variables must often be forecasts themselves.

Expected value. The expected value of a statistic is the mean of the distribution of that statistic; that is, the average of the values of the statistic that could be computed from a very large number of samples.

Ex post forecast.* "Forecasting" with past (known) values of the independent variables. Useful for evaluating forecasting models.

F-test.* An analysis of variance test. In regression analysis, *F*-tests are used to test the entire regression (whether the independent variables affect the dependent variable), part of the regression (whether a subset of the independent variables affects the dependent variables), whether estimated regression coefficients of the same equation computed from two different samples represent the same parameters (population values of the regression coefficients), and so on.

Functional form.* The mathematical form of the equation, such as linear in the variables, logarithmic, hyperbolic, and so forth.

Heteroscedasticity.* The converse of homoscedasticity. The variability of the disturbance term differs among sample observations.

Homoscedasticity.* The variability of the disturbance term is the same for each observation in the sample; that is, the variance of the disturbance term is of constant size.

Lagged variable.* If one of the variables on the right-hand side of a regression equation refers to a time period earlier than the time period of the dependent variable (on the left-hand side), it is a lagged variable. The meaning of a lagged variable is that its effect on the dependent variable is experienced in a later time period. A lagged variable can represent prior values of the dependent variable or of a causal independent variable.

Least squares.* A technique of fitting a regression function (a line for simple regression, a plane or hyperplane for multiple regression) to a set of observations, under the constraint that the sum of the squares of the deviations of the actual from the fitted values of the dependent variables are minimized.

Model. * A set of noncontradictory assumptions. Models relevant to this discussion may be statistical, economic, or econometric; a model may comprise a single equation or several (simultaneous) equations.

Multicollinearity. * A high degree of intercorrelation among independent variables. When two independent variables are highly correlated in a set of sample observations, the data do not permit precise estimates of the separate effects of the independent variables on the dependent variable; that is, the estimates of the regression coefficients are imprecise.

Normal distribution. The normal probability distribution or normal curve of error. The *t*-distribution and *F*-distribution apply to statistics derived from normally distributed variables. Tests of hypotheses and estimation procedures using the *t*-distribution and the *F*-distribution in regression analysis are based on the assumption that the disturbance term is normally distributed (that is, follows or is characterized by the normal distribution).

Null hypothesis. An assertion, to be tested, that there is no difference between two (or more) values, at least one of which is a parameter. In regression analysis, a common form of the null hypothesis is that a parameter minus a stated value equals zero. For example, $\sigma^2_{ut} - c = 0$; this means that the variance of the disturbance term is a constant for all observations. Another example is $B_2 - 0 = 0$, which states that the associated independent variable X_2 has no effect on the dependent variable. Null hypotheses can also be formed for combinations of regression coefficients, such as $B_2 + B_3 - 1 = 0$ which states that the sum of B_2 and B_3 has the value of one. Tests of significance of null hypotheses are made using *t*-ratios, *F*-statistics, Durbin-Watson statistics, and the like.

One-tail test. * A test made with an alternate hypothesis which states that the effect is in only one direction, either positive or negative (type a or b, *see* ALTERNATE HYPOTHESIS).

Parameter. * A constant population value which relates variables in the model to one another, such as a population regression coefficient, or describes the probability distribution of a variable, such as the variance of the disturbance term.

Partial correlation coefficient. A measure of the association between two variables when one or more other variables are held constant. The usual notation is $r_{12.3}$, which indicates the correlation between variable 1 and variable 2, when the effect of variable 3 is held constant.

Predetermined variable. Either an exogenous variable or a lagged value of an endogenous variable. Thus, all variables that are not determined by the model simultaneously, that is, in the same time period.

Reduced form. An alternative form of a simultaneous equation model, derived from the original, structural form. There is one equation in the reduced form for each endogenous variable in the model, in which the endogenous variable is related to the entire set of predetermined variables and disturbance terms. The endogenous variable is the dependent variable of the reduced-form equation, and only predetermined variables, disturbance terms, and regression coefficients appear on the right-hand side of the equation. If no structural change has taken place between the period of observation and the period of forecast, the estimated reduced-form equations can be used to forecast the endogenous variables.

Regression analysis. * A method of estimating the parameters of an equation with sample data, in order to show the separate effects of the independent variables on the dependent variable. Simple regression analysis is applied to an equation with one dependent and one independent variable. Multiple regression analysis is applied to an equation with one dependent and two or more independent variables.

Regression coefficient. * Shows the average effect of an independent variable on the dependent variable. In multiple regression analysis, this is the partial effect of the associated independent variable, when the other independent variables are held constant.

Residual. * This is the difference between an actual value of the dependent variable and a calculated value, thus the portion of a given value of the dependent variable not accounted for by the corresponding independent variables and the *estimated* regression coefficients. The residual is a statistic, while the disturbance is a parameter.

Serial correlation. * Time dependence in *any* variable. Most economic time series are serially correlated, because the values in successive periods are of similar value and are thus correlated with each other.

Simultaneity. When the dependent variable and one or more of the independent variables of a single equation are affected by the same forces and interact within the (time) period of observation. In such a case, the disturbance term will be correlated with the independent variable (or variables) so affected. A simultaneous equation model (containing two or more equations) would explicitly take the interaction into account. If regression analysis is applied to the single equation alone, the accuracy of the estimates is reduced. Joint estimation of all the equations in a simultaneous equation model (as by use of two-stage least squares) avoids the problem of simultaneity.

Simultaneous equation model. A model containing two or more equations; some of the variables in one equation interact with variables in at least one other equation.

Specification. * The construction of the model by stating the assumptions. In the case of a single-equation econometric model, specification entails listing the variables to be explicitly included, stating the functional form of the equation, and stating the probability distribution of the disturbance term. Specification errors are omission of important variables, using the wrong functional form, and the like.

Standard error of a regression coefficient. * A measure of the variability of estimates of a regression coefficient in repeated sampling.

Standard error of estimate. * The standard deviation of the residuals from a fitted re-

gression. This measure serves as an estimate of the variance of the disturbance term.

Statistic. * An estimation of a parameter which can be computed from sample data. Examples are the sample regression coefficient and the Durbin-Watson statistic.

Structural form. A simultaneous equation model in its original form, showing the theoretical relationships among the variables.

Test of significance. * A test of significance is made to determine whether an observed result could have occurred by chance at a specified probability level (the level of significance). For example, consider a test of the hypothesis that B_2 is zero. The test is made to see whether or not the calculated estimate of B_2 could easily have occurred as a result of random fluctuations in the sample data. At a 5% level of significance, the null hypothesis is rejected if the estimated value could have occurred at least one time out of 20 as a result of random fluctuations. A table of probabilities (of t-ratios, F-statistics, Durbin-Watson statistics, etc.) is consulted to learn the critical value for the specified level of significance and the number of degrees of freedom used in calculating the estimate.

Transformation. * Performing mathematical operations on the variables, such as squaring, taking logarithms or ratios, and so on.

t-ratio. * The ratio of an estimated regression coefficient to its standard error. The greater the t-ratio in absolute value (either positive or negative), the more precise the estimate of the regression coefficient. Used in tests of hypotheses, such as a test that the independent variable has no effect on the dependent variable.

Two-stage least squares. A technique for simultaneous estimation of simultaneous equation models. In stage one, each reduced-form equation is estimated separately by least-squares regression and the fitted values of the endogenous (dependent) variable of the reduced-form equation are calculated. In stage two, each structural equation is estimated separately by least-squares regression, but for any endogenous variables that appear on the right-hand side of the structural equation, the fitted values from stage one are used in place of the actual values in the regression.

A simple example may be helpful at this point.

Let Y_1 and Y_2 be endogenous variables
X_1, X_2, and X_3 be exogenous variables
u_1, u_2, v_1 and v_2 be disturbance terms
B's, C's, D's and E's be regression coefficients
e_1 and e_2 be residuals

Structural form of model

$$Y_1 = B_1 + B_2 Y_2 + B_3 X_1 + B_4 X_2 + u_1$$
$$Y_2 = C_1 + C_2 Y_1 + C_3 X_1 + C_4 X_3 + u_2$$

Reduced form of model

$$Y_1 = D_1 + D_2 X_1 + D_3 X_2 + D_4 X_3 + v_1$$
$$Y_2 = E_1 + E_2 X_1 + E_3 X_2 + E_4 X_3 + v_2$$

(Here the D's and E's are each equal to a combination of B's and C's, and the v's are each equal to a combination of u's. But this is not important for the question at hand.) In stage one, each of the two equations in the reduced form is estimated separately by least-squares regression and the fitted values of Y_1 and Y_2, $\hat{Y}_1$ and $\hat{Y}_2$, are calculated for each observation in the sample. In stage two, the n fitted values are first substituted for the actual values on the right-hand side of the two structural equations.

$$Y_1 = B_1 + B_2 \hat{Y}_2 + B_3 X_1 + B_4 X_2 + u_1$$
$$Y_2 = C_1 + C_2 \hat{Y}_1 + C_3 X_1 + C_4 X_3 + u_2$$

Then each structural equation is estimated separately by least-squares regression to produce the estimate of the structural form.

Estimated structural form

$$Y_1 = b_1 + b_2 Y_2 + b_3 X_1 + b_4 X_2 + e_1$$
$$Y_2 = c_1 + c_2 Y_2 + c_3 X_1 + c_4 X_3 + e_2$$

This technique is used to eliminate *bias* in the estimates of the regression coefficients that would result if least-squares regression were applied directly to each equation in the structural form. The bias would result from *simultaneity*; the first disturbance, u_1, is correlated with Y_2 in the first structural equation, and the second disturbance, u_2, is correlated with Y_1 in the second structural equation.

Two-tail test.* A test made with an alternate hypothesis which states that the direction of the effect is not known in advance (type c, *see* ALTERNATE HYPOTHESIS).

BIBLIOGRAPHY

Almon, Shirley, "The Distributed Lag Between Capital Appropriations and Expenditures," *Econometrica* (January 1965), pp. 178–96.

———, "Lags Between Investment Decisions and Their Causes," *Review of Economics and Statistics* (May 1968), pp. 193–206.

Chisholm, Roger K., and Gilbert R. Whitaker, Jr., *Forecasting Methods*. Homewood, Ill.: Richard D. Irwin, Inc., 1971.

Christ, Carl F., *Econometric Models and Methods*. New York: John Wiley & Sons, Inc., 1966.

Conference Board, *Quarterly Survey of Capital Appropriations*. Investment Statistics Series. New York: The Conference Board, Inc.

Durbin, J., and G. S. Watson, "Testing for Serial Correlation in Least-squares Regression," pts. I and II, *Biometrika* (December 1950 and June 1951), pp. 409–28 and pp. 159–77.

Fox, Karl A., *Intermediate Economic Statistics*. New York: John Wiley & Sons, Inc., 1968.

Goldberger, Arthur S., *Econometric Theory*. New York: John Wiley & Sons, Inc., 1964.

Hoel, Paul G., *Introduction to Mathematical Statistics* (2nd ed.). New York: John Wiley & Sons, Inc., 1954.

Johnston, J., *Econometric Methods* (2nd ed.). New York: McGraw Hill Book Company, 1972.

Klein, Lawrence R., *An Introduction to Econometrics*. Englewood Cliffs, N.J.: Prentice-Hall, Inc., 1962.

Malinvaud, E., *Statistical Methods of Econometrics*. Amsterdam: North-Holland Publishing Company, 1966.

Suits, Daniel B., "Use of Dummy Variables in Regression Equations," *Journal of the American Statistical Association* (December 1957), pp. 548–51.

Theil, H., and A. L. Nagar, "Testing the Independence of Regression Disturbances," *Journal of the American Statistical Association* (December 1961), pp. 793–806.

JULIUS SHISKIN & LEONARD H. LEMPERT

Indicator Forecasting

CHAPTER OUTLINE

It is helpful at the outset to provide some perspective on the indicator approach through a description of the concept of the business cycle.

I. THE BUSINESS CYCLE

The "business cycle" concept has evolved from the sequence of events discerned in the historical movements of economic activity. Though there are many cross currents and variations, periods of economic expansion appear to cumulate to peaks. As they cumulate, contrary forces tend to become dominant and ultimately bring about a contraction or retardation. As the weaker

phase proceeds, forces making for expansion gradually emerge until they again become dominant. This repetitive pattern of expansion and contraction may be seen in chart 1, which shows an index of economic activity covering the years 1885–1971. The regularities and some of the irregularities of the pattern are evident from the chart.

Monthly business cycle peaks and troughs have been dated by the National Bureau of Economic Research for the period 1854–1961. These peaks and troughs separate major upward and downward movements of the economy. The NBER peaks and troughs reveal that expansions have prevailed roughly 64 percent of the time, and contractions 36 percent.

For purposes of illustration, it is help-

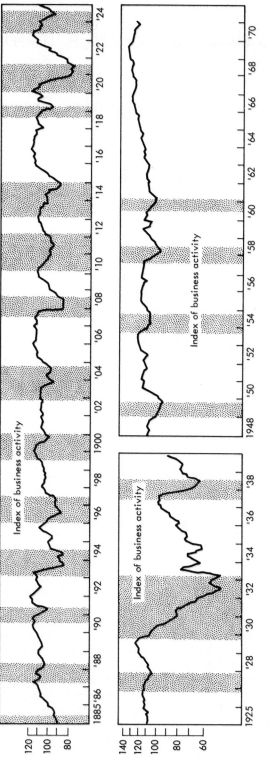

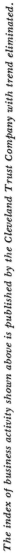

The index of business activity shown above is published by the Cleveland Trust Company with trend eliminated.

Chart 1   An Index of Business Activity, 1885–1971

ful to summarize the sequence of events during a business cycle as espoused some years ago by Arthur F. Burns and the late Wesley C. Mitchell, leading students of business cycles.

In the advanced stage of an expansion, business concerns frequently encounter obstacles. New supplies of materials and components become scarce; business loans are less readily available; interest on such loans is higher; and shortages of some types of labor occur. Even though costs, such as wages and interest rates, tend to rise more rapidly than in the early stages of the advance, competitive pressures make it somewhat hazardous to raise prices proportionally. The outlook for further expansion becomes less favorable and a "squeeze" on profits or profit rates develops. When this occurs, businessmen become cautious and reduce their commitments for the future. As the prospects for forward profits appear more uncertain, investment commitments—involving inventories, new orders for machinery and equipment, and contracts for commercial and industrial construction—are reduced. Sometimes the reaction is promptly apparent in the stock market, where changes in outlook can be registered quickly. Reductions in overtime and hours of work and the closing down of marginal activities are also symptoms which appear at this juncture.

However, current production and employment, which flow from earlier business commitments, continue to rise, often to all-time highs. Actual expenditures for plant and equipment, contracts for which were necessarily made long in advance, continue to go up even after the peak of production and employment has been passed. Thus, at the very time when forward commitments, in the form of new contracts and new orders, are being reduced and forces set in motion which lead to a reversal in business activity, production and employment are at full strength and plant and equipment expenditures continue to rise for some months. However, the decisions to reduce investment

commitments finally begin to affect production and employment, and a decline in aggregate economic activity sets in. During a recession, when facilities and supplies become more readily available, inventories tend to be low, costs often decline and, as future profit prospects improve, a reverse movement gets underway and the forces which lead to a new expansion gradually come to the fore. In this way, the effects of investment decisions by businessmen are spread over many months and among many different economic processes.

This highly generalized and oversimplified pattern is, of course, affected by international developments and by government policies and programs which in modern society play a significant role in the economy. The impact of "external" events must necessarily be considered carefully in any study of cyclical movements.

The extent to which these developments take place determines the relative magnitudes of contractions and of expansions.

II. LEADING, COINCIDENT, LAGGING, AND OTHER INDICATORS

Much historical evidence reveals that economic indicators tend to move through the cyclical course in consistent but different time sequences. Accordingly, economic indicators useful for business cycle studies have been grouped into three major categories and are designated as *leading, roughly coincident,* and *lagging.*

A basic principle behind this classification of indicators is that decisions to expand or curtail output take time to work out their effects.

The selection of indicators for each of these groups is based on extensive empirical tests conducted since World War I primarily by the National Bureau of Economic Research under the leadership of Wesley C. Mitchell, Arthur F. Burns, and Geoffrey H. Moore. Professors Edwin B. Frickey and Warren M. Persons of Harvard might be mentioned among many others at universities, research organizations, and government agencies who have made significant contributions to the study of business cycle indicators.

The group of economic indicators referred to as *roughly coincident* relates primarily to aggregate economic activity and includes such measures as gross national product, industrial production, employment,

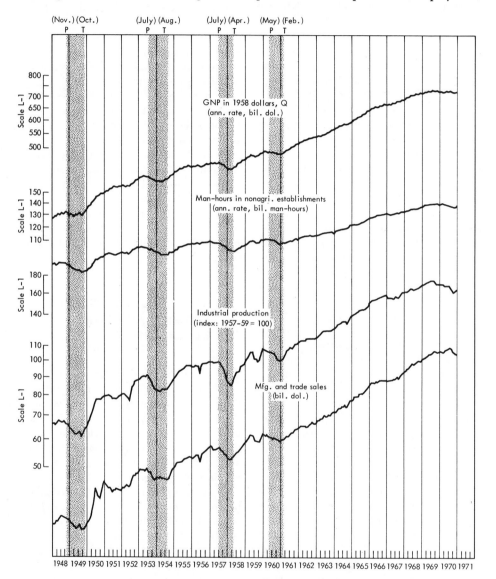

Chart 2   Recent Expansions and Contractions as Shown by Roughly Coincident Indicators

income, and manufacturing and trade sales. The movements of these activities tend to coincide with, and in a sense measure and define, the economy as a whole. Several of these series are shown in chart 2.

It is from these and similar measures

that dates are selected to represent turning points in the economy as a whole.

Individual indicators do not always "coincide" precisely with each other or with the chosen date. A composite of all indicators of aggregate economic activity would

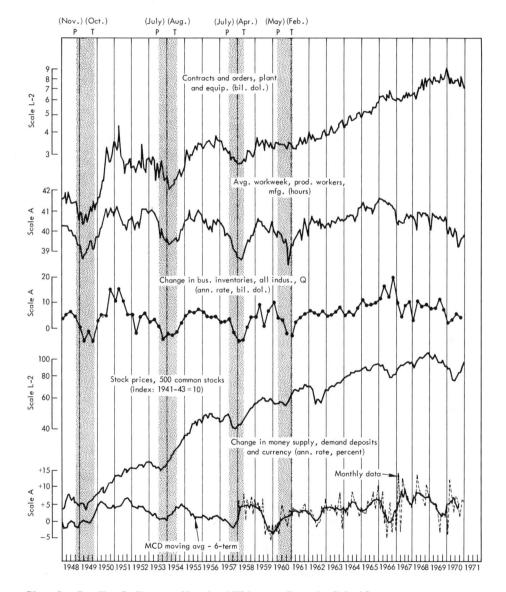

Chart 3   Leading Indicators: Signals of Things to Come in Coincident

tend to demonstrate a more faithful "coincidence." This emphasizes the importance of studying many indicators rather than a few in making judgments about the position of the economy and its prospects.

As noted earlier, certain activities frequently foreshadow changes in aggregate

economic activity. They reflect future production and employment. For example, new orders are placed, particularly for machinery and other types of equipment; contracts are let for the construction of new plants; investments in materials inventories are made; and new businesses are started. Statistical

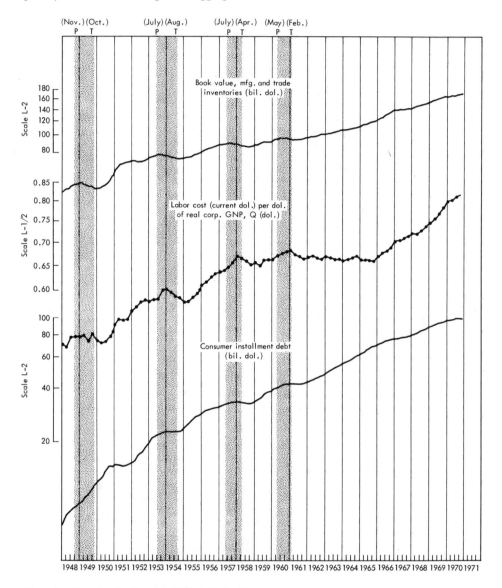

Chart 4   Lagging Indicators Follow Coincident

measures of activities which foreshadow changes in aggregate economic activity (illustrated in chart 3) are called *leading indicators*. They are signals of things to come.

In contrast to these advance signals, there are some activities which lag behind aggregate economic activity. Some of these relate to business costs (e.g., unit labor costs and bank interest rates) which respond sluggishly to changing business conditions. Others included are such statistical indicators as inventories of finished goods, consum-

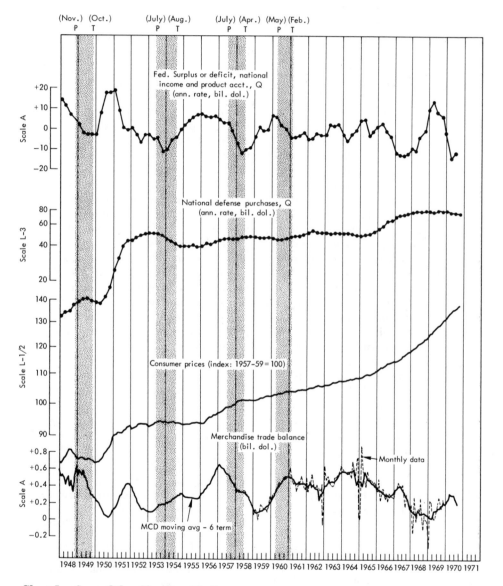

Chart 5   Some Other Significant Indicators

er debt, and long-term unemployment rate. Illustrative lagging indicators are shown in chart 4.

Students of the business indicator approach state that while the sequence of events varies from cycle to cycle, it is sufficiently orderly to enable one to make judgments about the pattern of the next stage of the cycle from developments during a given cyclical phase. The sequential arrangement of the series is aimed at assisting in this process. This applies to lagging as well as leading and coincident indicators. The "lagging" activities contribute to bringing about changes in the activities measured by the leading indicators. For example, as various business costs decline (e.g., unit labor costs), there is more incentive for business to place new orders. By the same token, when these costs rise during the latter part of an expansion, there is pressure to reduce or postpone new business commitments.

In order to improve judgments on short-term prospects, it is also essential to examine other measures of economic activity which do not behave in a manner sufficiently consistent to be classified into one of the three foregoing groups. These include such indicators as consumer prices, the federal surplus or deficit, military obligations, foreign trade, and the balance of international payments. As can be seen in chart 5, most of these do not move up and down with the business cycle in an orderly and repetitive fashion. Indeed, some represent factors which distort the normal course of the business cycle and suggest forces which may be harnessed to control it.

III. SELECTING THE MOST HELPFUL INDICATORS

The National Bureau of Economic Research published its first list of business cycle indicators in 1938. Compiled by Wesley C. Mitchell and Arthur F. Burns, the list was based on a study of nearly five hundred

monthly and quarterly indicators covering varying historical periods, but ending with the business cycle that reached its trough in 1933. Mitchell and Burns selected 21 "most trustworthy" indicators of cyclical revival, and presented a fuller list of 71 indicators which they said have been tolerably consistent in their timing in relation to business cycle revivals and at the same time of sufficiently general interest to warrant some attention by students of current economic conditions.[1]

About a dozen years later, in 1950, a second comprehensive review was made.[2] The new study was based on a larger number of indicators, about eight hundred, and utilized measures of cyclical behavior through 1938. This study went beyond the earlier report in several ways: indicators of contraction as well as of revival were covered; probability standards against which the historical records of timing and conformity could be judged were introduced; a comprehensive economic classification of the eight hundred series was used in making the final selection of indicators; and the selected indicators were classified into the three categories—leading, roughly coincident, and lagging—reflecting timing at business cycle peaks and troughs. The final 21 indicators selected included 8 leading, 8 roughly coincident, and 5 lagging.

This list was again revised in 1960.[3] The new list was based on a still larger num-

[1] Wesley C. Mitchell and Arthur F. Burns, *Statistical Indicators of Cyclical Revivals*, Bulletin 69 (New York: National Bureau of Economic Research, May 28, 1938). Reprinted in Geoffrey H. Moore (ed.), *Business Cycle Indicators*, Vol. I, Chap. 6 (Princeton University Press for National Bureau of Economic Research, 1961), p. 162.

[2] Geoffrey H. Moore, *Statistical Indicators of Cyclical Revivals and Recessions*, Occasional Paper 31 (New York: National Bureau of Economic Research, 1950). Reprinted in *Business Cycle Indicators*, Vol. I, Chap. 7.

[3] *Business Cycle Indicators*, Vol. I, Chap. 3, "Leading and Confirming Indicators of General Business Changes."

ber of series and on business cycle measures through 1958. Some indicators in the 1950 list were dropped and new ones were added. The 26 indicators finally selected included 12 leading, 9 roughly coincident, and 5 lagging. A supplementary list of additional indicators was also shown.

Another review of the cyclical indicators was completed in 1966, and the resulting new list is described in the NBER publication, *Indicators of Business Expansions and Contractions*.[4] This latest review covered 122 indicators. It included those indicators which previous studies suggested as most promising, as well as new indicators compiled since the earlier lists were issued. The principal features of the new list follow:

1. The major principle of classification is a fourfold grouping of U.S. indicators by cyclical timing: leading, roughly coincident, lagging, and other. The first three categories take into account timing at both peaks and troughs. The fourth group includes the economic activities which have an important role in business cycles but have displayed a less regular relation to them.

2. The type of economic process represented by the indicators is used as a secondary principle of classification, with emphasis on the eight processes that are important for business cycle analysis. The processes are (1) employment and unemployment; (2) production, income, consumption, and trade; (3) fixed capital investment; (4) inventories and inventory investment; (5) prices, costs, and profits; (6) money and credit; (7) foreign trade and payments; and (8) federal government activities. Each major process is subdivided into minor economic process groups that exhibit rather distinct differences in cyclical timing. For example, under fixed capital investment, new investment commitments are dis-

tinguished from investment expenditures. The cross-classification is summarized in table 1. (A ninth group, not included in the table, presents data on economic activity in other countries.)

3. The selection of indicators for this new list was facilitated by a plan for assigning scores to each indicator within a range of zero to 100. The scoring of each indicator reflects the desire not only to make the criteria for selecting indicators as explicit as possible, but also to increase the amount of information available to the user as an aid in evaluating their current behavior. The assigned scores must be considered rough rather than precise measures of the relative usefulness of different indicators. The scoring plan includes six major elements. The scores received by an indicator for each of the six elements indicate the particular merits and limitations of the indicator and are of special assistance to users of the indicators. When the subheads under these elements are included, some twenty different properties are rated. This list of properties provides a view of the many different considerations relevant to an appraisal of the value of a statistical indicator for current business cycle analysis. The six elements are:

   a. *Economic significance.* An indicator that broadly represents a strategic process was rated higher than one more narrowly defined, not only because its significance for business cycle analysis is likely to be greater but also because its significance is less likely to shift as a result of technological developments, changing consumer tastes, and similar factors.

   b. *Statistical adequacy* reflects the requirement that an indicator continue to measure the same economic process during future business cycle fluctuations when it is put to the hard test of current usage. Eight different factors were considered: type of reporting system, coverage of

---

[4] Geoffrey H. Moore and Julius Shiskin, *Indicators of Business Expansions and Contractions*, Occasional Paper 103 (New York: National Bureau of Economic Research, 1967).

TABLE 1. CROSS-CLASSIFICATION OF BUSINESS INDICATORS BY ECONOMIC PROCESS AND CYCLICAL TIMING

Economic Process \ Cyclical Timing	LEADING INDICATORS (36 series)	ROUGHLY COINCIDENT INDICATORS (25 series)	LAGGING INDICATORS (11 series)	OTHER SELECTED U.S. SERIES (16 series)
1. EMPLOYMENT AND UNEMPLOYMENT (14 series)	Marginal employment adjustments (5 series)	Job vacancies (2 series) Comprehensive employment (3 series) Comprehensive unemployment (3 series)	Long-duration unemployment (1 series)	
2. PRODUCTION, INCOME, CONSUMPTION, AND TRADE (8 series)		Comprehensive production (3 series) Comprehensive income (2 series) Comprehensive consumption and trade (3 series)		
3. FIXED CAPITAL INVESTMENT (14 series)	Formation of business enterprises (2 series) New investment commitments (8 series)	Backlog of investment commitments (2 series)	Investment expenditures (2 series)	
4. INVENTORIES AND INVENTORY INVESTMENT (9 series)	Inventory investment and purchasing (7 series)		Inventories (2 series)	

Minor economic processes and the number of series in each process are shown for each classification.

46

TABLE 1.   (CONT'D)

Cyclical Timing Economic Process	LEADING INDICATORS (36 series)	ROUGHLY COINCIDENT INDICATORS (25 series)	LAGGING INDICATORS (11 series)	OTHER SELECTED U.S. SERIES (16 series)
5. PRICES, COSTS, AND PROFIT (11 series)	Sensitive commodity prices (1 series) Stock prices (1 series) Profits and profits margins (4 series)	Comprehensive wholesale prices (2 series)	Unit labor costs (2 series)	Comprehensive retail prices (1 series)
6. MONEY AND CREDIT (17 series)	Flows of money and credit (6 series) Credit difficulties (2 series)	Bank reserves (1 series) Money market interest rates (4 series)	Outstanding debt (2 series) Interest rates on business loans and mortgages (2 series)	
7. FOREIGN TRADE AND PAYMENTS (6 series)				Foreign trade and payments (6 series)
8. FEDERAL GOVERN-MENT ACTIVITIES (9 series)				Federal government activities (9 series)

47

TABLE 2. SCORES FOR 25 ECONOMIC INDICATORS ON 1966 NBER SHORT LIST

Classification and Series Title*	First Business Cycle Turn Covered	Average Source	Scores, Six Criteria					
			Economic Signifi-cance	Statistical Adequacy	Conform-ity	Timing	Smooth-ness	Currency
(1)	(2)	(3)	(4)	(5)	(6)	(7)	(8)	(9)
Leading Indicators (12 series)								
1. Avg. workweek prod. workers, mfg.....	1921	66	50	65	81	66	60	80
4. Nonagri. placements, BES............	1945	68	75	63	63	58	80	80
12. Index of net business formation......	1945	68	75	58	81	67	80	40
6. New orders, dur. goods indus..........	1920	78	75	72	88	84	60	80
10. Contracts and orders, plant and equipment.................	1948	64	75	63	92	50	40	40
29. New building permits, private housing units	1918	67	50	60	76	80	60	80
31. Change in book value, mfg. and trade inventories...........	1945	65	75	67	77	78	20	40
23. Industrial materials prices........	1919	67	50	72	79	44	80	100
19. Stock prices, 500 common stocks.......	1873	81	75	74	77	87	80	100
16. Corporate profits after taxes, Q......	1920	68	75	70	79	76	60	25
17. Ratio, price to unit labor cost, mfg. ..	1919	69	50	67	84	72	60	80
113. Change in consumer debt............	1929	63	50	79	77	60	60	40
Roughly Coincident Indicators (7 series)								
41. Employees in nonagri. establ.........	1929	81	75	61	90	87	100	80
43. Unemployment rate, total (inverted)....	1929	75	75	63	96	60	80	80
205. GNP in constant dollars, expenditure estimate, Q	1921	73	75	75	91	58	80	50
47. Industrial production.............	1919	72	75	63	94	38	100	80

NOTE: Scores for the full list of 122 series covered in the study, and the weights used in averaging the different factors given above, are provided in *Indicators of Business Expansions and Contractions,* Occasional Paper 103, National Bureau of Economic Research, Inc., 261 Madison Avenue, New York, N.Y., 10016, 1967. NA = Not Available.

* Numbers preceding series titles are the identification numbers used in *Business Conditions Digest.*

48

TABLE 2. (CONT'D)

Classification and Series Title	First Business Cycle Turn Covered	Average Score	Economic Significance	Statistical Adequacy	Scores, Six Criteria Conformity	Timing	Smoothness	Currency
(1)	(2)	(3)	(4)	(5)	(6)	(7)	(8)	(9)
52. Personal income................	1921	74	75	73	89	43	100	80
56. Mfg. and trade sales.............	1948	71	75	68	70	80	80	40
54. Sales of retail stores............	1919	69	75	77	89	12	80	100
Lagging Indicators (6 series)								
44. Unempl. rate, persons unempl. 15+ weeks (inverted).............	1948	69	50	63	98	52	80	80
61. Bus. expend., new plant and equip., Q......................	1918	86	75	77	96	94	100	80
71. Book value, mfg. and trade inventories...................	1945	71	75	67	75	66	100	40
62. Labor cost per unit of output, mfg....	1919	68	50	70	83	56	80	80
72. Comm. and indus. loans outstanding ..	1937	57	50	47	67	20	100	100
67. Bank rates on short-term bus. loans, Q..................	1919	57	50	55	82	47	80	25
Summary Measures								
Average, 12 leading indicators		69	65	68	80	68	62	65
Composite index of 12 leading series	1931	NA	NA	NA	74	78	100	NA
Reverse trend adjusted composite index of 12 leading series, 1948–65	1948	NA	NA	NA	70	89	100	NA
Average, 7 coincident indicators	1948	74	75	69	88	54	89	73
Composite index of 6 roughly coincident series, 1948–65	1948	NA	NA	NA	90	91	100	NA
Average, 6 lagging indicators, 1948–65		68	58	63	84	56	90	68
Composite index of 3 lagging series	1948	NA	NA	NA	90	89	100	NA

49

process, coverage of time unit, measure of revisions, measure of error, availability of descriptive material, length of period covered, and comparability throughout the period.

c. *Conformity* measures the tendency of an indicator to exhibit upswings and downswings in accordance with past business cycles.

d. *Consistency* of its turning points relative to those in general business is obviously an essential quality of an indicator.

e. *Smoothness* of an indicator is important, since prevailing current trends, as well as the beginning of a new cyclical phase, can be discerned more promptly in an indicator which is smooth than in one which is irregular.

f. *Promptness.* For an indicator to be useful in current analysis, it must be up to date. Indicators that are released promptly, therefore, were assigned higher scores than those whose publication is late.

The new list of indicators includes 36 leading, 25 roughly coincident, 11 lagging, and 16 unclassified by timing, or 88 in all; 72 are monthly and 16 are quarterly. This list includes 13 not on the previous NBER list and omits 5. In addition, 14 indicators previously unclassified by timing were assigned a timing classification.[5]

---

[5] Since originally published, the 1966 list of indicators has been slightly modified. The full list, presently published in *Business Conditions Digest*, consists of 37 leading, 26 roughly coincident, 11 lagging, and 16 unclassified by timing. The short list consists of 12 leading, 8 roughly coincident, and 6 lagging. The series on average weekly overtime hours of manufacturing production workers was added to the full list of leading indicators. Changes in the short list of indicators include (1) substitution of the series on initial claims for state unemployment insurance in lieu of the nonagricultural placement series and (2) addition of the series on current dollar GNP.

A short list of 25 indicators having the relatively highest scores is also presented. This more selective list includes 12 leading, 7 roughly coincident, and 6 lagging indicators; 21 are monthly and 4 are quarterly.[5] The short list (table 2) involves little of the duplication in economic coverage that is provided, for various reasons, in the full list. Like the full list, it includes indicators representing the different timing and economic process categories.

Conformity and timing scores for the 88 indicators comprising the full list average 61. Average score for the 25 indicators on the short list is 72. These compare with conformity and timing scores for artificial indicators (i.e., cumulative random first difference indicators) approximately equal to zero. Some analysts have remarked that the scores for the selected economic indicators are not very high. They probably had in mind a bottom score of 50 rather than zero, the relevant comparison base.

The indicators included on the lists are cyclical indicators in the broad sense. They are intended to be helpful in measuring, anticipating, and interpreting short-run changes in aggregate economic activity. Although the indicators have been selected largely with reference to their behavior during periods marked off by a simple chronology of cyclical peaks and troughs in aggregate economic activity, their uses are by no means restricted to the identification of turning points from expansion to contraction and from contraction to expansion. The economic relationships and properties embodied in the set of indicators can be turned to account in analyses of various aspects of short-term economic developments, including acceleration or retardation in growth, inflation or deflation, the timing and magnitude of movements of particular economic aggregates such as the gross national product or nonagricultural employment, and so on.

IV. ANALYTICAL SUPPLEMENTS TO THE INDICATORS

Various analytical measures provide a further aid to understanding current and prospective business conditions. Some are designed to show how widespread and how fast movements are through the economy and others show summary or average behavior for the different types of indicators.

Diffusion Indexes and Rates of Change

Generally, the scope narrows and the rate of change moderates in the late stages of expansion and contraction. These phenome-

na are brought out by diffusion indexes and measures of rates of change. Diffusion indexes show how widespread an expansion or contraction is, and whether it is continuing to spread. Rates of change indicate the relative magnitudes of change.

Diffusion indexes show the percentage of companies, industries, or geographic areas which are experiencing rises over the time interval measured. For example, a diffusion index of employment in 30 nonagricultural industries would illustrate the percentage of these industries showing increases in employment in successive months.

Diffusion indexes are useful predictive tools because they almost always reach their highs and lows before the highs or lows in the corresponding aggregates, frequently leading by six months or more. They are also

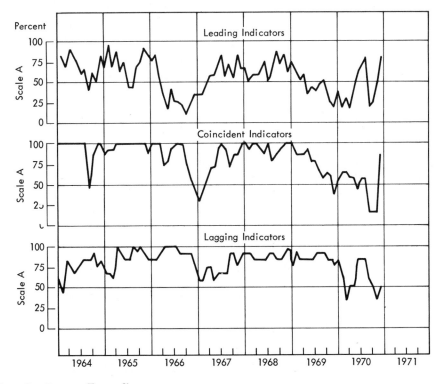

Chart 6   Percent Expanding

helpful in understanding business conditions, because they make clear that there is rarely a period, during either expansions or contractions, when business activities are all moving in the same direction. Crosscurrents are to be expected at all times. Activities that are moving counter to the general tide often provide a clue to the eventual reversal of the tide. Certain types of diffusion indexes show the percentage of businessmen expecting a rise in, say, sales or orders, as compared with the actual increase in these activities. Hence they show current opinion as to the state of business, and sometimes reveal widespread errors of optimism or pessimism.

One popular diffusion index shows the percentage of the NBER short list of leading, roughly coincident, and lagging indicators which are expanding from month to month (see chart 6). An individual indicator

is said to be expanding and is given a weight of 1 if its three-month moving average rises. An indicator showing no change is weighted as ½. The group percentages are based on simple arithmetic. If six and one-half of the twelve leaders are classified as expanding in a particular month, the percentage expanding for the leading group for that month is 54 percent. If six of the seven coinciders are expanding, the percentage expanding for the coincident group is 86 percent. If none of the six laggers is expanding and none remains unchanged, the percentage expanding for the lagging group is zero percent.

That the percentage expanding curves of even the coincident indicators should turn prior to general business is not unexpected. The individual coincident series do not move at precisely the same time. As soon as even one series changes direction from the

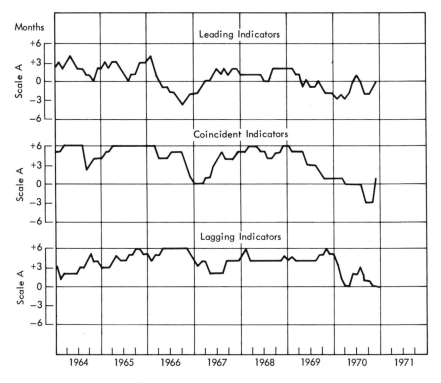

Chart 7   Average Monthly Duration

prevailing trend of the others, the percentage expanding curve also changes direction.

Because the simple percentage expanding diffusion index is rather erratic from month to month, a so-called duration of run diffusion index has been devised (see chart 7). The duration of run weighs the expansion and contraction of an indicator by the number of months the expansion or contraction has been under way. The duration of run for a single series is calculated simply by assigning a numerical value to the number of months the series has been continuously expanding or contracting.

After expanding (contracting) for six months, a series retains a value of +6 (−6). When a change in direction finally takes place, the run begins at −1 (+1). A leveling-off is considered a continuation of the previous month's classification.

The average duration of run for each of the three major groups of indicators is simply the sum of the duration of runs of the individual series in the group divided by the number of series in the group.

Rates of change for the principal business indicators show the magnitude of business changes from month to month. The average monthly change for any particular historical period provides a perspective against which to judge recent changes.

Cyclical Comparisons

Cyclical data can be compiled which compare the behavior of the indicators in

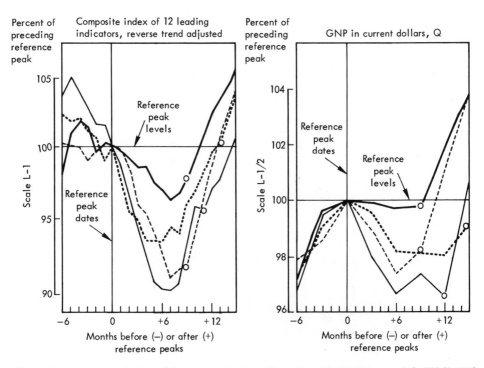

Note: Contractions beginning with reference peaks in November (IV Q) 1948 ——, July (III Q) 1953 - - - -, July (III Q) 1957 ....., May (II Q) 1960 ——.
° *Point at which this contraction reached a reference through.*

Chart 8   Contraction Comparisons

the current business cycle phase with their behavior during the corresponding phase of previous business cycles. Such data are helpful in placing a current movement in the historical perspective of previous cyclical developments.

Examples of such cyclical comparisons are illustrated in chart 8. The comparative courses of two statistical indicators are shown prior to, during, and shortly following the four periods of contraction in the economy since World War II. (The derivation of the composite index of twelve leading indicators used in chart 8 is described in the following section on composite indexes of leading, coincident, and lagging indicators.)

In making these comparisons, each monthly (quarterly) value of an indicator is shown as a percentage of the value at the previous peak. For example, six months following the NBER reference peak dates of November 1948, July 1953, July 1957, and May 1960, GNP was roughly 96.7%, 98.6%, 97.4% and 99.7% of its peak date value respectively.

Such comparisons may be helpful in providing a perspective on the implications of a current contraction. For example, it would be significant if GNP declined significantly more in the first three months of a current contraction than was typical during the first three months of previous contractions.

Similar charts are useful during recovery periods and can also be helpful in appraising the reasonableness of a forecast relative to historical experience. Illustrative

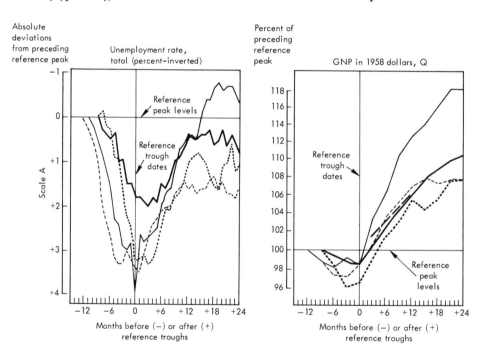

Note: Recoveries beginning with reference troughs in October (IV Q) 1949 ——, *August (III Q) 1954* ‑‑‑‑‑, *April (II Q) 1958* ....., *February (I Q) 1961*
1971 projections ooo

Chart 9   Recovery Comparisons

recovery patterns for the unemployment rate and GNP in constant dollars are shown in chart 9, along with a highly publicized forecast of the recovery pattern made at the beginning of 1971. These comparisons are made from business cycle peak levels and business cycle trough dates. In other words, the cyclical sectors of series are aligned at the trough dates so that, for example, the May 1958 and the February 1961 troughs are shown at the same point along the horizontal (time) scale. They are also aligned at their previous peak levels along the vertical scale so that, for example, the 1957 and 1960 peak values are shown at the same level. Previous peak levels are used as the comparison base so that differences in the severity of contractions, an important factor in the vigor of the subsequent rebound, are taken into account.

Because the cyclical experience is not one of all indicators moving neatly in prescribed patterns time after time, such comparisons are also useful in a more general way by bringing out relatively significant differences in a contemporary experience as it progresses.

Finally, they are helpful in forecasting future cyclical trends. Thus during the early stages of a current recovery, some judgments on its subsequent course may be made by reviewing the course of previous recoveries in the light of the severity of the preceding contractions and the economic policies to be followed.

Composite Indexes of Leading, Coincident, and Lagging Indicators

In studying the current economic situation, a broad view of the overall situation is available through the composite indexes. These indexes combine groups of indicators with similar timing behavior into a single series. Thus, leading indicators are combined into one index, coincident indicators into another, and lagging indicators into a third. While the indicators included in each composite index are heterogeneous in that they are not expressed in a common unit, they are homogeneous in the sense that they all have common timing behaviors. Thus each index provides a simplified measure of a significant complex of economic activities which experience cyclical fluctuations with roughly similar timing.

An amplitude-adjusted composite index can be constructed for any group of indicators in five steps: (1) compute the month-to-month percentage changes in each indicator; (2) proportionally adjust these percentage changes so that the average, without regard to sign, for each indicator over a period of years is equal to 1.0 percent per month; (3) average the adjusted percentages for each month for the several indicators, (4) adjust these averages so that they too will equal 1.0 percent per month over a period of years; and (5) translate these adjusted average percentage changes into a monthly index.

This procedure allows for the fact that some indicators, such as new orders, typically move in wide swings while others, such as the average workweek, experience narrow (but nevertheless significant) fluctuations. Thus, the impact of a change in an indicator is large or small *relative to its average movement.* For example, when an amplitude-adjusted percentage increase is 2.0, the indicator is rising twice as fast as its average rate of change over the base period used.

Weights based on the component indicators' values in identifying cyclical movements in aggregate economic activity are then applied. The weights used are the scores mentioned earlier.

The index for the leading group can also be adjusted further in order to make its long-run trend the same as that of the coincident index. This "reverse-trend-adjustment" has the effect of shortening leads at business cycle peaks and lengthening them at troughs, and thus makes the leads at peaks more uniform with those at troughs from

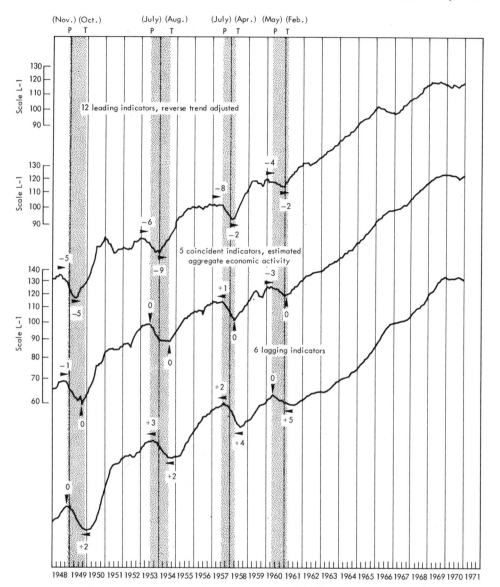

Note: *Reverse trend adjusted index of 12 leaders contains the same trend as the index of 5 coincident indicators. Shaded areas represent recessions as designated by the NBER.*

Chart 10   Composite Indexes of Leading, Coincident, and Lagging Indicators

cycle to cycle.[6] It removes much of the dif-

[6] Julius Shiskin, "Reverse Trend Adjustment of Leading Indicators," *Review of Economics and Statistics* (February 1967), p. 47.

ferences in magnitude among the leading, coincident, and lagging indexes, but retains the cyclical timing, with the leading index typically moving first, the coincident index next, and the lagging index last.

These leading, coincident, and lagging composite indexes are shown in chart 10.

Composite indexes that make use of the economic process groupings have also been compiled. Thus indexes are available for five of the economic process groups which are classified as leading. Each index is based on three or four indicators selected to provide broad coverage of the particular group without much duplication. The twelve leading indicators on the short list are all included, as well as seven additional leaders or nineteen in all. These indexes exhibit a rather striking family resemblance in timing as well as in general configuration, despite the variety of economic activities they represent. No one of them is likely to be mistaken for the index of coincident indicators or for the index of lagging indicators. These indexes are helpful in forecasting developments in the corresponding coincident indicators and lagging indicators sectors. Thus the index of capital investment commitments will be helpful in forecasting backlogs of investment commitments and investment expenditures.

Ratios of individual indicators to other indicators have frequently been devised to help in analyzing movements of economic activity. Thus, the ratio of manufacturers' prices to unit labor costs is a leading indicator in its own right. However, Geoffrey Moore has gone one step further and investigated the ratio of a coincident composite to a lagging composite and emerged with still another leading indicator.[7]

He explains the phenomenon as follows.

The ratio of coincident to lagging series gives concrete expression to the notion of cyclical imbalance or maladjustment. On each of the occasions when the leading indicators entered upon a general decline, the ratio of coincident to lagging

[7] Geoffrey H. Moore, "Generating Leading Indicators from Lagging Indicators," *Western Economic Journal*, VII, No. 2, (June 1969), p. 144.

series showed substantial declines paralleling, if not preceding, the declines in the leaders. Indeed, on two occasions, namely, in 1951 and 1966, when there was no general decline in the coincident indicators or in the economy as a whole, the ratio of coincident to lagging series declined, and so did the leading indicators. These situations of imbalance righted themselves before a recession got under way.

The lead times prior to the four post-World War II troughs in 1949, 1954, 1958, and 1961 were eight, eight, two, and two months respectively. The leads prior to the three peaks in 1953, 1957, and 1960 were seven, twenty seven, and thirteen months respectively.

V. FINDINGS BASED ON HISTORICAL BUSINESS CYCLES

The study of previous cycles over the past 100 years provides the basis for explanations of the sequence of events which permit us to make effective use of the different types of economic indicators. In addition to the knowledge that has accumulated about the timing sequence of economic processes and the behavior of diffusion indexes and rates of change, certain key findings, relevant to short-term analysis, emerge from studies of the successive ebb and flow of business activities. These can be summarized as follows:

1. Since 1854, peacetime business-cycle expansions have averaged about 26 months and contractions about 20 months. Since World War II, contractions have been shorter and milder, lasting only about a year from peak to trough. There is, however, considerable variation around these averages, and contractions have sometimes been longer than expansions.
2. The severity of a contraction in its early stages is often correlated with its ultimate severity. Historically, when

industrial production and employment have dropped sharply during the first six months of a contraction, the full decline has usually been large; when the initial declines were small, the contraction has usually been mild.

3. The rates of advance in aggregate economic activity during expansions have been more nearly uniform in different cycles than the rates of decline during different cyclical contractions. Thus a more accurate estimate can ordinarily be made of the rate of advance at the beginning of an expansion than can be made of the rate of decline at the beginning of a contraction.

4. The rate of expansion has usually been more rapid in its early stages—the first six to nine months—than in later stages.

5. The rate of rise during the early stages of an expansion has ordinarily been more rapid after a severe contraction than after a mild one.

6. Despite slower rates of expansion, previous peak levels have generally been regained much more quickly after mild contractions because the amount of ground to be recovered is smaller than that after a severe contraction.

7. There has been a dramatic improvement in economic stability during the post-World War II period, with a substantial decrease in the average monthly changes during both contractions and expansions. (This has been accomplished without adverse effects on the long-term rate of growth. In fact the long-term rate of economic growth was slightly higher in the 1960s than over the previous 60 years.)

VI. VARIATIONS OF THE TRADITIONAL BUSINESS CYCLE

The unusually long duration of economic expansion from 1961 through 1969 prompted business-cycle analysts to explore new ways of statistically describing the cyclical phenomena. Although obvious periods of contraction in the economy did not occur in the decade of the 1960s after 1961, there were periods when the economy as a whole definitely slowed its upward pace.

Such interruptions are variously referred to as subcycles, retardations, sluggishness, and in a recent paper by Ilse Mintz as "growth cycles."[8]

These interruptions do not imply that the forces which led to major reversals of the economy in the past are no longer operative. On the contrary, such periods are still characterized by actual contractions in some, but not all, of the cyclical indicators.

For example, there is an extra cyclical contraction phase in 1966–67 in both the money supply and the leading indicator composite index which is not included in the business cycle chronology. The absence of a corresponding business cycle movement can perhaps be explained by the actions taken to avert a major economic contraction after the leading indicators and the money supply started to decline.

The leading indicators, as a group, reached a peak in March 1966 and continued to decline for eleven months, reaching a low in February 1967 (see chart 11). The index of coincident indicators rose throughout 1966, leveled off at the beginning of 1967, and remained approximately level during the first five months of that year. GNP (in 1958 dollars) rose until the fourth quarter of 1966 and declined slightly in the first quarter of 1967. Industrial production did suffer a significant absolute decline.

These figures indicate that a serious threat to continued expansion developed in 1966 and early 1967, and that a short pause in real aggregate economic activity actually took place. But in terms of the effect upon

[8] Ilse Mintz, "Dating American Growth Cycles," paper prepared for the Colloquium on Business Cycles, National Bureau of Economic Research, September 24, 1970.

the national economy, the pause in expansion was neither of the magnitude, duration, nor scope required to qualify as a recession, and none was announced by the National

Bureau of Economic Research, the accepted authority in this field.

It is to be noted that both the rate of change in the money supply (considering

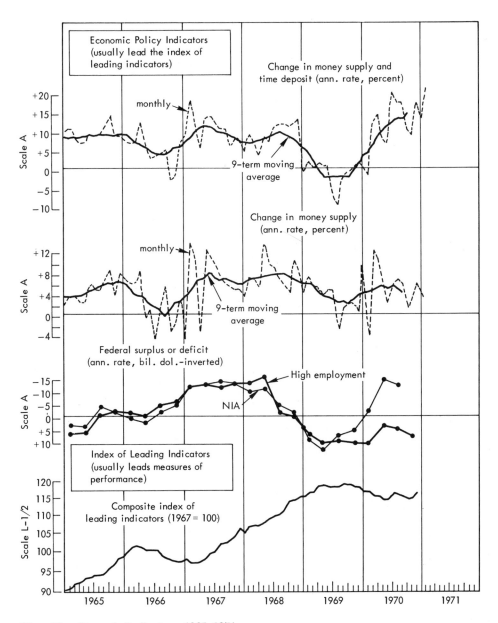

Chart 11 Strategic Indicators, 1965–1971

both the broad and narrow definitions) and the national income accounts deficit began to decline in late 1965, before the decline in the index of the leading indicators began in April 1966. The coincident index leveled off in the first quarter of 1967, but, as explained above, there was no contraction in the familiar sense. The reason appears to be mainly

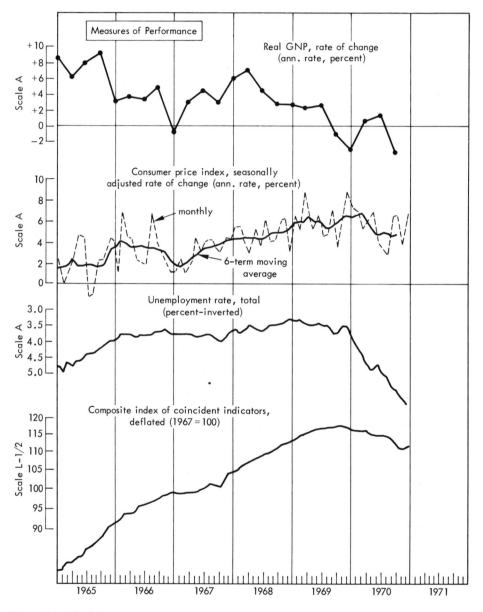

Chart 11   (Con't.)

that actions favorable to expansion in aggregate economic activity were begun a few months after the leading indicators started their decline. Thus the reduction in the rate of change in the money supply (considering both the broad and narrow definitions) was reversed sharply in the autumn of 1966 and the rate of increase reached a high level early in 1967. The budget deficit began to increase a little later. Late in 1966, after the rises in these economic policy variables had begun, the decline in the leading indicator index leveled off; and early in 1967 this index began to rise. The leads of the economic policy variables over the leading indicator index were unusually short at both turns, perhaps because money and the budget moved in conformity during this period. Other counter-cyclical measures were also taken during this period.

The indicator analyst clearly needs to be alert to recognize these expansions and contractions which may be too small or too short to be regarded as cyclical movements under the present NBER definitions. The work in the area is still of an exploratory nature. Various alternative ways of handling these episodes within the traditional business cycle concept are being studied.

Ruth Mack's work is more generally concerned with subcycles—or minor fluctuations, or extra cycles in specific indicators—as distinct from movements of the economy as a whole.[9]

In a technical paper, one of the authors discussed the 1961–69 cyclical expansion and its two periods of "retardation" in 1962 and in 1967.[10] For the most part, the retardations reflected periods of relatively slow rates of gain.

[9] Ruth Mack, *Information, Expectation, Inventory Fluctuation* (New York and London: National Bureau of Economic Research, Columbia University Press, 1967).
[10] Julius Shiskin, "The 1961–69 Economic Expansion in the United States: The Statistical Record," Technical Paper, *Business Conditions Digest* (Washington, D.C.: Bureau of the Census, January 1970).

In Mrs. Mintz's colloquium paper, a much more ambitious attempt is made to create a standardized method of measuring cycles in terms of deviations from a growth trend and in terms of relatively high and low rates of change.

In one approach, Mintz measures the monthly percentage deviations of an indicator from its 75-month moving average. The maximum positive or minimum negative deviations represent peaks; the minimum positive or maximum negative deviations represent troughs. In a second approach, monthly rates of change are classified as high or low relative to an average rate of change during three successive cycle phases.

Using these techniques, Mintz has tentatively designated seven unfavorable periods during 1948–70. Included are all four periods which have traditionally been considered cyclical contractions. Three additional unfavorable periods are added, 1951–52, 1962–64, and 1966–67. The amplitudes of three of the four contraction periods are twice as large as the average of all seven. Apparently 1960–61 is about average, and the magnitudes of the three added unfavorable periods are about half the average.

Two important findings have evolved from the Mintz work thus far:

1. All of the new cycles correspond to matching cycles in a composite of leading indicators. There are no instances when the leading indicators have had a significant upswing or downswing without a similar movement subsequently occurring in the deviation, or rate, cycle pertaining to the overall economy. That is when recessions and slowdowns are considered part of the same family of economic cycles; the leading indicators match one-to-one every cyclical peak and trough since 1945; lead at nearly every turning point; and do not lag at any, i.e., there are no false signals.

2. Moreover, every traditional contraction has begun within six months of the beginning of the downturn of a

rate cycle, or deviation cycle. Stated another way, if no contraction had begun within six months after the rate cycle downturn, then no contraction occurred. Such a hypothesis will help to appraise the significance of weakness in the leading indicators.

Work in the area of rate cycles and deviation cycles is still progressing. As additional relationships are examined and further hypotheses are formulated, new insight into probable future economic developments should become available.

VII. CONTEMPORARY INTERPRETATION AND USE OF THE INDICATORS

There are a great many important things which are not known about cyclical fluctuations. Thus, little is known about the factors determining the duration of different expansions and contractions. For this reason, the duration of these cyclical phases cannot be forecast reliably at the time they begin. Furthermore, during the late stages of an expansion, there is no historical basis for determining whether the weakening to follow will be mild or severe. Similarly, in the late stages of contractions, historical cyclical patterns do not indicate what the amplitude of the next expansion is likely to be.

Present statistical techniques are often inadequate for disentangling the more meaningful cyclical trends in the current statistics. For this reason we frequently can only guess when a current change is "cyclically significant." Sometimes months must go by before trends underlying the crisscross patterns in current figures become clear.

Caution must be exercised in using the leading indicators, not only because of the incomplete knowledge of their typical behavior and the statistical problems of measuring the current underlying trend, but also because different decisions reflected by

the leading indicators require different amounts of time to work out their effects. This is one reason why it is so difficult to forecast the amount of lead, and also why the lead is variable.

Economic Policy and Indicators

It is an important fact that the course implied by the leading indicators at any given time can be altered or reversed by subsequent events. This consideration is especially important during periods when monetary and fiscal policy actions exercise an important role in guiding the course of economic activity.

One of the liveliest controversies in economics today concerns the relative roles of monetary policy and fiscal policy in influencing changes in aggregate economic activity.

Although it is recognized that sequential relations alone do not demonstrate causality, studies of the records of conformity and timing of policy indicators during the past business cycles point to the following conclusions:[11]

1. The rate of change in the money supply has had a consistent record of leads and no lags at business cycle turns, a record that is not shared by the fiscal surplus or deficit indicators.
2. The mean leads of the money supply indicators are long, even when allowance is made for smoothing the indicators by moving averages; and the means substantially exceed the standard deviations.
3. The money supply indicators rarely skip a business cycle turn, but do exhibit a few extra turns not matched by business cycles. The fiscal indicators deviate more often in these respects.

[11] Julius Shiskin, "Economic Policy Indicators and Cyclical Turning Points," *Business Economics*, 5, No. 4 (Sep. 1970), p. 20.

An important characteristic of the timing of the money supply indicators is that the leads are occasionally so long that their meaning is ambiguous. For example, when a decline in the rate of change in the money supply occurs toward the end of a business expansion but stops even before the peak of the expansion is reached, both the money supply peak *and* trough antedate the contraction. Such long leads occur on several occasions when the rate of change in the money supply is compared to the business cycle chronology. The following procedure helps to resolve this problem.

Instead of trying to relate monetary or fiscal factors directly to bringing about changes in GNP, consider whether they affect something else which in turn affects GNP. It is plausible to suppose that these factors affect certain leading indicators, such as new orders, construction contracts, new business formation, and inventory accumulation, which in turn affect GNP. It is therefore appropriate to examine the timing of cyclical movements in the policy indicators with respect to those in the index of leading indicators.

The change in the money supply reached its turns earlier than the index of leading indicators on all but two occasions during 1920–70. The exceptions (both of which occurred in the 1920s) hardly damage the generalization, because the money supply indicator is very erratic and, when the leads are short, some coincidences or short lags are likely merely as a result of chance. The leads in the change in the money supply indicator over the index of leading indicators, are, of course, shorter than over the business cycle turns. There are no cases where the leads in the change in the money supply cross opposite turning points in the index of leading indicators. Furthermore, there are no extra cycles in the money supply indicator when it is compared with the leading indicator index. In general, the record for the change in the money supply is better when the comparison is made with the

leading index reference dates than with the business cycle dates. In short, when compared to the leading indicators, the money supply performs very much the way other leading indicators do when compared with GNP and other coincident indicators.

The budget indicators, on the other hand, match only about one-half and lead only about one-third of the turning dates in the leading indicator index. Thus, they do not meet the conditions required to qualify as leading, coincident, or lagging indicators when compared either to the conventional business cycle turning dates, or to the leading index turning dates.

At critical junctures, then, future changes *implied* by the leading indicators (as well as by other methods of economic forecasting) must be considered along with future changes *expected* as a result of economic policy actions.

Quantitative Forecasts of GNP Based on the Leading Indicators

Proceeding from the assumption that the reverse trend adjusted composite index of the leaders leads aggregate economic activity by six months, Geoffrey Moore has devised a formula for forecasting coincident indicators such as GNP or industrial production.[12]

The implication of the six-month lead is that the percentage change between *fiscal year* averages of the leading index should be closely correlated with the percentage change between the subsequent *calendar year* averages of the aggregates being forecast.

The percentage gain for a full fiscal year over the previous fiscal year does not become available until July; this is too long

[12] Geoffrey Moore, "Forecasting Short-Term Economic Change," *Journal of the American Statistical Association*, 64, No. 325 (March 1969), p. 15.

TABLE 3.   SUMMARY MEASURES OF ERROR IN SEVERAL SETS OF FORECASTS OF GNP

	Period Covered	Mean Absolute Error (%)	Correlation Coefficient, Forecast and Actual Change
1. Forecasts of annual percentage changes of GNP in current dollars			
a. Mean, 8 sets of business forecasts	1952–63	2.0	.78
b. Index of leading indicators	1952–63	1.8	.74
c. Extrapolation of preceding year's change	1952–63	4.1	−.43
d. Economic report.............................	1961–67	1.3	.34
e. Index of leading indicators	1961–67	0.8	.66
f. Extrapolation of preceding year's change	1961–67	1.8	−.04
2. Forecasts of annual percentage changes of GNP in constant dollars			
a. Suits's econometric model.....................	1952–67	1.5	.71
b. Index of leading indicators	1952–67	1.6	.71
c. Extrapolation of preceding year's change	1952–67	3.4	−.20
d. Economic report.............................	1961–67	1.1	.48
e. Suits's econometric model	1961–67	1.1	.12
f. Index of leading indicators	1961–67	0.4	.94
g. Extrapolation of preceding year's change	1961–67	1.6	−.44

Source: Moore, 1969. P. 18.

NOTE: The mean errors and correlation coefficients are calculated using the "actual" change the first official GNP estimates published in January or February following the year being forecast.

to wait to forecast the percentage gain for that calendar year. Therefore, a forecast is first made when the initial quarter of the new fiscal year becomes available.

In October, for example, the percentage change between the level of the leading composite index in the third calendar-quarter (which is the first quarter of the fiscal year) and the average level for the preceding fiscal year is obtained. This percentage is then used in the estimating equation derived from a linear regression fitted to percentage changes in the leading composite and in the aggregate being forecast.

Dr. Moore presents numerous tables comparing the results of the application of such a forecasting procedure with the results of using other well-known methods. One of his tables is reproduced here as table 3 in order to provide readers with an indication of the relative reliability of the leading indicator index approach.

It is clear from table 3 that this leading indicator approach compares favorably with the results of the other designated methods.

Dr. Moore comments, "The experiment suggests, therefore, that this mechanical use of the leading index can produce a standard of forecast accuracy which is not easy to surpass."[13]

Balances and Imbalances

It has been noted that in appraising the meaning of the movements of the statistical indicators, relationships between indicators are important, for example, the relationships between coinciders and laggers.

[13] Geoffrey H. Moore, "Forecasting Short-Term Economic Change," *Journal of the American Statistical Association*, 64, no. 325, (March 1969), p. 16.

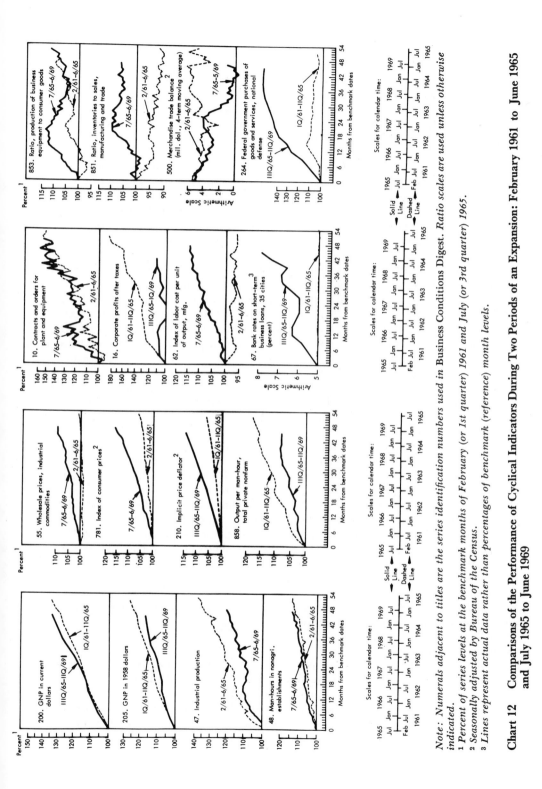

Note: Numerals adjacent to titles are the series identification numbers used in Business Conditions Digest. Ratio scales are used unless otherwise indicated.

[1] Percent of series levels at the benchmark months of February (or 1st quarter) 1961 and July (or 3rd quarter) 1965.

[2] Seasonally adjusted by Bureau of the Census.

[3] Lines represent actual data rather than percentages of benchmark (reference) month levels.

Chart 12   Comparisons of the Performance of Cyclical Indicators During Two Periods of an Expansion: February 1961 to June 1965 and July 1965 to June 1969

Relationships within individual indicators from one period to another are also important. The latter relationships often depict imbalances that may be occurring, such as excessive costs or excessive inventories.

In chart 12, a technique is portrayed which helps to visualize the development of such imbalances in the economy.

There are two starting points in the chart—February 1961, when an expansion got under way, and July 1965, when imbalances first began to appear.

The first panel shows several measures of aggregate economic activity. While there was not much difference in the performance of current-dollar GNP or total man-hours during these two periods, physical output behaved quite differently. Physical output (as measured by GNP in 1958 dollars) rose vigorously during the earlier period, at an annual rate of 5.7 percent, and more moderately, 4.2 percent per year, during the second period. The Federal Reserve Board's Industrial Production Index rose at a 7.4 percent annual rate in the earlier period and 4.8 percent in the later period. The differences are attributable to wholesale and consumer prices, which rose slowly during the first period, but rose rapidly and at an increasing rate in the later period. (See the prices indexes in the second panel of chart 12.) Prices, as measured by the implicit price deflator of GNP, rose slowly during the earlier period (at an annual rate of only 1.4 percent) and more rapidly (at 3.7 percent per year) during the second period.

Inasmuch as the increases in total man-hours were about the same during both periods (2.9 and 3.1 percent per year respectively), the slackening in the rate of increases of physical output could be attributed in large part to changes in productivity. This is borne out by the index of output per man-hour, which increased at an annual rate of 3.8 percent during the first period, but rose only 2.0 percent per year during the later period.

In the third and fourth panels, 1965–69 excesses and imbalances other than prices and productivity are shown.

The stability in labor cost and cost of business loans came to a halt in 1965, and both these indicators then rose vigorously. The ratio of inventories to sales, which at first had been declining fairly steadily as businessmen gained confidence in the prospects of continued business expansion, rose abruptly and very sharply from April 1966 to February 1967. Similarly, the ratio of production of business equipment to consumer goods, which had risen slowly during the earlier years, rose much more rapidly in 1965 and 1966. As these imbalances developed, more and more trouble spots showed up in the economy. The trade balance, which had been favorable for many years, declined sharply beginning in late 1967. National defense purchases, which were almost steady from 1961 to early 1965, rose very sharply towards the end of 1965 and through 1966 as U.S. participation in the Vietnamese conflict escalated. Corporate profits after taxes rose steadily during 1961–65, but from late 1965 through late 1969 there was virtually no improvement at all.

Thus the period of economic growth and stability which prevailed from 1961 to 1964 was replaced, starting in 1965, by the more familiar cyclical pattern of spreading imbalances throughout the economy.

These imbalances ultimately led to the sluggishness in the economy in late 1969 and 1970.

VIII. MAKING AN INDICATOR FORECAST

An initial step in making an indicator forecast, a step which will provide a broad statistical base for further investigation, is to utilize the leading indicator index-GNP forecast method devised by Geoffrey Moore.

A forecast devised by this method is regularly shown in the monthly *Statistical Bulletin* of the Conference Board.

It will be recalled that this method provides an annual forecast for the calendar year following the third quarter of a current year. All that is necessary in order to obtain the forecast is to obtain the percentage increase in the leading indicator index between its third quarter level and its average level for the four quarters preceding. The estimating equation will then provide the calendar year percentage change in GNP.

The results may then be appraised in the light of a comprehensive study of the movements of all pertinent indicators and policy considerations.

The further task of the indicator analyst, then, is to weigh the relative importance of favorable activities against those that are unfavorable. In doing this, he should carefully distinguish between activities that will have a future impact and those whose impact has already been felt.

To assist in making a comprehensive evaluation of current conditions, the scoresheet shown in table 4 has been devised.[14] The scoresheet is set up in such a way as to help spot an impending change in aggregate economic activity (output, employment, money flows, income, etc.)

In making use of the scoresheet, the analyst should bear in mind several general considerations.

Even the apparently simple designation of the trend of an indicator as being favorable or unfavorable is not really simple. One should at least take into account the direction of (1) the latest month's movement (2) the indicator's three-month average, or an even longer moving average if the indicator is especially erratic, and (3) whether a high or low appears to have been reached in the preceding six to twelve months. Many publications discuss the contemporary movements of the important indicators.[15]

Because the ascertaining of a current cyclical trend can be difficult and because the significance of the trend may vary, we suggest a weighting from $+1$ to $+3$ and from -1 to -3. The weighting procedure also helps to distinguish between long-lead and short-lead indicators. Thus, an uptrend should become discernible in the money supply indicator long before it appears in the average workweek. The assigning of merely a $+$ and $-$ respectively, would result in a simple canceling out of the effect of the two indicators for some time, whereas the weights enable changes to be evaluated more meaningfully.

The weighting also gives credence to the fact that at any point in time, data are not available for all the indicators through the same month or quarter. The average workweek, for example, is usually reported one month sooner than net business formation. If the workweek, then, has been moving upward for three months and net business formation for one month, it is reasonable to give the workweek a more positive weight than net business formation.

The weighting procedure is not intended to give greater weights to the "more important" indicators. The weighting procedure is designed simply to distinguish between more or less favorable trends.

Obviously, the value of the scoresheet is not solely in its one-time appraisal of conditions, but also in the change that occurs from one appraisal to the next.

[14] Julius Shiskin, "The 1961–69 Economic Expansion in the United States: The Statistical Record" Technical Paper, *Business Conditions Digest* (Washington, D.C.: Bureau of the Census, January 1970).

[15] The weekly *S.I. Reports* of Statistical Indicator Associates, and the monthly *Statistical Bulletin* of the Conference Board are two publications which specifically designate current trends of the indicators as favorable, unfavorable, or indeterminate.

TABLE 4. INDICATOR FORECASTING SCORESHEET

Developments to Appraise	Most Recent Cyclical Trend Favorable +1, +2, +3 Unfavorable −1, −2, −3	Comments
1. Change in Scope a. Diffusion indexes of individual leaders (Sec. E, D1, D5, D6, D11, D19, D23, D34) b. Diffusion indexes of individual coinciders (Sec. E, D41, D47, D54, D58) c. Diffusion indexes of short-list leaders as a whole (SIA percentage expanding, avg. duration of run, and trend summary) d. Diffusion index of short-list coincident as a whole (SIA percentage expanding, avg. duration of run, trend summary) e. Diffusion index of short-list laggers as a whole (SIA percentage expanding, avg. duration of run, trend summary) Score	_____ _____ _____ _____ _____ _____	**1. Change in Scope** In judging whether a change in scope (e.g., diffusion indexes) is favorable or unfavorable, it is necessary to keep in mind that the laggers must be treated in an inverted sense. As the scope of strength (weakness) in the laggers becomes widespread, the situation tends to become unfavorable (favorable) with respect to a change in the scope of the leaders, and subsequently in the scope of the coinciders. In interpreting the weights assigned to changes in scope, the timing sequence of inverted laggers, leaders, and coinciders must be kept in mind. The inverted laggers anticipate a change in aggregate economic activity by many months. The leaders anticipate such a change by several months. And the coinciders anticipate such a change by a few months. It must be remembered that diffusion indexes are erratic. This is especially true of a diffusion index of the components of an individual indicator. In addition to using statistical smoothing techniques, the interpreter needs to bring to bear on this appraisal any special information available which explains a movement as temporary.
2. Status of Summary Composite Measures a. Composite index of leaders (810, 811) b. Composite index of coinciders (820) c. Composite index of laggers (830) Score	_____ _____ _____	**2. Status of Summary Composite Measures** The inclusion of all three composites together here may seem unnecessary. However, corresponding movements in first the coinciders and then the laggers corroborate the movements in the leaders and add insight as to the length or magnitude of the movement being depicted by the leaders. Failure of the coinciders to respond, or a mild response, are signs of caution regarding the signal in the leaders. Failure of the laggers to respond could be similarly significant.

Source: Shiskin, *Business Conditions Digest*, January 1970.
NOTE: BCD indicates *Business Conditions Digest*; SIA indicates Statistical Indicator Associations; Numbers enclosed in parentheses are BCD indicator numbers, Section B unless otherwise noted.

TABLE 4. (CONT'D)

Developments to Appraise	Most Recent Cyclical Trend Favorable +1, +2, +3 Unfavorable −1, −2, −3	Comments
		The relative lengths of the leads (−) and lags (+) of the three composites in the post-World War II years provide a perspective for appraising the contemporary significance of the coinciders and laggers relative to the leaders. (Numbers in parentheses are indicator designations in *Business Conditions Digest*.)

	1948 Peak	1953 Peak	1957 Peak	1960 Peak
Leading (810)	−5	−6	−8	−4
Coincident (820)	−1	0	+1	−3
Lagging (830)	0	+3	+2	0

	1949 Trough	1954 Trough	1958 Trough	1961 Trough
Leading (810)	−5	−9	−2	−2
Coincident (820)	0	0	0	0
Lagging (830)	+2	+2	+4	+5

In the periods of sluggishness or slow growth in 1966-67 and 1969-70, relatively mild weakness in the leading composite was followed by very little response from the coincident and lagging composites.

3. *Excesses and Imbalances and Their Corrections*

The assessing of imbalances and their corrections as unfavorable and favorable respectively, is based on either the rate of change of the various indicators or their relative levels, or both.

Most of the measures of excesses are lagging indicators. Consequently, it is excessively high rates of increase and excessively high levels that are unfavorable. In this respect, it is important to have a fairly long-term history of the indicators' movements as a perspective for judging their contemporary status.

Such a perspective is especially important for judging the ratios included. The ratio of inventories to sales, for example, might be thought of as rising to unusually high levels prior to a contraction of

Developments to Appraise (cont.)	Trend
3. *Excesses and Imbalances and Their Corrections*	
a. Unit labor costs (62, 68)	——
b. Inventories (65)	——
c. Ratio of inventories to sales (Sec. E, 851)	——
d. Ratio of production of business equipment to consumer goods (Sec. E, 853)	——
e. Ratio of personal saving to disposable personal income (Sec. E, 854)	——
f. Consumer debt (66)	——

TABLE 4.   (CONT'D)

Developments to Appraise	Most Recent Cyclical Trend Favorable +1, +2, +3 Unfavorable −1, −2, −3	Comments
g. Ratio of coincident composite to lagging composite index (820 ÷ 830) h. Plant and equipment expenditures (61) i. Commercial and industrial loans (72) Score	——— ——— ——— ———	aggregate economic activity and dropping to unusually low levels prior to an expansion of activity. Much of the ratio rise, however, occurs during the contraction itself, and expansions generally have begun with the ratio at its high for the cycle, not its low. That is, the ratio of inventories to sales tends to lag at peaks. It is also true that the ratio of savings to disposable income has generally risen, not decreased, in the early stages of an expansion. For judging the ratio of the coincident composite index to the lagging composite index, the reader is referred back to the discussion at the end of section IV.
4. *Monetary Conditions* a. Short-term interest rates (67, 114) b. Long-term interest rates (115, 116, 117, 118) c. Free reserves (93) d. Money supply change (85, 98) Score	——— ——— ——— ——— ———	4. *Monetary Conditions* In appraising monetary conditions, it is imperative that one distinguish the varying timing sequences among the pertinent indicators. Bank rates on short-term business loans (67) among the short-term interest rates and mortgage yields (118) among the long-term interest rates are both lagging indicators. The other interest rate indicators are all classified as roughly coincident, as is the indicator of free reserves. With these indicators as others, it is important to realize what their timing classifications are with respect to their combined performances at both peaks and troughs of aggregate economic activity. For their favorable or unfavorable status at any specific time, it is wise to be aware of the timing differences that exist among them in their behavior at peaks and in their behavior at troughs. Remember, too, that the money supply change indicators are long-lead indicators with leads over business cycle turning dates of many months at both peaks and troughs; furthermore, as is explained above, they are useful in forecasting turning dates in the leading indicators.

TABLE 4.   (CONT'D)

Developments to Appraise	Most Recent Cyclical Trend Favorable +1, +2, +3 Unfavorable −1, −2, −3	Comments
5. Financing Activity		**5. Financing Activity**
a. Consumer installment debt change (113)	⎯⎯⎯	The acceleration or deceleration in the rate of raising funds by borrowing or by equity financing is depicted in measures of change which are all designated as leading indicators.
b. Mortgage debt change (33)	⎯⎯⎯	In more recent years, the indicators of change in the mortgage debt and the consumer debt have had considerably longer leads at peaks than at troughs. The change in bank loans in more recent years might better qualify as a coincident indicator.
c. Bank loans to business change (112)	⎯⎯⎯	Information on mortgage and consumer debt becomes available relatively late, and this should detract from the certainty of their favorable or unfavorable contemporary status.
Score	⎯⎯⎯	
6. Corporate Climate		**6. Corporate Climate**
a. Profit margins (15, 16, 17, 22)	⎯⎯⎯	All of the indicators included in this grouping are considered to be leading indicators.
b. Business failures (14)	⎯⎯⎯	The "Profit margin" indicators, in recent years, have led downturns in aggregate economic activity by many months but have been more coincident at troughs.
c. Common stock prices (19)	⎯⎯⎯	The prices-to-costs ratio has also tended to coincide at troughs in more recent years.
d. Ratio of prices to unit labor costs (17)	⎯⎯⎯	All of the corporate climate indicators have exhibited somewhat different longer-term trends in the 1960s than those previously in vogue. This behooves the appraiser of their current status to appraise their latest movements in the light of this new pattern of behavior.
Score	⎯⎯⎯	
7. Fixed Capital Investment		**7. Fixed Capital Investment**
a. New orders for producers capital goods (24)	⎯⎯⎯	The inclusion of plant and equipment expenditures, a lagging indicator, among what are mostly leading indicators stems from the fact that data on "anticipated" spending are available for this lagger. These
b. Construction contracts (8, 9, 10)	⎯⎯⎯	should not always be accepted at face value. Nevertheless, just as a
c. Housing permits and starts (28, 29)	⎯⎯⎯	

71

TABLE 4. (CONT'D)

Developments to Appraise	Most Recent Cyclical Trend Favorable +1, +2, +3 Unfavorable −1, −2, −3	Comments
d. New capital appropriations (11)		leading indicator may be given a favorable (unfavorable) status well before aggregate economic activity is expected to show a similar status, the anticipated plant and equipment spending figures may prompt the indicator analyst to give this indicator a more favorable (unfavorable) current status in spite of the spending performance to date.
e. Anticipated plant and equipment spending (61)		
f. Business formation (12, 13)		
g. Capital appropriations backlog (97)		The capital appropriations backlog is classified as a roughly coincident indicator, but it has led at peaks and lagging at troughs.
Score		
8. *Reflections of Demand for Goods*		8. *Reflections of Demand for Goods*
a. New orders for durable goods (6)		Many of these indicators frequently have movements which are of several months duration; involve changes of fairly large magnitude; and which are not preceded, accompanied, or followed by similar movements in aggregate economic activity. These movements cannot be dismissed as simply erratic; they are, on the contrary, well defined.
b. Buying for inventory (20, 31, 37, 245)		
c. Unfilled orders backlogs (25, 96)		
d. Vendor delivery schedules (32)		To designate all their ups and downs as "cyclically" favorable or unfavorable would in a very real sense distort their meaning. Their movements are actually cyclically irrelevant much of the time. But to designate all of their ups and downs as irrelevant would be to dismiss the movements which are relevant.
e. Length of buying commitments (26)		
f. Prices of sensitive materials (23)		
Score		One realistic answer, if not an especially objective one, is to judge or weight their movements in the light of what appears to be happening in indicators which are cyclically appropriate. Weakness or strength in indicators which accompanies similar weakness or strength in the cyclically appropriate indicators ought to be given greater cyclical significance.
		The indicator of prices of sensitive materials has had a rather checkered performance in the 1960s and its contemporary movements at this time probably should not be given too much cyclical weight.

72

TABLE 4.   (CONT'D)

Developments to Appraise	Most Recent Cyclical Trend Favorable +1, +2, +3 Unfavorable −1, −2, −3	Comments

9. *Labor Market Conditions*
a. Average workweek (1)
b. Layoffs (3)
c. Hirings (2, 4)
d. Help-wanted openings (46)
e. Initial unemployment claims (5)
Score
	_____
	_____
	_____
	_____
	_____
		9. *Labor Market Conditions*
		    The help-wanted indicator is a roughly coincident indicator in a grouping where all the remaining indicators are leaders. Actually, it does tend to lead at peaks, but it is consistently coincident at troughs. In recent years, its performance is very similar to that of the other indicators in this group designated as leaders.
		    The need to review an indicator's current movements within the perspective of its historical record should thus be repeated, as this caution is especially pertinent in appraising labor market conditions.

10. *Fiscal Considerations* a. Fed. surplus or deficit, NIA (Sec. D, 600) b. Fed. national defense purchases (Sec. D, 264) Score	_____ _____	10. *Fiscal Considerations* The empirical evidence discussed in the subsection entitled "Economic Policy and Indicators" (in section VI) would seem to suggest that the indicators considered in this grouping fall closer to the "outside influences" group (below) than to a separate grouping. This may seem inconsistent with the role which fiscal policy plays in current economic theory and in many of the econometric models designed to simulate the economy. Nevertheless, in their observable role as indicators, it is clear that their importance and timing varies from one major movement in aggregate economic activity to another. Appraisal of their status as favorable or unfavorable with respect to cyclical trends is difficult.
11. *Outside Influences* a. Strike threats, strikes, and their aftermaths b. Federal Reserve policy c. Federal budget policy d. War commitments	_____ _____ _____ _____	11. *Outside Influences* Far and away, labor disruptions in the steel industry have had the greatest effect on the course of aggregate economic activity in the post-World War II years. In the auto industry, General Motors strikes have had major repercussions, but they have not been nearly as persistent nor as pervasive as those related to a strike-threat or a strike in the

TABLE 4. (CONT'D)

Developments to Appraise	Most Recent Cyclical Trend Favorable +1, +2, +3 Unfavorable −1, −2, −3	Comments
e. International developments	___	steel industry. For purposes of the scoresheet, perhaps the impact can be oversimplified into the favorable impact of a strike-threat buildup, the unfavorable impact of a strike or no-strike letdown, and the favorable impact of a post-strike rebound.
f. Political developments	___	The two "policy" considerations included here refer not to the policy indicators as such, but to actions or contemplated actions of the Federal Reserve Board or the administration and Congress with respect to discount rates, interest rates, tax schedules, wage and price contracts, etc.
Score		The "war commitments" also refer to new or contemplated actions apart from those already reflected in the appropriate indicators.
12. Magnitude of Change		*12. Magnitude of Change*
a. Comparisons of movements with those in previous periods	___	The parentheses show the pertinent chapter section and subsection which discusses this consideration.
b. Severity of contraction in early stage (V-2)	___	Comparative movements and business cycle findings go hand in hand. Findings with respect to *relative* rates of change or of the time necessary to regain levels obviously require the calculations of comparative movements of the current experience and those of earlier experiences.
c. Rate of change in expansion and contraction (V-3, V-8)	___	
d. Rate of change over course of expansion (V-4)	___	The occurrence of such periods as 1962–64, 1966–67, and 1969–70 (at least through third-quarter 1970), which do not qualify as traditional cyclical movements, do not lend themselves directly to some of the business cycle findings. Yet, statistical comparisons of timing and magnitudes of movements of pertinent indicators within these periods alone and in contrast to the cyclical movements can provide helpful guideposts.
e. Rate of expansion in early stage (V-5)	___	
f. Regaining of peak levels in expansion (V-6)	___	
g. Ultimate level of expansion (V-7)	___	
h. Contractions with respect to growth cycle slowdown (V-9)	___	
Score		

IX. CONCLUSIONS

The difficulties of indicator forecasting are formidable. The interpreter of current change is confronted with false signals, pauses in underlying trends, variability in the performance of his most trusted series, shifts in attitudes arising from external events, and errors of measurement.

The contention that indicator forecasting is a mechanical manipulation of economic statistics is naive, in the light of the problems engendered by these difficulties.[16]

[16] It is true that phases of indicator forecasting such as the leading composite indicator-GNP forecast are essentially mechanical. Even here, however, numerous subjective decisions need to be made with respect to the derivation of the composite indexes involved. And in any case, the results yielded by this technique should be considered a first approximation rather than a final forecast.

It is obvious from the use of the scoresheet that while a framework of indicator relationships for use in current forecasting can be created, the decisions that are made within that framework are often subjective. The designation of the cyclical status of an indicator as favorable or unfavorable involves much more than simply deciding whether its latest month is up or down.

Moreover, even when the areas of economic activity covered by the framework have been filled in, no single unqualified answer emerges. The value of the scoresheet does not lie in a mere cumulation of the scores for the individual groupings. Rather than a printout of specific numbers, what emerges is an informed judgment on the part of the indicator forecaster on where the economy has been, where it probably is, and what the rough probabilities are of its moving in various directions, and the approximate speed of these movements.

EXPLANATORY NOTES FOR CHARTS

Shaded areas indicate business contractions as designated by the National Bureau of Economic Research. The months of cyclical turns are shown at top of charts with the designations P for peak, or T for trough.

Numbers in boxes near the right margin indicate the latest month (arabic numeral) or quarter (roman numeral) for which data are plotted or for which data are used in computing diffusion indexes and moving averages.

Diffusion indexes are placed at the center of the spans over which they are computed; e.g., a diffusion index comparing January and July data (6-month span) is plotted in April. Similarly, the rates of change and first differences are plotted at the center points of the spans involved.

Moving averages are also centered; e.g., a 4-term average for the months January through April falls between February and March on the time (horizontal) scale.

Quarterly series are identified by the letter Q after the title; the absence of Q indicates monthly data.

The scales are designated in the margin as follows: "Scale A" indicates arithmetic scale; "Scale L-1" indicates a logarithmic scale with 1 cycle in a given distance; "Scale L-2" indicates a logarithmic scale with 2 cycles in that distance; etc.

Short parallel lines drawn across the plotted lines indicate a break in continuity (data not available, changes in series definitions, extreme values, etc.)

MORRIS COHEN

Surveys and Forecasting

As a judgmental forecaster, I am exceedingly wary of magic formulas, no matter how prominent the formulator. In my view, the modern industrialized economy is a highly complex matter that cannot be captured in a simple equation, or a set of simple equations, or a simple system of relationships that happens not to be set in mathematical form. I am as leery of a monetarists's simplistic equations as I am of a neo-Keynesian.

For business purposes, it is not the name of the game merely to forecast total gross national product or the Federal Reserve's Industrial Production Index. Rather it is to forecast a whole host of variables which have a bearing on the success of the industrial or financial enterprise. That is why it is superficial to develop a set of four or five equations to yield the GNP in current or constant dollars.

SECTORAL FORECASTING

In plain words, I am a very strong advocate of forecasting procedures which involve sectoral forecasting. You do need to get a grand total. You do need the discipline of adding up all the pieces to see if you have

The author acknowledges the capable assistance of Mary Beth Seidenfeld in the preparation of this chapter.

a consistent whole. You have to do this, sector by sector, with as much disaggregation as is possible with available time and resources. This procedure should provide many checks and balances, and, hopefully, prevent you from falling into the trap that has lured so many eminent systems. I don't have to recount all those examples—from the Harvard barometers of the 1920s, to the postwar depression forecasts based on extrapolation of the simplistic Keynesian consumption function, to the more recent examples whether of the Keynesian or Friedmanite variety.

With regard to sectoral forecasting, I do not want to be in the position of denying the usefulness of developing statistical equations for each of the significant sectors. In the past, I have spent my own time doing this, and am always very interested in what is being done in the field. What worries me about these equations is that frequently the historical relationship breaks down in a critical period. Then the forecaster has to go back to the drawing board to redesign the equation or to manipulate the constant term, taking into account the last grievous error. Obviously, such a procedure is an integral part of the forecasting process. In a basic sense, we shall never develop the final system of equations which can then be frozen forever in the memory cores of the giant computers.

It has long been my position that surveys are a major input in judgmental forecasting. I refer, of course, to those surveys which are broadly called "anticipatory." In the business sector, the best anticipatory surveys are those which tap the planning process. The more objective the base, the better the survey. In the consumer sector, the best surveys are those which measure prospective actions and attitudes. The main emphasis should be on surveying the principal actor in the economic process. For example, I believe that it is more helpful in preparing a forecast to survey homebuilders on their building plans than to survey housing experts. Excluded by definition are surveys of economists, bankers, journalists, or other observers of the business scene. The principal interest is only with the key participants, those that are personally involved in decision making that affects the economy.

Surveys are needed because we cannot depend on the equations of the leading econometric models. We can never be certain that the equations aren't headed for a mistake because of a new development that was not contained in the historical relationships. This is particularly true for the consumer sector. Despite the vast amount of work that has gone on in the consumption function field, from Duesenberry and Modigliani to Houtthaker, I, for one, am unwilling to accept the equation results without question. I always want to know the results of the various consumer surveys before I make a final judgment in a consumer spending forecast. In the investment field, despite the recent spate of new research, I think it is fair to say that investment spending equations, particularly for fixed investment in the short-term, are subject to considerable error.

Simply put, anticipatory surveys are an indispensable tool of business forecasting which is concerned with sectoral analysis. Of course, if you are a monetarist, whether of the Friedman or neo-Friedman variety, surveys are almost useless. It seems difficult to develop surveys which have a monetarist

perspective. Perhaps some should be developed which would try to measure the impact of changes in monetary aggregates on consumer and business behavior. Surveys at present seem useful only to those who attempt to piece together the various sectors.

Anticipatory surveys, then, are essential because either the equations presently available are inadequate for the job, or as a check on those equations that are reasonably accurate. The surveys tell you what is actually happening in the marketplace. They are a hard discipline, since at times they contradict what everyone knows. Forecasters should recognize that there are fashions in methodology and in forecasts. Sometimes, influential forecasts emanating from key government agencies can have a very great impact. Every forecaster at times "knows" what is going to happen, particularly when Washington tells him so. Yet the economic agents in the real world may have different ideas. Anticipatory surveys enable the forecaster to tap this important source of information as an independent check on the forecasting community, whether public or private, and on forecasting methodology of whatever type.

Expectations play an important role in economics, in both theory and practice. From the Swedish economists to the present, some theoreticians have viewed the economy mainly from the standpoint of the expectations of the economic participants. (Professor Albert G. Hart of Columbia is a leading exponent.) It is the relationship of the expectation to the actual event that provides a better understanding. As for the business decision-maker, he is constantly subject to changing expectations in formulating plans for the future. How he views the future may provide a stronger foundation for capturing the dynamic interrelationships that at times may be too complex for even the most sophisticated model.

In this chapter I propose to discuss anticipatory surveys of plant and equipment spending, consumer attitudes and buying plans, inventory plans, and homebuilders' plans. Time and space do not permit an exhaustive analysis of all the anticipatory surveys now available. Specifically, I shall review the following:

1. Plant and equipment spending surveys
   a. Commerce-SEC survey of spending plans
   b. McGraw-Hill survey of spending plans
   c. The Conference Board capital appropriations surveys
   d. McGraw-Hill survey of new order expectations by nonelectrical machinery manufacturers
2. Consumer attitudes and buying plans
   a. Census Bureau survey of consumer buying plans
   b. Commercial Credit Company reports
   c. The Conference Board survey of consumer attitudes and buying plans
   d. University of Michigan Survey Research Center's index of consumer sentiment
3. Commerce surveys of expected sales and inventories by manufacturers
4. Housing surveys
   a. Fortune survey of homebuilders
   b. Commercial Credit Company findings on homebuying plans

PLANT AND EQUIPMENT SPENDING SURVEYS

The preeminent survey of anticipatory value is that conducted by Commerce-SEC on expected outlays for plant and equipment. In this connection, everyone in the field should be aware of the definitive articles which appeared in the *Survey of Current Business* in January and February, 1970. These articles represent a complete reconstruction of the plant and equipment spending surveys, which go back to 1948 (and on a quarterly basis, back to the second quarter of 1947). It is a seasoned survey and there is a great deal of information available to test its validity over all phases of the business cycle and over all phases of changing governmental policies.

Commerce-SEC Survey of Spending Plans

To review what everyone already knows, the Commerce-SEC survey reports quarterly anticipated spending for two quarters ahead, as well as now offering an annual projection both at the turn of the year and in March. Let me summarize my conclusions about the annual March survey figures. The survey has proved a reliable guide to spending for plant and equipment. There is, interestingly enough, a general tendency to overestimate outlays, but the range of error, I submit, is surprisingly small. In the 1950s, actual outlays proved to be 100% or more of those anticipated in two years. These were 1953 and 1955, when the error was 1%. In eight years actual outlays were less than expected. The worst year was 1958, when the shortfall was 6%. (Incidentally, in 1949, another recession year, the shortfall was also 6%.) During the 1960s, actual exceeded forecast in three years, and fell short in seven years. In 1963 and 1964, actual exceeded anticipated by 2%, and by 1% in 1965. The shortfall was 1% in 1961, 1966, and 1967; 3% in 1962 and 1969; 4% in 1968; and 5% in 1970. Thus, 1970 has proved the worst year since 1958 and 1949, and helps to explain why 1970 has been recorded as a year of recession.

The main source of error in 1970 was in the manufacturing sector. In manufacturing, actual outlays equaled or exceeded anticipated in four years of the 1950s, with 1955 some 7% over expected, 1953 some 3%, and 1951 and 1954 just 1% over the survey finding. In the shortfall category were 1956 and 1957, off 2%; 1952 and 1959, off 4%; 1960 (a recession year), off 5%; and 1958, the worst postwar recession year, off 9%. In the 1960s the breakdown was again the same as in the 1950s. The year in which actual outlays most exceeded expected outlays was 1964, with 5%. Then came 1965 with 3%, 1963 with 1%, and 1966 was right on the nose. The shortfalls came in 1961 and 1962 with 2%, 1967 and 1969 with 3%, 1968 with 5%, and again 1970 with 8%; 1970 was off the most since 1958. The shortfall in 1971 came to 2%.

There is a general tendency to overstate changes by broad industrial sector. In the 1950s, only in the mining and communications sectors actual outlays equaled or exceeded anticipated in the majority of years. During the 1960s, all broad sectors fell short a majority of the time. Year-to-year expected changes came closest, in general, to reality in the public utility sector, and were off the most in the railroad industry. In 1968–70 the overall survey shortfall averaged 4%; in 1966–70 it averaged 3%. In 1963–65 as well as in 1971 it came to 2%, and in 1956–62 it also averaged 3%.

In 1970, the first time the revised version of the survey had a chance to operate, the biggest error came in railroad spending, off 24% from expected (but similar to the shortfalls in 1966–68). Nonrail transportation outlays were 6% less than projected (matching the 1962–63 record), and public utilities were off 4%. Commercial firms outlay projections were quite accurate, while communications firms spent 4% more than expected. It is well known that 1970 was featured by relative strength in spending by public utilities and communications firms, yet the two survey errors were offsetting.

In 1971, the second year in which the revised survey operated, the shortfall was concentrated in the manufacturing sector, with the error amounting to almost 6%, with durables manufacturers finally reporting an 8% worse decline than anticipated in the prior March survey. While the nonmanufacturing sector's final figures were almost identical in total to the anticipated

number, there were wide differences among industries. The mining and commercial sectors spent a lot more than they had expected, while the railroads and airlines spent a lot less. The utilities came fairly close to their anticipated spending, as did other transportation companies, while there was a 4% shortfall in capital outlays by the communications group.

It is of major importance to recognize that the Commerce-SEC survey makes important adjustments to anticipated outlays, based on historical experience. All the private surveys in the field, including McGraw-Hill, do not make such adjustments. It may well be worthwhile to review for a moment what these adjustments have amounted to. On the average, Commerce-SEC adjusts the actual figures upwards by 5%. The bias correction factor has run as high as 8% in one year and as low as 4% in eight years. Reviewing the results for the twenty-three-year period from 1948 through 1970, one finds that the figures corrected for bias, i.e., the figures that are ordinarily cited, give better results in predicting the actual figures in eleven years. In ten years, however, the figures not corrected for bias give better answers, and in two cases there is no clear-cut difference. To repeat, the McGraw-Hill and other private surveys show only reported figures; they do not make any attempt to correct for systematic bias.

To be quite fair about this matter, it must be pointed out that the bias correction procedures have been a lot closer to reality in recent years. In the past decade or so, only the reported results for 1960, 1968, and 1970 were superior to those corrected for the bias factor. The failure of the bias correction factor to help the 1970 survey projections was particularly disappointing, since it represented the first year in which the thoroughly revised procedures were in full operation.

The correction factors in manufacturing are less important quantitatively than those in nonmanufacturing. Reported figures did better in thirteen years, while the bias-corrected figures were superior in five years, with the remaining five years a toss-up. Incidentally, the correction factor in manufacturing runs to 2% for the entire postwar period and just 1% in the past decade.

It is in the nonmanufacturing sector where the bias correction procedures assume greater significance. On average, Commerce-SEC has raised reported figures by 8% in the post-war period, and by 9% in the past decade. The bias correction works better in fourteen years, while the actual figures are superior in nine years. Again, in the most recent years, correcting for bias has helped. The biggest correction takes place in the category "commercial and other." Here the correction amounted to a whopping 16% on average in the postwar period, 17% in the past decade. In this subsector, the procedure helps, for the bias-corrected figures outperformed the reported results in nineteen years. Incidentally, the bulk of the entire survey correction factor is accounted for by this one group alone, over half in recent years and over 70% from 1955 to 1965. It must be noted, finally, that in actual practice the survey corrections are now shown only for the manufacturing sector and for all nonmanufacturing.

As noted, 1970 was the first year in which the new correction procedures operated without prior controls. For the total survey, the percent change from 1969 to 1970 reported in March 1970 was 5.7%; the "anticipated" figure was 10.6%, while actual turned out to be 5.5%. For manufacturing, the reported figure was 8.0%, "anticipated" was 9.8%, and actual a mere 0.9%. In nonmanufacturing, reported was 4.1%, "anticipated" was 11.1%, while actual was 8.8%. For 1971 the correction procedure proved to be quite accurate for the nonmanufacturing sector. For the manufacturing sector, however, the very small correction factor compounded the final error, since spending fell by over 6%, compared to a tiny "anticipated" decline. I leave it to the reader to

make the judgment whether it is all worthwhile. It may well be that if one is interested in individual pieces, the procedure is superior, but if one wants to know the total, it may get in the way.

The Commerce-SEC plant and equipment spending survey also reports anticipated spending for one and two quarters ahead. Space does not permit an exhaustive analysis of the errors involved in this procedure. That is just as well since large correction factors are introduced in the quarterly projections and the whole procedure was thoroughly revised in early 1970. A quick examination of the survey reported in March 1970, with the actuals reported in March 1971 (the first full year of the new procedures) indicates that the quarterly expectations must be treated somewhat more gingerly than the annual figures. For example, in March 1970 the survey reported anticipated spending in the second half of 1970 at a seasonally adjusted annual rate of $86.06 billion. Reality came to $80.26 billion, an error of $5.8 billion, or almost 7% within a period of less than a year.

The quarterly anticipations proved to be better in 1971, though they should still be judged inadequate. Compared to the March 1971 survey report, the actual first quarter was over $1 billion lower than expected and the second quarter a little under $1 billion lower, while the second half annual rate proved to be over $2.5 billion less than originally reported. The second half error in 1971 was half that for the second half of 1970.

It is clear that much more experience will be needed with the revised version of the quarterly projections before definite judgments can be made. In general, one can draw upon past experience to note that in periods of rising outlays, the quarterly anticipations tended to understate actual. As spending leveled off or declined, the reverse was true. The year 1970 qualifies as one in which spending leveled out, with the rate in the fourth quarter only a billion dollars higher than in the third quarter of 1969.

Again, 1971 spending actually leveled out in the second half of the year.

McGraw-Hill Survey of Spending Plans

While the Commerce-SEC spending plans survey can be regarded as the benchmark against which private surveys are measured, for important business forecasting purposes the information provided comes too late. Business firms have to prepare annual budgets for the following year before the year begins. For that purpose, the annual survey taken each fall by the McGraw-Hill organization provides critically needed information. The first of these surveys covered the year 1955 and it has been done every year since. This, too, is a seasoned survey, an indispensable tool for every forecaster. The earlier period was reviewed in a previous publication. Together with the data from 1964 through 1971 I can only repeat my earlier judgment that the McGraw-Hill preliminary fall survey of capital spending has proved to be surprisingly accurate.

A technical problem in appraising recent survey developments centers on the fact that the McGraw-Hill report ties in directly with the latest available Commerce-SEC survey. In practice, this means that the fall survey starts with annual current year data provided in the Commerce-SEC report issued in September of that year. Then the McGraw-Hill survey projects from these annual figures the following year's figures for its report, generally issued in early November. The revised version of the Commerce-SEC survey became available in early 1970, too late for the fall 1969 survey of 1970 spending plans. We shall have to use an estimate of the older version's 1970 spending plans. The earlier McGraw-Hill surveys shall have to be judged against the record of the prerevised actual Commerce-SEC results, rather than the latest revised version.

In the period 1964 to 1971, capital spending rose each year, and the McGraw-Hill early fall survey correctly forecast the direction of each year's change. In the period 1964 through 1966, the actual year's figures, however, averaged more than 10% higher than projected in the survey. In 1967 it overshot reality by 5%, and by 1% in 1968. It understated actual by close to 3% in 1969 and overstated it by 2% in 1970. Interestingly enough, for the period 1968 to 1971, the McGraw-Hill survey outperformed the reported Commerce-SEC anticipations in three out of four years: 1968, 1970, and 1971. In 1970, a difficult year for forecasters, the Commerce-SEC survey exceeded actual by 5%, compared to only 2% for McGraw-Hill. The reason, as we have learned, is that Commerce-SEC's correction factors proved to be inadequate. McGraw-Hill, which does not correct, came closer to the mark. For 1971, the early McGraw-Hill survey proved astonishingly accurate, so far as the total is concerned.

The early fall McGraw-Hill survey now has a competitor in the year-end survey regularly carried out by Commerce-SEC. Since there are only two observations, this latest survey cannot be deemed seasoned. It reported an increase of 9.3% for spending in 1970 over 1969; in the March survey, this was raised to 10.6%. Actuality proved to be an increase of 4.3%. As a matter of fact, the special McGraw-Hill survey taken in August 1969 came even closer than the others, having shown an increase of 4.9%. At the turn of 1971, the Commerce-SEC survey reported an anticipated increase of 1.4%, compared with actual of 1.9%, a far better performance than in the prior year. The moral is clear. The early fall McGraw-Hill surveys, including the occasional special earlier ones, are worthwhile inputs for forecasting purposes.

Mention should be made of the annual spring McGraw-Hill survey which usually comes out in April. The significance of this survey for forecasting purposes lies in the wealth of detail it provides on a variety of topics important for business forecasting. I refer specifically to matters such as capacity operation, changes in capacity, effects of changes in tax laws, special questions on spending for antipollution purposes and the like, as well as regional spending patterns. So far as the spending anticipations are concerned, they have overstated the actual year-to-year changes in 1966–71 by 2% to 4%. In 1969–70, the spring survey by McGraw-Hill was better than the March survey by Commerce-SEC. Again, this was probably due to the use of correction factors by the government agencies. For 1971, however, the spring survey overshot the mark by about the same proportion as the annual Commerce-SEC survey.

The Conference Board Capital Appropriations Surveys

Since the manufacturing sector is one of the most volatile spenders for capital goods, the capital spending surveys, whether Commerce-SEC or McGraw-Hill, must be compared with the Conference Board's capital appropriations surveys. As I have long argued, the capital appropriation represents the key capital spending decision. The capital budget, in effect, is the translation of the flow of capital appropriations. The capital budget data, of course, comprise the backbone of the capital spending surveys; they can be affected in total by financial considerations. Capital budgets can be pared when incoming cash flow is less than expected, for example. The capital appropriations, in large part, represent the pure capital spending decision. To be sure, the spending consequences of the appropriation are also influenced by other considerations like financial matters. In practice, what I am arguing for is a reconciliation of the capital spending surveys with the capital appropriation findings. If there is a conflict, I would tend to favor the capital appropriation results.

In recent years a great deal of work has been undertaken with the capital appropriation series, and I leave it to others to appraise the importance of this research. What is involved, really, is a forecast of the capital appropriation itself, since you need appropriations in future quarters to yield projections of capital spending as a consequence of previously approved appropriations. The basic research underlying the spending flows of the capital appropriation was done by Shirley Almon, who demonstrated an eight-quarter distributed lag between the approval and the expenditures which followed from the approvals. More recently, the Federal Reserve Bank of Cleveland has updated her work in their *Monthly Review* for October 1970.

For present purposes, I continue to use the capital appropriation as an indicator series for manufacturers' capital outlays, with particular emphasis on the backlog of unspent appropriations as perhaps the key series. In the more recent period, newly approved appropriations peaked in the second quarter of 1966, three quarters ahead of the peak in manufacturers' spending as reported by Commerce-SEC. It is more difficult to pick the trough in appropriations in 1967, since all the quarters that year were almost identical. Nonetheless I shall pick, subject to criticism I am sure, the first quarter of 1967. The trough in spending came in the fourth quarter of that year. Capital appropriations peaked again in the second quarter of 1969, with a peak in spending quickly following in the third quarter. After falling in the fourth quarter, spending leveled out through the third quarter of 1970, while appropriations ran at a substantially lower level.

The backlog of unspent appropriations is a smoother series than new approvals, and may therefore be more reliable. Once the backlog moves, it continues to move in the same direction for a number of quarters. Thus, in 1966 it peaked in the third quarter, two quarters ahead of the spending peak; it troughed in the second quarter of 1967, again two quarters ahead of the corresponding movement in spending.

It leveled out for a year starting with the third quarter of 1967, and this corresponded to a year of flat spending. The first major move up in backlogs came in the third quarter of 1968, and spending picked up appreciably two quarters later. The latest peak in backlogs came in the fourth quarter of 1969, and they fell all during 1970. By contrast, spending was stable during 1970, with a drop only in the fourth quarter of the year. Significantly, the appropriations backlog series fell further in the first half of 1971, and leveled out in the second half. Little wonder, then, that the Commerce-SEC survey for 1971 overstated manufacturers' capital outlays.

In recent years, the Commerce Department has been reporting figures that are roughly analogous to capital appropriations. I refer to the data on new starts of capital projects by manufacturers, and the carry-over of starts after taking spending into account. The starts series seems to lag the appropriations series by a quarter or two, and so does the carry-over series. In other words, peaks and troughs in the starts and carry-over series seem to come a quarter or two after the corresponding turns in the appropriations data. I would urge further research reconciling the two sets of data, since I feel confident that we could learn a great deal about the capital spending decision and the flow of actual capital outlays if we did. In the meantime, for indicator purposes, I would place greater reliance on the appropriations materials. Of course, one should now keep a watch on the Commerce data to check out the turns in the Conference Board's data.

McGraw-Hill Survey of Machinery Order Expectations

In general, I do not place a great deal of reliance on surveys of industry order expectations. Nevertheless, it is worthwhile to consider briefly one which has a bearing on capital spending. McGraw-Hill's economics department conducts a quarterly survey of nonelectrical machinery manufacturers covering the orders they expect to receive in the coming four quarters. McGraw-Hill also collects actual data in this field, and provides seasonally adjusted figures for actual and forecast, by quarters, or total nonelectrical machinery orders.

In recent years, the series has not behaved too badly. This has been particularly true when the forecasts showed little change. This has been followed by a roughly comparable real world. For example, in mid-April 1967 the survey showed little change for the next four quarters, and this was close to fulfillment. The same was true for the survey conducted in mid-November 1969. On the other hand, the survey conducted in mid-October 1967 projected a sharp rise in orders, which proved to be way off since orders remained virtually stable. In mid-February 1968 the survey once again showed a sharp rise in orders; reality turned out to be a rising trend, but a more moderate one. In mid-May 1968 the forecast for four quarters ahead showed a sizable drop; the actual drop in orders in that quarter turned out to be a third of that forecast. In mid-February 1969 the forecast turned out to be too low in projecting a rising trend in orders, and the same was true for the forecast reported in mid-May 1969. By mid-November 1969 the producers had caught up to the situation, and projected only a bit too much of a rise. The surveys conducted in 1970 all showed a sizable upswing for the fourth quarter of 1970, which didn't happen. All in all, I find the McGraw-Hill survey of nonelectrical machinery order expectations of limited value in forecasting capital spending. Perhaps those forecasters who are actually engaged in this business have developed correction factors which would make the survey more useful to those outside the nonelectrical machinery industry.

In summary, the capital spending and appropriation surveys are highly useful inputs in forecasting because they are based on the business planning process, which is taken very seriously by management. Capital budgets and capital appropriation approvals are reviewed at the highest company levels. Forecasters would be making a mistake to ignore them. However, as I have discussed, even these survey results cannot be taken at face value and must themselves be subject to judgment by the judgmental forecaster. This is true whether you want to accept the Commerce-SEC correction factors, or want to modify the survey projections for manufacturing because of developments in capital appropriations or the Commerce Department's figures on new starts and carry-over. Simple survey results should not be used directly in the forecast model.

CONSUMER ATTITUDES AND BUYING PLANS

Census Bureau Survey of Consumer Buying Plans

There has been a revival of interest in consumer surveys in recent years, a development which I welcome. The most imaginative new work has been done by the Census Bureau in its quarterly survey of consumer buying indicators. With a conscious and clear break from previous work which owes its main thrust to the pioneering activities of George Katona, the Census Bureau has significantly extended the boundaries of this field. In the limited space available, I could not do justice to this new survey. It does require careful analysis in the professional journals, and a lot more attention than it has received.

Much could be said about the bureau's new techniques. In practice, no matter how critical one can be about the nature of the questions asked and the nature of the statistical adjustments made to the raw data, the payoff will come in actually using the data in a real world forecasting setting. The new

Census Bureau survey was introduced in September 1967, and so cannot be considered a seasoned survey in the same sense as the capital spending surveys. My comments necessarily will have to represent preliminary judgments about the usefulness of their findings. It goes without saying that these surveys provide a wealth of information on actual purchases and income changes in the consumer sector, a body of data that is yet to be mined by analysts.

Since the Census Bureau survey is continuously undergoing revisions in methodology, one will have to confine attention to the most recent period, namely, 1968 through 1970. The basic thrust of the bureau's survey is to provide buying plans data which can be directly inserted into a GNP model. In reports issued in 1970, the bureau has shown indexes of expected unit purchases based on average of 6-month and 12-month buying plans (mean purchase probabilities) for cars and homes, as well as the actual purchase probabilities for 6- and 12-month buying horizons for both items. For homes, the bureau also uses a 24-month planning horizon. For furniture and carpets, major appliances, and home improvements, it reports buying plans on a 12-month horizon. All this, of course, is done on a seasonally adjusted basis. Since this material is incorporated in the reports issued by the Commercial Credit Company, I shall defer comment until I review them shortly. The Census Bureau, however, does show household automobile purchases, actual and anticipated, for six-month periods in a series of quarterly reports beginning with 1968. Thus, in the report issued in mid-February 1971, they showed the number of anticipated car purchases, seasonally adjusted annual rate, for the first half of 1971.

A review of the data for 1968 through 1970 does not leave one with a great deal of confidence in the results so far reported. In 1968 and the first half of 1969, they survey understated actual auto purchases. This happens to be one of the critical periods in forecasting consumer behavior, since it will be recalled that the tax surcharge was supposed to dampen spending. The 8% error for anticipated purchases in the second half of 1968, shown in the survey taken in July and reported in late August, is particularly damaging. I must quickly add, however, that the next survey taken in October 1968 and reported in November, had caught up with the changed situation; the shortfall for the six months ending with the first quarter of 1969 was only 1%. But the damage was done, since the surge in car buying in the summer of 1968, along with the whole consumer sector, demonstrated one of the major errors in forecasting in recent times on the part of so many analysts. Starting with the report covering anticipated purchases for the second half of 1969, the surveys have overshot the mark, with the greatest error coming in the figures for the first half of 1970. Survey results for the second half of 1970, to be sure, must be appraised in the light of the General Motors strike.

In all candor, I find the recent Census Bureau survey findings disappointing so far as projected car buying is concerned. True, the bureau is using a system of correction factors in the form of regression equations. In other words, the bureau does not simply rely on direct reports of buying plans, but prefers to adjust them considerably. The answer, hopefully, to the question of using the data for forecasting purposes may well be the accumulation of many additional observations to provide the appropriate correction factors.

Commercial Credit Company Reports

The Commercial Credit Company issues quarterly reports, now called "Economic Prospects" (formerly "Consumer Buying Prospects"). The basic inputs for these reports are the Census Bureau surveys just discussed. The principal editor of the Commercial Credit reports is the same person who has played a major role in the Census Bureau's revamped procedures. What the Commercial Credit Company reports do is to translate the implications of the Census Bureau surveys directly into dollar figures which are appropriate for a GNP model. Indeed, as noted, that was the main thrust behind the Census Bureau's surveys, but evidently it was deemed inappropriate for the bureau, as a government agency, to carry out itself the full implications of its surveys. The private Commercial Credit Company feels no such restrictions. Thus, in commenting on the Commercial Credit reports, one is also talking about the Census Bureau approach.

For the forecaster, the consumer buying reports provide a gold mine of information. If these reports could live up to expectations, a major part of the short-term forecasting problem would disappear. Available are seasonally adjusted data for new auto expenditures, appliances, and other durables (i.e., the whole consumer durable sector), as well as unit sales for autos. In addition, spending on new home purchases is shown, along with single-family homes in units. The quarter in which the report is issued, for which there is limited data, is projected along with the next two quarters. I shall confine my attention to the consumer durable sector, leaving the housing part for later review. The full array of forecasts—three, six, and nine months ahead—is available in great detail only for 1970 and 1971. Spending on new autos, aside from parts, was shown for only a portion of 1969.

The auto and parts forecasts for 1969 were wide of the mark. Those made for three quarters ahead fell short of the mark by as much as $5 billion annual rate. The six months ahead forecasts were somewhat better, and the three months ahead projections were best of all. The shortest projections were only close to the mark in the second half of the year; they were off considerably for the first half.

Spending projections for new autos alone in 1970 were better. They overshot the mark for the first quarter by a little more than a billion-dollar rate. They fell short in the second quarter by as much as \$2 billion. For the third quarter they were off just as much, except for the projection three months ahead which proved quite accurate. The fourth quarter of 1970, of course, was way off, but that was the result of the General Motors strike and should not be counted as a test.

For 1971, three-month projections were a lot better than six- or nine-month forecasts. Spending for automobiles in the third quarter, of course, was missed badly owing to the significant impact of President Nixon's proposed lifting of the excise tax. Once that was known, the next forecast caught the change.

Turning now to the household durables and appliance sector, an important group which needs help from surveys, the errors were considerable, considering the fact that fluctuations here are somewhat less dramatic than they have been for cars. For example, the closest forecast for the second quarter of 1969 came in the nine months ahead projection. The closer one came to reality, the worse the projection for a quarter when spending rose sharply. The comparisons for the rest of 1969, it must be noted, were rather good. But then, in the first quarter of 1970 when spending again rose sharply, the survey failed to catch it, even looking ahead three months. As actual spending leveled out in 1970, the predictions for the second quarter were better than for the first, but still understated. It was not until projections for the third quarter that the survey caught up with the level of outlays, and even here, those for the next three months shot way ahead of actuality. For the fourth quarter of 1970, predictions for nine months ahead were closer to the mark than those made six and three months ahead. In 1971, the survey projections tended to run ahead of actual outlays.

To repeat, the Census Bureau and Commercial Credit reports are still too new to be subjected to a full and comprehensive analysis. Many more observations will be needed. The desired end result is ideal from the forecasters viewpoint, namely, dollar figures for consumer spending. But these require a series of questions, correction factors, and statistical interpretation which needs to be considerably improved. In the meantime, one should view these projections cautiously.

The Conference Board Survey of Consumer Attitudes and Buying Plans

Finally, to round out the publicly available comprehensive consumer surveys, one should consider the bimonthly Conference Board survey of consumer attitudes and buying plans. Unlike the Census Bureau, the Conference Board has renewed the approach it started in earlier years. Since 1967 the board has been providing bimonthly readings on six-month buying plans on autos, homes, a series of major appliances, carpets, and vacations. Except for seasonal variations, no attempt is made to adjust these data.

To appraise these data, one must compare changes in the buying plans indicators with changes in consumer spending for autos and for household equipment and appliances. Perhaps the most damaging critique of the survey is the complete failure to catch the auto boom of 1968. Spending rose sharply in the first half of the year and still more in the second half. From a high level of plans reported in the 1967 surveys of May-June, July-August, and September-October, the rate ran lower right through the report for July-August 1968. It rose moderately in the next bimonthly report and again in the final 1968 report, but the damage had been done. Spending then essentially leveled out in 1969, close to the fourth-quarter 1968 rate. Auto buying plans ran at a lower rate in the first two bimonthly reports for 1969 and then rose sharply to a new high sustained level for the series. Reality, as noted, bore no resemblance to these fluctuations in plans. In 1970, buying plans rose sharply in the March-April report, after two reports with much lower figures. In the first three quarters of 1970, spending on autos ran at a much lower level than in 1969, a fact not captured by the surveys. For 1971, the survey failed to catch the gyrations caused by the proposed lifting of the auto excise tax. The report for September-October, in particular, showed a weakening in auto demand at a time when sales were running at very high levels.

Neither did the buying plans for major appliances appear helpful in projecting movements in spending on household equipment and major appliances. Spending rose sharply in 1968, but buying plans, then not seasonally adjusted, did not rise sharply, say compared to the year-ago level. In the six reports for 1968, only the January-February survey reported plans up from a year earlier. Starting with the report for July-August 1969, figures are now shown on a seasonally adjusted basis. In 1969 spending rose moderately, and then quite sharply in the first quarter of 1970. It leveled out for the last three quarters of the year. Buying plans fluctuated a lot more, rising sharply in the last bimonthly report for 1968, even stronger in the reports for March-April and May-June 1969. In late 1969 and 1970, it is difficult to interpret them as signaling a leveling out. Indeed, in the September-October and November-December reports for 1970, there was a much lower level of buying plans, which proved to be an incorrect signal. Indeed, spending on furniture and household equipment rose quarter by quarter starting with the fourth quarter of 1970 and throughout 1971. True, plans rose in the March-April 1971 report, but then fell back in the following two reports. In the last two reports for 1971, there was a moderate rise in buying plans.

To sum up the relatively short period in which the Conference Board's buying plans survey has been in operation in recent

years, it seems to add little that a forecaster could use in practice.

University of Michigan Index of Consumer Sentiment

No analysis of anticipatory surveys would be complete without at least a mention of the work done at the University of Michigan's Survey Research Center under the direction of one of the pioneers in this field, George Katona. My position here is to review those surveys that are publicly available, and in recent years only subscribers have received the full reports. To be sure, after each year the Survey Research Center publishes the reports, still abridged, but these cannot be used for forecasting. The only figures publicly available from the Survey Research Center is its Index of Consumer Sentiment,[1] and it can be found in

[1] The Survey Research Center uses the answers to five questions to calculate the Index of Consumer Sentiment. The questions are:
1. "We are interested in how people are getting along financially these days. Would you say that you and your family are better off or worse off financially than you were a year ago?"
2. "Now looking ahead—do you think that a year from now you people will be better off financially, or worse off, or just about the same as now?"
3. "Now turning to business conditions in the country as a whole—do you think that during the next twelve months we'll have good times financially, or bad times, or what?"
4. "Looking ahead, which would you say is more likely—that in the country as a whole we'll have continuous good times during the next five years or so, or that we will have periods of widespread unemployment or depression, or what?"
5. "About the big things people buy for their homes—such as furniture, house furnishings, refrigerator, stove, television, and things like that. For people in general, do you think now is a good or bad time to buy major household items?"
The index is calculated by using a relative

the Census Bureau's *Business Conditions Digest*. Each quarter's report receives wide attention.

How should one interpret the findings? Two possibilities exist, one as a guide to significant changes in the personal saving ratio (the percent of post-tax incomes that is saved), the other as an indicator of changes in spending on consumer durable goods. In the recent period, two years stand out when the personal saving ratio increased sharply, as these things go—in 1967, and again in 1970. The Michigan index ran at a sustained high rate through most of 1966 and all of 1967, after having fallen sharply from the peak levels reached in 1965 and early 1966. It is difficult to cite this as a case when the abrupt rise in the saving ratio was predicted. The more recent case yields more satisfactory results. The index dropped quarter by quarter from the peak reached in early 1969, and this continued through the second quarter of 1970. Indeed, it is my impression that the recent case represents one of the forecasting coups of the Michigan index.

The record is somewhat less favorable for 1971. After leveling out in the second half of 1970, the consumer sentiment index rose moderately in the first half of 1971, and then leveled out in the second half. The average index for 1971 was higher than for 1970. Yet the saving ratio for 1971 was a bit higher than for 1970, though it did show a drop in the second half of 1971 compared to the first half.

When it comes to usefulness in predicting consumer durable outlays, the record is also mixed. As noted earlier, consumer spending on durables rose sharply in 1968. In 1967 and 1968, the index remained on a

fairly high plateau. Spending rose more moderately in 1969, and essentially leveled out in 1970. Again, as pointed out, the index dropped sharply starting with the second quarter of 1969. One is tempted to argue that the Michigan index overstated the case with its sharp drop. On the face of it, it might be reasonable to ask why spending didn't actually decline.

This necessarily cursory review of the Index of Consumer Sentiment is far too brief and quite unrepresentative of the vast amount of work in the field of consumer surveys going on at Ann Arbor for many years. Yet, as a practical matter, it does suggest that the index is useful as an overall test of consumer confidence, without advocating that it be used in a precise way to forecast consumer durable outlays.

For the record, mention must be made of a vast body of anticipatory data provided by Albert E. Sindlinger and Company in its reports to its private clients. Since these materials are not generally available to the average forecaster, no comment can be made one way or the other about its usefulness. Suffice it to say that a number of important business firms, especially the auto companies and large retailing and consumer durables organizations, seem to find the flow of data provided by weekly telephone interviews of considerable help. One may express the hope that these data will become available for further research and analysis.

It is safe to say that despite major efforts in the field, the consumer surveys have not been as good predictors of the future as have the investment surveys. In investment, surveys tap actual formal planning procedures that are taken very seriously by large companies. For consumers, the planning process is obviously quite informal. The decision time horizon for consumers may represent a more difficult problem that has so far escaped the techniques used. Consumer surveys now use various time horizons, from one month to two years, but results thus far are not as good as forecasters require. Yet the potential payoff still seems large, and

---

score for each question separately, taking the percentage giving favorable or optimistic answers and subtracting the percentage giving unfavorable answers, and adding 100. See *1970 Survey of Consumer Finances* by George Katona, Lewis Mandell, and Jay Schmiedeskamp, University of Michigan, Survey Research Center, Institute for Social Research, pp. 247–248.

additional resources should be devoted to existing efforts. The work of the Census Bureau in developing correction factors through regression techniques is certainly a step in the right direction. Perhaps other outside groups and analysts should join in this research in the needed effort to improve the usefulness of consumer anticipatory surveys.

COMMERCE SURVEYS OF MANUFACTURERS' INVENTORY AND SALES EXPECTATIONS

One area where forecasters can make major errors is in predicting inventories. It is therefore incumbent to consider in depth the major new survey in anticipations of recent years: the Commerce survey of manufacturers' inventory and sales expectations. For forecasting purposes, the inventory part is of course far more important, though sales expectations are needed for a proper perspective on inventories. This survey is now in its twelfth year; although methodology has changed somewhat in preparing the expectational data, the whole period should be reviewed. In my judgment, this survey is not receiving the attention it deserves from either the press or the forecasters. It is the only short-term expectational survey of business operations that is carried out by the government, with a broad sample, and directly tied to the data reported as actuals by the Census Bureau.

Each quarter, the survey reports manufacturers' expected inventory levels for the end of the quarter, for which one month's information is usually available, and for the next quarter ahead, as well as corresponding data for sales expectations. Separate totals are available for both durables and nondurables manufacturers.

I have examined the full record of this survey, starting with the report issued in December 1961 and going through the report issued in March 1972. In the early years of

1961 and 1963 the survey sometimes overstated the inventory change and sometimes understated it. On the whole the record is good, with the largest error occurring in March 1964, when the inventory change two quarters ahead overstated reality by almost $1 billion, at quarterly rates. Starting with September, 1964, the survey consistently understated the inventory change through practically all of 1966. The errors here were larger than before and on numerous occasions the error exceeded $1 billion. Starting with the September 1965 report and continuing through the September 1966 report, the survey failed to catch the changes three and six months out, and by relatively large amounts. Beginning with the June 1967 report, the survey has consistently overstated the changes in manufacturers inventory levels, but the errors have been relatively small. The biggest discrepancies were reported in the September 1968 survey, when the three months projections understated the change by over $1 billion (one of the few such cases of a minus sign in the four-year period), and the six months projection overstated the change by almost $1 billion. In most other cases, the error can be measured in terms of tenths. Interestingly enough, the survey overstated inventory change each quarter in 1971, one and two quarters out, with but one exception.

On the whole, so far as total manufacturers' inventory change is concerned, the survey has earned an important role in any forecaster's toolkit. In a review of the survey prepared by the Federal Reserve Bank of Cleveland in its weekly *Economic Commentary* of May 11, 1970, calculations were made of the average differences between anticipated quarterly changes and actual changes. For the first anticipation, the average absolute difference was ±$1.9 billion and for the second anticipation ±$1.5 billion. The corresponding root mean square difference was ±$2.6 billion for the first anticipation and ±$2.1 billion for the second. The bank concluded from its review that "although the differences between anticipated changes and actual changes in manufacturers' inventories are sizable, the surveys of manufacturers' inventory expectations continue to be useful aids to economic forecasters and public policymakers. The survey results appear to be fairly reliable during periods of inventory adjustments."

When it comes to separate forecasts for durables and nondurables, however, the record is not quite as good. In other words, there are compensating errors, a fact of life that many forecasters are grateful for. In general, the pattern of error noted above for total projected inventory change is also applicable to the durables sector. The pattern is less comparable for the nondurables sector. In 1969 and 1970, broadly speaking, frequent understatements of change by nondurables manufacturers compensated for the overstatements by the durables sector. As expected, the nondurables group came closer to the mark than did the hard goods group, since as everyone knows, their changes are less volatile. For the decade under review, in ten cases the soft goods group hit the change exactly on target, compared to seven times for the hard goods group.

Turning to the sales expectations, surely a desirable thing to know not only for appraising inventory changes but for the trend of the manufacturing sector itself, comparison was made between actual and projected in terms of percent deviations from actual percent changes in sales. Again, the survey results seemed to run in cycles. Generally speaking, in 1963–65 sales expectations were understated more often than not, with the biggest errors coming in the March 1965 report for the second quarter ahead, namely, that spring, and for the second quarter ahead reported in December 1965. In both cases the underestimation was at least 2½%. Starting with the September 1966 report, however, the survey swung to overstating sales changes on average. This then went back to understatements with the June 1968 report, a trend which lasted almost all through 1969. In 1970, by contrast, the trend had swung back to overstatements.

For 1971, understatements about equaled overstatements. Eighty-one observations were available for the totals, and separately for the durables and nondurables sectors.

Confining attention to those cases where the error in predicting the quarter-to-quarter sales change was 1% or more, this happened six times for all manufacturing when projecting one quarter ahead, with projected falling short of actual; seven times for durables; and surprisingly, 13 times for nondurables. Two quarters ahead occurred under these circumstances six times for all manufacturing, but thirteen times for durables companies and nine times for nondurables companies. In cases where sales were overstated by 1% or more, the record shows nine occurrences for all manufacturing, fourteen times for durables, and nine times for nondurables. For two quarters ahead, this happened eight times for the total group, twelve times for the durables sectors, and ten times for nondurables.

The Federal Reserve Bank of Cleveland in its weekly *Economic Commentary* for May 18, 1970 also reviewed these manufacturers' sales expectations. It tested the survey in terms of the percentage point difference between anticipated quarterly change and actual change. For the first anticipation, the average absolute error was ±1.3%, and for the second anticipation ±0.8%. The corresponding root mean square errors were ±1.7% and ±1.2% respectively. The bank concluded its review of the sales expectations series as follows.

> Surveys of manufacturers' sales expectations appear to underestimate sales during periods of economic expansion and to overestimate sales during economic slowdowns. On balance, it appears that the annual estimates provided by the surveys of manufacturers' sales are subject to considerable error. Nevertheless, quarterly estimates produced by the surveys are considerably more accurate than naive forecasts of manufacturers' sales.

All in all, this is not a bad record. More positively, I would state that the Commerce survey of manufacturers' expectations deserves more attention than it gets. The errors are frequently rather small, as these things go, and the projections require some care, particularly to determine whether or not you are in a particular cycle of error, up or down, as noted in several examples. The manufacturers' inventory survey has earned its keep. I, for one, now always pay the closest attention to its findings in real world forecasting, and I would suggest that all sectoral forecasters do the same.

HOUSING SURVEYS

Changes in housing starts and the consequent changes in outlays for residential building represent one of the major forecasting problems that still seem difficult to solve. This is an area that has long been ripe for a major effort by anticipatory surveys.

Fortune Survey of Homebuilders

The only publicly available survey in the field is that conducted by *Fortune* magazine twice a year, reported in the April and October issues. Unfortunately, the record of this survey suggests that much more work has to be done before it can be used as a major input by forecasters.

In the April 1964 issue, *Fortune*'s homebuilders' survey reported builders' projections for the current year of 1,740,000 private nonfarm housing starts. It actually turned out to be 1,525,000, or a decline from the 1963 level. This had followed a period in which "builders projected an average rise of 12% in the past three years (1961–63) and while the actual rise averaged 8%, they were closer to the mark than most projections which looked for little or no change."[2] In April 1965 the homebuilders again reported

[2] "Business Roundup," *Fortune* (April 1964), 28.

an expected increase, and again an actual decline took place. In 1966 the same sequence occurred but the error was even larger. Thus in October 1965, the projected rise for 1966 was 3%, which became 8% in the April 1966 report. Actually the decline was almost 20%.

The upturn in the housing market was caught accurately by the survey reported in the April 1967 issue. In the October 1967 issue, the further rise in 1968 that actually took place was also projected but not quite as fully as reality. Even with the April 1968 report, the full rise was missed. But when housing starts dipped by 3% in 1969, the survey failed to catch the change in trend. A sharp rise was projected both in the October 1968 and April 1969 issues. By October 1969 the survey for the current year had caught up with events, but it then went ahead to predict a further moderate rise for 1970 as compared with a slight dip. It should be noted that in the October 1970 issue, a major rise was projected for 1971, and by April 1971 this was confirmed and a succeeding large advance was projected for 1972.

From the record, it would appear that the *Fortune* homebuilders' survey catches upturns, but seems to miss a leveling out or declines. Obviously, the findings have to be used with caution in forecasting housing starts.

Commercial Credit Company Homebuying Findings

Are the consumer surveys of any help in this forecasting problem? Looking at the Commercial Credit Company reports which cover single-family homes only, it doesn't seem so. The experience here is limited, of course, and the fluctuations in single-family housing in 1969 and 1970 were not as dramatic as in the earlier years that proved so troublesome for the *Fortune* surveys. Single-family housing sales, according to these reports, fell throughout 1969. The declines were first caught in the survey one quarter ahead for the third quarter of the year. Similarly, only the three months ahead projection for the fourth quarter of the year caught the flavor of actual developments. In 1970, the trend of actual home sales was the reverse image of 1969, i.e., they rose quarter by quarter. Again, the survey failed to catch the upswing. For example, all the reports for the second quarter of the year missed the actual upturn in that quarter. It was really not until the three months ahead projection for the fourth quarter of 1970 that the survey caught the sharp upturn which was taking place. Even for 1971, which was surely a boom year in housing if there ever was one, it was not until the projections for the final quarter of the year that the survey began to signal the significant advance.

It is regrettable that the anticipations surveys in the housing field do not yet live up to their promise. I would strongly urge that a major effort be made in this field to improve the anticipatory surveys, with particular emphasis on home and apartment builders. The Census Bureau should be encouraged to use its field operations to survey the builders covered in its monthly reports.

CONCLUSION

In summary, after reviewing the performance record of the major anticipatory surveys in recent years, I remain optimistic about their usefulness for forecasting. Since I believe that forecasting is a difficult business in which humility is a notably desirable trait, I advocate a judicious application of anticipatory surveys, including those where the record has not been totally satisfactory. There are few techniques that have been totally satisfactory, and each technique goes through a fashionable period in which it is proclaimed as the new saviour.

Anticipatory surveys, even the best ones, must be used with care. They cannot be taken at face value; they should not be taken at face value. Arithmetical or regression correction techniques should be used, and more work needs to be done in this area by both the data-supplying agencies and the individual forecasters.

Anticipatory surveys should not be used as the only technique, or even the principal technique. But they do represent a major forecasting input which all forecasters should use. Those who ignore the results of anticipatory surveys do so at great peril. The more important the forecast, i.e., turning points or unusually large changes, the more carefully should the survey materials be analyzed in sectoral forecasting. Finally, anticipatory surveys which are so close to the marketplace itself aid the forecaster in better comprehending the complexities of the modern economic world as well as in appreciating the possibilities of abrupt change from previous historical relationships.

BIBLIOGRAPHY

Adams, F. Gerard, "Consumer Attitudes, Buying Plans and Purchases of Durable Goods: a Principal Component, Time Series Approach," *Review of Economics and Statistics* (November 1964), 347–55.

———, "Prediction with Consumer Attitudes; Time Series—Cross Section Paradox," *Review of Economics and Statistics* (November 1965), 367–78.

Almon, Shirley, "The Distributed Lag Between Capital Appropriations and Expenditures," *Econometrica* (January 1965), 178–96.

———, "Lags Between Investment Decisions and their Causes," *Review of Economics and Statistics* (May 1969), 193–206.

An Appraisal of Data and Research on Businessmen's Expectations about Outlook and Operating Variables, Report of Consultant Committee on General Business Expectations, organized by the Board of Governors of the Federal Reserve System, at the request of the Subcommittee on Economic Statistics of the Joint Committee on the Economic Report (September 1955).

Burch, S. W. and H. O. Stekler, "Forecasting Accuracy of Consumer Attitude Data," *Journal of the American Statistics Association* 64 (December 1969), 1225–33.

Byrnes, James C., "An Experiment in the Measurement of Consumer Intentions to Purchase," *1964 Proceedings of the Business and Economic Statistics Section, American Statistical Association,* 265–279.

Campagna, A. S., "Capital Appropriations and Investment Decisions," *Review of Economics and Statistics* (May 1968), 207–14.

Cohen, M., "The Capital Goods Market: A New Survey of Capital Appropriations," *The Conference Board Business Record* (October 1956), 418–34.

———, "Forecasting Capital Goods: The Eclectic Approach," *Business Economics* (September 1970), 66–72.

———, "The NICB Survey of Capital Appropriations," *The Quality and Economic Significance of Anticipations Data.* (Princeton, N.J.: Princeton University Press, 1960), 299–320.

———, and M. R. Gainsbrugh, "Consumer Buying Plans: A New Survey," *The Conference Board Business Record* (November 1958), 449–67.

Consumer Survey Statistics, Report of the Consultant Committee on Consumer Survey Statistics, organized by the Board of Governors of the Federal Reserve System, at the request of the Subcommittee on Economic Statistics of the Joint Committee on the Economic Report (July 1955).

Crockett, Jean, Irwin Friend, and Henry Shavell, "Impact of Monetary Stringency on Business Investment," *Survey of Current Business* (August 1967), 10–27.

Eisner, R., "Realization of Investment Anticipations," in *The Brookings Quarterly Econometric Model of the United States,* ed. J. S. Duesenberry et al. (Chicago: Rand McNally, 1965), 95–128.

Evans, Michael, and Edward W. Green, "The Relative Efficacy of Investment Anticipations," *Journal of the American Statistical Association* 61 (March 1966), 104–16.

Federal Reserve Bank of Cleveland, "The Relationship between Capital Appropriations and Expenditures," *Economic Review* (October 1970), 3–11.

Ferber, R., "The Role of Planning in Consumer Purchases of Durable Goods," *American Economic Review* (December 1954), 854–74.

Ferber, R., and R. A. Piskie, "Subjective Probabilities and Buying Intentions," *Review of Economics and Statistics* (August 1965), 322–25.

Foss, M., "Manufacturers' Inventory and Sales Expectations: A New Survey," *1961 Proceedings of the Business and Economic Statistics Section, American Statistical Association,* 234–51.

———, "The Structure and Realization of Business Investment Decisions," *The Quality and Economic Significance of Anticipations Data.* (Princeton, N.J.: Princeton University Press, 1960), 387–403.

———, and V. Natrella, "Ten Years Experience with Business Investment Anticipations," *Survey of Current Business* (January 1957), 16–24.

Friend, Irwin, "The Predictive Ability of Consumer Intentions to Purchase," *1964 Proceedings of the Business and Economics Statistics Section, American Statistical Association,* 178–85.

————, and F. Gerard Adams, "Predictive Ability of Consumer Attitudes, Stock Prices and Non-attitudinal Variables," *Journal of the American Statistical Association* (December 1964), 987–1005.

————, and Robert Jones, "Short-Run Forecasting Models Incorporating Anticipatory Data," *Conference on Research on Income and Wealth, Models of Income Determination*, Princeton, N.J.: Princeton University Press, 1964.

————, and W. Thomas, "Predictive Ability of Plant and Equipment Anticipations," *Journal of the American Statistical Association*, 6 (June 1970), 510–19.

Freund, W. C. and R. A. Kavesh, "Seasonal Patterns in Business and Consumer Attitudes," *1962 Proceedings of the Business and Economic Statistics Section, American Statistical Association*, 11–24.

Greenberg, E., "Appropriations Data and Investment Decision," *Journal of the American Statistical Association* (June 1965), 503–15.

Gruber, A., "Purchase Intent and Purchase Probability," *Journal of Advertising Research* (February 1970), 23–27.

Hart, A. G., "Capital Appropriations and the Accelerator," *Review of Economics and Statistics* (May 1965), 123–36.

Jorgenson, D. W., "Anticipations and Investment Behavior," in *The Brookings Quarterly Econometric Model of the United States*, ed. J. S. Duesenberry. (Chicago: Rand McNally, 1965), 95–128.

————, "Capital Theory and Investment Behavior," *American Economic Review* (May 1963), 247–59.

————, and J. A. Stephenson, "Anticipations and Investment Behavior in U.S. Manufacturing 1947–1960," *Journal of the American Statistical Association* (March 1969), 67–89.

Juster, F. Thomas, "Anticipations and Purchases: An Analysis of Consumer Behavior," Princeton University Press for the National Bureau of Economic Research, 1964.

Juster, F. T., "Anticipatory and Objective Models of Durable Goods Demand," *American Economic Review* (September 1972), 564–79.

————, "Consumer Anticipations and Models of Durable Goods Demand: The Times Series Cross Section Paradox Re-examined," in *Economic Forecasts and Expectations*, ed. Jacob Muneer. New York: National Bureau of Economic Research, 1969.

————, "Consumer Anticipations Surveys: A Summary of U.S. Postwar Experience," Paper presented to the 9th CIRET Conference, Madrid, September 1969.

————, "Consumer Buying Intentions and Purchase Probability: An Experiment in Survey Design," *Journal of the American Statistical Association* 61 (September 1966), 658–96.

————, *Consumer Expectations, Plans and Purchases: A Progress Report*, Occasional Paper No. 70, New York: National Bureau of Economic Research, 1959.

————, and Paul Wachel, "University, Expectations and Durable Goods Demand Model," *Human Behavior in Economic Affairs: Essays in Honor of George Katona*, Amsterdam: North-Holland Publishing Company, forthcoming.

Katona, George, "Anticipations Statistics and Consumer Behavior," *American Statistician* (April 1967), 12–13.

————, "Federal Reserve Board Committee Reports on Consumer Expectations and Savings Statistics," *Review of Economics and Statistics* (February 1957), 40–45.

————, *The Powerful Consumer*. New York: McGraw-Hill Book Company, 1964.

————, *Psychological Analysis of Economic Behavior*. New York: McGraw-Hill Book Company, 1951.

————, et al. *Survey of Consumer Finances*, University of Michigan, annual issues 1960–70.

Keezer, D. M., R. P. Ulin, D. Greenwald, and M. Matulis, "Observations on the Predictive Quality of McGraw-Hill Surveys of Business Plans for New Plants and Equipment," *The Quality and Economic Significance of Anticipations Data*. (Princeton, N.J.: Princeton University Press, 1969), 369–85.

Liebling, H. I., and J. M. Russell, "Forecasting Business Investments by Anticipation Surveys and Econometric Models in 1968–1969," *1969 Proceedings of the Business and Economic Statistics Section, American Statistical Association*, 250–60.

Maynes, E. Scott, "An Appraisal of Consumer Anticipations Approaches to Forecasting," *1967 Proceedings of the Business and Economic Statistics Section, American Statistical Association*, 114–23.

Modigliani, F., and H. M. Weingarten, "Forecasting Uses of Anticipatory Data on Investment and Sales," *Quarterly Journal of Economics* (February 1958), 23–54.

Mueller, E., "Effects of Consumer Attitudes on Purchases," *American Economic Review* (December 1957), 946–65.

————, "Ten Years of Consumer Attitude Surveys: Their Forecasting Record," *Journal of the American Statistical Association* (December 1963), 899–917.

Okun, A., "The Value of Anticipations Data in Forecasting National Product," *The Quality and Economic Significance of Anticipations Data*, (Princeton, N.J.: Princeton University Press, 1960), 407–51.

Pashingian, B. P., "Accuracy of the Commerce-SEC Sales Anticipations," *Review of Economics and Statistics* (November 1964), 398–405.

The Quality and Economic Significance of Anticipations Data, Princeton, N.J.: Princeton University Press, 1960.

Reports of Federal Reserve Consultant Committees on Economic Statistics. Hearings before the Subcommittee on Economic Statistics of the Joint Committee on the Economic Report, 84th Cong., 1st sess., July 19–26, October 4–5, 1955.

Shavell, Henry, and John T. Woodward, "The Impact of the 1969–70 Monetary Stringency on Business Investments," *Survey of Current Business* (December 1971), 19–32.

Sindlinger, A. E., "Techniques for Measuring Buying Plans with Consumer Confidence," *1962 Proceedings of the Business and Economic Statistics Section, American Statistical Association*, 158–68.

Statistics on Business Plant and Equipment Expenditure Expectations. Report of the Consultant Committee on Business Plant and Equipment Expenditure Expectations, at the request of the Subcommittee on Economic Statistics of the Joint Committee on the Economic Report (July 1955).

Survey Research Center, University of Michigan, "Fifteen Years of Experience with Measurement of Consumer Expectations," *1962 Proceedings*, 169–72.

Theil, H., and R. F. Kosobud, "How Informative Are Consumer Buying Intentions Surveys," *Review of Economics and Statistics* (February 1968), 50–59.

Tobin, J., "On the Predictive Value of Consumer Intentions and Attitudes," *Review of Economics and Statistics* (August 1959), 1–11.

White, W. H., "Lags Between Actual and Reported Fixed Investment," *IMF Staff Papers* (July 1969), 240–66.

Wimsatt, G. B., and J. T. Woodward, "Revised Estimates of New Plant and Equipment Expenditures in the United States, 1947–69," *Survey of Current Business* (January 1970), 25–40 and (February 1970), 19–39.

NANCY H. TEETERS

Federal, State, and Local Budgets

The purchase of goods and services by government—federal, state, and local—absorbed nearly 23 percent of total output in 1970. Nine percent of personal income was derived from government transfer payments to persons. A forecast of government expenditures is therefore frequently crucial in making projections of economic developments. Equally important are forecasts of government revenues. Government revenues, at least in the long run, tend to set limits on government spending and in the short run permit calculation of the current surplus or deficit.

Because so much of our total output or gross national product is channeled through government, decisions concerning the size, composition, and sources of both revenues and expenditures directly affect the operation of the economy. In the past ten years, the aggregate relationship of federal receipts and expenditures has played an increasingly important role in efforts to attain the national economic goals of full employment and price stability. This use of the federal budget for stabilization purposes is called fiscal policy, and the debate about what is appropriate fiscal policy has increased markedly in recent years. Rapidly

rising state and local expenditures have put pressure on state and local revenues and have resulted in not only higher tax rates but expansion of federal grants-in-aid. This chapter covers data sources for government expenditures and receipts; the interrelationships between federal, state, and local expenditures; and methods currently in use for forecasting expenditures and receipts in both the short run and the long run.

BASIC DATA

The amount of information available on government receipts and expenditures, especially for the federal government, is prodigious and frequently confusing. A more detailed discussion of the various data sources is contained in appendix A. However, a brief description of data is presented here.

The main source of information on federal receipts and expenditures is *The Budget of the United States Government*. It is published each year in late January or early February. If read carefully and used correctly, the budget document is a gold mine of information. It sets forth in both summary and detail what has been spent in the fiscal year just ended, what is expected to be spent in the current year, and what is requested for the coming fiscal year. This is all set forth program-by-program within each agency and by function in the summary tables.

There are many different types of information available in the budget documents.[1] The information used depends on what the analyst is interested in. The budget sets forth the overall spending requests of the administration and the proposed methods of financing those expenditures. The aggregates of expenditures, receipts, and net borrowing express the federal government's proposed fiscal policy for the next eighteen months. There is usually a discussion of the economic developments that the proposed fiscal policy is to help achieve.

In addition to the aggregates there is a wealth of detail, both on a functional and broad program basis, that is relevant for persons interested in specific areas. Obviously, the projected expenditures for defense procurement are of direct interest to the defense suppliers, but there is also detailed information on expenditures for health, manpower, education, and construction, to name a few of the areas covered by documents. The program area can be found both in the part of the official document that discusses federal programs by function and in the *Special Analysis* volume. Even greater detail is given on an agency basis in the *Appendix* volume. For example, the status of the interstate highway system is given in considerable detail on a state-by-state basis in the *Appendix*.

Information concerning receipts by type is presented in the revenue section of the official document and in greater detail in the summary tables. The revenue section of the budget discusses proposed changes in tax rates and presents estimates of the impact on fiscal year revenues. The economic assumptions on which the revenue estimates

are based are included in the discussion of revenues.

The budget as originally presented is submitted to Congress six months in advance of the fiscal year that it covers. It presents the President's *proposals* for government expenditures. The budget process within the executive branch is a decision-making process. In producing the budget, decisions have to be made on which programs are to be expanded, which held down and which are to be held back. Congress, of course, can and does make changes in the programs proposed by the administration. The estimate for the current fiscal year in the budget reflects the effect of congressional action on the previous year's proposal.

A frequent source of confusion in using the federal budget arises over the relationship between authorizations, authority, obligations, and outlays (cash payments).[2] A federal program must first be authorized; frequently the total amount of money that can be spent for the program is specified in the substantive legislation. Authorization can be for one year, for a given number of years (e.g., five), or indefinitely. Authorization, however, does not usually provide the authority to obligate funds. In many cases, annual appropriations must be voted by Congress. Appropriations cannot exceed the authorizations, but they can be less. The budget authority granted by Congress is authority to obligate funds. In many programs, obligations and outlays for any given fiscal year are similar, reflecting primarily an end-of-year difference between when a liability is incurred and when the checks are made out. In other programs, construction projects for example, funds obligated in one year may be paid out over a number of years in the future.

In evaluating the effect of congressional action on the budget proposed by the administration, care must be taken to distin-

---

[1] In addition to the official budget document, three others are published simultaneously at the time the budget is sent to Congress: the *Budget in Brief, Special Analysis,* and the *Appendix.*

[2] See the glossary in appendix A for more precise definitions of the terms.

guish the categories to which the funds belong.

After the budget has been released, the fiscal year totals must be monitored not only for congressional changes in the estimates but for increases in the so-called uncontrollables. A substantial part of federal expenditures is relatively uncontrollable in the short run. Many of these expenditures (such as social security, veterans benefits, and unemployment benefits) occur automatically when individuals meet eligibility requirements. Others, like interest, are contractual agreements. If interest rates rise, maturing debt has to be refinanced at those higher rates and interest expenditures will rise.

Data on federal government receipts and expenditures are available on two different reporting bases: (1) on a cash basis and (2) as translated into the federal sector of the national income accounts. The major differences are:

The cash basis records expenditures when paid and revenues when received. The federal sector records expenditures when goods are delivered and revenues, generally, on an accrual basis.

Lending and certain financial transactions are included in the cash accounts and excluded in the government sectors.[3]

With the introduction of the unified budget for the federal government in 1968, the conceptual differences between the federal sector data and the cash basis have been reduced but not completely eliminated.

The choice of which basis to use depends on the purpose of the forecast. If the forecast is being done for financial analysis, the unified (cash) budget data should be used, because the main purpose would be to estimate the borrowing requirements—both the magnitude and timing—of the federal government.

[3] This does not include all the differences. Appendix B gives a more detailed description of relationships between the reporting bases.

The Treasury Department and the Federal Reserve System both make projections of federal receipts and expenditures on a cash basis not only in connection with the debt operations of the federal government but as part of the process of managing the treasury's cash balances. The treasury's cash balance, the bank accounts from which expenditures are made, are held in the Federal Reserve banks. In order to prevent sudden drains of funds from the banking system into the Federal Reserve banks such as would occur after a major tax settlement date (e.g., April 15) or a substantial debt operation, federal monies are left on deposit in tax and loan accounts in commercial banks. As the funds are needed to meet expenditures, the money is called into the treasury's cash balances at the Federal Reserve banks. Large banks sometimes make cash projections in order to estimate when the federal tax and loan accounts are likely to be drawn down.

If the purpose of the forecast is to evaluate the general economic outlook, the federal sector of the national income accounts is more appropriate because the expenditures and receipts have been adjusted to be consistent with the other elements in the accounting system used for making estimates of total income and output. Each year, Special Analysis A, "Federal Transactions in the National Income Accounts," translates the unified budget estimates into national income account terms. Special Analysis A contains a discussion of the national income accounts concepts and a reconciliation between unified budget totals and federal sector totals.

SHORT-TERM FORECASTING OF FEDERAL RECEIPTS AND EXPENDITURES

A short-run forecast usually requires that the data be projected for shorter periods than a year. Quarterly estimates are the ones most commonly used, but the financial analyst may want a shorter time period, such as a month. Developing a time-phased projection that totals to the official fiscal year estimates provides a standard against which current developments can be measured and in one of the methods of evaluating the official estimates.

PROJECTING THE UNIFIED BUDGET OVER TIME

One way of projecting the timing of unified (cash) expenditures is to use seasonal adjustment factors to distribute an annual total. This requires, of course, that seasonal adjustment factors be developed by putting historical data on either a monthly or a quarterly basis through a standard seasonal adjustment program.[4] The seasonal adjustment factors indicate how great the deviation usually is from one-fourth of the year's total. Total expenditures have a surprisingly mild seasonal pattern but outlays of particular programs frequently have marked and stable seasonal patterns. Projecting in more detail than just the total makes it possible to spot program areas where expenditures are either exceeding or falling short of the amount expected for the year.

There are also other sources of information that permit the analyst to evaluate the validity of expenditure estimates as the year progresses. For example, it is possible to compare the projected increase in welfare recipients with actual experience to date and to make some judgment as to whether or not actual expenditures will exceed the projected totals.

Projections of expenditures must be adjusted for the timing of proposed legislation. For example, the 1972 budget proposed a $5 billion program at annual rates

of general revenue-sharing with state and local governments. However, the program was not expected to start until three months after the beginning of the fiscal year. Therefore, no money at all would be expended in the first quarter, and only three-quarters of the proposed $5 billion would be expended in the remainder of the year.

A projection of cash expenditures is useful even if the analyst's main purpose is to project on a national income accounts (NIA) basis, because there is monthly reporting on unified budget expenditures by program. Deviation from the official projections can be spotted sooner than they can in the federal sector.[5] The monthly data on unified expenditures are the source of the current quarterly estimates on an NIA basis.

Projecting expenditures on an NIA basis differs somewhat from projecting cash expenditures. In the federal sector, expenditures are classified within five major categories, two of which are further subdivided. Each year, the Office of Business Economics presents a reconciliation not only of total unified expenditures to NIA expenditures, but of expenditures by function to NIA categories.[6] It is possible in general terms to classify unified expenditures into NIA categories.

The NIA quarterly estimates of federal expenditures are seasonally adjusted and are at annual rates. Using the $5 billion general revenue-sharing proposal as an example, a quarterly cash projection and an NIA projection for that program would be as shown in table 1 (assuming it was paid in equal installments).

As with the unified expenditures, developing a quarterly projection that totals to the official fiscal year estimates is a useful starting point. The process of monitoring the fiscal year totals for congressional action

[4] Data on both expenditures and receipts are available in the *Monthly Treasury Statement* and the *Treasury Bulletin*.

[5] Data on both expenditures and receipts are available in the *Monthly Treasury Statement* and the *Treasury Bulletin*.

[6] See table 3.10, "Government Expenditures by Type of Function" in July issues of [50].

TABLE 1.   EXAMPLE OF HOW EXPENDITURES ARE ANNUALIZED

	Calendar Quarter				Fiscal Year Total
	III	IV	I	II	
		(in millions)			
Unified budget		$1,250	$1,250	$1,250	$3,750
Federal sector		5,000	5,000	5,000	3,750

and overruns in open-ended or uncontrollable programs is similar, as is making adjustments for the timing of new proposals.

Attempts have been made to forecast federal expenditures using regression analysis. Most of the work has concentrated on projecting defense expenditures, which is the subject of another chapter. An attempt has been made to forecast total unified civilian expenditures by structuring the equations to reflect the budget process.[7] Thus, the equations use new obligational authority, unobligated balances, and obligations to project expenditures. The equations were relatively good at predicting expenditures based on the second estimates (the ones for the current fiscal year) of authority, unobligated balances, and obligations but were of limited usefulness in forecasting expenditures more accurately than the budget eighteen months into the future. The reason it does not work is the same as for one that requires the user of the official estimates to monitor them—the appropriations for the coming fiscal year have not yet been legislated and Congress almost inevitably modifies the administration's proposals. This research did develop useful information concerning the lags between congressional authorization and expenditures. Because expenditures are the result of prior obligations, it takes time for reductions in budget authority to lead to reduced expenditures.

Two types of problem arise in projecting federal receipts. The analyst has to decide whether the underlying economic as-

sumptions seem reasonable. If they do seem reasonable, a time-phased pattern can be developed. Because taxes are due on particular dates, there is a very strong seasonal pattern to federal revenue collections. The historical data for the major categories of receipts can be used to develop a rough idea of the timing of receipts during a year. However, tax rates have changed so frequently in recent years that historical patterns provide only a starting point.

The table in the revenue section of the budget can be used to adjust a projection for changes in the law. A quarterly projection of receipts should reflect not only the change in revenue due to legislative action, but the effective date.

For example, the recent surcharge became effective on July 1, 1968. However, it was made retroactive to January 1 for corporate income taxes and to April 1 for individual taxes. The corporations had to make special payment in July of that year to bring collections more in line with their liabilities. Although the withholding rate for the individual income tax was raised on July 1, no extra provision was made to cover increased liability between April 1 and July 1. Most of this extra liability was collected in April of the following year when the final settlements were made. On a unified budget basis, all of the revenue from the increase in calendar year 1968 liability was collected in fiscal year 1969. A revenue projection made at that time would have had to be modified to reflect the extra corporate tax collection date and the unusual size of the final settlements in April of 1969. The actual collec-

---

[7] See [5].

tion of receipts lags behind the accrual of liability. A number of steps have been taken to shorten these lags but individuals have until April 15 and corporations until June 15 of the following year to file their tax returns and pay any unpaid liability or apply for a refund.

Most of the federal receipts on an NIA basis are reported on an accrual basis. Thus, if corporate profits are rising, the corporate profits tax accruals (NIA) would tend to exceed unified corporate tax collections. On an NIA basis, changes in corporate tax rates are applied evenly to all four calendar quarters, regardless of when the tax rate change takes effect. For example, the five percent corporate surcharge applicable for the first half of calendar 1970 appears in the NIA accounts as a two and a half percent tax for all four quarters of calendar 1970.

Withheld individual income taxes are reported essentially on accrual basis in the NIA but the nonwithheld part (quarterly payments and final settlements) are on a collections basis. Consequently, in forecasting revenues on an NIA basis, it is necessary to know which of the tax changes affect withholding rates and which affect the nonwithheld taxes. The differential treatment of the two parts of individual income tax in the national income accounts is of importance because it makes it difficult to fit an equation to the historical data that can be used in developing independent forecasts of receipts.

Under the social security tax laws, taxes are paid only until the employee's earnings reach the ceiling ($10,800 in 1973). Payments then stop, which is what accounts for strong seasonal pattern in these receipts on a unified basis. Due to the seasonal adjustment process, social security taxes on an NIA basis do not show this pattern. When the wage ceiling is raised, the increased liability and collections do not occur until incomes exceed the old ceiling, generally in the latter half of the calendar year. On an NIA basis, the full amount of the expected annu-

al increase in revenue expected from increasing the wage ceiling is included in the first quarter of the calendar year, even though none of the liability accrues or is collected until later in the year. No way has yet been figured out to show this phenomenon in the annualized seasonally adjusted quarterly date.

If the analyst wishes to make an independent estimate of revenues, he can either develop estimating equations of his own, or utilize those that have been developed by others, usually on an NIA basis. Most of the large econometric models have equations for federal revenues by type. For example, in the fiscal policy model of the United States developed for the Office of Business Economics, federal corporate profits tax accruals are a simple function of corporate profits and the effective tax rate.[8] Federal personal taxes are a function of the effective tax rate on median family incomes and personal income. Somewhat more complicated, but similar, equations were developed for indirect and social security taxes.[9] Although putting in the effective tax rates solves the problem of fitting the equations to past data, it leaves the person using them for projection purposes the problem of determining current and future effective rates. In some cases that is not difficult, at least under existing laws. It presents a problem, however, for personal taxes, where the average effective tax rate rises over time due to the progressive rate structure. It has been estimated for the period from 1954 to 1964 (when the individual income tax laws remained virtually unchanged) that a 100 percent increase in personal income resulted in a 1.4 percent increase in personal taxes. There is some evidence that this elasticity has been increased somewhat under the rate schedules in effect after 1963.[10]

[8] See [11].

[9] The tax equations in other models are similar. Some use dummy variables to pick up the effect of changes in the tax rates.

[10] See [44].

BASIC DATA

State and Local Government Receipts and Expenditures

Unfortunately, there is no summary document like the U.S. budget that provides specific information on future spending plans of state and local governments. Each state and most of the big cities produce budget documents, but collecting and collating the material is difficult. Most analysts therefore use material from either the *Census of Governments* collected by the Census Bureau, or the state and local sector of the national income accounts. The census data are on a fiscal year cash basis by function (i.e., education, highways, etc.). The NIA data are divided into the same categories as the federal sector: purchases, transfers, personal taxes, etc.

The choice between projecting on a census or NIA basis again depends on the purpose of the projection. Much more interest has developed recently in both short-range and longer-range projections of state and local receipts and expenditures on a cash basis because of the proposals to share federal revenues with state and local governments.[11] The projections of the needs of state and local governments use the census data. One of the reasons that the census data is used is because the data is presented state by state. It is only from the census figures that data on expenditures by type, on a per capita basis, or relative to state income can be derived.[12] The census data are also used to develop estimates of state and local tax effort. Tax effort is defined as how much state and local governments are willing to tax themselves relative to their levels of income. It varies widely from state to state and

[11] For a more thorough discussion of revenue sharing, see [22].

[12] Personal income estimates, which are the only income estimates on a state-by-state basis, are published annually in the August issue of the *Survey of Current Business.*

is one of the factors frequently included in the formulas proposed to distribute federal funds.

Every five years (1962 and 1967, for example) a full census of governments is taken. In addition to the data for aggregate state and local government receipts and expenditures, some data are available on a county, municipality, and special district basis.

The NIA concepts of state and local receipts and expenditures, like the federal sector, are usually used if the purpose of the projection is to develop a forecast of the economy in general. One major difference between census and NIA data is their treatment of two items: (1) unemployment benefit expenditures and taxes and (2) the pension funds. Unemployment expenditures and receipts are classified as a federal program in the national income accounts and as a state program in the *Census of Governments.*[13] The gross receipts and expenditures of the state and local retirement systems are recorded in the NIA accounts, whereas only the net contribution of state and local governments is recorded in census data.[14]

FORECASTING STATE AND LOCAL GOVERNMENT EXPENDITURES

Short-term forecasting on an aggregate basis tends to be undertaken primarily as

[13] The tax receipts under the unemployment compensation program are deposited in the federal treasury and the benefits are paid by the treasury. However, the states determine the tax rates (within limits), the eligibility for and size of benefits, and administer the program. For a thorough discussion of the unemployment compensation program see [15].

[14] State and local governments tend not to regard employee-employer contributions to social insurance as tax receipts nor the benefit payments as expenditures.

part of an evaluation of the economics outlook. Therefore, the national income concepts of state and local receipts and expenditures is used. Usually such forecasts do not develop the state and local sector explicitly but the components are estimated, at least implicitly, in any projection that develops the income as well as the product side of the national accounts.

Since there are no projected totals available, short-term projections are generally based on past trends, whether fitted mathematically or by more simple intuitive methods. Several econometric models have fitted equations for certain categories of the state and local sector. The "Fiscal Policy . . ." model[15] has, for example, an equation that relates state and local government purchases of goods and services to per capita gross national product, to the ratio of school-age population to total population, and to per capita federal grants-in-aid. The model also has equations for estimating state and local taxes, similar to the ones developed for federal tax revenues. In other models (for example, the quarterly model developed at the University of Michigan), state and local purchases are exogenous (i.e., not determined by the model), and state and local taxes are estimated implicitly in tax functions that estimate total government revenues by type.[16]

Estimating state and local government receipts and expenditures on a census basis has, so far, been done mainly for longer-term projections. One method of projecting is called component analysis. Component analysis of the aggregate state and local financial position evolved as a way of summarizing the detailed projections that were made during the 1960s as part of a large study on national economic growth called Project '70.[17] In that study, estimates were developed on a state-by-state basis, with the same basic methodology applied to each state.

William H. Robinson defines component analysis as follows:

> Component analysis postulates a simplified model of public expenditure determination. It isolates three generic factors which influence the changes in spending for any given program:
> 1. *Work load*, usually gauged by changes in total population or some relevant subset (e.g., children between the ages of 5 and 17 for elementary and secondary education);
> 2. *Prices*, which influence the money costs of a specified level of service units per capita;
> 3. *Policy decisions*, which extend the scope and/or improve the quality of services provided—above and beyond changes in work load and price. For convenience, this factor assumes the truncated terminological form of "scope-and-quality changes."[18]

Projections of work load are based on population projections (usually one of the census series). If the projection is for ten or fifteen years into the future, alternate population projections are significant. One of the major differences between alternate population projections is the assumption about fertility rates. If high fertility rates are assumed there will be more school-age children five to fifteen years from now than if low fertility rates are assumed. Since educational expenditures account for close to forty percent of state and local expenditures, this work load assumption is crucial. For medium-term projections, the next five years, the alternative population projections are less crucial because that population is already born. Projections for the decade of the seventies are heavily influenced by the decline in the birthrate between 1957 and 1968. Not only has the birthrate per thousand population dropped, but the actual number of live births declined for seven

---

[15] [11], p. 62.

[16] See [8].

[17] See [17].

[18] See [20].

years.[19] If a realistic level of per capita public services is to be provided, changes in work load adjusted for price changes should yield estimates of state and local expenditures. Comparison of estimates of state and local expenditures by type based only on increases in work load and prices over the past fourteen years with actual expenditures reveal that expenditures have risen much more rapidly than those two factors would indicate. Reischauer estimates that approximately seventy percent of the increase in state and local expenditures between 1955 and 1969 was due to work load or price.

The remainder—30%—was related to the improved Quality and Scope of public services. This reflects the substantial expansion in the functions of state and local governments during this period. In 1955 few would have regarded job training, all inclusive medical care for the poor, day care centers, rat control, or Shakespeare in the Park as normal state and local undertakings.

The picture varies considerably from program to program. The increase in expenditures on local schools was related primarily to rising prices and only secondly to the expansion in the school-age population–there was little improvement in quality or scope. In higher education, on the other hand, almost 37% of the increased expenditures could be attributed to a broadening of scope. Not only were a higher percentage of persons aged 18–24 enrolled in institutions of higher education, but a greater fraction of those enrolled were attending schools supported by state and local governments. During the 1955–1969 period, the workload for public welfare—the poor population—decreased about 40% but a significant expansion in the fraction of the poor receiving aid (scope) transformed what would have been a relatively small increase in expenditures into a whopping 282 percent rise. . . ."[20]

Reischauer found that projections of future levels of state and local expenditures are quite sensitive to the assumptions about scope and quality. If the scope and quality of state and local expenditures were held at 1969 levels, the total state and local expenditures projected for 1976 are $90 billion less than total expenditures assuming that the expansion of scope and quality of state and local expenditures continued at the 1965–69 pace.[21]

The definitions of expenditures and receipts used by Reischauer are those developed by W.H. Robinson.[22] Debt retirement and addition to liquid assets are included on the expenditure side. New debt issued and federal grant-in-aid are included on the revenue side. It is a definition that ex post always makes expenditures and revenues equal. It illustrates one of the major problems in forecasting state and local expenditures. The state and local governments have a number of options open to them in dealing with their financial situation. If the demand for public services exceeds the resources available, they can reduce the level of public services demanded, they can finance some of them through borrowing, or they can increase tax rates. State and local borrowing is often restricted to capital projects—schools, public buildings, parks, sewage treatment plants, etc. They attempt to meet their current expenses out of general revenues. As the demand for public services has risen, so have state and local tax rates. State and local revenues have risen from ten percent of gross national product in 1959 to more than twelve and a half percent in 1969.[23] Accompanying the rise in tax rates

[19] Both the birthrate and the number of live births increased somewhat in 1969, reflecting the increase in the number of people of childbearing age, in turn a reflection of the high birthrates in the 1947 to 1957 period.

[20] Reischauer, Robert D., "The State and Local Fiscal Crisis in Perspective." Unpublished paper, Brookings Institution, 1971.

[21] Reischauer, *op.cit.*

[22] Robinson, *op.cit.*

[23] See [48], various issues.

TABLE 2.   GNP ELASTICITY OF MAJOR STATE AND LOCAL TAXES

Type of Tax	Nitzer	Tax Foundation	Comm. for Eco. Develp.	Robinson	Reischauer
Property tax	1.0	0.9	1.0	0.9	0.86
General ratio tax	1.0	1.1	1.0	1.0	1.0
Selective sales tax	...	0.7	0.7	0.7	0.7
Personal income tax	1.75	1.7	1.7	1.7	1.7
Corporate income tax	1.15	1.2	1.2	1.2	1.2
Other	...	0.7	0.7	0.7	0.7

Source: Data from Robinson, 1969 and Reischauer, 1971.

was the expansion of federal grant-in-aid programs. Counting the grant-in-aid programs, the resources available to state and local governments have expanded from just under eleven and a half percent of GNP in 1959 to nearly fifteen percent in 1969.

Projecting revenues for state and local governments thus requires a projection of revenues both from their own sources and from federal grants-in-aid. Most projections of state and local revenues assume elasticities (i.e., the percentage change in revenues associated with a one percent change in GNP) for each type of tax. The elasticities assumed in different studies are shown in table 2.

The revenue projections usually assume constant tax rates because generally one of the purposes of the projection is to obtain, at least in general terms, some notion of how large a gap exists between state and local projected expenditures and receipts. The projections of federal grants-in-aid are taken from longer-range projections of federal expenditures and receipts.

LONGER-RANGE FORECASTING OF FEDERAL EXPENDITURES AND RECEIPTS

In recent years more attention has been given to longer-term projections of federal expenditures and receipts. A greater awareness has developed that programs proposed today commit resources available in the future and sometimes that commitment is at an increasing rate over time.

The methodology for projecting federal expenditures is similar to that used for state and local governments. Since more detail is known about specific federal programs, the projections tend to be done on a program basis using the unified budget. The projections can then be translated into the NIA basis to become part of a larger long-term economic projection.[24]

The concept of work load is basic to these projections. However, here the work loads are the number of social security beneficiaries, the number of recipients of veterans' benefits, the number of people in the armed forces. Three approaches have been taken to the problem of price. One approach is to estimate future expenditures in today's prices, in effect making allowance only for increases in work load.[25]

A second method prices out the expenditures that are uncontrollable under present law. Federal civilian and military pay raises are determined each year on the basis of a survey of comparable wages in the private sector. Some programs already include automatic adjustment for increases in the cost of living and under consideration

[24] See "Future National Output and the Claims Upon It" in [27], pp. 78–89.

[25] See table 13 in [27], p. 79.

are proposals to extend these automatic adjustments to other programs. Projections on this basis have been presented for two years in the federal budget.[26] Assumptions are made about future wage and price increases for programs where they are applicable. The expenditure levels for programs other than the uncontrollable ones are held at the current year's level.

A third method takes into account not only pay and price increases that legally must be met, but the effect of pay and price on other programs as well. In effect, this method assumes that the real level of existing programs will be maintained.[27] The purpose of various projections of federal expenditures is to estimate the fiscal dividend.

In the early 1960s, it was recognized that the automatic growth in federal revenues tended to exceed the automatic growth built into federal expenditures. The automatic growth in revenues was partially obscured by the impact of the business cycle on federal revenues. Corporate profit tax receipts, in particular, are sensitive to recession and expansion, but all receipts are lower in a recession than they would be if the economy were operating at full employment.

The concepts of potential output (GNP), full employment revenues, and the fiscal dividend were developed. They were first officially discussed in the *1962 Annual Report of the Council of Economic Advisers.* Potential GNP was defined as the rate of growth in real terms needed to maintain unemployment at four percent.[28]

With the passage of time, the unemployment rate will remain constant only if

output rises. Because the labor force grows over time, constancy in the unemployment rate means a rise in the number of employed workers and thus requires an increase in total output. Because output per worker also tends to rise —with advances in technology, improvements in skills, and additions of new capital equipment—production must increase faster than employment.[29]

The rate of potential growth needed to maintain full employment is thus based not only on increases in the labor force, but on productivity. Potential GNP is, then, estimated by applying the derived rates of growth from base periods in which there was full employment.[30] Given potential GNP, it is then possible to estimate revenues on either a unified or NIA basis. The fiscal dividend was originally defined as the increase in federal revenues associated with full-employment growth.

The concept tended to fade into the background after 1965 because actual and potential GNP were very similar in the 1965 to 1969 period, and full employment and actual surpluses told similar stories. But as was pointed out in "The Full Employment Surplus Revisited," one of the uses of the concept is as a delineator of fiscal dividend or drag:

The increases in annual revenue associated with economic growth provide a useful bench mark in fiscal planning. In the early sixties, it was important to stress in public discussions that, because of this annual fiscal dividend, the budget becomes tighter if expenditures and tax laws stand still. If allowed to operate, fiscal drag would tend to hold the economy below its potential growth. Today the fiscal drag message lingers only in nostalgia. The relevant current lesson is that no more than the annual fiscal dividend can be added to spending (or given away as

---

[26] See [52], *1972 Budget,* pp. 58–68.

[27] See [34].

[28] Four percent rate of unemployment was defined as full employment. It was established as an interim goal, with the hope that once it was reached manpower training programs and other policies could reduce the unemployment rate still further without creating inflationary pressures.

[29] [25], p. 26.

[30] There are alternate ways of determining potential GNP.

tax cuts) without making fiscal policy more stimulative. And a further caveat is required—that much of the dividend has been committed in advance through built-in increase in expenditures or already enacted tax cuts.[31]

The fiscal dividend today is defined as the difference between the growth in full-employment revenues and of built-in expenditures, however defined.

Doing the projections in real terms (i.e., with no allowance for the impact of price increases on either expenditures or revenues) focuses on the allocation of resources between the public and private sectors.[32] Making allowance for only mandatory increases in pay and price can be justified on the grounds that executive and legislative decisions must be made on the other programs. This method may overstate the fiscal dividend somewhat because part of it will be used to maintain the real program level of the so-called controllable programs. Making full allowance for expected pay and price increases may understate the dividend somewhat because, in a few cases, real program levels have been reduced by not raising the current dollar funding.

USE OF THE FISCAL DIVIDEND

The fiscal dividend is therefore the amount that growth in federal revenues, at full employment, exceeds the growth in federal expenditures. Although the different methods of estimating it result in somewhat different estimates as to its size, none of them is so large that all of the proposed uses for that dividend could be met.[33] The fiscal dividend is the amount by which federal

programs could be expanded, taxes reduced, or debt repaid. Various interests desire priority for each of these three alternatives. People interested in achieving the national housing goals feel a full employment surplus is necessary in order to free resources for the homebuilding sector. Others feel that taxes are too high and that lowering tax rates should be given first priority. Still others feel that the need for public services is of paramount importance. Within the latter group there is sharp competition for increased funds. For example, to fully meet the demands of the proponents of revenue-sharing to ease state and local financial problems would leave less for national health insurance or education.

The fiscal dividend is limited; choices have to be made between competing priorities. The economic analyst cannot establish national priorities. This is the choice of the President, the Congress, and ultimately the electorate working through the democratic process. What the analyst can do, however, is to estimate the costs and the resources available to achieve certain priorities.

APPENDIX A

Federal Budget Documents: Their Contents and Usage

Each year in the presentation of its budget, the federal government prepares and publishes four budget documents. In increasing order of size, they are *Budget in Brief*, *Special Analyses*, *The Budget of the United States Government*, and the *Appendix*.

The Budget of the United States Government is the official budget document. The other documents either summarize (*Budget in Brief*), analyze (*Special Analyses*), or expand (*Appendix*) on the information contained in the official document.

The Budget in Brief is a 70- to 75-page

---

[31] See [42].

[32] Such a projection understates revenues, because inflation affects revenues more than expenditures. See [34], pp. 329–31.

[33] See [26].

summary of the main document, designed primarily to inform the public on overall budget trends. It contains a lucid account of the budget process that is helpful in understanding the relationships between authorizations, appropriations, and outlays. The glossary on the following page, reproduced from *The U.S. Budget in Brief*, should help the reader not only in using the various budget documents but also in reading and interpreting newspaper accounts of congressional and presidential actions on the budget.

GLOSSARY

Fiscal Year   Year running from July 1 to June 30 and designated by the calendar year in which it *ends*.

Expenditure Account   The portion of the budget consisting of (1) budget receipts, and (2) budget authority and outlays for all nonlending programs, lending programs not classified in the loan account, and the administrative and other net expenses of programs in the loan account.

Loan Account   The portion of the budget consisting of the principal amounts of disbursements and repayments for domestic loans subject to definite requirements for full repayment and for foreign loans made on commercial terms.

Authorization   Basis substantive legislation which sets up a Federal program or agency. Such legislation sometimes sets limits on the amount that can subsequently be appropriated, but does not usually provide budget authority.

Budget Authority (BA)   Authority provided by the Congress—mainly in the form of appropriations—which allows Federal agencies to incur obligations to spend or lend money. While most authority is voted each year, some becomes available automatically under permanent laws—for example, interest on the public debt. Budget authority is composed of:

New   Obligational   Authority   (NOA),

which is authority to incur obligations for programs in the expenditure account; plus

Loan Authority (LA), which is authority to incur obligations for loans made under programs classified in the loan account.

Obligations   Commitments made by Federal agencies to pay out money for products, services, loans, or other purpose—as distinct from the actual payments. Obligations incurred may not be larger than the budget authority.

Outlays   Checks issued, interest accrued on the public debt, or other payments made, net of refunds and reimbursements. Budget outlays are composed of:

Expenditures (Exp.)   Outlays relating to the expenditure account; plus

Net Lending (NL)   Gross loan disbursements minus repayments in the loan account.

Budget Receipts   Money collected because of the sovereign or other compulsory powers of the Government, net of refunds. (See offsetting receipts.)

Budget Surplus or Deficit   The difference between budget receipts and outlays, representing the expenditure account surplus or deficit plus net lending.

Federal Funds   Funds collected and used by the Federal Government, as owner. The major federally owned fund is the general fund, which is derived from general taxes and borrowing and is used for the general purposes of the Government. Federal funds also include certain earmarked receipts, such as those generated by and used for the operations of Government-owned enterprises.

Trust Funds   Funds collected and used by the Federal Government, as trustee, for specified purposes, such as social security and highway construction. Receipts held in trust are not available for the general purposes of the Government. Surplus trust fund receipts are invested in Government securities and earn interest.

Offsetting Receipts   Composed of (1) proprietary receipts from the public derived from Government activities of a business-type or market-oriented nature which are offset against related budget authority and outlays; and (2) intrabudgetary transactions between one Government agency or fund and another which are offset to avoid double counting.

Undistributed Intragovernmental Transactions Composed of (1) payments to trust funds by Government agencies, as employer, for their employees' retirement; and (2) interest paid to trust funds on their investments in Government securities. To avoid double counting, these transactions are deducted from the budget totals.

The 1972 budget of the United States government consisted of eight parts, although the number of sections varies somewhat from year to year.[1] Part 1, "The Budget Message of the President," presents the overall budgetary and fiscal program of the administration. It usually discusses major new programs being proposed and existing programs that are to be expanded.

The message sometimes contains information about the timing and full-year costs of proposed programs. For example, the 1971 budget message said:

> For the Family Assistance Program, I have included outlays of $500 million in the budget for 1971. This estimate is significantly lower than the $4.4 billion first full-year cost of this program for a number of reasons. Time is required. . . .[2]

With a $4.4 billion annual cost, if the program were expected to be in effect for even a full quarter it would have had a fiscal year cost of $1.1 billion. Therefore, the 1971 budget assumption seemed to be that the family assistance program would go into effect late in the fiscal year. It turned out that this inference about the timing of the program was partially wrong. In the 1972 budget, in which welfare reform was again proposed, the welfare reform was expected to become effective at the beginning of the following fiscal year (1973) and the $500 million in the 1972 expenditures was to establish the administrative machinery needed to carry out the program.[3]

Part 2 of the 1972 budget was a discussion of one of the major new programs proposed in that year—revenue-sharing. General and special revenue-sharing were defined. General revenue-sharing proposed to share "a portion of Federal revenues with State and local governments without any program or project restriction.[4] Special revenue-sharing proposed the consolidation of existing grant programs into broad functional areas. The size of the proposed programs, both in terms of budget authority and outlays was presented in part 2.

Part 3 of the 1972 budget, "Perspectives," is a section that was started in the 1971 budget. The material included has varied. In 1971 there was a discussion of the controllability of federal expenditures. In the 1972 budget this section discussed the relationship of budget surplus and deficit to the federal debt. Of most interest to the analyst interested in forecasting is the discussion of the long-range outlook. Estimates are presented of aggregate receipts and expenditures for the fiscal year five years in the future.

Part 4 of the budget, "Revenues," summarizes the budget receipts by source.[5] Data in the budget tables are for three fiscal years—the year just completed, the current fiscal year, and the coming fiscal year. Thus, the actual receipts and expenditures for 1970 appear in the 1972 budget. Not only are the revenue estimates of interest to the forecaster, but the economic assumptions on

---

[1] The format of the budget has varied over the years. The present format and the four documents have been developed since 1963. Analysts seeking earlier data will find that the official budget prior to fiscal 1963 looks like what today is the *Appendix*.

[2] See [52], *1971 Budget*, pp. 30–31.

[3] See [52], *1972 Budget*, p. 162.

[4] See [52], *1972 Budget*, p. 33.

[5] A more detailed presentation of receipts by source is presented in [52], Part 8, "Summary Tables."

which they are based appear in the revenues section. In addition, proposed and enacted changes in tax laws are discussed and estimates of their fiscal year revenue effects are presented.

Part 5, "The Federal Program by Function," is a discussion of expenditure programs on the official functional basis. There is a good deal of information in the functional program discussion. The information on the family assistance plan in the 1972 budget cited above was found in the discussion of income maintenance programs rather than in the message section, where it had been the previous year. In the 1972 budget, a summary of active military personnel and forces appears in the discussion of national defense programs; the number of recipients of public assistance by type is included in the discussion of income security programs. Information of this type is often useful in evaluating the reasonableness of projected expenditures.

Part 6, "The Federal Program by Agency and Account" (commonly called the sidewise table) is the section most useful to the analyst in search of information on specific federal programs. There are two general reasons for seeking information on specific programs. Information on a particular program may be of direct interest to an industry or a firm within an industry. A second reason for seeking information on a program level is to be able to evaluate the reasonableness of the estimates and to subsequently follow the progress of receipts and expenditures in greater detail. The *Monthly Treasury Statement* reports receipts and expenditures using the same format as the sidewise table, but in a more summary form. The sidewise table presents information on new obligational authority (NOA) expenditures, net lending, type of funds, and usually a brief description of the program. The 1971 budget for water quality and research is reproduced as table 3.

Knowing how to use the sidewise table is important in dealing with specific pro-

grams. The table is in thousands. The new obligational authority is in boldface, the expenditures in lighter type, and each is appropriately labeled down the side. The "construction grants for waste treatment works" in the Federal Water Pollution Control Administration is an example of the types of information valuable to the analyst. The message refers to seeking " . . . legislation for a 5-year program providing grants to communities for construction of sewage treatment plants."[6] In the functional discussion of natural resources, the following is said about the program:

> Proposed legislation would authorize $4 billion of contract authority to be used over 5 years for grants to localities for construction of waste treatment facilities. Of that amount, $800 million will be allocated to the States in 1971 and in each of the next four fiscal years. Coupled with State and local financing, the Federal share will stimulate about $10 billion of construction."[7]

Looking at the sidewise table, the 4,000,000 is the $4 billion referred earlier in the budget (the table is in thousands). Of the $4 billion in new obligational authority requested, only $40 million would be spent in fiscal 1971. The numbers at the end of the account title are the functional codes (401). By reference to the summary functional tables in Part 8, it can be determined that this program is classified under "water resources and power." If the analyst wishes to know what other programs are in this category, he can scan the sidewise tables for other 401 codes. Because these water programs did not have any loan programs, the notations of LA (loan authority) and NL (net lending) do not appear in the table. As the glossary indicated total outlays are divided into expenditures and net lending. The reasons for this are explained in Appendix B.

---

[6] See [52], *1971 Budget*, p. 28.

[7] *1971 Budget, op.cit.*, p. 111.

TABLE 3.   ANALYSIS OF BUDGET AUTHORITY AND OUTLAYS BY AGENCY (in thousands of dollars)

Account and functional code		1969 enacted	1970 estimate	1971 estimate	Increase or decrease(−)	Explanation
		DEPARTMENT OF THE INTERIOR				
WATER QUALITY AND RESEARCH						
Office of Saline Water						
Federal Funds						
General and special funds:						
Saline water conversion 401	NOA	24,547 }	25,000	F29,373	4,373	Increase provides for construction of a new desalting module.
Reappropriation...............	NOA	96 }				
	Exp.	28,177	27,853	27,000	−853	
Prototype desalting plant 401	NOA	1,000	...	...	...	(Expenditures are for liquidation of prior year obligations.)
	Exp.	290	460	...	−460	
Construction, operation, and maintenance 401	Exp.	241	9	...	−9	
Total Federal funds Office of Saline Water.	NOA	25,643	25,000	29,373	4,373	
	Exp.	28,708	28,322	27,000	−1,322	
Trust Funds						
Cooperation with foreign agencies (permanent).............401	NOA	759	1,528	...	−1,528	Funds provided in 1970 by the Government of Saudi Arabia to finance a desalting plant.
Liquidation of contract authority (permanent, indefinite).		(7,626)	(6,072)	(1,500)	(−4,572)	
	Exp.	8,741	8,384	1,500	−6,884	
Federal Water Pollution Control Administration						
Federal Funds						
General and special funds:						
Construction grants for waste treatment works: 401						

B Proposed for separate transmittal under proposed legislation.

F Recommended to carry out authorizing legislation to be proposed.

TABLE 3. (CONT'D)

Account and functional code		1969 enacted	1970 estimate	1971 estimate	Increase or decrease (—)	Explanation
Contract authority............	NOA	...	...	B4,000,000	4,000,000	Proposed legislation would provide $4 billion of contract authority to stimulate $10 billion of waste treatment works over a 5-year period.
Liquidation of contract authority.		...	...	B(40,000)	(40,000)	
Appropriation................	NOA	214,000	800,000	...	−800,000	
	Exp.	134,530	158,000	322,500 B40,000	204,500	
Pollution control operations and research............401	NOA	86,675	86,124	98,018 B2,500	14,394	Increase is primarily for surveillance, enforcement, training, and aid to State and interstate agencies.
	Exp.	79,002	96,940	98,075 B2,200	3,335	
Buildings and facilities 401	Exp.	1,125	2,700	2,000	−700	(Estimate provides for alterations, extensions, and repairs of existing laboratory facilities.)
Intragovernmental funds: Advances and reimbursements .401	Exp.	95	400	200	−200	
Total Federal funds Federal Water Pollution Control Administration.	NOA	300,675	886,124	4,100,518	3,214,394	
	Exp.	214,752	258,040	464,975	206,935	
Trust Funds						
Cooperative funds (permanent) .401	NOA	3	...	...	...	(State contributions were formerly used for alewife control measures on Lake Michigan.)
	Exp.	189	2	...	−2	
Total Federal funds water quality and research.	NOA	326,318	911,124	4,129,891	3,218,767	
	Exp.	248,460	286,362	491,975	205,613	
Total trust funds water quality and research.	NOA	762	1,528	1,500	−1,528	
	Exp.	8,930	8,386	1,500	−6,886	

Part 7 of the 1972 Budget is an explanation of the budget system and concepts. Part 8 contains the summary and historical tables.

The Special Analyses volume of the Budget is the second most useful of the four documents to the analysts. The 1972 Special Analyses volume had nineteen analyses. Eight were economic and financial analyses; seven were analyses of federal social programs; three dealt with special aspects of federal programs; and one with the analytic program structure of the budget.

Special Analysis A contains the translation of the unified budget estimates into the categories of the federal sector of the national income accounts. In addition to presenting the projections on an NIA basis, there are descriptions of the NIA categories and reconciliation of the unified budget with the federal sector.

Special Analyses B (funds in the budget), C (borrowing and investments), and E (federal credit programs) are of special interest to financial analysts. The total amount of public debt subject to limitation is determined by the federal funds surplus or deficit,[9] but the total amount of debt held by the public is heavily influenced by the amount of public debt held by the government agencies. The federal funds surplus or deficit can be obtained from Special Analysis B, and the expected increase in agency holdings of public debt is presented in Special Analysis C. In addition to public debt, certain government agencies are empowered to issue debt. Agency debt can be held by the public or by other agencies. The expected changes in agency debt are shown in

Special Analysis C. These data are of interest to financial analysts in developing projections of the federal demands on the money and credit markets. There is also information in Special Analysis C on net borrowings of government sponsored enterprises and net borrowing by nonfederal entities through debt instruments guaranteed by the government. This latter category has been growing rapidly in recent years. Insured mortgages account for the bulk of the outstanding debt guaranteed by the government.

Special Analysis E presents the data on direct federal credit programs. Many federal programs make loans for a particular purpose and receive repayment overtime. Net lending in the loan account was expected to total $946 million for fiscal 1972. But it was composed of $9.7 billion of new loans granted, offset by $8.5 billion of repayments.[10] Because of the loan programs, the federal government has rather extensive holdings of financial assets. If, for example, a veteran defaults on his guaranteed mortgage, the federal government pays off the balance of the mortgage to the lender and takes over ownership of the house. The house is then resold and a new mortgage created. Since there is a market for mortgages, the federal government can sell the new mortgage to a private investor. The net sale of such assets can be substantial. The data for sales of such financial assets are presented in Special Analysis E as well as for the expected net change in outstanding loans of government sponsored credit programs. All of this information is an input to studies of the credit markets.

Special Analysis P, federal aid to state and local governments, is of direct interest to analysts making projections of state and local receipts and expenditures.[11] Federal

[8] All of the special analyses used to be published as part of the main budget. As the number of special analyses increased, not all were printed in the main document. Starting with the fiscal 1970 budget, all the analyses were removed from the main document. A separate document containing all the special analyses had been available for several years prior to the 1970 budget.

[9] See appendix B.

[10] A more detailed account of the loan programs is contained in a table in the *Appendix*.

[11] The letter (e.g., P) designating the grants analysis changes from year to year.

grants are, of course, a major source of state and local revenue and influence the type of expenditures these governments make. Estimates are available in Special Analysis P not only for total grants but for grants by type. By looking at grants by type, some judgments can be made as to which state and local expenditures will be affected.[12]

The *Appendix* is the largest and most detailed of the budget documents. If more detail than is presented in the budget is wanted on particular programs, the analyst must use the *Appendix*. A person using the *Appendix* should start by reading the explanation of the estimates which appears in the front of the book. One of the most important (and most confusing) differences between the material presented in the *Appendix* and the official budget is that data are on an obligation basis, while the official budget is on an expenditures (outlay) basis. Intrabudgetary transactions are not netted out of the material in the *Appendix*, as they are in the budget. Offsetting receipts (fees paid to the government for a government produced good or service, such as fees charged for use of government owned grazing land) are not deducted from individual schedules unless those receipts are earmarked by law for use in revolving funds. The *Appendix* includes the annexed budgets. These are the budgets of the government sponsored enterprises that are outside the budget process. These government sponsored enterprises are credit programs, and their budgets may be of interest to financial analysts.

APPENDIX B

Budget Concepts

The fiscal 1969 budget was the first to

[12] There are three measures of federal grants: the budget definition, the Census Bureau definition, and the NIA definition. The 1972 grant analysis has a reconciliation of the three concepts.

be presented on the unified basis. Prior to that, three budget concepts were in general use, the administrative budget, the consolidated cash budget, and the federal sector of the national income accounts. The budget messages and documents have emphasized one or the other at various times. The budget is a complicated document, even now, but the variety of budget concepts only added to the confusion.

In 1967, the President appointed a commission on budget concepts. The unified budget now in use incorporates most of the recommendations of that commission.

Until the mid-1930s almost all federal expenditures were financed from general revenues, that is, income taxes (corporate and individual), excise taxes, and customs. Most receipts were paid into the general fund of the treasury and expenditures made from that fund. As the operations of the government became more complex, a variety of specialized funds were established. The unified budget concept in current use includes not only the general fund but most of the specialized funds.

The two major funds are the federal funds and the trust funds. Federal funds are defined as those owned by the federal government; trust funds are defined as receipts held in fiduciary capacity by the government. The distinction is a legalistic one.

The federal funds consist of the general fund, special funds, public enterprise funds, and intragovernmental and management funds.

The *general* fund is credited with receipts not earmarked by law, and is charged with payments from such revenues and from general borrowing. *Special* funds account for Federal receipts earmarked for specific purposes, other than carrying out a cycle of operations. *Public enterprise* (revolving) funds finance a cycle of operations in which outlays generate receipts, primarily from the public. *Intragovernmental revolving and management* funds facilitate financing operations within and between Government agencies.[1]

The federal funds budget is the one closest to (but not identical with) the former administrative budget concept.

Major use of the trust funds began with the establishment of the social security system.[2] Supposedly, the trust fund was to hold the "contributions" employers and employees made to the retirement system in trust for future payment of benefits. In reading through the legislative history of the establishment of the social security system, it is obvious that in order to secure passage it became necessary to call the new system "insurance" and to create the trust fund mechanism. This has subsequently created many problems, both conceptual and political.

The "contributions" are mandatory and the coverage (i.e., workers subject to tax) is now almost universal. If tax receipts exceed benefit payments, by law that surplus must be invested in U.S. government securities, so that any surplus flows into the general fund of the treasury in exchange for debt instruments. Any deficit financed by redeeming debt is a net drain on the general fund. Although the retirement trust fund was the first of the large trust funds, there are now eight other large funds and numerous small ones. In fiscal 1970, trust fund receipts totaled $59 billion and outlays $49 billion.

As the commission on budget concepts pointed out, the trust fund technique is a mechanism for earmarking certain programs for financing by specific taxes or other revenue sources.[3] The distinction between a trust fund and a special fund in the federal funds is unclear. What it seems to come down to is that a trust fund is a trust fund because the law says it is.

The budget concepts commission recommended that a new budget concept, the unified budget, including both federal and trust funds become the official budget of the government.

There has never been a question of the Federal Government's responsibility for determining the size and shape of major trust fund programs, or for altering or redirecting these programs by appropriate changes in legislation.... With the passage of time, trust fund activities have loomed larger in both absolute and relative magnitude in the total picture of Federal Government receipts and expenditures. Receipts, expenditures and the surplus or deficit in Federally owned funds, therefore, have correspondingly less significance. It is clear to the Commission that the current surpluses of trust funds must be considered in calculating the effect of Federal Government activities on the level of income and employment, in managing Treasury cash balances, in deciding on Treasury cash borrowing needs, and in program evaluation.[4]

The commission did not recommend elimination of the trust funds, because they serve some purposes quite well.

The unified budget is similar but not identical to the older consolidated cash concept. Because of the various funds and because the trust funds have sizable holdings of U.S. government securities that earn interest, there are numerous intrafund and interfund transactions. Both the consolidated cash budget and the unified budget net out the intragovernmental transactions, although items netted are not identical in the two concepts.[5]

[4] See [43], pp. 26–27.

[5] The employer's share (federal government payment) of retirement taxes for both OASDI, where applicable, and the federal retirement system are netted in the unified budget and not the consolidated cash budget. The District of Columbia budget is no longer included in the federal budget, as it was formerly.

[1] See [52], *1972 Budget*, p. 508.

[2] Trust funds had existed earlier but were minor in amount.

[3] See [43], p. 26.

The other major difference between the consolidated cash budget and the unified budget is the netting of proprietary receipts. Proprietary receipts are those that arise from business-like activities of the federal government. Examples of these receipts are interest earned, sale of property and products, and rents and royalties. In the unified budget the proprietary receipts are netted against outlays at the agency level, whereas under the consolidated cash concept they were considered revenues.

Two of the commission's recommendations have not yet been implemented. These are the recommendations that (1) both receipts and expenditures be moved to an accrual basis and (2) that the present value of subsidy element in federal loans be shown as an expenditure in the year the loan was made.

The commission recognized the problem of budget coverage quite clearly.

A full discussion of issues involved in delineating the outer boundaries of the Federal Government could easily carry into quite esoteric matters of philosophy and political theory.[6]

The problem of what programs to include or exclude in the budget arises primarily in the loan or credit area. Economic theory differentiates between fiscal and monetary policy. In practice, the border line between fiscal and monetary affairs is blurred. It is clear that open market operations of the Federal Reserve System should not be included in the federal budget. But there are a large number of credit programs or so-called credit programs either sponsored or directly run by the federal government. These credit programs extend across a broad spectrum. At one end of this spectrum are the operations of the Home Loan Banks, with functions closely related to monetary policy. At the other end are the nonrecourse loans. A nonrecourse loan is one which, if

not voluntarily repaid, has no mechanism for forcing payment. Thus, nonrecourse loans are frequently just expenditures by another name. Certain of the credit programs were established by issuing capital, some of it provided by the federal government, and some raised by selling debt or equity instruments to the private sector.

The commission recommended that the credit operations in the federal budget be distinguished from the expenditures. Total unified outlays are thus broken into expenditures and net lending. Total outlays are the sum of expenditure and loan accounts. The nonrecourse loans, however, are included in the expenditure account.

The problem of the government sponsored enterprises, those with banking-like functions and partially owned by the private sector, is more difficult to solve. The general rule that has evolved is that if the federal government owns less than 50 percent of the capital, the program is not included in the budget.

The exclusion of the government sponsored enterprises led to an adjustment in budget totals at the time of the adoption of the unified budget. There was a subsequent adjustment when more than 50 percent of the stock of the Federal National Mortgage Association became privately owned. These adjustments not only confuse the data on federal expenditures but raise the question as to what constitutes a federal expenditure.[7]

The introduction of the unified budget reduced but did not eliminate the confusion generated by the existence of several different concepts. Public debt subject to limitation is still a function of the federal funds surplus or deficit. The expenditure account is similar but not identical to the expenditures in the federal sector of the national income accounts.

[6] See [43], p. 25.

[7] See [34] for a fuller discussion of this problem.

TABLE 4.   RELATIONSHIP OF THE BUDGET TO THE FEDERAL SECTOR NIA

	Fiscal Year		
	1968 actual	1969 actual	1970 actual
	(In billions of dollars)		
Receipts			
Total budget receipts	153.7	187.8	193.7
Government contribution for employee retirement (grossing)	1.9	2.1	2.7
Other netting and grossing	1.1	1.3	1.5
Adjustment to accruals	4.6	1.7	0.9
Other	−0.2	−0.2	−0.1
Federal sector, NIA receipts	161.1	192.7	198.7
Expenditures			
Total budget outlays	178.9	184.6	196.6
Loan account	−6.0	−1.5	−2.1
Financial transactions in the expenditure account	−1.6	−1.0	−1.8
Government contribution for employee retirement (grossing)	1.9	2.1	2.7
Other netting and grossing	1.1	1.3	1.5
Defense timing adjustment	−2.1	0.7	1.5
Other	0.2	0.6	−0.5
Federal sector, NIA expenditures	172.4	186.7	197.9

Source: Special Analysis A, various years.

Relationship of the Unified Budget to the Federal Sector of the National Income Accounts

The federal sector receipts and expenditures differ from the unified budget in several ways. First, there are differences as to what is included and excluded. Second, there are differences as to the recording of transactions (accrued versus cash). Finally, the data are classified differently.

Table 4 shows the reconciliation covering the first two sources of differences for the fiscal years 1968, 1969, and 1970.

Two of the reconciliation items are identical for both receipts and expenditures —"Government contribution for employee retirement" and "Other netting and grossing." They affect the level of receipts and expenditures but not the surplus or deficit. The adjustments to accrual accounting ("Adjustment to accruals" on the receipts side and the "Defense timing adjustment") are two of the largest differences between the two concepts. Accruals of tax liabilities usually exceed payments in a growing economy. However, in the early stages of recession the reverse may occur, especially if corporate profits have declined. The defense timing adjustment reflects the difference between cash payments and the delivery of finished goods. If defense expenditures are rising rapidly, or if very long-lead time items are being constructed (such as an aircraft carrier), the defense timing adjustment tends to be negative. If defense expenditures are declining or if large defense items are delivered, the adjustment is positive.

The NIA excludes the entire loan account on the grounds that they are financial transactions; some of the loans in the expenditure account are also excluded on the same basis.

The federal sector differs from the

TABLE 5.   DOMESTIC TRANSFER PAYMENTS

Fiscal Year	Total	Retirement and Disability	Medicare	Veterans	Unemployment Insurance	All Other
			(In billions of dollars)			
1960	20.6	13.1		4.4	2.7	0.3
1961	23.6	14.4		4.6	4.2	0.4
1962	25.1	16.4		4.6	3.6	0.5
1963	26.4	18.0		4.7	3.1	0.5
1964	27.3	19.1		4.6	2.9	0.6
1965	28.3	20.2		4.7	2.5	0.8
1966	31.8	23.9		4.7	2.1	1.3
1967	37.3	25.3	3.2	5.3	2.1	1.3
1968	42.7	27.9	5.1	5.5	2.2	1.8
1969	48.5	32.0	6.3	6.2	2.3	1.8
1970	54.9	35.5	6.8	6.9	3.0	2.7
1971	67.5	42.2	7.5	8.0	5.7	4.1
1972[a]	77.0	47.3	8.5	9.1	7.1	5.1

Source: Special Analysis A, *1973 Budget*, p. 14.

[a] Estimated.

unified budget by grouping receipts and expenditures into categories. The receipts are grouped as follows:

Unified Budget Title	*NIA Category*
Individual income tax	Personal tax and nontax receipts
Estate and gift taxes	
Corporate profits tax	Corporate profits tax accruals
Federal Reserve earnings	
Excise taxes	Indirect business taxes
Miscellaneous receipts (other than Federal Reserve earnings)	
Customs	
Social insurance taxes and contributions	Contributions for social insurance

The expenditures are grouped into the following categories: purchases of goods and services (defense and nondefense); transfer payments to persons (domestic and foreign); grants-in-aid to state and local governments; net interest paid; and subsidies less current surplus of government enterprises. Unfortunately, the classification of expenditures is not as straightforward as that of receipts.

Purchases include the goods and services (mainly labor) consumed directly by federal operations. Defense purchases include most of the expenditures of the Defense Department (except military retirement), military assistance programs, the Atomic Energy Commission, and other defense-related activities. Nondefense purchases include such programs as space exploration; construction of flood control projects; maintenance of national forest, park, and recreational areas; operation of federal airway system; etc.

Transfer payments consist of expenditures for which no current services have been rendered. Included in the transfer payments are such expenditures as old age, survivors, and disability benefit payments; medicare payments, veterans' compensation and pensions; military retirement; and unemployment benefits. Table 5 shows the growth in domestic transfers by major type over the past ten years.

Foreign transfers are expenditures for economic assistance and payments to individuals living abroad for social security and similar programs.

TABLE 6.   FEDERAL GRANTS-IN-AID

Fiscal Year	Total	Public Assistance	Health	Education and Manpower	Trans-porta-tion	Community Develop-ment and Housing	Revenue Sharing and Other
				(In billions of dollars)			
1960	6.8	2.3	0.2	0.5	3.0	0.1	1.8
1961	6.9	2.4	0.3	0.5	2.6	0.1	0.9
1962	7.6	2.6	0.4	0.6	2.8	0.2	1.0
1963	8.4	2.9	0.5	0.7	3.0	0.2	1.0
1964	9.8	3.1	0.7	0.8	3.7	0.2	1.4
1965	10.9	3.2	0.7	0.1	4.1	0.4	1.5
1966	12.7	3.3	1.3	2.2	4.0	0.4	1.6
1967	14.8	3.3	2.0	3.2	4.0	0.6	1.6
1968	17.8	4.6	2.8	3.9	4.3	0.8	1.5
1969	19.4	4.8	3.5	3.9	4.4	1.1	1.8
1970	22.6	5.7	4.1	4.3	4.6	1.7	2.1
1971	27.0	8.1	4.6	5.0	4.9	1.9	2.4
1972[a]	36.2	11.2	5.9	6.0	5.1	2.1	5.8

[a] Estimated.

Source: Special Analysis A, *1973 Budget*, p. 15.

The grants-in-aid category groups together the many programs that either assist state and local governments to provide public services, or to assist their financing of benefit programs for needy people. The public assistance grants are channeled into the national income via state and local transfer payments. The grants for transportation, which are primarily highway trust fund monies, enter the national accounts as a state and local purchase of goods and services. Table 6 shows growth in the grants by type.

The grants have been the fastest growing category of NIA expenditures in recent years, and most of the new domestic programs being proposed involve grants to state and local governments.

Net interest in the NIA accounts is the same as the interest function in the unified budget *less* interest received by the trust funds. Subsidies less the current surpluses (or deficits) of government enterprises are combined.

A subsidy is a monetary grant to a unit engaged in commercial activities (mainly businesses and farms). Examples of subsidies are Government payments to farmers for land retirement, payments to air carriers, and the operating differential subsidy of the Maritime Administration.

Government enterprise is the term applied to those functions of Government ... for which operating costs are to a great extent covered by the sale of goods and services to the public. ... The largest of these enterprises are the Commodity Credit Corporation (CCC), the Postal Service, and the Tennessee Valley Authority.[8]

The distribution of expenditures by function into NIA categories is published each July. Unfortunately, the distribution is done on a calendar year basis instead of a fiscal year as in the unified budget. In addition, the NIA functions do not correspond exactly with the unified functions.

[8] Special Analysis A, *1972 Budget*, p. 17.

BIBLIOGRAPHY

Short-Term Projections

1. Brown, Murray, and Paul Taubman, "A Forecasting Model of Federal Purchases of Goods and Services," *Journal of the American Statistical Association* (September 1962), pp. 633–47.
2. Galper, Harvey, "The Timing of Federal Expenditure Impacts," *Staff Papers and Other Materials Reviewed by the President's Commission on Budget Concepts*, Washington: Government Printing Office, 1967, pp. 416–64.
3. ———, and Edward M. Gramlich, "A Technique for Forecasting Defense Expenditures," *Review of Economics and Statistics* (May 1968), pp. 143–55.
4. ———, and Helmut F. Wendel, "Progress in Forecasting the Federal Budget," *Proceedings of the American Statistical Association*, 1968, pp. 86–98.
5. —————, "The Measurement and Implication of the Federal Expenditure Process," Mimeographed. Washington: Federal Reserve Board.
6. Gramlich, Edward M., "The Behavior and Adequacy of the United States Federal Budget 1952–64," *Yale Economic Essays*, 6 (Spring 1966), pp. 99–159.
7. ———, "Measures of the Aggregate Demand Impact of the Federal Budget," *Staff Papers and Other Materials Reviewed by the President's Commission on Budget Concepts*. Washington: Government Printing Office, 1967, pp. 431–45.
8. Greenberg, Edward, "Employment Impacts of Defense Expenditures and Obligations," *Review of Economics and Statistics* (May 1967), pp. 186–98.
9. Hymans, Saul H., and Harold T. Shapiro, *The DHL-III Quarterly Econometric Model of the U.S. Economy*. Ann Arbor, Michigan: University of Michigan, Research Seminar in Quantitative Economics, 1970.
10. Pantuliano, Camille B., "Alternate Budget Concepts for Forecasting Defense Impact," *Staff Papers and Other Materials Reviewed by the President's Commission on Budget Concepts*. Washington: Government Printing Office, 1967, pp. 349–76.
11. Thurow, Lester C., "A Fiscal Policy Model of the United States," *Survey of Current Business*, Office of Business Economics, Department of Commerce (June 1969), pp. 45–64.
12. Weidenbaum, Murray, "Impact of Vietnam War on American Economy," in *Economic Effect of the Vietnam Spending*. Joint Economic Committee, 90th Cong., 1st sess. Washington: Government Printing Office, 1967, p. 210.

State and Local Financing

13. Advisory Commission on Inter-governmental Relations, *Sources of Increased State Tax Collections: Economic Growth vs. Political Choice*. Washington: Government Printing Office, October 1968.
14. ———, *Fiscal Balance in the American Federal System*. Washington: Government Printing Office, 1967.
15. Haber, William and Merrill G. Murray, *Unemployment Insurance in the American Economy*. Homewood, Ill: Richard D. Irwin, Inc., 1966.
16. Kegan, Lawrence R., and George P. Roneger, "The Outlook for State and Local Fi-

nance," *Fiscal Issues in the Future of Federalism.* Committee on Economic Development, Supplementary Paper No. 23. New York: CED, 1968.

17. Muskin, Selma, and Gabrielle Lopo, "Project '70: Projecting the State-Local Sector," *Review of Economics and Statistics* (May 1967), pp. 237–45.

18. Netzer, Dick, "State-local Finance in the Next Decade," *Revenue Sharing and Its Alternatives: What Future for Fiscal Federalism,* Vol. III of a compendium prepared for the Joint Economic Committee, U.S. Congress, 1967.

19. ———, *Economics of the Property Tax.* Washington: Brookings Institution, 1966.

20. Robinson, William H., "Financing State and Local Government: The Outlook for 1975," Paper presented before New York chapter, American Statistical Association, April 24, 1969.

21. Runyon, Herbert, "Federal Grants, Welfare, and Income Equalization." Federal Reserve Bank of San Francisco, 1969.

22. Schultze, Charles L., Edward R. Fried, Alice M. Rivlin, and Nancy H. Teeters, *Setting National Priorities: The 1972 Budget,* Chapters 6 and 7, "General Revenue Sharing," and "Special Revenue Sharing" with Robert D. Reischauer. Washington: Brookings Institution, 1971.

23. Smith, David L., "The Response of State and Local Governments to Fiscal Grants," *National Tax Journal,* 21, No. 3 (September 1968), pp. 349–57.

24. Tax Foundation, *Fiscal Outlook for State and Local Governments to 1975.* New York: Tax Foundation, Inc., 1966.

25. *Annual Report of the Council of Economic Advisers, 1963.* Washington: Government Printing Office.

Long-Term Forecasts

26. *Annual Report of the Council of Economic Advisers, January 1969,* "Report to the President from the Cabinet Coordinating Committee on Economic Planning for the End of Vietnam Hostilities," pp. 187–211. Washington: Government Printing Office.

27. *Annual Report of the Council of Economic Advisers, February 1970,* Chapter 3. Washington: Government Printing Office.

28. *Budget of the United States Government, Fiscal Year 1972,* Part 3. Washington: Government Printing Office.

29. Committee for Economic Development, *The National Economy and the Vietnam War.* New York: CED, 1968.

30. Joint Economic Committee, *U.S. Economic Growth to 1975: Potentials and Problems,* Joint Committee Print of the 89th Cong., 2d sess. Washington: Government Printing Office, 1966.

31. National Planning Association, *National Economic Projections to 1975–76.* National Economic Projections Series, Report No. 65-2. Washington: NPA, 1965.

32. *Revenue Estimates Relating to the House, Senate and Conference Versions of H.R. 13270: Tax Reform Act of 1969.* Prepared by the staff of the Joint Committee of Internal Revenue Taxation. Washington: Government Printing Office, December 1969.

33. Schultze, Charles L., Edwards K. Hamilton, and Allen Schick, *Setting National Priorities: The 1971 Budget.* Washington: Brookings Institution, 1970.

34. ———, Edward R. Fried, Alice M. Rivlin, and Nancy H. Teeters, *Setting National Priorities: The 1972 Budget,* Chapters 16 and 17, "Expenditures Outside the Budget," and "The Fiscal Dividend Through 1976." Washington: Brookings Institution, 1971.

35. Teeters, Nancy H., "Trends in Federal Receipts and Expenditures," paper presented before New York chapter, American Statistical Association, April 1969.

Fiscal Dividend

36. Brown, E. Cary, "Fiscal Policy in the Thirties: A Reappraisal," *American Economic Review*, 46 (December 1956), pp. 857–79.
37. Committee for Economic Development, *Taxes and the Budget: A Program for Prosperity in a Free Economy*, New York: CED, November 1947, pp. 22–25.
38. ———, *A Stabilizing Fiscal and Monetary Policy for 1970*, New York: CED, December 1969, p. 10.
39. Knowles, James W., "Staff Memorandum on the Relationship of the Federal Budget to Unemployment and to Economic Growth," *1961 Joint Economic Report*, 87th Cong., 1st sess. Washington: Government Printing Office, 1961, pp. 119–25.
40. Lusher, David W., "Some Key Economic Variables in the 1960's," in *Planning and Forecasting in the Defense Industries*, ed. J. A. Stockfisch. Belmont, California: Wadsworth Publishing Company, Inc., 1962.
41. "National Income Issue," *Survey of Current Business,* Office of Business Economics, Department of Commerce (July, 1972).
42. Okun, Arthur M., and Nancy H. Teeters, "The Full Employment Surplus Revisited," *Brookings Papers on Economic Activity*, Vol. 1. Washington: Brookings Institution, 1970, pp. 77–100.
43. *Report of the President's Commission on Budget Concepts.* Washington: Government Printing Office, 1967.
44. Waldorf, William H., "The Responsiveness of Federal Personal Income Taxes to Income Changes," *Survey of Current Business,* Office of Business Economics, Department of Commerce (December 1967), pp. 32–45.

Data Sources

45. Council of Economic Advisers, *Annual Report*. Washington: Government Printing Office.
46. ———, *Economic Indicators*. Monthly. Washington: Government Printing Office.
47. Federal Reserve Board, *Federal Reserve Bulletin*. Monthly. Washington: Federal Reserve Board.
48. U.S. Department of Commerce, Bureau of the Census, *Summary of Governmental Finances*. Annual. Washington: Government Printing Office.
49. ———, *Defense Indicators*. Monthly. Washington: Government Printing Office.
50. U.S. Department of Commerce, Office of Business Economics, *Survey of Current Business*. Monthly with annual revisions in the July issue. Washington: Government Printing Office.
51. ———, *Supplement to the Survey of Current Business: The National Income and Product Accounts of the United States, 1929–1965*. Washington: Government Printing Office.
52. U.S. Office of Management and Budget, *The Budget of the United States Government*. Annual. Washington: Government Printing Office. Consists of

The Budget of the United States Government
Appendix
Special Analysis
Budget in Brief

53. U.S. Treasury Department, *Monthly Treasury Statement of the United States Treasury.* Washington: Government Printing Office.

54. ———, *Treasury Bulletin.* Monthly. Washington: Government Printing Office.

JUSTINE FARR RODRIGUEZ

Sources of Data

Introduction
Output and Income
  Gross National Product
  National Income
  Labor Market Indicators
  Education, Capital, and Productivity
Components of Demand
  Government Expenditures
  Business Fixed Investment
  Residential Construction
  Inventories
  Foreign Trade
  Balance of Payments
  International Data
  Population
  Consumer Income, Assets, and Attitudes
  Consumer Expenditures
Industry Statistics
  Business Population
  Industrial Production
  Prices
  Overall Measures and Input-Output
  Manufacturing
  Mining
  Agriculture
  Trade and Services
  Transportation
  Utilities
Finance
  Money Supply and Bank Debits
  Monetary Policy
  Banking
  Other Savings Institutions
  Insurance Companies
  Pension Funds
  Other Financial Institutions

124

Money Market Instruments
Other Short-term Credit
Governments and the Capital Markets
Structure of Financial Markets
Profits
Stock Market
Conclusion

Statistics, to paraphrase an old saying, are the root of all forecasting. What is forecast is the future level of a specific series, and the figure is set on the basis of historical behavior and relationships with other specific series. That is the *raison d'être* of this chapter discussing available statistics.

An enormous volume of statistics is published in the United States. Additional figures are produced but are less accessible. To get a feel for this vast information system, take a moment to consider why it has grown up.

1. In the first place, the United States is characterized by a multitude of decision-making units. There are thousands of governments and millions of corporations, partnerships, proprietorships, and households. Each of these units needs facts on which to base its decisions. In view of the variety of their vantage points, that mounts up to a lot of facts!

2. Important, too, have been the increasing size, complexity, and interdependence of our economy. Gone are the days when people could observe for themselves most of the forces influencing their economic lives. Less and less sufficient are words and examples to summarize and weigh the trends. Thus, the value of statistics as a framework for description and a tool for analysis has been rising.

3. Last, but surely not least, are the needs of the policymakers. The federal government has taken an active and increasingly deliberate role in shaping economic activity. This requires, on one hand, a backlog of empirical study to provide understanding of the way our economy works, and, on the other, extensive up-to-date information on the current situation and outlook.

A sight along the broad sweep of the history of economic statistics clearly shows that such needs have tended to call forth the required data. Since colonial times, statistics have been collected in proliferating numbers. Particularly notable growth in our information system has taken place in periods of great stress, such as world war and depression, and in periods such as the present, that are marked by the confluence of change.

In specific terms, too, new series and systems have been developed in response to particular problems. Thus, the commonly used measures of industrial production and wholesale prices were begun during World War I when attention was directed at mobilizing supplies and containing inflationary pressures. The much-quoted series on the labor force, employment, and unemployment were initiated during the Great Depression, as were our basic national accounts, the familiar gross national product. From input-output to flow of funds, from balance of payments to unemployment, statistics have been initiated, detailed, and strengthened to answer the pressing questions of the day.

Let us turn now and look at some of these specific series. What do they measure? How much detail is available? Where can they be found? How frequently and how promptly are they issued? How far back do they go?

Naturally, this discussion will have to be highly selective. Background studies, such as are noted in the other chapters, will not be covered. The focus will be on the regularly-issued series most frequently used for general business forecasting with some mention of those helpful in detailing particular markets, industries, or areas. A bit of extra attention has been devoted to information from nongovernment sources since these are the most difficult for the newcomer to discover for himself.

Before setting forth these sources, a note on the quality of the available statistics is in order. "He who begins to count begins to err" goes the Roman saying. Anyone who has heard the title of the book *How to Lie with Statistics,* and most certainly anyone who has read Oskar Morgenstern's *On the Accuracy of Economic Observations,* may wonder at the massive effort which has been expended on gathering and publishing these numbers. Surely much can be said for the Morgenstern argument; the list of potential and probable errors and biases is indeed horrifying.

Those who work with such statistics every day soon learn that to keep from multiplying error it is necessary to study carefully the definitions and concepts, the origins and methods of compilation behind each series. From time to time, a fine-print footnote becomes the key to an analysis.

It is helpful, too, to read the very thorough critiques which have been done on federal statistics, particularly The National Accounts Review Committee report on the national income and product accounts, flow of funds statements, balance of payments tables, input-output tables, and national balance sheets. A special President's Committee to Appraise Employment and Unemployment Statistics reported on these important indicators. Consultant committees from the Federal Reserve examined plant and equipment expenditures, savings statistics, consumer survey data, inventory figures, and information of general business expectations. The Office of Management and Budget studied profit data and international statistics. Price indices have been vigorously dissected. The Joint Economic Committee, which published most of the other studies, has examined the statistics on the size distribution of income. And more recently the President's Commission of Federal Statistics has issued a two-volume study of the current issues and opportunities for improving federal statistics.

Reading these studies, the user gradually comes to know how this figure, given so precisely, is pieced together and how that one, previously taken for granted, is based on concepts open to various interpretations. Revisions, for example the one in money supply, can sometimes be jolting. Series meant to measure the same or similar facts sometimes cannot be made to jibe. It becomes obvious that the changing structure of the economy, the introduction of new products, and the improving or deteriorating quality of products all have an adverse impact on the continuity of statistics.

Yet further study reveals that many series, obtained from different sources and by different methods, do indeed jibe—sometimes in "just" a reasonable way, and sometimes with higher precision. Moreover, it becomes clear that most decisions are made by a margin which is greater than any likely error in the key statistics. In practice, therefore, the numbers we possess have proven extremely useful to public and private policymakers.

The Statistical Policy Division in the Office of Management and Budget and the Joint Economic Committee of Congress have worked tirelessly to improve our statistical reporting system. They have been very effectively aided in this endeavor by a private organization, the Federal Statistics Users' Conference, which has pointed out many opportunities for data improvement and helped to set up priorities for further efforts. The massive improvement which has been achieved in the quantity, quality, and sophistication of our economic data is the basis of the trend toward a "science" of economics.

OUTPUT AND INCOME

Gross National Product

The broadest measure of the nation's economic activity, and perhaps the one best suited to forecasting general business, is gross national product. GNP, itself, is an unduplicated total of the market value of goods and services produced throughout the economy during the time period specified—in other words, the sum of final products ready for their ultimate use. It stands at the head of a system of national accounts setting forth expenditures on and income derived from current production, and is actually the sum of the expenditure side.

The breakdown of expenditures which is currently available on a quarterly basis outlines the major sources of demand for the nation's output and the broad types of goods and services being produced. The largest component is personal consumption expenditures, divided among outlays for durable goods, nondurable goods, and services. Second in size are government expenditures for goods and services, including state and local outlays, federal national defense, and other federal outlays. The third main category, gross private domestic investment, consists of residential construction, other construction, producers' durable equipment and change in farm and nonfarm business inventories. (The sum of other construction and producers' durables is called business fixed investment.) The final category in this breakdown of GNP is net exports of goods and services with exports and imports shown separately. Two series helpful for analysis can be calculated from these figures: (1) final sales, which is GNP minus change in inventories and is a measure of total demand, and (2) final sales minus government expenditures, which is a measure of demand from the private sector.

A second breakdown of GNP is now prepared which shows total production, inventory change, and final sales of durable goods; there are the same three series for nondurable goods, along with output of services and of construction. These series as well as those listed above are released not only in current dollars but also in constant dollars of 1967 purchasing power.

Many of these figures first become available as preliminary estimates around the middle of the month following the close of the quarter. Likewise, annual preliminary estimates with some additional detail come out in the latter part of January. The Bureau of Economic Activity in the Department of Commerce has responsibility for the official estimates and their revision. It publishes the advance estimates in its news releases and the January *Survey of Current Business*. And it publishes the official estimates one month later in both the news releases and the *Survey*.

Every July the *Survey of Current Business* carries revisions of the annual and quarterly data for the preceding year and three to five years before that. These revisions, which are based on the accumulation of income tax, census, and other data, can be quite sizable. The July issues also carry many additional series—including, for example, details of consumer, government, and investment spending—and are well worth careful examination.

Historical data may be obtained from a supplement to *Survey: The National Income and Product Accounts of the United States 1929–1965*. Comprehensive data on the definitions and the sources used in the accounts are available in *Readings in Concepts and Methods of National Income Statistics* distributed by the National Technical Information Service. The new Department of Commerce *Dictionary of Economic and Statistical Terms* is also helpful. These repay extensive study. GNP itself, in 1954 prices annually from 1870 is available on page 110 of *Output, Input and Productivity Measurement,* volume 25 of Studies in Income and Wealth, National Bureau of Economic Research. Also see the new *Historical Statistics of the United States* and the sources cited therein.

National Income

National income is theoretically the other side of the gross national product coin, but according to the definitions used in the U.S. accounts, is actually a somewhat smaller total. Thus, capital consumption allowances and indirect business taxes must be added to national income and some smaller adjustments made to reach the GNP figure.

To present a positive definition, national income is the aggregate of earnings by labor and property from the current production of goods and services, or factor income. It includes compensation of employees, proprietors' income, rental income of persons, net interest, and corporate profits with inventory valuation adjustment.

Preliminary figures for all but the profits are released by the Commerce Department in the month following the quarter close. Official estimates, now including a preliminary figure on profits, are released the following month in Commerce Department news releases and the *Survey of Current Business*. They are revised in the July *Survey*. Historical data and definitions appear in the same publications noted for GNP above.

Labor Market Indicators

The most promptly issued labor market indicators are the familiar monthly ones on the labor force, total employment, and unemployment. These come out early in the following month in a Bureau of Labor Statistics news release, *The Employment Situation*. Included are figures on agricultural, nonagricultural, and part-time employment and on unemployment by age, sex, race, occupation, industry, and duration—all on

both a seasonally adjusted and unadjusted basis.

This group of indicators is based on a sample survey of households. Respondents are classified as employed when they have a job and as unemployed when they fit into a range of situations which have in common the respondent's opinion that he or she is able and willing to work. Employed workers by industry, their hours, and their wages are also reported based on a survey of establishments. Some additional information is published in *Monthly Report on the Labor Force*, a Department of Labor magazine. But the largest volume of additional detail on the labor market situation is carried in another Labor Department publication, *Employment and Earnings*. This has the establishment data on employment, hours, and earnings by very fine industry detail. It also has state figures on employment by major industry, and totals for the 150 major labor market areas. For these areas, the number of unemployed covered by insurance is also included. Historical data are published in *Employment and Earnings Statistics for the United States, 1909–72*, with area figures in a companion volume, *Employment and Earnings Statistics for States and Areas, 1939–69*. The annual *Handbook of Labor Statistics* is another source of back data.

Speaking of area statistics, there is a publication called *County Business Patterns* issued by the Census Bureau and based on social security reports. It started in 1946, came out every three years from 1953 to 1962, and then every year beginning with the issue for 1964. This publication has employment, payrolls, and number of reporting units by employment-size class by industry for states, counties, and standard metropolitan areas.

Returning to *Employment and Earnings*, it also carries job vacancy and labor turnover data for manufacturing, gathered from employers. The figures, including job vacancies, accessions, new hires, total separations, quits, and layoffs, are published first, however, in a Bureau of Labor Statistics release, *Job Vacancies, Hires, Quits and Layoffs in Manufacturing,* about 40 days after the end of the month to which they pertain. The total, but not the industry breakdown, is seasonally adjusted.

Finally, a related sensitive labor market indicator is the index of help-wanted advertising compiled by The Conference Board and B. K. Davis and Bro. Advertising Service. Separate figures for 52 cities in 9 regions are issued in a release, *Help-Wanted Advertising,* by The Conference Board (New York) about two weeks after month-end. Seasonally adjusted monthly data for the national index from 1945 are in the December 1970 *Business Conditions Digest of the Department of Commerce.* Historical data for all cities and a discussion of the compilation and behavior of the series are in Technical Paper Number Sixteen, *The Conference Board's New Index of Help-Wanted Advertising.*

Education, Capital, and Productivity

What about the other factors related to the supply side of GNP? Here the data are mostly annual, if that, and less detailed. To start with education, the *Manpower Report of the President* contains data on the training and the formal educational attainment of the labor force. Statistics on the educational attainment of the population as a whole are issued by the Bureau of the Census in its *Current Population Reports* Series P-20. These also have prompt annual figures on school enrollment. The rest of the information on education comes from the Department of Health, Education, and Welfare, chiefly in the annual *Digest of Education Statistics and Projections of Educational Statistics,* the latest of which is to 1979–80. These are extensively quoted in the *Statistical Abstract.*

On research expenditures, the sources are the National Science Foundation's *Reviews of Data on Science Resources, Federal Funds for Research, Development, and Other Scientific Activities* and *Research and Development in Industry.* These have annual figures by the sources of funds and the performers of the research. Linked to the business research expenditure component here are the figures on current and planned research outlays in a special annual survey taken by McGraw-Hill, Inc.

McGraw-Hill also has a survey of anticipated plant and equipment spending. This is discussed more fully in the section on business fixed investment below. It has indices of actual and expected capacity, along with annual operating rate figures by industry. The government's plant and equipment survey, also described below, has a percent distribution of manufacturers according to whether they feel their capacity is inadequate, adequate, or excessive. The *Economic Report of the President* has annual and quarterly figures on manufacturers' operating rates and an index of capacity. And there are quarterly estimates of the percentage utilization of industrial capacity starting with 1946, computed by the Econometric Research Unit, Wharton School of Finance and Commerce at the University of Pennsylvania. Related work has been done by Chase Econometric Associates, the Federal Reserve Board, The Conference Board, and *Fortune* magazine.

On the stock of capital goods, data are difficult to find and interpret. Estimates of the gross stocks of business capital for selected years were published in the April 1970 issue of the *Survey of Current Business.* Similar figures were computed by the Machinery and Allied Products Institute and published in their *Capital Goods Review.* But most of the data on capital are to be found in books: *Institutional Investor Study Report of the Securities and Exchange Commission,* Supplementary Volume I; Raymond W. Goldsmith's *The National Wealth of the United States in the Postwar Period;*

his prior *A Study of Savings in the United States;* Simon Kuznets' *Capital in the American Economy;* and the related volumes in the National Bureau's series.

Another National Bureau book, Kendrick's *Productivity Trends in the United States,* is the magnum opus in the field of productivity. It was updated in the Bureau's 1962 *Annual Report.* Within government, responsibility for data on output per man-hour is vested in the Bureau of Labor Statistics. The BLS issues figures for the major sectors of the economy in a quarterly release entitled *Productivity, Wages, and Prices.* This publication continues the figures in their Bulletin 1249, *Trends in Output per Man-Hour in the Private Economy, 1909–1958* and their *Index of Output per Man-Hour for the Private Economy, 1947–1969.* The BLS also annually issues *Indexes of Output per Man-Hour for Selected Industries* covering 1939 and the years since 1947.

More frequent indications of the movements in productivity are available in *Business Conditions Digest,* a Department of Commerce publication. Here are monthly figures on unit labor cost in manufacturing, a monthly ratio of prices to unit labor cost in manufacturing, and a quarterly series on unit labor cost for the whole economy measured as a ratio of labor cost to real GNP. Historical figures for the first two are in the August 1970 issue.

COMPONENTS OF DEMAND

Government Expenditures

There are several commonly used sources in which for the federal government, the prime source is *The Budget of the United States Government* which the President sends to Congress each January and which contains actual figures for the past year and estimates for the current and forthcoming years. Some historical data are avail-

able in a *Budget* appendix; earlier figures (from 1789) for the major items are in *Historical Statistics.* For deeper analysis of expenditures see the *Combined Statement* which accompanies *The Budget.* For receipts see *Statistics of Income* of the Internal Revenue Service. Both are annual.

Current figures can be found in a Treasury Department release, *Monthly Statement of Receipts and Expenditures of the United States Government.* More on defense expenditures can be found in the *Monthly Report on Status of Funds* put out by the Financial Analysis and Control Division of the Defense Department. And, of course, much valuable information emanates from the Congress via hearings, the *Congressional Record,* and the press. Quarterly figures on a seasonally adjusted basis are included in *The Survey of Current Business, Economic Indicators,* and the Commerce Department's *Business Conditions Digest.* Closely related but unadjusted figures on "deposits and withdrawals" are in every *Daily Statement of the United States Treasury.*

For state and local governments, similar figures have been available only on an annual basis in the Bureau of the Census release, *Governmental Finances in 19——,* issued in preliminary form in August and in final form in October of the following year. Back data (from 1920) appear in *Historical Statistics,* and also in *Historical Statistics on Governmental Finances and Employment,* part of the 1967 Census of Governments. Again there are sources of additional detail: a series of Census Bureau releases on state finances dating back to 1915 and one on city finances dating back to 1898. Now, the Census Bureau has a *Quarterly Summary of State and Local Tax Revenue* which comes out about three months after quarter close. The figures begin in the first quarter of 1962. And the Bureau issues a quarterly series on expenditures and intentions to spend for construction and other items.

Finally, for federal, state, and local

governments, there is a full statement of receipts and expenditures on a national income accounts basis beginning in 1929. It is designed to provide a measure of the direct impact of government fiscal activity on the nation's current flow of income and output. For example, it excludes purely financial and asset transactions, and shifts the timing to a tax accrual and delivery of goods basis. These series also are available quarterly from 1946, seasonally adjusted, in the *Survey of Current Business* along with the GNP figures, and in greater detail in the July *Survey*.

A good source of assistance in this area is the Tax Foundation, which has several publications including an annual compendium of *Facts and Figures on Government Finance*.

Business Fixed Investment

When used specifically, business fixed investment refers to the total of "other construction" and producers' durable equipment in the GNP accounts. These are available with GNP in the sources cited above. The construction figures (which cover private construction except for residential, with the addition of oil and gas well drilling) are basically the same as the Census Bureau statistics on construction put-in-place for this sector.

These put-in-place figures (which are also calculated for residential and public construction) are issued monthly in the Census Bureau *Construction Reports* release C-30—unadjusted, seasonally adjusted, and in dollars of constant 1957–59 purchasing power. Each has a 28-category breakdown by type of building and public or private ownership. In mid-1964, there was a revision of these figures back to 1946. Annual data for construction put-in-place from 1915 (and monthly figures from 1939) are available in *Construction Statistics 1915–1964* (a supplement to the government's *Construction Review*).

Returning to the subject of business investment, to get an industry breakdown it is necessary to go to a different source and a slightly narrower concept. The Securities and Exchange Comission jointly with the Commerce Department issues quarterly data on business expenditures for new plant and equipment. The figures leave out farm investment, expenditures of institutions and professional people, and plant and equipment outlays charged to current account, all of which are included in the business fixed investment.

The plant and equipment figures are first issued in a Department of Commerce news release in the midst of the third month of each quarter. This gives actual outlays for the preceding quarter, anticipated outlays for two quarters, and anticipated outlays for the current year as a whole—all by industry, both seasonally adjusted and not adjusted. This is generally followed by an article in the *Survey of Current Business*. Back data from 1947 may be traced through various issues of the *Survey* or through the *Business Statistics* supplement.

Two interesting innovations have recently been made to this Commerce Department release. A regular table has been added, with data from the end of 1962, on carry-over at end of quarter, or expenditures yet to be incurred on plant and equipment projects already underway. There is also a companion table on starts of new plant and equipment projects. And then there is the previously mentioned tabulation on manufacturers' replies to the query: "Taking into account your company's current and prospective sales . . . how would you characterize your (year-end) plant and equipment facilities?——More needed,——About adequate, ——Existing exceeds needs."

Another survey of businessmen's intentions to spend for plant and equipment, also mentioned above, is that done each April and November by the economics department of McGraw-Hill, Inc., the publishers. The November survey offers a preliminary look at plans for the forthcoming year. The April survey has current-year plans and preliminary figures for the three succeeding years by industry. It also has two-year anticipations for each region by industry, sales expectations, capacity indices, and operating rates; a separation of outlays for modernization vs. those for expansion; figures on outlays for research and development; and other special tabulations. These April results are issued as a separate pamphlet; the chief findings are also usually reported in *Business Week* and other McGraw-Hill publications. These comprehensive surveys were begun in 1947.

A third valuable source in analyzing business investment is The Conference Board, which runs quarterly surveys of capital appropriations. The one on manufacturing, which started at the beginning of 1953, presents seasonally adjusted figures for net appropriations, expenditures, and change in backlogs for all manufacturing, durables industries, and nondurables industries. A separate survey provides capital appropriations figures for 38 metalworking industries producing capital goods and consumer durables. Seasonally adjusted quarterly back data are in the August 1967 *Conference Board Quarterly Survey of Capital Appropriations*. The Board also surveys investor-owned gas and electric utility companies and manufacturers' capital appropriations for foreign facilities.

There are other leading indicators in this field. One is the F. W. Dodge series on construction contracts awarded for commercial and industrial building (in terms of square feet). Seasonally adjusted figures for this series are published in *Economic Indicators* and the *Business Conditions Digest*. But the original statistics are part of the Dodge service which includes detailed data on the value of contracts awarded by type and location. (A few of the main national figures are included in the statistical section at the back of every *Survey of Current Business*, and some annual data from 1925 are in

Historical Statistics.) Then there is the series on the value of new orders in the machinery and equipment industries, that is part of the manufacturers' shipments, inventories, and orders release discussed below. Related to these are the figures on orders and shipments issued by the National Machine Tool Builders Association.

Residential Construction

The other large item in the gross private domestic investment account of GNP is residential construction. Both the census figures on construction put-in-place and the Dodge data on contract awards include figures on housing. Besides, there are five series of Census Bureau releases. Series C-20 gives monthly data on housing starts—private and public; farm and nonfarm; one-, two-, three-, or more unit; metropolitan and nonmetropolitan; northeast, north central, south, and west. The figures on total private and private nonfarm housing starts are seasonally adjusted. In mid-1964 the data received very substantial revisions back to 1945. Figures going back to 1889 (from private sources before 1920) are in *Historical Statistics*.

The C-20 release also has a series on housing units authorized (building permits) from 1959—monthly, seasonally adjusted, by region and type of structure. The overall series has been linked to earlier monthly figures from 1946 and published in the June 1970 issue of *Business Conditions Digest*. The housing authorization figures have their own releases: C-42 for the compiled series and C-40 for the actual counts in individual permit-issuing places. And starting with January 1968, there are also statistics on housing units completed.

Vacant housing units, their proportion and characteristics, are detailed quarterly in the Series H-111 release of the Census Bureau. Separate figures are available for rental and homeowner housing by location, number of rooms, condition of housing, and amount of rent or price of house. Figures are available from 1955. Annual figures on the housing inventory are included. And starting at the beginning of 1962, a Series C-25 release has been issued on sales of new one-family homes. This is a monthly release setting forth the number of new homes sold by stage of construction at time of sale, number for sale, time from start, and median value. Quarterly supplements present cross-tabulations.

Information about existing housing units, including their characteristics and condition by location, can be found in the decennial Census of Housing volumes. These figures are available for 1940, 1950, 1960, and 1970. A special National Housing Inventory was taken in 1956 for the first time. The 1970 census included a survey of residential finance.

There are two compendiums containing much of the above information. *Housing and Urban Development Trends*, published monthly by the Department of Housing and Urban Development, provides comprehensive current information on housing production and financing, as well as program activities of the department. There is also the annual HUD *Statistical Yearbook. Construction Review*, now issued by the Business and Defense Services Administration, covers all kinds of construction. It reprints figures on construction put-in-place, housing starts, contract awards, and housing permits, along with data on nonresidential permits, costs, employment, and construction materials.

Inventories

Net change in business inventories is the final and most volatile item in domestic investment. Aside from the figures in the GNP accounts themselves, the key figures here come from the Census Bureau. The initial release, which is issued with a one-month lag, is called *Current Industrial Reports: Manufacturers' Shipments, Inven-*

tories, and Orders. It contains seasonally adjusted and unadjusted data both by industry and by market category for shipments, inventories, new orders, and unfilled orders. Also included for the industry breakdown are ratios of inventories to shipments, of unfilled orders to shipments (i.e., months of backlog), and a table giving inventories by stage of fabrication (i.e., materials and supplies, work in process, finished goods). Back data for these series are published in two booklets put out by the Census Bureau called *Manufacturers' Shipments, Inventories, and Orders: 1947–1963 Revised* and *Manufacturers' Shipments, Inventories, and Orders: 1961–1970*.

Linked to these statistics are the series on manufacturers' anticipations of inventories and sales for the current and forthcoming quarters put out in Commerce Department news releases and then discussed regularly in the March, June, September, and December issues of the *Survey of Current Business*. The data are given both seasonally adjusted and unadjusted for durable and nondurable goods makers. Also available are quarterly figures from the beginning of 1959, again with the durable-nondurables division, showing the proportion of manufacturers' inventories which, relative to sales and unfilled orders, are felt to be too high, about right, or low.

Some ten days after the figures for manufacturing come out, a news release is issued with figures on manufacturing and trade sales and inventories. This gives separate figures not only for durable and nondurable goods manufacturers but also for durable and nondurable goods retailers and merchant wholesalers. Monthly figures from 1948 can be obtained from the Bureau of Economic Activity.

Part of this body of statistics, though not actually including any inventory figures, is the advance release on durable manufacturers' shipments and orders (new and unfilled, seasonally adjusted and unadjusted) which comes out two and a half weeks after the end of the month in Commerce Department news releases. Related are the figures for ten-day spans on automobile inventories published in *Ward's Automotive Reports*. Other related material is the monthly data on sales of both domestic and imported cars and auto inventories, seasonally adjusted and unadjusted, issued by the Bureau of Economic Activity (see December 1970 *Survey of Current Business* for data from 1958).

Finally, it is useful in this connection to study the monthly releases of the National Association of Purchasing Agents.

Foreign Trade

One of the earliest (1790) and most elaborate bodies of statistics deals with foreign trade. The first figures available each month come out after a 30-day lag in a pair of Census Bureau releases, Series FT 990. Exports with and without Department of Defense shipments; and with and without reexports, general imports, and imports for consumption are presented along with broad commodity breakdowns. Two figures are seasonally adjusted: total exports excluding defense and general imports. These releases also include a finer commodity breakdown of exports of domestic merchandise and imports for consumption, and breakdowns of export trade by country of destination and import trade by country of origin. There are also data by customs district and by means of transportation.

In effect, these are all summaries of the extremely detailed reports with fine cross-classifications by country by commodity and vice versa for imports and exports in the Series FT 135 and 410. In using the commodity figures in these reports, it is necessary to realize that, beginning with the monthly data for January 1963, the fine U.S. import and export commodity classification Schedules A and B respectively, were rearranged to fit into the broader Standard International Trade Classification, for comparability

with the trade statistics of other nations. And there is a discontinuity in the import figures beginning in September 1963, when the Schedule A for imports was replaced by the Tariff Schedules of the United States, Annotated, also arranged to fit into the broader SITC groups.

Since 1957, trade statistics on an annual basis have also been put together according to the U.S. Standard Industrial Classification for comparison with figures on domestic production by industry. These are published in the Census Bureau's *U.S. Commodity Exports and Imports as Related to Output*.

The repository of back data for trade figures is *U.S. Foreign Commerce and Navigation*, an annual book which resumed publication in 1962 after a lapse of fifteen years. A *Guide to Foreign Trade Statistics* has been issued annually since 1967. The main series can be found in *Statistical Abstract* or in the *Business Statistics* supplement to the *Survey of Current Business*. Another *Survey* supplement, *U.S. Exports and Imports Classified by OBE End-Use Categories, 1923–1968*, is very helpful for analysis. Also helpful is *Index Numbers of U.S. Exports and Imports, 1919–1969*, which has volume and price series.

Balance of Payments

The *Survey* is also the chief reference for the significant balance of payments accounts. They are published regularly in the March, June, September, and December issues. Another *Survey* supplement, *Balance of Payments* published in 1963, contains back data occasionally from 1870, annually from 1919, quarterly from 1945, and quarterly with seasonal adjustment from 1950. There are also balances with principal areas annually from 1946 and quarterly from 1948.

In addition, this supplement is a gold mine of related data. It has import and export figures by categories, chosen for their analytical significance and in many cases going back to 1923. It has a section on international transportation. Another section on international travel is updated annually by the June issue of the *Survey*, giving figures on the number and expenditures of U.S. travelers abroad and of foreign travelers in the U.S. There are sections on miscellaneous services and private remittances.

Another section deals with U.S. government transactions including defense expenditures and foreign aid. Other sources of information on this subject are *Foreign Aid by the United States Government 1940–51* and a quarterly report issued by the Bureau of Economic Activity entitled *Foreign Grants and Credits by the U.S. Government*. The Agency for International Development issues an annual report on *U.S. Economic Assistance Programs* as well as a quarterly *Operations Report*.

In the field of investment, the *Balance of Payments* supplement has tables on U.S. investments abroad (both direct and other), foreign investments in the U.S., and related items. These statistics are regularly updated in the August issue of the *Survey of Current Business* and in the quarterly balance of payments articles there. Other booklets from the Bureau of Economic Activity on this subject include: *Foreign Business Investments in the United States* (1962), *U.S. Business Investment in Foreign Countries* (1960), *U.S. Investments in the Latin American Economy*, and *U.S. Direct Investments Abroad*.

On financial investments, much more detail is available in the *Federal Reserve Bulletin* and the *Treasury Bulletin*. Here are banks' short-term liabilities to foreigners by type and country, banks' short-term claims on foreigners by type and country, and banks' long-term liabilities to and claims on foreigners on a monthly basis. Here, too, are foreigners' purchases of long-term securities by type—including treasury bonds and notes, corporate securities, and foreign secu-

rities. These last are given monthly with some country data in the *Federal Reserve Bulletin* and with more detail in the *Treasury Bulletin*. The supplemental *Statistics of Income* includes data both on foreign incomes received by U.S. corporations and foreign taxes paid.

These publications also have more detail on gold than the *Balance of Payments* supplement. There are figures on gold reserves by country; holdings of gold and short-term dollar liabilities and of U.S. government bonds by country; gold production; earmarked gold; and Federal Reserve Banks' holdings of convertible foreign currencies. All these statistics are monthly. Much back data is in *Banking and Monetary Statistics*. For current data on silver as well as gold, the monthly Census Bureau release FT 2402 gives exports and imports of the metals by form and country.

For definitions of the balance of payments items and a discussion of the way the accounts are constructed, see the older *Balance of Payments 1949–51* supplement. For an explanation of the different concepts of balance, see *The United States Balance of Payments in 1968* by Walter S. Salant et al., published by the Brookings Institution.

The first estimates of the balance of payments by the Department of Commerce are discussed within a few weeks of the end of the quarter by the Balance of Payments Group of the National Foreign Trade Council. The official preliminary figures come out in Commerce Department news releases about a month and a half after quarter-end. And the full detail in the *Survey of Current Business* has a three-month lag.

International Data

There are many sources of statistics about other nations. The United Nations' *Statistical Yearbook* and the other publications of that organization are helpful. Its *Monthly Bulletin of Statistics* has data relating to population, manpower, earnings, prices, production in many industries, international trade, national income, and finance. *The Growth of World Industry* is but one example of the valuable information available from the U.N. There are two volumes, each with data for a decade. Volume I covers industrial activity in 70 countries; Volume II has statistics on commodities. The United Nations is particularly noted for its efforts to coordinate the statistical reporting methods and definitions in the different countries. This is especially clear in its extensive international trade reporting (*Yearbook of International Trade Statistics, Commodity Trade Statistics*) and its work with gross national product and national income (*Yearbook of National Accounts Statistics*).

International Financial Statistics, issued monthly by the International Monetary Fund, contains some of the same statistics but with much heavier emphasis on finance. Reserves, foreign exchange holdings, gold holdings, Fund gold tranche positions, and Fund total tranche positions are given along with such items as the money supply, prices, exchange rates, interest rates, and data on financial institutions and instruments. This has an annual supplement with historical statistics.

Main Economic Indicators of the Organization for Economic Cooperation and Development, *General Statistical Bulletin* of the European Economic Community, and the numerous other publications of these two organizations give detailed information on Europe, covering its industries particularly well. And many individual governments, for example that of Japan, compile considerable economic data.

On financial markets, central bank discount rates and open market rates for some countries may be found in the *Federal Reserve Bulletin* along with a table of arbitrage on treasury bills versus United Kingdom and Canada. As indicated above, some rates and other financial data are in *International Financial Statistics*. The O.E.C.D. *Main Eco-*

nomic Indicators, which includes charts, has call money and other short-term rates. An historical volume is available with data for 1959 to 1969. And the O.E.C.D. has a periodical *Financial Statistics*, issued several times a year, with detailed statistics on money, capital, and equity markets.

For much foreign financial information, however, one must go to individual sources for the countries involved. The *Monthly Report of the Deutsche Bundesbank*, which is printed in English, has much data for the Federal Republic of Germany and some interest rates for other countries. *Financial Statistics*, available from Her Majesty's Stationery Office, and *Canadian Statistical Review*, available with its weekly and historical supplements from the Dominion Bureau of Statistics, cover the United Kingdom and Canada.

For the most current information, of course, one must go to the newspapers or directly to the financial community. Much of their data does not get published, though there are some exceptions. For example, Chase Manhattan Bank's bi-weekly *International Finance* contains a regular table on interest rates in various financial markets around the world.

Population

Having discussed the labor force in relation to the supply side of GNP, we turn now to discuss population itself in relation to the demand side—specifically, consumer markets. Population estimates are prepared by the Bureau of the Census and issued in its *Current Population Reports*. Monthly estimates of the total population are published a month and a half after the day to which they pertain, in Series P-25 of the *Reports*. This series also contains annual estimates of the components of population change; of the age, sex, and color breakdown of the population; of the population by state, and later by age by state; and of the population of selected metropolitan areas as well as periodic detailed projections by age and sex for several decades into the future. In Series P-20 the bureau publishes annual data on the number and characteristics of households and families, on education, and on mobility.

Marriage, birth, and death statistics are compiled by the Department of Health, Education, and Welfare and published with a two-month lag in *Monthly Vital Statistics Report*, which includes a state breakdown. These figures are reprinted in *Health, Education, and Welfare Trends* with seasonal adjustment and marriage and birth rates per thousand women age 15–44. *Trends* also contains a broad age breakdown of the population on a quarterly basis.

A convenient reference for much of the above population data when timeliness is not important, and a fairly good source of back figures, is the *Statistical Abstract of the United States*, which has a relatively large section on this subject. *Historical Statistics* carries earlier data. And of course, the decennial Census of Population volumes are crammed with detail, not only for fine geographical locations, but for many cross-classifications of characteristics of people and families.

Consumer Income, Assets, and Attitudes

Turning to income, there are monthly figures, seasonally adjusted, on receipts of personal income by source, released about three weeks after the close of the month in another Commerce Department news release. And the after-tax figures (disposable income) on a quarterly basis are included in the national income release. Linked as they are with the national income figures, both personal and disposable income are revised in the July issues of the *Survey of Current Business* and are carried back and discussed in the supplement, *The National Income*

and Product Accounts of the United States, 1929–1965.

Personal income statistics are also compiled annually on a state basis, including per capita figures and an industry breakdown of income sources. Historical data from a supplement entitled *Personal Income by States since 1929* are updated in the August issues of the *Survey of Current Business*, beginning with 1959. More recently, quarterly statistics on personal income by state were issued in the *Survey*. From time to time, there are other analytical articles in the *Survey*, such as the one in August 1970 on "Geographic Trends in Personal Income in the 1960's." Monthly indications of the movement of income by state can be found in a featured series in *Business Week* magazine. Income data for metropolitan areas also have been developed by the Department of Commerce and are published in the May issue of the *Survey*.

Another concept which has been found useful in studying consumer markets is discretionary income—what is left over after necessities have been purchased. One definition of discretionary income is quantified on a quarterly basis, seasonally adjusted, by The Conference Board. It is released about two months after the end of the quarter and discussed in the *Conference Board Record*. Back data quarterly from 1946 and a discussion of the series are in an annual release available to Conference Board associates on request.

On the distribution of income, the prime source is now the Bureau of the Census in its *Current Population Reports* Series P-60. This has cross-classification of the income distribution by many other characteristics of consumer units. Annual data are issued in preliminary and then final form about June and October respectively. Historical figures are convenient in *Trends in the Income of Families and Persons in the United States, 1947–60.* For a finer breakdown of the topmost bracket, the tax data issued by the Internal Revenue Service in an annual publication, *Statistics of Income*, might be helpful. Another source is the *Survey of Consumer Finances* done by the Survey Research Center at the University of Michigan.

On consumer assets, there is a variety of information. In addition to its detail on residences, the Census of Housing has some data on ownership of consumer durables. Some of these figures are in the Census of Population volumes. Each year one of the February issues of *Merchandising Week* carries figures on ownership of appliances. *Automobile Facts and Figures*, issued annually by the Automobile Manufacturers Association, has car ownership statistics. And *Current Population Reports* Series P-65 are an additional source.

A quarterly tabulation of individuals' saving comes out in the Securities and Exchange Commission's *Statistical Bulletin*. The July issue carries a reconciliation between these figures and the savings figures in the GNP accounts. The SEC table works back to a book, *Individuals' Saving: Volume and Composition* by Irwin Friend with Vito Natrella. The annual figures to 1929 are in *Historical Statistics*. Many related figures are included below in the section on finance: notably deposits in savings institutions, insurance and pension reserves, consumer credit, and statistics from the household sector in the flow of funds.

As for cross-tabulations, the March 1964 issue of the *Federal Reserve Bulletin* carried the first in a series of reports on a survey of financial characteristics of consumers. Similar data are collected by the Survey Research Center of the University of Michigan and released, first as part of their quarterly service to subscribers, and later in an annual book entitled *Survey of Consumer Finances*. In the late forties and fifties, this Survey Research Center material was published in the *Federal Reserve Bulletin*.

The Michigan service and the books also contain the results of their regular survey of consumer attitudes and intentions to buy. These likewise used to be included in the *Federal Reserve Bulletin*. Since 1959, however, the Bureau of the Census has made a survey of buying intentions for automobiles, housing, and selected household equipment on a quarterly basis and issued it in *Current Population Reports*, Series P-65.

Consumer Expenditures

For analysis of spending patterns associated with consumer characteristics, perhaps the best source is Fabian Linden's monthly article in the *Conference Board Record*. The basic data come from the survey of consumer expenditures done periodically to update the "market basket" of goods and services on which the Consumer Price Index is based. Some results of the 1960–61 survey are discussed in the *Monthly Labor Review*; the Bureau of Labor Statistics analyses are in a report Series 238; and the figures themselves are in a report Series 23. There are separate tabulations for 66 metropolitan areas and urban places; for regions; and for the United States as a whole for urban, rural nonfarm, farm, and all areas. The 1950 survey was thoroughly analyzed at the University of Pennsylvania and published under the title *Consumption and Saving* along with a multivolume tabulation of the figures themselves. This covered urban families only, but it included all characteristics found in the 1960–61 survey—income, family size, home tenure, race, age, occupation and education of head, family composition, number of earners, and location. A new survey to update the "market basket" is being undertaken in 1972–73.

Turning to consumer expenditures themselves, the quarterly measures and annual detail which are part of the gross national product accounts are discussed above. Besides this, there are four series of retail sales figures including: (a) weekly figures by broad kind of business, not seasonally adjusted and issued with a one-week lag; (b) preliminary monthly figures with seasonal adjustment for the total and the durable goods and nondurable goods stores which come out ten days after the month-end; (c) the final figures on monthly sales and accounts receivable by type of store both adjusted and unadjusted (and including a table on percent change in department store sales in over 90 metropolitan areas and cities); and (d) unadjusted sales by broad group for regions, and totals for nine states and five cities. These are issued by the Bureau of the Census in its *Current Retail Sales Reports.*

Four sources are of specific interest in the volatile consumer durables area. These are (1) the ten-day figures on automobile sales, which come out in the weekly service of *Ward's Automotive Reports*; (2) the monthly figures on sales of specific household appliances released by the National Electrical Manufacturers Association and (3) by the American Home Laundry Manufacturers' Association; and (4) the monthly figures on shipments of furniture released by the accounting firm of Seidman and Seidman.

For analysis of geographical areas of smaller dimensions than those separated out above, there are two annual publications with population, income, and retail trade figures for counties and towns: *Editor and Publisher Market Guide* and *Sales Management.*

INDUSTRY STATISTICS

Business Population

Information on the number of proprietorships, active partnerships, and active corporations by industry and size are available, with a lag, in the tax return tabulations, *Statistics of Income.* The Federal Trade Commission annual figures on mergers and acquisitions by industry are published in *Statistical Abstract.*

For monthly figures, three seasonally adjusted series are among the leading indicators carried in *Business Conditions Digest*: the number of new business incorporations, the total liabilities of business failures, and the number of business failures with liabilities exceeding $100,000. The source of all three, however, is Dun and Bradstreet. They publish a *Monthly New Business Incorporations* release giving the number of incorporations starting in mid-1945, with a state and regional breakdown. Then they have weekly, monthly, quarterly, and annual releases on failures. *Weekly Failures* has only the number of failures and some commentary. *Monthly Business Failures* has numbers and liabilities of failures by some 39 lines of business, by states and regions, and by size of liability, along with a seasonally adjusted series on the rate of failure per 10,000 business. *Quarterly Analysis of Failures* has a much finer line-of-business breakdown. The annual, *The Failure Record Through 19——*, has totals on the number and liabilities of failures from 1920; figures by line of business for 1940, 1950, and the last six years; and an analysis of the reasons for failures and the age of failing businesses. Annual totals are available back to 1897, monthly and state figures to 1900, and approximately the current breakdowns back to 1934. Some of the annual figures are available in *Statistical Abstract* and *Historical Statistics.*

Industrial Production

Perhaps the most widely used set of statistics on an industry basis is the Federal Reserve Board's Index of Industrial Production and its components. These are designed to measure changes in the physical volume of output in the manufacturing, mining, and electric and gas utilities sectors of the economy. Monthly series on twenty industries are compiled. These are combined into two alternative groupings which are seasonally adjusted. The first is the family industry classification with durable manufactures, non-durable manufactures, mining, and utilities as the main categories. The second is a market classification based on type of end use, with consumer goods, equipment, and materials as the chief breakdown.

Preliminary figures for the total FRB Index and most of the major breakdowns are available about the fifteenth of the following month in Federal Reserve release G.12.3. This same release also carries a revision of the previous month's major series and figures for the individual industries, virtually all for the previous month, as well as some revisions of back data. The indices were revised and updated to a 1967=100 base in 1971. An article discussing the changes back to 1939 was in the July 1971 *Federal Reserve Bulletin* and historical data was published in *Industrial Production: 1971 Edition*. Annual figures for manufacturing and mining output back to 1870 are available in *Output, Input and Productivity Measurement*. Other back data can be found in *Historical Statistics*.

Prices

In turning from real volume to prices, one goes to a set of statistics with a long and venerable history. The monthly Wholesale Price Index was inaugurated in 1902 and later carried back monthly to 1890 and annually to 1749 by linkage with private sources. *Historical Statistics* carries much of the earlier data.

Today, the WPI is a most extensive system. More than 2,450 different commodities are priced. Indices for them, and in many cases also actual prices, are published in a Bureau of Labor Statistics monthly pamphlet, *Wholesale Prices and Price Indexes*. This has final figures with a lag of three months, and preliminary figures with a two-month lag. However, the Bureau puts out a news release containing figures for eighteen major categories and 102 subgroups

within twenty days of month-end. In addition, since 1932 the Bureau has issued weekly indices for five main groups. Over the postwar periods, the weekly figures have been computed on the basis of the changes in price from the previous month for a sample of 260 items and issued in a separate series of news releases within a few days of the week's end.

For a description of the method of calculating the Wholesale Price Index, see *Handbook of Methods for Surveys and Studies,* Bulletin 1458. Helpful also is an article from the February 1962 *Monthly Labor Review* entitled "Weight Revisions in the Wholesale Price Index 1890–1960." Weights used in computing the indices are changed every five years with data from the Censuses. Each January some adjustments are made to more accurately reflect current production and marketing patterns.

The Wholesale Price Index, incidentally, is meant to measure price changes at the primary market level, i.e., the first important commercial transaction for each commodity. Besides the regular commodity grouping, several special groupings are available. The Bureau of Labor Statistics includes in its monthly pamphlet tables showing price indices by stage of fabrication and by durability of product. And the Federal Reserve has a monthly release Series G.8 with a third special recombination of the BLS figures for analysis.

Another major price system is the Consumer Price Index, which is often inaccurately called the cost of living index. This is supposed to measure the changes in price of a specifically described market basket of goods and services, typical of the purchases of urban wage-earner and clerical-worker families (and now including single individuals) in the weight period.

This, too, is calculated by the Bureau of Labor Statistics and issued in its own monthly release containing about 50 group indices. A quarterly supplement provides additional detail on services and goods other than food and fuel. Indices and actual prices (monthly) for food and fuel items are in a separate release.

Historical Statistics carries earlier data for the Consumer Price Index, which was initiated in 1913, and similar figures from other sources for previous years. The Bureau's Bulletin 1458, noted above, carries a description of the concepts and calculation. The Index underwent a revision in 1964, at which time weights derived from the 1960–61 survey of consumer expenditures were incorporated and other changes were made. Several helpful memos were then put out including *An Abbreviated Description of the Revised Consumer Price Index, Major Changes in the Consumer Price Index*, and *Consumer Price Indexes for Individual Cities*. The base has since been changed to $1967 = 100$. In the mid-1970s the market basket will be updated to take account of 1972 expenditure patterns. Indices are available for some cities in the U.S. For five cities these are monthly, for 18 they will be quarterly, and for four semiannual. They are included in the regular monthly releases. It should be noted that these indices show the relative rates of increase in prices in these cities and tell nothing about the relative levels. Some work on relative levels has been done by The Conference Board, which has issued several technical papers on the subject as well as an article in the January 1964 issue of The *Conference Board Record.*

Back data for each individual series in both the Wholesale Price Index and the Consumer Price Index on the 1967 base are available from the Bureau of Labor Statistics. Requests should be specific since each single series is a separate release. The revised back data are also convenient in *The Handbook of Labor Statistics* or they may be traced through the *Survey of Current Business* to the most recent *Business Statistics* supplement.

There are several additional sources of price information. The implicit price deflators, derived from the calculation of constant dollar gross national product accounts, are available in the *Survey of Current Business* and the *National Income and Product Accounts of the United States 1929–1965*. Then, the Bureau of Labor Statistics issues a weekly summary of its *Daily Spot Market Price Indexes and Prices* giving primary market figures for foodstuffs and raw industrial materials. Data on prices paid and received by farmers are included in the publications noted in the section on agriculture below. Figures on construction costs are in *Construction Review*. Finally, monthly data on used car prices are in *Automotive News.*

Overall Measures and Input-Output

There is a vast array of additional material on industries. This section sets forth some of the other sources with industry breakdowns but fairly broad overall coverage.

Many statistics with industry detail are put out in conjunction with the GNP accounts. There are annual figures on the national income originating in each industry by some 66 divisions in the July *Survey of Current Business;* there are quarterly figures for the 10 major groups in the February, May, August, and November issues. In addition, the July issues carry, for the detailed industry divisions, annual data on the following: total compensation of employees, wage and salary payments, number of employees on a full-time equivalent basis, average number of employees, average annual earnings per employee, average number of people engaged in production, and corporate sales. Supplements to wages and salaries are included for the 10 major groups. Back figures are in *National Income and Product Accounts of the United States.*

Starting with the October 1962 and September 1963 issues, the *Survey of Current Business* presents an addition to the tables related to GNP. The tables contain annual figures from 1947 on gross product originating in 18 industries by type of income. Dollar figures and indices for the industry gross product originating totals are also included.

A detailed input-output table with figures for 1963 based on census and other data came out in the November 1969 *Survey of Current Business* and in a three-volume opus, *Input-Output Structure of the U.S. Economy 1963*. Tables for 1958 in somewhat less detail were published in the November 1964 and other issues of the *Survey*.

It is presently planned for the Bureau of Economic Activity to calculate input-output matrices, showing sales by (and purchases from) every industry by every other industry and sector, every five years with some annual updating in betweentimes. Roughly similar input-output tables for 1939 and 1947 were done by the Department of Labor. The 1947 table in summary was printed in the May 1952 issue of the *Review of Economics and Statistics*. Tables for these and other years were discussed in *The Structure of American Economy, 1919–1939* (2nd edition) and *Studies in the Structure of the American Economy* by Wassily W. Leontief. Forecasts using these input-output statistics as well as other data, to predict employment by industry to 1980 were published in the Bureau of Labor Statistics bulletin, *Patterns of U.S. Economic Growth*.

Censuses of different areas of business activity underlie not only the input-output tables, but to a greater or lesser extent also most other industry statistics. They can be called the keystone of the whole industry information system. In addition to those listed below, there are census data on other sectors such as the construction industry and commercial fisheries.

Manufacturing

The Census of Manufactures is the oldest of business censuses, dating from 1809. It was taken at 10-year intervals until 1899, at 5-year intervals until 1919, at 2-year inter-

vals to 1939, in 1947, in 1954, and then at 5-year intervals from 1958. Statistics covered include the quantity and value of products made, materials used, value added by manufacture, employment, payroll, capital expenditures, and fuel and electricity consumed. These are published for 80 groups of related industries. The main figures are given for industries by states and the large standard metropolitan areas; they are also given for industries of consequence in important counties.

Since 1948 an Annual Survey of Manufactures has been taken in the intercensal years. These contain data on shipments, employees, payrolls, man-hours worked, value added, materials, inventories, and capital expenditures by industry and for states and large metropolitan areas. *Industry Profiles* is a handy summary of these surveys for the past decade.

For current data in addition to the statistics on manufacturers' shipments, inventories, and orders discussed above, there are two sources of reports on individual industries in manufacturing. The Bureau of the Census issues separate releases on 104 industries of which 40 are on a monthly basis, 19 are quarterly, 2 are semiannual, and 43 are annual. These contain statistics on production, shipments, orders, and inventories for some 3,000 manufactured commodities. The overall title for these releases is *Current Industrial Reports*. They may be purchased as a group, or the industries may be purchased individually.

The second source, the Business and Defense Services Administration, also issues several monthly or quarterly *Industry Reports*. Its broadest effort, however, is devoted to a series of nearly one hundred *Outlook Studies*. These knowledgeable industry summaries contain various statistics on the value and volume of shipments, imports, exports, employment, and product detail. Their distinguishing characteristic is the inclusion of specific estimates for the year ending and projections for the forthcoming year. The

Outlook Studies are released individually over the winter months and then combined into a book, *The U.S. Industrial Outlook for 19——*, which comes out in the spring. The 1971 edition has a preface discussing the overall economic outlook and appendices containing projections of value added for nearly 450 industries, for all the states, and for 40 metropolitan areas. It also has projections of gross product originating and persons engaged in production for the major sectors of the economy, and some selected productivity data.

A variety of private sources, helpful in many industry inquiries but particularly applicable in the manufacturing area, might be mentioned here. For one thing, it is frequently timesaving to start by reading one of the many current analyses of the industry in question. These are issued by many publishers and financial institutions; perhaps the best-known service is *Standard and Poor's Industry Surveys*. And The Conference Board has booklets with collections of available statistics on some industries.

Trade associations and kindred organizations are an excellent source of information. The Electronics Industries Association, for example, provides data not available from the government, which has no electronics category in its standard industrial classification. The same is true to some extent of the Aerospace Industries Association. Other associations such as the American Iron and Steel, the Textile Manufacturers', and the Petroleum Institute all have strong statistical programs. And often information on fine product lines is available only from a trade group. The standard reference for finding the relevant organizations is the *Encyclopedia of Associations*, volume I, by the Gale Research Company.

Specialized periodicals can be useful. Magazines such as *Iron Age*, *Modern Plastics*, *Steel*, *Engineering News-Record*, and others have recognized expertise in their fields. A directory in which such publications may be found is the *Ayer Directory* of newspapers and periodicals. A final reference covering government, associations, and the periodicals, and leading directly to the originators of data, is the Gale Research Company's *Statistical Sources*.

Mining

Turning to mining, a Census of Mineral Industries was started in 1839 and taken at approximately ten-year intervals to 1939, and then in 1954, and at five-year intervals starting with 1958. Included are statistics on production, number of companies and mines, persons engaged, pay, supplies, capital expenditures, man-hours, and productivity.

Current statistics on minerals are compiled by the Bureau of Mines in the Department of the Interior. Every year since 1882 the Bureau has published a *Minerals Yearbook*. This gives annual data on the quantity and value of all minerals produced in the U.S. along with prices, employment, foreign trade, foreign production, and consumption and inventory figures for important minerals. It is issued in three volumes: the first with chapters on individual minerals, the second with chapters on specific fuels, and the third with area reports. The individual chapters are available in the spring as separate reports before publication in book form, and some of the statistics come out in releases in the winter.

The *Yearbook* chapters contain discussions of trends, changes in technology and consumption patterns, and an introductory section on the overall picture. In addition, about every five years the Bureau issues a volume called *Mineral Facts and Problems* reviewing longer-run developments. This has analysis of the structure of the industry, reserves, costs, productivity, taxes, tariffs, and transportation.

The Bureau of Mines also issues a number of weekly, monthly, and quarterly reports on important minerals giving production, consumption, shipments, and inventories. Deserving of specific mention for its prompt publication of statistics for the metal industries is the daily *American Metal Market*, whose publisher also issues an annual book of *Metal Statistics*.

Agriculture

The third area of commodity production also has been covered by census since 1839. A Census of Agriculture was taken every ten years to 1919; every fifth year thereafter. Acreage per farm, tenure, land use, production and sales of products, characteristics of farmers, and data from balance sheets and income statements are covered.

A very extensive current reporting service is carried out by the Department of Agriculture. Perhaps the best brief and up-to-date source for those with a less intensive interest is a monthly release from the Statistical Reporting Service entitled *Agricultural Statistics*. This contains the latest crop estimates for the current year, monthly livestock and products production, prices of farm products, indices of prices received and paid, and the first available monthly figures on cash receipts by type and by state.

For those with a more detailed interest, the Statistical Reporting Service issues two monthlies: *Crop Production*, with past and expected yield per acre and production figures by product by state, and *Crop Values*.

Another section of the Department of Agriculture, the Economic Research Service, issues a quarterly analysis of the *Demand and Price Situation* and one of the *Marketing and Transportation Situation*. This service also issues the interesting quarterly, *Farm Income Situation*, with a summer supplement containing state estimates. Other publications cover *Farm Real Estate Market Developments* (three times a year); the *Balance Sheet of the Farming Sector* and *Agricultural Finance Review* (both annual); and

the *Farm Cost Situation, Changes in Farm Production and Efficiency*, and *Farm Costs and Returns* (all annual). The service also issues the monthly *Foreign Agricultural Trade of the United States*, and annually the *World Agricultural Situation* with supplements.

Extensive though this list is, it by no means exhausts the publications of the Department of Agriculture. For example, there are regular publications on many individual commodities. The best general source of historical material is the department's annual *Agricultural Statistics*.

Trade and Services

Moving away from the commodity area, there is the so-called Census of Business. Despite its broad title, this covers just retail and wholesale trade and a variety of service establishments. Data were collected for 1929, 1939, 1948, and approximately every five years thereafter, with special reports for 1933 and 1935. Sales, payroll, employment, size of firm, and establishment information are included. For wholesale trade additional data were collected on receivables, bad debt losses, sales by class of customer, and sales by commodity line. In the 1963 Census of Business, for the first time since 1948, sales by merchandise line were also collected from retailers.

A characteristic particularly notable in the Census of Business is the geographic detail. Statistics are presented for states, metropolitan areas, incorporated urban places, central business districts of the larger cities and other important retail centers in metropolitan areas, and counties.

Current material on trade and services comes mostly from the Bureau of the Census. The four parts of the *Current Retail Trade Reports* were discussed in the section on consumer expenditures. A single-part *Monthly Wholesale Trade Report* is also released giving sales and inventories with a one-month lag for the preliminary figures and final data the following month.

Starting in 1962 the Census Bureau has collected monthly data on the receipts of seven service trades: hotels and motels, personal services, business services, automobile repairs and services, other repair services, motion pictures, and other amusement and recreation services. A publication, *Monthly Selected Service Receipts Report* Series BS-72, began in November 1966 with data starting in October 1965. Hotel figures have been compiled by the accounting firms of Horwath and Horwath, and Harris, Kerr and Forster.

Transportation

In 1963 a Census of Transportation was undertaken for the first time. It was designed as a four-part supplement to the considerable information already available from regulatory agencies on transport. One part is a national travel survey covering patterns of national, regional, and home-to-work trips. A second part is a commodity flow survey covering manufacturers' shipments by tons, ton-miles, means of transport, distance, origin and destination, commodity, size of shipment, and shipper group. A third part is a census of bus and truck carriers not subject to regulation by the Interstate Commerce Commission. Included are statistics on form of ownership, type of service, revenues and expenses, employment, capacity, and passengers and freight carried. The final part is a truck inventory and use survey describing the characteristics, distribution, and utilization of trucks. This whole Census of Transportation will now join the five-year schedule of economic censuses.

The Interstate Commerce Commission in its annual *Transportation Statistics in the United States* covers the operations, employment, equipment, and finances of rail,

motor, and water carriers; oil pipelines; freight forwarders; and others. The commission also publishes the monthly *Transport Economics.* The Association of American Railroads releases weekly carloading figures by region and type of commodity, and a quarterly forecast of loading collected from regional shippers' advisory boards. Likewise, the American Trucking Associations, Inc. issues weekly releases on intercity truck tonnage and quarterly reports with breakdowns by region and by commodity for common and for contract truckers.

For commercial airlines, the Civil Aeronautics Board publishes statistics on traffic, operations, and finances. It issues an annual *Handbook of Airline Statistics*; a quarterly *Air Carrier Financial Statistics* with income, expense, and other data; and a monthly *Air Carrier Traffic Statistics* with mileage, traffic, and load factor information. In its *FAA Statistical Handbook of Aviation,* the Federal Aviation Agency provides additional annual data covering not only carriers but general aviation facilities and operations, aeronautical production, and some state breakdowns. The FAA also issues annual five-year forecasts of indicators of aviation activity.

Among the other series related to transport are: the Census Bureau figures on international trade by air and ship, and movements of vessels in U.S. ports; the Army Corps of Engineers figures on domestic cargo movements by water; the Maritime Administration data on vessel ownership, construction, and utilization; and the Bureau of Public Roads statistics on motor vehicle registrations, characteristics, traffic, fuel consumption, and other items.

Utilities

Finally, for utility companies there is no census because complete figures are available annually from regulatory agencies. The

Federal Communications Commission publishes *Statistics of Communications Common Carriers* with financial and operating data on telephone and telegraph companies along with two monthly releases covering 42 telephone companies and large telegraph companies. The FCC also issues the annual *Final AM-FM Broadcast Financial Data* and *Final TV Broadcast Financial Data*.

Electric and gas utilities are covered in reports of the Federal Power Commission. It publishes a pair of annual volumes on *Statistics of Electric Utilities in the United States*; one volume has financial and operating figures on privately-owned and the other on publicly-owned companies. Up-to-date detailed figures are published in the FPC's monthly *Electric Power Statistics*. *Statistics of Natural Gas Companies*, another FPC annual, gives financial and operating data on natural gas pipelines. The Edison Electric Institute and the American Gas Association are also very active in compiling current statistics.

FINANCE

Money Supply and Bank Debits

The broad area of money and finance is covered in massive detail by statistics. This section must therefore be more in the nature of a survey of the series and accounts than a more complete enumeration.

One of the most important financial series is the money supply, or the total of the public's holdings of coin, currency, and demand deposits. This, together with the closely related figures on time deposits in all commercial banks, is published weekly in the Federal Reserve Board's statistical release H.6. Included are unadjusted weekly figures, and seasonally adjusted semimonthly figures issued with a one-week lag. These figures also come out in the *Federal Reserve Bulletin*. Revised semimonthly data from 1947 were published in the June 1964 issue.

The revised data from 1964 were in the November 1971 issue. These figures differ only in minor technical respects from those included in the Consolidated Condition Statement for Banks and the Monetary System, which is carried monthly in the *Federal Reserve Bulletin* and annually back to 1892 in *Historical Statistics*. There is also a weekly *Summary of Banking and Credit Measures*, H.9.

Another Federal Reserve release, G.6, contains monthly figures on bank debits and deposit turnover for New York and 343 other centers around the country, individually and with totals, seasonally adjusted and unadjusted. And there are annual figures in C.5. The totals are also carried in the *Federal Reserve Bulletin* and seasonally adjusted postwar data are available from the board. A discussion of the last major revision of the series, which began in present form in 1943, is in the April 1953 *Bulletin*. Another series, not wholly comparable but going back to 1919, is in both *Historical Statistics* and *Banking and Monetary Statistics*. Along with debits, the *Federal Reserve Bulletin* also carries data on the velocity or annual rate of turnover of demand deposits in New York, 6 other leading centers, and 337 other reporting centers. These are monthly, seasonally adjusted, and unadjusted.

As currently defined, debits are the sum of withdrawals from demand deposits, except for interbank and U.S. government payments. They are the direct measure of deposit activity in contrast with the figures on clearings, which do not include all withdrawals and which are affected by changes in the banking structure. However, clearings figures do go back further: annual data for the United States back to 1882 and for New York to 1854 are in *Historical Statistics*. And clearings figures are available weekly for 26 cities collected from the local clearinghouses and published by Dun and Bradstreet, Inc. Finally, the Federal Reserve has a monthly release, G.15, on clearings between Federal Reserve districts.

Both the clearings and especially the debits figures are valuable indicators of local business activity. In this connection, there are biennial figures produced by the Federal Reserve in cooperation with the other bank supervisory agencies and published under the title *Distribution of Bank Deposits by Counties and Standard Metropolitan Areas.*

Monetary Policy

The Fed, of course, also provides much information bearing on monetary policy. It has a weekly release, H.4.1, which gives weekly averages of daily figures on factors affecting bank reserves, along with changes from week-ago and year-ago and Wednesday figures. Here, too, is a consolidated statement of condition of the twelve Federal Reserve Banks, a maturity distribution of their loans and securities, and statements for the individual banks. There is also a weekly release, H.7, containing deposits, reserves, and borrowings of reserve city banks and two groups of country banks by district, along with demand and time deposit figures for country banks in small places by state.

Turning to the *Federal Reserve Bulletin*, the tables start with one like the first page of release H.4.1 above, showing factors supplying and absorbing reserve funds, with monthly and weekly averages of daily figures, end-of-month, and Wednesday figures. This is following by a table of monthly and weekly reserves (required, excess, and free) for New York, Chicago, other reserve city banks, and country banks.

In each issue are several presentations on discount rates, reserve requirements, margin requirements, and maximum interest rates payable on time and savings deposits. Also there is a four-week version, similar to H.7, with deposits and reserves of member banks. Another table, new in mid-1964, sets forth the transactions of the Federal Reserve System on open market account by security and type of transaction. Finally, there are

the statements of condition of the Federal Reserve Banks and the maturity distribution of their loans and securities.

Back data may be traced through older issues of the *Bulletin*. The open market table traces to the *Annual Report* of the board. Most of the other series noted can be found in the Fed's historical compendium, *Banking and Monetary Statistics* (1943 with a supplement issued in sections in 1964 and thereafter), usually starting in 1914 when the Federal Reserve System was established. For example, the figures on the factors affecting bank reserves are published there in terms of annual averages, end-of-month, and call dates from 1914; in terms of monthly averages from 1917; and in terms of weekly averages from 1922. The Fed's *Annual Report* provides authoritative discussion of its monetary policies.

Banking

Turning to the banks themselves, frequent and detailed information is available. Most frequent are the figures on the weekly reporting member banks. Release H.4.3 has breakdowns of assets and liabilities of such banks in New York and Chicago; H.4.2 has figures for reporting banks in leading cities with separate figures by Federal Reserve district. These figures are reproduced in the *Federal Reserve Bulletin* and may be traced back therein to *Banking and Monetary Statistics*, which has the series starting with 1919. There are two significant discontinuities in mid-1946 and mid-1959. On both occasions coverage was improved, and in the latter case classification of loans and deposits was changed.

A smaller group of the member banks report in detail their commercial and industrial loans by industry. These are issued, in total and by district, in H.12 and in the *Bulletin*. Month-to-month changes in the series are seasonally adjusted by the Commerce Department and published in *Business Condi-*

tions Digest. Begun in 1951, the series changed successively to exclude agricultural loans in 1956, loans to finance institutions in 1959, and bankers' acceptances for the creation of dollar exchange in 1963. It now includes all loans for commercial and industrial purposes except those secured by real estate and those for purchasing or carrying securities. Still another revision was published in the *Federal Reserve Bulletin* of February 1967.

Partly based on the weekly reporting member bank figures, since 1947 the Federal Reserve has calculated monthly (and now biweekly) figures on the principal assets and liabilities of all banks in the United States. Commercial banks and member banks, as well as New York, Chicago, and other reserve city and country banks are shown separately. These statistics first appear in release H.8, and then are published on a monthly basis in the *Bulletin.* The Fed also compiles the same balance sheet information for member banks by district, monthly, and releases it in G.7.1. Semiannually in E.3.4, the same items are released by state for all banks, all commercials banks, and all mutual savings banks.

The *Bulletin* also carries a special seasonally adjusted monthly series covering all commercial banks for loans, U.S. government securities, and other securities, with a total. A discussion of the series was in the July 1962 issue and revised figures from 1948 in the June 1964 issue.

The Federal Reserve also issues a quarterly release, E.2, with a distribution of bank rates by size of loan with weighted averages for 19 cities—New York, 7 northern and eastern cities, 11 southern and western cities. Annual figures back to 1929 are in *Historical Statistics.* Monthly rates for the period 1928 through 1938 plus quarterly rates through 1941 are in *Banking and Monetary Statistics,* which also has rates on "customers' loans" monthly from 1919 to 1929. (The prime rate for leading city banks is in the Fed's weekly G.13 release discussed below.)

Turning to actual summations of bank balance sheets, there are three sources. Arrayed in order from the lease inclusive to most inclusive, and also from the longest series to the shortest, they are: the Comptroller of the Currency, the Federal Reserve Board, and the Federal Deposit Insurance Corporation.

The Comptroller is responsible for federally chartered banks and has compiled data on them since 1863. Such banks now comprise 47 percent of all bank resources. Quarterly the Comptroller issues an *Abstract of Reports of Condition* with balance sheets for national banks by class, state, and district. His *Annual Report* also carries the quarterly state balance sheets along with annual income statements by state and district. Midyear earnings are issued in a press release.

All national banks and those state-chartered banks which care to join are member banks of the Federal Reserve System, set up in 1914. Assets of member banks now constitute 72 percent of all bank resources. A *Summary Report* (formerly *Member Bank Call Report*) is issued with the balance sheet data by class of bank, state, and district. This was done on a quarterly basis until June 1963 and then semiannually, as reporting changes for national banks made them not quite comparable with those for the state banks. Prior to the issuance of the *Summary Report,* release E.3.1 comes out with preliminary asset and liability figures and E.3.4 appears with loan details. There is also a semiannual E.5 release with member bank earnings, detailed annually in the Fed's *Annual Report.*

Finally, all member banks and those nonmember banks which choose to be are insured by the Federal Deposit Insurance Corporation, founded in 1933. This agency issues *Assets, Liabilities and Capital Accounts,* semiannually, with quarterly figures to June 1963. It contains balance sheet data by class of bank and state, not only for the insured banks which constitute 98 percent of the total, but for all banks. Much of this data is reproduced in the *Annual Report* of the FDIC, along with additional analytical tables (for example, by size of bank) and annual income statements for insured banks.

Though the Comptroller's figures cover only national banks, they are the best available for tracing bank balance sheets from the earliest official data, 1863 to 1895. One should next turn to *All-Bank Statistics, U.S. 1895–1955*, a book issued by the Federal Reserve after thorough research into available information. Since 1947, when an agreement was reached among the regulating agencies on definitions and reporting forms, these figures are almost identical with those found in the current periodicals, particularly those by the FDIC. As noted above, only after mid-1963 is there again some divergence; after this point the Fed and the FDIC make some adjustments to the Comptroller's national bank series to keep them comparable with the figures for nonnational banks. The main series are in *Historical Statistics*.

The *Federal Reserve Bulletin* also carries a table compiled by the National Association of Mutual Savings banks and originally issued with a one-month lag in a monthly release, *Balance Sheet of Mutual Savings Banks*. Along with its *Annual Report*, this association since 1960 has issued a booklet called *National Fact Book of Mutual Savings Banking* with some statistics going back to 1900 but most for the postwar period.

Other Savings Institutions

Other savings institutions have similar associations which collect and publish industry information. The United States Savings and Loan league, for example, issues an annual *Fact Book* crammed with statistics on savings and loan associations. This industry is organized similarly to commercial banking in that the institutions are either federal- or state-chartered; may or may not be insured (by the Federal and Savings and Loan Insurance Corporation); and may be either members (of the Federal Home Loan Bank system) or nonmembers. Since 1954 the Federal Savings and Loan Insurance Corporation has issued monthly balance sheet estimates based on monthly reports from insured associations and annual reports from the others. These are reprinted in the *Federal Reserve Bulletin*. Monthly, the Federal Home Loan Bank Board issues figures on the inflow of savings. Annually they issue in two parts the *Combined Financial Statements* containing balance sheets and income statements with figures by type of association, size, state, and metropolitan area. The Board also publishes the *Savings and Home Financing Source Book*.

Another locus of individual savings is credit unions. For these there is an *International Credit Union Yearbook* issued by the Credit Union National Association. This contains figures not only for the United States and its 50 states, but also for Canada and its provinces and for the other countries of the world. Since federal chartering was established in 1934 the Bureau of Federal Credit Unions has collected data on this segment of the savings industry. In 1952 it took over from the Bureau of Labor Statistics the job of keeping statistics on the state chartered unions. These are published in the *Report of Operations of Federal Credit Unions*.

Now that most of the related sectors have been discussed, this might be a good place to mention a convenient table in *Economic Indicators*. This has monthly and seasonally adjusted figures on selected liquid assets held by the public—meaning not only individuals but also businesses, state and local governments, corporate pension funds, nonprofit institutions, foreign and other holders outside the U.S. government, government agencies, the Federal Reserve, and the commercial banking system. Annual data back to 1946 are in the *Supplement to Economic Indicators*.

Insurance Companies

Returning to the rundown of financial institutions, the life insurance industry also has a trade-supported agency that publishes an annual *Fact Book* with extensive statistics. In addition, this Institute of Life Insurance issues two monthly publications: *The Tally*, with statistics on benefits, investments, and related subjects, and *Insurance Facts*. One of the supporters of the ILI is the industry trade association, the Life Insurance Institute of America. It issues several releases of its own including prompter monthly figures on assets, liabilities, and acquisitions covering a somewhat smaller group of companies; a quarterly cash flow report; a monthly write-up of forward investment commitments; and a monthly release on average yields on directly placed corporate bond authorizations. Life insurance is thoroughly covered in *Historical Statistics of Life Insurance*. Best and *The Spectator*, noted below, also have data on life insurance.

Annual data on fire and casualty companies are available from A. M. Best Company covering premiums written by type, with overall loss and expense ratios. *The Spectator*, a Chilton publication, gives separate loss ratios by type of liability. Then there are several sources of relevant statistics: the Bureau of the Census for motor vehicle deaths; Travelers Insurance Company for injuries; the National Bureau of Casualty Underwriters for average claims for injury and property damage resulting from auto accidents; and the National Board of Fire Underwriters for fire losses. Best has figures on the investments of fire and casualty companies.

Best also has some figures on health insurance companies. More on this can be obtained from the *Source Book of Health Insurance Data* issued by the Health Insurance Institute. But the main figures come from the Department of Health, Education, and Welfare in its *Social Security Bulletin* and other publications.

Pension Funds

On pension funds, there are three sources of data in addition to the figures on private insured funds included with the life insurance data above. The Securities and Exchange Commission periodically in its *Statistical Bulletin* shows the asset composition of all private noninsured funds. For the corporate funds, which exclude nonprofit organizations and multiemployer plans and comprise 91 percent of the total, they present asset composition, industry, receipts, and expenditures. Then there is a table on total assets of all types of pension systems, and a pair showing net purchases of stocks and corporate bonds by pensions and by other groups.

The *Social Security Bulletin* presents much information on social security and other government pension systems. This can be supplemented by a few items from the *Treasury Bulletin*, the *Annual Report of the Secretary of the Treasury*, the *Budget*, and, for state and local pension systems, the *Governmental Finances in 19——* along with the releases on state and city finances and the Census of Governments. Besides, the *Social Security Bulletin* contains tabulations of coverage, contributions, beneficiaries, benefits, and reserves of all types of systems both public and private. Finally, the Department of Labor now issues *Welfare and Pension Plan Statistics* giving the asset composition of the 100 largest and all other plans.

Other Financial Institutions

Investment companies have a trade association, the Investment Company Institute. Their *Fact Book* covers not only the open-end companies commonly known as mutual funds, but also closed-end and other investment companies. For mutual funds alone, they have *A Statistical Summary* with figures from 1940. Also there is a periodical, *Investment Company News*, and a series of monthly and quarterly releases with asset and share figures on the funds.

For the other financial institutions as such, there is little in the way of current statements. However, it is possible to get a picture of their activity by bringing together the available information on the instruments which comprise their principal sources and uses of funds. On finance companies, for example, one can gather the weekly reporting member bank figures on loans, the commercial and financial paper placements, and the many statistics on consumer credit noted below.

For brokers and dealers, there are more data. Again, there are weekly reporting member bank loans as well as loans on securities of all banks. For dealers specifically, there are the figures on federal funds loans, and the three tables in the *Federal Reserve Bulletin* on transactions, positions, and financing of U.S. government securities dealers. This first comes out in a weekly release from the Federal Reserve Bank of New York, which contains additional detail on treasury bills and federal agency securities as well as transactions, positions, and financing of dealers in negotiable certificates of deposit and dealer holdings of bankers' acceptances. And for brokers, there are the tables on credit to and from stockbrokers described below, and the well-known volume-of-trading figures.

Money Market Instruments

Turning to money market instruments, in mid-1964 a new release was begun by the Federal Reserve to report on the federal funds market and related transactions. The substance of this H.5 release is then reprinted regularly in the back of the *Federal Reserve Bulletin*. Back data may be traced through older issues to that of August 1964, which has the series beginning with September 1959.

On the new negotiable certificates of deposit, there are two sources besides the dealer data just noted. There are footnotes at the bottom of the weekly reporting member bank releases H.4.3 and H.4.2 and at the bottom of the corresponding table in the *Federal Reserve Bulletin* showing C/Ds outstanding at such banks. There is also an E.8 release with the results of a quarterly survey of the maturity of such certificates of the weekly reporting banks.

The *Federal Reserve Bulletin* also carries monthly figures on bankers' acceptances outstanding by holder and by basis for issuance. Release H.12 and the corresponding table on commercial and industrial loans in the *Bulletin* give bankers' acceptances held by weekly reporting member banks. The *Bulletin*, too, has monthly series on commercial and finance company paper outstanding, placed through dealers and directly placed.

Leaving the discussion of treasury bills and brokers' loans for later, let us conclude this money market section by noting that weekly data on yields, mostly of money market instruments, are available in a Federal Reserve release G.13; these are of course reprinted in the *Bulletin*. Moody's also has a release on short-term yields, and daily figures are printed in many newspapers. Perhaps this would be a good place to mention that most of these financial series are conveniently observed in the *Federal Reserve Chartbook*, traced back in the *Historical Chartbook*, and pinpointed in an accompanying volume of statistics. *Historical Statistics* and *Banking and Monetary Statistics* also carry many of the earlier series.

Other Short-Term Credit

The Federal Reserve is also the main source of consumer credit information. Its *Bulletin* carries monthly data on credit outstanding, installment and noninstallment by type and by holder, along with extensions and repayments of installment credit by type and holder, seasonally adjusted and unadjusted. Descriptions of the series are in the April 1953 issue; revised data from 1955 are in the issue for December 1961. Annual figures to 1929 are in *Historical Statistics,* and other back data are available from the Federal Reserve on request.

Most of this data comes out in releases several weeks before the issuance of the *Federal Reserve Bulletin.* Release G.22 deals with loans at consumer finance companies. G.20 covers sales finance companies and includes business as well as consumer credit, extensions, and the number of motor vehicles financed. G.18 deals with installment credit at commercial banks, including the division between purchased and direct auto paper, and giving total credit outstanding and extensions by Federal Reserve districts. Release G.19 gives total credit outstanding by type, installment and noninstallment, details of installment credit by type and holder, and seasonally adjusted extensions and repayments by type. A related release is the monthly *Delinquency Rates on Bank Installment Loans* of the Installment Credit Committee of the American Bankers Association. It gives percentage of loans delinquent by six types of loan, three terms-to-maturity, and ten regions of the country along with charted comparisons to prior years.

On trade credit less is available. But there is one relevant source—the Securities and Exchange Commission. They put out a quarterly release and periodically publish in their *Statistical Bulletin* figures on working capital of all U.S. corporations except banks and insurance companies. On the assets side the *Bulletin* lists cash, U.S. government securities, receivables from the government, notes and accounts receivable, inventories, and other current assets. As for liabilities, there are government advances and prepayments, notes and accounts payable, federal income tax, and other current liabilities.

Governments and the Capital Markets

Federal obligations by type, holder, and term-to-maturity are also covered on a monthly basis in the *Federal Reserve Bulletin.* Much more detailed statements are to be found in the *Treasury Bulletin.* Included here are data on specific securities, intragovernment holdings, fine reports on issuance and other transactions, and more information on ownership, as well as quotations on treasury securities at month-end and bond yield series. A much prompter source of monthly reports on public debt outstanding, issued and retired, along with obligations of government corporations and agencies held by the treasury, is the month-end *Daily Treasury Statement.* Regular issues of this have summary tables of changes in the public debt, certain debt transactions, and treasury cash balances. A much prompter source of yields is a weekly Federal Reserve release H.15 with daily averages by maturity. The *Weekly Bond Buyer* has daily quotations in detail and many quotes are available in newspapers.

Incidentally, the *Federal Reserve Bulletin* has one table on federal agency debt outstanding and another giving key asset and liability items for such agencies. The *Treasury Bulletin* has statements of condition of federal corporations and certain other business-type activities. And the *Bond Buyer* gives quotes on federal agency securities.

State and local government security issues by type, issuer, and use of proceeds on a monthly basis are carried in the *Federal Reserve Bulletin.* The figures originally come from a release of the Investment Bankers Association of America, where they are available sooner. Each month this gives a cross-tabulation by issuer by purpose, a finer division by type, and tables on bond elections scheduled and the election results. The quarterly version gives authorizations yet unsold, municipal bond sales by state, sales by delivery date, and principal managing underwriters.

Both Standard & Poor's Corporation and Moody's Investors Service, Inc. rate municipal and corporate bonds for quality.

Both also issue historical series of average prices and yields for the various categories of bonds. A few of these are reprinted in the *Bulletin* and in *Historical Statistics*. A weekly index of municipal bond yields is calculated by the *Bond Buyer*.

The Securities and Exchange Commission *Statistical Bulletin* carries monthly data on gross proceeds from new securities offered for cash in the United States by issuing agency and registration status. This includes not only corporate offerings but also those of the U.S. government, federal agencies, state and municipal governments, foreign governments, and international and nonprofit institutions. On corporate offerings alone, there are gross proceeds by industry and type of security, and net proceeds by industry and proposed use of funds. Quarterly statistics are presented on net change in corporate securities outstanding by type of security and industry. Included also are monthly figures on registered securities indicating cost of flotation and method of offering, and quarterly figures on block distributions of stocks. Back data to 1933 with additional detail are published in the SEC *Annual Report,* and more is available on request. Some of these series are reprinted in the *Federal Reserve Bulletin* and *Historical Statistics*. In addition to these sources (Moody's, Standard & Poor's, and the *Bond Buyer*), there are yield figures for corporate bonds in a weekly *Bond Market Roundup* put out by Salomon Brothers & Hutzler. The same firm has a historical record of monthly figures in *An Analytical Record of Yields and Yield Spreads.*

The *Federal Reserve Bulletin* also assembles considerable information on real estate credit. There is an overall compilation on a quarterly basis showing mortgage debt outstanding on farm, nonfarm, one- to four-family residential, and multifamily residential and commercial properties held by financial institutions and others. There are quarterly estimates of bank holdings of mortgages by type, and monthly figures

taken from the Institute of Life Insurance and the Federal Home Loan Bank Board for life insurance and savings and loan holdings. And there are three tables with monthly data on federal activities in the field; these cover FHA insurance, VA guarantees, and Federal National Mortgage Association and Federal Home Loan Bank holdings and transactions.

The *Bulletin* also carries data on home mortgage debt outstanding by holder and by form of financing. These statistics originally come from releases of the Federal Home Loan Bank Board which appear about five months after quarter-end; they are subsequently included in the board's *Housing Statistics*. This last publication also contains considerable information relating to the initiation of mortgages. There are figures on nonfarm mortgage recordings of $20,000 or less (which are reprinted in the *Bulletin* and additional detail on the number, average amount, and type of such recordings. Then, there are seasonally adjusted figures on FHA applications and VA requests on existing and proposed homes, along with additional data on the progress and type of such applications and requests. Incidentally, the series on mortgage loans made by savings and loan associations carried here has an interesting breakdown by purpose showing the sharp increase in mortgage use for other than construction or home purchase.

At the other end of the process, *Housing Statistics* carries statistics on FHA and VA defaults and default rates and on nonfarm mortgage foreclosures by type. The Mortgage Bankers Association of America issues a quarterly release on delinquency by number of installments past due and foreclosure numbers and rates by type of mortgage on one- to four-family homes.

The FHA issues a monthly release on prices of FHA-insured mortgages by region, along with a brief table on interest rates on conventional first mortgages on new and existing homes by region. A much more detailed release on conventional *Home Mort-*

gage Interest Rates and Terms is put out by the Federal Home Loan Bank Board. This gives monthly interest rates, fees and charges, term-to-maturity, loan/price ratios, and prices for conventional mortgages on new and existing homes. Each of these items is given separately for five types of institutions which are major lenders and for eighteen cities in the U.S. For the current month there are percentage distributions for each of the items by lender.

Structure of Financial Markets

An overview of capital formation, saving, and credit during the year can be found each May in the *Survey of Current Business*. This has semiannual figures on the sources and uses of corporate funds, a similar annual table with a four-way industry breakdown (also discussed on a June-to-June fiscal year basis in the November issues), tables on personal investment, financial asset accumulation and debt operation, and a complete enumeration of public and private net and gross debt. Back data on the corporate sources and uses are in the *National Income and Product Accounts of the United States* and the July issues of the *Survey*. The debt figures are in *Historical Statistics*.

The most comprehensive picture, however, comes from the flow of funds accounts compiled by the Federal Reserve Board quarterly and published, with a four-month lag, in the *Bulletin*. These cover the income, expenditures, capital outlays, borrowing, lending, and other acquisition of financial assets for eighteen separate sectors of the economy, with emphasis on the financial institutions. Two pages tight with figures depicting saving, investment, net financial flows, and principal financial transactions by instrument and sector have seasonally adjusted data.

Flow of funds is a relatively recent major accounting system based on Morris Copeland's 1952 book, *A Study of Money-*

flows in the United States. The Federal Reserve first began to publish annual figures in 1955, carrying them back to 1939 in *Flow of Funds in the United States, 1939–1953*. This was partly revised by *Flow of Funds Accounts, 1945–1968 Supplement*. Publication of quarterly tables was begun in August 1959, and that issue of the *Bulletin* is still a good reference for descriptions of the sectors and transactions. The data, however, have been revised in *Flow of Funds Accounts, Unadjusted Quarterly Data, 1952–62* and seasonally adjusted in the *1963 Supplement* noted above. Recently the Federal Reserve began releasing preliminary supplements— one with annual, one with quarterly, and one with seasonally adjusted data. These more than cut in half the lag in publication of the data. Bankers Trust Company and Salomon Brothers & Hutzler both issue annual analyses and forecasts based generally on this flow of funds format.

The year-end statement, now in the April *Bulletin*, is accompanied by a summary of the assets and liabilities of each sector shown. A more comprehensive set of statements is shown in *Studies in the Nation Balance Sheet of the United States*, another book published by the National Bureau of Economic Research. The list of publications of the National Bureau should be examined particularly by researchers in finance, for many of these books and papers originate historical data and detail not available elsewhere. Two examples are Saul Klaman's figures on mortgage yields and David Durand's on corporate bonds.

Profits

Turning to profits, there are five major sources. First, annual tax return data are available starting with 1926. Figures are issued for all corporations and for a fine industry breakdown in the *Corporation Income Tax Returns* volume of *Statistics of Income* by the Internal Revenue Service.

Even finer industry detail can be obtained in the microfilm *Source Book*. Included are income statement items for all corporations and balance sheet items for most. Some tabulations are also presented by asset size categories. The chief back series are conveniently collected in *Historical Statistics*. In another volume, *U.S. Business Tax Returns*, there are income statement items for unincorporated enterprises. One drawback of these figures is the publication delay, which runs more than two years despite recent improvements. And, especially for industry work, there are problems of definition, classification, consistency, and continuity.

A second source of profit data is the familiar GNP accounting system. The July issues of the *Survey of Current Business* (along with the National Income and Product Accounts) have annual figures dating from 1929 with considerable industry detail on corporate profits, tax liability, profits after taxes, net dividend payments, undistributed profits, and corporate depreciation. Again, there is a lag—amounting to two and a half years. However, these figures are available with a half-year lag for the broader industry classifications; on the same timing, there are annual figures on net income of unincorporated enterprises.

As part of this system, there are quarterly figures starting with 1939 on all of the above listed items for all corporations with a two-month lag reported in the *Survey* and in *Economic Indicators*. The fact that these sometimes change significantly with later revision does pose a problem. There are also quarterly figures in the *Survey* on the total corporate gross product and its components in the recent quarterly discussions of GNP. Historical figures from 1947 were in the July 1964 issue. And there is a monthly series of news releases with an industry breakdown of publicly reported cash dividends paid in the previous month. All of these originate with the Bureau of Economic Activity.

A third source of profit data is the *Quarterly Financial Report for Manufactur-*

ing Corporations issued by the Federal Trade Commission. As the title indicates, this covers a narrower sector than the sources above but plans are underway to broaden it to include nonmanufacturing sectors. Its great advantage is that it gives income and balance sheet information for some 30 industries and for 9 asset-size groups on a quarterly basis within less than four months of the quarter-close. Unlike the two sources above which are rooted in tax reports, this source and the two noted below are based on statements to shareholders. The series, started in 1947, has several discontinuities resulting from changes in the sample and in the industry classification. The series on profits per dollar of sales in all manufacturing from this source is seasonally adjusted and printed in *Business Conditions Digest*.

Fourth, since 1923 the First National City Bank has compiled quarterly figures on net income of corporations with an industry breakdown. They are reported in the May, August, November, and March issues of the bank's *Monthly Economic Letter*. Among the advantages of these figures are their prompt availability and their broad coverage. One disadvantage is the inconsistency of the sample from quarter to quarter; a partial remedy for this is the seasonally adjusted link-relative index of net income available from the bank on request. Another disadvantage is the absence of any data related to the quarterly figures. However, in the April issues with the annual data are book net assets, return on net assets, and margin on sales, along with percentage change in net income, dividends, retained income, depreciation, and cash flow for the broader industry groups and total figures.

Finally, the Federal Reserve has quarterly figures for sales or operating revenue, profits before and after taxes, and dividends for a consistent sample of large corporations. Railroad, electric power, telephone, durable and nondurable goods manufacturing companies, and six manufacturing industries are distinguished. Preliminary figures come out in a release series E.6 and final figures are in the *Federal Reserve Bulletin*.

Stock Market

Since stock prices are a leading indicator, *Business Conditions Digest* carries Standard & Poor's index based on 500 stocks. This links with their earlier series based on 90 stocks which runs from 1957 back to 1918 and, before that, to the Cowles Commission index back to 1871. These are in *Historical Statistics*, which also carries indices for the three main subgroups: industrials, rails, and utilities. The composite and the three subgroups now are actually computed every five minutes during trading on the New York Stock Exchange; the results are available for transmission, and records are kept at Standard & Poor's. Averages for each hour from 11:00 to 3:00 along with high, low, and closing figures are printed in the Daily News Section of their *Standard Corporation Records*. Daily high, low, and closing figures for these four indices are available in their *Current Statistics* going back a year, and historical data are in their *Security Price Index Record*.

These two publications also carry quarterly figures on earnings per share, seasonally adjusted and unadjusted; dividends per share; price/earnings ratios; and yields for the composite and the three main groups. Price/earnings ratios and yields for the four are also available weekly there.

In addition, Standard & Poor's calculates weekly stock price indices for 101 industry groups. These come out first in *The Outlook*, with back data in *Current Statistics* and *Security Price Index Record*. Publication of the *Analysts Handbook* began in 1965. It contains annual figures for the same 101 industry groups on such items as equity, sales, operating income, depreciation, earnings, taxes, dividends, plant and equipment expenditures, and year-end working capital. Quarterly figures on dividends and earnings may also be published.

Three other sources of stock price information are widely distributed. There are many imitators of the original stock price index started in 1897, the Dow Jones. Averages for the composite, based on 65 stocks, and the industrials, rails, and utilities groups are computed for opening, high, low, and closing prices and for each hour from 11:00 to 3:00. Daily figures are in the *Wall Street Journal* and weekly ones in *Barron's*. Moody's issues weekly stock price indices for these three subgroups, for banks, and for fire insurance companies. For the same five categories, Moody's issues monthly data on dividends per share, yields, and quarterly earnings. These are carried in the *Survey of Current Business* along with prices from Standard & Poor's and Dow Jones. But the original data are in Moody's weekly *Stock Survey*. And finally, the Securities and Exchange Commission issued *SEC Indexes of Weekly Closing Prices of Common Stocks on the New York Stock Exchange* with figures from 1939 to mid-1964. The chief advantage of these figures was a 32-industry breakdown according to the Standard Industrial Classification by which all government statistics are arranged. The service of Crandall, Pierce & Co. seems to be continuing these series.

The Securities and Exchange Commission in its monthly *Statistical Bulletin* does continue to publish weekly data on round- and odd-lot transactions on the New York and American stock exchanges by transactor, market value, and volume of sales on registered and exempt exchanges. For the other exchanges it publishes monthly volume and value data.

The New York Stock Exchange, which now accounts for nearly three-quarters of all shares traded on registered exchanges and six-sevenths of the dollar value, compiles daily figures on the volume traded going back to 1900; monthly figures on the shares of short interest outstanding; monthly figures on customers' net debit balances and free credit balances from 1931; member borrowings from 1918; and distributions of percentage changes in the prices of individual stocks from a month ago, a quarter ago, and a year ago. The Exchange also keeps track of the number and market value of shares listed, and the dividend records. This information is released to the press, and published in their *Monthly Review* or their annual *Fact Book*. The Exchange also runs and publishes an annual *Census of Shareholders* and special studies, for example, on institutional holders.

The Exchange's debit, credit, and borrowings figures, supplemented by the Fed's own tabulations for some June and December dates, are the basis for a regular table in the *Federal Reserve Bulletin*. This shows customer borrowings and net borrowings from stock exchange members with U.S. government and other securities as collateral. Then there are two columns on people's borrowings from banks for purchasing and carrying securities, U.S. government and other, as reported by the weekly reporting member banks. The rest of the table shows the financing of the stock exchange members themselves, including borrowings against U.S. government securities, other customers' securities, and other securities belonging to the firms, as well as customers' free credit balances. In addition, the *Survey of Current Business* carries a series on New York Stock Exchange members' cash on hand and in banks. The main back figures are in *Historical Statistics*.

CONCLUSION

Out of this vast amount of material, how should someone with a small amount of space and money begin a collection which will best serve his needs? For most people, the first purchase should be a copy of the *Statistical Abstract of the United States*. Not only will this volume answer many questions entirely, but it will also provide back-

ground, assist in visualizing the available data, and refer the user to supplementary sources in the footnotes and appendix. Thus, even those on a very limited budget should get a copy every other year.

Purchase number two should be a subscription to the *Survey of Current Business*. This is the main source for many of the nation's important statistics. It also has a massive statistical appendix reprinting series from other government and private sources, and including much industry data. With the *Survey* comes a weekly supplement entitled *Business Statistics*, which contains the series in the statistical appendix as they are released throughout the month. With this weekly supplement, most users will find it unnecessary to subscribe to the press releases of the Department of Commerce. The time gap is only a couple of days; whenever this is significant, newspapers usually supply the necessary information.

For those who do find it necessary to be up to the minute, the news releases are listed in the text. Such people will also find helpful the *Business Conditions Digest* publication of the Commerce Department. This is so partly because it has a short printing time, and partly because its whole framework is oriented to sensitive indicators with regular tendencies to lead, coincide with, or lag behind turns in general business activity.

Another way to keep up to the minute is to follow some of the weekly indicators such as: automobile production and ten-day reports of sales and inventories in *Ward's Automotive Reports*; electric power distributed from Edison Electric Institute; steel production from the American Iron and Steel Institute; paperboard production from the National Paperboard Association; railroad freight carloadings and intercity truck tonnage from the Association of American Railroads and the American Trucking Association respectively; retail sales from the Census Bureau; the Wholesale Price Index from the Bureau of Labor Statistics; insured unemployment from the Bureau of Employment Security; the number of industrial and commercial failures from Dun and Bradstreet; federal receipts and withdrawals (daily) from the Treasury Department; stock prices (daily); the treasury bill rate (daily); the money supply (with seasonally adjusted figures biweekly); commercial and industrial loans; and free reserves of member banks.

Returning to the needs of those who can get only a few publications, most will find it useful to get two of the supplements to the *Survey of Current Business*: (1) the latest of the biennial *Business Statistics* volumes with historical data to match the appendix series and (2) the latest national income volume. The next recommendation would probably be a subscription to the *Federal Reserve Bulletin*. If several people will be using such publications, it is probably better to get one of each in order to have access to more data and articles and to improve slightly the timing of data receipt, though this may mean sharing around.

For a small office, this "short shelf" may be sufficient. In one of these publications, most of the available types of data can be found, brought reasonably close to date. The other publications mentioned in the text, however, provide much additional detail, description, timeliness, and historical background. To find the right person to answer inquiries on any of the federal statistics, a copy of the *Federal Statistical Directory*, compiled in 1970 by the Office of Management and the Budget, is valuable. It lists all U.S. government personnel who create and analyze data.

One type of information not covered at all in the above brief list is state and city data. For this one must go to the individual subject publications. Throughout this chapter, some attention has been paid to noting the availability of local area figures. For ex-

ample, sources are noted for employment, unemployment, hours, earnings, local government budgets, construction contracts and permits, status of existing housing, much population data, personal income, retail sales, automobile registrations, business incorporations and failures, consumer prices and cost-of-living; information on manufacturing, mining, agriculture, and other business including that found in the Annual Survey of Manufactures, *Minerals Yearbook,* and the current Department of Agriculture publications; statistics on utilities, bank debits, loan rates, and balance sheets; and data on savings and loan associations and credit unions.

The index of the *Statistical Abstract* will give additional clues under "states," "cities," and "standard metropolitan statistical areas." A supplement to the *Abstract,* called *County and City Data Book*, which comes out every four years, provides not only suggestions of sources but also much data in convenient form. The government has issued many guides to help in locating area information: *Directory of Federal Statistics for Metropolitan Areas*; the Advisory Commission on Intergovernmental Relations, October 1962, which also has references for counties, cities, and other places; the more recent *Measuring Metropolitan Markets* of the Business and Defense Services Administration; the *Directory of Federal Statistics for Local Areas*, 1966; the *Directory of Federal Statistics for States*, 1967; and the *Directory of Non Federal Statistics for States and Local Areas*, 1970. The prime sources of additional data for a specific state or area are state and city government departments, local development organizations and chambers of commerce, transportation companies, communications firms, utilities, banks, and universities.

Part Two

MAJOR APPROACHES
TO BUSINESS FORECASTING

Tools are to be used. But how? Forecasts must be framed in a model of economic behavior. But the models used by business forecasters are of two types. They either rely on formal mathematical representations of the economy or they are essentially intuitive.

Chapters 1 and 2 illustrate the two most widely used formal models. The first chapter is an overview of the econometric approach to business forecasting: its structure, its rationale, its uses, and its abuses. This is followed by a chapter on a completely different approach to formal economic model building in which the focus is upon the interindustrial framework of the economy.

In contrast, the "intuitive" approach in its most sophisticated form—the sectoral method—is described in the subsequent chapter. Variations of this approach are illustrated in Part 3 and throughout the book, and are among the most widely used by the economics profession. Part 2 closes with a survey of the many varied techniques which are used in the rapidly growing field of technological forecasting.

MAJOR APPROACHES
TO WEATHER FORECASTING

MICHAEL K. EVANS

Econometric Models

INTRODUCTION

Econometric models have had a short but checkered history when compared to the ancient and sometimes honorable art of forecasting. Initially billed as *the* answer to man's age-old wish to foresee the future, then in many cases cast aside when they failed to fulfill this wish, econometric models are returning toward an equilibrium position in the forecaster's portfolio. For better or worse, econometric models are here to stay—in assisting businessmen to improve their forecasting decisions at the macroeconomic, industry, and company level. Yet a subtle difference in the blend between science and art has become apparent in this latest generation of econometric models. The raw power of advanced computer technology and econometric methodology untempered by judgment is fast becoming the exclusive province of academe, while the refined blend of these essential elements is spreading rapidly throughout the sophisticated business community.

It is this blend of statistics and judgment, of art and science, that can be used to best advantage in designing forecasting models. Inability to accept this fusion has led to many econometric forecasting disasters. The reluctance of many forecasters even tentatively to explore the improvement which could result from the use of statistical methods has led to consistently poor forecasts for many companies and industries. Thus, besides discussing the statistical and mathematical methods of forecasting, where appropriate I will show how judgment enters the forecasting process. I will also show how the presence or absence of judgment may have affected other econometric forecasts. For it is only with this balance that we maximize the probability of generating the most accurate forecasts.

Strictly speaking, econometrics is defined as the use of statistical and mathematical techniques to measure results hypothesized by economic theory. An econometric model incorporates functional relationships estimated by these techniques into an internally consistent and logically self-contained framework. All such models contain some variables which are used as inputs into the system but are themselves determined outside the model; these variables, which include policy variables and uncontrolled events, are known as *exogenous* variables. All models also contain variables which are determined within the system; these are known as *endogenous* variables. The equations which comprise the model may be either *stochastic*, which means that they include some error term and thus do not hold exactly at every moment in time, or they may be *identities*. Although macroeconomic models have received the most attention, many suitable models have been built for a

161

specific sector, region, industry, firm, or individual product. It is likely that the bulk of econometric model building during the next decade will occur in these areas.

To some people, the term "econometric model" rings of esoteric formulas and technology which will never be useful to the practical businessman. To others, it suggests mountains of computer output untouched by human hands—or, in extreme cases, by human minds. Yet it may be fairly stated that every intelligent business forecaster in effect goes through an informal econometric exercise every time he generates a prediction. He determines the principal factors which affect the variable he is forecasting and tries to estimate their relative importance. In many cases it is just common sense to put these relationships in a quantifiable framework. In order to do this, however, it is necessary to be familiar with the general methods of building, testing, and forecasting with econometric models. These are discussed in the next section.

APPLYING ECONOMIC THEORY

The first step in building any econometric model should be to apply relevant portions of economic theory to the problem at hand. The theory may not be very detailed or esoteric; few economists who have tried to estimate functions based on the pure theory of the firm or consumer behavior have wanted to talk about it afterward. It is usually sufficient for the would-be model builder to have some idea of the principal independent variables which will be important in the various equations. One of the surest ways to fall into the pitfall of bad forecasting is to summon one of the many large economic data bases presently available, select a few hundred variables, run correlations on all possible sets of pairs, triplets, or larger subsets, and then select the equation with the best fit as the one to be used

for forecasting. In the great majority of cases the equation with the best sample period statistics will *not* give the best forecasts.

While this caveat may sound overly simplistic, it will at least eliminate the two most common pitfalls in estimating equations for which the errors in the forecast period are much worse than in the sample period. The two pitfalls avoided are:

1. It minimizes the possibility of including spurious variables which just happen to be correlated with the dependent variable during the sample period but in fact have no underlying relationship. Elementary statistical textbooks usually quote allegedly humorous examples, such as the correlation between the number of schoolteachers and the amount of alcohol consumed, or the number of births and the amount of highway construction. However, mistakes are seldom so obvious in actual empirical investigation.

2. It reduces the possibility of correlating a variable with itself. Stated in such bald terms, this also seems like an impossible mistake. However, the variable can be camouflaged in various ways. For example, someone searching a data bank for series with high correlations might decide to "explain" aggregate investment as a function of total savings, without realizing that they differ only by the statistical discrepancy. In one study which I have seen, new car sales are a function of the personal savings rate as well as other variables. Evidently the economist in question was unaware that on an ex post basis the main cause of change in the savings rate is the change in new car sales. Thus the relationship gave an excellent sample period fit, but in the forecast period the economist could not predict the savings rate unless he knew the level of new car sales, and vice versa.

Misspecification of the underlying equations occasionally happens to the most sophisticated econometricians and forecasters. One should at least make every attempt to avoid the simple pitfalls.

A Typical Macroeconomic Model

As an example of how one would construct a model from relevant economic theory, we might consider the example of a typical macroeconomic model. While the example is somewhat well-worn, it does offer a clear-cut example of how one might proceed. Furthermore, the great bulk of econometric application to date has been in the field of short-run macroeconomic models. As we will want to examine the accuracy of these forecasts later in the chapter, it may be useful to outline the type of models which have been utilized.

The basic outline of the generalized Keynesian system can be presented as follows:

$$C = f(X, i)$$
$$I = f(X, i)$$
$$C + I + \bar{G} = X$$
$$X = f(E, K, \bar{t}) \text{ or } E = f(X, K, \bar{t})$$
$$\frac{\delta X}{\delta E} = \frac{w}{p} \text{ or } p = \frac{w}{\delta X/\delta E}$$
$$\Delta w = f(\Delta p, Un)$$
$$\bar{M}_s = M_d = kpX - \lambda pi$$
$$Un = \bar{L} - E$$

where C = consumption expenditures
I = investment expenditures
G = government purchases
X = total income or output
i = interest rates or other financial variables
E = employment
K = capital stock (weighted average of past investment)
t = trend for technology
w = wage rate
Un = unemployment rate
M_s = money supply
M_d = demand for money
p = price level
Barred variable denote exogenous inputs

Stated very briefly, this set of equations posits that consumption expenditures are a function of output (or income) and financial variables; investment expenditures are also a function of output and financial variables; and consumption plus investment plus government expenditures, which are assumed to be exogenous, equals gross national product. On the supply side, output is a function of labor and capital inputs and the state of technology. Alternatively, we can write that the demand for labor is a function of output, the existing capital stock, and the state of technology. Prices are assumed to be some constant proportion of wages divided by the marginal product of labor; this relationship comes directly from the conditions for cost-minimization by the firm. The change in wage rates is a function of the changes in prices and the rate of unemployment. The money supply is assumed to be exogenous, while the demand for money is a function of output, the price level, and the rate of interest. Finally, unemployment is the difference between the labor force (assumed to be exogenous) and actual employment.

This simple model contains all the elements of the fundamental Keynesian system, which has become the basis for virtually all of the large-scale econometric models which have been built in the last decade. However, this model if estimated directly would not be useful for either forecasting or analysis. First, the model contains too few variables to present accurate forecasts. Second, the variables themselves must be quantified (such as the difference between income and output). Third, a specific lag structure must be included, since we all know that the economy does not react instantaneously to changes in government policy. We will now briefly explain how this is accomplished.

The first major step in the transformation of this outline to a workable theoretical model is the expansion of the components of aggregate demand. Consumption of durables is a cyclically volatile component of GNP, with a short-run income elasticity substantially in excess of unity. Furthermore, it is heavily influenced by attitudinal variables, which can be adequately measured and represented by the rate of unemployment and the rate of inflation, and by monetary variables such as the cost and availability of credit. Most of the other components of consumption have short-run income elasticities which are much less than unity and are heavily influenced by previous as well as present income. In addition, income distribution may be important for some components of consumption. So-called luxury goods are likely to rise more rapidly when nonwage income increases, while necessities are likely to show little response to such a change.

Investment should be disaggregated by plant and equipment expenditures, residential construction, and inventory investment, since these have widely differing patterns over the business cycle. Inventory investment is quite volatile and has accounted for over half of the total fluctuations in GNP during postwar recessions. Plant and equipment investment is influenced primarily by lagged variables and hence tends to lag the cycle. Residential construction is countercyclical because it receives residual factors of production from other sectors of the economy. Credit rationing is extremely important in determining residential construction, somewhat less important for nonresidential construction, and has relatively little influence on purchases of producers' durable equipment. On the other hand, changes in depreciation tax lives or the rate of investment tax credit are quite important in determining equipment purchases, but have virtually no direct effect on the remainder of investment.

The net foreign balance is completely exogenous in the simplest Keynesian model. However, imports clearly depend on domestic income and prices, while exports depend at a minimum on domestic prices as well as a variety of foreign incomes and prices. While government purchases are properly treated as exogenous, there is a great difference in the impact of changes in defense expenditures, government construction, pay increases, or changes in farm supports.

The second major addition which is needed is the distinction between GNP, national income, and personal disposable income, since consumption depends on the latter, whereas plant and equipment and inventory investment depend on total output or some close variant. To do this it is necessary to explain the intermediate variables in the identities linking these terms. Separate functions are needed for depreciation, taxes and transfers, and corporate savings. Taxes and transfers should be separated into functions for personal income taxes, corporate income taxes, indirect business taxes, and transfers. Corporate savings depend on after-tax corporate profits, which can be estimated either directly or as a residual. If the latter is done, it is then necessary to estimate equations for other factor shares; wages, unincorporated business income, and rentier income.

A third major addition is the expansion of the monetary sector to include the prediction of several different interest rates, some measure of the availability of credit, and the endogenous components of the money supply. While it is true that the Federal Reserve does control monetary conditions closely through open market operations, there is sometimes a substantial lag between changes in free reserves and changes in the money supply. The demand for money, often disaggregated further into equations for currency, demand deposits, and time deposits, is a function of income, interest rates, and various components of aggregate demand. The short-term interest rate is a function of monetary policy (as represented by changes in free reserves, the discount rate, and the required reserve ratios) and of the demand for funds by category. The long-term rate is a function of a weighted average of past short-term rates, a weighted average of expected rates of inflation, and the percentage of financing done in the bond market. An identity is then used to link the relationship between free reserves, required reserve ratios, and the actual money supply.

A model which is disaggregated along these lines would probably have approximately 30 to 50 stochastic equations. Several models of this approximate size exist and are currently being used for actual forecasting. These include the Wharton, Michigan, Office of Business Economics (OBE), and IBM models. It is also possible to expand the models considerably by including much greater detail in both the aggregate demand, aggregate supply, monetary, and wage and price sectors. Such expansion might take place, for example, by predicting ten to fifteen components for each of the major sectors of aggregate demand. Further equations could be added on the supply side by considering various sectors separately rather than working with aggregate production, wages, employment, and unemployment. The monetary sector could be expanded to include the demand for assets held by a variety of financial intermediaries and their corresponding interest rates. Finally, we could treat separately the price deflator for each individual component of aggregate demand, rather than estimating just one overall price level. Several models have also been constructed along these lines, including the FRB-MIT model, one by this author, and several others built by commercial economic consulting firms. The Brookings model, the pioneering work in this area, was originally structured in this way but original plans were never completed and the revised model included little of this detailed disaggregation.

Because of the proliferation of macro-econometric models, it is no longer useful, as perhaps it was in the earlier edition of this book, to list one or more of these models in toto. However, in order to give a flavor of the type of equations commonly used in these models, I have included equations for (a) new passenger car sales, (b) single-family housing starts, and (c) demand deposits, which are taken from the model which I have most recently estimated. While these equations are somewhat more complicated than others I could have chosen, they are indicative of the degree of sophistication contained in most macroeconomic models.

Some Actual Equations

New Passenger Car Sales

$$C_{NCS} = 7.43$$
$$+ \underset{(2.7)}{0.0141} \sum_{i=0}^{4} (0.6)^i (DI - TR)_{-i}$$
$$+ \underset{(1.3)}{4.83} \sum_{i=0}^{4} (0.6)^i (Y_{DIST})_{-i}$$
$$- \underset{(3.7)}{0.422} {}^{1}\!/_{4} \sum_{i=1}^{4} (CRED)_{-i}$$
$$- \underset{(2.9)}{0.0975} \left(\frac{p_{CAMP}}{p_{CI}} \right) - \underset{(6.7)}{0.565} UN$$
$$+ \underset{(2.6)}{0.883} d_{ASTR}$$
$$- \underset{(1.0)}{0.0196} \sum_{i=0}^{4} (0.6)^i (K_{NCS})_{-i-1}$$
$$\bar{R}^2 = 0.923$$
$$d = 1.46$$

where C_{NCS} = new passenger car sales, millions

DI = personal disposable income, billions of constant dollars

TR = transfer payments, billions of constant dollars

Y_{DIST} = ratio of nonwage personal income to wages and salaries

$CRED$ = credit rationing variable

p_{CAMP} = average monthly payment for new cars, dollars/month

p_{CI} = Consumer Price Index

UN = unemployment rate

d_{ASTR} = dummy variable for auto strikes

K_{NCS} = stock of new cars

T-ratios are given parenthetically directly below each coefficient

$\bar{R}^2$ is the coefficient of determination, adjusted for degrees of freedom

d is the Durbin-Watson statistic

In general, this equation follows our earlier remarks about the equations for consumer durables. As the independent variables, we have included disposable income less transfer payments, income distribution, credit rationing, the average monthly payment, the rate of unemployment, the previous stock of cars, and a dummy variable for auto strikes. In most cases the independent variables are lagged up to one year, which represents a fairly short adjustment period. The lag in income can be compared to the functions for nondurables and services, where the lags on income and income distribution are as long as sixteen quarters.

While this equation is fairly complex, an equation to explain new car sales which was part of a model for the automobile industry would undoubtedly contain additional terms for the supply of cars and for inventory adjustments. We have not attempted to do this in the macroeconomic model.

Single-Family Housing Starts

$$IH_{S1} = 4.392 + \underset{(4.8)}{0.00210}DI$$

$$-\underset{(7.1)}{0.1420}\frac{1.0}{\dfrac{2.5 - 3CRED + 2CRED_{-1} + CRED_{-2}}{6}}$$

$$-\underset{(12.9)}{0.1537}\frac{3VAC_{R-5} + 2VAC_{R-6} + VAC_{R-7}}{6}$$

$$-\underset{(7.2)}{3.911}\left[\left(\frac{p_{IHNF}}{p_{CIR}}\right)_{-2} + \left(\frac{p_{IHNF}}{p_{CIR}}\right)_{-3}\right]$$

$$+\underset{(5.6)}{0.0247}\,\tfrac{1}{4}\sum_{i=1}^{4}(UN_C)_{-i}$$

$$+\underset{(2.8)}{4.056}\,\tfrac{1}{4}\sum_{i=5}^{8}\left(\frac{N_M^{20-24}}{N_M^{25-54}}\right)_{-i}$$

$$\bar{R}^2 = 9.13$$
$$d = 1.02$$

where IH_{S1} = millions of single-family housing starts

DI = personal disposable income, billions of constant dollars

$CRED$ = credit rationing variable

VAC_R = vacancy rate of residential units

p_{IHNF} = implicit deflator for nonfarm residential construction

P_{CIR} = Consumer Price Index for rent

UN_C = unemployment rate in construction industry

N_M^{20-24} = number of males ages 20–24

N_M^{25-54} = number of males ages 25–54

It is clear from this equation that housing starts are a function of both supply and demand factors. On the supply side, credit rationing, the relative availability of labor, and the price of factors of production relative to a rent index are all quite important. On the demand side, the vacancy rate and the proportion of males between the ages of 20 and 24 are also key variables. The unlagged disposable income term represents a modifications term. As income rises, more units are built for a given level of available resources and demand, which means that more units are built for speculative purposes.

Demand Deposits

$$\Delta DD = -2.87 + \underset{(4.0)}{0.0300 DI\$}$$
$$- \underset{(1.0)}{0.0292 I_p\$} - \underset{(1.3)}{0.0237 I_i\$}$$
$$- \underset{(6.1)}{0.873} \sum_{i=0}^{3} (0.4 - 0.1^*i) r_{cp-i}$$
$$- \underset{(2.7)}{1.103} \frac{(r_{TD-1} + r_{TD-2})}{2}$$
$$- \underset{(2.9)}{0.552} \left[\frac{d_{CD} + d_{CD-1}}{2} \right.$$
$$\left. - \frac{1}{4} \sum_{i=2}^{5} (d_{CD})_{-i} \right]$$
$$- \underset{(4.6)}{9.02} \frac{E_{D-1} + E_{D-2}}{2}$$

where DD = demand deposits, billions of current dollars

$DI\$$ = personal disposable income, billions of current dollars

$I_p\$$ = fixed business investment, billions of current dollars

$I_i\$$ = inventory investment, billions of current dollars

r_{cp} = commercial paper rate

r_{TD} = interest rate on time deposits

d_{CD} = dummy variable for introduction of certificates of deposit

$E_D = \delta(r_{CP} - r_{CL}) - \delta(r_{CP} - r_{CL})_{-1}$

r_{CL} is the commercial loan rate

δ is the Kronecker delta, which is 1 if $r_{CP} > r_{CL}$ and 0 otherwise

As mentioned above, demand deposits are a function of disposable income, interest rates, and various components of aggregate demand. We have also included a variable to represent the introduction of certificates of deposit into the banking system, which had a once-and-for-all effect of lowering demand deposits although the effect was spread over several quarters. The single most important variable for explaining quarterly fluctuations, however, is the variable denoted by the symbol E_D. This is a "flash point" variable which in effect measures the response to disintermediation. When the commercial paper rate rises above the commercial loan rate, certain funds flow out of the banking system into directly placed securities and stay there until the rates return to normal levels. It is nonlinear terms such as these which do much to distinguish the most recent econometric models from their predecessors.

DATA SOURCES AND PROBLEMS

It is quite unlikely that anyone has ever built an econometric model of a given degree of reliability without having data which were at least as reliable. The sources of data have been covered thoroughly in the previous chapter. This brief section will be concerned with possible pitfalls in some of the most commonly available data. We limit ourselves here to a discussion of the generally available government statistics. In my experience, data from private and industry sources are much worse that the government statistics.

The main problems are as follows:

1. Timeliness. This may be important if one is engaged in monthly or even quarterly forecasting. For example, quarterly series which do not appear for several months until after the quarter has ended are apt to be less useful than up-to-date series. For this reason, many forecasters tend to use components of the national income accounts which appear promptly, rather than more exact series which appear with a lag of several months.

2. Revisions. The usefulness of many

data series is seriously impaired if the revised numbers are significantly different from the preliminary releases. A major example of this is the weekly series of retail trade, which were found to be so unsatisfactory that they are no longer publicized, although the numbers are still available. Unfortunately, there is some tradeoff between timeliness and amount of revision, so one must choose with this in mind.

One quirk in the revisions centers on the investment figures. Figures for fixed business investment are available both in the national income accounts (NIA) and as tabulated jointly by the Office of Business Economics and the Securities and Exchange Commission (OBE-SEC). The NIA figures are based primarily on the OBE-SEC figures, but when the NIA figures are first released the OBE-SEC figures are not final and do not appear in final form for another month and a half. However, the NIA figures are not revised again, even after the final OBE-SEC figures appear, until the next annual revision of the national income accounts. Thus the NIA figures may contain substantial errors for as long as a year. In this case one is well advised to use the OBE-SEC figures as regression inputs; both sets contain the preliminary errors, but the NIA figures are not adjusted until as much as a full year later.

In addition, note that many of the NIA numbers are not finalized until three years have passed. While the majority of these series change very little after the first year, the corporate profits numbers three years earlier are often revised substantially. The figures for industry shipments by two-, three-, and four-digit industries are also not available in final form until three years afterward. This particular problem stems from the time lags inherent in compiling the raw data used in the *Annual Survey of Manufacturers.*

3. Comparability. When a series in the national income accounts is revised (because of a change in either definition or benchmark), the series is usually available for previous years on a revised basis; at a minimum a factor is provided which allows one to link the old and new series. This is emphatically not the case for many other government series. The most outstanding culprit is the *Quarterly Financial Report for Manufacturing Corporations* (QFR), where a change of companies in the sample usually does not even rate a footnote, let alone a splicing factor. No adjustment factors are provided when companies change their method of accounting or when a given company switches from one industry to another. Unfortunately, the QFR at present provides the only source of data for industry profits.

4. Methodology. Many series are not what they purport to be. One of the main examples of this is the respected Federal Reserve's Index of Industrial Production. The monthly movements in many of the components in that index, particularly for the smaller industries, are not based on shipments but rather are little more than employment statistics adjusted for some arbitrary measure of productivity. A different type of problem exists with the unemployment rate, since the labor force statistics are based on a household survey, while the employment statistics are tabulated on an establishment basis. Sometimes the series do not move in the same direction, so that the residual, which is the number of self-employed, fluctuates wildly from month to month. In reality this series should be one of the most stable employment series, since individual entrepreneurs do not fire themselves if there is a short-run decline in business.

5. Seasonality. The Bureau of the Census has developed very sophisticated methods for treating seasonal factors. Unfortunately, these methods do not always work. Several types of problem may occur. First of all, these arguments assume that the seasonal factors

are multiplicative, which means that the same percentage seasonal occurs each year. While this is the single best assumption if one must be restricted to one method, it does not hold in all cases. For example, prices increase proportionately more in the fourth quarter in a year of high inflation than low inflation; conversely, they sag more (on a seasonally adjusted basis) in the third quarter. This has recently led to considerable difficulty in analyzing inflationary trends during the 1969–71 period. To choose another example, there has been either a steel strike or a threat of one in more than half of the last fifteen years. As a result, in the off years, third quarter steel production on a seasonally adjusted basis has been recorded about ten percent too high. As a final example, if one uses additive instead of multiplicative factors to adjust unemployment, the unemployment rate during postrecession years turns up sooner in the year than has been reported. There are many other similar examples where the seasonally adjusted series have masked underlying movements.

The practical business economist, faced with the existing plethora of data and worried about which variables to choose in the first place, can hardly be expected to spend a great deal of time weighing which series he should choose on the basis of the reliability of the data. However, as a start, it is often worth examining the lags with which the data appear, the record of revision over the past few years, and at least a brief introduction on the methodology. Otherwise the economist may find himself spending his time predicting quirks, seasonal factors, and revisions in the data instead of his company's sales.

Estimation Techniques

There are many different estimation techniques which are used by the experi-

enced statistician and econometrician. However, one method — least squares — has proven so useful and durable that it still accounts for the great majority of empirical work undertaken in the social sciences today. As explained in the chapter by John G. Myers on basic statistical methods, this method minimizes the sum of the squares of the residuals—the difference between the actual value and predicted value—over the sample period.

Shortly after World War II, a group of research economists at the Cowles Commission (now Cowles Foundation), led by T. C. Koopmans, focused their attention on what has become known as the *simultaneity bias*. This states that least-squares estimates are inconsistent if some of the independent variables are determined simultaneously with the dependent variable. Probably the major example of such a function at that time was the simplistic relation in which consumption was a function of unlagged income. It was pointed out that although income is clearly a determinant of consumption, consumption is the major component of total income. This two-way causality causes a spuriously high coefficient for the income term and may lead to poor forecasts.

During the postwar period a number of methods have been developed which would theoretically eliminate this bias. The most common of these methods include two-stage least squares, limited information, and full information. While we will not cover the details of these methods, the basic methodology can be summarized here very briefly:

1. In calculating regression parameters for two-stage least squares, one first regresses the unlagged independent variables (such as income) on the lagged and exogenous variables of the complete model.[1] The values of income

---

[1] If the number of variables exceeds the degrees of freedom, one usually chooses a subset of the lagged and exogenous variables by using principal components. This is discussed later in this section.

and other simultaneous variables *predicted by these first-stage regressions* are then used as the independent variables in the second-stage regressions. Further detail on this method is given in the appendix to the Myers' chapters.

2. If one uses limited or full information methods, he must estimate the whole model simultaneously. This involves maximizing the likelihood function, which means that one is maximizing the probability of estimating the true population parameters. The main difference between limited information and full information is that in the latter case one must know the complete specification of every equation in the model, while for limited information one must know all the other variables in the system but need not know the form in which they enter the equations.

While these methods should eliminate the simultaneity bias, there are several possible drawbacks. First, the methods are computationally cumbersome. While this problem has been somewhat reduced by third generation high-speed computers, it is still ridiculous to have to specify a complete model in order to estimate one equation. Furthermore, the cost factor is still significant; estimation of a single equation by simultaneous equation methods can cost between 50 and 1,000 times as much as estimating the same equation using ordinary least squares.

However, if cost and complexity were the only factors, it would still be worthwhile to experiment with simultaneous equation methods once one had formulated a model. There are much more compelling reasons why they may result in poorer parameter estimates. The misspecification of a single variable in a complete model may cause biases and distortions which are worse than those caused by simultaneity bias. In addition, it is usually impossible to estimate today's large-scale models by these methods

because one soon runs out of degrees of freedom. In order to use any simultaneous equation methods of estimation without further modifications, the number of observations must be greater than the total number of variables in the model. With over two-hundred variables in most modern macroeconometric models, this is impossible. This has led to various modifications of these methods to circumvent the situation. One method used is to divide the model into blocks and then assume that all variables in a given block depend only on other variables in that block and in blocks for which the solution has already been completed. For example, investment would depend only on lagged variables, consumption would depend only on investment, and so forth. This method, known as the block-recursive system, is seriously defective because it negates one of the most important facets of econometric models —the interaction between aggregate demand and supply, and between the real and monetary sectors.

Another method commonly used is to choose a certain subset of exogenous variables which is smaller in number than the degrees of freedom. In order to avoid an arbitrary choice of exogenous variables, the method most commonly employed consists of calculating a certain number of principal components (usually between four and twelve) from all the exogenous and lagged variables and then using them as the exogenous instruments for the first stage of regressions. While this method is the least offensive of the available choices, it is still seriously deficient in the sense that we are no longer specifying the particular exogenous variables which enter the complete system. Thus we are increasing the probability of misspecification and hence of biased and distorted parameter estimates from that source.

The silliest case of all is clearly that of full information, where by definition no shortcuts (such as block-recursive or principal components) can be used, so that the total number of variables—jointly determined, lagged endogenous, and exogenous—must be less than the number of observations. In addition, the complete model must be linear, thus eliminating the various non-linearities and asymmetries which have proved to be so important in modern-day forecasting models.

There are thus substantial drawbacks to using simultaneous equation methods. Yet it is possible that there are substantial biases caused by using single-equation methods. On balance the question of which source of error is greater is an empirical one. While the subject has not been tested extensively, we can draw on the two available tests which have been performed.

Several years ago this author constructed and estimated a model of the agricultural sector of the U.S. economy. This model was quite detailed, containing eighteen sectors and over one hundred jointly determined variables. The model was, however, particularly adaptable to simultaneous equation estimation because in many cases individual subsectors (such as dairy, food grain, etc.) could be treated as separate blocks. Furthermore, of all the areas of econometrics, it is most likely that the agricultural sector could benefit most from the use of simultaneous equations, since price and quantity are often determined simultaneously. This is not the case with industrial commodities, where the price is set and the quantity to be sold at that price is then determined.

This model of the agricultural sector was estimated by ordinary least squares, two-stage least squares with various numbers of principal components, and limited information. The model was then used to generate ex post forecasts one and two years beyond the sample period, using a variety of different assumptions about the type of constant adjustments. It was indeed found that the ordinary least squares equations produced the best predictions. However, we also found that in certain cases the limited information estimates would not even reach a convergent solution, let alone give reasonable predictions.

In the second study designed to test the relative efficacy of different methods of

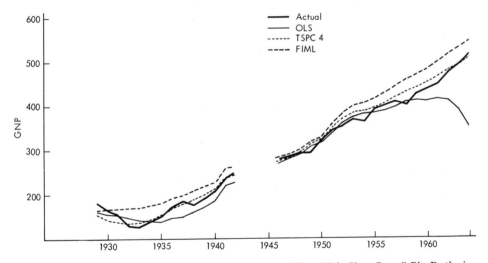

Adapted from Morris Norman, "The Great Depression and What Might Have Been," Ph. D. thesis, University of Pennsylvania, 1968.

Chart 1

estimation, Morris Norman, in his Ph.D. thesis at the University of Pennsylvania, estimated an updated version of the Klein-Goldberger model.[2] Because this model was of modest size and contained no nonlinearities, he was able to estimate it using full information as well as all the other methods mentioned above. He then simulated the model over the sample period, 1929–65, which included the Great Depression. The results are so striking that they are reproduced in chart 1, where it can be seen that the full information estimates show *no downturn at all* during the Great Depression.

These results have led me to believe that, in spite of the dangers inherent in using ordinary least squares, the hazards are smaller than if one uses simultaneous equation methods.

One final point might be mentioned on this matter. When econometricians were still estimating aggregate consumption as a function of national income, the possibilities for upward bias in the slope coefficient were substantial. We now estimate consumption of clothing as a function of a weighted average of eight quarters of personal disposable income, income distribution, and relative prices; the possibility of simultaneity bias seems indeed remote. Much more sophisticated uses of econometrics have led away from aggregate functions and hence have bypassed the problem which led to the formulation of simultaneous methods in the first place. While econometricians will still make bad forecasts on occasion, I doubt very much if it will be due to the fact that they used ordinary least squares.

Testing the Model

As I have pointed out many times in the past, the best test of the usefulness of

any econometric model is its true ex ante forecasting record. However, if this were the only test, no models would ever see the light of day. Some pretesting on known data is essential if we are to have any idea of the type of accuracy which can be expected in the future. There are three usual steps to testing the model: (1) examination of equation residuals, (2) sample period simulations, and (3) ex post forecasts. We will now consider each of these in turn.

Checking single-equation residuals is, of course, by far the most common and time-honored method of starting econometric research. Virtually all economic statisticians, even if they claim otherwise, do most of their empirical work by formulating an equation, staring at the biggest residuals which occur when they first estimate it, and then rerunning the function to reduce the size of these residuals. If this approach is kept within bounds, it is a reasonable and even necessary ingredient of empirical investigation. There are, of course, many other criteria which need to be examined. These include the overall fit of the equation, the autocorrelation of the residuals, the signs of all of the parameter estimates, the reasonableness of the values of the coefficients, the behavior of the function at turning points, and the levels of significance of individual variables.

The fit of the overall equation can be measured either by the multiple coefficient of determination adjusted for degrees of freedom $(\bar{R}^2)$[3] or by the standard error of estimate over the sample period (S_e).

The measure of $\bar{R}^2$ may well be the most misused statistic in practical econometrics. Unfortunately there is a widespread convention to relate the highest $\bar{R}^2$ to the "best" equation for forecasting purposes. In an earlier chapter, John G. Myers has already shown by example how this need not be true. In all of the thousands of equations

[2] Morris Norman, "The Great Depression and What Might Have Been," Ph.D. thesis at the University of Pennsylvania, 1968.

[3] The *F*-ratio, another statistic commonly used, is simply calculated as $R^2(n-k)/(1-R^2)(k-1)$ and thus contains no additional information.

which I have estimated for predictive purposes, probably less than five percent of those selected for forecasting were those with the highest $\bar{R}^2$. The reason is simple. If one calculates several regression equations in order to determine the best one, it is likely that certain variables will appear to be significant when in fact they have only a spurious correlation. If one leaves these variables in the equation, he is likely to generate a very poor forecast, both because the false variable has no real relationship with the dependent variable and because including it in the sample period reduces the importance of variables which are actually significant.

If we use the conventional 95 percent confidence level for deciding whether to include a variable in a regression, then by definition the chance is only one in twenty that an unimportant variable will sneak in by mistake. However, hardly anyone runs only one regression and accepts the first result, and in fact to do so would be a serious methodological mistake. Thus several functions, many of them independent of one another (in that they represent alternative or competing hypotheses), are tried. If 20 functions are tried, the probability that a mistaken variable will be included is raised to 0.64; if 50 are tried it is 0.92; and if 100 equations are tried, it is 0.994. Thus if large numbers of alternative formulations are tried, the probability is almost unity that one or more spurious variables (or lags) will enter the function. The major question then is no longer how to raise $\bar{R}^2$, but rather how to avoid terms that don't really belong but appear to satisfy the conventional statistical criteria. What is to be done?

Part of the answer to this question goes back to my earlier remarks about the importance of choosing a reasonable theory as a guide toward estimating the best forecasting equation. Having done this, one must examine the other criteria mentioned at the beginning of this section. One of the statistics which is regularly examined is the Durbin-Watson statistic, which, as was explained in the Myers' chapter, measures the autocorrelation of the residuals.

The use of the Durbin-Watson statistic has become curiously convoluted in much of the econometric literature. The statistical properties associated with this statistic are clear; if positive autocorrelation exists, the $\bar{R}^2$ of the equation is overstated and the standard errors of the coefficients are understated. What should be equally as clear but is often left unsaid is that positive autocorrelation means that the equation is misspecified because one or more significant variables are missing. A Durbin-Watson statistic of 1.4 or less should serve as a red flag warning that additional work is needed on the equation. Since $\bar{R}^2$ tells one very little, this is one of the few tests which signals that there may be large errors in the forecasting period if the equation is not respecified.

Having one or more variables missing is not a very pleasant state of affairs, but sometimes nothing can be done about it. It may be that the data themselves are collected in such a way that errors of measurement are built into the series, or perhaps the missing effect is important but unquantifiable (such as general business optimism) and needs to be added in at the appropriate time by the forecasters through fine tuning. In any case, misguided econometricians have sometimes been known to "cure" the situation by adding the lagged dependent variable to the right-hand side of the equation. While this will in most cases improve both the fit and the Durbin-Watson statistic, it almost certainly makes for worse forecasts if one is forecasting for more than one period. The reason for this is quite straightforward. Suppose, for example, that we are predicting consumption as a function of income and lagged consumption, which we can write simply as

$$C_t = a_0 + a_1 Y_t + e_t$$

where e_t is the residual at time t.
In the first quarter of the forecast period our prediction is likely to contain some error.

This error will then be included in the lagged dependent variable and will affect the second period forecast as well. In general, this error will continue to grow over time until the forecast becomes ridiculous. If this equation is part of a simultaneous system, it is likely to create poor forecasts for all the variables in the system. However, this problem is well recognized, at least in theory, to the point that if someone uses the lagged dependent variable in a regression, he apologizes for it and does not try to defend it on the grounds that it improves the fit and reduces autocorrelation.

Consider again an equation for which autocorrelation of the residuals is present, and assume that we are unable to find any other reasonable variable which would eliminate this problem. According to classical statistical theory, we should then reestimate the equation to reduce the $\bar{R}^2$ and eliminate the biased standard errors. This is done very simply. If we have an equation

$$C = a_0 + a_1 Y + e_t$$

and

$$e_t = p e_{t-1} + u_t$$

(where the u_t are now serially uncorrelated) then transform the equation to

$$C - p C_{-1} = a_0' + a_1(Y - pY_{-1}) + u_t$$

This method, known as the Cochrane-Orcutt transformation, should produce unbiased standard errors and goodness of fit statistics, which should satisfy everyone.

However, just as in the case of simultaneous equation bias, classical statistical theory fails again. This time it is the problem of multiperiod forecasting which causes the problem. For if we rewrite this equation as

$$C = a_0' + a_1(Y - pY_{-1}) + p C_{-1} + u_t$$

it is almost indistinguishable (except for the lagged income term) from the one above which we dismissed out of hand. We have managed to put the lagged dependent variable back on the right-hand side of the equation, which is exactly the thing which should be avoided. In some experiments with the Wharton model, we used the Cochrane-Orcutt transformation to adjust those equations which had positive autocorrelation. In virtually every case the adjusted equations gave worse predictions than the unadjusted equations, and for exactly the reason given above.

In fact, the whole area of multiperiod forecasting is one which is sadly neglected in the econometric literature, although it is of immense practical importance in business forecasting. Theoretical econometricians would do well to devote themselves to a serious examination of the statistical properties of multiperiod forecasting instead of developing still more ways to estimate systems of simultaneous equations, which can never be used anyway because of practical limitations. It is because this theory has not yet been developed that it is essential to test the equations by using sample period simulations and ex post forecasts. While these methods of testing are important in any case, the multiperiod aspects are particularly critical.

After the econometrician has examined the fit of the equations, the autocorrelation of the residuals, and the signs and values of all the parameter estimates, there are still several additional tests which should be performed. First, he should try to determine, on a single-equation basis, how well the equation or model will forecast. The standard error of estimate for each equation is often an unreliable measure of the magnitude of error which can be expected in the forecast period. There are three reasons why this might be the case:

1. The data probably have been searched for the best sample period fit, hence the equations probably include some variables which have only a spurious correlation. This point has already been discussed.

2. In general, it will not be possible to predict the independent variables in

the equation with perfect accuracy, whereas in the sample period it is assumed that these values are known. This may sound something like the simultaneous equation bias, but it is not; in the forecast period the values of the exogenous variables are not known either.

3. When we consider multiperiod forecasting, the standard error is an even less reliable guide, since it is essentially a measure of single period error. The function may drift farther and farther off the track as the number of forecasted periods increases. This is almost sure to be the case if one has included the lagged dependent variable on the right-hand side of the equation; however, it may also occur even if this error has not been committed. Theoretically, the multiperiod single-equation forecast error is no greater than the single period error if the residuals are not autocorrelated, but in practice I can attest to the fact that this is not the case. Searching the sample period for the "best" result is almost as likely to bias the autocorrelation coefficient downward as it is to bias the $\bar{R}^2$ upward.

While there are no foolproof methods for guarding against proportionately larger errors in the forecast period, there are some fairly stringent methods of testing which are often employed. The first involves using ex post forecasts to examine the behavior of the model outside the sample period. The only drawback to this approach is that it is necessary to omit several data points in the sample period, and it is often the case, particularly in industry or company models, that there is scant data history. Furthermore, the problem becomes even more serious if one wants to perform this analysis for multiperiod forecasting. However, there is a way around the problem.

After the form of the function has been chosen, reestimate it with a truncated sample period (e.g., by omitting the last five years). Such a method probably won't work unless at least ten years of data are available. Assuming, however, that at least this much historical data is available, use the truncated sample period to reestimate the function, and then measure the forecast error for the next t quarters, where t is the number of periods the function will be used to predict. Examine the forecasts errors, with particular reference to the amount they increase over time. Then reestimate the function, including one more time period in the sample. Note whether the coefficients change and by how much. The process should be *repeated* until the end of the sample period has been reached. It is then possible to tell whether there are cyclical or secular patterns in the fluctuation of the parameter estimates as well as in the forecast errors themselves. By examining factors like this it is possible to gain a great deal of additional information about the type of function which will yield the best ex ante predictions. On the basis of this kind of testing, it may be reasonable to introduce new cyclical variables, or possibly even to use weighted regressions or dummy variables which make certain parameters more important in one part of the sample period than elsewhere. In addition, one obtains a much better measure of both single period and multiperiod forecasting error.

Another widely used method of testing is the use of sample period simulations for the entire model; this is a necessity when we have simultaneous equation models. For example, we might find a very close relationship between investment in equipment and new orders for durable goods. However, this would be of little use unless we were able to explain the patterns of new orders themselves. Fluctuations in the money supply might be a function of the spread between two interest rates, but it might turn out that these rates usually move together and the major differences in the spread were due to random events which could not be accurately predicted. Simulation of the complete model also guards against errors of the type mentioned earlier, such as putting the same variable on both sides of the equation. Even if this mistake is not noticeable in the single-equation estimation, it will become quite clear whenever anyone tries to predict the complete set of endogenous variables simultaneously.

There are various methods of conducting such sample period simulations. Probably the most straightforward and most widely used is simply to gather all the correct lag values, insert the actual values of all the exogenous variables on a period-by-period basis, and then just let the model run for as many periods as the longest multiperiod forecast. Sometimes the simulation is extended over the whole sample period in order to test the long-run dynamic properties and stability of the model. However, there are also some other ways to structure these simulations.

Expanding on the test which we proposed for single equations, the complete model could be estimated over a truncated sample period and then used to predict the next t periods. However, this is probably too stringent a test. Although it could be claimed that this is really the way we make forecasts, since in practice the functions are used outside the sample period, all actual ex ante forecasts include certain adjustments made to keep the model on track. This is explained in some detail in the next section. For this reason I don't think that this particular test has ever been tried, although it might be an interesting experiment.

A more common simulation experiment is the one which tries to simulate actual forecast conditions a little more closely by adjusting the constant terms by the average residual error in the previous period. This will tend to keep the errant functions from straying too far and may also provide a better estimate of the forecast error which one is likely to encounter. Besides using the adjustments as a self-serving tool which make the sample period simulations look better, this method may provide valuable information, for it may indicate the best way to de-

termine the constant adjustments during the actual forecast period.

USING THE MODEL

If the reader has followed the instructions in the previous sections and has performed all the indicated tests, he probably has a fairly good model. All that remains is to use it to make good forecasts.

The first thing we have to consider is an efficient solution algorithm. Fortunately this is no longer a problem. However, it used to be; when I first started making forecasts with an econometric model in 1963, I used a desk calculator. The model in question had about 30 stochastic equations, was largely recursive, and had few nonlinearities. Even so, the process took two days. Within two years we had developed a solution algorithm for nonlinear models, and today several such algorithms are available.

It has long been realized that if the model is linear there is no problem with the solution; one simply solves a system of linear equations, which involves only one matrix inversion that remains unchanged over time. Or, alternatively (what is really the same thing), the equations can be rewritten in the *reduced form*, which means that the model is solved so that each endogenous variable is a function of only exogenous and lagged variables.

A minor complication arises if we have the lagged dependent variable on the right-hand side of one or more of the equations. Then we have to invert a different matrix for each time period if multiperiod forecasting is required, since the multipliers (the change in an endogenous variable per unit change in an exogenous variable) are different over time. Even so, this involves only one matrix inversion per unit time period. Early multiplier analysis, such as that done by Goldberger with the Klein-Goldberger model, essentially used the reduced form.

All of the simplicity disappears when the models become nonlinear, which is the case for any realistic model. The nonlinearities may occur for a number of different reasons. The simplest example would be a price times quantity term in the national income account identities. Another example might be the use of ratios of different variables, such as relative prices or the income distribution variable (wage/nonwage income) used in the consumption function given above. Still another use might be variables of the type $1/(1 - x)$ where x is some ratio between 0 and 1. We might estimate a function, such as the production function, in logarithms, or we might estimate wage and price functions in percentage terms. There are many other similar terms in today's models.

The first method to be developed for solving nonlinear econometric models was the Newton-Raphson method. The basic idea of this method is to divide each equation into linear and nonlinear parts, and then to solve the nonlinear parts by an iterative procedure. For example, if the equation contained a term pq, the idea would be to hold q constant (at some assumed value) while solving for p, then to hold p constant while solving for q, and to continue this in an iterative fashion until some desired level of tolerance was reached. In somewhat more exact language, any nonlinear equation can be approximated by a linear portion plus the partial derivative of the function with respect to the endogenous variables around any given point. We then linearize the partial derivatives and solve the resulting linear system.

This method will give an exact answer if the nonlinearities of the model are all in simple multiplicative form. To illustrate this point, consider a model which can be separated into a "price" (including wage) and "quantity" block, i.e., all equations can be usefully classified as belonging to one block or the other. If nonlinearities arise only in the form pq or p/q, then the derivatives of each of the terms are linear expressions in one of the two blocks. Since there is no approximation involved at this stage of the calculation, the degree of precision will be determined only by the convergence criterion. Since the matrix of partial derivatives with respect to prices will all be linear functions of quantities, and analogously for the other block, we are able to solve the system of equations exactly.

The convenient feature of exactness disappears, however, if the model contains certain other kinds of nonlinearities, such as those found in logarithmic production functions. In that case, for example, it is necessary to replace $\log y_t$ by

$$\log y_t \simeq \log y_{t-1} + \frac{y_t - y_{t-1}}{y_{t-1}}$$

Similar problems will arise if the equations contain other nonlinear terms of the exponential or asymptotic variety. For example, the partial derivative of $\frac{1}{1 - x}$ is $\frac{1}{(1 - x)^2}$ which if anything is even more nonlinear. The buildup of error due to these additional approximations could be substantial in multisector models or where simulations are calculated over many periods. In practice, moreover, this method has proved cumbersome to program and relatively slow for computational purposes, since it involves inversion of 50×50 or even 100×100 matrices.

Because of these drawbacks of the Newton-Raphson method, virtually all econometric models are currently solved by the Gauss-Seidel method. While at least the first part of the name would indicate that this is not a particularly new method, it has only recently been adapted to solving econometric models. In a very broad sense, this method is an extension of the Newton-Raphson method in the sense that the model is divided into blocks. However, in the Gauss-Seidel method, *each equation* is treated as a separate block. This omits the need to solve multiequation systems and thus to take partial derivatives. No matter how complex, as long as it can be expressed algebraically, each equation can be solved exactly. The user guesses at starting estimates for all of the jointly determined variables (in practice, setting them equal to the preceding period's values is a very close guess). These estimates are then used as values for the dependent variables on the right-hand side of each equation. When the first iteration has been completed, a new set of all simultaneous variables is available. These values are then used to re-solve the system one equation at a time. This process continues until a preassigned degree of precision is reached. Algebraically, this method of solution can be expressed as follows:

Let the jth equation be expressed by

$$y_{jt} = f(y_{1t}, y_{2t}, \cdots, y_{jt}, \cdots, y_{nt};$$
$$x_{1t}, \cdots, x_{mt})$$
$$j = 1, \cdots, n$$

We first evaluate

$$y_{jt}^{(1)} = f(y_{1t}^{(0)}, y_{2t}^{(0)}, \cdots, y_{jt}^{(0)}, \cdots, y_{nt}^{(0)};$$
$$x_{1t}, \cdots, x_{mt})$$
$$j = 1, \cdots, n$$

and continue to iterate until we obtain

$$y_{jt}^{(n)} = f(y_{1t}^{(r-1)}, y_{2t}^{(r-1)}, \cdots, y_{jt}^{(r-1)},$$
$$\cdots, y_{nt}^{(r-1)}; x_{1t}, \cdots, x_{mt})$$
$$j = 1, \cdots, n$$

such that

$$\left| \frac{y_{jt}^{(r)} - y_{jt}^{(r-1)}}{y_{jt}^{(r-1)}} \right| < \varepsilon,$$

where ε is any desired degree of tolerance (usually 0.001)

It would be possible to substitute values already calculated in the rth iteration for $y_{1t}, \cdots, y_{j-1,t}$ when solving for y_{jt}. It would also be possible to use $y_{jt}^{(r)} = y_{jt}^{(r-1)} + \lambda(y_{jt}^{(r-1)} - y_{jt}^{(r-2)})$ where $0 < \lambda < 1$. While both these shortcuts reduce the length of time needed for computation, they may lead to a diver-gent solution for certain orderings of the equations. Thus we usually avoid it when solving the model, since the method is quite fast, at least ten times as fast as the Newton-Raphson algorithm.

Thus in practice, solving the model represents no real problem. Now we have to make the forecast, which involves several potential problem areas. The first step is choosing the values for the exogenous inputs, which may be a considerable task. In fact, it has often been said that, over the lifetime of a model, generating the forecasts and properly maintaining the model will be more expensive and time-consuming than the original estimation. Choosing the best estimates of all the exogenous variables is clearly a major part of generating the forecasts.

In general there are four distinct classifications of exogenous variables: policy variables; exogenous sectors; demographic and other trend variables; and other miscellaneous inputs, mainly dummy variables.

Policy variables, which are probably the most important of the exogenous inputs, include the instruments of fiscal and monetary policy. In most macroeconomic models, fiscal policy variables include government purchases by sector, transfer payments by type, various tax rates, government employment and wage rates, and changes in tax laws such as the investment tax credit and the length of accounting tax lives for depreciation. Monetary policy variables include the discount rate, unborrowed reserves, ceiling rates on certain types of deposits, and the required reserve ratios on demand and time deposits. Different values of many of these variables are often used to generate alternative forecasts.

Exogenous sectors are principally those parts of the economy for which one could estimate equations but which are either unimportant to the total economy or are almost impossible to predict accurately. Examples of the former would include the farm sector and certain foreign sector variables. The main example of the latter is the stock market.

Demographic and trend variables would be endogenous in a truly long-run model, but can be taken as exogenous for short-term forecasts, with no loss in accuracy and some saving in efficiency. The main example of this type of variable is population, either for the entire economy or disaggregated by age/sex classification. Long-run technological trends also fit into this group.

Other miscellaneous variables are primarily dummy variables for strikes or for introduction of new legislation (such as a wage-price freeze). These variables should always be used sparingly and should not be used in place of events caused by economic phenomena, such as credit crunches.

As previously mentioned, determining the values for all of these variables for the forthcoming forecast period can be quite a demanding job. The model I am currently using for short-term forecasting has 100 exogenous variables, over 40 of which are policy variables. While it could be claimed that most of these do not differ much from one period to the next, such logic does not hold very well in times of New Economic Plans.

We now come to an area which continues to be among the most controversial in the area of econometric model building and forecasting. That is the question of constant adjustments.

By this time I am sure it is no secret that virtually everyone who uses an econometric model for forecasting does so only after he has adjusted the constant terms in some or even all of the stochastic equations. These adjustments may be made for a variety of reasons:

1. There may be short-term exogenous disturbances due to variables not included in the model, such as a strike or a natural disaster.
2. As discussed earlier in this chapter, it is more often the rule rather than the exception that the data have just recently been revised. Usually these revisions are minor, so it would be counterproductive to reestimate the function every time the figures were revised. This is best handled by adjusting the constant term.
3. There may be a change in institutional structure. The wage-price freeze is an outstanding example of this. Other examples which are not as striking might include a change in the way the government influences the housing market, or the influx of small imported cars.
4. The function may not work very well. While presumably all the equations in the model have been carefully checked by the method outlined above, there may still be some bloopers. In that case the obvious indicated cure is to reestimate the equation. However, in the short run it is usually impossible to tell whether the divergence between actual and predicted values is due to reason 1, 3, or 4.

Over the years, several methods have evolved for adjusting the constant terms in forecasting equations. We next list and discuss the four main methods.

1. Adjust the constant terms by the amount of the residual during the previous period. While this may seem like a crude and unrealistic method, it is in fact the method implicitly used whenever one predicts with an equation estimated in first differences. While it is true that the constant terms of first difference equations can also be modified, this rather harsh assumption has led in most cases to the abandonment of first difference equations for an entire model, although they are still used in various equations in the model (such as prices) where theory would appear to warrant such a choice.
2. Adjust the constant terms by the average residual during the previous several periods (usually four to six). This method, while similar to the previous one, has the distinct advantage of ironing out quirks due to one-quarter aber-

rations in the data or the economy. Even so, it is quite mechanical in nature.

3. Adjust the constant terms by some proportion of the average residual. If we assume that the regression coefficients in the forecast period are drawn from the same population as the regression coefficients in the sample period, it may be reasonable to assume that the distribution of the errors in the forecast period is the same as in the sample period. In particular, this would mean that the autocorrelation coefficient for the forecast period would be the same as it was during the sample period. Thus, if the residuals have autocorrelation coefficient ρ in the sample period, that would also be the case in the forecast period. This line of reasoning therefore suggests that the average residual should be multiplied by $\rho, \rho^2, \cdots, \rho^n$ for forecasts of $1, 2, \ldots, n$ periods. This line of reasoning was first developed by Goldberger.

4. Adjust the constant terms, incorporating as a guideline the average residuals of the previous period, but using judgment to adjust the residuals further. In addition, if there seems to be a clear increasing (or decreasing) trend in the residuals, continue this trend into the future at the same rate. If this problem continues for very long, the function should probably be reestimated.

There is also a pathological case of method 4 which consists of adjusting the constant terms using judgment based on not only the previous residuals but on what the forecast "ought" to be. This method has become known as adjusting the model by the use of "add factors." Such a method is clearly not econometric forecasting; it is judgmental forecasting dressed up in an econometric framework. This method may work (although in practice it has not) but in any case should be discussed further under the judgmental forecasting section.

It can, however, be argued that method 4 is also judgmental forecasting dressed up in an econometric framework. This could be construed as a serious objection. Econometric models are clearly costly to build and operate, particularly when compared to judgmental forecasts. If in fact they give no better results, perhaps the econometricians are all wasting our time. This suggests that it is important to examine the forecasting record of econometric models. It is true that no test is conclusive. Even if the model forecasts appear to be better than the consensus forecasts, it may just be that those forecasters who build econometric models would have made superior forecasts without the models. Conversely, econometricians could conceivably be just plain lousy forecasters. However, if in fact the forecasting record of econometric models is no better than average, their usefulness will be severely limited.

Before progressing to the actual forecasting record, we should settle at least one issue. When we refer to econometric models, the only kind of models of any real interest are those which are living, working documents continuously subject to change. They are not carved in stone. Any attempt to use the same model over an extended period of time (certainly as much as five years) will certainly lead to bad forecasts after a while. After all, having one's feet firmly implanted in cement really ought not to be the hallmark of the successful econometrician. In keeping the model current, then, all econometricians must consider several problems.

The first problem which any econometric model builder faces is the problem of data revision. We have already mentioned this problem several times. Several things need to be taken into account. First, the national income accounts, employment and earnings data, and money supply figures are adjusted to new benchmarks each year. In addition, almost all of the data are preliminary for the first year; profit figures are subject to revision for three years.

There are also the problems of complete revision. We must, however, distinguish between rebasing and revision. For example, early in 1971 all the consumer price indexes began to appear on a base of 1967 = 100 instead of 1957–59 = 100. However, the figures at that time were not reweighted. Instead, every component of the consumer price index was simply divided by its 1967 price on the old basis. On the other hand, when the Industrial Production Index was changed from a 1957–59 base to a 1967 base, the complete series was revised and a different set of weights was used. In the first case, no recalculation of equations was indicated; in the second, the equations had to be reestimated. In any case, the model ought to be reestimated every year or two *if only because of data revisions.*

The second problem faced by any econometric forecaster is that the model must be "managed" to a certain degree. This does not mean wholesale substitution of "add factors" to compensate for the underlying lack of economic structure. It does mean constant awareness of changes in structure, shifts in the application of monetary and fiscal policy, exogenous disturbances such as strikes, even changes in seasonal patterns. Most of these have been mentioned before. The point to be stressed, however, is that the econometrician cannot use the coefficients of the model as a substitute for judgment. In fact, because of the greater variety of exogenous inputs and stochastic equations, he must use *more* judgment than the purely judgmental forecaster. The value of the model stems from the exercise of forcing the forecaster to go through each and every assumption in a rigorous and logically consistent manner. The equations of the model will then express the interactions between sectors in a way that no judgmental forecaster can do, if only because of the complexities. However, this works only if the structure is sound. If it is not, the forecasts will be poor, and respecification of the equations is needed—which is the third and most vital problem faced by econometric model

builders who keep their systems current.

Every econometric model which was ever estimated is, almost by definition, based on the events of the past. For some people this is enough to dismiss econometric models out of hand. Only judgmental forecasters, they say, can take into account the effect which changes in institutional structure will have on the economy. If I had ever met anyone who was able to do this on a consistent basis, I might tend to agree. In fact, I would even hire him to make my forecasts. But I have had no luck so far.

Having said this, the fact still remains that econometric models as such cannot incorporate changes in institutional structure. Thus, in addition to reestimating the equations every year or two because of data revisions and other minor inconsistencies, the model must occasionally be respecified, which involves changing the functional form of the equations and possibly adding or dropping variables.

In order to give some idea of the magnitude of the changes which have occurred during the past five years, we might usefully consider what happened between the time I last respecified the Wharton model, which was late 1965 and early 1966, and the model I am currently using, which was estimated in late 1969 and early 1970. There were complete changes in virtually every sector. The monetary sector had to be completely changed to reflect the fact that up until 1966 the Fed had not used monetary policy as a very vigorous tool, whereas after that they completely changed their method of operation and it became the most important policy tool.[4] The emerging importance of credit rationing, ceiling rates on different types of deposits, the increase in certificates of deposit and commercial paper, the federal

---

[4] Actually, the monetary sector had to be added, since the old Wharton model had a two-equation monetary sector. This compliment was perhaps unwittingly repaid when the St. Louis Fed built a model with a two-equation real sector.

funds rate as a key indicator of monetary policy, and greater emphasis on monetary aggregates instead of interest rates were only some of the changes in the monetary sector. In the real sector, credit rationing became important as a determinant of housing, non-residential construction, and consumer durables. Bottleneck variables reappeared in the investment functions. Multifamily housing and mobile homes appeared as significant factions of the housing market with different cyclical and secular patterns than traditional single-family houses. Consumption patterns changed as the savings rate shifted to a much higher level and income distribution, the rate of unemployment, and the rate of inflation all assumed much more importance than previously. In the foreign sector there was a shift in imports. This shift was away from mostly food and crude and semimanufactured products to finished goods produced in plants of U.S. companies set up abroad in order to take advantage of cheaper labor. In the price and wage sector, nonlinearities and asymmetries became much more important than previously, since these equations were previously based on a sample period which was dominated by the 1954–64 experience. While there were many other changes, these are some of the main ones. Furthermore, it is a safe bet that the econometric models which are estimated five or ten years from now will differ from today's versions as much as the 1970 models differ from those of the 1960s.

Thus if we are to analyze the forecasting properties of econometric models, we should do so within a framework which allows the models enough flexibility to reflect exogenous and structural changes. Tests of the properties of models which utilize only mechanical adjustments tell us very little about the real forecasting ability of the system. The best test of any model is its actual forecasting record. In the remainder of this chapter we analyze this record for several models and then draw some conclusions on how it might be improved.

FORECASTING RECORD OF EXISTING MODELS

It is true that while there are many different kinds of econometric models which can be built, the state of the art is most highly developed for the macroeconomic model. Where ten years ago there were perhaps two or three econometric models of the U.S. economy, there are now literally dozens which are in various states of repair. The list includes those created by research organizations, such as the Brookings Institution and the Federal Reserve Board; those produced by academic institutions, such as the Wharton School and the University of Michigan; those built by private corporations, such as IBM and General Electric; those estimated by government institutions, such as the Office of Business Economics; and those built by economic consulting firms. For example, this author has personally been responsible for three different econometric models of the U.S. economy. Clearly it would be impossibly lengthy and ridiculously boring to describe each of these even briefly. However, we may note the various types of models which currently exist.

First we have the very small models in which the money supply is the principal independent variable. Such models have been developed primarily by the Federal Reserve Bank of St. Louis; the ill-fated Laffer model is a direct relation of these models. These are not true forecasting models and have not been presented as such by their developers, although their use has become distorted in transmission. These models filled a void left by the failure of traditional economics to predict the continued boom during the 1968–69 period of easy money. This failure is discussed in some detail later in the chapter. However, these models have done extremely poorly since then, predicting a very severe recession in 1970 and an equally sharp recovery in 1971, and in my opinion they have been discredited. We do not discuss them in detail in this chapter, although the reader will find a more sympathetic treatment in Part VI.

The second level of model predicts the aggregate variables of the economy but does not include any sectoral disaggregation. The best known example is probably the Wharton School model; others are the Michigan model and the IBM macroeconomic model (IBM also has a separate industry model). The basic structure of these models was discussed in an earlier section.

The third level of model is one which uses the same basic structural approach as the medium size model but in addition includes substantial sectoral detail on both the demand and supply side. As mentioned earlier, the Brookings model was the first attempt to build such a system, but it never got off the ground. The Federal Reserve Board model, which was jointly developed by Massachusetts Institute of Technology and later by the University of Pennsylvania, has recently been programmed to reach a convergent solution, but only after the original theoretical structure had been severely modified. Although not yet conclusive, the evidence to date suggests that beyond a certain size, econometric models can no longer be handled adequately by the economists, although computationally size is no longer a problem. Since none of these supermodels has anything like a track record, we do not discuss them further in this chapter.

In spite of the recent proliferation of econometric models, only two, those developed and maintained by the University of Michigan and the Wharton School, have long enough published track records to permit some sort of meaningful analysis. IBM has used various versions of their macro-model to generate forecasts since 1963, and the Office of Business Economics has used theirs since 1966. While these forecasts are not released publicly, I can state that in general their records have been better than average, although they were somewhat low in 1968 and 1969 (as was almost everyone else)

and a little high in 1970 and 1971. However, these forecasts, if included, would on balance give evidence favorable to the forecasting ability of econometric models.

I have compared the forecasts from these two econometric models with the actual data, the consensus forecast (which is an average of about 50 forecasts as compiled by the Federal Reserve Bank of Philadelphia), the predictions issued by the Council of Economic Advisors, and two naive models. The other common method of forecasting, which is the use of leading indicators, has been discussed extensively in the Platt chapter in Part II. The first naive model simply states that the change this year will be the same as the change last year. The second one is based on a similar idea but is an extrapolation of the change between the first quarter and third quarter GNP through the following year, the third quarter representing the latest data available to most economists when they forecast the following year. This naive model is calculated as follows. Let GNP for the first quarter of year $t - 1$ equal x_1; let GNP for the third quarter of year $t - 1$ equal x_2. Then using simple extrapolation and projecting the same trend,

GNP_t, 1st quarter $= x_2 + 1.0(x_2 - x_1)$

GNP_t, 2nd quarter $= x_2 + 1.5(x_2 - x_1)$

GNP_t, 3rd quarter $= x_2 + 2.0(x_2 - x_1)$

GNP_t, 4th quarter $= x_2 + 2.5(x_2 - x_1)$

so that for the yearly average

$$GNP_t = x_2 + 1.75(x_2 - x_1)$$

which is naive model II.

The forecasting record generated by these various methods for current dollar GNP during the last ten years in given in table 1. While a correct forecast of GNP could very easily mask offsetting errors in the prediction of real growth and inflation or components of aggregate demand, it would not be possible to construct a table with even this much detail if we were to consider a detailed breakdown of GNP. In addi-

TABLE 1.   COMPARISON OF ALTERNATIVE FORECASTING METHODS

(In billions of current dollars)

	Actual, Revised Data	Actual, Prelim. Data	Con-sensus Forecast	Error	Michigan Model	Error	CEA Model	Error	Wharton Model	Error	Naive Model I	Error	Naive Model II	Error
1961	520	519	512	−7	521	2	…	…	…	…	522	3	511	−8
1962	560	556	560	4	560	4	570	14	…	…	535	−21	559	3
1963	591	584	573	−11	578	−6	578	−6	585	1	594	10	582	−2
1964	632	623	616	−7	619	−4	619	−4	625	2	612	−11	614	−9
1965	685	666	656	−10	652	−14	660	−6	662	−4	661	−5	663	−3
1966	750	732	725	−7	725	−7	722	−10	728	−4	724	−8	721	−11
1967	793	781	785	4	794	13	787	6	784	3	791	10	788	7
1968	865	861	841	−20	840	−21	846	−15	842	−19	830	−31	835	−24
1969	931	932	915	−17	909	−23	921	−11	914	−18	941	9	941	9
1970	977	977	986	9	990	13	985	8	980	3	1,003	26	1,002	+25
1971	1,050	1,049	1,047	−2	1,043	−6	1,065	+15	1,046	−3	1,022	−27	1,032	−17
Average absolute error	…	…	…	8.9	…	10.3	…	9.5	…	6.3	…	14.6	…	10.0

tion, ability to predict GNP is still the most common yardstick for measuring forecasting accuracy, and it would indeed be difficult to build much of a case for a forecast which consistently missed GNP.

Several salient points may be noted about the results listed in table 1:

1. All of the forecasts, econometric and noneconometric alike, are substantially better than the naive models I have listed here and several others I have tried but have not included. Economic forecasters are still assured a useful role in society for the time being.

2. The forecasting record of the Council of Economic Advisors, who might be expected to make the best forecasts since they have access to all the methods of forecasting including several econometric models, top econometric talent, and supposedly the inside word on the assumptions, has been worse than the consensus forecast. This has led to the feeling that the Council forecast is used more for a target than an actual prediction as such, particularly in 1962 and 1971.

3. During the period 1961–66, the two econometric models listed here did substantially better than the consensus forecast, although the Wharton record is superior to the Michigan record. However, this ranking was reversed in the next few years, when most forecasts were far wide of the mark but the econometric forecasts were worse than the others. In 1970 and 1971 the Wharton model (and others) again tracked quite well, although the Michigan model seems to have been permanently derailed.

THE FAILURE OF ECONOMETRIC MODELS

There are several ways to interpret the apparently erratic forecast record of econometric models. One possibility is that the structure of the models was correct, but they predicted poorly because erroneous inputs for key exogenous variables such as monetary and fiscal policy were used. This view might possibly receive some corroboration from the fact that the noneconometric forecasts were also very poor for 1968 and 1969. It is also possible that the underlying structural relationships of the models are sound, but short-run exogenous disturbances were incorrectly adjusted for. As mentioned previously, all econometric model forecasters do a considerable amount of adjusting the constant terms in each equation before actually completing the forecast. However, there is little reason why these adjustments should have been so much more confusing in 1968 and 1969 than at other times.

A much more plausible hypothesis is that the models work very well during periods of slack capacity, substantial unemployment, and little inflation (that is, when the functions are linear) but perform much more poorly when the economy is near full employment and capacity. One could object that 1966 and 1967 were certainly full employment years, and at least the Wharton model seemed to do well during that period. However, in this case the annual averages disguise more than they reveal. As was mentioned at the session where the chapters for this book were originally presented, the forecast made by the Wharton model in mid-1966 (and prominently featured in *Business Week*) called for no slowdown at all in the coming months, an error which became painfully obvious soon afterward. Similarly, the 1967 forecast had too high a first half and too low a second half. It was also suggested at the same session that econometric models may work well at predicting trends but fail at turning points. However, the Wharton model predicted the 1970 recession well and in fact anticipated it by several quarters. It is more likely that the models failed to capture the nonlinearities near full employment and full capacity, and since the economy usually reaches a turning point when it bumps the ceiling, the models missed the turning point as well.

The only study which will permit us to examine these alternative hypotheses in detail is one in which I participated as part of a much larger project sponsored by the National Bureau of Economic Research. The purpose of this study was to examine the actual forecasting records of econometric models, and then determine the causes of forecast error by substituting the exogenous variables, and different methods of adjusting the constant adjustments. In order to do this it was necessary to have access to the complete records of all of the forecasts generated by a given model. This was available only for the Wharton model and, to a lesser extent, the Office of Business Economics (OBE) model. This study was done for the period 1964–68 for the Wharton model and 1966–68 for the OBE model. While the study is fragmentary, it is the only one to date which can shed important light on the question of why econometric models make errors.

The principal conclusions of the study are as follows:

1. The true ex ante forecasts—the forecasts actually issued by the respective groups—are much better than the ones which would have resulted if any of a variety of arbitrary methods had been used to adjust the constant terms. Judgment is clearly an important element in good econometric forecasting.

2. Various types of mechanical adjustments for the constant terms were examined, but no one method was superior in a significant number of cases. There is some evidence that the method where the average residual is multiplied by the factor ρ^n, where ρ is the autocorrelation coefficient, is slightly better. However, all mechanical methods tried were quite inferior to the actual adjustments.

3. With very few exceptions, the true ex ante forecasts are *superior* to the ex post forecasts with the original constant adjustments but the *actual* values

of the exogenous variables. This result is really quite surprising. It means that when the actual values for government expenditures and monetary policy were put into the forecasts and nothing else was changed, the models gave substantially worse forecasts. Furthermore, this result holds across time periods and across models, and in most cases the differences are quite substantial.

4. For both models and forecasts examined, about half of the ex ante forecasts with mechanical adjustments have smaller errors than the respective ex post forecasts. Thus, even if we use a mechanical method of adjusting the constant terms, we still get worse forecasts by putting in the correct exogenous values. The significance of this point will become apparent later.

The first point above is easily explained and provides substantive evidence for the widespread belief that there is a considerable amount of fine tuning of econometric models when they are used for true ex ante forecasting. This point also explains why the true ex ante forecast errors for econometric models are much *lower* than the sample period errors. One would have expected that finding to be reversed. Since the data have been searched for good sample period fits, the sample period standard error is likely to be understated relative to the actual forecast error. However, this tendency is more than offset by using fine tuning methods.

It is not possible to draw any definite conclusions about the second point, since the two models analyzed present conflicting evidence. However, in terms of our hypotheses above, they do disprove one point rather effectively. If in fact it could be demonstrated that the mechanical adjustments improved forecasts in certain cases, then one would be warranted in drawing the conclusion that the forecasters overreacted to certain short-run exogenous events. But the evidence does not support this view, since the fine tuning adjustments are much better than any mechanical method.

We next consider the third point, potentially the most damaging to the econometric technique. It was originally thought that the subjective adjustment of constants was in large part a method of offsetting bad guesses for the exogenous variables. For example, suppose that the econometric forecaster expects government expenditures for the next quarter to increase by $5 billion, and inserting this assumption in the model generates a $20 billion increase in GNP for the next quarter. However, given his "feeling" about the economy, strengthened perhaps by information about new orders, construction starts, and other leading indicators, the forecaster thinks that $15 billion will be a better estimate. This would lead to a downward adjustment in the constant terms of the consumption and investment functions until the GNP forecast is reduced to a $15 billion increase. Later, the actual figures reveal that government expenditures increased by only $2 billion; the rise in GNP is in fact $15 billion. Since most econometric models have impact multipliers for government purchases of approximately 1.5, this would reduce the increase in GNP which was predicted on an ex post basis to only $10 billion. If the additional constant adjustment had *not* been made, the ex post forecast would have been about a $15 billion increase, which was the right number. However, it was much lower because of the attempt to adjust for an erroneous government expenditure estimate. In this case the ex post forecast would be inferior to the ex ante forecast when the ex ante constant adjustments are used.

However, this example illustrates only a conjecture. There may be other reasons why the ex ante forecasts are better than the ex post forecasts. If we introduce the evidence summarized in the last conclusion, that conjecture must be rejected, for the ex ante forecasts are superior to the ex post forecasts in almost half the cases *even when*

the same method of constant adjustment is used. While seeming to be less powerful than the third conclusion, this result is potentially a much more damaging argument for the use of econometric models for forecasting and policy analysis than the prior conclusion. Even if we eschew all judgment in the adjustment of the constant terms, the forecast error increases almost as often as it decreases when we introduce the correct values of the exogenous variables into the solution. The first conclusion could be explained by offsetting errors; the forecaster is able to gauge the change in the economy accurately for the next one or two quarters, so he offsets his bad guesses for the values of the exogenous variables by adjusting the rest of the model. With the mechanical constant adjustments, this is no longer an admissable argument. Inserting the correct exogenous values often pushes the solution farther away from the true value. This could occur either because the actual data series are faulty or because the fiscal policy multipliers are overstated and are offset by the forecaster's choice of the exogenous values that will yield "reasonable" forecasts. Each of these possiblities is considered in turn.

The only exogenous variables for which the differences between estimated and actual values make much difference are government expenditures, tax rates, and monetary policy variables (mainly the discount rate and open market policy). Of these, only the ex post figures for government expenditures are likely to be subject to distortion or revision. While it is true that the recent data on the money supply leave a great deal to be desired, the reserve figures themselves are usually not revised very much. However, defense spending may be entered in the national income accounts as inventory investment while the goods are being produced and become government purchases only when they are finished and are transferred to the military authorities. There is some evidence that this did in fact occur, particularly around the time of rapid buildup in defense expenditures associated with the Vietnam war, but even this would not completely explain the results.

There is substantial evidence, then, that the impact multipliers for fiscal policy were overstated and the monetary policy multipliers were understated for the great majority of econometric models used during the 1963–69 period. Further examination leads to the conclusion that these errors fall into several groups. The adjustments which have been made to overcome these errors are discussed in the final section of this chapter.

NEW DEVELOPMENTS IN ECONOMETRIC MODELING

The interaction of the real and monetary sectors has been completely reestimated. While the structure which we outlined earlier in the chapter allowed for substantial links between monetary variables and the consumption and investment functions, these links were seldom implemented on an empirical basis. Interest rate variables were usually given lip service in the investment functions, but the much more important effects of nonprice credit rationing were not included at all. This omission has been rectified through the inclusion of an explicit credit rationing variable which has been specifically designed to measure the degree to which loans are not available to small businessmen and consumers. This variable has been found to be quite important in the equations for housing starts, nonresidential construction, and consumer durables. As might be expected, it often enters these functions in a nonlinear form.

The short-term fiscal multipliers have been reduced, particularly near full employment. Their overstatement was due in large measure to an overestimate of the short-run marginal propensity to consume, which was in turn caused by two principal factors.

First, the absence of monetary variables in the consumer durables equations led to an overstatement of the effect of income on purchases of durables. Secondly, most consumption functions for nondurables and services were estimated in the form

$$C = f(Y, C_{-1})$$

which means that unlagged income is assumed to have a larger effect on consumption than any of the other income terms. This formulation does not allow for the possibility that the response of certain types of consumption to a change in income may follow a pattern other than one with geometrically declining weights. When further disaggregation of the consumption function was undertaken and the weights of income on consumption were allowed to vary more freely, it was found that in certain cases the time pattern of income was closer to an inverted U, which is to say the weights were smaller at the beginning, larger in the range four to eight quarters out, and then declined after that.

In addition, the functions for fixed business investment were incorrectly specified. In particular, the relationship between investment and capacity utilization was treated badly. Previously it had been thought that there was a strong positive partial correlation between these two variables. However, after further examination and experience with the 1966–70 pattern of investment, it has become apparent that the strong partial correlation is between investment and output, with capacity utilization entering the function in a much different manner. First it was determined that over time there is hardly any relationship between investment and capacity if output is already included in the equation. However, when the capital goods sector of the economy approaches its peak and bottlenecks are reached, there is a short-term *negative* relationship between capacity utilization and investment, since the demand for new investment increases but all the goods cannot be delivered or built immediately. Existing orders are thus stretched out much longer than they would be under ordinary circumstances. Thus we use a term of the form $1/(1 - Cp)$ with a set of coefficients which are negative for the first few quarters and then positive. Thus when capacity utilization is near 100 percent, investment is lower than would be expected for the given level of output, but deliveries are then extended over a much longer period of time than would ordinarily be the case. This sort of analysis explains why investment stayed high in 1969 even though the boom was over, and then collapsed in 1970. It also has the effect of reducing the value of the short-term fiscal multiplier near periods of full employment and peak capacity.

The wage and price terms have been reformulated to include the necessary nonlinearities and asymmetries. Previous omission of these terms resulted in a twofold problem. First, the degree of inflation was severely underpredicted by econometric models during the 1968–69 period. Second, as the economy approaches full utilization of its resources, the real multipliers become smaller and the price multipliers become larger, but a model which has a linear set of wage and price functions does not capture this effect. In addition, several asymmetries were introduced into the price functions to reflect the fact that prices rise much more easily than they fall. While this is an easily observable phenomenon of the real world, it has previously failed to make its way into econometric model estimation. Use of these asymmetries undoubtedly accounts for successful predictions by models during the past two years that the economy would grow slowly, but that inflation (until the wage-price freeze) would continue almost unmolested.

There have been many other subtle modifications and improvements in econometric models during the past five years, but these areas indicate where the most striking progress has taken place.

CONCLUSION

Econometric analysis and forecasting remains a valuable implement in the business economist's bag of tools. Of that I am convinced. Whether it can improve on the predictions generated by the superior judgmental forecasters remains to be seen. Certainly the last ten years have offered no evidence to support this hypothesis. However, there have been widespread advances during the past ten years both in econometric technique and in estimation of macroeconomic models. With what might be called the incurable optimism necessary to survive as an econometrician, I am hopeful that the combination of superior judgment and econometric technique will produce forecasts which are better than those produced by superior judgment alone.

ROBERT B. PLATT

Input-Output Forecasting

I. INTRODUCTION

The business forecaster's primary focus of concern is the gross national product and its various income and expenditure components. These aggregate economic measures are important since they describe the environment within which an individual firm operates, and informed judgments on their future direction and magnitude are essential to organized planning of production, capital expansion, diversification, sales promotion efforts, and indeed all those activities which require the significant allocation of a firm's resources.

But how are these various uses of forecasts of the aggregate economy to be achieved in practice? To be of concrete use to the business decision-maker, the forecaster must be able to relate accurately his estimate of the aggregate economy to its specific implications for his industry and his firm. This is not an easy task, and there is no unique set of procedures by which it can be accomplished.

One of the reasons that it is so difficult to relate industry and firm forecasts to forecasts of general economic activity is that all sectors of the economy are interrelated. Within this context, many firms, both large and small, are simultaneously engaged in forecasting their sales, production, and resource needs. If all of these forecasts were

compared, it is quite unlikely that they would be consistent. Should it be surprising, therefore, that company decisions based on such forecasts so often prove disappointing?

In order for the industry or firm forecaster to accomplish his task adequately, he should take into consideration many factors not related directly to his firm's or industry's operations. Take, for example, the problem of a forecaster in the steel industry attempting to determine the implications for his industry of a particular forecast of the GNP. Virtually none of the demand for steel is for final use, but rather for use as an intermediate product in the production, construction, or fabrication of other products. To properly assess the implications of a particular value of the GNP on the demand for steel, the forecaster should concern himself not only with a measure of total final demand, but also with the question of how this demand is distributed among different business sectors, and how it will affect the sales and production plans of industries which are important users of steel, such as the automobile industry. Furthermore, once this has been accomplished, the forecaster is faced with the additional problem of converting the estimates of final demand for steel-using industries into specific estimates of their steel requirements.

To properly evaluate all of these considerations, the forecaster should work within some general equilibrium framework where all of the interrelationships among the various industries in the economy are taken into account. One approach to this very formidable task is by the use of input-output analysis, a technique pioneered by the economist Wassily W. Leontief in the late 1930s.[1]

On the surface, input-output appears merely as an elaborate system of economic accounting—a more detailed form of the gross national product accounts. From this viewpoint, input-output is a tabulation of the flows over some particular time period of the value of goods and services used and produced by different industry sectors. Specifically, it is a breakdown of the total *output* of different industries into the portion which is sold to other industries for use as *inputs* in their production, and the portion which is sold to final users of the product. It is this latter portion, equal to the so-called value added by industry, which is measured in the GNP accounts. But input-output is also more than an aggregate accounting system.

Unlike the GNP accounts, input-output is also an analytical tool by which a forecaster can convert estimates of aggregate final demand into forecasts of both final and intermediate demand by each of the industry sectors represented on the input-output table, and also into estimates of the various resources, or inputs, that will be needed by each of these industries to produce their total product. This conversion of input-output from an accounting system to a forecasting tool results from the unique tabular relationship of the sectoral input-output flows that was developed by Leontief, and from the application of certain crucial assumptions with regard to how the production of goods is related to each of the industry's input requirements.

It is this use of input-output as a forecasting technique, and the related use of input-output as a tool of corporate planning, that are the principal topics of this chapter. The next section describes how input-output flows in the economy are presented in tabular form, using for illustration a much aggregated three-industry (approximate) representation of an input-output table for the United States economy.[2] This is then followed by a section showing how an input-output table can be converted into a tool for forecasting the total output and input requirements of individual industries, once we have available a forecast of aggregate final demand. Following this there are two sections which describe the uses of input-output in forecasting and other related aspects of corporate planning, as well as some of the limitations of the technique. Also included in these sections is some discussion of the forecast accuracy of the input-output approach, and some discussion of the methods which have been used by economists to overcome the limitations of input-output forecasting.

II. INPUT-OUTPUT ACCOUNTING

In order to illustrate input-output accounting, a very simple economy is assumed, in which there are three industry sectors: agriculture, manufacturing, and services. Some part of the output over some specified period of time, in practice it is usually one year, of each of these industries may be sold to any industry or industries as raw materials or semifinished goods to be used by them as inputs in their production. The bal-

---

[1] For a useful compendium of Professor Leontief's writings on input-output, see Wassily Leontief, *Input-Output Economics* (New York: Oxford University Press, 1966).

[2] The most recent input-output table published by the Department of Commerce has the economy divided into 370 industry sectors. For a discussion of this table see "Input-Output Structure of the U.S. Economy: 1963" *Survey of Current Business* (November 1969), pp. 16–47.

ance of the output not sold as intermediate demand is sold to final users of the product. These final users may be individuals buying consumer goods; they may be business firms buying investment goods, such as plant and equipment or additions to inventories; or they may be federal, state, or local governmental units.[3]

To produce its output, each industry requires some intermediate goods purchased from other industries (and perhaps uses some of its own product as well), and pays out to the "primary" factors of production (in the form of wages, interest, rents, and profits) their contribution to the industry's total output. In dollar value, each industry's total output equals its total inputs. This equality can be visualized by analogy with the familiar accounting profit and loss statement. From the P&L statement, the value of a firm's sales plus its additions to inventories of its finished product, i.e., its total output, is equal to the sum of the costs of production (including the value of any goods used

in production, plus wages, interests, rents, and the value of capital consumed in production) and profits. Profits are the residual and balancing item in the P&L statement and likewise they are the balancing item in the input-output accounts.

The input-output flows of our highly simplified economy are illustrated in table 1.

The first three rows of table 1 show the total output of the three industries broken down into the portion being used by each industry for further processing, i.e., as inputs, and the portion going to final demand. Notice that in the example, each of the industries represented in the table uses part of its own product as inputs. For example, $15 billion of the total output of $90 billion of the agricultural sector is used by that industry as input in its production. An example of such a situation would be the use of farm produce on the farm for animal feed. In cases where the input-output table was less aggregated than in our example, there would be many instances in which particular industries use neither their own products nor the products of certain other industries. In these cases the appropriate cells in the table are blank. The final demand for each industry's product is broken down in the table into the portions representing consumption goods, investment goods, and the demand of governments for goods and services.

The first three columns of table 1 show the inputs for each of the three industries. The manufacturing sector (column 2), for example, purchased as intermediate products $50 million of agricultural goods, $215 billion of manufactured goods, and $100 billion of services. In addition, this industry paid out a total of $215 billion in the form of wages, interest, rents, and profits. The total of its inputs, $580 billion, equals the total value of the manufacturing industry's output (row 2). The same is true for each of the other industries.

The totals of the columns under the general heading of final demand indicate ag-

---

[3] For the purpose of keeping this example simple, a "closed economy" is assumed in which there is no foreign sector. In actual input-output tables, exports are treated as sales to final demand by each of the producing industries. Imports are treated in two ways. If there is a domestic industry producing the same product, the value of the imports are added to sales of these industries to the purchaser of the imported goods. If there is no domestic equivalent, the purchases of the imports, whether for intermediate or final demand, are handled by adding another row to the input-output table, usually entitled "Directly Allocated Imports." The addition of imported goods to domestic sales where equivalent products are produced domestically is designed to avoid a misleading distinction between goods which are physically identical. This procedure, however, has the unfortunate consequence of inflating the output of the industries involved. The total value of all imports, in addition, is usually entered as a negative item in the export column of input-output tables so that the sum of this column will equal the appropriate GNP category, "net exports," i.e., gross exports minus imports.

TABLE 1. INTERINDUSTRY TRANSACTIONS, 1963

(In billions of dollars at producer's prices)

Purchases from \ Sales to,	Intermediate Demand				Final Demand				Total of Rows
	Agriculture	Manufacturing	Services	Total	For Consumption Goods	For Investment Goods	By Governments for Goods & Services	Total	
Agriculture	15	50	5	70	20	0	0	20	90
Manufacturing	20	215	55	290	130	80	80	290	580
Services	10	100	100	210	230	0	60	290	500
Subtotal (Intermediate inputs)	45	365	160						
Primary inputs (Value added)	45	215	340						600
Total of columns	90	580	500	570	380	80	140	600	600

193

gregate expenditures in the economy on consumption goods, investment goods, and by governments. The sum of these three expenditure components equals the gross national product. As is well known, in addition to arriving at the GNP by aggregating expenditures by sectors, you can calculate the sum of income payments plus depreciation and certain indirect business taxes. These amounts, which in aggregate are often called value added, are all included in the primary input row of our simple input-output table, and indeed the sum of the items in this row of table 1 is $600 billion, which is equal to aggregate final demand.

Thus, the input-output table gives the same information, although in somewhat less detail, that is provided by the GNP accounts. But, in addition, it provides considerably more. It also gives an industry breakdown of output, both intermediate and final, and provides details on each industry's use of intermediate products and primary inputs.

The input-output flows illustrated in table 1 are all in dollar values. It is of course possible, at least in theory, to construct an input-output table in terms of physical quantities. Indeed, the original theoretical work of Leontief which underlies the construction and use of input-output tables was based on just such a concept.[4] In practice, however, tables in physical quantities are seldom constructed. There are several reasons for this. One is that physical production and input data are often difficult to obtain since most standard accounting records are in value terms. In addition, and probably most importantly, few industries, and indeed few large firms, make a single homogeneous product. There is no simple way that different physical quantities can be aggregated, and any such aggregation would undoubtedly have very little meaning.

[4] We will see a little later in this chapter why this is so. For a discussion of the theoretical basis of input-output, see Leontief, *op. cit.*, pp. 134–45.

III. INPUT-OUTPUT FORECASTING

Input-output flows, such as those shown in table 1, provide much interesting information, but they are, by themselves, of little direct use to the forecaster. What makes an input-output table a useful forecasting device is the application of a very bold assumption with regard to how an industry's production is related to its use of various inputs. Specifically, as the level of an industry's output changes, the levels of all of the inputs it uses are assumed to change proportionately. This implies, of course, that there is no substitution in production among the various inputs available to each of the industry sectors.

This assumption appears contrary to what is usually assumed in economics in the theory of production, and contrary to the practical experience of most businessmen. Actually, the assumption is more justifiable than it would at first appear. The situation that it describes can be considered as one in which each industry has available to it a number of alternative productive processes, and each process requires some particular fixed combination of inputs. Based on technological considerations and relative costs, one of these processes is "best" at any point in time for each of the industries, and this productive process is adopted. From this point of view, the input-output table simply shows the combination of optimal productive processes that exist in the economy at the time the table was constructed.

Once an industry adopts a particular mode of production, it will usually be retained for some time. It will, of course, change with changes in technology and relative costs, but the use of input-output analysis assumes—and this is crucial—that the changes take place very slowly, and perhaps even predictably. The implications of this assumption for forecast accuracy will be discussed later in the chapter. But first, it will be shown how the assumption of fixed pro-

TABLE 2.   DIRECT REQUIREMENTS

Purchases from \ Sales to,	Agriculture	Manufacturing	Services
Agriculture	0.17	0.09	0.01
Manufacturing	0.22	0.37	0.11
Services	0.11	0.17	0.20
Primary inputs	0.50	0.37	0.68
Total	1.00	1.00	1.00

portions of inputs can be used to convert a forecast of aggregate final demand—the gross national product—into a forecast of total demand for each industry's product, and a forecast of each of the inputs required by that industry to produce its total output.

The first step in this procedure is to calculate the fixed proportions of input requirements.[5] These are known in the jargon of input-output analysis as the technical input-output coefficients, or more simply as the technical coefficients. To calculate these, you take the first three columns of table 1, which represent the inputs required by each of the three industries to produce its total product, and divide each element in that column by the total output for the industry. The results of these calculations are shown in table 2, under the heading "direct requirements" (since the table gives the direct inputs needed from each industry to produce one unit of output).

The sum of the technical coefficients in each column of table 2 is one. This, of course, merely demonstrates in a different way what already was seen in the previous section—that the sum of the value of all the

[5] Since the assumption of fixed factor proportions refers to a technical aspect of production, a pure application of the theory would require that we use physical quantities of inputs and outputs in these calculations. We shouldn't be too concerned, however, about this departure from the pure theory, since tables in physical units and money units are readily converted into each other if the prices of the various goods are known.

inputs used by an industry equals 100 percent of the value of its total output.

While the technical coefficients (or direct requirements) in the columns of table 2 refer to the inputs used by each industry per unit of its output, each of the rows of table 2 represents the proportions of the total output of the three industries which will constitute intermediate demand for one of the industry's products. For example, row one indicates that the agricultural industry will use seventeen percent of its own total products in producing agricultural goods, while the manufacturing industry will use in production an amount of agricultural products totaling nine percent of the value of total manufacturing output. Likewise, services will use in production agricultural products totaling one percent of the value of services output. Hence, if we knew the value of each industry's total output, these technical coefficients could be used to arrive at an estimate of each industry's demand for agricultural products. The sum of these demands for agricultural products, plus the final demand for agricultural products, equals the total demand for the products of the agricultural industry. Each of the other rows of table 2 is to be interpreted in the same way.

Considering the information in the rows of table 2, it is possible, therefore, to represent the output of the three industries in the form of three simple linear equations.

Agriculture:
$$0.17 \times 90 + 0.90 \times 580 + 0.01 \times 500 + 20 = 90$$

Manufacturing:

$$0.22 \times 90 + 0.37 \times 580 + 0.11 \\ \times 500 + 290 = 580$$

Services:

$$0.11 \times 90 + 0.17 \times 580 + 0.20 \\ \times 500 + 290 = 500$$

To see more clearly the implications of these output equations for forecasting, we can put them in somewhat more general form. Let the symbol Y_1 represent the total output of agricultural products; Y_2, the total output of the manufacturing industry; and Y_3, the total output of services. The demand for the products of each of these industries by final users is represented by the symbols D_1, D_2 and D_3. Using this notation the three output equations can be written in the form.

Agriculture:

$$0.17Y_1 + 0.09Y_2 + 0.01Y_3 + D_1 = Y_1$$

Manufacturing:

$$0.22Y_1 + 0.37Y_2 + 0.11Y_3 + D_2 = Y_2$$

Services:

$$0.11Y_1 + 0.17Y_2 + 0.20Y_3 + D_3 = Y_3$$

These equations can be rearranged into a form which is more convenient for analysis by moving to the right-hand side of the equations all of the terms in Y that appear on the left. This rearrangement gives us the following equations:

Agriculture:

$$D_1 = (1 - 0.17)Y_1 - 0.09Y_2 \\ - 0.01Y_3$$

Manufacturing:

$$D_2 = -0.22Y_1 + (1 - 0.37)Y_2 \\ - 0.11Y_3$$

Services:

$$D_3 = -0.11Y_1 - 0.17Y_2 \\ + (1 - 0.20)Y_3$$

These are three simultaneous equations for the total output of the three industries (Y_1, Y_2, Y_3) in terms of the demand for each industry's product by the final users (D_1, D_2, D_3). We have now reached an im-

portant step in the conversion of an input-output table to a forecasting device. If we had a forecast of final demand (gross national product)—perhaps by using the producers discussed elsewhere in this volume—and if we could estimate the portions of this final demand relating to each of the three industries, we could then use these three output equations as a basis for estimating the total demand (both intermediate and final demand) for each industry's product. This could be done by solving the three output equations for the three unknowns (Y_1, Y_2, Y_3) in terms of the three (estimated) knowns (D_1, D_2, D_3). This can be done using any of the standard mathematical techniques for solving a system of simultaneous linear equations.[6] The result of this mathematical exercise for our sample problem gives us the following three equations:

Agriculture:

$$1.26D_1 + 0.185D_2 + 0.04D_3 = Y_1$$

Manufacturing:

$$0.49D_1 + 1.725D_2 + 0.24D_3 = Y_2$$

Services:

$$0.08D_1 + 0.40D_2 + 1.32D_3 = Y_3$$

The coefficients in these three equations play a very important role in input-output analysis, and they are often presented in tabular form, under the heading "direct and indirect requirements per unit of final demand." These coefficients are shown in Table 3.[7]

[6] The solving of input-output systems is most easily handled using a branch of mathematics called matrix algebra. For a good introduction to matrix algebra, particularly those topics useful for input-output analysis, see Clopper Almon, *Matrix Methods in Economics* (Reading, Massachusetts: Addison-Wesley Publishing Company, 1967).

[7] These coefficients considered as a group, and arranged in rows and columns as they are in table 3, are sometimes referred to as the *Leontief inverse matrix*. The use of the term inverse matrix comes from the method of calculation of the coefficients using matrix algebra.

TABLE 3.   DIRECT AND INDIRECT REQUIREMENTS PER UNIT OF FINAL DEMAND

	Agriculture	Manufacturing	Services
Agriculture	1.26	0.185	0.04
Manufacturing	0.49	1.725	0.24
Services	0.08	0.40	1.32

The title of table 3 comes from the fact that each column shows how much the total output of each industry will be affected by a unit increase in the final demand for one of the industry's products. Thus, column 1, row 1 indicates that $1.00 of final demand for agricultural products will eventually mean an increase of $1.26 in the total output of the agriculture industry. Included in this figure is the $1.00 of final demand for that industry's product plus the $0.17 of agricultural products (see table 2) needed to produce this amount of output. The $0.17 constitutes the direct requirements of agriculture inputs needed to produce a unit of final demand.

In addition, however, agriculture required $0.22 of manufactured goods and $0.11 of services to produce this unit of final demand (column 1, rows 2 and 3 of table 2). In order to produce this $0.22 of output, manufacturers had to buy $0.09 \times $0.22 = $0.02 worth of agricultural products, and the service industry, in order to provide this $0.11 of its product, had to use $0.01 \times $0.11 = $0.001 of agricultural goods. Moreover, in order to produce its $0.17 of direct requirements, agriculture used an additional $0.17 \times 0.17 = $0.03 of its own output. These *indirect* feedbacks on the demand for agricultural products resulting from the unit increase in final demand are also in the figure of $1.26. But this is only the first round of the feedbacks. The $0.02 feedback increase in demand for agricultural products resulting initially from the use of manufacturing inputs by the agriculture industry, for example, requires still more inputs of manufactured goods and services. To make these goods, the manufacturing and service industries require still more agricultural goods, and so on. The sum total of all of these direct and indirect (feedback) effects on demand for agricultural products resulting from a unit increase in final demand for its product are included in the figure of $1.26. The other cells in table 3 have similar interpretations.

Table 2 (Direct Requirements) and table 3 (Direct and Indirect Requirements Per Unit of Final Demand) are the basic tools of the input-output forecaster. Armed with these tools and an estimate of final demand by industry sector (D_1, D_2, D_3), he can forecast total demand for each sector's output (Y_1, Y_2, Y_3), as well as all of the inputs required by each industry to produce that value of total output. In short, he can calculate the amounts in each cell of table 1.

He would do this first by multiplying each column of table 3 by his estimate of final demand for the appropriate industry. The total of each row, once this multiplication has been carried out, gives the total demand, both intermediate and final, for one of the industry sectors. Once total output of an industry is known, this amount can be multiplied by the technical coefficients in the appropriate column of table 2. This will give the total dollar inputs from each industry needed to produce that amount of total demand. The difference between the value of total output and the sum of these intermediate product inputs is the total value added by that industry. This is, of course, the same amount that appears in the primary input row of table 1. This calculation can be continued until each of the first four rows and three columns of table 1 are completed. While we have gone through these

TABLE 4.   FINAL DEMAND COEFFICIENTS

	Consumption	Investment	Government
Agriculture	0.05	0	0
Manufacturing	0.34	1.00	0.57
Services	0.61	0	0.43

calculations step by step in order to illustrate how a forecast would be produced using input-output tables, in practice the preparation of the forecast can be produced almost instantaneously through the use of high-speed digital computers.

The use of input-output tables provides a great deal of forecast information based only on an estimate of final demand by industry sector. In practice, however, the input-output forecaster rarely has even this amount of data initially available to him. Typically, he will begin his analysis only with a forecast of aggregate demand, perhaps broken down into broad expenditure sectors. For example, he might begin only with an estimate of aggregate consumption expenditures, total investment expenditures, and aggregate expenditures by governments. Is it possible to use an input-output table for forecasting when we initially have only an estimate of aggregate demand and perhaps its components? The answer is affirmative, if we are willing to make one additional assumption. This assumption is that each sector has a fixed share of the final demand in each expenditure category. We will have something more to say in the next section with regard to the forecasting implications of this assumption.

Look at the columns headed "final demand" in table 1. If it is assumed that the proportion of each expenditure category going to each industry is stable, ratios can be calculated which are analogous to the technical coefficients by dividing the amount in each cell by the appropriate column total.[8] The results of these calculations are shown in table 4.

Using the final demand coefficients, three equations can be constructed to explain the total final demand for each industry in terms of the estimates of aggregate consumption expenditures (C), aggregate investment expenditures (I), and aggregate government expenditures (G).[9] These three equations are:

Agriculture:
$$D_1 = 0.05C + \quad 0I + \quad 0G$$
Manufacturing:
$$D_2 = 0.34C = 1.00I + 0.57G$$
Services:
$$D_3 = 0.61C = \quad 0I + 0.43G$$

Once final demand for each industry sector is determined, we can then forecast total industry output and input requirements using the procedures described earlier in this section.

[8] The use of these final demand coefficients, along with the technical coefficients of table 2, provide the basis of a form of input-output analysis which is known in the literature as the *closed Leontief system*. For some of the technical aspects of this system, see Robert Dorfman, Paul Samuelson, and Robert Solow, *Linear Programming and Economic Analysis* (New York: McGraw-Hill Book Company, 1958), chapter 10.

[9] Actually, in practice some attempt is often made to link final demand by industry categories to aggregate final demand components using statistical techniques such as regression analysis and using data from a number of past periods. This is done to minimize the effects on forecasts of purely random factors which in any time period might have influenced the industry distribution of final demand.

IV. SOME USES OF INPUT-OUTPUT

So far, the discussion in this chapter has concentrated on the technical considerations involved in using input-output tables as a bridge between the very general forecast of aggregate demand and the implications of that forecast for total industry output and resource needs. This discussion, although not entirely rigorous, was on a rather abstract level. In this section, we will be concerned with the more concrete issue of how input-output can be used by the business forecaster.

Before beginning, perhaps one point should be emphasized. Not all firms or industries can make good use of input-output analysis. One of the key advantages of input-output to the business forecaster is that this technique enables him to forecast not only final demand for his firm's or industry's product but also intermediate demand by other businesses. For those business organizations which are primarily suppliers to final demand, there is thus little advantage in using input-output analysis, compared with the use of some traditional tools of the sales forecaster such as market research. But for those firms where demand comes in large part from other businesses purchasing goods for further production, input-output can be a very important addition to the forecaster's kit of tools.

Even in such instances, however, the limitations of input-output as a forecasting tool are substantial. One very important difficulty in its use is that input-output tables are completely static in the sense that the time sequence of adjustments in industry output and resource use is ignored. All of the effects on output and resource use of a change in final demand are assumed to take place entirely within the period being forecast. This assumption is far too gross to enable us to use input-output tables with any substantial degree of confidence for forecast-

ing over short-run time horizons. What is meant by short-run in this context is not altogether clear, since it depends on how rapidly the various economic markets adjust. Some attempts are now being made to integrate input-output forecasts with the output of quarterly econometric models of aggregate demand components.[10] However, the most frequent and probably the most successful application of input-output forecasting has been for long-run predictions, often involving forecast lead times of several years and even decades.

The purposes for which long-run economic forecasts are prepared often differ substantially from the purposes for which the more usual quarterly or annual forecasts of sales, aggregate demand components, interest rates, etc., are constructed. Over the short run, economic forecasts are prepared, updated, and revised in an almost continuous process. In most instances, they are prepared with no specific purpose or need in mind, but rather they are used in only a general way to provide the background data for a wide range of managerial decisions. Long-run forecasts, however, are more typically prepared in business organizations when there is some specific need associated with a particular problem or managerial decision. It is in this context of long-run corporate planning that input-output has had its most important impact on business forecasting.

In a sense, then, to describe input-output forecasting is to catalogue a number of specific corporate planning uses that have

---

[10] For some discussion of how input-output forecasts have been integrated with the output of GNP forecasting models, see Dusenberry, James, et al., eds., *The Brookings Quarterly Econometric Model of the United States* (Chicago: Rand McNally and Company, 1965), particularly chapter 17. Also see Otto Eckstein, Edward Green, and V. Sundarajan, "New Approaches in Input-Output Analysis," a paper delivered at the September 1970 meeting of the National Association of Business Economists held at Boston, Massachusetts.

been made of input-output analysis. We will consider a few simple examples in the following paragraphs in the hope that these give some flavor of the potential range of uses of input-output analysis.

Consider the following highly simplified and hypothetical problem. A firm is a leading domestic steel producer about to initiate a capital expansion program. The decision on the size of total new steel capacity, and the capabilities of the new plant to produce various specific steel products (such as sheet, wire, and various specialized alloys) depends importantly upon estimates, for a specific number of future years, of total demand for steel products, and also upon how this demand is distributed among different industry sectors. This problem is potentially ideal for the application of input-output techniques.

The first step in the solution of this problem is to obtain forecasts of aggregate final demand components with suitable lead times. This, of course, is not an easy problem to solve, but the issues involved in long-run GNP forecasting go well beyond the scope of this chapter. For our purposes it will be assumed that such forecasts are available to the input-output analyst.

The next step for the analyst is to see if the available input-output tables are in sufficient detail to meet the needs of the project. The existing tables available from government sources (we will have more to say about the availability of input-output tables later) separate out the input-output flows of the "primary iron and steel manufacturing industry" and, in the most recent version of the table, the input-output flows of well over 300 other industry categories. If this is sufficient detail for the purpose at hand, the input-output analyst's job is then rather straightforward.

Given the forecasts of aggregate final demand components, he can convert them into forecasts of final demand by industry sectors through use of the final demand coefficients (a suitably enlarged version of table

4). By applying each industry's coefficient of direct and indirect requirements (enlarged version of table 3) for the products of the "primary iron and steel manufacturing industry," he can estimate each industry's total need for iron and steel products.

At this point an alert analyst should recognize his opportunity to make a couple of extra points with his boss, since the input-output tables readily provide still more information which might be very pertinent to management's decision. Once an estimate of total output of iron and steel is obtained by the methods described above, the input-output analyst can estimate the resources needed to produce this output, both in terms of intermediate products and in terms of primary inputs, by multiplying aggregate output by the column of technical coefficients (from an enlarged version of table 2) for the iron and steel industry. This might prove to be useful to management for obtaining advanced warning of possible bottlenecks in the supplies of certain specific raw materials, or in the recognition of favorable or unfavorable changes in the distribution of resource use. This information, in turn, may motivate changes by the firm in its production techniques or expansion plans for the purpose of attaining a greater degree of vertical integration.

Clearly, underneath this naively simple statement of the solution to this problem are many complexities which might hamper the successful application of input-output techniques. Some of these as indicated previously, such as the problems of long-run GNP forecasting, are really beyond the subject of this chapter, but others—particularly the availability of suitably detailed input-output tables and the reliability for forecasting of the direct and indirect requirement and final demand coefficients for forecasting—are crucial to our discussion. In the next section these problems will be discussed in greater detail. But first, a few more examples of the uses of input-output analysis.

The previous example illustrated how input-output can be used for long-run forecasting and to highlight possible future supply bottlenecks. In addition to these forecasting uses of input-output, the tables themselves provide much direct information which might be of substantial use to the corporate planner. Specifically, by considering a number of input-output tables constructed at different time periods, the corporate planner and the input-output analyst have at their fingertips a capsule summary of changes in industrial mix, the structure of the economy, and technological change.[11] This information is embodied in the changes which occur over time in the industry distribution of output, and the changes that take place in the technical coefficients and the coefficients of direct and indirect requirements. By considering these changes, the corporate planner is able to uncover industries undergoing rapid growth and which may represent suitable opportunities for company diversification.

For example, as a first step in a company's search for diversification opportunities, the input-output analyst can provide useful and easily obtainable information by merely calculating average rates of change in output by industry categories using input-output flows from tables constructed over a number of past periods. The various industries could then be ranked by their average growth rates. To make these calculations more meaningful to management, the input-output analyst can go further and isolate some of the causes of the patterns observed in this initial experiment.

The changes which take place in output flows result from a number of causes. In part they reflect the impact of inventions and innovations in the technological conditions of production. But in addition they reflect the impact of cyclical and trend changes in the overall level of operations of the aggregate economy and the distribution of final demand among different components of GNP. These various effects on the rate of change in output can be isolated by designing suitable input-output experiments. For instance, suppose management wishes to highlight that portion of growth in various industries that has resulted from technological factors. This could be done by calculating (using the input-output tables) industry output in each period, given some fixed "menu" of final demand by industry category. By holding final demand and its distribution constant in each period, the output figures used in the calculation of average growth rates would give a purer measure of technological change.

The previous examples have only scratched the surface of potential uses of input-output techniques. Many more uses could be listed. For example, some firms have used input-output as a means for examining the implications for firm output and resource use of various alternative assumptions with regard to changes in aggregate demand, and its distribution among different demand sectors. Input-output has also been used as a marketing tool. A suitably detailed table provides a capsule summary of the distribution of a company's or industry's sales by various industrial categories. Armed with such information the marketing executive can pinpoint weaknesses and strengths in its sales efforts, and this can help in the more efficient allocation of the firm's advertising budget and sales promotion efforts by allowing him to concentrate on those industrial markets that offer the greatest potential.

One area of marketing and diversification planning that has been a productive area for input-output is in examining the

---

[11] For a detailed treatment of how input-output tables can be used to analyze technological change, see Anne Carter, "Changes in the Structure of the American Economy, 1947 to 1958 and 1962," *The Review of Economics and Statistics* (May 1967). Also see Anne Carter, *Structural Change in the American Economy* (Cambridge, Massachusetts: Harvard University Press, 1970).

potentials of foreign markets. More than 60 countries have some type of interindustry input-output table, although many of them are of questionable value because of poor data or because the tables are too old to be reliable. However, about 20 countries, half of which are located in Western Europe, have reliable and up-to-date input-output tables. These tables provide easily accessible marketing information for (1) possible export expansion, (2) recognition of growth areas for possible investment, and (3) recognition of possible suppliers of raw materials. The examination of foreign input-output tables as well as regional tables for the United States economy has also been useful in the selection of plant location sites.

More uses could be given, but even this short catalogue should give some idea of the uses which business firms have made of input-output analysis, and also some idea of the enormous potential of the technique. Unfortunately, many of the benefits of input-output have not been fully realized in practice. Some of the reasons for this are the subject of the next section.

V. SOME PROBLEMS OF INPUT-OUTPUT

A full realization of the benefits of input-output as a forecasting device or as a tool of corporate planning often depends upon the availability of very disaggregated tables, with frequently updated and reliable estimates of the technical coefficients and the coefficients of direct and indirect requirements.

For the United States economy, however, published input-output tables are infrequently prepared, and when they are prepared the new tables are released only with a substantial time lag. Moreover, until the most recent table, the degree of disaggregation typically was far less than that required for use by most business forecasters and corporate planners.

The first input-output table for the United States economy designed for general use was published by the Office of Business Economics of the Department of Commerce in 1949. It was based on interindustry data for the year 1947. Subsequently, all work along these lines was discontinued until 1962, when the Department of Commerce, in cooperation with other government agencies, published a new table based on data for the year 1958. These data were later updated to 1961. In November 1969, a new interindustry table, using data for 1963, was released by the government. Over the year, then, the frequency with which new tables have been prepared, or old tables updated, has increased markedly. Despite this improvement, at the present time the business forecaster who wishes to use published input-output tables must rely on data which describes the interindustry flows and the technology of the economy of about eight years ago. This is a serious deficiency since the economy and its technology are not static.

How serious a problem is this for the forecaster? It is hard to say without a detailed analysis of a large number of input-output tables, a project made difficult by the infrequent publication of tables for the United States economy. We can, however, get some idea of the magnitude of the problem in forecasting caused by the gaps in the availability of published data on interindustry transactions by considering the results obtained by Dutch econometricans in forecasting input-output flows with tables prepared for the Netherlands.

In the Netherlands, input-output tables have been prepared annually since 1948. In a careful analysis of the forecasts made using the tables for the 1948–57 period, Henri Theil, a noted Dutch econometrician, reached a number of interesting conclusions.[12] A few of these can be summarized briefly.

[12] Henri Theil, *Applied Economic Forecasting* (Chicago: Rand McNally and Company, 1966), pp. 168–255.

1. Prediction errors, not surprisingly, were on average larger in absolute value the larger the difference between the year of the input-output table and the prediction year.
2. The magnitude of the mean square forecast error[13] also increased with the "age" of the table, and relationship between the magnitude of the forecast error and the time span of the forecast was only slightly less than proportionate.
3. The magnitude of the average root mean square error for a forecast of the changes in total industry output one year beyond the age of the table was about 8 percent of the actual changes, a not insignificant forecast error.
4. The use of aggregate final demand rather than each individual sector's final demand raised the average root mean square error to about 10–15 percent of the actual change.

It would be wrong to use these results directly to reach conclusions with regard to the forecast accuracy of input-output tables for the United States economy. For one thing the Dutch tables are far more aggregated,[14] and this tends to reduce the volatility of the technical coefficients. Moreover, there are vast differences in the industrial mix of the two countries, and based on Thiel's results, significant differences exist in forecast accuracy among different industry sectors. Nevertheless, the Dutch results are suggestive, and point to the possibility that the infrequency of published input-output tables for the United States economy is a serious drawback in their use for forecasting or planning.

Another difficulty in using input-output is the inadequacy in industrial detail. The 1947 table had interindustry flows grouped into 42 major sectors. This was expanded to 86 industries for the 1958 table. The 1963 table includes nearly 370 industries. Despite this impressive increase in size, the published input-output tables seldom give all of the detail desired by the business forecaster since most often he wishes to go beyond total industry classification to an analysis of the implications for his particular firm, and often even for divisions and departments within that firm.

Many large business organizations, recognizing the potentials of input-output but faced with the deficiencies of the existing tables, have either developed their own input-output tables or have further disaggregated the pubilshed tables.[15] While these activities have significantly expanded the potentials of input-output, the results have not in all cases been entirely satisfactory. A number of problems exist for the analyst attempting to disaggregate or construct input-output tables.

Among these problems, perhaps the most important are related to the availability and reliability of the data used in the calculations. In approaching the task of disaggregation, or building a new input-output table, an economist will use a variety of data sources, including internal sales records of individual companies, records of purchases by the firm of their input requirements, and

[13] The mean square error is the average of the sum of squares of the differences between actual and predicted values. Unlike the average absolute difference between actual and predicted values, this measure of forecast accuracy gives greater weight to the large forecast errors. The root mean square forecast error is simply the square root of the mean square forecast error. For a full discussion of the use of these and other measures of forecast accuracy, see the chapter in this volume on statistical measures of forecast accuracy.

[14] The tables used in the analysis were comprised of 32 industry sectors, compared with 370 industry sectors in the most recent table for the United States economy.

[15] A useful summary of some of the developments in the use of input-output tables by individual firms is provided in the papers presented at the symposium on the "Use of Input/Output as a Marketing and Economic Tool," held by the American Chemical Society in Chicago, Illinois in September 1967.

a variety of shipment and sales data collected and published by trade associations. Much of these data are of doubtful quality, and often important gaps are left in the input-output tables because certain information—information which is often very important to the firm using the input-output table—was unavailable.[16] Moreover, the disaggregation of existing tables or the construction of new tables is an expensive, laborious, and complex job which can be tackled only by the larger business, management consulting, or research organizations. It has been said before, and probably is not too much of an exaggeration, that the future of input-output as a forecasting technique depends upon the development of simple and inexpensive methods of disaggregation.

To overcome the difficulties in using input-output when the tables have become too old, forecasters frequently attempt to update existing tables by estimating changes which have taken place in the technical coefficients. As is the case in disaggregating or constructing input-output tables, there is no unique way that the analyst can approach

the task of estimating changes in technical coefficients. In practice, he will typically use an eclectic approach, including the study of various engineering data to determine any trends which may be apparent in resource availability or use, and in the technical conditions of production. In the absence of such information, he may rely instead on mathematical extrapolation of past observed trends in the magnitudes of the technical coefficients, and on informed judgments about changes in consumer taste, product mix, etc.[17]

Probably the most ambitious attempt at estimating changes in technical coefficients (which relied on all of these procedures, and more) was the work of Anne Carter, her colleagues of the Harvard Research Project, and the staff of Arthur D. Little, Inc., using the 1958 Department of Commerce table. This work provided the basis for Clopper Almon's forecasts of interindustry output through the year 1975.[18]

VI. CONCLUDING COMMENTS

In this brief survey of input-output, some attempt was made to strike a balance between the pros and cons of using the technique for forecasting. It is important to do this since over the years there have been many over-enthusiastic claims about what input-output can accomplish for the business forecaster and corporate planner, and equally strong denunciations by its critics.

Input-output is not a panacea for the business forecaster and corporate planner,

[16] The unavailability of data often results in certain peculiarities in actual empirical input-output tables. One common result of data scarcity is the existence of so-called dummy industries. Their use results from the fact that in some instances it is impossible to identify precisely the industry furnishing a particular input. As an example, the 1963 Department of Commerce table included the dummy industry, "Office Supplies." This inclusion was necessitated by the fact that office supplies are made from the products of a number of different industries and it is difficult, if not impossible, to separate out each industry's contribution. For example, paper used in office work belongs with the work products industry and paper clips with some metalworking subdivision of manufacturing. However, it is a rare firm that keeps detailed records on the portions of its total office supply expense represented by paper and paper clips. In order not to inflate one sector's output, office supplies were kept together as the output of a separate, hypothetical industry.

[17] For some of the problems and methods of forecasting technological change see the chapter by Arthur Gerstenfeld in this volume.

[18] Clopper Almon, *The American Economy to 1975* (New York: Harper & Row, 1966). Recently, Almon and his research group at the University of Maryland have extended these forecasts to 1980.

nor is it simply a useless addition to their kit of tools. Like all forecasting techniques it has certain advantages and disadvantages. The decision by the business forecaster as to whether or not to use input-output should depend on his analysis of its advantages and disadvantages compared with alternative methods, the goals of his forecasting activity, and the relative costs of using different techniques to achieve these goals.

The adoption of input-output forecasting is fairly extensive in industry, but to be candid, its use is less widespread than most analysts initially expected. The reason for this is that the costs of implementing an input-output system, especially in view of the previously discussed inadequacies of the published tables, are high. Only the largest, most diverse organizations can justify such expenditures by the gains achieved with input-output compared with alternative forecasting techniques.

Ultimately, the use of input-output on a broad scale by industry depends on two things. First, it depends on the activities of the government in publishing frequent, up-to-date, and highly disaggregated tables. Second, it depends on the activities of government and private economists in carefully analyzing the forecasting performance of input-output tables compared with forecasts obtained using alternative approaches.

While the existing tables have many deficiencies, the Office of Business Economics has recently made vast strides in overcoming them. And based on various statements of government officials, more progress can be expected in the future. In addition, early indications are that the publication of the 1963 table has greatly stimulated research activities in the field of input-output in the government, as well as by academic and business economists. These factors would lead me to forecast, with a high subjective probability, that the future will see a substantial increase in the use of input-output by the business forecaster.

BIBLIOGRAPHY

Almon, Clopper, *The American Economy to 1975*. New York: Harper & Row, 1966.

Almon, Clopper, *Matrix Methods in Economics*. Reading, Massachusetts: Addison-Wesley Publishing Company, 1967.

Carter, Anne, "Changes in the Structure of the American Economy, 1947 to 1958 and 1962." *The Review of Economics and Statistics*, (May 1967), pp. 209–224.

Carter, Anne, *Structural Change in the American Economy*. Cambridge, Massachusetts: Harvard University Press, 1970.

Dorfman, Robert, Paul Samuelson and Robert Solow, *Linear Programming and Economic Analysis*. New York: McGraw-Hill Book Company, 1958.

Duesenberry, James, et al., eds., *The Brookings Quarterly Econometric Model of the United States*. Chicago: Rand McNally and Company, 1965.

Eckstein, Otto, Edward Green, and V. Sundarajan, "New Approaches in Input-Output Analysis." Paper delivered at the September 1970 meeting of the National Association of Business Economists held at Boston, Massachusetts.

"How Good is Input-Output." Papers delivered at the December 1967 Meeting of the Business and Economic Statistics Section of the American Statistical Association held at Washington, D.C.

"Input-Output Structure of the U.S. Economy: 1963," *Survey of Current Business* (November 1969), pp. 16–47.

"Input-Output Structure of the U.S. Economy: 1963; Volume 1, *Transactions Data for Detailed Industries;* Volume 2, *Direct Requirements for Detailed Industries;* and Volume 3,*Total Requirements for Detailed Industries.* Washington: U.S. Government Printing Office, 1969.

Leontief, Wassily, *Input-Output Economics.* New York: Oxford University Press, 1966.

Symposium on the "Use of Input/Output as a Marketing and Economic Tool." American Chemical Society. Chicago, Illinois, September 1967.

Theil, Henri, *Applied Economic Forecasting.* Chicago: Rand McNally and Company, 1966.

Yan, Chio-shuang, *Introduction to Input-Output Economics.* New York: Holt, Rinehart and Winston, Inc., 1969.

WILLIAM F. BUTLER & ROBERT A. KAVESH

Judgmental Forecasting of the Gross National Product

The purpose of this chapter is to describe a technique for forecasting the gross national product for a year or so ahead and to appraise the many problems associated with this operation. And problems there will be, for the task of estimating the future course of overall business activity involves a complicated combination of quantitative and qualitative elements—with a heavy emphasis placed upon the exercise of judgment.

The approach to be followed here will be the sectoral analysis procedure, in which the various components of the gross national product are separately evaluated and then combined to form a total. Specifically, the terms *intuitive* and *judgmental* have been applied to the type of analysis that will be utilized, in that the approach lacks much of the precision associated with formal econometric models and does not restrict itself to a single set of "indicators."[1]

[1] This lack of precision is, in many respects, more apparent than real. Model builders, after all, must exercise discretion and be selective in *specifying* and *estimating* the factors to be included in their equations. Furthermore, there is always the nagging problem of providing values for the *exogenous* variables in econometric models. Most models, in fact, are constantly being adjusted to bring them more into line with the actual pattern of events. Even so, no one who works with econometric forecasting models would claim that his equations incorporate all the *elements* influencing the course of business activity. At most, he would assert that the

Clearly, subjective elements play an important part in judgmental forecasting, and as a result this method is often criticized as lacking the elegance and the methodological exactness of the econometric approach. What is often lost sight of by the critics is that the judgmental approach ultimately relies as much on macroeconomic theory as do the econometric models. In the judgmental approach, however, the forecaster is less bound by specific coefficient values estimated entirely from past occurrences. The judgmental forecaster is constantly juggling the weights attached to specific causal variables in making his forecasts, based on his intuitive conception of the special circumstances which are then affecting the economy. In fact, this flexibility in approaching the ever-changing conditions underlying economic activity is the greatest strength of the judgmental approach, and has probably contributed most to its continued good performance compared with econometric forecasting.

Perhaps a better way of describing this technique is to borrow William Fellner's

relationships describe fairly accurately the major economic variables relating to the forecasting target. Similarly, the list of "leading" indicators has been revised on occasion, and rare is the economist who hitches his forecast to this one measuring rod alone, although most would scrutinize the indicators quite carefully.

207

phrasing: "looser frameworks of a quasi-mathematical character." In less esoteric terms, this means the application of common sense and economic theory to the available statistics and forces.

Whatever the term used, the challenges involved are significant. It is safe to say, nevertheless, that the bulk of general business forecasting is carried out in approximately the fashion to be described and will probably continue to be done this way in the foreseeable future. For no other technique is as useful in immersing the analyst in his job and in furnishing a basic understanding of the way the economic system functions. *Flexibility* is the byword in this approach and, practiced by an expert, the results can be surprisingly accurate for periods ranging up to roughly a year or so ahead.

Almost every business forecaster is required to try his hand at estimating the gross national product. In corporate work, GNP becomes the starting point; from there the analyst can narrow his focus more sharply to the industry and, ultimately, to his firm. To be sure, a given industry or firm may well prosper while the economy dips, but this is the exception and not the rule. Thus, knowledge of general trends represents a firm foundation upon which to build a sales or profit forecast.

In government, forecasts of the GNP are painstakingly assembled by several agencies. The Council of Economic Advisers carries on a continuing survey of business activity, and makes known its estimates in January, when the Economic Report of the President and the Budget Message are delivered. These figures furnish the basis for an evaluation of how well or how poorly the economy is performing and are useful for anticipating possible shifts in administration policies. Similarly, economists in the treasury prepare GNP forecasts (with results that at times are somewhat different from those of the CEA) as a means to project federal tax receipts and to anticipate developments in the balance of payments as well as

to provide guidance on other economic matters to treasury officials.

In other areas of the government GNP estimates are also prepared. The Department of Commerce (the major collector of the relevant component statistics) gauges movements in GNP by use of its own econometric model as well as by less formal techniques. Similarly, the Department of Agriculture incorporates an overall business forecast into its appraisal of the future course of farm activity.

To these must be added the detailed analyses undertaken by economists in the Federal Reserve System, to be adapted into a monetary policy framework for stability and growth. Nor can one ignore the independent (and often controversial) estimates furnished by the Office of Management and Budget.

Finally, most speeches on "the business outlook" focus for the most part on GNP and its several sectors.

What is it then, that is the subject for so much analysis and concern? What is GNP, and how is it put together?

In a sense, GNP is a sprawling aggregate that sums up the output of the economy. Put more precisely, it is a part of the conceptual apparatus that demonstrates the process by which goods and services are produced and incomes generated. Income and output, after all, are merely different ways of looking at the same basic process—and these concepts are linked together in a framewrok called the *national income and product accounts.*[2]

[2] A complete description of the anatomy of these accounts may be found in *The National Income and Product Accounts of the United States, 1929–1965* (Department of Commerce). In addition, periodic revisions and updatings are provided in the July issues of the *Survey of Current Business.* Every forecaster is deeply indebted to the economists and statisticians who aided in the conceptualization and implementation of this framework. Without these data, forecasting—by any form—would be far less accurate, if

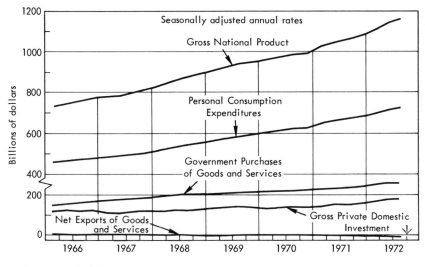

Source: *Department of Commerce.*
[1] *Preliminary.*

Chart 1   Gross National Product or Expenditure

Gross national product is the most widely used and publicized of these related concepts and will be the focus of our attention. It measures the market value of the final goods and services produced by the nation. Looked at another way: it comprises the total expenditures of consumers, business, and government, as well as our net export balance with foreigners. Statistics are issued quarterly, on an annual rate basis, and are adjusted for seasonal variations.

Table 1 presents data on GNP and its major components in current and constant dollars for recent years. A picture of how the economy has performed since 1947 is illustrated in chart 1. Here we see evidence of the forecasting problem in a nutshell—several cycles superimposed upon a rising trend. What can the analyst do to anticipate the rate of cyclical advance or decline, and what

not impossible. The value to the business community in having data readily available in comprehensive form cannot be precisely measured, but it is enormous.

can he do to judge when turning points will appear?[3]

Economists approach forecasting problems in a variety of ways. Some, indeed, use what amounts to no technique at all, merely stating in general terms some vague notions about the possible course of business activity. They seem motivated more by what they think their superiors want to hear than by independent analysis and judgment. This fear or hesitancy on the part of the forecaster is lamentable (but understandable).

[3] This chapter (and most of the others in this book) is concerned almost exclusively with techniques for *short-run* forecasting. That is, the emphasis is upon cyclical movements that might be anticipated in the period of a year or so ahead. Even the term *cycle* has been under question, however. The indicator-oriented publication, formerly called *Business Cycle Developments* changed its title to *Business Conditions Digest* during the long, sustained advance of the 1960s. The reemergence of the cycle, in the form of the recession of 1969–70, stayed the voices of those who believed the business cycle was obsolete.

For discussion of long-run projections, see the chapter by Lawrence Mayer in this book.

TABLE 1. GROSS NATIONAL PRODUCT OR EXPENDITURE

Billions of dollars; quarterly data at seasonally adjusted annual rates

Period	Total Gross National Product in 1958 Dollars	Total Gross National Product	Personal Consumption expenditures	Gross Private Domestic Investment	Net Exports of Goods and Services	Government Purchases of Goods and Services						Implicit Price Deflator for Total GNP 1958 = 100[2]
						Total	Federal				State and Local	
							Total	National Defence[1]	Other			
1962	529.8	560.3	355.1	83.0	5.1	117.1	63.4	51.6	11.8	53.7	105.78
1963	551.0	590.5	375.0	87.1	5.9	122.5	64.2	50.8	13.5	58.2	107.17
1964	581.1	632.4	401.2	94.0	8.5	128.7	65.2	50.0	15.2	63.5	108.85
1965	617.8	684.9	432.8	108.1	6.9	137.0	66.9	50.1	16.8	70.1	110.86
1966	658.1	749.9	466.3	121.4	5.3	156.8	77.8	60.7	17.1	79.0	113.94
1967	675.2	793.9	492.1	116.6	5.2	180.1	90.7	72.4	18.4	89.4	117.59
1968	706.6	864.2	536.2	126.0	2.5	199.6	98.8	78.3	20.5	100.8	122.30
1969	725.6	930.3	579.5	139.0	1.9	210.0	98.8	78.4	20.4	111.2	128.20
1970	722.1	976.4	616.8	137.1	3.6	219.0	96.5	75.1	21.5	122.5	135.23
1971	741.7	1,050.4	664.9	152.0	.7	232.8	97.8	71.4	26.3	135.0	141.61
1972	789.5	1,151.8	721.0	180.4	−4.2	254.6	105.8	75.9	29.9	148.8	145.89

Source: Department of Commerce.

[1] Preliminary.

[2] Gross national product in current dollars divided by gross national product in 1958 dollars.

Still others emphasize pure statistical techniques in their approach to forecasting, eschewing any reliance at all upon economic theory (theory, you will recall, is the basis for econometric model building). This "mechanical" method literally avoids any exercise of judgment at all. In a real sense it isn't forecasting, but rather extrapolation.

Both of these techniques are largely frivolous. But they do indicate a perennial problem in the profession—forecasters who refuse to forecast, or who try to play it safe.

Another group of economists rely very heavily upon one or two statistical series in framing their forecasts. New orders for durable goods are frequently used as the sole basis for overall GNP patterns; so, too, is the series on capital expenditure anticipations. Nobody should underestimate the importance of these indicators; they are clearly of prime significance in describing key aspects of business behavior. However, sole reliance upon either one or both is no true substitute for the scrutiny of the entire "indicator" series. Furthermore, both of these factors—and many more—are almost certainly considered by the forecaster who utilizes the complete intuitive approach.

How then does the intuitive technique operate?

While the actual procedure will vary according to the skills, habits, and experience of the economists, in general the similarities outweigh the differences. The process involves moving from the "known" to the "unknown" or "less known," sector by sector. That is, the forecaster will set up the structure of the GNP accounting framework (see table 1) and will methodically attempt to fill in the empty boxes with his own estimates. Some of the figures will be fairly easy to approximate to a high order of accuracy; others will involve careful weighing and appraisal of a myriad of quantitative and qualitative forces.

Like any craftsman assembling a product, he will try to make sure that each piece fits together into a unified, consistent whole.

And if the total seems unrealistic or somehow wrong, he will adjust and adapt the parts until the artist in him is satisfied. Thus, the forecaster is like an artist or a craftsman: he will ponder, appraise, and improvise until he feels satisfied with his final product.

In doing his job he will use tools: often years of seemingly impractical (but, in truth, eminently useful) studies in economic theory and analysis. These represent his basic investment in knowledge and technique; they are the foundation of sound analysis. In addition, he will be steeped in the elements of statistics, for a great deal of the piecing together of a forecast involves statistical consistency checks. Most importantly, he should have a deep understanding of how the economy and its sectors operate and interact in practice. This latter quality is the most elusive and generally serves to set apart the superior forecaster from his inferiors. Experience and study may help acquire this understanding, but in many cases they do not. And perhaps it is because the ultimate tool—the one that combines and synthesizes all the others—is that indefinable "judgment." Without it, the forecaster may become mired in a swamp of statistics; with it he may be able to create order and form.

Judgment, however, is not totally independent of knowledge. It stems from it in varying degrees, depending upon how well the forecaster has mastered the tools of his trade and upon his ability to separate the relevant from the irrelevant.

But let us move on to the actual forecasting process itself—the integration of the relatively known information with what is less well known.

First and foremost, before setting down any figures, the economist must state his basic, underlying assumptions. That is, he must describe in broad terms the overall environment in which business activity will be taking place. Since many external forces may have a substantial bearing upon the economy, the forecaster should cite some of the political, diplomatic, and sociological assumptions under which he is operating. Thus, in setting up the forecast for a year ahead, the analyst will ordinarily assume that:

1. No major war or heating up of international tensions will occur. Obviously, such developments would have an overpowering impact upon the pace of business activity. The disruptive effects of the war in Vietnam on the American economy after hostilities escalated in late 1965 is a case in point.

2. Relationships between government and the business community will not be sharply altered. An example of this type of shift occurred in 1962 when President Kennedy took a strong stand in opposition to the attempted steel price rise. A crisis of confidence developed, which served to slow down the rate of economic advance.

3. Crippling strikes will, by and large, be averted. Collective bargaining patterns are difficult to anticipate precisely. Strikes occur from time to time and are part of the normal economic process. Major strikes, however, such as the one in the steel industry in 1959 that lasted almost four months and had a major effect upon business, cannot readily be predicted. The prolonged shutdown by General Motors in the latter part of 1970, which strongly affected the pattern of business activity, is another example of an "unusual" occurrence.

4. Sociocultural patterns will not produce inordinate strains. An example of this would be if racial tensions erupted so violently as to cut heavily into sales or output, either through major boycotts or outbreaks of violence.

5. Taxes will not be raised or lowered in any significant fashion. Most forecasts prepared in early 1963 presented two sets of estimates, based upon whether or not the tax cut was passed by Congress. Clearly, tax changes play a major

role in the business outlook; a surprising act by Congress would probably render a forecast obsolete.

6. Monetary policy will not produce a climate of undue credit stringency. The credit crunch of 1966, in which the financial faucet was literally turned off, influenced the economy significantly. An even greater impact occurred during late 1969 and early 1970, when interest rates reached all-time highs and when the availability of funds was sharply restricted.

7. It goes without saying—a sudden imposition of a wage-price freeze (such as in August 1971) will not take place.

To these could be added any number of reasonable assumptions relating to the external environment in which business activity would be taking place.[4]

Once the assumptions have been stated, the forecaster can then turn to the numerical estimates themselves. Some economists prefer to begin by predicting total GNP and then working backwards to supply the details. This technique is a handy one, in that it is much easier to estimate GNP within a small range of error than it is

---

[4] At this point some skeptics may scoff and claim that the list of assumptions could be so extended as to obviate the necessity for a formal forecast. There is some truth in this, in that one may hedge so much that he is guilty of plugging into his model the very things he supposedly is seeking to determine. At its worst, this technique is employed by some who will present an analysis filled with "if this happens, if that occurs . . . then business will rise (or fall)." What they fail to recognize (or perhaps it is rather a convenient ploy) is that they're really not forecasting, but are merely describing the way in which the economy operates—and that is not a substitute for forecasting.

It should be noted that one of the great advantages of formal econometric models is that different assumptions may be tested by varying the values for the exogenous variables. Thus, an econometric model may produce literally hundreds of "forecasts"—each based upon different sets of assumptions.

to do as well on each (or even on most) of the sectors. Compensating errors have frequently given the lie to the old saw that the total is merely the sum of the parts. However, this "working from the top down" approach merely delays the detailed effort required to supply the sector accounts. In practice, many forecasters work with a rough overall total in mind as a kind of index to the business environment they anticipate. This total figure, however, is not a constant; if the sum of the sectors is higher or lower, the forecaster will analyze and reappraise all of his estimates.

This brief description of the "top down" method serves to highlight a frequently voiced criticism of the entire intuitive school. It is claimed that forecasts of the various sectors are not independently derived because in the process of making these estimates the forecaster is working within a framework of the overall level of business activity and is merely adapting each sector to the predetermined total pattern. Thus, it is averred, the component estimates are simply tailored to fit the cloth and should not be taken seriously.

This claim misses the point. Forecasting total GNP without analyzing the sectors is merely a guessing game, for it overlooks the interactions and stresses that only a more detailed study would furnish. Similarly, it would be absurd to fix rigidly a total for GNP and then mechanically or unimaginatively juggle the sectors until the parts equaled the whole. Rather, the process that is generally followed consists of a series of successive approximations in which the parts add up to a whole that has been roughly approximated in advance. Flexibility provides the key, as the sectors and the totals evolve into a final shape.

After all, this is really what should be expected. The forecaster is not operating in a vacuum. He generally has a pretty good idea of what is happening in the economy at the moment; he knows much more about development of the past few months. He has studied the cyclical behavior of GNP and its parts. Thus, he has a feel for what he anticipates will happen, and that feel extends to both the overall level of the economy and to many of its sectors. In practice, he will usually balance totals and parts until he reaches what he considers to be a unified forecast. This is what is meant by an intuitive approach.

But intuitive does not mean nonanalytical. What specific techniques will the forecaster utilize in deriving his GNP forecast? Let us approach this through the "bottom up" approach; that is, the estimation of each sector separately, beginning with the easier sectors and moving on to the more difficult ones.

Government expenditures on goods and services (not to be confused with total governmental outlays, which would also include, among other things, transfer payments) may be approximated in a variety of ways. At the *state and local* level, where forecasting materials are quite limited,[5] extrapolative techniques are mainly used. Since 1960, for example, state and local expenditures (on the GNP account basis) have increased by roughly ten percent per year—a substantially faster rate than that of overall GNP. Indeed, these outlays are quite a bit higher than federal expenditures.

It is interesting to note that the ten percent trend line is amazingly smooth, with only minor deviations. Soaring municipal bond rates, inflationary cost increases and stepped-up demands for services—somehow, all of these elements have been incorporated into the basic trend. This is not to negate the notion of a municipal crisis; it simply describes the facts on expenditures.

The forecaster should keep close tabs on discussions and developments in the area

---

[5] Although spending commitments and plans are matters of public record, there is no central collection agency to consolidate the combined totals of the more than 100,000 governmental units in the state and local complex.

of revenue-sharing and grants-in-aid. In the short run, however, they rarely influence the predictions in any marked away.

So, the first set of empty boxes—those for quarterly estimates of state and local spending—may now be filled in. The job is under way.

At the federal level, the data have displayed substantially more variation, so that the forecasting problem is somewhat more difficult. The following chapter presents a detailed procedure for estimating this sector; consequently, the discussion here will be brief. The *Budget of the United States* furnishes the major source of information, although it relates to the July 1–June 30 fiscal year rather than the forecaster's conventional calendar year. While the budget is useful in terms of roughly gauging total expenditures, it is not too helpful in anticipating the quarterly patterns which must be placed into the GNP framework. Then too, the budget is not that "tight" a document; for political purposes, expenditures (and even more, receipts) may actually be far off the mark. Additional information may be gathered from *The Economic Report of the President*, the *Midyear Budget Review* and the February issues of the *Survey of Current Business.*

An invaluable way to supplement these official reports is to hold informal discussions with governmental officials and economists. They are very close to the day-to-day happenings and frequently can assist in clarifying matters and in furnishing clues about evolving developments. These people are interested in cooperating with other economists (many of them also prepare forecasts). Trading ideas and insight is part of the business; however, it should be clearly understood that the kind of material these governmental economists discuss does not compromise their positions of trust. Generally, they help in furnishing details and in serving as sounding boards against which the business economist can try out his own ideas.

Of particular importance in the federal sector is the level of *national defense expenditures*, accounting for about 70 percent of purchases of goods and services. Here the forecaster should keep a close watch over international developments, disarmament conferences, and the like. In the short run, however, major swings in spending are unlikely unless cold war tensions mount. For the longer run, developments in defense spending could have a major impact upon the level and composition of economic activity.

Complications occasionally arise in federal finance which may complicate the forecasting problem. The national debt ceiling periodically comes up for congressional discussion, and if delays occur in adapting to fiscal realities, governmental payments should be slowed down abruptly. To some, this was a major factor in the recession of 1957–58. There is no simple way to anticipate a happening of this type; in general, steps are taken before any adverse effects are felt by the economy.

One additional matter the forecaster should examine in the overall government sector is the trend of transfers, interest, and subsidies. These items are excluded from GNP proper, but they do have an influence on overall spending. Here, the pattern has been one of uninterrupted advance. From 1960 to 1971 government purchases of goods and services rose from $99.6 billion to $232.8 billion, an increase of 134 percent. During the same period governmental transfers, interest and subsidies rose from $36.5 billion to $108.0 billion.

Thus, the sectoral analysis approach to government spending would tend to rely upon past trends (for state and local), budget information, discussions, and a general appraisal of developments that might occur in the next few months. Clearly, the federal government cannot simply be regarded as a dependent factor, fixed regardless of the state of the economy. Rather, it can play a major role in controlling the cycle; although, surprisingly enough, during the postwar era it has minimized its direct, discretionary role in countercyclical policies. Nevertheless, as a starting point in preparing a forecast, the government sector provides a fairly solid foundation.

The next sector to be incorporated into the forecasting framework relates mainly to business spending. *Gross private domestic investment* includes expenditures for plant and equipment, residential construction, and changes in business inventories. As such, it encompasses the most difficult areas in GNP forecasting. These are truly the volatile parts of the economy; the bulk of the decline in GNP during the postwar recessions can be accounted for by declines in capital spending and in inventory liquidation.

Detailed explanations of how to forecast each of these sectors are presented in subsequent chapters on capital spending, housing and other construction, and inventories. Accordingly, the procedure outlined here will cover only the highlights.

Capital spending (plant and equipment outlays) involves a whole host of judgments. How are profits doing, in the aggregate and in terms of margins? At what level of capacity is the economy operating? (Capacity is a crucial factor, but there is still no completely satisfactory way to analyze it.) What is the overall competitive environment? How are prices moving? Some economists attempt to link capital spending to one or more other variables by constructing a model, but the results have generally not been too useful for short-term predictions.

Far and away the most widely used tool in forecasting capital spending is the survey approach. Periodically, McGraw-Hill, Inc., as well as the Department of Commerce and the Securities and Exchange Commission, measures the capital spending anticipations of American businesses. These figures are translated into GNP counterparts and provide estimates for the period ahead. Admittedly, these forecasts are rarely perfectly accurate; they are based upon data supplied by the respondents and these figures are subject to revision in light of actual developments. Thus, when business conditions are uncertain, plant and equipment expenditure plans may be somewhat low. But as the economy moves up, expectations change and plans are revised upward, and vice versa.

Therefore, the forecaster should use judgment in accepting the preliminary surveys as a guide to what may actually occur later on. If he believes that the state of the economy is going to improve, he will tend to scale the survey results upward; he will do the reverse if he feels that a recession may be in the offing. From time to time, economists may speak with corporate officials who respond to these surveys in an attempt to ascertain whether the estimates have been changed. A periodic check of this sort may prove to be quite illuminating in presaging increases or decreases in the aggregate.

In addition to using the above mentioned surveys, further insight into capital spending may be derived from studying the reports of the Conference Board, which supplies data on capital appropriations.

Surveys are quite useful in this area, but the forecaster must also try to anticipate the climate of monetary policy in making his evaluations. Too fast a rate of advance in business activity may bring about tight money conditions, which could serve to slow down the rate of capital spending. This caveat would also apply in the case of residential housing and inventories.

What emerges, then, from this rundown of forecasting capital spending is the great reliance placed upon the anticipations surveys. At best, the analyst is quite nervous about estimating this area; the surveys provide at least a useful first approximation.

With regard to *housing*, the forecasting problems are complicated by the fact that the residential housing cycle has frequently followed a pattern quite distinct from that of the overall economy. In certain respects, housing seems to relate more close-ly to changes in the availability and cost of mortgage money than to changes in disposable income. Nevertheless, economists generally attempt to set up estimates of the structure of demand for new homes by analyzing census reports on family formation, adjusting for undoubling, estimating second-house demand (a rapidly rising area), and studying migration patterns and vacancies. To this are added demolitions, condemnations, and accidental losses. The total provides a useful approximation of the demand side—when combined with estimates of disposable income.

On the supply side, credit factors are of prime importance—so much so that more emphasis is generally placed upon this factor than on all the others (at least in the short run). The role of governmental financing is a complicating element, in that changes in FHA and VA regulations can bring about sharp changes in the housing picture, as can the actions of FNMA, GNMA, and the Department of Housing and Urban Development. Conventional financing is a much more stable element; but here, too, clues must be sought by examining mortgage rates in comparison with other money and capital market movements.

All in all, the forecaster usually finds that this field presents an overwhelming combination of seemingly contradictory patterns. He may look at the F. W. Dodge figures on residential construction contract awards, as well as at some of the housing surveys. All too frequently, however, he will find himself asking the advice of specialists in this area, and will feel less certain about his estimate for housing than for almost any other sector.

The exception is the *inventory* forecast. This is truly the frustrating part of the forecasting profession—the giant question mark in the sectoral analysis approach to GNP. It would not be an exaggeration to state that errors in anticipating inventory movements constitute the blackest element

in the forecasters' record. Indeed, when two economists compare GNP estimates, the similarities are often more striking than the differences—with the exception of their inventory figures.

The problem stems in part from the fact that what is being measured is not the total level of inventories, but rather the changes that occur in these totals. Consequently, inventory accumulation is registered as a plus, liquidation as a minus. Furthermore, in terms of impact on the economy, a slowdown in the rate of accumulation (say from an annual rate of $6 billion per year to $3 billion) results in a lower flow of income and output—other things being equal. But they are rarely equal. In the example given, the slower rate of accumulation might stem from a sudden surge in consumption, which would reflect improving business conditions. Under these circumstances, firms might attempt to adjust their inventory positions to higher levels.

What we find, then, is that it is difficult to pinpoint the pattern of inventory movements. In general, stocks are built up during the upward phase of the cycle and are reduced during the decline. The problem is the interpretation of changes occurring near turning points in general business activity. It may be, for example, that as the economy bottoms out of a recession and begins to move upward, inventories will continue to be liquidated as buying moves goods from the shelves, even though orders have been placed with suppliers. This is involuntary liquidation. The reverse might occur during the upper turning point; goods previously ordered or being processed would accumulate in the face of sagging sales—an instance of involuntary accumulation.

The confusion is sometimes so complete that competent forecasters may be very close in terms of total GNP and many of its components, but will have altogether different inventory estimates—even with regard to the sign.

In approaching the inventory sector,

the forecaster must rely upon a number of devices—some analytical, others less so. For one thing, he can refer to the monthly series on manufacturers', wholesalers', and retailers' inventories collected by the Department of Commerce. These statistics are useful in understanding and evaluating past and current developments. He can appraise these movements in light of shifts that may be occurring in sales and new orders. In addition, he will study inventory/sales ratios in an attempt to anticipate gluts or shortages. Here, however, he will frequently and frustratingly find that slight changes in the denominator may completely alter what seemed like a simple set of relationships. Finally, he can get some idea of the businessman's view by referring to the quarterly survey of manufacturers' inventory anticipations issued by the Department of Commerce.

In practice, forecasters tend to rely most heavily upon the inventory/sales ratio. Although cause and effect are clearly interrelated, the analyst would estimate a level of final demand for the economy and gauge the level of inventories that would correspond to this figure. In doing this, he would appraise price pressures, the means to finance inventories, and the like. Finally, he would judge what pattern the ratio would follow and translate these results into a rate of change.

It might be said that a simpler method could merely involve the plugging in of past cycles in inventory/sales ratios. However, the patterns have tended to shift somewhat; in general, the ratio has become lower. This stems in part from early postwar conditions in which inventories were often hoarded. Delivery times were longer, inflation tended to validate the decision to amass excess amounts of material and goods, and interest rates for financing inventories were fairly low. More recently, however, the economy as a whole has operated at less than full capacity, thus reducing delivery times. Also, borrowing costs have been higher than the

rates that prevailed during the earlier period.

In addition, better inventory management controls are being utilized in industry, often in conjunction with a computer program. As a result, less inventory seems to be needed per unit of sales. Whether this is a permanent development or not remains to be seen.

Gross private domestic investment—that complicated amalgam of capital spending, housing, and inventory change—stands as the real obstacle in the way of successful forecasting. Each part presents difficult challenges against which analytical procedures so often prove inadequate. What distinguishes the successful forecaster is the insight and judgment he can bring to bear in estimating these areas.

A particularly troublesome aspect of GNP forecasting is the sector headed *net exports of goods and services*. This measures the extent to which exports exceed imports. In order to avoid double counting, the figures are reduced to a "net" basis.

The forecasting problem centers around the fact that exports and imports are subject to many forces, including the vagaries of the business cycle. For instance, a strong advance in economic activity in the United States might lead to a demand for increased imports. Price pressures, in addition, might serve to hold down our exports, particularly if Europe were experiencing a recession. Thus, the net export balance would decline or become negative.

The balance of payments also enters into the picture. The net export totals do not account for other elements that comprise the broader concept of the balance of payments: investment, capital flows, and transfer payments. In recent years these have swung the overall totals decidedly to the deficit position—with a corresponding buildup of foreign dollar claims and a movement of gold. Steps have been taken, ranging from devaluation, and cooperation among central banks, to tax adjustments and encourage-

ment to exporters in addition to import sur-
charges and the suspension of convertibility.
"Hot money" flows have resulted in a greater
similarity between central bank rates among
the industrialized nations.

In assembling the net exports sector,
forecasters usually look at the monthly patterns of exports and imports prepared by the
Department of Commerce as well as current
developments in the balance of payments.
It is particularly difficult to prepare quarterly patterns for net exports; indeed, many
GNP forecasts incorporate a constant figure
on the assumption that it is too difficult to
do much more. Fortunately, the total is usually $5 billion or less, so that minor errors
will not unduly affect the overall GNP total.

The final sector of the national accounts is far and away the largest: consumer
purchases of goods and services. *Personal
consumption expenditures* currently account
for over 60 percent of GNP and consist of
outlays for durable and nondurable goods
as well as services. Two of these components,
services and nondurables, are relatively
smooth in their cyclical patterns, while durables (particularly automobiles) fluctuate
widely.

While it is possible to utilize a variety
of procedures to estimate each portion of
consumption (and this will be done shortly),
the reason for considering consumption last
is because it is generally considered to be less
of a dynamic factor than many of the others
in making for cyclical change. That is, consumption adapts to the other forces rather
than vice versa. This is not always the case,
nor is this assumption necessarily an integral feature of the sectoral analysis approach. For example, during 1970 and 1971
the rate of personal savings jumped sharply;
this is merely another way of saying that
consumption patterns showed a marked departure from "normal."

However, most judgmental forecasters
first fill in their worksheets with estimates
for government, gross private domestic investment, and net exports—and save the
consumption sector for last.

How, then, to estimate this huge aggregate? The procedure that is generally followed segments personal consumption expenditures into two parts: (1) automobiles
and (2) all other outlays.[6]

Automobile spending has displayed
considerable volatility over time. A detailed
description of how to forecast this area is set
forth in the chapter by Robert Eggert. Briefly, the factors to be considered include: car
production, inventory changes, exports and
imports, average price paid, sales of accessories and parts, and dealer markups on
used cars. The forecaster would also have to
take into account such elements as: credit
terms and financial conditions, scrappage
rates, demographic forces (teen-age demands), income and age distributions, and
the like. From these considerations he would
enter a total for the automobiles and parts
sector—often with a good deal of hesitancy.

For the balance of the consumer spending forecast the procedure is a good deal
easier. These outlays consist of durable
goods (minus automobiles), nondurables,
and services. This total has tended to bear a
very close relationship to disposable personal income for most time periods in the post-
World War II era—again, subject to the
variations that always must be anticipated
by the judgmental forecaster.

The relative constancy of the relationship between personal consumption expenditures (less automobiles) and disposable
personal income may be extended to derive
relationships between personal income and
GNP; disposable personal income and personal income; and, consequently, disposable

---

[6] A clear exposition of this approach is
detailed in J. P. Lewis and R. C. Turner,
Business Conditions Analysis (New York:
McGraw-Hill Book Company, 1967); particularly pp. 479–90 and 540–49.
It should be noted that "personal consumption expenditures" as used in the GNP accounts are lower than "total personal outlays," which also include interest paid by
consumers and personal transfer payments to
foreigners.

personal income and consumption. Used in conjunction with previously derived estimates for the other sectors of the national accounts, these ratios produce totals for personal consumption expenditures less automobiles and parts.[7]

Details for durable, nondurable, and service expenditures by consumers may then be apportioned on the basis of further judgmental processes. *Durable* outlays, while they tend to be heavily influenced by the automobile component, accounted for approximately the same proportion of consumer spending (14 percent) in 1971 as in 1960. *Nondurable* expenditures (food, clothing, gasoline, drugs, household goods) have experienced a decline from 46 percent in 1960 to 43 percent in 1971. As for *services* (housing, personal business, utilities and telephones, cleaning, transportation, recreation, medical care, religious and educational activities), these expenditures have taken an increasing share of the consumer dollar, rising from 40 percent in 1960 to almost 43 percent in 1971. It should be noted, however, that the services sector has exhibited the greatest amount of inflation in recent years.

At this stage of the sectoral analysis forecasting approach, entries will have been made for all the GNP components following the familiar Keynesian framework, for, say, four quarters ahead. In amassing these entries, the economist will have referred to volumes of data, will have performed numerous statistical measurements and comparisons, will have tapped his storehouse of economic theory, and may have conferred closely with many of his fellow analysts. The forecast may appear complete, except for adding up the several sectors to derive total GNP. In practice, however, it is far from finished and must be regarded merely as a first approximation.

---

[7] The algebraic derivation of these relationships is set forth in Lewis and Turner, *op. cit.*, pp. 548–49.

For now the real difficulties begin—the seesaw process of making the parts consistent with a more carefully considered whole. Here is where the talents, insight, and judgment of the forecaster are truly tested. Rare is the economist who simply aggregates and stops at that. Generally, a considerable amount of time is spent on balancing, weighing, and appraising in order to derive a set of estimates the forecaster is willing to accept as a final verdict. And he must always remember that a change here means a change there—in the matrix of interrelationships.

Several procedures can be followed in refining a forecast. One involves working through the income side of the national accounts by estimating the flow of wages, salaries, profits, interest, rent, and taxes which would result from the projected GNP. From the income side, the forecaster can run a series of important checks: Will profits suffice to call forth the investment in new plant and equipment in the GNP estimates? Is the savings rate reasonable? Will government fiscal results stimulate or retard the private economy? In general, is the supply of funds and the probable rate of interest consistent with the demand patterns in the economy? These tests frequently lead the forecaster to modify his estimates of consumption or investment.

The forecaster will also ask himself if the magnitudes of the changes he has posed are in keeping with past experience. This requires detailed knowledge of past business cycle patterns. A basic judgment underlying the determination of any business forecast is the phase of the business cycle covered during the forecast period. The projected movements of GNP and of its components should be consistent with experience in the comparable phase of past business cycles. While the exhaustive research of the National Bureau of Economic Research shows that no two business cycles are alike, there are general similarities which can provide useful checks for any forecast.

Study of the business cycle is also important in meeting the major challenge a forecaster confronts—that of calling a business downturn, or an upturn, in advance. The GNP framework is not particularly useful in forecasting major turning points because it does not take explicit account of such factors as changes in credit policy or cost-price trends. Thus, GNP forecasts must be supplemented by, and to a considerable extent based on, studies of past business cycle patterns.

But past experience cannot be wholly relied upon. Intuition and detective work must be used as supplements. The forecaster will try to judge the tone of business activity, knowing that here too, even in the midst of a balanced advance, he could, by selecting certain series, compile a glossary of gloom. Picking the relevant measures—and these would vary—represents the true exercise of skill and judgment. Should he focus upon questionable aspects of the quality of credit or should he emphasize a sudden surge in new order? Choosing the accurate guides from a myriad of indicators is a chancy but necessary process. As Solomon Fabricant has stated, ". . . to look is not necessarily to see," and accurate forecasting requires twenty-twenty vision with regard to distinguishing between relevance and irrelevance.

Judgment, consequently, must take over where mechanics leaves off. After all, the data are not uniformly accurate—many series are substantially revised after their initial release. Some are late in appearing; others may show conflicting trends. So the forecaster will look for evidence of emerging stresses and bottlenecks in determining how far the advance will carry, and for early signs of improvement in deciding upon the lower turning point.

Thus, the final step consists of refining the tentative estimates and seeking a set of GNP components that square with the total as the forecaster sees it. This process of successive approximations gives the ultimate stamp to the forecast.

When it is all done the forecaster will have a detailed picture of the course of business activity as he sees it during the year ahead. It should be clearly noted, however, that there may be a difference between what the economist predicts and what he would like to see happen. A forecast of a recession means simply that the forces are shaping up in that direction—not that the forecaster wishes it to happen, as some corporate officials believe.

And after all is said and done, the forecast may turn out to be wrong! If this happens, the practitioner has no recourse but to analyze what went wrong and to revise his estimates. When to change a forecast—when to abandon a given line of reasoning—and reshape the entire framework, is truly one of the forecaster's nightmares. Econometricians have it easy; they simply plug in new values for the exogenous variables and generate new forecasts. Judgmentalists, however, must reconsider the entire range of variables. In deciding upon the need for a revised forecast the judgmentalist will seek out sudden or unanticipated developments: an imposition of wage and price controls, a long strike, a major shift in monetary policy.

Sticking to an obsolete forecast is out of character for a good forecaster. By Labor Day, when the forecasting system gets under way, he recalls that "pride goeth before the fall." Pride in one's talents: yes. Arrogance in refusing to give ground in the face of obvious errors: no! As Bertrand Russell noted, ". . . whenever you find yourself getting angry about a difference of opinion, be on your guard; you will probably find, on examination, that your belief is getting beyond what the evidence warrants."

Some will insist that the judgmental forecast is nothing more than a set of mystical guesses—that it lacks replicability. Perhaps so, but it's astonishing how competent judgmentalists, working independently, frequently come up with very similar estimates. And the results may well be better than those generated by a complex econometric model.[8]

[8] One of the authors remembers a heated session with economists at the Department of Commerce. The OBE econometric model had just been explained and the forecast distributed. Louis J. Paradiso, who worked in that office for many years and is a master of the "yellow sheets and pencil (with eraser)" judgmental approach, was asked if he concurred. He shook his head slowly and offered his own—less formal—comments. Memory serves that he was closer to the mark.

Forecasts will continue to be made—some better than others. The task is arduous yet fascinating, and it is clearly important. In a universe of uncertainties, business decisions have to be made, and the forecaster can play a major role in furnishing useful perspective. But in rolling up his sleeves and getting down to work, he should be guided by the forecaster's motto: "The best is to be positive and right; next best is to be positive and wrong!"

BIBLIOGRAPHY

Chambers, J. C., S. K. Mullick, and D. D. Smith, "How to Choose the Right Forecasting Technique," *Harvard Business Review* (July–August 1971), pp. 387–399.

Chisholm, R. K., and G. R. Whitaker, Jr., *Forecasting Methods*. Homewood, Illinois: Richard D. Irwin, Inc., 1971.

Dauten, C. A., and L. M. Valentine, *Business Cycles and Forecasting*. Cincinnati: Southwestern Publishing Company, 1969.

Enzler, J. J., and H. O. Stekler, "An Analysis of the 1968–69 Economic Forecasts," *Journal of Business*, 44 (July 1971), pp. 416–431.

Evans, M. K., *Macroeconomic Activity: Theory, Forecasting and Control*. New York: Harper and Row, 1969.

Lewis, J. P., and R. C. Turner, *Business Conditions Analysis*. New York: McGraw-Hill Book Company, 1967.

Mincer, J., ed., *Economic Forecasts and Expectations*. New York: National Bureau of Economic Research, 1969.

Moore, G. H., "Forecasting Short-Term Economic Change," *Journal of the American Statistical Association*, 64 (March 1969), pp. 117–134.

Silk, L. S., and M. L. Curley, *A Primer on Business Forecasting*. New York: Random House, 1970.

Stekler, H. O., *Economic Forecasting*. New York: Frederick A. Praeger, 1970.

Theil, H., *Applied Economic Forecasting*. Chicago: Rand McNally and Company, 1966.

ARTHUR GERSTENFELD

Technological Forecasting

Technological forecasting's function is to aid management in peering into the future. It differs from traditional planning techniques in that it involves the scheduling of undeveloped products or processes. A technological forecast either predicts that new processes or products will be discovered or that the potential of the process or product will be recognized at a certain time. Technological forecasting is becoming formalized in many organizations in the hope of anticipating new product developments in today's rapidly changing markets.

Technological forecasting is important to the business economist since it is now essential that new technologies be taken into account for planning purposes. When the rate of change was slower, the business economist could forecast based on existing technologies. In today's world and in tomorrow's world, if new technologies are not included in the forecast then the plans lose much of their validity.

Perhaps this can best be understood by considering the new technologies in terms of degrees of importance to the firm. In the past the business economist could consider the present technologies and simply add a small factor for some new products or processes when predicting the future. Now the new products or processes become the heavy parts of the scale and when predicting the future the business economist must often give more weight to yet undiscovered products and processes than to existing ones.

Ninety percent of all the scientists who ever lived are now alive. New scientific discoveries are being made every day. The time between original concept and practical use has been radically reduced. It was 2,000 years between the discovery of conic sections and their application to engineering problems. Similarly, it was centuries between the discovery of ether as an anesthetic and the time it began to be used for that purpose. Technological forecasting was clearly not called for.

It was found that for a group of appliances introduced in the United States before 1920, the average span between introduction and peak production was 34 years. The groups of appliances that appeared more recently including television, and washer-dryer combination, the span was only 8 years. The lag had shrunk by more than 76 percent and is becoming shorter every year. Each new machine changes all existing machines by permitting us to put them together in new combinations. We now begin to recognize why the business economist must take into account technological forecasts when planning for the future.

A survey conducted by this author in 1969 asked for information on the usage of five leading techniques of technological forecasting.[1] These five techniques are: Delphi,

[1] Arthur Gerstenfeld, "Technological Forecasting," *Journal of Business of The University of Chicago,* XLIV, No. 1 (January 1971), 10–18.

trend fitting, PATTERN, time-independent technological comparisons, and PERT.

DELPHI

The Delphi technique developed and discussed by Olaf Helmer has been widely publicized.[2] In this technique, the technological forecasters form a panel of experts to study a particular question, but with a carefully designed sequence of questionnaires replacing direct debate. The following cases illustrate the method:

First round. The members of the panel were asked, by letter, to name inventions and scientific breakthroughs which appeared to them to be both urgently needed and realizable within the next 50 years. A list of 49 items was compiled from their answers.

Second round. The participants were asked, again by letter, to situate the fifty-fifty probability of realization of each of the 49 items in one of the time periods into which the next fifty years had been divided.

Third round. Letters announced to the participants the items on which there was a consensus. Those who did not agree with the consensus were invited to state their reasons. In the case of those items where there was no significant consensus, the participants were asked to give the reasons for the widely dissenting estimates. Several panel members reevaluated their time estimates and a narrower time range resulted.

Fourth round. To narrow the range of time estimates still further, the procedure followed in the third round was repeated. Thirty-one items were included in the final list of those on which reasonable consensus had been obtained.

Instead of using the traditional approach toward achieving a consensus

through open discussion, the Delphi technique eliminates committee activity altogether. Helmer and Rescher point out that this reduces the influence of certain psychological factors such as persuasion, unwillingness to abandon publicly expressed opinions, and the bandwagon effect of majority opinion.[3]

Modified Delphi plans can be utilized where the panel consists of members both within and outside of an organization. A particular firm may be interested in a seven-year horizon. The forecasters would then appoint a panel of knowledgeable people for the specialty under study. (An important use of Delphi is in situations where each member of the panel is an expert on some aspect of a problem, but no one is an expert on the whole problem.) The initial questionnaires would establish the general products under inquiry. Second and third rounds would feed back to the panel some of the results of the first round, and an attempt would be made to reach a consensus. The final round would then try to home in closer on the expected new product parameters.

The next Delphi example studies the role of automation in the future. A group of experts knowledgeable in this field were selected and answered four sequential questionnaires spaced approximately two months apart.[4]

The predictions by the panel regarding major developments in the field of automation are summarized in figure 1. Each bar extends from the lower to the upper quartile of the responses and peaks at the median.

In addition to technological progress in automation, the panel was asked to give some thought to the problem of unemployment resulting from automation. In general, the respondents felt that the problem is a

---

[2] Olaf Helmer, *Social Technology* (New York: Basic Books, Inc., 1966).

[3] Olaf Helmer and Nicholas Rescher, "On the Epistemology of the Inexact Sciences," *Management Science*, 6, No. 1 (October 1959), 25–52.

[4] Olaf Helmer, *Social Technology* (New York: Basic Books, Inc., 1966).

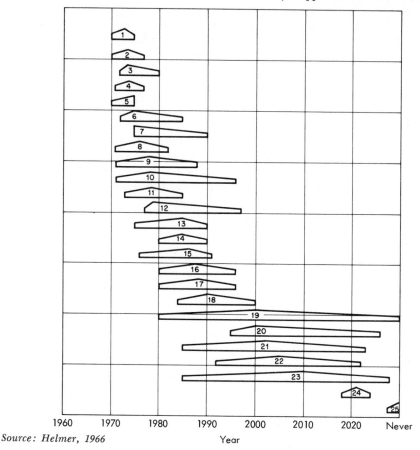

Source: Helmer, 1966

Figure 1   Consensus of panel on automation (medians and quartiles)

1. *Increase by a factor of 10 in capital investment in computers used for automated process control*
2. *Air traffic control—positive and predictive track on all aircraft*
3. *Direct link from stores to banks to check credit and to record transactions*
4. *Widespread use of simple teaching machines*
5. *Automation of office work and services, leading to displacement of 25 percent of current work force*
6. *Education becoming a respectable leisure pastime*
7. *Widespread use of sophisticated teaching machines*
8. *Automatic libraries, looking up and reproducing copy*
9. *Automated looking up of legal information*
10. *Automatic language translator—correct grammar*
11. *Automated rapid transit*
12. *Widespread use of automatic decision-making at management level for industrial and national planning*
13. *Electronic prosthesis (radar for the blind, servomechanical limbs, and so forth)*
14. *Automated interpretation of medical symptoms*
15. *Construction on a production line of computers with motivation by "education"*
16. *Widespread use of robot services, for refuse collection, as household slaves, as sewer inspectors, etc.*

very serious one. They felt that social up-
heavals will accompany automation but
that suitable countermeasures would fore-
stall severe social disruptions.

TREND FITTING (S-CURVES)

Envelope curves are hypothetical
curves that describe the maximum perform-

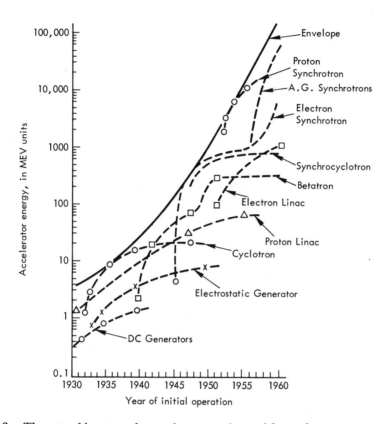

Figure 2   The rate of increase of operating energy in particle accelerators

17. *Widespread use of computers in tax collection, with access to all business records—automatic single tax deductions*
18. *Availability of a machine which comprehends standard IQ tests and scores above 150 (where "comprehend" is to be interpreted behavioristically as the ability to respond to questions printed in English and possibly accompanied by diagrams)*
19. *Evolution of a universal language from automated communication*
20. *Automated voting, in the sense of legislating through automated plebiscite*
21. *Automated highways and adaptive automobile autopilots*
22. *Remote facsimile newspapers and magazines, printed in home*
23. *Man-machine symbiosis, enabling man to extend his intelligence by direct electromechanical interaction between his brain and a computing machine*
24. *International agreements which guarantee certain economic minima to the world's population as a result of high production from automation*
25. *Centralized (possibly random) wire-tapping*
Source: Helmer, 1966.

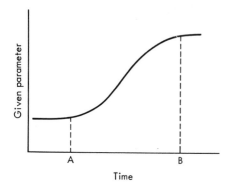

Figure 3   S-curve

ance available for any particular functional characteristic. They are extremely valuable tools for the technological forecaster.

Figure 2 plots the maximum energy available from high-energy particle accelerators (atom smashers).[5] Each new type of machine takes the lead for a short period and then it reaches the end of its phase of rapid

[5] Erich Jantsch, "Technological Forecasting In Perspective," Paris: Organization for Economic Cooperation and Development, 1967, p. 161.
[6] *Ibid.*

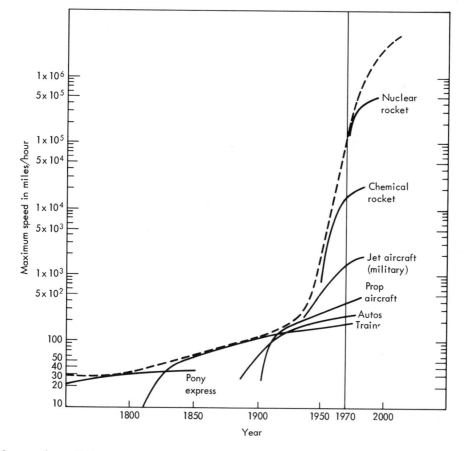

Source: Ayres, 1966.

Figure 4   Trend fitting (S-curves)

improvement while a newer invention escalates to a higher level. The "envelope" is a curve which approximates the general trend and is tangent to the individual performance trends.

Individual growth curves are often referred to as S-curves since the plot of a given parameter over time generally conforms to the approximate shape of a letter S. In figure 3, it may be seen that from time zero to time A there is a little change in a given parameter. The second portion of the S-curve (A to B, fig. 3) shows a large increase in the given parameters over time. The final portion of the S-curve again flattens out, as shown in the figure.

This pattern may be applied to more than just the individual technology. Figure 4 shows how S-curves could be applied to predict the maximum speed for transportation, going from the pony express to the nuclear rocket. By connecting the tangents of each individual growth curve, an envelope S-curve may be developed. The upper limits of the envelope S-curve may be recognized as the absolute or natural limits, such as the velocity of light or the exhaustion of some fixed resource.

PATTERN

PATTERN (Planning Assistance Through Technical Evaluation of Relevance Numbers) was developed by Honeywell, Inc.[7] The system features a scenario which is descriptive information on which the forecasters' value judgments are made. The scenario describes the broad objectives of the United States and its goals for a specific time period. It brings together the common background of knowledge and opinions

[7] J. V. Sigford and R. H. Parvin, "Project PATTERN: A Methodology for Determining Relevance in Complex Decision-Making," *IEEE Transactions on Engineering Management*, 12, No. 1 (March 1965), 9–13.

of the various members of the forecasting groups, and of the national experts consulted for this purpose.

The scenario then forms the basis for the construction of a relevance tree, as shown in figure 5. The relationship between technological deficiencies and the national objectives now becomes clear. Figure 5 shows an eight-level relevance tree. The elements of the eighth level list the nation's critical technological deficiencies.

With the completion of the relevance tree based on the scenario, the forecasters acquire a knowledge in depth of how our national goals would be advanced with improvements in various technological deficiencies. Now the task is to assign relevance numbers to each element on the tree. To assign a relevance number, each forecaster votes secretly according to his own judgment and then has the opportunity to state his case if he so desires. The total relevance number for each element on the tree is the assigned relevance number for that element times the relevance number of each element in line above it. Hence, a high relevance for "active hostilities" would be reflected in the relevance of all elements below it. This opportunity to compare the relevance of all elements by computer readouts results in the PATTERN methodology contributing substantially to the generation of useful information.

TIME-INDEPENDENT TECHNOLOGICAL COMPARISONS

The most obvious method of technological forecasting is to assume that a past trend will continue into the future. However, the trend of a technical parameter which is complex and difficult to predict by itself may be more easily expressed as a result of its relationship to another trend. In order to use one trend to determine another, the forecaster must have available a

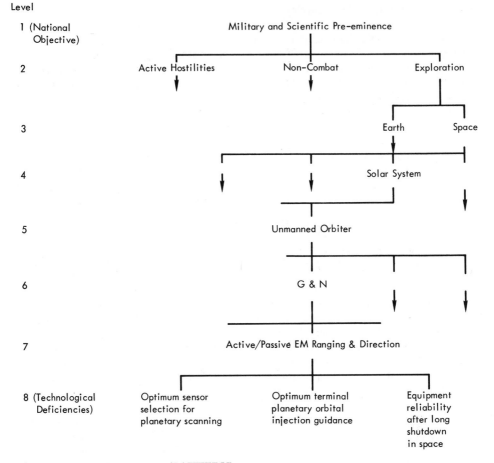

Figure 5   The relevance tree (PATTERN)

primary trend which is related to the technical field of interest. To this, the forecaster must add a knowledge of the relationship between these two trends. The prediction is then completed by plotting the primary trend and then projecting the unknown on the basis of the relationship between the two.

The technological comparison method uses the correlation between two developments, one of which is leading the other. For example, the growth of future fast reactors can be cited as logically dependent on plutonium production. A simple correlation

of two trends is valuable for forecasting only insofar as the leader-follower relationship between the two developments is maintained.

Cetron and Monohan describe this technique as follows:

> The trend of a technical parameter which is complex and difficult to predict by itself may be more easily expressed as a result of its relationship to two or more other trends. Whereas time-dependent trend extrapolation attempts explicit forecasting, interrelationships between parameters can be explored on a much

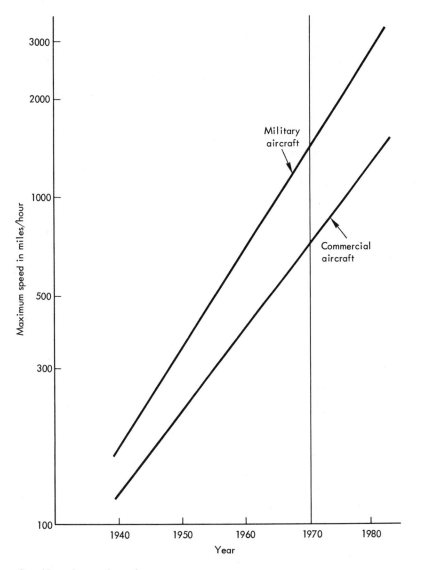

Figure 6   Aircraft speed vs. time

more general level if they do not have to fit into an explicit time frame. Nevertheless, they may represent extrapolations of reality beyond present capability or estimates, in the instance of future technologies.

In order to use two or more trends to determine a third, the predictor must have available a number of primary trends which are related to the technical field of interest. To these he must add a knowledge of probable relationships that might arise from combinations of such variables. The predictor may then select the relationship and the primary variables which influence the desired technical improvement. The trends of the primary variables may be projected on the basis of any techniques which appear appropriate. The prediction is then completed by projecting the unknown variable on the basis of the relationship between the primary variables.[8]

An interesting and plausible example of technological comparisons can be observed by comparing the maximum speed of military aircraft and transport aircraft as shown in figure 6. The two speed trends are logically related. The R & D effort applied to military aircraft also influences commercial aircraft. The slope of the military aircraft speed trend corresponds to a doubling of speed every ten years. By way of comparison, the slope of the commercial aircraft speed trend indicates a doubling in speed every twelve years.

PERT

When used in technological forecasting, the usual PERT (Program Evaluation and Review Technique) network is applied over a long time period. The R & D events which must be accomplished prior to a technological breakthrough are scheduled by estimates from the forecaster. The network indicates every critical event and shows the activity time needed between sequential events. The activities should be broken down into the smallest unit to be scheduled. The logical analysis required to draw up the lists of activities and to establish their sequential relationships provides good insight into the required steps leading toward a future technology.

Figure 7 shows a PERT chart diagram for technological planning. The upper half

of the chart is concerned with the development of lasers and technologies related to pulsing, recording media, and achieving intensity and coherence. The top of the lower half traces developments in production techniques. The lower quarter is concerned with the development of projection techniques and the requirements associated with exhibiting the movies.

The advantage of the PERT system is that uncertainty is taken into account by using probability distributions for activity time estimates. For technological forecasting with highly uncertain activity times, one can develop a probabilistic critical path.[9]

USE OF TECHNOLOGICAL FORECASTING IN 162 COMPANIES

In order to determine the degree of acceptance and the particular technological forecasting techniques in use today, questionnaires were sent to the top 425 companies listed in *Fortune*'s "500."[10] There were 162 returns, a response rate of 38 percent. The companies that responded may have been more likely to be using technological forecasting than the nonresponders, which could bias the findings. Most survey research (where there is less than 100 percent response) could have biases present and the reader should bear this in mind when examining the results.[11]

Table 1 shows the four questions used

[8] Marvin J. Cetron and Joel D. Goldhar, "The Science of Managing Organized Technology," Gordon and Breach, Science Publishers, New York, 1970, p. 857.

[9] Warren Dusenbury, "CPM for New Product Introduction," *Harvard Business Review*, 45, No. 4 (July–August 1967), 124–39.

[10] This study was performed in 1969 and can be found in Arthur Gerstenfeld, "Technological Forecasting," *Journal of Business of the University of Chicago*, XLIV, No. 1 (January 1971), 10–18.

[11] Paul Berger, "Statistical Report—Fact or Fancy?" Boston University Working Paper, January 1971.

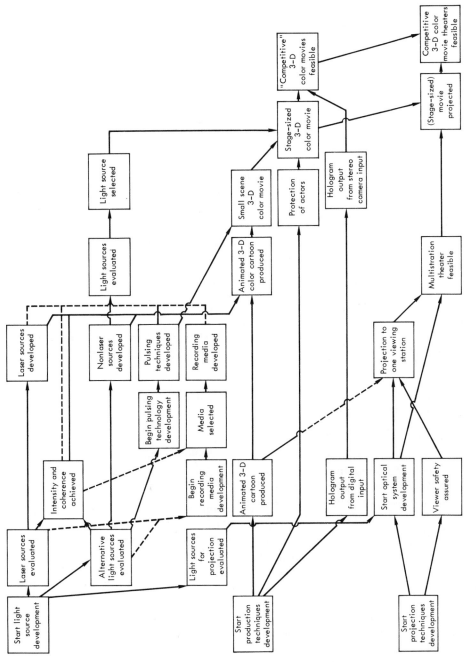

Figure 7 PERT network for the development of 3-D color holographic movies

231

TABLE 1.   QUESTIONS AND ANSWERS

1. Does your company use a formal system of long-range planning or technological forecasting?

115	(71%)	Yes
47	(29%)	No
162	(100%)	

2. Have you ever had the occasion to use:

23	(11.3%)	Delphi;
68	(33.6%)	Trend fitting (S-curves);
24	(11.8%)	PATTERN;
25	(12.3%)	Time-independent technological comparisons;
39	(19.2%)	PERT (for technological forecasting);
24	(11.8%)	Others (please name)
203	(100.0%)	

(Of the 162 respondents, ninety-five firms indicated that they use at least one specific method of technological forecasting. Most of the firms stated that they use more than one method of technological forecasting.)

3. Please circle the average number of years into the future that you perform technological forecasting:

0 1 2 3 4 5 6 7 8 9 10 11 12 13 14 15
Average answer: 7.06 years

(Ninety-three of the ninety-five firms that indicated a specific technological forecasting method showed the number of years into the future that they perform technological forecasting. The other two firms stated that they used no fixed time periods.)

4. How many people are in your technical forecasting or related group?
Average answer: five

(Ninety of the ninety-five firms that indicated a specific technological forecasting method showed the number of people in the technological forecasting group. Five firms indicated that they had no formal group, and the work was performed by various people as needed.)

and summarizes the answers. The first question shows that 115 of the 162 respondents (71 percent) indicated that they use a formal system of long-range planning or technological forecasting. Uses of specific methods of technological forecasting, as opposed to long-range planning in general, are covered in question 2. Here, 95 of the 162 companies (59 percent) indicate the use of at least one specific technological forecasting technique. It was assumed that the reason that 20 firms answered "yes" to question 1, but did not cite a technique in question 2, was that these firms are using some form of long-range planning, but no specific method of technological forecasting.

Some of the companies who indicated that they did not employ any formal technological forecasting technique did state that they were in the midst of installing a technological forecasting function. Some specific quotations, taken from the bottom of the questionnaires follow:

Establishing it now.

We are just beginning a technological forecasting program. Two men are assigned. We will probably use all of the techniques mentioned except Delphi, which is a clerical burden.

Technological forecasting, which is inherent to our planning program, is still relatively crude. With time and development of expertise, this phase of the planning program is expected to increase significantly.

Just starting.

The second question in table 1 shows that the trend fit (S-curve) is the most popular method of technological forecasting in use today. The least used method is Delphi, probably because of its high cost and inherent delays in securing information from panels of experts. (In a follow-up study described later in this chapter, the use of Delphi is shown to now be gaining wide acceptance.)

Twenty-four responses to question 2 listed "other methods." Of these, five firms stated that they used multiple-regression analyses, and three stated that they used a simulation analysis. Several firms listed their own designed technological forecasting systems such as "Boeing-developed system" or inhouse names such as "planalog." The balance of the responses that cited other methods varied from "matrix analysis" to "input-output forecasting." Therefore, in 1969 there is evidence of a large number of methods used by firms today and little agreement on a standard methodology.

The remaining questions and answers as shown in table 1 require no additional comment.

Industry Analysis and Responses

Do industries differ in their use of technological forecasting? To study this, the 162 companies that participated in the 1969 survey were divided into twelve industry categories in accordance with the standard industrial classifications (SIC).[12] The results are shown in table 2. Column 3 shows that firms in the scientific instruments industry are the most likely to use technological forecasting, with four out of the five companies (80 percent) in our sample indicating the adoption of at least one specific technological forecasting technique. The next largest user of technological forecasting is the electrical machinery and equipment industry, with fifteen of the twenty-one companies

[12] Bureau of the Budget, U.S. Office of Statistical Standards, *Standard Industrial Classification Manual* (Washington: Government Printing Office, 1967).

indicating the employment of at least one specific technological forecasting technique.

Those industries where the smallest percentage of firms have adopted technological forecasting are primary metals and textile mill products. Perhaps textiles and primary metals are used for such diverse purposes that forecasting may not be as important or feasible for them as for those industries which need to design specific facilities or products for a relatively small number of end uses.

There is a positive relationship between an industry's growth rate and the likelihood that its firms will use some technique of technological forecasting. Using the data from table 2 and dividing industries at the medians for growth rates and the percentage using forecasting, the array of table 3 was obtained. Five of the six high-growth industries were high users of technological forecasting. Five of the six low-growth industries were low users of technological forecasting. Given that there was indeed no relationship between industry growth and use of technological forecasting, the Fisher test of significance shows that these results would occur by chance less than 5 times out of 100.

The reasons for this association are not obvious. Because technological forecasting is in the early stages of development, it is safe to assume that the effect of its adoption is not yet reflected in growth figures. Perhaps what is currently being witnessed is the embracing of new techniques by progressive managements. It has also been suggested that the growth industries are faced with such rapid technological change that they are forced to use forecasting techniques.

Table 2 also shows industry breakdowns of responses to the last question in table 1, that dealing with the mean number of years covered by forecasting efforts. Although the average number of years is seven, the petroleum industry uses an average future time horizon of ten years. This is understandable, since extremely long time spans exist from product conception to the

TABLE 2.   NUMBER OF COMPANIES, BY INDUSTRY, USING TECHNOLOGICAL FORECASTING, AS RELATED TO GROWTH

Industry (1)	No. of Company Respondents per Industry (2)	Companies Using at Least One Specific Forecasting Method (3)		Industry Growth Rate* (4)	Mean No. of Years into the Future (5)
		No.	% of Industry		
Transportation equipment..........	13	8	(61.5)	5.0	7.15 (N = 8)
Chemicals and allied products......	27	18	(66.6)	8.3	6.52 (N = 17)
Electrical machinery, equipment, and supplies....	21	15	(71.5)	6.4	7.75 (N = 15)
Fabricated metals.................	10	7	(70.0)	4.7	5.50 (N = 7)
Primary metals...................	7	1	(14.3)	3.6	5.00 (N = 1)
Food and kindred products	27	14	(52.0)	3.2	7.15 (N = 13)
Paper and allied products..........	8	5	(62.5)	4.9	7.00 (N = 5)
Scientific instruments	5	4	(80.0)	5.5	5.25 (N = 4)
Machinery, except electrical........	18	11	(61.0)	5.8	7.69 (N = 11)
Petroleum refining and related industries	14	7	(50.0)	3.2	10.00 (N = 7)
Stone, clay, and glass.............	4	2	(50.0)	3.5	7.50 (N = 2)
Textile mill products..............	8	3	(37.5)	3.5	5.00 (N = 3)
Total..........	162	95	...	...	7.06† (N = 93)

Source: Bureau of the Census, Long-Term Economic Growth, 1966.
* 1957–60 to 1960–65 (annual %). Growth rates based on Federal Reserve Production Indexes for Industries, U.S. Department of Commerce, Bureau of the Census.
† Average years.

TABLE 3.   RELATION BETWEEN GROWTH INDUSTRIES AND USE OF FORECASTING

	High-Growth Industry	Low-Growth Industry	Total
High use of forecasting..........	5	1	6
Low use of forecasting	1	5	6
Total	6	6	12

marketed product in the petroleum industry. A recent statement by a firm that manufactures power generating equipment is as follows: "Since our business involves large capital equipment with lead times from 4 to 7 years, our forecasts involve 10 to 20 years in the future."

The textile mill products and primary metals industries use the shortest future time horizons. These industries have not only expressed a lack of interest in technological forecasting, but the very few firms in these two industries that have adopted forecasting methods are planning over shorter time periods.

It is interesting that the scientific instruments industry, which showed very high adoption of technological forecasting, uses relatively short time horizons. The two decisions are apparently somewhat independent. The firm must first decide on the importance and feasibility of technological forecasting. As a subsequent decision, the firm must then determine the mean number of years into the future which can be forecast in order to be of most value to the organization. In the case of scientific instruments, these results might be explained by pointing out that instruments must be tailored to the changing needs of their users, but need not anticipate users' needs by a very long time.

A Follow-Up Study

Two years after the original study, fourteen organizations were contacted who had indicated in the 1969 study that they use technological forecasting. During these years (last quarter 1969, 1970, and first quarter 1971) the general business economy was in a recession, so that it was possible to examine how technological forecasting performed over time, and also whether or not it survived a business recession.[13]

Of the fourteen corporations who participated in this follow-up study, six firms contended that their methods, uses, and applications of technological forecasting are as yet experimental. They are unsure of the use and value of technological forecasting, and have made no effort to expand their use of this tool.

The remaining eight firms contend that they are serious in their uses and applications of technological forecasting. They are convinced of the value of the technique and are attempting to expand its uses and applications in various areas throughout the firm. Four of these eight firms have recently completed a Delphi forecast. This is somewhat surprising since the original findings showed very little acceptance of this technique. Delphi is becoming more accepted and more organizations are switching to this system. The firms find that Delphi provides an objective method of achieving a consensus which eliminates the biases that are always present in group interactions.

The 1971 follow-up study also provides the following facts concerning technological forecasting:

[13] The author wishes to thank N. James Barletta, research assistant at Boston University, for his assistance with this section.

1. Most of the technological forecasts are being performed by small ad hoc committees as opposed to formal forecasting staffs.

2. Most technological forecasting is being performed for a specific problem or project. Few firms are engaged in exploratory forecasting done merely to enlighten and guide the firm.

3. The main areas of use for technological forecasting are in R & D planning and product development.

4. Although there are instances in which technological forecasts have been the basis for strategic corporate planning, technological forecasting has yet to have had more than experimental or token use in high-level corporate planning.

5. Most firms are continuing to use a five- to ten-year time horizon.

6. Most firms are optimistic as to the future of technological forecasting. This optimism is often expressed by middle management while top management is still expressing its reservations.

In general, the Delphi technique is gaining wider acceptance, although it is still too early to be able to measure the results of the forecasts. Consider the following quotations from various companies as substantiation for both of those points:

For the most part we have used a Delphi technique, aiming at both short- and long-term events. We have not done any work analyzing the accuracy, more due to lack of passage of time since the forecasts were made. In all, we think this is becoming a very valuable asset and we plan on expanding its use.

We at _____ have conducted three Delphi-type technological forecasts since the end of 1969. With respect to accuracy, our endeavor is too new to assess its reliability. However, we are maintaining a file of technological developments in our areas of interest so that we can begin to audit our results.

Since your last survey, we have been engaged in the use of technological forecasting as a significant input to our R & D planning process. We have conducted two major Delphi studies in an effort to forecast technological developments which would have an impact on our research and development activities.

A FORECAST ON FORECASTING

Technological forecasting is a new management discipline that is rapidly gaining acceptance among the more innovative firms. With the rate of change ever increasing, organizations are recognizing that it is too late to cope with change when it occurs; rather, they must anticipate it. The effective firms of the future will be those than can adapt to change. Forecasting is a tool to aid them in this adaptation.

We have examined many different methods of technological forecasting and find no agreement on "the accepted technique." The art is young, and one may expect that combinations of available techniques will occur in the future. As firms work more with Delphi, trend fits, and PATTERN, there may be an integration of the strong points from the various methods. The area of weakness will start to decay. Before this fusion takes place, however, there will be widespread use of many of the various systems available today.

The future will see increased integration of social goals with technical goals. Clearly, the effect of one on the other is inescapable. Technical feasibility without due consideration of social goals will only serve to blur the vision. (A case in point is the SST: within grasp technically, but highly debatable as to its social desirability.) Social goals will play an ever increasing role as man's technical abilities progress. Industry is capable of accomplishing enormous technical feats limited more by potential payoffs than by physical constraints. Forecasting

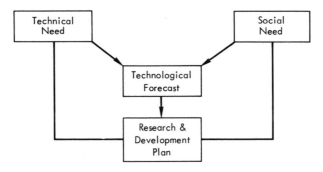

Figure 8   A systems concept model for technological forecasting

may be expected to place increased emphasis on the nontechnical aspects of future development.

As in other areas of management, one may expect that technological forecasting will advance toward a total systems concept. Clearly, views toward the future involve all facets of the firm and go beyond organizational boundaries. The systems approach may be expected to become the bedrock of effective forecasting. The systems concept will include both social needs and technical needs, as shown in figure 8. Both technical and social needs will influence the technological forecast. The forecast will largely determine the R & D plan. The R & D efforts then feed back to the needs, since current research is a large determinant of future capabilities. Thus there is a closed loop linking technical and social needs, the technological forecast, and the R & D plan.

It is technological forecasting that will largely influence the allocation of R & D resources. Decision-makers must use every tool they can to aid them in these most critical decisions. Management is in a position to determine the R & D direction only after a most through consideration of the future.

BIBLIOGRAPHY

Ayres, Robert U., *A Technological Forecasting Report*, HI-484 DR, Rev. Harmon-on-Hudson, N.Y.: Hudson Institute, January 17, 1960.

Bender, A. Douglas, Alvin E. Strack, George W. Ebright, and George von Haunalter, "Delphic Study Examines Developments In Medicine," *Futures* (June 1969), pp. 289–303.

Bennis, Warren G., *Changing Organizations*. New York: McGraw-Hill Book Company, 1966.

Berger, Paul, "Statistical Report—Fact or Fancy?" Boston University Working Paper, January 1971.

Bureau of the Budget, U.S. Office of Statistical Standards, *Standard Industrial Classification Manual*. Washington: Government Printing Office, 1967.

Bureau of the Census, U.S. Department of Commerce, *Long-term Economic Growth*. Washington: Government Printing Office, October 1966.

Cetron, Marvin J., and Joel D. Goldhar, "The Science of Managing Organized Technology," New York: Gordon and Breach, Science Publishers, 1970.

Dusenbury, Warren, "CPM for New Product Introduction," *Harvard Business Review*, 45, No. 4 (July–August 1967), pp. 124–39.

Forrester, Jay W., "Advertising: A Problem in Industrial Dynamics," *Harvard Business Review* (March–April 1959), pp. 100–110.

Gerstenfeld, Arthur, *Effective Management of Research and Development*. Reading, Massachusetts: Addison-Wesley Publishing Company, 1970.

———, "Technological Forecasting," *Journal of Business of the University of Chicago*, XLIV, No. 1 (January 1971), pp. 10–18.

Helmer, Olaf, *Social Technology*. New York: Basic Books, Inc., 1966.

Helmer, Olaf, and Nicholas Rescher, "On the Epistemology of the Inexact Sciences," *Management Science* 6: 4B (October 1959), pp. 25–52.

Jantsch, Erich, *Technological Forecasting in Perspective*. Paris: Organization for Economic Cooperation and Development, 1967.

Lenz, R. C., Jr., "Forecasts of Exploding Technologies by Trend Extrapolation," *Technological Forecasting for Industry and Government*, Englewood Cliffs, N.J.: Prentice-Hall, Inc., 1968.

Mansfield, Edwin, "The Speed of Response of Firms to New Techniques," *The Quarterly Journal of Economics*, 77 (May 1963), pp. 290–311.

———, *Industrial Research and Technological Innovation*. New York: W.W. Norton & Company, Inc., 1968.

Quinn, J. B., "Technological Forecasting," *Harvard Business Review* (March–April 1967), pp. 89–106.

Schon, Donald A., "Forecasting and Technological Forecasting," *Daedalus* 96, No. 3 (Summer 1967), pp. 759–70.

Sigford, J. V., and R. H. Parvin, "Project PATTERN: A Methodology for Determining Relevance in Complex Decision-Making," *IEEE Transactions on Engineering Management*, 12, No. 1 (March 1965), pp. 9–13.

Part Three

AGGREGATE FORECASTING IN PRACTICE

The most widely used concept for describing the overall level of business activity is the gross national product and related accounts. Some may argue about certain of the elements GNP includes (or omits), but there is little doubt that it represents the focal point for any discussion of general business conditions. For the forecaster, the GNP estimates he prepares (or utilizes) provide the basis for a more detailed survey of the industry or firm he may be interested in analyzing.

Prior to the 1930s there was a paucity of data on the operation of the aggregate economy. Since then, statistics have been collected and pieced together to provide a valuable framework for analyzing and interpreting change and growth.

The chapters in this section demonstrate techniques for forecasting various components of GNP and related economic measures.

The first five chapters focus upon several of the more volatile sectors of economic activity and how they are forecast.

Following these are discussions of some more specialized but nevertheless important issues that confront the practicing forecaster and the techniques he employs to contend with them.

MURRAY L. WEIDENBAUM

Forecasting Defense Expenditures

INTRODUCTION

Defense expenditures — technically, the purchases of goods and services by the Department of Defense and related agencies —account for about seven percent of the gross national product of the United States at the present time. However, it is not the size but the volatility of military spending that makes this area of the economy both so important and so challenging to the forecaster. These outlays, together with gross private domestic investment, provide the major dynamic elements in the changing direction of business activity in the United States.

For example, purchases for national security rose by $10.6 billion, or over twenty percent, between 1965 and 1966. They rose by $11.7 billion, or another twenty percent, between 1966 and 1967. For the two-year period, military spending directly accounted for twenty percent of the growth in GNP.

Basic to preparing forecasts of future changes in GNP resulting from military spending is an understanding of the process through which such spending is made.

THE FEDERAL GOVERNMENT SPENDING PROCESS

As a starting point, we may take the federal budget which is usually transmitted by the President to the Congress each January and covers the twelve-month period beginning the following July 1. The presidential budget recommendations are subjected to many months of detailed congressional scrutiny and to numerous revisions before the funds are appropriated. Following quarterly apportionment of the funds by the Office of Management and the Budget, the various federal agencies commit the funds appropriated to them for their various authorized activities. Thus the funds are "obligated." For many government programs, disbursements (checks issued) follow rather quickly. Pension payments to veterans, interest payments to holders of the national debt, and wage and salary payments to government employees are made at the time funds are obligated or very soon afterward.

However, obligations for major items of equipment purchased from the private sector are in the form of orders awarded or contracts placed; such transactions are not soon followed by equivalent amounts of expenditure. Particularly in the case of military weapon systems (which are mainly produced by private industry), a considerable amount of time is necessary for the design, production, and delivery of the items ordered. On the larger items, "progress payments" and occasionally "advance payments" or outright loans are made to provide working capital; these preliminary payments are typically about 20 to 30 percent

241

TABLE 1.   LAG BETWEEN ORDERING AND PRODUCING TYPICAL MILITARY ITEMS

Item	Years[a]
Military uniform	½
Medium tank	1¼
Recoilless 57mm. rifle	2
Destroyer DD692	2
Transport plane	2
Bomber	2¼
Jet fighter	2¼

Source: Based on materials contained in *Defense Production Record*, May 15, 1952.

[a] The time shown for each item represents the span from the end of contract negotiation until the first unit comes off the production line set to deliver at the scheduled rate.

less than the total cost of the resources currently being utilized by the defense contractors. Also, these partial payments lag behind the actual disbursements by government contractors to their employees, suppliers, and subcontractors.

The delays involved are hardly trivial. The lags in the early stages of the government procurement and spending process are primarily administrative. It takes time for the federal agencies to prepare and obtain approval of their apportionment requests, for specifications to be drawn up for individual orders, and for contracts to be awarded. The length of this period may be attributed to the time-consuming nature of planning. The lag may depend in part on the newness in design of the equipment in the program and the necessity for establishing new procedures.

A later and more important lag is technological, the lag between the letting of contracts and the beginning of quantity production. This is a period of makeready, which may range from a few weeks to more than a year. In the typical case of a complex new military item, hundreds or even thousands of additional engineers and supporting personnel are hired and trained for the specific task; many thousands of detailed drawings are made; production lines are laid out and production personnel are hired; material requirements are computed; schedules are prepared for deliveries of material and compo-

nents to be procured; and subcontracts are negotiated.

Table 1 shows an estimate of the number of years which may elapse between contract negotiation and quantity production for typical military items. During the Korean War, this stage varied from approximately one-half year in the case of military uniforms to over two years for bombers and jet fighters. Following quantity production, there is the delay between delivery to the government and final payment for the goods delivered. This includes the time needed for inspection, processing vouchers, and making disbursements. The lead time for procurement of aircraft for Vietnam has been estimated by the Department of Defense at eighteen months. The estimate for ammunition is six months.[1]

An examination of major federal equipment contracts casts some light on the total lag in the military spending process. It is the heavy equipment with long production time that accounts for the great bulk of the lag. As shown in figure 1, of the total appropriations for a hypothetical procurement program in the fiscal year 1967, only twenty percent was spent in that year. Fifty percent was spent during the following year, and

[1] U.S. Senate Committees on Armed Services and Appropriations, *Supplemental Military Procurement and Construction Authorizations, Fiscal Year 1967* (Washington: Government Printing Office, January 1967).

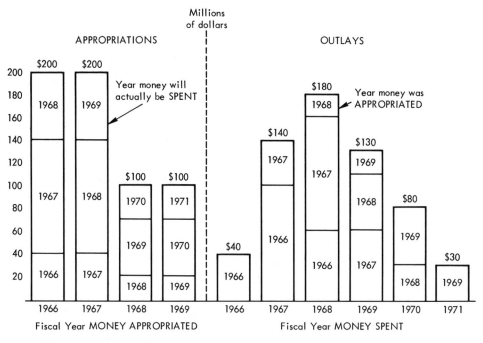

Executive Office of the President, Bureau of the Budget.

Figure 1   Relation of authority to outlay, hypothetical major equipment contracts

the remaining thirty percent during the third year. It is more than coincidental that these figures generally correspond to lags in the total air force budget during the period 1951–53.[2]

As would be expected, purchases of soft goods and services do not evidence such a time-consuming lag. In the case of salaries and wages, travel, and similar items, the total lag between obligations and expenditures is usually no more than a few weeks or a few months.[3]

In the case of military procurement programs, it is clear that the placement of orders with defense contractors and their commencement or expansion of production generates directly or indirectly demands for resources. This is evidenced by the hiring of manpower and the acquisition and utilization of raw and semiprocessed material. However, all such activity initially shows up in the private sector and not in the public sector.

Table 2 shows the impact of a hypothetical government expenditure program involving the purchase of $50 million worth

[2] U.S. Senate Committee on Appropriations, *Hearings on Department of Defense Appropriations for 1953* (Washington: Government Printing Office, 1952).

[3] Irving H. Licht, "Government," in Conference on Research in Income and Wealth, *Input-Output Analysis*, Technical Supplement (New York: National Bureau of Economic Research, 1954), pp. 2–13. In 1957,

the Bureau of the Budget estimated the lag for personal services, printing, travel, and transportation expenses at from 15 to 140 days. Michael S. March, "A Comment on Budgetary Improvement in the National Government," *National Tax Journal* (June 1952), p. 173.

TABLE 2.   ILLUSTRATIVE IMPACT OF THE MAJOR STAGES OF
            THE GOVERNMENT SPENDING PROCESS

Stage	Government Purchases	Business Inventory Accumulation	All Other	GNP
($50 million military procurement program)				
1. Appropriation	...	...	...	...
2. Contract placement	...	...	...	...
3. Production	...	+50	...	+50
4. Delivery	+50	−50	...	...

Source: Adapted from M. L. Weidenbaum, "The Timing of the Economic Impact of Government Spending," *National Tax Journal*, March 1959, p. 82.

NOTE: Only direct effects are shown.

of military equipment produced in the private sector of the economy. For purposes of simplicity, the gross national product is divided among *government purchases, business inventory accumulation,* and *all other.*

The process begins with a congressional appropriation of $50 million. No direct effect occurs on the level of economic activity. The federal agency receiving the appropriation then places a contract with a private firm, which prepares to produce the order. (This may affect expectations of the firm, in terms of its planning, financial arrangements, etc., even prior to production.)

Actual production then follows. The total cost (including profit)—here estimated at $50 million—initially shows up in the business inventories of the defense contractor. Progress payments by the Department of Defense to the contractor do not change this because they are not entered into the GNP accounts. Such payments are excluded because they are not considered to represent the flow of resources but are merely financial transactions. When the work is completed and the items are delivered to the government, the $50 million transaction is then recorded as a government purchase, and a corresponding decline occurs in business inventories.

As will be shown consequently, the extent to which the placement of contracts by the Defense Department leads the actual production and subsequent military expenditure may provide a useful basis for developing a methodology for forecasting defense spending.

FORECASTING METHODOLOGY: SHORT TERM

Many of the techniques used for forecasting military spending, particularly in the short run, boil down to taking the available data and adding adjustments essentially based on judgment and on qualitative evaluation.

For example, the estimates of future-year military expenditures contained in the budget document can be taken as anticipations survey data, and adjustments made for such items as the unwillingness of the Congress to appropriate funds for some of the new weapon systems and other programs recommended by the President, as well as the addition by the Congress of projects not included in the President's original budget.

Instead, or in addition, the estimates of appropriations or obligations incurred may be used as lead indicators to gauge the future trend of expenditures. The very length of the spending process makes the early stages of value for projecting ahead, but is possibly primarily valuable in terms of providing broad directional guidance.

Also, forecasts of government expenditures can be prepared by making assumptions as to the availability of government funds, the extent to which they will be committed during the period under study, and the resulting expected delivery or expenditure rates. The major question involved, at least in short-term forecasting, is the extent to which the lead time coefficients remain constant over time—a problem related to the product mix of the weapon systems or other procurement on order.

For example, the Department of the Navy has found that expenditure rates for the major categories of long-range procurement have many characteristics of the logistics or S-curve.[4] By estimating the availability of funds for a given program and the expenditure rates experienced on similar programs in the past, expenditure forecasts can be made for the next several years.

The rationale for the S-curve is that production on long lead time items is slow in getting started, hits its stride with quantity production, and tapers off as the order nears completion. In a more general way, changes in the level of new authorizations and/or new commitments can be used to gauge the future course of expenditures. This can be done in a manner similar to that by which business analysts use fluctuations in new orders to estimate future sales and production trends.

Hence, when the current level of new obligational authority and/or obligations incurred exceeds the level of expenditures, the indications are strong that expenditures will rise in the future. Conversely, if the lead series are lower than the current level of payments, the future expenditure rate is likely to be lower. Unexpended balances of prior authorizations play a role analogous to that of unfilled orders in the private economy. Even during a cutback in new authoriza-

tions and new commitments, it is possible for expenditures to hold steady or even to rise if they are made out of preexisting balances.

One very promising method of forecasting defense expenditures in the short run is based specifically on the lags in the government spending process. Harvey Galper and Edward Gramlich have developed models for forecasting defense spending on income and product account using equations estimated by regression techniques. A detailed treatment of the Galper-Gramlich approach is included in the following chapter.

FORECASTING METHODOLOGY: LONG TERM

The simplest method—and perhaps still the most popular way of making long-term forecasts—is to take military expenditures as a constant percentage of GNP. A slightly more sophisticated approach, somewhat in line with recent experience, is to estimate the military expenditure level as a declining percentage of GNP.

However, the realities are certainly more complex than that. Military expenditures have been a major part, but only a part, of the federal budget and certainly an important but smaller proportion of GNP. Within the constraint of a budget which is approximately in balance over an extended period of time (if only on a "full employment" basis), the GNP and its growth is far more of a limitation on federal revenues than on military spending directly. A fairly extended model of the federal budget is needed. Given the tax structure, the revenues generated are a function of the level of economic activity—and hence so are total expenditures. Within the budget total, defense programs compete with other uses of federal funds, including a growing variety of nondefense programs and possibly tax

---

[4] U.S. Department of the Navy, *Statistical Approach to Forecasting Expenditures,* NAVEXOS P-1571.

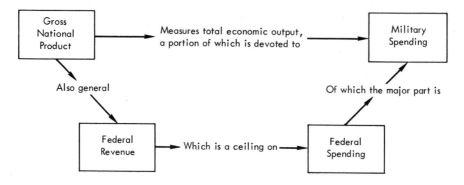

Figure 2   Relationship between GNP and military spending

and debt reductions over the period (see figure 2).

However, for more detailed purposes, such as industry market research and business planning, resort should be made to what may be termed the "top-down versus bottom-up" approach. The top-down approach is essentially that shown in figure 2, with the analyst working from gross national product down to military spending. The bottom-up aspect involves arriving at the military budget total by building up from cost estimates of each of the individual weapon systems which are likely to be included in the budget during the forecast period. Often the bottom-up approach yields a higher total than the top-down approach during the first few years of a projection. Then, as the analyst tends to run out of new systems, the bottom-up curve tends to show a strong downward trend.

Essentially, the top-down versus bottom-up approach is a series of successive approximations which involves adjustments to the "top line" resulting from phasing of specific key systems as well as adjustment in the bottom-up items as a result of funding limitations or availability.

Underlying any statistical methodology which may be used, it is essential to bring to bear an underlying qualitative analysis of the forces that determine military expenditure levels. Such a budget philoso-

phy shows that, in the absence of major active hostilities, neither sputniks nor economy drives result in the sharp shifts in military spending levels which occur at the beginning or ending of wartime periods. Also, although we cannot forecast necessarily the specific weapon systems which will be funded in the coming decade, the continuation of the underlying threat in international affairs requiring defense outlays and the degradation of any military system over time point in general to a rising trend of military spending. Of course, recent experience indicates that even the same weapon systems might cost more, due to general inflationary factors.

Over the years, I have found the following quotation from the work of a distinguished analyst and practitioner of federal budgeting to be an extremely useful guide:

> Outlays for defense . . . have been stimulated by a number of unforeseen shocks and have exhibited an erratic step-like upward growth in the post World War II period in response to [external] challenges. . . . This step-like movement may well be the pattern over the long-run future, as long as the cold war remains with us, but there need not be upward steps every year.[5]

[5] Samuel M. Cohn, "Problems in Estimating Federal Government Expenditures," *Journal of the American Statistical Association* (December 1959), p. 719.

Possibly with tongue in cheek, I have described my approach to military budget analysis and forecasting as resting on an unpatented blend of statistical data, historical relationships, heroic assumptions, and a sufficient mixture of past boners and good guesses usually referred to as experience.

SOME USES OF PROJECTIONS OF MILITARY EXPENDITURES

To sum up, projections of military expenditures are clearly a necessary part of forecasting the level and changes in direction of the national economy. Military purchases of goods and services are a large and volatile component of GNP.

In addition, projections of defense expenditures and the various components of the military budget are essential planning inputs for a very wide variety of regions, industries, and organizations. For companies who are major suppliers to the Pentagon, changes in the amount and composition of government expenditures which result in purchases from private industry are critical planning and market research data. This is emphasized by the fact that, for many individual firms in a variety of industries and in many localities, the government often represents the major and dominant customer.

In the case of many companies, a great deal of effort is devoted to developing the maximum relationships between the limited pertinent budgetary data available and the resultant business potential they may represent. In the case of the major defense equipment suppliers, for example, estimated budget expenditures for aircraft or missiles or space systems or ships represent the best available guide to the very size of the markets in which they are competing.

Current and historical budget data which reveal military purchasing patterns and trends provide important starting points or bench marks for market research and planning by private industry. Company investments in plant and equipment and research and development are often strongly influenced by the outlook for overall levels of defense expenditures, as well as for very specific types of purchases.

TABLE 3. USEFUL PUBLICATIONS ON DEFENSE SPENDING

Issuing Agency	Publication Title	Where Available
Department of Commerce, Bureau of the Census	*Defense Indicators*	Government Printing Office
Department of Commerce, Office of Business Economics	*Survey of Current Business*	Government Printing Office
Department of Defence	*Monthly Report on Status of Funds by Functional Title*	Office of Assistant Secretary of Defense (Comptroller)
Department of Defense	*Military Prime Contract Awards and Subcontract Payment or Commitments*	Office of Assistant Secretary of Defense (Installations and Logistics)
Department of Defense	*Military Prime Contract Awards by State*	Office of Assistant Secretary of Defense (Installations and Logistics)
Department of Defense	*Defense Industry Bulletin*	Office of Assistant Secretary of Defense (Public Affairs)

Those companies which are closely related to defense contractors—suppliers and subcontractors, banks and other investment sources, and firms which supply goods and

TABLE 4.   INDICATORS OF MILITARY SPENDING

Type of Data	Series	Department	Frequency	Current Publications
Leading Indicators				
Manpower	Draft calls	Selective Service	Monthly	Press releases
	Average weekly overtime hours in defense industries	Labor	Monthly	*Defense Indicators*
Material	Defense set-asides for copper, steel, aluminum	Commerce	Quarterly	Press releases
Business	Military contract awards: actual data	Defense	Monthly	*Military Prime Contract Awards . . .* (both publications)
	Military contract awards: seasonally adjusted	Commerce	Monthly	*Defense Indicators*
	Manufacturers' new orders for defense products	Commerce	Monthly	*Defense Indicators*
Financial	Defense obligations: actual data	Defense	Monthly	*Monthly Report on Status of Funds by Functional Title*
	Defense obligations: seasonally adjusted	Commerce	Monthly	*Defense Indicators*
Coincident Indicators				
Manpower	Armed strength	Defense	Monthly	*Defense Indicators*
	DOD civilian employees	Defense	Monthly	*Defense Indicators*
	Employment in defense industries	Labor	Monthly	*Defense Indicators*
Business	Defense industry inventories	Commerce	Monthly	*Defense Indicators*
	Unfilled defense industry orders	Commerce	Monthly	*Defense Indicators*
Financial	Defense Department net outlays: actual data	Defense	Monthly	*Monthly Report on Status of Funds by Functional Title*
	Defense Department net outlays: seasonally adjusted	Commerce	Monthly	*Defense Indicators*
	Outstanding progress payments	Defense	Monthly	*Defense Indicators*
Lagging Indicators				
Business	Shipments of defense products	Commerce	Monthly	*Defense Indicators*
	National defense purchases	Commerce	Quarterly	*Survey of Current Business*

services to the employees of defense contractors—also follow very closely changes in spending patterns. In the case of suppliers of such major components as aircraft power plants, missile guidance, and shipboard equipment, the firms involved must go through essentially the same analytical process as the prime contractors. They must then carry the work a step forward and relate the likely purchases of end products to the resultant market potential for the component portions.

As in the case of firms selling directly to the Department of Defense, these related companies frequently adjust their long-range planning and investment patterns to likely trends in the military budget. Input-output data systems may provide some general and rough guides to military subcontractors and suppliers.

DATA SOURCES

Several governmental publications are particularly useful for keeping abreast of short- and medium-term developments in military programs. Table 3 contains a listing of those monthly and quarterly publications which are both fairly readily available and which cover an important segment of defense spending trends. The Census Bureau's monthly report, *Defense Indicators*, is clearly the most useful single source of data for the forecaster of defense spending. This publication was specifically initiated in response to requests by potential users.

As in most areas of the economy, it is far too easy for the uninitiated forecaster to become overwhelmed by a plethora of data and statistical series. Table 4 is an attempt to indicate the basic categories of data and the most useful series in each area. By themselves, these series can be used in a modified fashion of the "National Bureau" approach to leading, coincident, and lagging indicators (and they are arranged in that form, although the categorizations are my own). For those using and/or developing more formal models, table 4 indicates the type of data that are available.

In addition, the Office of Business Economics of the U.S. Department of Commerce has developed input-output tables which can be used as a starting point in estimating industry production and manpower requirements to support a given level of defense spending.[6] It needs to be emphasized that such statistics are still mainly rough approximations but may be useful supplements to the relatively limited amount of "hard" industry data now available.

[6] "Input-Output Structure of the U.S. Economy: 1963," *Survey of Current Business* (November 1969) pp. 16–47; Richard P. Oliver, "Increase in Defense-Related Employment," *Monthly Labor Review* (February 1970), pp. 3–16.

HARVEY GALPER & EDWARD GRAMLICH

A Statistical Approach for Forecasting Defense Expenditures in the Short Run

I. GENERAL METHOD

A useful method for forecasting defense spending in the short run is to adapt a technique that has been developed in other areas of economic forecasting, namely relating final outlays to earlier stages of the spending sequence.[1] This approach can be attempted when data on the earlier stages are available and when fairly long lags exist between final expenditures and these earlier stages.

In the case of defense spending, both of these conditions are satisfied. Time series on defense obligations or contract awards are publicly available, and for defense products the time-consuming nature of the production process guarantees a fairly long lag between the time of contract awards and the time of subsequent spending, at least as reflected in the national income accounts. If these lags are sufficiently predictable, contract awards can serve as accurate forecasters of the defense spending which will follow.

It should be noted that a *predictable* lag structure is not necessarily equivalent to a *stable* lag structure. The timing relationship between contract awards and expendi-

tures may be highly variable, but if the sources of this variation can be found, useful forecasting equations may still be developed. Thus, statistical efforts at developing such equations should be directed toward not only finding the *basic* lag structure between contract awards and defense spending but also toward determining the sources of whatever variation may exist in this basic lag structure.

II. EQUATION SPECIFICATION AND ESTIMATION

In our work,[2] two separate equations have been developed: one for the compensation component of national defense purchases and one for goods, services, and construction. The latter involves a much more complex lag structure relating contract awards to expenditures and, hence, will be discussed in more detail in this chapter. A basic specification for relating contract awards to defense goods is

$$(1) \quad DG = f_0 + f_1 \, \text{time} + \sum_{i=0}^{n} a_i CA_{-i}$$

---

[1] Such an approach has been successfully developed for capital expenditures. See Shirley Almon, "The Distributed Lag Between Capital Appropriations and Expenditures," *Econometrica* (January 1965), pp. 178–196.

[2] Harvey Galper and Edward Gramlich, "A Technique for Forecasting Defense Expenditures," *Review of Economics and Statistics* (May 1968), pp. 143–155.

where DG = defense goods, services, and construction purchases in the national income accounts, CA = contract awards, and *time* and the constant term capture coverage differences between these two series.[3] We then assume that the basic lag structure as reflected in the a_i are influenced by three additional factors:

1. K, the aggregate capacity utilization rate, a proxy for supply factors.
2. A, a proxy representing the urgency of military demands, the level of the armed forces in t divided by the level in $t - 1$.
3. L, a variable reflecting the composition of contract awards and represented by contracts for aircraft, ships, missiles, and construction divided by total contract awards. Thus,

$$a_i = f(K, A, L)$$

This formulation indicates that the lag structure is not constant but varies in response to outside forces. In the cases of K and A, furthermore, we expect that the values of these variables over the entire period from the time of the contract awards until the time of the final expenditure should influence the a_i. To capture this effect, each a_i is assumed to vary according to the average K and A over the relevant time period. This will not be the case with the awards composition variable L since once a contract award has been made, subsequent values of L will not change the rate at which previous awards are transformed into expenditures. Illustrating these ideas for a particular a_i, say a_4, we may write

$$(2) \quad a_4 = b_4 + c_4 \sum_{j=0}^{4} \frac{K_{-j}}{5} + d_4 \sum_{j=0}^{4} \frac{A_{-j}}{5} + e_4 L_{-4}$$

On this basis, the complete estimating equation may be written as

[3] See table 4 for a listing of the data and their sources.

$$(3) \quad DG = f_0 + f_1 \text{ time} + \sum_{i=0}^{n} b_i CA_{-i}$$
$$+ \sum_{i=0}^{n} c_i \left[\frac{\sum_{j=0}^{i} K_{-j}}{i+1} \right] CA_{-i}$$
$$+ \sum_{i=0}^{n} d_i \left[\frac{\sum_{j=0}^{i} A_{-j}}{i+1} \right] CA_{-i}$$
$$+ \sum_{i=0}^{m} e_i L_{-i} CA_{-i}$$

As a result of statistical testing, we have adopted an eight-quarter span for n (the period over which aggregate contract awards K and A affect expenditures) and a ten-quarter span for m (the period over which long-lag items as reflected by $L \cdot CA$ affect expenditures). The resulting regression equation may be summarized as follows:[4]

$$(4) \quad DG = 14.460 - \underset{(0.0401)}{0.1644} \text{ time}$$
$$+ 0.8461 \sum_{i=0}^{10} w_i CA_{-i}$$

$$\bar{R}^2 = 0.943 \quad SE = \$0.680 \text{ billion}$$
$$DW = 1.720$$
$$Fit: 1953\text{-IV}\text{---}1965\text{-IV}$$

This equation shows only the *sum* of the coefficients on current and lagged contract awards when K, A, and L are all held at their mean values over the estimating period. Table 1 indicates the entire lag structure as well as the mean values and forms the basis for using such an equation for forecasting purposes.

A much simpler equation may be used to estimate the compensation component of national defense purchases. Using the same reasoning behind the goods equation, we have related total defense compensation—military and civilian—to military personnel

[4] The equation was estimated using the Almon polynomial technique for estimating distributed lags. We employed a third-degree polynomial with zero points fixed on both ends. See Almon, *op. cit.*, pp. 178–196.

TABLE 1. COEFFICIENTS OF CONTRACT AWARDS

Contract Award Period	Expression for Coefficient of CA_{t-i}*	Coefficients of CA_{t-i} at means of K, A, and L†
CA_t	$0.3923 - 0.0993L_t \quad - 0.1533K_t \quad - 0.1260A_t$	0.0787
CA_{t-1}	$0.4934 - 0.1596L_{t-1} - 0.2377\bar{K}_{t-1} - 0.0785\bar{A}_{t-1}$	0.1249
CA_{t-2}	$0.3798 - 0.1872L_{t-2} - 0.2557\bar{K}_{t-2} + 0.0880\bar{A}_{t-2}$	0.1443
CA_{t-3}	$0.1280 - 0.1884L_{t-3} - 0.2239\bar{K}_{t-3} + 0.3188\bar{A}_{t-3}$	0.1426
CA_{t-4}	$-0.1856 - 0.1695L_{t-4} - 0.1829\bar{K}_{t-4} + 0.5595\bar{A}_{t-4}$	0.1253
CA_{t-5}	$-0.4842 - 0.1366L_{t-5} - 0.1173\bar{K}_{t-5} + 0.7554\bar{A}_{t-5}$	0.0983
CA_{t-6}	$-0.6915 - 0.0962L_{t-6} - 0.0516\bar{K}_{t-6} + 0.8519\bar{A}_{t-6}$	0.0670
CA_{t-7}	$-0.9309 - 0.0545L_{t-7} - 0.0005\bar{K}_{t-7} + 0.7946\bar{A}_{t-7}$	0.0372
CA_{t-8}	$-0.5259 - 0.0177L_{t-8} - 0.0216\bar{K}_{t-8} + 0.5288\bar{A}_{t-8}$	0.0144
CA_{t-9}	$- 0.0078L_{t-9}$	0.0044
CA_{t-10}	$+ 0.0158L_{t-10}$	0.0090
	Total	0.8461

* $\bar{K}_{t-1} = (K_{t-1} + K_t)/2$, $\bar{K}_{t-2} = (K_{t-2} + K_{t-1} + K_t)/3$, $\bar{K}_{t-3} = (K_{t-3} + K_{t-2} + K_{t-1} + K_t)/4$, and so on through $\bar{K}_{t-8}$. Similar expressions define $\bar{A}_{t-1}$, $\bar{A}_{t-2}$ through $\bar{A}_{t-8}$.

† The mean values of K, A, and L respectively are 0.852, 1.006, and 0.567.

obligations using the constant and a time trend to capture differences in coverage of the two series. The equation is

$$(5) \quad DC = 5.046 + 0.8179PO$$
$$\quad \quad \quad \quad \quad \scriptstyle(0.0504)$$
$$\quad - 0.2976(PO - PO_{-1})$$
$$\quad \scriptstyle(0.0935)$$
$$\quad - 0.1159(PO - PO_{-2})$$
$$\quad \scriptstyle(0.0705)$$
$$\quad + 0.0743 \text{ time}$$
$$\quad \scriptstyle(0.0044)$$

$\bar{R}^2 = 0.991 \quad SE = \$0.185$ billion

$DW = 1.489$

Fit: 1953–III—1965–IV

DC = defense compensation

PO = personnel obligations

The lag pattern is:

t: $0.8179 - 0.2976 - 0.1159$
$\quad \quad = 0.4044$

t–1: $\quad \quad 0.2976$

t–2: $\quad \quad 0.1159$

steady state $\quad \overline{0.8179}$

Although the lag is short, there is still much to be gained from information already available and, in any case, defense compensation is not difficult to predict even by fairly straightforward extrapolation.

III. FORECASTING DEFENSE SPENDING: AN HISTORICAL EXAMPLE

As noted, both equations have been estimated through the end of 1965. The year 1966 was intentionally omitted from the estimation period to test the usefulness of the equations for forecasting purposes. After four years of stable defense spending at the level of $50 billion, defense spending increased by over twenty percent in 1966 to an annual rate in excess of $60 billion. This provided a demanding test of the usefulness of the technique.

Although both equations (and especially the goods equation) imply that the defense spending of each quarter is for the most part determined by past levels of all the variables (contract awards K, A, L, and personnel obligations), assumed values for these variables must nonetheless be entered for the forecasting period. The further into the future that the forecasts are to be made, the more crucial these assumptions become. In the short run, however, these assumptions do not significantly affect the results.

TABLE 2.   DATA FOR 1963-III THROUGH 1965-IV AND ASSUMPTIONS FOR FORECASTING DEFENSE SPENDING IN 1966

Quarter	CA		PO		K	A	L
			(Billions of $)				
Actual							
1963-III	30.9		13.9		0.840	1.004	0.554
IV	23.4		14.5		0.841	0.997	0.552
1964-I	25.7		14.4		0.849	0.997	0.548
II	27.4		14.9		0.859	1.005	0.540
III	28.1		15.2		0.866	1.000	0.532
IV	22.5		14.7		0.866	0.995	0.523
1965-I	21.3		14.8		0.888	0.991	0.500
II	29.6		15.2		0.887	0.992	0.460
III	31.7		16.3		0.889	1.007	0.441
IV	32.6		16.7		0.890	1.036	0.420
*Forecast**	*Conserva-tive*	*Moderate*	*Conserva-tive*	*Moderate*			
1966-I	33.0	33.5	17.0	17.0	0.890	1.036	0.400
II	34.0	35.0	17.5	18.0	0.890	1.036	0.400
III	35.0	36.5	18.0	19.0	0.890	1.036	0.400
IV	36.0	38.0	18.5	20.0	0.890	1.036	0.400

* The actual quarterly pattern of contract awards and personnel obligations in 1966 were *CA*: 32.9, 38.8, 41.1, 39.1; *PO*: 17.3, 18.6, 20.0, 19.9.

TABLE 3.   FORECASTING RESULTS FOR DEFENSE SPENDING IN 1966

	1966-I	*1966-II*	*1966-III*	*1966-IV*	*Year 1966*
			(Billions of dollars)		
Actual NIA defense expenditures*	55.1	58.4	63.0	65.6	60.5
Conservative forecast	54.6	57.3	60.1	62.8	58.7
Error	+0.5	+1.1	+2.9	+2.8	+1.8
Moderate forecast	54.7	57.4	60.5	63.4	59.0
Error	+0.4	+1.0	+2.5	+2.2	+1.5

* From the July 1967 issue of *Survey of Current Business.* These figures have since been revised slightly.

Two sets of assumptions with respect to contract awards and personnel obligations were used to forecast defense spending for 1966. For K, A, and L, 1966 values were based on 1965 experience along with information presented in the January 1966 *Economic Report of the President*. These assumptions along with historical data from 1963-III through 1965-IV are presented in table 2.

When these assumptions along with the appropriate historical figures are entered into the expressions shown in table 1 and in equation (5), 1966 forecasts for defense spending may be obtained. Calculation of the coefficients of CA_{t-i} and multiplication of the coefficients by the appropriate contract award values is quite laborious by hand. However, the relationships may be programmed for the computer without difficulty.

The forecasting results and actual defense spending as published in the July 1967 issue of *Survey of Current Business* are

TABLE 4.   VARIABLES AND THEIR SOURCES FOR FORECASTING DEFENSE SPENDING

Variable Name	Variable Symbol	Source
1. Defense compensation	DC	U.S. Department of Commerce, Office of Business Economics, *Survey of Current Business*, July, various years. This series is interpolated quarterly from data presented in table 3.11 under "National Defense, Compensation of Employees."
2. Defense goods, services, and construction (noncompensation)	DG	Table 3.2 of above source under "Purchases of Goods and Services, National Defense" gives total defense expenditures. The values found for DC above are then subtracted from this total to derive DG.
3. Contract awards	CA	U.S. Department of Commerce, Bureau of the Census, *Defense Indicators*, series #625 entitled "Defense Department Military Prime Contract Awards for Work Performed in the U.S., Total, Seasonally Adjusted."
4. Capacity utilization rate	K	Board of Governors of the Federal Reserve System, release E.5 entitled "Capacity Utilization in Manufacturing."
5. Rate of growth of the armed forces	A	The military labor force as defined in U.S. Bureau of Labor Statistics, *Employment and Earnings and Monthly Report of the Labor Force*. The military labor force is the difference between the civilian and the total labor force.
6. Ratio of long lead time contract awards to total contract awards (composition variable)	L	*Defense Indicators* (see variable 3). The sum of series #626, "Defense Department Military Prime Contract Awards, Aircraft"; #627, "Defense Department Military Prime Contract Awards, Missile and Space Systems"; #628, "Defense Department Military Prime Contract Awards, Ships"; and #634, "Defense Department Military Prime Contract Awards, Construction," all divided by total military prime contract awards (variable 3). All series for this calculation are available on a seasonally adjusted basis except for series #628, ships.
7. Personnel obligations	PO	Office of the Assistant Secretary of Defense (Comptroller), *Monthly Report on Status of Funds by Functional Title*, series entitled "Obligations DOD Total, Military Personnel."

shown in table 3.[5] As expected, however, the further into the year the equations forecast, the larger are the errors. For the first half of 1966 the errors average about $0.75 billion, but in the second half they are over three times as large. Thus, the equations provide quite accurate results for six-month forecast-

ing and passable results for up to one year ahead, but they are less reliable beyond that. Yet, even the more remote forecasts still did very well in comparison to other forecasts in this period.[6]

[5] These defense spending figures have been revised slightly by the Office of Business Economics of the Department of Commerce in subsequent publications. However, the data used in the regression equations themselves have also undergone revision. See the next section for modifications of these equations for forecasting defense spending in the future.

[6] Illustrative of this are the estimates of defense spending for fiscal years 1966 and 1967 in the *Economic Report of the President* of January 1966. The defense spending figures for the last half of calendar 1966 implied by these fiscal year estimates are $5.5 to $6.0 billion below our last half of 1966 forecasts, and this despite the fact that our own forecasts were about $2.5 billion too low. See table 7 in Council of Economic Advisors, *Economic Report of the President*, January 1966, p. 59.

IV. MODIFICATIONS FOR FUTURE FORECASTING

As they are presented here, neither equation (4) (or its more complete presentation in table 1) nor equation (5) are likely to predict successfully for 1971 and beyond. First, the equations, as noted, were estimated only through 1965, and more recent experience should be incorporated into the regression equations to use them for current short-term forecasting. Secondly, several of the data series used in estimating the original equations have been refined or otherwise changed. This includes not only the basic defense purchases data which undergo periodic revision by the Department of Commerce, but also other series such as contract awards data.[7] Nevertheless, the same basic

approach can be used to derive more up-to-date estimates of the lag structure between contract awards and defense spending.[8]

To assist the practitioner in developing equations along these lines for future forecasting work, table 4 indicates the basic variables we have used and the current sources of each.

---

[7] As now published in *Defense Indicators,* this series includes intragovernmental contract awards and awards to educational and nonprofit institutions, whereas these were ex-

cluded in the series originally available to us. Also, subsequent testing yielded better results from the use of the Federal Reserve Board capacity utilization rate of primary products rather than the aggregate capacity utilization rate. Furthermore, a quarterly series for the composition variable L was originally interpolated from annual data but is now available on a quarterly basis from data in *Defense Indicators.*

[8] For an example of a more recent equation based on this same approach, see Harvey Galper, "The Impacts of the Vietnam War on Defense Spending: A Simulation Approach," *The Journal of Business* (October 1969), pp. 401–415. This article also uses a different approach to the forecasting of defense compensation.

LAWRENCE P. HAWKINS

Plant and Equipment Outlays

The outlook for business investment holds the interest of economists and business planners because of its instrumental role in determining the shape of the economy. Of the five postwar recessions, capital spending led the march down in two (1948–49, 1957–58) and was a large contributing element in two others (1953–54 and 1960–61). In addition, booms in investment spending helped power the vigorous expansions of the mid-fifties and the decade of the sixties. (see chart

1.) The influence of plant and equipment spending on the business cycle is traced to the fact that swings in investment outlays are usually exaggerated, and often out of line with levels warranted by economic conditions. Thus capital spending booms normally extend well beyond their time and result in overbuilding capacity. Likewise after business recessions, investment outlays continue at a subdued pace for some time. Finally, confidence is restored and the pau-

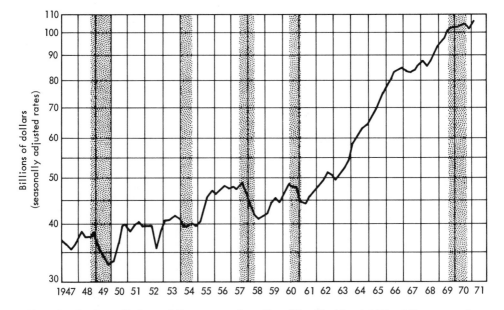

Chart 1   Business Cycles and Investment Spending (Non-Residential Fixed Investment)—
Billions of Dollars—Seasonally Adjusted Annual Rates

city of capital is fully realized, triggering a new investment boom.

DUAL ROLE OF INVESTMENT

Business capital spending plays a dual role in the economy: creating productive capacity and generating income. By affecting the net additions to the stock of capital, investment spending also affects the potential volume of output flowing from that capital base. In addition, spending on plant and equipment generates income for the producers of investment goods (wages to labor, and profits and interest to management and capital). These income flows affect spending patterns in consumer goods and other areas of the economy, in turn generating another round of income. By generating fresh income flows through successive rounds of spending, changes in capital outlays have feedback effects throughout the economy— the well-known investment multiplier.[1]

FORECASTING METHODS

The full flavor of investment forecasting would not be achieved if this chapter dwelled solely upon my own techniques. Consequently, a thumbnail sketch of the basic theory of investment demand will be presented, as well as a treatment of major forecasting methods. All techniques fall into one of three methodological categories:

1. *Anticipations and intentions*, where the forecaster uses surveys of investment intentions and other anticipatory data to derive his estimate of future capital spending. Major surveys

of investment plans include the Mc-Graw-Hill survey, and the Plant and Equipment Spending Survey conducted jointly by the Department of Commerce and the Securities and Exchange Commission (referred to as the Commerce-SEC survey). In addition, a quarterly survey of funds appropriated for investment projects of manufacturing and utility corporations is conducted by the Conference Board.

2. *System models*,[2] where the investment sector is a subset of a broader analysis of the economy (general equilibrium analysis). System models are usually statistical or econometric (using simultaneous equations) but can also be subjective, employing a "feel for numbers" that every good business forecaster must develop.

3. *Sector models*, where the investment sector is analyzed by itself without reference to behavioral relations in other sectors, (partial equilibrium analysis). Sector models can be statistical, econometric, or subjective.

SUBJECTIVE INFLUENCES

All methods of investment forecasting are influenced by subjective elements, including those developed by the solons of scientism—the econometricians. These elements—which I like to call judgmental inputs—supersede and modify the statistical results of a formalized approach. In so doing the forecaster is saying that the unique combination of business profits, costs, sales, and expectations will yield a rate of investment different than the model run indicates. The hooker here is "expectations," which are crucial in investment behavior but are

---

[1] The reader can find mathematical illustrations of the investment multiplier among the many available books on macroeconomic theory.

[2] Usually, but erroneously, referred to as "econometric models." Many system models are statistical rather than econometric, and some "econometric" models do not fully address themselves to econometric problems.

never directly measured. Instead, expectations appear in investment equations through proxy variables (profits, sales growth, etc.). Thus by modifying his forecast output, the economist is implicitly saying that the expectations proxies are not fully reflecting what he deems to be the true tone of business expectations.

Examples of such tinkering are widespread. In late 1968 a large midwestern university released its 1969 economic forecast, derived from their well-known econometric model. The research director freely admitted that the model run generated an investment forecast of "no change" in 1969. But that output did not suit the director, so it was raised to four percent growth—obviously influenced by the eight and nine percent gains then being projected by the investment surveys. (The actual rise in capital spending that year was twelve percent.) Perhaps it is not widely known, but model builders are constantly changing parameters (usually the intercept) so that the model run will more closely approximate the forecaster's subjective and intuitive feelings. Indeed, a noted econometrician once freely admitted that he wasn't ". . . going to let a 25-bit computer upstage me."

A NOTE ON DATA

There are two major investment series used by economists. One is the business plant and equipment spending series from the Commerce-SEC survey; the other is the nonresidential fixed investment series from the GNP accounts. The Commerce-SEC plant and equipment series is an estimate of business investment based on a sample of about 8,000 respondents, most of them corporations. The national income accounts series (nonresidential fixed investment) uses the Commerce-SEC data and adds investment estimates for the following sectors: agriculture, real estate, professionals (doc-

tors, lawyers, etc.), and nonprofit institutions (including schools).

My own preference is to use the investment data in the national income accounts, but only because we are closely involved in forecasting GNP. Actually the choice is somewhat arbitrary because the Commerce-SEC series is a very large subset of nonresidential fixed investment. Hence, any statement about one is, by definition, a statement about the other. At any rate, the difference will be narrowing. At this writing Commerce-SEC has undertaken to include the real estate, professional, and nonprofit institution sectors in its quarterly survey.

INVESTMENT DETERMINANTS

Theory of Investment

The theory of the firm postulates that investment will expand until the marginal physical product of capital equals the marginal physical product of labor. This theory operates in the rather unreal framework of a static state, with perfect substitution of capital for labor. Investment is included in the fixed and marginal cost schedules in the profit maximizing equation.

Obviously this approach is of little value for the business forecaster because of its pedagogic cast. But even more realistic theories of company behavior are limited in usefulness, because some causal relationships are not additive. In other words, the determinants of total activity in a system can be different than the determinants of activity of any single unit.

Classical theory was formulated in terms of demand for investment and the supply of savings, both of which varied with the rate of interest. If investment exceeded savings in the classical system, interest rates would rise causing increased savings (reduced time preference of current consumption) and lower investment (declining profitability). This would continue until investment equaled savings. Thus, investment is determined by the savings schedule and the rate of interest. But classical theory makes no provision for unemployment in the economy, thus limiting its usefulness.

The modern Keynesian theory of aggregate investment is based on the marginal efficiency of capital and the rate of interest. The marginal efficiency of capital denoted by r in the equation is the rate used to discount the expected future returns in order to equate them with the cost of capital, or:

Cost of capital
$$= \frac{Q1}{1+r} + \frac{Q2}{1+r^2} + \cdots + \frac{Qn}{1+r^n}$$

where the Q_i's represent the expected returns to capital in the ith year. If r exceeds the going rate of interest, the project is profitable. (What this all means in today's parlance is that an investment project is profitable if the present value of discounted cash flow exceeds the cost of the project.) By aggregating over the system, an investment demand function is formulated. Thus the rate of interest and the marginal efficiency of capital together determine the rate of investment. Note well, however, that the future return of an investment project is an expectation, subject to uncertainties. And expectations can change dramatically with the state of business confidence.

Empirical Determinants

Theoretical underpinnings are important for a complete understanding of investment processes, but empirical specification of such theory is another matter. This is particularly true when theory is formulated in a static framework. In addition, many dynamic theories bear little resemblance to the dynamic elements in the real world. For example, the marginal physical products of labor and capital in the theory of the firm

are not directly measurable but must be estimated—thus becoming influenced by expectations. Even if they were measurable, these marginal physical products would not be aggregated for the economy as a whole involving heterogeneous products and industries.

For Keynesian income theory, which already is formulated in aggregate economic terms, measurement of the marginal efficiency of capital schedule is all but impossible, since by definition it is expected that future returns and expectations are a fragile psychological state. As a result, empirical proxies are often used as a stand-in for expectations. Traditional investment theory places little importance on financial variables, except the rate of interest. But modern investment analysis is incorporating large financial blocks into its models.

The empirical approach tries to adapt theoretical constructs to the data at hand. The proxies used for the nonmeasurable theoretical determinants can appear in several forms in the investment equation. The most commonly used statistical determinants include capacity utilization, used as a stock adjustment variable. Utilization rates attempt to quantify the relationship between current output and the capital stock. Businessmen tend to adjust for any excesses or deficiencies in the capital stock, and these adjustments are effected by varying the rate of investment. However, utilization rates are calculated by abysmally elementary methods (trend lines are drawn through peak periods of output) which may hamper their statistical effectiveness. Output is another variable often used, though it is related to capacity utilization.[3]

Sales expectations enter in as a determinant of market requirements, and are usually represented by lagged values of sales or

[3] Covariation among explanatory variables, called multicollinearity, can lead to inefficient estimates of the parameters. This is but one of many statistical and econometric problems in which any good business economist must be well grounded.

a conditional forecast. The interest rate, as we have seen, plays a significant theoretical role in determining investment. Empirically, interest rates represent financing costs and the opportunity cost of capital. And there is a growing belief that the rate of interest is also a proxy for credit conditions (high bond yields=restricted credit availability). Profits and cash flow are very significant determinants of plant and equipment outlays. Besides acting as a gauge of financing ability, cash flow has a profound influence on business expectations—perhaps the single most important determinant of investment outlays.

FORECASTING METHODOLOGIES

Anticipations and Intentions

Economists are very much interested in how businessmen feel about the investment climate, and therefore closely follow the various surveys of investment intentions. Those forecasters who have not formalized their methods (the so-called seat of the pants approach) rely heavily on such surveys. Perhaps the most widely followed is the Commerce-SEC Plant and Equipment Expenditures Survey, a sample survey with about 8,000 respondents polled quarterly on what they expect to invest. Note that this survey is not a forecast, but an aggregation of investment plans.

Chart 2 shows the investment survey errors from Commerce-SEC's January-February survey of each year. (These errors are not based on the original estimates, since Commerce has gone back and adjusted the numbers for systematic biases.) The survey record has been pretty fair. It has called the right direction in every year but one (1950). However, the Commerce-SEC survey has a tendency to overestimate; it was too high in 16 of the last 23 years. The average absolute error of this survey was 3.1 percent. Since 1966, Commerce-SEC has been estimating investment intentions in the next calendar year in its November survey. To date its record has been extremely spotty.

The survey also estimates quarterly rates of investment a half year ahead. A look at these projections reveals several systematic tendencies. First, the surveys usually miss the

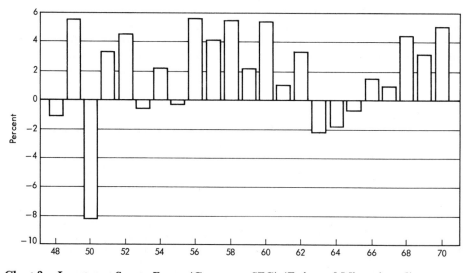

Chart 2   Investment Survey Errors (Commerce-SEC) (Estimated Minus Actual)

turning points, often lagging by one or two quarters. This is understandable since businessmen (the survey's respondents) tend to formulate near-term expectations by extrapolating current developments over the short run. As a result, the surveys usually don't show a change in direction until after the corner has been turned.

The second tendency—one familiar to most business economists—is that in periods of accelerating investment the survey understates the actual capital spending, while in periods of sluggish activity the spending plans overshoot the mark. This can readily be seen in chart 3 which shows the average percentage error after turning points in the investment cycle, based on Commerce-SEC expectations two quarters ahead. During capital spending declines, the error goes from near zero at the peak, then rises steadily to a substantial +5.1 percent three quarters later before trailing off slightly. This clearly illustrates the survey's overstating tendency during investment declines. The pattern was consistent for each cycle, and the average error over the period was +3⅓ percent.

The case is less clear during early stages of expansion. A very large error at the trough (remember it overstates on the way down) gives way to an underestimate by the third and fourth quarters after the low. Averages here may not be meaningful, for in

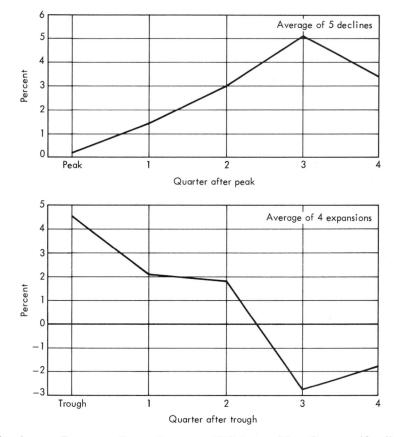

Chart 3   Average Percentage Error, Commerce-SEC Survey (Two Quarters Ahead)

the last two expansions the errors were very small, and for the year after the turn the average errors just about cancel out.

Since corporate planners need economic forecasts before the calendar year begins, economists cannot wait until March when the Commerce-SEC survey results appear. And the December survey results are as yet unreliable. Fortunately, McGraw-Hill, Inc. has been conducting surveys of investment intentions and industrial capacity in both the autumn and spring. Table 1 shows the results of these surveys along with actual plant and equipment spending. The spring survey shows about the same results as Commerce-SEC—an average error of 3.4 percent with a consistent upward bias (13 of 15 years). However, the fall survey has a downward bias, with an average error of 4.9 percent. McGraw-Hill's largest errors occurred in 1964–66, when the survey failed to pick up the full strength of the investment boom. Otherwise the average error is a respectable 3.5 percent. There is every good reason why the fall surveys are less accurate. For one

thing, much of the capital budgeting has traditionally taken place around year-end, so that later surveys reflected the formal plans. With respect to all investment surveys, the fact that they record intentions, which are later reformulated as conditions unfold, explains the systematic biases (negative in periods of strength, positive in periods of weakness) that are well recognized.

The Conference Board also collects investment data on capital appropriations in its quarterly survey. Estimates of its survey universe (1,000 largest manufacturing companies and investor-owned gas and electric utilities) account for about 80 percent of manufacturing and 90 percent of utility plant and equipment spending. Together they comprise about 45 percent of total business fixed investment. The Conference Board's survey does not estimate investment plans, but records actual spending plus newly appropriated investment funds. However, some empirical work has been done using distributed lags on appropriations to estimate future spending, as well as the influ-

TABLE 1.   PLANT AND EQUIPMENT SPENDING

	Actual	McGraw-Hill Estimates	
		Fall Survey	Spring Survey
		(Percent change)	
1956	21.0%	13%	30%
1957	6.2	11	12
1958	−15.9	−7	−12
1959	5.2	1	7
1960	9.5	10	16
1961	−2.3	−3	−1
1962	6.9	4	11
1963	6.2	3	7
1964	15.2	4	12
1965	15.9	5	15
1966	16.7	8	19
1967	3.1	5	6
1968	3.5	5	8
1969	11.5	8	13
1970	5.5	8	9

Source: U.S. Department of Commerce and McGraw-Hill, Inc.

ence of the backlog of unspent appropriations on spending rates.

Surveys of investment intentions have a real influence on a business economist's subjective input. This applies perhaps as much to the econometricians as to those who use less sophisticated methods. In this respect, the knowledge of the survey's systematic errors is helpful. For example, if a model run predicts a three percent decline in investment spending and the surveys come out with three percent gain, the forecaster feels assured. He knows that surveys overstate spending in a weakening investment climate. But if the survey results indicated a nine percent gain, the forecaster would take a hard look at his model to try and see what he may have overlooked. As indicated earlier, he would even fiddle with the model parameters to change the results, since he would probably be unprepared to accept a twelve percent survey error.

System Models

System models refer to the structure of an entire economic system usually expressed statistically. These are referred to as simultaneous equation systems, containing behavioral equations of the major sectors as well as identities. Variables are classified as predetermined (determined outside the system, e.g., government spending) and endogenous (determined within the system, e.g., investment). There are a number of conditions to be satisfied for the equations in the system to be identified, and if they are not met the system approach cannot claim any superiority over the sector approach regarding the structure of the equations.[4]

Within a system model framework, plant and equipment spending is viewed as a subset of a system. In estimating the parameters, the investment equation is trans-

[4] For a good exposition of identification and its conditions, see Christ, chapter 8.

formed into its "reduced form," meaning that substitutions are made with other equations in the system until the dependent variable (investment) is a function of predetermined variables only. The parameters are then estimated and put back into the original equation. The results are used for prediction by plugging in the predetermined variables in the forecast period. Note that some of the predetermined variables are only predetermined in the sample period, but in the forecast period must be estimated. This makes the forecast a conditional one. Of course the econometrician then makes adjustments for unusual events (strikes, tax changes if cash flow does not appear in the equation) either directly or through the use of dummy variables. Then a final adjustment may be made if the tone of expectations is not adequately accounted for by the estimating equation.

System models do have the advantage of providing a disciplined framework, thus making for consistency. The average system model has performed somewhat better than the average nonsystem forecast, but only because the average nonsystem forecast is weighed down by unknowledgeable practitioners. Yet the record of the system model approach has been disappointing—particularly in view of the substantial resources necessary to build and sustain such models. Their strong point seems to lie in the substantial industry and product detail they can produce. But in terms of aggregate economic forecasting, top business economists using the simpler sectoral approaches have consistently outperformed the system models. It probably boils down to the fact that forecasting accuracy depends in large measure on the final adjustments based on subjective judgment (knowledge of economic processes and a feel for the industry and situation). Many of the system models have not been in existence long enough to establish a reputation, and some have gone off-track so badly the last few years that their once substantial influence has dissipated sharply. Today the trend in econometric work is toward greater emphasis on sectoral approaches.

Sector Models

Formal sector models cover a wide range of statistical sophistication. Some are econometric models well grounded in theory, while others are merely naive correlations. The final result depends, of course, on the accuracy of the forecaster's judgment in making adjustments, but the best statistical results come from models that are simple and properly transformed. Simplicity is desirable for several reasons. Complex formulations, with many explanatory variables, limit the number of degrees of freedom in the sample, which in turn affects the significance of variables. It also compounds potential estimating errors of conditional forecasts, i.e., the explanatory variables are to be estimated and the investment forecast is conditional upon it. In addition, complex formulations often introduce a serious degree of multicollinearity (covariation among explanatory variables) which can distort the relative influence of variables by increasing the sampling variances. This problem becomes meaningful from a forecasting point of view when the covariation is not constant.

Proper transformation of the data is necessary in order to minimize the risks of serial correlation, which lead to inefficient estimators. In addition, most economic time series contain strong trend elements. As a result, if the data are not first transformed, correlations will often reflect only the co-movement of the time trends. In other words, the correlations are spurious.

Some business economists use yearly models while others use quarterly data. However, many quarterly models miss turning points and have misleading standard error values because of serial correlation and a large sample. It is often useful when working with quarterly data to back it up with a reliable annual model. For marketing study purposes, some forecasters break down the investment estimate into the plant and the equipment component. One note of caution —plant component is more erratic than equipment and also appears to have a larger random error.

Typical Sectoral Formulation

A typical sectoral formulation is presented using annual data in order to illustrate that with a little care in specifying the sector model, it is not overly difficult to obtain acceptable results. The equation is in the following form:

$$(1) \quad I_t = \sum_{i=0}^{1} \beta_i CFLO_{t-1} + \beta_2 GP8_t + \beta_3 + e_t$$

The variables have all been transformed into percent changes and expressed in real terms.

I_t = percent change nonresidental fixed investment, 1958 dollars
$CFLO_t$, $CFLO_{t-1}$ = percent changes in corporate cash flow, adjusted for investment price deflator
$GP8_t$ = output variable, percent change GNP in 1958 dollars
β_i ($i = 0 \ldots 3$) equation parameters (coefficients)
e_t = error term

Ordinary least squares yields the following results:

Variable	Coefficient	Standard Deviation	t-Value
$GP8_t$	1.016	0.34	2.99
$CFLO_{t-1}$	0.319	0.10	3.07
$CFLO_t$	0.299	0.08	3.77
$R^2 = 0.79$	DW = 1.64		

Chart 4 shows a comparison between the actual and the predicted changes. The fit is pretty good; the average error is less than the surveys and yet it doesn't have the "stage-of-cycle" bias the surveys exhibit.

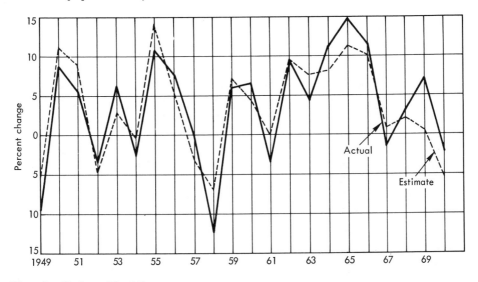

Chart 4   Business Fixed Investment

Among the independent variables, output ($GP8_t$) is not too difficult to estimate for a good business economist. Cash flow is more problematic but one of the cash flow variables is already determined (lagged value of an endogenous variable). It should be noted that when a fourth variable, capacity utilization, is added its high intercorrelation with the output variable makes the latter's coefficient insignificant at the five percent confidence level. The fit actually deteriorates because of the loss of an additional degree of freedom.

Capital Stock Approach

One of several approaches used in determining investment requirements at Chase Manhattan Bank is the capital stock approach developed by this writer. The capital stock approach is in the form of a stock adjustment model. In theory it holds that for a given level of output, businessmen desire a certain stock of capital assets to produce that output. But business plans in this regard suffer from all the inaccuracies of expectations that plague other decision-mak-

ing processes. So businessmen do not always realize the required capital stock, but only approximate it. And that approximation may be formulated as a "realization function." In this framework, the rate of new investment is dependent upon the overall capital stock requirements and the depreciation rate.

Keep in mind that this approach specifies the economic requirements for investment. Whether these requirements are financeable is another question concerning the fiscal and monetary authorities. In other words, corporate cash flow (in large measure determined by the tax structure) and credit availability should be sufficient to meet the economic requirements of net capital stock additions plus replacement of depreciated capital.

The Commerce Department has generated estimates of the capital stock in constant 1958 dollars. (For the reader's reference, this study uses the net capital stock series, declining balance depreciation using Commerce's constant cost-2 formulation.) With these data, and taking business fixed investment from the GNP accounts, we can derive table 2.

TABLE 2.   NET CAPITAL STOCK

	Net Capital Stock	Business Fixed Investment	Depreciation* (Implicit)	Depreciation as % of Capital Stock Previous Year
	(1958 dollars)			
1947	161.8	36.2	21.1	14.4
1948	176.2	38.0	23.6	14.6
1949	185.1	34.5	25.6	14.5
1950	195.1	37.5	27.5	14.9
1951	205.5	39.6	29.2	15.0
1952	213.7	38.3	30.1	14.6
1953	223.2	40.7	31.2	14.6
1954	230.9	39.6	31.9	14.3
1955	241.6	43.9	33.2	14.4
1956	254.0	47.3	34.9	14.4
1957	265.3	47.4	36.1	14.2
1958	270.3	41.6	36.6	13.8
1959	277.9	44.6	37.0	13.7
1960	287.3	47.1	37.7	13.6
1961	294.3	45.5	38.5	13.4
1962	304.4	49.7	39.6	13.5
1963	315.1	51.9	41.2	13.5
1964	329.7	57.8	43.2	13.7
1965	350.2	66.3	45.8	13.9
1966	375.1	74.1	49.2	14.0
1967	395.8	73.2	52.5	14.0
1968	415.5	75.5	55.8	14.1
1969	437.3	80.8	59.0	14.2
1970	454.0	79.2	62.5	14.3

* Includes minor amounts of net sale or purchases of used equipment from the business sector.

Using this capital stock series and relating it to output in the economy (GNP in 1958 dollars) we arrive at the results in chart 5. If we view the residuals in the bottom panel as "errors" in business planning, then we may attempt to explain them by some realization function. In other words, we are trying to explain the deviations of the actual from the required capital stock levels. This appears to be empirically justified since these residuals are positively correlated with the index of capacity utilization, as shown in chart 6.

One possible hypothesis is that businessmen never fully anticipate the magnitude of large swings in investment requirements. For this purpose we introduce a new variable, the change in the required capital stock (defined as the required capital stock in period t minus the actual capital stock in period $t-1$). We can expect the change in the required capital stock ($CRCS$) to be negatively correlated with the capital stock residuals ($CSRES$), since very large increases in $CRCS$ will lead to an underestimate by the business community and a negative residual ($CSRES$ defined as actual capital stock minus required capital stock). A correlation using this simple expectations error structure yields an R^2 of just under 60 percent.

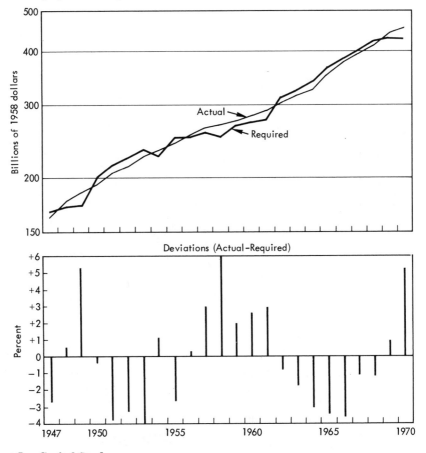

Chart 5   Capital Stock

When the coefficients are adjusted for systematic tendencies in the error term, the equation structure explains much of the variation in *CSRES*, as shown in chart 7.

Evaluation

Although some work has been done using quarterly proxies of the capital stock, this approach seems to be more effective using annual data. Thus its use is limited in formulating a near-term investment outlook. However, the capital stock approach, by looking at investment as both capital additions and capital replacement, is very good

at gauging conditions that lead to big swings in investment spending. It is also useful to have this approach, in addition to quarterly models, to measure the capital requirements of the economy a year or more ahead.

Longer-Term Forecasts

The capital stock approach is particularly useful for calculating longer term investment requirements, because near-term deviations of the actual capital stock from capital requirements tend to cancel out over time. This was the approach I used in 1970 to calculate investment requirements

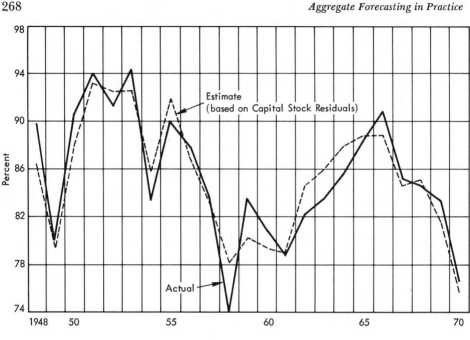

Chart 6   Capacity Utilization

through 1975, as part of a Chase Manhattan planning study. It was estimated that the economy would aproach full employment during 1973 and then track approximately along a full employment growth path (as represented in column 1 of table 3). This is not strictly in the form of an assumption, but is more of a probability statement. At those levels of activity, capital stock requirements are calculated in column 2. Column 3 indicates what the capital stock is likely to be—it converges on "required" capital series sometime in 1972 and then tracks together. Column 4 is the normal depreciation on the capital stock. Using the net capital stock additions and the depreciation, we arrive at investment requirements for the five-year period (column 5).

The estimates are extremely revealing, for it is strongly indicated that after moving essentially sideways through 1971 and much of 1972, a new capital spending boom would take hold. Indeed, in the three-year period 1973–75, real investment outlays would ex-

pand about 35 percent, with 1973 in particular being a very big year.

SUMMARY

It was not the intention to lobby for any one approach to forecasting capital spending, but to suggest the strengths and weaknesses of various approaches. Other factors enter in, including the time horizon of the forecast, the magnitude of acceptable errors, and—needless to say—cost factors. I do feel that the most promising work is in applying econometric methods to sector models. From this we can see that the successful business economist needs two things: a thorough grounding in statistics and econometrics, and experience in forecasting in order to sharpen his understanding of the economy as well as his instincts of subjective judgmental inputs.

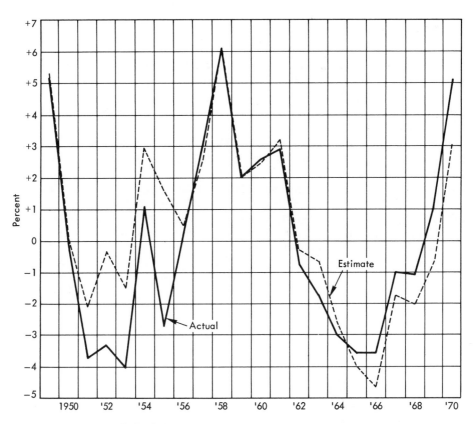

Chart 7   Capital Stock Deviations—Actual Minus Required as a Percent of Actual Capital Stock

TABLE 3.   CAPITAL STOCK REQUIREMENTS 1971-75

	Gross National Product	Required Capital Stock	Estimated Capital Stock	Depreciation	Fixed Investment
	(Billions of 1958 dollars)				
1971	744	443	466	65	77
1972	781	467	477	67	78
1973	830	498	497	68	88
1974	885	530	523	71	97
1975	925	555	554	74	105

BIBLIOGRAPHY

Christ, Carl F., *Econometric Models and Methods.* New York: John Wiley & Sons, Inc., 1966.

Domar, Evsey D., "Expansion and Employment," *American Economic Review,* 37, No. 1 (March 1947), pp. 34–55.

Ferber, Robert, ed., *Determinants of Investment Behavior.* New York: National Bureau of Economic Research, 1967.

Johnston, J., *Econometric Methods.* New York: McGraw-Hill Book Co., 1960.

Keynes, John Maynard, *The General Theory of Employment, Interest and Money.* London: Macmillan & Co., 1936.

Wasson, Robert C., et al., "Alternative Estimates of Fixed Business Capital in the U.S., 1925–1968," *Survey of Current Business* (April 1970), pp. 18–36.

Wimsatt, Genevieve B., and John T. Woodward, "Revised Estimates of New Plant and Equipment Expenditures in the U.S. 1947–69," Parts I & II, *Survey of Current Business* (January and February 1970), pp. 25–40 and 19–39.

ROBINSON NEWCOMB

Housing and Other Construction*

INTRODUCTION

Forecasting construction requires that attention be paid to seven major aspects of the industry: (1) Construction is a durable goods industry whose end products have an unusually long life; (2) Construction serves the entire economy: production distribution, consumption, and both public and private sectors; (3) Construction is not a growth industry in the sense that it grows faster than the economy as a whole. It accounted for about 11% of GNP in the twenties and now accounts for under 10% (9.9% in the five years 1967–71); (4) Its efficiency, both direct and indirect, is increasing; (5) Its market is heavily affected by governmental actions, again both directly and indirectly; (6) Its markets can change dramatically over time: residential construction has varied from 0.8% to 6.4% of GNP in particular years; (7) Changes in engineering can have tremendous impact on markets—as when new traffic control methods increase highway lane capacity manyfold at a small fraction of the cost of equivalent additional lanes or overpasses.

1. Because the end products of construction have a relatively long life (averaging possibly 60 years or more for hous-

* This chapter was written in 1970 and the spring of 1971.

ing), construction does not add 3% to the stock of existing facilities in major categories in any one year. A change in demand of 3% for the end product could nearly wipe out a market, or double it—in any category and in any location.

2. Because construction serves the entire economy, its volume reflects what is happening to the entire economy. If one category in the economy is weakening but another is becoming stronger, construction for the first category may weaken, but at the same time it is likely to be getting stronger for the second category. So the ratio of construction to the entire economy does not change greatly from year to year, except when drastic changes occur in the economy itself, as in the thirties and in wartimes.

3. Possibly because relatively modest increases in the demand for an end product of construction (as housing or highways) can cause a boom in the demand for construction of that end product, construction has been thought of as a growth industry. It has tended to overbuild at times, but this is followed by periods of relatively low activity. Construction overbuilt, in market terms, during 1925–29, reaching 12.5% of GNP in 1925, then it stopped rising as a proportion of GNP. It dropped in physical terms, though GNP was still rising, in 1928 and dropped to 10.5% of the economy in

271

1929 (a drop of 2.2 points and over 20%). High employment needs for the products of construction were not met in the thirties and the early forties, so it was not until 1946 that the industry began to attack the backlog of market demand that developed in these years. Construction reached about 11.4% of GNP while attacking this backlog. The attack was interrupted by the Korean War, and it was not until roughly 1963–65 that the backlog was largely taken care of. Then the ratio of construction to the economy dropped toward what may be its long-term relationship. Should the GNP approximate $1.255 trillion in 1973, and construction remain at its 1967–71 ratio of 9.9%, it would total about $123 billion in 1973. But even that high figure would be 10% less than it would be under the 11% ratio of the 1920s. The fact that construction is somewhat erratic should not be interpreted to mean that it is a growth industry. That can lead to serious marketing difficulties. This is illustrated by chart 1.

Variations in the relationship of construction to the economy are of course a result of the adequacy of the current stock of facilities for the current level of economic activity, of changes in standards of adequacy, changes in the economy which alter standards of adequacy, changes in the cost of construction, and of competition from other claimants. As adequate data are not available on several of these variables, it has not been possible to secure good forecasting results from econometric models alone.

4. The direct efficiency of the construction industry is increasing. This means that decreasing amounts of manpower and material but greater amounts of equipment are used per unit of end product. This is happening in part through osmosis—improvements in technology and techniques developed in other industries are picked up by contractors, engineers, and architects. It is also an indigenous development.

As firms get large (several are in the billion dollar category) it becomes necessary for them to increase their efficiency to survive. They are doing so very effectively, and smaller firms are copying them—or at times, leading them.

Efficiency is increasing indirectly. If a new machine will turn out twice as many widgets per hour as its predecessor and take up less space, a tripling of output of widgets could be accomplished with a 50% increase in the factory space devoted to the fabrication process. Less factory construction is needed year by year per unit of FRB capacity added.

5. The market for construction is heavily affected by governmental actions. It is heavily affected directly because government expenditures tend to be about half of private expenditures. But they are not a constant 50%. They were 51% of private expenditures in 1967 and 45% in 1960. Public hospital construction rose 60% between 1966 and 1969, while miscellaneous public building outlays rose 50%. Meanwhile conservation expenditures dropped 32%. If formulae for public construction are put into a computer, it must be on a judgment basis.

The market for construction is heavily affected indirectly because governments change rules affecting construction. Rules on depreciation allowances, subsidies, investment credit, savings and loan reserve ratios, FHA processing, etc., are changed from time to time, and occasionally with a large impact on the market for construction.

6. Markets can change dramatically over time. The variation of 700% in the proportion of GNP accounted for by residential construction is not a unique phenomenon. Office building may go in spurts city by city. Airports and highways may displace railroads and railroads displace canals. Microwave relay stations may displace overhead telephone lines. What sold in the past may not sell in the future.

7. Engineering developments may result in important changes in construction volume. This is similar to the last point, but whereas that point relates to the impact of outside technology, this one relates more to technology within the industry itself. Two such examples are the competition of ultra-sonic vibrators with pile drivers, and of prestressed concrete with steel beams. When Hoover Dam was built, expensive cooling pipes were installed in the dam to absorb most of the heat of crystallization. Now ice is mixed with cement (a trick the Russians knew 75 years ago) and expensive piping need not be installed or left in the dam. As Mr. Barnes showed in Baltimore and New York, a bucket of paint may add as much capacity to the street system as would a new street. Such things do not mean just more efficient construction, they may mean breakthroughs which multiply—or diminish—markets. They made it possible to forecast a cessation to the growth in highway expenditures (in constant dollars) in 1965, even while the vast new interstate system was getting under way. A good forecaster should have at least an acquaintance with developments in engineering.

RESIDENTIAL LONG-RANGE FORECASTING

My grandmother used to tell about the days when women's skirts got longer and

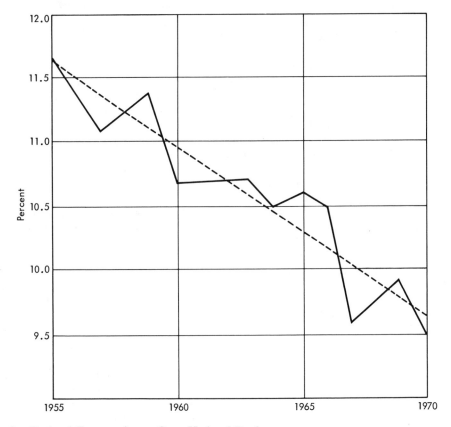

Chart 1   Ratio of Construction to Gross National Product

longer, and trailed the floor for greater and greater distances. Finally a friend of hers had her dressmaker make a dress with a three-foot train. But by the time the dressmaker delivered the dress the style had changed, and ankle length skirts were in again. Housing markets may not change quite that dramatically, but housing is a consumer good, and as such is subject to very marked changes in demand. People change their aspirations as well as their actions over time.

This can be illustrated by one of the most basic of human phenomena—the birthrate. The birthrate dropped 50% from 1910 to 1933, then rose 37% from 1933 to 1954.[1] It dropped over 30% between 1954 and 1968. It started to rise again in 1969, but turned down again in 1971.

Such changes in aspirations and actions may have major erratic impacts on particular markets and institutions, including housing, even though GNP as a whole rises steadily. Personal consumption expenditures were at an all-time peak in 1947, but housing expenditures as a percent of total expenditures hit a 20-year low (9% as compared with 15% in 1929, a drop of 40% in 20 years). But by 1967, 20 years later, expenditures for housing were 14.5% of all consumer expenditures, up 60%. Specific markets, including housing markets, can fluctuate greatly. Do not assume a constant ratio of the housing market to any other market, or to anything else.

However, changes may fluctuate around a norm or a trend. The 1971 annual report of the Council of Economic Advisers showed that 14.9% of personal consumption expenditures went to housing in 1970, almost the same as the 15% that went for housing in 1929.[2] The reported ratio fluctuated very widely, as did the ratio of new residential construction to consumer expenditures. Both may continue to fluctuate in the seventies, but barring major economic difficulties the fluctuation may be comparatively minor.

The forecaster must remember that people change, that the changes may affect housing, and that the changes may fluctuate around a norm even though the norm may be changing slowly.

The forecaster must remember also that people—workers and students alike—feel frustrated by the boredom that now seems to accompany the repetitive operations necessary to mass production and its resulting abundance. An obvious result of this is continued emphasis on more sophisticated production equipment, and less emphasis on unskilled and semiskilled labor. This trend will encourage unemployment among lower skilled workers and make housing markets in the central city, and other areas with largely unskilled workers, more hazardous. Either we train people—and that means we train them for service jobs and give service jobs status—or we will have uncomfortably large unemployment, a heavy dole, and a poor rental housing market (though possibly a large government underwritten market), particularly in central cities.

In addition, the forecaster must remember that the economy will have to offset the effects of both a high standard of living and crowded conditions on the environment. That means more dispersal, more suburban and exurban living. Smog in some cities is affected to a large degree by city stop-and-go driving. A car traveling rapidly on a freeway may omit only 10% of what it emits on a crowded stop-and-go city street. Sewage disposal can be handled more cheaply in small dispersed centers than in large centralized operations. Such things will encourage suburban living. Dispersal to the suburbs and to exurbia will be further encouraged by lengthening vacations and long weekends. In the suburbs it is easier and safer to keep a boat or a sports car, it is easier to get the kids to a swimming pool, it is easier to have

[1] Department of Health, Education, and Welfare, *Vital Statistics Analysis*, Series 21, #19, 1970.

[2] 1971 *Annual Report*, table C-10.

an impact on the board of education or the police department or the department of streets and lighting.

Studies at the Michigan Survey Center and elsewhere show that many times as many people want to move even farther out as prefer to live downtown. With rising incomes, they can afford space around them and they will get it. They want to get away from riots and the frustration of crowded streets. Despite efforts to gild the ghettos and protect central city values, industry and people will continue to move to the country, as will housing.

The forecaster must also remember that inflation will encourage investment in suburbs. Even if inflation drops to less than 2% per year by 1980 and averages 2.25% in the decade, that inflation will mean a 25% price increase over 10 years. It will help keep ownership cheaper than renting and prove a check to the growth of rental living. It will also possibly be a stimulus to cooperative and condominium housing.

With these caveats in mind, the long-range forecaster will examine the prospects for five things in particular: (1) the economy, (2) household formation, (3) the proportion of household and public income allotted to housing, (4) the types of housing the market will support, and (5) public and private funds available for new home financing and at what cost.

The Economy

The state of the economy is basic to the demand for housing. It is as important as demographic conditions. If incomes are rising, a given size and mix of the population will pay for far more new housing than it will pay for if incomes are falling. The reported number of new units started in 1933 was only 10% of what it had been eight years earlier and 12% of what it had been five years earlier. The decline was due only to a small degree to the oversupply which

existed in 1928, in terms of 1928 incomes. It was due largely to the 47% decline in per capita incomes.

The ratio of private residential construction outlays to total consumer expenditures during the years 1929–70 varied from 1% to 7.5%. In the sixties the ratio varied from 4.8% to 6.7%, a range of 40%. And in the last two decades the number of nonfarm conventional starts per year varied from 1.17 to 1.95 million, a range of 67%. The ratio of private expenditures for residential construction to total consumer expenditures on housing alone also has varied greatly. It was 23.4% in 1929, 4.4% in 1933, 42.5% in 1947, 23.5% in 1967, and about 22.7% in 1970. The variation in the last decade alone was from 23.1% to 32.7%, a range of 39%.

A study made for the National Planning Association sometime ago indicated that with housing starts at 100 for an annual growth in GNP of 1.8%, a GNP growth of 2.4% per year could yield a housing starts figure of 110, and a 3% GNP growth could yield a starts figure of 121. The forecaster must have a clear concept of the coming economy, or work in terms of a well-understood range for that economy.

Household Formation

The next problem that must be tackled is the probable volume of household formation in the light of the anticipated income and age and sex distribution of the population in the period for which the forecast is made. Household formation will of course be affected not only by the economy but also by attitudes toward children, responsibility toward society, etc. It depends on age and sex distribution, income and income distribution, proclivity to marriage and divorce, and the tendency to set up or keep separate quarters in each age group.

Forecasting household formation has proved much more difficult than might be expected. It is relatively easy to project population by age and sex in the household formation ages. Those who will form households in the next decade have already been born. Only a relatively few unknown factors of significance exist (for instance, the size of the armed forces at home and abroad). But it is difficult to estimate how many other than husband and wife households will be formed, because this varies markedly over time, and with changes in income. Even sophisticated projectors missed much of this. The projected B series put out by the census in 1962 gave an increase for 1960–65, in the number of primary individuals, of 1,200,000. The increase reported in the 1965 Census Report, P-20, No. 140, was 1,640,000. The increase in three years was 37% greater than forecast. The Series B projections for primary families other than husband-wife households were 31% too low, and for husband and wife households, about 10% too high. The census was in error again from 1965 to 1970. The lowest increase projected in 1967 for 1967–70 on the increase in the number of husband-wife households was a third too high. The highest increase for the number of primary individuals was a third too low.

Some of the error in the number of husband–wife households was due to the increase in the armed forces, particularly in the number of men stationed abroad. But a major part of the error was due to a shift in the tendency of individuals to set up their own households early in life, and of the tendency of widows and widowers and other older people to maintain separate quarters rather than to move in with children or relatives at ages at which this was commonly done in previous decades.

Despite the difficulty, the forecaster must estimate the market. One of the factors mentioned earlier, a tendency to fluctuate around a norm even if the norm itself is moving, may be helpful. The sharp increase in other than husband–wife households may not continue in the seventies. The possibilities must be evaluated for each age group

and a projection made by household type—including widows and widowers, as well as by other types of single person and nonmarried couple households.[3]

As this book is not a forecast but a study in techniques of forecasting, the following example is given for illustrative purposes only. It is not a forecast. However, using the techniques suggested the forecaster may decide that the proportion of the market taken by husband–wife households may not drop as much this decade as it did in the last decade. The age distribution will favor the married couple household more. The sharp rise in "other households" such as we saw particularly from 1950 to 1960, and a trifle less dramatically from 1960 to 1970, could be moderated somewhat in the seventies. If the proportion of husband–wife households does not drop much below 70% by 1980, the July 1980 count could be as much as 53.7 million, for an increase of 9.1 million over the 1970 figure. Other households could increase about 4.7 million. The growth from 1970–75 could be about 6.5 million (an average of 1.3 million per year of which about two-thirds could be married couples and one-third other households). From 1975 to 1980 under these premises the total growth could be 7.3 million, with 4.8 married couples and 2.5 other households.

Migration of households has a major impact on local markets but a smaller impact on national markets. If the estimate of the average increase in net households for a given period is 1.1 million per year, the fact that there may be a decline in the number

---

[3] Basic source data are to be found in the Census Bureau P-20, pp. 25, 60, and related series. Analytical studies such as *Marriage and Divorce* by Hugh Carter and Paul Douglas (Washington: Howard University Press, 1969) are helpful in forming judgments. Housing goal projections of HUD must be used very cautiously. Original data in them are useful, but the selection of and use made of these data can be misleading. The census publication, *The Methods and Materials of Demography* is very informative.

in some communities or even states will not mean an appreciable increase in total demand. It will mean that replacements for abandoned housing (a subject discussed later) will be built in growing rather than in declining areas. But the amount of additional housing needed to replace units left idle in declining communities because out-migration in these communities is greater than in-migration plus natural increase, is very small for the country as a whole. But the effect on the market may be appreciable in a particular locality where rent control or other factors discourage maintenance, or where migration to the suburbs or out of the state helps reduce the central city population. The resulting local market is not a function of household growth, but more a function of local social and economic developments and their impact on migration. Net migration from the farm is dwindling, while migration from the cities to exurbia is growing. Abandonment and replacement of substandard rural housing will therefore be less important in the seventies than it has been in the last several decades.

Private and Government Income Allocations to Housing

A third controlling factor is the amount and proportion of personal and governmental income allotted to housing. The simplest way to illustrate this may be to relate residential construction to GNP. The ratio has varied greatly over time. Private investment in housing has varied from 3.5% of GNP in 1929 to 0.8% in 1933, 6.4% in 1950, 4.3% in 1960, and 3.5% in 1970. The proportion in 1970 was about 6% lower than it had been in 1966. Fluctuation in the seventies need not be as great as this, and at least for long-range forecasting for this decade, it probably will be safe to assume that, on the average, funds invested in residential construction will not be far from the 3.5% of GNP that they were in 1929. They aver-

aged about 3.7% in the sixties, but that was a period in which housing standards were increased very markedly, and in which construction costs rose faster than other costs. As will be discussed later, housing costs in the seventies may be restrained by the competition of industrialized housing, such as mobile homes. If the forecaster reaches the conclusion that the market may not require an average of over 2.1 million units per year from 1970 to 1975, and as about 1.8 million units (including mobile and public housing units) were added in 1970, he will reach the conclusion also that the market will grow more slowly on the average from 1970 to 1975 than the GNP. The fact that the average unit size will be less from 1970 to 1975 than it was from 1965 to 1969 will help support this view.

If the analysis indicates also that the market may not grow as much from 1975 to 1980 as the economy, 3.5% of GNP may be an adequate figure on the average for residential construction in the seventies. This is a smaller proportion of the economy than it was in the fifties and sixties. It is a figure the economy can support. And the cost for the decade as a whole, though not in every year, will be competitive. Whether the structure of financial institutions and the savings habits of households will be as well or better adapted to this market as they were from 1945 to 1965 must be brought into the analysis.

Undoubling need not be taken into account for long-range national projections. Some doubling is bound to occur for other than income reasons, and the early 1970 volume may be representative of the average amount during the current decade.

Types of Housing

The fourth controlling factor is the types of housing the market will support. Housing types may be categorized in many ways. For the purposes of this analysis they are categorized as follows:

1. New
   a. Single family
   b. Multifamily
   c. Owner occupied
   d. Rental
   e. Expensive
   f. Moderate
   g. Low cost
   h. Second home
2. Rehabilitated
   a. Central city
   b. Other.

The above categories overlap and compete with each other as well as with other markets.

The market for new housing is the outcome of (1) changing standards and changing urban patterns which result in the net abandonment of more existing units than pure physical wear and tear would cause; (2) replacement of less from calamities, as well as of loss resulting from changing land use, and from governmental action; (3) second house demands; and (4) changes in vacancy rates. The market for second homes is small but growing, and to date has been affected by the availability of rental housing and trailer units.

Standards vary with changes in community size and organization, income, and distribution of family sizes. The percentage of rental units tends to rise with city size and density. But the growth of urban areas has been declining, particularly the central part of urban areas. This has been forecast for years.[4] The Census Bureau reported an annual metropolitan growth rate of 2.0% for metropolitan areas under 250,000 for the years 1960 to 1966[5] and of 1.6% for areas over 250,000. But its projections from 1965 to 1975 call for an annual growth rate for all metropolitan areas of only 1.1%.[6] The areas in the northeast and north central

parts of the country, which are projected as having 55% of the metropolitan population by 1975, are indicated as likely to grow only 0.7% per year. Areas in the west, which are projected as having 20% of the metropolitan population, are indicated as likely to grow by 2.25% per year, a drop of about 50% from the 1950–60 rate, and 25% of the 1960–65 rate. This decline in rates of growth, combined with a tendency for suburbs to grow faster than central cities, may reduce the rate of growth of rental versus owner occupied units. On the other hand, the increase in the proportion of young and old families will push in the other direction. The forecaster must weigh the impact of such trends before predicting the market for the two types of new units.

The average cost of units built is reported to have risen over 25% during the sixties for both private and public housing, despite the shift toward apartments. About 63% of all new housing sales in 1963 were for less than $20,000, and only 9% brought over $30,000 in that year. But by 1969 only 26% (41% as large a proportion) sold under $20,000. That year 35% (four times as large a rate) sold for over $30,000. The median price rose 42%. But that does not mean that prices will continue to rise at this rate during the seventies. The change in the age distribution will bring a curb to the rise. Both the young and old families can accept two or three rather than four or five bedrooms, for instance. The reported average cost per single family privately financed house started down in the second half of 1969, and has continued to drop to the time this is written (March 1970).[7] In projecting the size and price distribution of housing in the seventies, the forecaster must weigh changes in family and household size, age, income, and attitude toward housing.

[4] See, for instance *Appraisal Journal* (July 1964), pp. 376 *et seq*.

[5] Metropolitan Area Statistics, tables 1 and 2, Bureau of the Census.

[6] Series P-25, #415, table A, Bureau of the Census.

[7] Note: As this goes to press in the winter of 1972 the data show a resumption of the rise in prices in January 1971, which was interrupted early in 1972. See *Housing and Urban Development Trends,* Sept. 1972, tables A-10 and A-11.

Two social rather than economic trends need to be kept in mind. The difficulty in securing tenant cooperation in apartment maintenance is raising the cost of that maintenance, and to some extent it is raising construction costs. It also is discouraging, at least to some degree, the construction of moderate or low income rental housing in central cities. It has not discouraged such construction as much in the suburbs. And at least partially because of maintenance problems, condominiums are receiving increased attention. Apartment type units are more readily adapted to condominium management than are single units, so this will encourage apartment—but not necessarily apartment-for-rent—construction.

The replacement market is difficult to quantify. Studies by the National Association of Home Builders suggest it is approximately 700,000 per year and growing.[8] The 1970 census suggests a total loss of existing units during the sixties of 5.5 million, or about 550,000 per year on the average. But this figure too must be an estimate, as many second homes were not counted. Few studies have been made of the effective life of mobile homes. Those that have been made are rough guides only, as mobile homes are becoming more substantial and their life-span may be increasing. It may be at least two years before good data are available on the loss from the housing stock from all causes during the sixties. The analyst can keep abreast of reports on governmental demolition for development, for transportation facilities, and for other reasons, and keep abreast of the somewhat scattered demolition permit data that are available. However, for long-range forecasting purposes he may feel that it will be unnecessary to use a more detailed allowance than a figure of 1% of the existing stock as being removed from the market each year.

Second homes are probably a growing market. Unfortunately, instructions given

census enumerators caused them to ignore many second homes in the 1970 count. The latest data we have are taken from 1967 surveys, and these data indicate the market is growing. Several corporations have made private studies which support this judgment. The market still is small and relatively localized. Anyone interested in it should secure some of the private studies, or at least discuss their implication with those familiar with them.

The rehabilitation market as distinguished from the new market is a melding of a barrel of monkeys and a kettle of worms. It is amorphous, messed up, slippery, changing and, to be conservative, difficult to predict. When good new housing becomes unusable in five years or so, but from an engineering standpoint could be readily rehabilitated, it is not likely to be rehabilitated. What is the use of fixing it up if the plumbing will be torn out and sold in a few months or weeks? And neither is it likely to be replaced. The occupants, however, will move to other units as they make existing ones uninhabitable. The previous occupants of the units they take over will move to still other units, usually better ones. The result tends to be a spreading of slum areas and a migration of the middle and upper income groups to the suburbs or to government subsidized upper income enclaves such as L'Enfant Plaza.

This type of urban decay will not be halted until the occupants of the decaying neighborhoods feel that they have a stake in their neighborhood and in their city. This is a social and a political problem and one that the housing forecaster cannot be expected to reduce to numbers. Nor can he be expected to forecast when present trends will be changed. Again, he may find his results just as accurate if he assumes no increase in the proportion of the total market to be served by rehabilitation, as they will be if he makes elaborate studies of what is being done.

In part this will be true because the rehabilitated market is a semantic term. What was good housing in 1949 may not be

[8] See also "Financing Housing for the Next Decade," 1966, *NAHB Index* 30.07, p. 10.

considered good housing in 1969. Standards change. I never lived in a unit with an indoor water closet until I went to college. And I did not consider myself or my family imposed upon. But were I to go back to that type of house today, I would "rehabilitate" it before moving in. And as Twentieth Century FUND studies[9] showed, many well-maintained units exist in decayed neighborhoods. If the neighborhoods are to be rehabilitated, many good units will be destroyed in the process. The rehabilitation market for central cities is largely a political, not an economic market.

The market outside of central cities is more nearly a free market. Farm output per man-hour rose 80% in the sixties (6% per year compounded annually) and farm income on viable farms increased, while the number of farms dropped. Some of the units vacated by death or migration of farmers offer opportunity to families leaving the city, and some are rehabilitated. But the number is decreasing. The long-range forecaster may be as accurate if he makes no allowance for this figure as if he computes it carefully on the basis of reports from the Department of Agriculture. Of course, specialists (such as certain groups of real estate brokers) need good data on the subject. But, their needs are for specific relatively local data, and rarely for long-range data.

This has major implications for the number of vacant units the market can accept. If vacancies are a result of rising standards, 700,000 a year may leave the market, without reducing the effective demand for new units. But if vacancies are a result of neglect, of tenant refusal to treat his unit with respect, vacancies may rise at the same time that crowding rises and standards drop. Vacancy figures of any given size must be checked against the reason for the vacancy, before they are used as a guide to housing markets.

[9] *America's Needs and Resources*, 1955, chapter 7.

Home Construction Funding

The last category, availability and cost of public and private funds for new home financing, may be somewhat easier to forecast in the seventies than in the sixties. With the main backlog of demand met and with the average size of new units declining rather than rising, the proportion of savings going into housing may drop in this decade. And with the federal agencies (FHA, FNMA, HLBB and its subsidiaries) available and more than willing, mortgage funds will be competitive with at least second-grade bond issues. At times they will carry lower rates than some first-grade issues.[10] For the long run, therefore, mortgage money will not be the problem in the seventies it was at times in the sixties.

Two qualifications should be made to this statement. The first is that money may be subsidized at times, as was the case in 1971 and 1972. This will accelerate construction temporarily, and reduce the volume later on. Careful analysis is needed of the rate at which construction is being accelerated or hindered by government operations for short-term analysis, and for judgments as to how such governmental intervention may modify long-term trends over two- or three-year periods.

The second qualification is more illusive. Governmental subsidy of middle income housing will reduce quality or increase costs or both, and will create neighborhood tensions. The "free" market is far from perfect, but governmental intervention makes it more arbitrary and frustrating. This will boomerang on Congress and the administration and cause changes in policy and administration which will have further reverberations in the market. This will mean more distortions and possibly a smaller margin in the long run.[11]

[10] This was true when this was written in April 1971.
[11] Supra.

Long-run forecasting of the housing market may be a simpler task than short-range forecasting, but it is still not an easy task.

SHORT-RANGE RESIDENTIAL FORECASTING

Short-range forecasting in this context is assumed to mean forecasting one year ahead. This is a more ticklish operation than long-range forecasting. The same types of data which are used in long-range forecasting are used to the extent that they are available. The most important use of the data is as a basis for making adjustments for short-run deviation from long-time trends in any one or all of the forces at play. Short-range changes in money supply and price, in government policies, and in economic conditions all have important short-range impacts.

Serious difficulties will come from the unavailability or delayed availability of data, as well as from the difficulty in interpreting data which we do have. If a forecast is being made in November for the volume of housing expected in the following year, census data for instance will be at hand as to number of households found by the sample census only through March of the current year. There will be no data on the increase in the number of households during the current year, and equally important, the data on the increase in households over the year ending in March of the current year will not be usable. Figures on the increase in households in any one year are derived by subtracting the previous sample estimate from the current year's sample estimate. If the estimate for the preceding year was 1% too high and the estimate for the current year 1% too low and the actual growth in households is 2%, the census report would indicate little or no increase in the number of households, not 2%. On the other hand, if

the previous year was 1% too low and the current year 1% too high, the census report could show a 4% increase in one year. Obviously this is an extreme illustration, but the point is valid. The P-20 series on household formation gives no valid data or even clues as to the increase in the number of households in any one year. Projection of the probable volume of household formation must depend on current trends in income, analysis of the age distribution at the time, and current changes in trends in marriages and deaths.

Elaborate statistical efforts have been made to work out formulae for short-run forecasting. The problems that we have been discussing suggest that a mathematical approach faces at least three almost insurmountable difficulties. First, data on which projections might be based are not available in time; second, the data that do become available are highly questionable; and third, the significance of the data varies sharply year by year.

The safest technique for short-run forecasting in the residential field depends on the use of averages for long-run trends, and a modification of these averages by what is believed to be the impact of the changing politics, economy, and financial conditions of the year ahead. If, for instance, at the point in the cycle at which the forecast is being made, the average household annual formation projection is 1,400,000, but money will be relatively scarce and expensive in the year ahead, and the marriage rate will have been checked because of the slow rate of growth in the economy, and deaths are rising, it may be safe to assume that household formation will not be over 1,300,000 in the coming year, and it may be lower, even though census data last year suggested that household formation was rising.

It may be helpful to remind ourselves of the dangers in the use of marriage data. Married couples account for from 60% to 75% of the increase in occupied units, but the proportion changes from year to year. A marriage may mean a reduction in the number of households. With a high proportion of single people occupying their own units, a marriage may mean that where there were two occupied units now there is only one. And a death may not mean a unit is being abandoned—the widow or widower may stay on—or it may mean that a unit is being abandoned. So year-to-year changes in the number of marriages need bear no direct relationship to year-to-year changes in the number of housing units being occupied or being built. Marriage data are clues to attitudes, demands for housing, and family formation, but they are not exact indexes of trends.

The proclivity to household formation, and to changes in housing standards, will be affected year by year not only by the state of the economy and by basic demographic factors, but also by federal intervention in the market. Section 608 starts rose from 51,000 in 1947 to 143,000 in 1950. FHA 235 and 236 starts rose from 1,388 in 1968 to 228,544 in 1970. Government subsidy was granted to 47,000 new units in 1957 and to 430,000 new units in 1970. The number to be subsidized was projected in the 1972 budget submission to reach 680,000 in 1972.[12] The short-term forecaster must keep abreast not only of administration plans but also of congressional support for these plans.

Once the impact has been measured of governmental, general economic, and demographic factors on the demand for housing for the coming year, the next step is to analyze the supply probabilities.

One of the first things to look at, of course, is the availability and price of money. Advice of financial experts is important here. Is the flow of funds to savings and loan associations likely to continue during the coming year? Will commercial banks be in a position to invest a larger or smaller proportion of their assets in home and apart-

ment financing next year? What are they likely to do? Similarly, what are insurance companies likely to do?

Projection of the flow of savings into institutions which emphasize home mortgage financing is a very ticklish business. The flow of such savings may be relatively higher in downswings than in upswings in the economy. It is not safe to assume that because the economy is improving, savings and loans will have appreciably more money. Nor is it safe to assume the reverse. Comparative dividend rates, aggressiveness, ability to shift funds from the east to the west, and vice versa must all be taken into consideration in projecting the flow of funds available and used for home mortgage financing by savings and loan associations and mutual savings banks.

The growth of FNMA, GNMA, the HLMC, the Farmer's Home Administration, etc., is now a major factor in home mortgage financing. During 1969 and 1970 these institutions accounted for 28% of the growth of the home mortgage debt. From 1965–1970 their holdings increased by over 230% while commercial bank holdings grew by less than 30%. And in addition to their holdings, these governmental intermediaries had sold a large volume of home mortgages to institutions whose purchases would otherwise have been much smaller.

In addition to being important suppliers of funds, federal and federally regulated intermediaries such as the Home Loan Bank Board are important regulators of the supply of funds. They can turn on the spigot, even when it is done at a loss, as at times in 1970. Or they can turn off funds as happened in 1966. Judgment as to the volume and price of mortgage money that will be made available by conscious decision rather than by the free working of the market place, is necessary to any short-run forecast.

This judgment must be related to the amount and type of subsidy, such as the 235, 236, and GNMA subsidies previously men-

[12] 1972 *Budget*, Special Analysis, table N-3, p. 212.

tioned that will be made available in the coming year. This, of course, is more a function of congressional decision than is the unsubsidized FNMA and HLBMC operation. The combination of conscious control of the volume and price of funds supplied through governmental and governmentally regulated intermediaries, and of federal subsidy, can determine the short-range volume of housing starts within relatively small limits.

That does not mean, however, that governmental forecasts will be accurate. These forecasts may be indicators of administration hopes rather than administration capacity. The competent forecaster must decide what the government actually can accomplish as distinguished from what he believes the government wants to accomplish, hopes to accomplish, and expects to accomplish.

An implicit assumption in the long-range forecast analysis was the expectation that housing would be competitive with other goods, costwise. The supply and cost of home mortgages will be more competitive in the seventies than they were in the late sixties, for instance. The use of industrial technology, as developed in the production of mobile housing, will help hold down construction cost. More urban highways will increase the amount of available land and help check the rise in land prices. But such developments do not come all at once or at steady rates. The short-run forecaster must judge whether or not adequate accommodations will be made in the coming year. It took builders several years after World War II to learn that more three-bedroom than two-bedroom houses would be needed. It has recently taken a long time for builders to learn that two-bedroom units are again in demand. A development that seems obvious to the analyst may not be as obvious to the builder, so there may be a lag between the development and the satisfaction of a new or a modified market. This tends to reduce the volume of starts as the new market de-

velops, then to result in a rush, and possible overbuilding as the new market is recognized. Fluctuations in supply will be greater than fluctuations in demand.

It is necessary therefore to watch the psychology and the actions of builders. What are builders and mortgagees telling the National Association of Home Builders and the mortgage trade associations? Is usable evidence coming from the Census Bureau or elsewhere suggesting that the houses being built are selling more rapidly or less rapidly than usual? Is there evidence that FHA offices are tougher or slower than usual, or are they operating more rapidly than formerly?

Such attitudes are more important than might appear at first glance, because the home building industry is being composed of larger and larger firms; that is, the home builders who are succeeding tend to put up more houses per builder than they formerly did. A small group puts up expensive custom-built houses, but a higher percentage of residential construction is now handled by men turning out over 20 units per year. This means advance arrangements must be made for land, materials, and financing. Attitudes in the fall, therefore, are likely to be reflected in the starts in the spring, if not in the starts in the fall of the next year.

The National Association of Home Builders publishes a monthly magazine which is useful in indicating builder attitudes, actions, and expectations. The NAHB also puts out frequent economic analyses which report on the latest data in the field, such as starts and savings flows, as well as builders' plans and expectations.

The experience of real estate dealers also reflects what is happening in the field. The National Association of Real Estate Boards releases monthly data on volume, by price breakdown, of sales of existing housing. These data show by major geographic regions how much is being sold at what price. As two to three existing houses are sold for each new house sold, this gives early clues to market trends. And NAREB's quarterly review of mortgage availability and price is useful in indicating how smoothly the market is functioning and where changes seem to be developing.

Of course, the monthly data for starts and building permits published by the Census Bureau, as well as the Dodge data, must be watched regularly. It is safer to use the data themselves without seasonal adjustment, as the seasonal adjustment is based on the calendar rather than on the weather. The seasonal adjustment is affected by what the weather was in the past, rather than by what the weather is this year. If demand is good but the weather bad, the current seasonally adjusted figures may suggest a serious decline in starts (but not necessarily in permits). The fact that the number of starts is below projected averages may in this case mean there is a big backlog of demand, not that housing is proving unprofitable. The building permit series is safer to use than the starts series, because weather has less effect on the issuance of permits than it does on starts, and, of coure, because the sample from which the permit figures are derived is bigger than the sample from which the starts series is built up. Also, the permit series suggests what starts may be, the starts series what they have been.

Except for appropriation bills, not much allowance need be made for changes in legislation, for short-run forecasting. It usually takes more than one year for even an important change in legislation to have much impact. There are exceptions, of course. When 608 fell out of favor with the government, this had a big impact on multi-family starts. But usually changes in legislation affect the availability of funds and terms on which the funds may be made available only over a somewhat extended period. It takes both contractors and financial groups time to make the adjustments the government wants. The effort to reduce residential construction in 1950 was successful in cutting back residential construction in 1951.

Actually, 1950 was the biggest year on record until 1971. The revised housing starts series for 1950 is 1,952,000 million units.

Of course, it is not always safe to assume that intervention by the government will be followed by results which are the opposite of those which the government intends. But it is at least safe to assume that the results which the government wants to achieve probably will not be achieved in the immediate future.

Little has been said in this discussion about mobile homes. Shipments of mobile homes increased from 7.4% of the total number of residential units provided in 1960 to 21.6% in 1969. They accounted for most of the sales in the under $15,000 bracket. Their success was due to many factors: less rigid building code restraints, small down payments, small monthly payments, provision of furniture, low maintenance problems, low taxes, and availability of financing even when builders of houses were having difficulty finding mortgage money. The very success of mobile homes may result in their becoming less important as a distinct class. The industrial techniques they developed will be made available to conventional houses. Many mobile home builders will become builders of modules which conventional builders can buy, or which will be installed by the manufacturer as part of a conventional home package. So the significance of the mobile home may not be in the number produced under the mobile home label, but rather in how they help reduce or at least check the rise in the cost of producing conventional homes. Whether the number sold per year rises to 500,000 or to a larger or a smaller figure may be a matter of definition. The industry is making its impact now, regardless of how that impact is counted.

Rental markets differ from sales markets. While all ages and incomes, and all types of households are represented among renters, the distribution is not the same as it is among buyers. Nevertheless, the techniques to use in forecasting rental are similar to those used in forecasting single-family housing. We must ask: What is the break between multifamily and single-family this year? Is it out of line or about what is to be expected? Is it likely to swing back because it has swung too far? Is the demand next year likely to be relatively stronger for one than for the other?

Somewhat better data are available on multifamily markets than on single-family markets. The National Association of Real Estate Boards, for instance, compiles careful reports on multifamily structures selected from among those managed by some of the more competent management firms. The reporting is well handled, so that the documents yield valuable evidence about the rates of return for the types of structures being reported upon. It may be, of course, that different types of buildings, or buildings located elsewhere, would yield higher returns in each city. With the movement of rental and multifamily housing to the suburbs, it is necessary to break the data down by area in the city as well as by price and type, before judgments can be reached as to whether the market is saturated or not. But at least as long as the buildings being reported on yield good returns, no matter what the census vacancy data may suggest, it may be that well-managed structures are paying. When these buildings fail to yield good returns, that may be evidence that the existing market is in trouble—though even then other markets might be profitable.

The market for rental housing is much greater than it used to be as a result in large part of the sharp change in age distribution. It is probable that 35% to 40% of the net growth in occupied housing units in the 1970s will be rental units. But this does not mean that each city will continue to build the same proportion of rental units. This is a big country, and things tend to go by spurts in section after section. New York had a tremendous spurt, and then its volume dropped. The volume in Chicago dropped in 1963, but the volume in Cleveland that year rose as much as it dropped in Chicago. The market tends to be discovered city by city. A big drop in New York and Chicago need not discourage construction in Cleveland or Dallas. It is not necessary to get concerned about the prospects for apartment construction in the following year just because some cities are reporting overbuilding this year.

Another point to bear in mind is that the construction of rental units is shifting from downtown to the suburbs. Suburban multifamily construction is now much larger than it was a decade ago. It is necessary to look at reports on suburban construction rather than on downtown construction, in judging whether or not the market is becoming saturated in any area or in any price group.

Dodge and census data do not follow each other over short periods. One series can go up while the other series goes down, and vice versa. But over the long run, the two series behave in very similar fashion, and for the short run, the Dodge multifamily series is a better clue to the latest happenings than are the census data. For very detailed work, of course, the Dodge series provides local data much more promptly than does the census.

If a decision is reached that certain markets are saturated and others are not saturated, it is not safe to assume that the unsaturated market will pick up promptly. It may be that there is a big demand for certain types of multifamily structures, but this does not mean that those in the business will recognize this new demand promptly, or, if they do recognize it, will be able to get the financing and other resources necessary to meet the demand promptly. There tends to be a lag between the development of the demand and its recognition, and a further lag between the recognition of the demand and its satisfaction. A forecaster works under the hazard of forecasting that something which is likely to happen will happen sooner than will be the case. He sees the situation as it is or at least as he believes it is. This does not mean that others will see it that way at once. The cultural lag, or the institutional lag, or whatever it should be termed, must be allowed for in situations of this sort. A market which is already overbuilt may continue to overbuild for some time. A market which is sadly underbuilt may remain underbuilt for some time. Allowance for inertia is one of the essentials of successful forecasting.

In some respects, this allowance for inertia may be more important than it was formerly. As consumers build up their stockpile of goods, the pressure to make an immediate decision to buy something new weakens. When a family of six with an adequate income lived in a two bedroom house, almost any three- or four-bedroom unit could be sold to it. When a family of six is already living in a three- or four-bedroom house, the new opportunity must be good indeed to draw them from their present location. As highways in and around the cities improve, existing locations become more accessible to jobs throughout the entire metropolitan area. If the wage earners take new jobs, it may be less necessary than it formerly was to buy or rent a new unit.

Factors which formerly did not weigh heavily in the planning of builders must now be given more consideration by them. For instance, some families prefer to live nearer their recreation than their work. It is more important to some husbands, for instance, to be able to get to the golf course easily on Saturday morning than to get to work readily on Monday morning. New standards of value will mean that new types of housing location can be put on the market successfully. But it will take time for these new developments to be accepted by builders and by mortgagees. Construction may proceed as it used to proceed, on the assumption that sales will soon pick up—when only sales of something new may pick up.

Over the long run, the fluctuations in single-family housing may be relatively minor in the future, and fluctuations in multifamily housing may also tend to be reduced. It is possible that errors in short-range forecasting can be held within the ranges of $\pm 10\%$ in almost every year.

Revised data will come out in the spring for the previous year, and it is always a temptation to modify a short-range forecast in the light of revisions in data which have become available since the forecast was made. However, unless the revisions in the data are rather sharp, and unless developments are appreciably different than anticipated, it may be inadvisable to change the forecast. Quite often a perspective in time permits a better forecast than one made in the midst of the situation. A forecast made in November for the following year, even with less accurate data, may be more reliable than a forecast made in April using the latest data, because the tendency in April will be to project what is happening then. And what is happening then may be a reflection in considerable part of weather or strikes or other short-range phenomena whose effects will be offset by the forces weighed more carefully last November. There are times, of course, when it is obvious that a serious mistake has been made. Once this is recognized it should be accepted and corrections made.

For very short-run forecasting of, say, three or four months, and as a check on the long-run forecasting, the relationship between permits and starts can be watched. If permits with or without seasonal adjustments are holding up, the probabilities are good that the starts will pick up. If permits have been dropping and starts have not been dropping, the backlog may be smaller than anticipated, and it may be advisable to watch for either an upturn in permits or a decline in starts below the range previously expected. But this should be done separately for single-family and multifamily homes.

In essence, short-term forecasting of residential construction is a task of estimating how far the coming year will deviate from the trend. Is it getting out of line on the high or the low side, or is it about where it should be—and how long is it likely to stay that way?

COMMERCIAL AND INDUSTRIAL CONSTRUCTION

Long-Range Forecasts: Commercial Construction

Long-range forecasting of commercial construction is a more difficult art than long-range forecasting of residential construction. In the early 1920s, when the quality of automobile paint was relatively poor and cars were somewhat harder to start, garages were very important. But when paint and waxes improved, when closed cars replaced open cars, and when automatic starters became the rule, garages lost much of their importance. Cars could be parked in the street or driveway. Demand for commercial construction is affected by economic and technological changes of this sort which are not reflected in the available statistics.

The word "commercial" covers a wide range of structures, and the importance of these structures changes with time. Nevertheless, such construction can be divided into two main groups: (1) structures for trade—retail stores, recreational facilities, restaurants, garages, warehouses and (2) structures for services—office and related building construction.

The volume of construction of stores, warehouses, restaurants, etc., that will occur in the next decade will depend largely on (a) trends in the amount and composition of personal consumption and (b) space required per sales transaction.

If the volume of wholesale and retail sales rises appreciably, obviously store and similar commercial construction will be required over and above the volume needed to meet the needs of replacement and modernization. But even if there should be no increase in total sales, new construction still would be required if each sale took more floor space on the average. It might take more space, for instance, because competitive conditions required more display. And even if there were no increase in total space actually used, new construction above that needed for maintenance and replacement purposes would still be needed if migration (as from central cities to suburbs and satellites) brought significant declines in the demand for store space in some areas, and increased requirements elsewhere.

The first step in a study of the probable construction volume required to handle trade, therefore, is a projection of consumer expenditures. The relationship of consumer expenditures to GNP depends, among other things, on the volume of governmental and investment expenditures. In general, the higher either of these is, the lower the proportion left over for consumers. Assumptions must be made, therefore, about the nature of the economy during the period for which the forecast is made, and the proportion of the economy that will take the form of consumer expenditures. Ideally, the assumptions should cover expenditures for durables, nondurables, and at least some types of services, such as medical care.

In projecting consumer expenditures, it helps to remember that trends change here as in other portions of the economy. It is not safe to project the past, or even past relationships, or lags or leads. Expenditures for services accounted for about 39% of total consumer outlays in 1929, dropped to less than 31% after World War II, and are reported currently as being over 42%. A change in the trend with changes in the age and household composition of the population could affect sales volume and the market for commercial space.

Primary families accounted for about 61% of the net increase in households from 1965 to 1970.[13] They may account for over 70% of the increase from 1970 to 1975, and over 75% of the increase in the next five

[13] U.S. Census Bureau, Series P-20, #218, March 23, 1971 and earlier P-20 reports.

years. The increase in the number of households averaged 1.12 million per year from 1965 to 1970. It may exceed 1.2 million from 1970 to 1975, and approximate 1.4 million from 1975 to 1980. These are relatively modest increases, but they will affect total consumer outlays for goods, as well as the outlay mix.

There is little immediate direct relationship between the reported volume of net household formation and total reported consumer expenditures for goods in any one year. There are many reasons for this. For instance, annual reported changes in net household formation are very erratic (and subject to great errors). And net household formation in any one year averages only about 2% of the total number of existing households. So slight variations in the expenditures of existing households have more impact on sales than does the change in the number of households year by year. See table 1.

Or, shown somewhat differently, using 1964 as 100, the basic data for 1964 and succeeding years are as shown in table 2.

Nevertheless, over the long run changes in the number and composition of households does have an impact on the market demands for commercial space.

TABLE 1.   INCREASE IN EACH YEAR AS PERCENT OF INCREASE IN THE PREVIOUS YEAR

	Consumer Expenditures*		Reported Net Household Formation[†]	Sq. Ft.[‡] Commercial Contracts*
	Current Dollars	Constant Dollars		
1964	132	137	157	158
1965	121	118	67	119
1966	106	85	90	85
1967	77	59	212	33
1968	169	185	85	382
1969	95	69	79	50

* Calendar year.
† Year ending March 31 of following calendar year.
‡ Special copyrighted F. W. Dodge Corporation tabulations made for this type of analysis, of store and warehouse construction.

TABLE 2.   COMPARISON OF CONSUMER EXPENDITURES, SQ. FT. COMMERCIAL CONTRACTS AND THE NUMBER OF HOUSEHOLDS

	Consumer Expenditures*		Sq. Ft. Commercial Contracts[†]	No. of Households[‡]
	Current Dollars	Constant Dollars		
1964	100	100	100	100
1965	108	107	107	101
1966	117	113	113	103
1967	121	115	115	105
1968	132	121	121	108
1969	141	126	125	110

* For goods only.
† Calendar year, store and warehouse area.
‡ Year ending March of following calendar year.

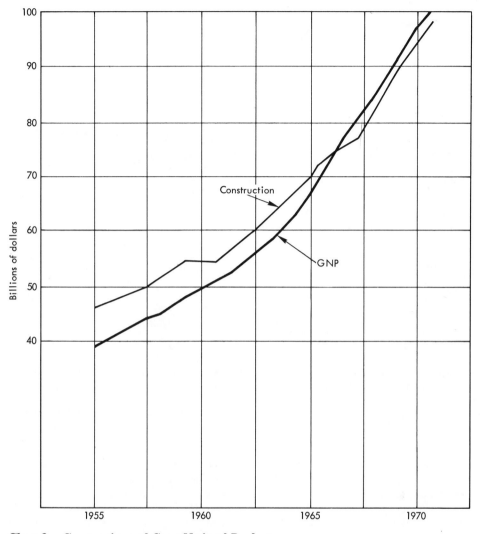

Chart 2   Construction and Gross National Product

Charts[14] three and four compare the volume of Dodge contracts for stores and warehouses, in current dollars and in square feet, with residential starts (including shipments of mobile homes), and with increase in consumer purchases of goods. Chart 3 shows that contracts rose relative to residential starts until 1968. The relationship to consumer expenditures is shown in chart 4. When related to constant dollar consumer purchases, store contract volume fell until 1966, then rose sharply. When related to current dollar purchases, store and warehouse

[14] As year-to-year fluctuations are very great, the household and residential starts figures used are for three years average growth ending in the year shown; store data are for two year averages starting in the year shown. Other ways of smoothing the curves could be used, but similar results would be secured.

Includes mobile units. Three-year moving average starts versus two-year moving average contracts, third year starts matching first year contract series.

Chart 3   Ratio of Dodge Store and Warehouse—Contracts Per Housing Unit Produced, 1960=100

contracts fell until 1966, then more or less leveled off. This suggests that the backlog of demand for store space was about taken care of by 1966 and that from 1967 to 1970 store space was added about proportionately to the rise in consumer expenditures.

Store construction is more clearly related to residential construction than to household formation, but of course household formation and residential construction are related over the long run, though not very closely over the short run. The number of conventional residential units started from 1960 through 1969 is reported as having exceeded 14.4 million. That number plus reported mobile unit shipments came to over 16.8 million (see table 3). But net household formation was reported as 11.1 million.

Over 50% more units than households were built during the decade. About a third of the construction was for replacement purposes. If a family moves from any area with plenty of stores to an area without an adequate supply, that movement increases the demand for commercial space. But the new community to which the family moves may have been provided with stores before the subdivisions around the new shopping center were filled. Or if the family moves to a new apartment, there may be no increase in the market for store space.

Residential construction is a clue to consumer expenditures, and so to the probable volume of store construction, but major attention should be given to consumer purchases. Contracts run more consistently with

290

TABLE 3. COMPARISON OF RESIDENTIAL STARTS WITH COMMERCIAL CONTRACTS LET

	Conventional Private Housing Starts	Conventional Plus Mobile Home Shipments	Commercial Contracts*
1964	100	100	100
1965	96	98	107
1966	76	80	113
1967	84	89	115
1968	99	108	121
1969	96	106	125

* As reported by F. W. Dodge.

the growth in current dollars than with the growth in constant dollar sales, on both a square foot and a dollar basis. This may be true in part because more sophisticated goods are being sold which require more space per unit of sale, and in part because current rather than constant prices determine how much can be sold. But whether current prices or constant prices are used in the calculations, it appears that the decline in store and related contracts per unit of growth in retail sales ended about 1966. The backlog of demand may have been met by that time. If the forecaster expects a rise in retail sales of the order of magnitude suggested by the NPA and many other forecasters, he may project an appreciable increase in store contracts in the seventies. A return of a sales growth rate of 3.5% or more per year in real terms might well hold contracts to approximately the 1967–69 ratio to increases in consumer purchases in current dollars.

Changes in living and commercial patterns could change this. More store space is built per 100 single-family units than per 100 multifamily units, and the peak in the ratio of apartment to total residential construction may have been approached if not reached. And trends toward computer control of inventories may already be reflected in construction volume for both stores and warehouses; some trends toward less space per sale are noticeable. But unless a major breakthrough (such as a major shift to vend-

ing machines, television shopping, or catalogue shopping) develops soon, then store, restaurant, and similar construction may grow by almost the rate maintained by consumer expenditures in constant dollars.

The analysis of this market must be made on the basis of Dodge contract data. The Commerce Department does not publish data on store or warehouse activity. But Dodge publishes detailed data monthly and with geographic breakdowns adequate for almost any purpose.

Office and Related Construction

The volume of office building and related construction over the long run will be a function in large part of white-collar employment. Such employment, as defined below, rose 80% faster than total employment from 1920 to 1960, and 100% faster from 1960 to 1970.

For the purpose of this analysis, office workers include professional and technical employees (except teachers), managers, officials, proprietors (except farm), and clerical workers. Sales personnel and service workers are not included. Some of the labor force included do not use office space, and some sales and service people do use it. But the trends over time, as suggested by these series, are indicative of the demand for office space.

Office workers increased in numbers by 2.8 million from 1920 to 1930. Their numbers were swollen by the postwar boom in 1920, and depressed by the onset of the depression in 1930. If these atypical years are excluded, the number probably grew at an annual average rate of about 380,000.

In 1957–59 dollars, office and similar construction, as reported by the Department of Commerce, averaged $1,079 million a year from 1920 to 1930. Adjusting, however, for the fact that the occupational statistics were distorted by the special situations existing in both 1920 and 1930, and using an average growth figure of 380,000 office workers per year, gives a construction volume of $2,850 per net new office worker added during the twenties.

The data suggest that the number of office workers as defined here increased by about 850,000 per year from 1959 to 1969. It may increase by 950,000 per year from 1970 to 1980. Office construction was reported by Dodge as totaling about 145 square feet per additional white-collar worker employed from 1960 to 1970. Should building proceed at a rate of 145 square feet per net new worker, an average growth of only 950,000 in the number of office workers would require a construction volume of over 135 million square feet per year, a figure 10% above the 1961–70 average, but 20% below the 1968–70 average.

These figures may understate the actual construction of office space, since some space is provided in other than office buildings which is not reported as office space. But they are indicative of the volume and the trend.

If the forecaster expects a larger or smaller increase in office employment, or in the historical rate of replacement of existing units, or a change in the amount of space provided per worker, he can adjust his forecast accordingly. Changes of this sort may already be occurring. As the available space becomes more nearly adequate, vacancies have started to rise, and the quality and appointments of new buildings and the utilities in them is rising. Instead of providing

a reported 145 square feet per net new worker, it may be necessary to provide appreciably more.

But the major increase in office space required by our changing economy is behind us. It came as a result of the shift toward white-collar employment. Only 13.1% of those employed in 1900 were white-collar workers requiring office space (as calculated here). By 1920 the proportion had risen to about 19%. It was over 25% in 1950, 37.5% in 1970, and may soon be not far from 40% —three times the 1900 ratio. But the major growth is past, and the major rate of expansion in office space may be behind us.

However, booms in particular cities may continue for some time, even with a steady or declining total. Activity in any particular city may start rather suddenly and continue until the demand in that city has been fairly well met or more than met. Then the activity may die down in that city and switch to another city, so that for the country as a whole, the volume of office building and related construction will not fluctuate as widely. Any conclusion about both the overall level and local rates will depend on judgments in both cases as to the growth in white-collar employment, quality of space provided per new employee, and the amount of rehabilitation or replacement of space for those already employed.

The conclusions must make allowance for cultural lags. Local enthusiasm may result in overbuilding in several localities. Other localities may not awaken to their markets until quite a backlog has developed. A study made in 1968 indicated a market demand for 1968–70 of only 70% of that later reported as started in those years. The estimate may have been low, although its assumptions on office employment turned out to be good. The resulting difference between the estimated real demand and the actual supply may be followed by a decline in new construction until demand catches up. Judgment as to how soon such a slackening may come and how long it will last requires real skill—more skill than required by long-range forecasting.

For such short-range forecasting, the conventional data on corporate investment (including McGraw-Hill and Industrial Conference Board reports) and plans and information on work on architects' boards (such as ENR tables on new plans) are useful. But as in short-range housing forecasting, short-range forecasting of office building construction is largely that of judging short-run deviations from long-run trends.

Industrial construction is undertaken for three purposes: (1) to replace or expand capacity to produce what is already being produced; (2) to cut costs or change styles or otherwise change existing plant capacity for cost or sales purposes connected with existing markets, rather than to secure capacity for new markets; (3) to produce new types of goods.

Moderate changes in, or additions to, existing equipment can often increase output strikingly, as illustrated by what has been happening in steel. So, to the extent that the proportion of outlays declines for replacing or expanding capacity for existing types of output, outlays necessary to increase plant output (that is, to raise the FRB index) will increase. But new types of goods may need new types of plant and equipment. As the McGraw-Hill studies have been showing for several years, the percentage of expenditures made for the purpose of increasing capacity has declined. This would tend to suggest that the spread between construction outlays for industrial plant and the increase in the FRB index may not be as great in the seventies as it was in the sixties.

The second category, modernizing to cut costs or change product designs rather than to expand capacity, also means above-average construction outlays per unit of increased production. Only 30% to 35% of the total outlays in the McGraw-Hill studies are for expansion as such. But 65% to 70% are for other purposes. The automobile companies, for instance, spent over $1 billion in 1957 and $700 million in 1959 on plants, but the total number of autos produced in 1960 was less than the number produced in 1955.

The third category, investment for the purpose of producing new products, may require more construction per unit of capacity added than does expansion of existing capacity to produce for current markets. There are exceptions of course. Some entirely new categories of goods can be produced from existing plants with only modest changes in the equipment. But more commonly, new products mean new equipment or at least the relocation of equipment in plants, if they do not mean new buildings themselves. Unless the new product is replacing existing products, the chances are that the new equipment means new structures or rebuilt structures in whole or in part.

Projections cannot be exact. For instance, if one product is replaced entirely by another product which uses completely different equipment (say, a plastic extrusion replaces a machined metal part), new construction will take place with no necessary increase in the total output. If the plastic is cheaper than the metal part it replaces, the reported value added figure may drop. Or one chemical may replace another but be produced with the same equipment. Because of changes in the processes and the catalysts, a much larger output may be possible in this situation with no construction at all, or with only very minor amounts of construction.

Then there is the perennial question: What is construction and what is equipment? An increasing proportion of outlays for plant and equipment seems to be going for equipment, and a declining proportion for construction. So the relationship of construction to production may be a declining one.

About 55.6 million square feet of manufacturing floor space were reported by the F. W. Dodge Corp. as started from 1956 through 1960, for each additional unit of capacity reported by the Federal Reserve Board from 1957 through 1961 (1967 output =100). About 48.9 million square feet were reported from 1960 through 1964 and 34.7 million square feet for each unit of capacity added from 1965 through 1970. This was a drop of about 12% in the number of square feet per unit of capacity added between 1956–60 and 1961–65 and 29% between 1960–64 and 1965–69.

The decline in dollar outlays per unit of capacity added has been less. Dodge figures show a drop of about 24% from the first to the second half of the sixties in dollar outlays per unit of capacity added.

Commerce Department figures show a dollar drop of under 7%. The Commerce figures include office buildings constructed as part of a manufacturing operation, whereas Dodge puts such buildings in the office building category. The Commerce figures are misleading for both market and for material use analysis. They indicate a smaller growth in office building outlays and occupancy and a larger growth in outlays and in expenditure per added capacity than has actually occurred in the general market. Unless he is working in very crude terms, the forecaster must depend on Dodge data. Though, of course, if his objective is to forecast what Commerce will report, he must adjust his analysis to the Commerce concept that office space built in connection with a factory is a factory.

The forecaster must recognize that the downward trend in floor space contracted for per unit of capacity added will continue. More productive equipment, more unsheltered equipment, and shifts in processing techniques and in end products will continue to reduce manufacturing floor space requirements. It is, however, questionable if the decline in the next decade will be as abrupt as it was in the last. This large drop in the latter part of the 1960s was due in part to rising construction costs and a corresponding increase in remodeling and improving existing facilities, and in part to a

change in the mix. While both of these influences will be at work in the 1970s, the forecaster who must prepare a forecast with any precision will want to work with the Dodge reports on Construction Contracts for Manufacturing Plants by Industry Classification. If he expects a decline in types of contracts costing $30 per square foot, and an increase in others costing $15 or less, or an increase in outlays for certain types of chemical plants with no covered floor area at all, for instance, he can develop defensible judgments as to what is happening more readily than if he has to rely on more general data.

A relatively detailed industry-by-industry analysis is therefore necessary before any valuable judgment can be reached as to how much the volume of construction will rise or fall during the seventies, per unit of capacity added. Even with a detailed study, it will be difficult to be specific about what new markets may mean to different types of plant construction in the coming decade. If the iron and steel industry makes a breakthrough in the construction market, that would require a sizable increase in steel capacity for fabrication of light joists and panels, and it would mean outlays for these products, if not for ingots. Or if the aluminum industry really makes a breakthrough in mass construction, a similar development could occur there. On the other hand, if the chemical industry begins to capture a sizable part of the construction industry, the types of equipment it will use for production and for erection would be quite different from those used by other metal processors, and the impact on construction might be less. And cost cutting in many industries may stimulate new construction, irrespective of capacity needs.

It is hazardous to forecast what types of plant or industry construction are likely to expand how much. The particular detailed areas that expand will depend on the whims of consumers as well as on the skills of managers and engineers. The forecaster

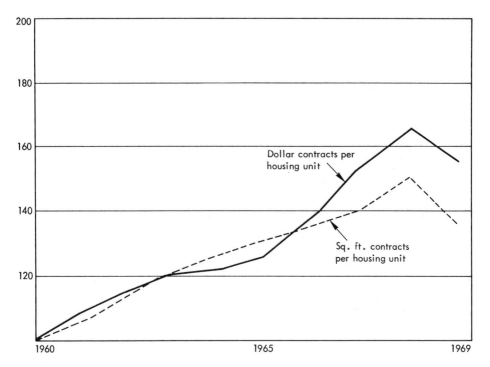

Three-year moving average of increase in sales, two-year moving average of contracts, third year of sale and first year of contract series matched.

Chart 4   Ratio of Dodge Store and Warehouse—Dollar Contracts to Growth in Consumer Purchases of Goods (In Current Dollars, 1960=100)

may or may not believe that unless steel makes a breakthrough in construction, for instance, its expansion of fabrication capacity may slow down. Automobile capacity may be adequate for the volume of output likely to be reached in the near future, but the forecaster may find that automobile and other expenditures will occur for construction in large part for design changes or cost-cutting purposes. However, should industry as a whole emphasize mass production of goods already being marketed, other than style changes, new capacity may de-emphasize construction.

The impact of the purpose of the expenditures for factory building on costs is illustrated when costs per square foot, de-

rived from Dodge data, are compared for manufacturers' nonrefrigerated warehouses and for other than manufacturer owned warehouses. The other than manufacturer owned warehouses, whose costs were identical with manufacturer nonrefrigerated warehouses in 1963, cost 19% less than manufacturer warehouses in 1970. And their costs rose only 23% as much as did those for factories. By keeping design and the erection process simple and efficient, owners and contractors of these buildings were able to hold costs down until 1969. Factory costs too were held to a rise of about 2% per year until 1967. But shifts in mix and purpose, increased emphasis on remodeling, and to factories without covered areas (as some

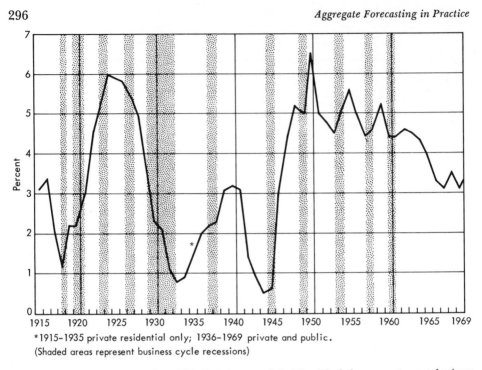

*1915–1935 private residential only; 1936–1969 private and public.
(Shaded areas represent business cycle recessions)

1915–35 private residential only; 1936–69 private and public. (Shaded areas represent business cycle recessions.)

Chart 5   New Residential Construction as a Percentage of Gross National Product 1915–69

chemical plants) along with increases in wage rates and material prices, sent costs soaring in 1970.

Factory construction costs varied erratically. They rose in 1964, dropped in 1965, leveled off in 1966, rose in 1967, dropped in 1968 and 1969, and shot up precipitously in 1969. The rise from 1963 to 1970 was over 50%, and the two-year smoothed average rose nearly 4% per year.

Rising costs were offset surprisingly well through 1968 by efficiency and improved technology. This will be more difficult to do in the seventies, but with factory costs over 50% above 1963 levels, the forecaster will probably expect vigorous efforts to hold down expenses in the coming decade.

This may actually increase costs per square foot for factory construction by putting more emphasis on improving existing

facilities rather than building new. It may be easier to forecast dollar outlay than area to be built. This will have an impact on the type of material to be bought and the trades used. It will make forecasting more hazardous and require more detailed industry-by-industry analysis. And it will require the purchase of more detailed Dodge data than is frequently used, not only as clues to trends in remodeling versus expansion, but as clues to costs by types of structure, and clues to expenditures by detailed industry classifications.

However, despite the fact that strong efforts are being made to control costs, newer plants have much better facilities for maintaining a comfortable working environment for people, and for maintaining better conditions for the processing operations themselves. Not only is temperature, humidity, and dust controlled better for the workers' satisfaction, it is controlled better for purposes of finer tolerances in the goods produced, and for lower costs in the plant operations themselves. This may tend to encourage new construction and to increase costs.

Another long-term development that will affect the overall environment of plant construction has already been noted. The ratio of white-collar workers to blue-collar workers is rising. The new plants and the new processes have higher ratios of white-to-blue-collar workers. So the companies and operations being expanded now and to be expanded during the decade may add about one white-collar for every two net additional blue-collar workers put on the payroll.

Each worker gets more space today than he used to get, whether he is blue-collar or white-collar. The blue-collar worker, on the average, is operating or servicing bigger machines than were formerly handled. Machines turn out more per cubic foot of space occupied, so the cubic feet of factory space does not rise directly with production, but it rises more than does employment. And the proportion of the space used by management, by sales staffs, and by other white-collar employees will continue to rise.

Factors such as these suggest that forecasters may lean toward the upper rather than the lower end of a probable range. If it is assumed that the FRB capacity index will rise 4% per year, but square feet only 3%, on a constant dollar basis costs might rise another 1% or more because of additional amenities built into the new plants. If inflation is assumed to average 4% per year in factory construction costs, this could bring a projected 8% increase in outlay on the average, or a doubling of the current volume in less than a decade. Different assumptions, such as assumptions regarding major changes in the mix, yield different results, but forecasts can be built around this general framework.

Short-term forecasting depends on conventional short-term data sources. The Commerce-SEC and McGraw-Hill data on projected capital expenditures, and reports from the Industrial Conference Board are particularly useful. Such material must be used cautiously, however. If business sentiment improved after the inquiries were mailed, for instance, actual outlays could exceed the limits suggested by the reported figures. And the figures should be examined industry by industry. Some industries—as possibly railroads—may not have their next year's programs ready at the time of the inquiry. The forecaster's knowledge of trends and specific developments in certain industries may enable him to weigh the validity of some of the detailed projections before he puts them into his analytical framework. Even though a series released in November cannot be a perfect guide for the following year or even quarter, it can be very enlightening and can serve as a useful building block in developing industrial construction figures industry by industry in the process of reaching totals.

Manufacturing profits and cash flow figures also are useful guides. In general, industries and firms whose income position is improving will tend to be more liberal in their investment policy than firms or industries with low profits. But even this is not always true. The steel industry found that it had to increase its investment program because it was not making the profits it thought it should make. Investment for cost cutting was necessary because of the unsatisfactory profit position. So each industry must be examined in the light of its problems, not by an overall formula. The business press will usually provide clues which will suggest which industries need special attention for reasons of this sort.

PUBLIC CONSTRUCTION

There are at least two areas in which the volume of public construction is important and in which variations may be significant. The first is nonresidential building, primarily education, and the second is highways. Other categories such as hospital and institutional, administration, service, public residential, sewer and water, and conservation and development have fluctuated relatively little, or until recently at least could be forecast within moderate limits of error with relative confidence.

Schools

In the analysis of this market written in 1963 for the first edition of this book, the statement was made that these categories "fluctuate relatively little, or can be forecast ... with relative confidence." As priorities change, this becomes less true of some categories. Public educational building rose relatively steadily through 1965, spurted in 1966, rose slowly in constant dollars until 1967, and has dropped since then. The fluctuations in 1966 and 1967 may be explicable largely on the basis of the availability and cost of money. But the decline in real terms since then, and in current dollars since 1968, may be due to an increasing extent to changes in social priorities and to uncertainties about educational techniques and goals as well as to the increasing cost of the educational process. Despite cutbacks in private expenditures for school construction (as in church school outlays) public outlays have dropped, in current and constant dollars, since 1967.

School construction is now a political, social, and economic matter. It is not predominantly a matter of the shift in the number of children in each age group, and of local and national income. While political decisions are being debated as to who will pay for what (downtown and in the suburbs; locally, and from state, and from national sources) and under what rules, there can be little growth in school building expenditures. And while social considerations as to what type of education is best for whom are still under serious, and even violent debate,

little expansion is probable. And with teachers reaching for higher incomes than the median taxpayer earns the amount the taxpayers are willing to underwrite for structures is under serious constraints. The long-range forecaster can no longer assume fairly constant relationships between changes in the number of children of specific age groups and changes in real per capita income, and expenditures for school buildings. He must make political, social, and economic decisions before he starts to calculate funds available for education, and the proportion of these funds available for buildings.

The census, HEW, and National Education Association publications are still the best sources of data on trends in school populations and expenditures, and in expenditures by income categories and per student. But it is not as easy to use such data as it used to be.

Short-term trends are of course affected even more sharply than long-term trends by changes in the availability and cost of funds, and by current political debates. The *Money Manager*, the *Wall Street Journal*, and the F. W. Dodge Corporation are better sources of information as to short-term trends than are demographic and educational sources.

Expenditures on private educational facilities have not been keeping pace with those on public schools. Private outlays were reported as 31% of public in 1929. In 1955 they were 20% of public, and in 1970 only 17.3%. There are difficulties in holding them at even this rate. Religious institutions are finding it increasingly hard to sustain current expenditures, and the movement of students to college from high school has increased the pressure. However, it may be possible that public funds may be made available directly to students or their families for expenditure in private schools. This could change the mix of reported public and private expenditure on school buildings without necessarily increasing the total.

Highway Construction: Long-Range Forecasts

The next large public construction category is highways. In most respects, this is a very unsatisfactory area in which to work, as the data are very unclear and are made available relatively late.

Highway construction is a function, among other things, of growth in the proportion of traffic which rides on rubber rather than on rail or the airways, and on the proportion which is urban rather than rural. This makes forecasting highway construction a particularly difficult problem in economic, statistical, and political analysis.

Traffic grew faster than the economy for many decades, but the differential in growth has been dropping, and currently traffic as a whole by rail, road, water, and air appears to be growing but little if any faster than the economy. This is due in part to a shift in the generation of energy from coal to electricity, gas, and oil. And it is due in part to the fact that production of finished products is tending to move toward distribution centers, and industry and trade are tending to move to the suburbs where people live. The trends, of course, are not all in the same direction. While some delivery service is being reduced—a smaller proportion of milk or groceries may be delivered today than was delivered 30 years ago—on the other hand, people go to visit their doctor or may travel several miles to the grocery store instead of walking several rods. But in general, the trend may be toward a lower rate of growth in traffic in relation to the growth of GNP.

The proportion of traffic shifting to the roads also is dropping. During the 1920s, highway traffic was reported to have grown about ten times as fast as the economy. In the 1930s it grew something like three times as fast as GNP. But from 1958 on, the published data indicate little growth in relation to GNP. Reported vehicle miles traveled dropped from 1.49 in 1958 per 1958 dollars of GNP to 1.44 in 1956. They stayed at 1.44

through 1968, rose to 1.47 in 1969, and are estimated to have risen to 1.55 in 1970, when the constant dollar GNP dropped. The ratio of vehicle miles to constant dollar GNP was reported to be the same in 1969 as in 1959, but the fact that the ratio dropped until 1965, but rose in 1969 and 1970, may indicate that highway traffic in relation to GNP will not decline appreciably in the future and may rise slowly. After the interstate highway system is open along its full length, and when urban projects now under way are open, it is possible that a rate of growth relative to GNP will be resumed. The forecaster must form a judgment on this, and his judgment should be broken down by growth in urban as well as rural traffic.

The forecaster must form some judgment as to the impact of efforts to stimulate mass transportation on the use of rubber-tired vehicles. It is possible that most of the increase in mass transportation that does occur will be on rubber-tired vehicles. For instance, buses on reserved lanes are now carrying 30,000 persons per lane per hour. The capital cost per person per mile is far less by bus than by rail. So even in mass transport, relatively little of the increase may be by rail. But this is a judgment each forecaster will have to make.

After a judgment has been reached as to how much traffic, urban and rural, may be expected over the period for which the forecast is to be made, the next step is to estimate how much it will cost to provide the capacities needed to serve the projected traffic.

With the approaching completion of the interstate system as modified from time to time, future additions to its mileage will be smaller. But increased attention will be placed on improving traffic capacity within and around metropolitan areas, and to some extent to resort areas. The first emphasis will require more structures and traffic control systems. The structures, bridges, overpasses, etc., will be construction as conventionally understood. But expenditures on traffic control devices, which will yield several times the increase in traffic capacity per dollar of outlay that investments on structures or roads can yield, will not involve as much in the form of conventional materials, equipment, or labor skills. The forecaster should be careful not to apply historical material use trends or factors to his projections, without a careful check on their validity for his purposes.

Analysis of the potential growth in urban areas and in the population in cities during the 1970s, as compared to the growth in the 1950s and early 1960s, indicates that the growth in area will be relatively smaller in the future. Much of the recent growth in area has been due to increased land use per capita. This trend is declining. So the increase in urban highway mileage may not be as great, relatively, in the 1970s as it was in the 1960s. Also, the utilization of intercity routes will probably be more efficient in the 1970s than the 1960s. Should this prove to be the case, there will be an increase in the proportion of construction that will be in the form of replacement. Replacement expenditures may provide a greater capacity per dollar of investment than the original highway. And as new highways are more efficient (carrying more vehicles and more passengers per lane per hour than older highways), the forecaster may come up with a conclusion that we have about reached the end of rapid growth in highway expenditures.

This view may be reinforced by the fact that the tax rate on gasoline and other aspects of highway use may be approaching its practical limits. (This may be less true of the tax on diesel fuel.) Automobile users have been a favorite source of new tax revenues, because the auto is visible and because taxes can be indirect. It may not be safe to assume that the tax per vehicle mile of use will rise anywhere nearly as much in the future as it has in the past. This too may suggest a restraint on highway expenditures.

Anti-pollution attacks may exert a temporary restraint on highway construction, but in the end may result in an increase in outlays. Rail cannot serve a dispersed population, as New Jersey, Boston, Chicago, and other metropolitan areas have demonstrated. Increasing family incomes mean willingness to pay for a more open environment for children, whether the structure be a garden apartment or a single-family house. But an increasingly dispersed population enjoying a more open environment must depend on the bus, the truck, and the auto for transport of goods and people. Rubber-tired vehicles can be made as pollution-free as the public is willing to pay for. So the rubber-tired vehicle will remain the principal transport vehicle and the highway the principal route. But efforts to improve the environment may well result in more aesthetics being built into the highways. More noise restraining techniques, more bypassing of areas felt particularly worthy of protection, more sunken routes and tunnels, may be the practice of the 1970s. This will add to costs per lane mile though not necessarily to per passenger mile.

Other things must be examined too. For instance, the forecaster must analyze the proportion of highway revenues that goes to debt service, operation, maintenance, policing, and other overhead, as well as the proportion of highway-user revenues that is diverted. For instance, in 1969 total receipts by state governments for highway purposes approximated $15 billion. Of this, about $8 billion was spent for capital outlay, $1.8 billion for maintenance, over $1.4 billion for administration and policing, about $525 million for bond interests, and $675 million for bond retirement. Proceeds from bond sales approximated $1.3 billion, but the cost of servicing and retiring bonds came to almost $1.2 billion.

Some construction, including toll road work, is of course going ahead outside of the regular federal and state highway operations. A forecaster must form his judgment as to how long toll road construction will continue, and at what rate. Tolls collected by states and toll authorities totaled almost $775 million in 1969, and came to about 5% of total receipts in that year. This is a sizable sum, but still a very small proportion of total receipts from highway users for highway purposes.And the difference between net receipts from bond issues and the cost of bond interest and retirement was only $150 million, or 1% of total highway expenditure in 1969.

There is another problem which appears more significant. Nearly 30% of state receipts for highway purposes have been coming from the federal government, largely for construction of the interstate system. This is 90% money, that is, the federal government puts up 90% of the construction costs, the state government 10%. So state governments have tended to emphasize the federal system at the expense of other systems in which the federal government puts up less, or in which the states or the local governments have to put up all the money. As the adequacy of the interstate system grows, the relative pressure for expenditures on some of the other systems may increase. The probability that the rules for federal aid financing will be changed must be weighed carefully.

There are many other types of problems, for instance, the relative ratio of right-of-way costs to construction costs. The interstate system now puts heavy emphasis on urban highways, where the relative cost of rights-of-way is high. But the ratio may not rise much above current levels. Later urban construction may include a higher proportion in the suburbs, where rights-of-way will be somewhat less costly per mile than they are in downtown sections. Should there be a decline in the proportion of total outlays that has to go for rights-of-way, this would increase the funds available for construction itself. This is a particularly ticklish problem in short-range forecasting. It may be less ticklish for long-range forecasting,

but it is one of the problems that must be examined.

All of this means that long-range forecasts for highway construction must put heavy consideration on political and social as well as on economic and technical factors.

Highway Construction: Short-Range Forecasts

Short-range forecasting suffers from the fact that there are relatively few good current data. The Federal Highway Administration puts out data on state highway contracts by states, with a delay of approximately two months. The Department of Commerce puts out data on contracts let by state and local agencies. This series is broken down by federally aided and non-federally aided state projects, by local projects, and by contracts let directly by the federal government. The F. W. Dodge Corporation puts out each month, with a delay of about a month, contract data on highways and bridges. The series do not fluctuate in exact harmony. For instance, in 1969 and 1970 Dodge reports for highways and bridges averaged $7.5 billion. The Federal Highway Administration reported capital outlays (including engineering costs) of $8.9 billion in 1970.

For short-range forecasting purposes, obviously an examination should be made of plans of state highway authorities, as well as the bond issues proposed and voted on or otherwise accepted by other authorities. Checks should be made of the highway trust fund to see whether revenues are exceeding expectations, whether it may be necessary to slow down on the rate at which it can accept new projects, and whether the administration is releasing or is likely to release all the funds available. And an examination of the difference between federal approval of projects and federal outlays on these projects may suggest short-range changes in trends of expenditures. A check on the relative relationships between site and construction costs on recently approved projects may also be informative.

Every fall, *Engineering News-Record* publishes a summary of a study which its reporters make of programs of various state highway offices for the coming year, and an analysis of the resources available to these state highway departments. Some states may be running close to the limits of the money they can spend from federal aid or from other sources. Other states may have a big cushion. These cushions vary from time to time.

Occasionally, federal legislation is changed to support anticyclical construction in general or specific areas. More often the policy of the administration toward encouraging or restraining highway construction may shift.

After allowing for such factors, the backlog of contracts, plans, and resources can be projected to show the rate at which the forecaster expects contracts to be let in the next six to nine months. Then this contract series can be translated into an activity series, and the total for the volume of construction next year developed. This total should be reported in relation to the current year's totals, because before many weeks or months go by, the figures for the current year may change. The only forecast of any significance here is a forecast of an increase or a decrease of a given amount, not a forecast of the figure itself, because there is no good base from which to work. This needs emphasis. The forecaster should be very careful to make clear he is indicating how much he expects highway construction to rise or fall, what it will be next year in relation to this year. He cannot give a judgment of what the final figure will be.

There are many other types of public construction which have to be forecast. In general, techniques similar to those outlined for school buildings and highways can be followed in these other areas. The relative importance of local or federal decision making and of civilian or military decision making varies, of course, category by category. The political influence may be more strongly and more erratically felt in the so-called "conservation and development" category in which pork barrel appropriations may be more important than they are elsewhere. But this is a matter of degree and not of absolutes. Here, as in other fields, the forecaster basically wants to say whether next year will be above or below trends. And he must know the reason why, in order to make a reasonable judgment for most of the smaller public construction categories. He will want to judge, for instance, how fast and how much ecological lobbying will affect expenditures, and in what direction.

When the forecaster is finished, he may find that his total for the coming year will vary only slightly from that of the current year. He might have been able to do almost as well by forming a judgment as to whether private construction and/or public construction is going to go up or down next year by simply multiplying his estimated GNP for the coming year by 9.5% or a figure he believes appropriate for the coming year. But once he has worked out his reasons detail by detail, and done the job detail by detail, he can be much more confident of his results, and of some importance, he is more likely to be right.

LOUIS J. PARADISO

Inventories

Inventory movements reflect shifts in the volume of goods needed to support changing rates of business operations. Consequently, inventories normally conform closely with movements of orders, production, and sales. Hence, to forecast inventory changes it is necessary first to develop the short-term pattern of business prospects. However, variations from those associated with the business pattern occur from time to time, due to the influence of special factors such as threats of strikes and shifts in price movements. In these periods inventory investment may become quite distorted in relation to actual requirements or to the rate of business operations. Thus, an inventory forecast must take into account the effects on inventories of any foreseeable temporary disturbances.

There is no easy road to forecasting inventory changes, particularly over the short term. Because the factors influencing these changes are so numerous and may shift in their impact and importance, a reliable relationship between inventory movements and the various determinants of such movements is difficult to obtain. Much progress has been made in this direction, especially since computer programs have become more widely available. But at the moment the most fruitful technique is to utilize information from all possible sources. Consequently, this chapter will deal with various approaches, with the thought that the inventory forecast would reflect results obtained by the judicious use of several approaches, modifying such results, if need be, by judgmental considerations.

NATURE AND SIZE OF INVENTORIES, AND A FRAMEWORK OF REFERENCE FOR THE FORECAST

Before detailing the various methods for forecasting inventories, we shall set forth the framework under which inventories and their forecasts will be considered. First, the inventory analysis will be considered within the framework of the national income and product accounts and the measurement of inventories as set forth in those accounts. This item is designated "change in business inventories" and is published quarterly by the Department of Commerce as part of the gross national product statistics. The data are available both in current dollars and in constant dollars, and are seasonally adjusted.

The change in business inventories measures, in effect, the change in physical volume of stocks between two periods valued at the average inventory price which prevails during the period. The method of arriving at such a measure is, in simple terms, to derive a "volume" or deflated value figure from the book value of inventories re-

303

ported by business firms by adjusting for the appropriate price movements. The relevant prices are obtained by utilizing lags to conform with those prevailing at the time when the inventories were purchased.

These derived "deflated" book values represent a physical volume of stocks valued at base period prices, and the difference between the levels at two points of time yields the change in physical volume of inventories during the period. This change in physical volume in converted to current dollars by applying the index relationship of average current prices to those in the base period. The result then conforms with the current market valuation of output as measured in the GNP accounts.

Inasmuch as the changes in inventories of companies that employ LIFO (last-in, first-out) reporting are already substantially on a current valuation basis, LIFO inventories are not subjected to the general deflation procedure outlined above. The total inventory change is derived by summating the changes calculated from a detailed breakdown for manufacturing, trade, and other industries.

The main sources of information on inventory book values are the Bureau of the Census, the Federal Trade Commission, and the Internal Revenue Service. The bureau's quinquennial censuses and its annual and monthly samples for manufacturing and trade provide the basic sources of information for deriving both the inventory levels and changes in the nonfarm sector. These manufacturing and trade data are supplemented by information obtained from various agencies to cover inventories held by mining, construction, transportation, agriculture, and other industries.

It is not the purpose of this chapter to describe in detail the procedures used for estimating inventories. These are given in various publications of the Department of Commerce, in particular the National Income Supplement (1954 edition) and the later supplement, The National Income and Product Accounts of the United States, 1929–1965. However, it should be pointed out that the change in business inventories is probably one of the most difficult components to measure in the GNP accounts.

Because of the different accounting procedures used by business firms and the fact that many, particularly small companies, do not have adequate inventory records, there is a considerable margin of error involved in the estimates. However, it is believed that the general movements from quarter to quarter reflect with reasonable accuracy the shifts occurring in inventory investment. A detailed analysis of the problems involved in inventory measurement and of the accuracy of the estimates is included in a study made by the Federal Reserve Board.[1]

VOLATILITY OF INVENTORY MOVEMENTS

Inventory investment is probably the most volatile of all the segments of GNP. Over the postwar period inventory movements at times have had an important effect on the quarterly movement of total GNP. Comparison of the change in inventory investment with changes in the major components of GNP clearly shows that while inventories usually have not been the cause of business fluctuations, their position (whether high or low) and shifts have at times accentuated downturns or helped to bolster recoveries. In each of the four postwar recessions, shifts in inventory investment have been important in determining the shape and duration of the business cycle.

Table 1 shows the impact of inven-

[1] See "Statistics of Business Inventories" prepared for the Subcommittee on Economic Statistics of the Joint Committee on the Economic Report, 1955. Also see the Joint Economic Committee materials referred to in footnote 2.

TABLE 1.   CHANGES IN INVENTORY INVESTMENT AND GNP

(Billions of 1958 dollars, seasonally adjusted at annual rates)

Quarter	Change in Inventory Investment*	Change in GNP	Quarter	Change in Inventory Investment*	Change in GNP	Quarter	Change in Inventory Investment*	Change in GNP	Quarter	Change in Inventory Investment*	Change in GNP
1948–1	1.2	2.6	1954–1	1.4	−5.9	1960–1	3.4	9.8	1966–1	1.4	12.5
2	1.3	5.8	2	−0.7	−0.8	2	−5.8	−0.4	2	4.6	5.9
3	1.1	2.9	3	1.1	5.1	3	−0.8	−2.4	3	−4.2	5.2
4	−1.4	2.9	4	3.4	8.5	4	−5.6	−3.6	4	7.4	7.9
1949–1	−4.9	−4.2	1955–1	4.1	12.3	1961–1	−0.8	−1.1	1967–1	−9.4	−1.5
2	−5.8	−2.0	2	1.7	7.4	2	5.5	10.2	2	−4.8	5.0
3	3.8	3.6	3	−0.3	6.7	3	1.7	8.7	3	4.0	7.3
4	−4.0	−2.8	4	1.2	4.3	4	1.7	10.3	4	0.9	4.7
1950–1	10.0	16.3	1956–1	−1.4	−2.8	1962–1	1.0	7.8	1968–1	−6.8	9.9
2	2.5	8.9	2	−1.6	2.0	2	−0.6	8.2	2	7.1	11.9
3	0.0	14.3	3	−0.5	−1.1	3	−0.6	5.7	3	−2.1	7.2
4	11.6	7.3	4	0.3	5.8	4	0.9	4.9	4	1.1	4.9
1951–1	−6.9	4.7	1957–1	−2.3	3.1	1963–1	−1.6	2.9	1969–1	−2.4	4.6
2	5.3	6.7	2	0.3	−0.2	2	0.2	4.8	2	0.5	4.0
3	−4.4	7.2	3	0.6	2.0	3	1.1	8.7	3	3.3	4.8
4	−6.2	0.0	4	−5.5	−7.0	4	2.2	7.4	4	−3.8	−1.7
1952–1	0.3	2.7	1958–1	−3.1	−10.7	1964–1	3.3	9.0	1970–1	−4.8	−5.4
2	−8.2	−1.8	2	0.6	2.0	2	1.3	7.5	2	1.6	1.1
3	6.7	4.3	3	5.3	11.2	3	−1.3	7.3	3	1.7	2.5
4	1.5	11.4	4	4.0	10.9	4	2.8	2.7	4	−1.5	−7.1
1953–1	−2.6	6.8	1959–1	−0.5	7.0	1965–1	2.4	13.1	1971–1	−1.9	12.4
2	0.7	4.3	2	5.1	11.3	2	−1.7	3.8			
3	−2.6	−2.7	3	−8.4	−4.9	3	0.3	12.1			
4	−5.5	−4.9	4	5.7	5.4	4	0.7	14.1			

Source: U.S. Department of Commerce, Office of Business Economics; based on revised data shown in Survey of Current Business, July 1968, July 1969, July 1970, and May 1971.

* Quarter-to-quarter change in the change in business inventories.

tories on the changes in GNP in the postwar recessions. Perhaps the only clear-cut case where a shift in inventory demand was a causative factor in a business downturn was in the 1948–49 period. At that time, business firms had replenished their stocks of civilian goods which had been depleted during the war period. As businessmen found their inventories to be adequate in relation to sales and orders in the second half of 1948, they halted their accumulation. This had repercussions on incomes and employment which resulted in further liquidation; this was a major factor in precipitating the 1948–49 recession. In other recessions of the postwar period, however, inventory movements were the consequences of changes in other basic demands.[2]

It is important to understand this point with regard to the role of inventories in the business cycle, since the evidence suggests that in general, inventories seem to lag business activity. In other words, inventory shifts occur about six months after a turn has occurred in general business activity, and this is a basic consideration in forecasting inventory movements over the short term.

The sequence is as follows. Prior to the point where business turns down, orders are placed for inventories in the rising phase of business activity. Many of these orders are for delivery at some time in the future. After the downturn, however, deliveries of previous commitments continue to be made. As a result, businessmen find themselves with rising inventories at the very time when business is declining. Thus, it takes some time for the adjustment to take place and for liquidation to begin. As indicated earlier, this lag period is around six months for all

manufacturing industries and for total trade. Obviously the lag varies from industry to industry; for example, for food the lag is probably no longer than one month, whereas for some machinery items the lag might be over one year. The reverse situation takes place in an upturn when deliveries cannot be made as quickly as desired to meet rising demand. Thus liquidation continues for some time after the business upturn occurs.

However, in periods when there is some economic slack and the demand-supply situation is not tight, deliveries can be made much more quickly. Consequently, the lag between inventories and changes in business activity has been diminishing somewhat. This point is also important in short-term forecasting. An additional consideration is that in recent years businessmen have increasingly followed the practice of letting the supplier hold the stocks. The result has been that inventories in relation to sales have been kept rather low, since some of the duplication in stockholding has been eliminated. However, a disadvantage of this practice is that the final user sometimes has to await delivery from the primary holder of the goods.

In forecasting total business inventories in the GNP accounts, it is essential that the analysis be based on an examination of the inventory position and trends by industries, and, in manufacturing, by stages of fabrication, that is, raw materials, goods-in-process, and finished goods. Inventory movements vary widely and are affected by different considerations, industry by industry. In some industries the movement is closely associated with the current level of activity, whereas in other industries inventories must be accumulated long before sales are made. The latter is particularly true of seasonal industries such as apparel, toys, and so on.

Of particular interest is the movement of inventories in the automobile industry. Here, inventories are for a time partially independent of automobile sales. Initially,

---

[2] For a detailed discussion of the role of inventories in the business cycle, see materials prepared for the Joint Economic Committee, Parts I–IV, 1961–62. Also hearings before the Subcommittee on Economic Stabilization, Automation, and Energy Resources of the Joint Economic Committee, July 9–13, 1962.

Inventories 307

the industry generally produces new models at high rates so as to provide dealers with an adequate number of cars of different makes, styles, and colors. Inventories are adjusted after the test of the market has come about through sales performance. Thus, in forecasting total inventories it is essential to consider separately the movement of automobile stocks, since their fluctuations are so important in the overall fluctuations of inventories.

The basic data for analyzing the detailed inventory movements are compiled by the Department of Commerce. Manufacturers' inventories are published in the Bureau of Census, October 1970 release series M3-12 and the monthly report, "Manufacturers' Shipments, Inventories, and Orders,"

TABLE 2. **CHANGES IN BOOK VALUE OF BUSINESS INVENTORIES COMPARED WITH CHANGES ON THE GNP BASIS**

			Inventory Changes		
Quarter	Manufacturing* and Trade (Book Value)	Total Business (GNP Basis)	Quarter	Manufacturing* and Trade (Book Value)	Total Business (GNP Basis)
	(Billions of dollars, seasonally adjusted at annual rates)				
1958–1	−5.7	−5.4	1965–1	10.6	8.7
2	−6.1	−5.1	2	8.5	6.7
3	−0.8	0.1	3	9.5	9.4
4	4.0	4.1	4	9.3	9.9
1959–1	4.1	3.9	1966–1	13.5	11.3
2	10.3	9.1	2	17.5	16.2
3	0.5	0.4	3	14.9	11.9
4	5.0	6.3	4	18.4	19.9
1960–1	11.0	9.9	1967–1	7.9	9.6
2	3.3	3.9	2	2.5	4.5
3	0.8	3.1	3	5.2	8.7
4	−3.7	−2.4	4	9.8	10.0
1961–1	−4.2	−3.5	1968–1	6.5	2.6
2	−0.1	2.1	2	11.8	10.4
3	4.3	3.8	3	8.6	8.2
4	3.6	5.5	4	10.6	9.3
1962–1	7.3	6.7	1969–1	11.9	7.4
2	5.5	6.1	2	11.5	7.9
3	6.2	5.2	3	13.2	11.3
4	2.8	6.4	4	12.3	7.2
1963–1	2.7	4.5	1970–1	4.9	1.6
2	3.9	4.7	2	4.9	3.1
3	5.9	5.8	3	10.6	5.5
4	5.0	8.1	4	4.4	3.6
1964–1	4.9	3.3	1971–1	4.6	1.4
2	5.4	4.1			
3	6.7	3.8			
4	6.8	7.5			

Source: U.S. Department of Commerce, Office of Business Economics and Bureau of the Census.

NOTE: The difference between book value and GNP basis is due to the inclusion in the GNP basis series of the inventory valuation adjustment and inventories of industries other than manufacturing and trade.

* Change end of quarter from beginning of quarter.

M3-1. Inventories and sales for retail and wholesale trade by major lines are published by the bureau in its monthly retail and wholesale trade reports. Total manufacturing and trade sales and inventories are available in a monthly release of the Office of Business Economics. All these series are published in the *Survey of Current Business*.

The detailed industry breakdown of manufacturers' inventories is in terms of book value. These data provide a valuable guide to the underlying movements, particularly when price changes are relatively small, at which time book value changes move closely with the physical volume changes. The correspondence between the two series is, of course, much looser in periods of wide price movements. Table 2 compares the quarterly changes for 1958–71 in the book value of total manufacturing and trade inventories with changes in business inventories on a GNP basis. In periods of relative price stability the book value inventories can be safely used to mirror changes in the GNP measurement of inventories. The advantage of using book values lies in the wealth of information available by detailed industries, both for inventories and sales.

A DO-IT-YOURSELF METHOD FOR FORECASTING INVENTORIES

Two major steps must be taken in making an inventory forecast. First, it is necessary to appraise the quarterly pattern of demand for the major types of goods. This may be done by studying the chapters in this book where such forecasts are described. The major groups involved are outlays for business plant and equipment and consumer goods. An expansion in fixed investment outlays is always accompanied by increased inventory buying, not only by the major steel consumers but also by most other durable goods manufacturers. A decline in such spending has a decided effect on inventories as most major producers, feeling the impact

of reduced ordering, trim their inventories.

The next large group to forecast is consumer goods. This should be considered in three parts: (a) auto sales and output; (b) other consumer durables such as furniture, appliances, books, etc.; and (c) nondurable goods, with particular emphasis on apparel. As is indicated in another chapter, the forecast of auto demand is one of the more difficult to make. However, the surveys of consumers' intentions to buy may be considered in obtaining some clues.[3] Other durables such as furniture are related in part to residential construction, which may be determined for the short term ahead by the trend of residential starts and building permits. The 1971 housing boom, for example, has been accompanied by a spurt in furniture and household equipment sales.

The next step is to evaluate the prospects for price changes. When overall prices move in an orderly fashion and at a moderate pace (one to two percent increase per year), the influence on inventory buying is not significant. If prices rise significantly, the effect on inventories should be gauged by considering the supply-demand situation. For example, if at the same time that prices are rising, supplies appear to be ample in relation to foreseeable demand, the effect of the price increase on inventory policy would be of secondary importance. In this case, since prices of goods sold and inventory replacement costs would also rise, the incentive to accumulate inventories to a greater extent than needed to support higher production or sales rates would be small. On the other hand, if price movements were to accelerate at a relatively fast pace, and if at the same time demands were to become tighter relative to supplies, then there would be a move to accumulate inventories beyond operating needs.

The effects of price changes on inven-

---

[3] For an appraisal of the reliability of these surveys see Eva Mueller, "Ten Years of Consumer Attitude Surveys: Their Forecasting Record," *Journal of the American Statistical Association* (December, 1963), pp. 899 ff.

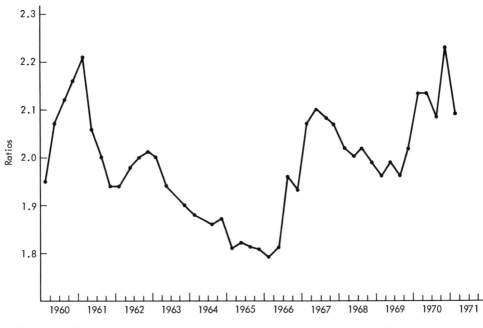

Chart 1   Manufacturing Durable Goods Industries: Inventory-sales Ratios—Quarterly averages

tory investment are frequently hidden by other developments — some temporary — which are more dominant in influencing inventory policy. Often inventory accumulations in one major area of the economy are offset by liquidations elsewhere. Even so, it is of utmost importance that an evaluation be made of the three elements—demand, supply, and prices—in order to make a sound judgment on prospective inventory movements.

The next phase of the forecasting process is to examine the course of inventory-sales ratios for manufacturing and trade and their major subgroups of industries. Inventory-sales ratios which are widely used as indicators of the relative inventory position are quoted in press releases and in business reports. Such ratios are of some value and should be analyzed for whatever guides they may provide, not only regarding the current inventory position but also as to the trend. In 1970, for example, the ratio of nonfarm inventories (in 1958 dollars) to real GNP in-

creased steadily by quarters. This occurred even though business firms pursued a generally conservative inventory policy. The rising ratio developed mainly as a result of a sluggish rate of economic activity.

In using inventory-sales ratios as guides, it is important to ascertain how the ratio changed: through a change in inventory holdings, a change in total output or sales, or a combination of both. Unless this procedure is followed, an examination of the ratios alone may not throw much light on the nature of the change in the inventory-sales relationship. Indeed, as will be described below, a more fruitful approach is to examine the pattern revealed by a scatter diagram depicting inventories at the end of a period against sales during the period.

Inventory-sales ratios are especially useful in determining developments in specific industries. They quickly reveal aberrations due to unusual and nonrecurring events such as threats of strikes or actual strikes. In such periods, inventories of the strike-affected commodities are often built up and subsequently liquidated. If the industry is unable to produce enough for stock building purposes, the sequence may be reversed: liquidation of inventories first occurs and a buildup follows. For example, in the spring of 1963 steel users accumulated a large volume of finished steel items—three million tons. When the threat of a steel strike was removed, these inventories were liquidated—a process which continued until the end of the year. During the liquidation period, other industries, however, were increasing their inventories, so that for all industries the inventory change was about in line with the rise in GNP. More recently, during the General Motors strike auto stocks were reduced in October and November of 1970 and then were sharply built up by dealers in February and March of 1971.

Chart 1 shows the inventory-sales ratios for the volatile inventories held by durable goods manufacturing industries. The ratio declined sharply in the period 1961 through 1965. Note the effect of the large accumulations in 1966 and the adjustments over the next two years. They also suggest that excessive accumulations occurred in 1970 and an inventory adjustment followed thereafter.

In estimating inventory change through the use of the inventory-sales ratio two forecasts must be made: (a) the overall inventory-sales ratio and (b) sales for the industries considered. The principal guides for projecting the ratio have been discussed. In addition, it should be kept in mind that when the economy is operating at less than full capacity so that supplies are generally adequate in relation to demand, this is an important factor restraining inventory buying. If this condition should change and the supply of certain items should become tight, the inventory appraisal would have to take into account this changed situation. The product of the sales forecasts derived from the component groups and the projected inventory-sales ratio yields an estimate of inventories for the forecast period.

The procedure, however, does not end here. Other influences should be considered and may require a modification of the results obtained by the method outlined above. The amount of adjustment is often a matter of judgment on the part of the analyst. Are profits rising so rapidly that labor would make large wage demands, and are strike threats indicated? If so, some allowance may be required for this contingency. Are demands increasing so fast that shortages of certain goods may occur? If so, there may be an inventory flurry which would probably affect the subsequent movement. Is an incipient inflationary price spiral indicated? This may affect inventory investment decisions. Is money getting tight so that borrowing for inventory needs may become more costly or may need to be limited? If so, the initial inventory calculation may require modification.

Thus, it becomes clear that this approach is far from mechanical. At every step judgment is required—in the projection of the inventory-sales ratios, in the projection of sales, and in allowance for the effects of other anticipated influences. Despite the uncertainties involved, however, this is the procedure most commonly used by economists for forecasting inventories. On the whole, forecasts obtained by this approach generally have been reasonably good, although at times the predictions have missed the mark by a wide margin and on some occasions even the turning points have not been correctly called. But if an appropriate lag between inventories and sales is taken into account, if a judicious projection of the inventory-sales ratio is made, and if other factors are evaluated, this method will yield a forecast as good as, and frequently better than, that obtained by other techniques.

ANTICIPATIONS SURVEYS

A second approach to inventory forecasting makes use of a representative sample of businessmen's projections of their own stocks. That a survey approach of this type is both practical and fruitful is demonstrated by the survey of manufacturers' inventory anticipations which has been conducted by the Office of Business Economics of the Department of Commerce on a quarterly basis since 1958.

Cooperating manufacturers are contacted about the middle of a calendar quarter and report on a voluntary basis the book value of their inventories at the end of the preceding quarter and their anticipated values at the end of the current and following quarters. Thus the surveys provide a first anticipation of inventories, made 4½ months in advance, and a second anticipation, 1½ months ahead, which can be subsequently compared with the actual book values. Sales expectations for the corresponding periods are also collected.

In addition, each reporting company provides an evaluation of its inventory condition at the beginning of the forecast period. Taking into consideration sales and unfilled order backlogs, manufacturers rate their inventories as "high," "about right," or "low." This supplementary information has been useful in evaluating the effects of the size of inventory holdings at stages of the business cycle. Additionally, it has provided an important means (described below) of preparing accurate estimates of inventory anticipations.

The monthly inventory and sales series, published by the Department of Commerce since 1939, provide the "actual" data from which the forecasts are projected and against which the accuracy of the anticipations may be measured. The anticipations survey sample covers about 1,300 manufacturing companies accounting for more than half of total factory inventories. From the sample data, estimates of anticipated inventories are prepared for total manufacturing, for the durable goods industries as a group, and for the nondurable goods group.

The inventory anticipations of manufacturing firms, as compiled in the 30 quarterly surveys up to the end of 1970, reveal a systematic tendency toward understatement. In only two instances did first anticipations exceed actual inventories, and second anticipations were always below actual levels.

Analysis of probable factors accounting for the systematic bias or "error" in the raw anticipations points to the condition of inventories at the beginning of the period as a prime influence. It was found that the larger the proportion of inventories considered to be "high," the smaller the understatement of the forecast level of inventories for both first and second anticipations. It was also noted that when inventories were rising, the degree of underestimate in the anticipations tended to diminish, and vice versa. Variables such as sales and prices did not appear to affect the "error" to any significant extent. Unfilled orders held by the durable goods industries, however, proved to be a significant factor in explaining part of the "error."

Relationships were developed between the "errors" and the explanatory factors. These relationships provided the basis for computing "correction factors" to be applied to the "raw" anticipations. In the case of the durable goods industries, the correction factor was based upon a regression between the "error" as the dependent variable and two independent variables—inventory condition at the beginning of the forecast period, and unfilled orders. The square of the coefficient of correlation, or R^2 for this relationship, was 0.87 for the first anticipation and 0.93 for the second. This implies that all but seven percent of the variance in the "error" factor for the second anticipation was accounted for by these two independent variables. For the nondurable goods group, best results were obtained from a regression involving inventory condition and the seasonal pattern in the error. Here the corresponding R^2's were 0.82 and 0.87. In each case the "raw" anticipations were divided by the factors derived from the regression equation to obtain the anticipations corrected for bias.

The corrected anticipations have yielded fair results, as may be seen in table 3. From 1964 to 1970, the average absolute error between actual quarter-to-quarter change in inventories and the first anticipation change for all manufacturers was $0.6 billion. For anticipations one quarter ahead,

the average error was improved somewhat, $0.4 billion. In a few quarters the "errors" are substantial, but on the whole the survey does forecast reasonably well the inventory movements, particularly in periods of wide swings.

Similar surveys have not been at-

TABLE 3.   QUARTERLY DOLLAR CHANGE IN TOTAL MANUFACTURERS' INVENTORIES

Year & Quarter		Expected		Difference Between Actual and Expected	
	Actual	1st Q Ahead*	2nd Q Ahead†	1st Q Ahead	2nd Q Ahead
	(Billions of dollars)				
1964–1	0.5	0.3	0.4	0.2	0.1
2	0.4	0.4	1.0	0.0	−0.6
3	0.7	0.4	0.7	0.3	0.0
4	1.8	1.2	0.7	0.6	1.1
1965–1	0.7	0.7	0.6	0.0	0.1
2	1.1	0.7	0.9	0.4	0.2
3	1.5	0.9	0.8	0.6	0.7
4	1.4	0.4	0.5	1.0	0.9
1966–1	1.8	1.0	0.4	0.8	1.4
2	2.6	1.3	1.3	1.3	1.3
3	2.9	2.4	1.6	0.5	1.3
4	2.7	2.6	1.2	0.1	1.5
1967–1	1.9	1.8	1.9	0.1	0.0
2	0.9	1.3	1.3	−0.4	−0.4
3	0.6	0.6	1.2	0.0	−0.6
4	1.1	1.7	2.0	−0.6	−0.9
1968–1	1.0	2.0	0.7	−1.0	0.3
2	1.7	2.1	1.9	−0.4	−0.2
3	1.5	1.3	1.8	−0.2	−0.3
4	1.5	2.1	2.4	−0.6	−0.9
1969–1	1.8	1.3	1.9	0.5	−0.1
2	1.8	2.5	2.4	−0.7	−0.6
3	2.0	2.3	2.3	−0.3	−0.3
4	1.7	2.2	2.3	−0.5	−0.6
1970–1	1.1	1.1	1.5	0.0	−0.4
2	0.7	1.4	1.8	−0.7	−1.1
3	1.0	1.1	0.9	−0.1	0.1
4	0.9	1.2	1.3	−0.2	−0.3
1971–1	−0.2	0.0	1.6	−0.4	−2.0
2	...	0.6	1.3	...	...
3	...	...	0.9	...	...

Source: U.S. Department of Commerce, Office of Business Economics.
NOTE: Data are seasonally adjusted and anticipations are adjusted for systematic biases.
* Reported 1½ months in advance.
† Reported 4½ months in advance.

tempted for industries other than manufacturing. In trade, for example, the survey approach would be practically impossible since many retailers pursue an inventory buying policy of playing it by ear, i.e., ordering is based mostly on the rate and trend of sales in the recent period. In some lines of trade there is seasonal inventory buying, and the seller must make a judgment about requirements for the season ahead. But in view of the wide variety of practices by lines of trade, reliance in forecasting overall trade inventories must be placed on the method described in the preceding section.

Total nonfarm inventories at the end of 1964 amounted to nearly $172 billion (in 1958 prices). Of this total over one-half was held by manufacturers, nearly one-quarter by retailers, about fifteen percent by wholesalers, and the remainder (about seven percent) by other groups. These proportions are typical, but of course may vary somewhat quarter-by-quarter and over the cycle. The results of the manufacturing survey thus provide a guide to the change in inventories for a sector of the nonfarm economy that normally holds more than half of total stocks. As explained earlier, auto stocks can be forecast by appraising the strength of the auto market and the schedules of output of the automobile industry.[4] In other lines of trade it is necessary to examine the trend of the stock-sales ratios and the strength and general direction of the economy, as these may affect sales, as well as other factors mentioned earlier.

Farm inventory data are published only on a quarterly and annual basis. The farm series is based upon physical quantity data for crops and livestock as estimated by the Statistical Reporting Service of the Department of Agriculture. From 1959 to 1963, farm inventories, with few exceptions, have risen on a quarterly basis. Increases, however, have been relatively small—averaging about $0.5 billion per quarter (at annual rate) in the past decade. Changes in farm stocks are considerably smaller and much less volatile than the changes in nonfarm stocks.

Forecasting changes in farm inventories requires painstaking examination of Commodity Credit Corporation operations, including the effects of price supports for various commodities, of shifts in exports and in farm production programs, a consideration of trends in demand for farm products, and of the rate of buildup or reduction of live animal stocks. Here, only experts in these areas can provide reliable guides. For working purposes, however, a small adjustment for farm inventories may be made and then modified by any relevant, available information.

THE ECONOMETRIC APPROACH

In many ways the econometric approach to the problem of inventory estimation is the most solid and fruitful procedure. The method in theory involves the development of a complete econometric model for the economy as a whole, consisting of a set of equations which involve explicit relationships among the economic variables for the system. The equations can be many or few, depending upon the purpose of the model and the degree of detail required. One model being developed involves a system of more than 300 equations; another model already in use contains over 30; and some condensed models make use of only a handful of equations.

An important advantage in using a model for forecasting inventories is that the

---

[4] A complete statement of auto sales, stocks, and production is given in "Automobile Output in the Postwar Period," *Survey of Current Business* (February 1963), where a GNP for the automobile sector of the economy is developed in detail. This information is brought up to date in the quarterly GNP and national income data in the *Survey of Current Business*, Office of Business Economics, U.S. Department of Commerce.

results obtained are consistent with projected changes in variables representing other phases or activities in the economy. Thus, if consumer expenditures for goods are rising at a relatively slow pace, while business purchases of plant and equipment are rising at a rapid rate, the inventory forecast yielded by a model containing these variables would reflect the effects of, and be consistent with, these movements. Furthermore, various interesting and useful experiments can be made with the use of a model by arbitrarily assuming certain conditions with respect to the variables. For example, given an assumption that inventories remained stable throughout the postwar period instead of fluctuating as they actually did, the model would yield the effect of this assumption on the course of total economic activity, on the other major sources of demand, and on other variables in the system. A simulation along these lines was presented to the Joint Economic Committee[5] in order to throw light on the basic effects of inventory changes on the course of the postwar economy.

For most do-it-yourself enthusiasts, the development of an econometric model is out of the question, since in addition to the expertise required, it is time-consuming and must be constantly modified, tested, and evaluated. In the absence of an econometric model, a more direct and simpler approach can be used—the development of a single relationship between inventories and the "explanatory" factors which will yield a forecast of inventories associated with assumed or known values of these factors. An equation can be derived to "explain" inventories for quarterly, semiannual, or annual periods depending on the need.

It should be emphasized at the outset that no single equation has been developed that is completely and consistently reliable.

Every analyst working in this field has tried his hand at developing one or more equations for use in forecasting inventories. There have been literally hundreds of equations produced in attempts to explain inventory changes.[6]

From this extensive effort, no one has produced an equation which has continued to yield accurate forecasts. Some equations do produce reliable forecasts for a time, but then break down at other times. Others simulate past experience reasonably well, but do not work for the forecast period. The problem seems to be that inventory movements are often the result of deliberate decisions by management to build up inventories, maintain them at existing levels, or reduce them. These decisions often result from management's appraisal of the future course of demand, orders, price movements, cost of borrowing, competitive position, and a host of other factors. If the appraisal of some of the basic factors turns out to be erroneous, management may be caught with an undesirable inventory position in relation to current sales or incoming orders. Often the response to such an unexpected development is a drastic adjustment of inventories.

Also, an unforseen spurt in sales usually results in sales being made by drawing down stocks to dangerously low levels. At other times, certain industries may deliberately buildup stocks as a strikehedge; such a development must be taken into account in the forecast. However, even when it is known that stockpiling for strike-hedging purposes of such items as steel and copper will occur, estimates of the amounts involved may be difficult to judge. The timing of the stockpiling process may vary—in one period companies may start to build up stocks six or more months before the date

---

[5] See Lawrence Klein, Joint Committee Print, *Inventory Fluctuations and Economic Stabilization*, Washington, 1961.

[6] Some of these equations were presented in materials prepared for the Joint Economic Committee, Congress of the United States, *Inventory Fluctuations and Economic Stabilization, Part I, Postwar Fluctuations in Business Inventories*, Washington, 1961.

of the contract expiration; in another period stockpiling may begin only a couple of months sooner. Also, depending on cost considerations and financial position, companies may build-up stocks of one item for strikehedging, but trim inventories of other items so that total inventories may not reveal the effect of the hedging.

Thus, it is clear that even if an econometric equation contains all of the major factors relevant to inventory demand, the forecast obtained from such an equation may require modification so as to take into account special factors—in other words, there would still be a judgmental phase involved in obtaining the final usable forecast.

For purposes of illustration, two equations will be presented. These generally have given fairly good results, although at times they have yielded poor forecasts mainly due to the influence of special factors which the equations could not or did not take into account.

The objective in this approach is to find a formula which combines a set of factors known to be causative, i.e., determinants of inventory movements. The form of the equation is predetermined on logical or empirical grounds—usually being linear, either arithmetic or logarithmic.[7] The variables may be used either in the form of actual amounts or as changes from one period to another. The latter type of formulation is more logical for short-term forecasting and has certain other advantages.

As a rule, however, the correlation based on changes is not so high as the corresponding one using the actual levels.

The correlation technique—usually consisting of the least squares method[8] applied to historical data covering a sufficiently long period—yields the weights or coefficients to be applied to the determining factors (the so-called independent variables) and results in an estimating equation that will produce the "best fit" between the values calculated from the equation and the actual historical series. This equation is then utilized to forecast the dependent variable from the values of the independent factors for the forecast period.

An equation that contains only lagged values of the independent variables can be used directly to yield computed values for the forecast period. Where the variables involved are all concurrent, however, forecasts of these must first be obtained.[9]

The first illustration involves an analysis of the *annual* change in the physical volume of total inventory investment (GNP basis), that is, the change in the current year change in business inventories from the previous year change, expressed in 1958 dollars.

The major factors affecting the change in inventory investment are considered to be: (1) change in final goods sales, excluding nonresidential investment; (2) change in business inventories during the preceding year; and (3) change in plant and equipment outlays (producers' durable equipment plus new construction other than nonfarm

---

[7] These linear types are of the form: $Y = a + bX_1 + cX_2 + \cdots$, or $\log Y = A + B \log X_1 + C \log X_2 + \cdots$; These two forms have quite different properties. For example, the first form implies that for a given *absolute* change in one of the X variables, the *absolute* change in Y is independent of the levels of the other variables. The logarithmic equation implies that for a given *percentage* change in one of the X variables, the *percentage* change in Y is independent of the levels of the other variables; the *absolute* change, however, does depend on the levels.

[8] For an explanation of the types of equations used in regression analysis and the method of least squares, see any standard textbook on statistics; for example, *Methods of Correlations and Regression Analysis*, Mordecai Ezekiel and Karl A. Fox, third edition, John Wiley & Sons, Inc. New York. 1971.

[9] This procedure is not used when the equation is immersed in a complete econometric model which permits the simultaneous solution of concurrent variables.

residential). The regression was based upon
the eighteen-year period, 1953–70. The data
are expressed in billions of 1958 dollars.[10]
The least squares regression is as follows:

(1) $\Delta I = 0.57 + 0.1675\Delta FS$
           $- 0.6834I_{-1} + 0.6252\Delta PE$

where ΔI = change in inventory investment
            from the preceding year
    ΔFS = change in final goods sales from
            the preceding year (excluding
            plant and equipment outlays)
    I_{-1} = inventory investment in preced-
            ing year
    ΔPE = change in plant and equipment
            outlays from the preceding year
            (GNP) basis

This equation gives a fairly close approximation of the actual change in inventories.
Only in 1953 does the formula miss the
direction of the movement from the preceding year. In periods of wide swings, the
values calculated from the equation are
similar in direction and reasonably close in
value to the actual movements. In fact, the
average annual absolute deviation or "error" of the formula (average of differences
between actual and calculated values without regard to sign) is only $1.3 billion, with
the maximum "error" of $4.2 billion occur-
ring in 1953. Also, the square of the correlation coefficient $\bar{R}^2$ is 0.75, a remarkably
high value for a regression involving
changes.

Equation (1) can be used to forecast
changes in business inventories for a year
ahead. The use of this equation will be
illustrated by forecasting the change in
business inventories for 1971. All data are
in 1958 dollars.

The final goods sales reported in the

[10] The basic data are from OBE *Survey of
Current Business*: Supplement, August 1966,
*The National Income and Product Accounts
of the United States, 1929–65*; and the
monthly issues of the *Survey*, for July, 1968,
July, 1969 and May 1971.

May *Survey of Current Business* amounted
to $386 billion (1958 dollars); nonresiden-
tial structures and producers' durable equipment were $79 billion. Thus, for 1970 *FS*
equals $307 billion. We shall assume that
this total will increase 3.5 percent in 1971
over 1970. This is a realistic assumption
based on an assessment of federal and state
and local government programs, on consumer intentions to spend, and on prospective residential construction activity
deduced from anticipatory data. The detailed procedures for forecasting these components are described in other chapters of
this book.

The 1971 estimate of final goods sales
excluding plant and equipment is $318 bil-
lion and the change is $11 billion ($\Delta FS$); the
change in business inventories in 1970 was
$3.0 billion ($I_{-1}$).

The survey of businessmen's intentions to spend on plant and equipment,
reported by the government in March 1971,
showed a 4.2 percent rise in 1971 over 1970
and was subsequently revised to 2.7 percent.
This latter forecast implies a decline in
physical volume of about 2.0 percent, since
prices of capital goods are rising at the
annual rate of 4.5 to 5.0 percent. Since
plant and equipment outlays (1958 dollars)
in 1970 were $79.2 billion, the survey re-
sults suggest a 1971 projection of $77.6
billion. Thus ΔPE equals −$1.6 billion.

Using these values for the variables in
eq. (1) yields a calculated change in investment (ΔI) of −$1.6 million (1958 prices).
Adding this to the inventory investment in
1970 ($3.0 billion) results in a calculated
inventory investment in 1971 of $1.4 billion
(1958 prices). To convert this figure into its
equivalent in 1971 prices, we utilize the
movement of the implicit GNP price deflator. For 1970 the implicit price is estimated at 134.9 (1958=100); it is assumed
that in 1971 the price increase would moderate to 4.8 percent over 1970, giving an
implicit price index in 1971 of 141.4 (1958=
100). An approximation of inventory change

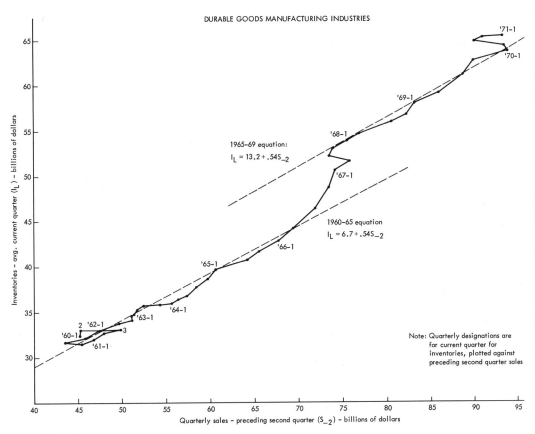

1965–69 equation:
$$I_L = 13.2 + .54S_{-2}$$

1960–65 equation
$$I_L = 6.7 + .54S_{-2}$$

Note: Quarterly designations are
for current quarter for
inventories, plotted against
preceding second quarter sales

Chart 2

in 1971 in current prices may be obtained by inflating the constant dollar figure by the 1971 price index, thus yielding a calculated change in inventories of about $2.0 billion. This may turn out to be low; but the annual rate of increase in the first quarter of 1971 was only $1.4 billion and preliminary results for the second quarter suggest about the same magnitude of change.

The second type of equation is much simpler and perhaps more revealing as to the nature of the underlying relationship between inventories and sales. It is essentially a little more sophisticated version of the inventory-sales ratio. The example is for book value inventories held by durable goods manufacturing industries. Recognizing that inventories tend to change after a change in sales occurs, the following form of the relationship was used:

$$(2) \qquad I_L = a + bS_{-2}$$

where I_L = inventory average for the current quarter, seasonally adjusted, in billions of dollars

S_{-2} = sales for the second preceding quarter

Chart 2 shows the quarterly pattern of producers' durable goods inventories related to sales for the period 1960 through first quarter 1971. It is apparent from the chart that there are two distinct relationships—the first fitting the observations from 1960 through 1965, and the second fitting those from 1967 through 1969. The second relationship is at a higher level and parallel to the first, suggesting that inventories in the earlier period may have been low in relation to sales. In any case, after the inventory boom year of 1966, producers ad-

317

justed their inventories along a new pattern parallel to that prevailing in the period prior to 1965.

The two equations depicting this pattern are:

For the period 1960 to 1965, by quarters,

$$(3) \qquad I_L = 6.7 + 0.54S_{-2}$$

For the period 1967 to 1969,

$$(4) \qquad I_L = 13.2 + 0.54S_{-2}$$

It may be noted that after mid-1970, inventories became excessively high relative to the previous pattern that had developed, thus suggesting future attempts by durable goods producers to bring them back in line. This did occur in the first quarter of 1971 when sales increased 6.4 percent over the fourth quarter of 1970, but inventories showed little change.

The forecast for several quarters ahead may be made on the assumption that equation (4) would prevail and computations of inventories for the second and third quarters of 1971 would be given from the actual sales for fourth quarter 1970 and first quarter 1971. It may be noted that 1971 is a year when steel consumers were buying steel as a strikehedge, so that an allowance for this distortion must be made in the forecast obtained from the relationship.

CONCLUDING REMARKS

Inventory investment usually fluctuates rather widely and often shifts direction from quarter to quarter. Over the long run, inventories are self-correcting, that is, pronounced accumulations or liquidations cannot continue for very long. But in the short run, shifts in inventory investment can have extensive economic repercussions, affecting the demand for labor, pricing policies, industrial operations, and final markets. Stated quantitatively, changes in inventory investment often have been important in their influence on the quarterly movements of GNP. Thus, a short-term economic forecast must include a careful evaluation of the probable course of inventory investment.

Although the quantitative approach through the use of regression equations which express inventory investment in terms of the causative factors is promising, this should be regarded as the starting point from which a final forecast is derived. In the end, the forecast must encompass an appraisal of a variety of factors and a consideration of businessmen's current inventory policies. Basic to a reliable forecast is a thorough knowledge of business developments in their major aspects and some detailed considerations of the inventory-sales trends by major industries and commodities.

BIBLIOGRAPHY

The literature on inventories is quite extensive. The following is a partial list of references relating to the problem of forecasting inventories.

Abramovitz, Moses, "The Role of Inventories in Business Cycles," Occasional Paper 26. New York: National Bureau of Economic Research, 1948.

Ackley, Gardner, "The Multiplier Time Period: Money, Inventories, and Flexibility," *American Economic Review* (June 1951), pp. 832–847.

Arthur, Henry, "Inventory Profits in the Business Cycle," *American Economic Review* (March 1938), pp. 142–163.

Bassie, V. L., *Economic Forecasting*. New York: McGraw-Hill Book Co., 1958.

Blodgett, Ralph H., *Cyclical Fluctuations in Commodity Stocks*. Philadelphia: University of Pennsylvania Press, 1935.

Brennan, Michael J., "Model of Seasonal Inventories," *Econometrica* (April 1959), pp. 216–237.

Clark, J. M., *Strategic Factors in Business Cycles*. New York: National Bureau of Economic Research, 1934.

Coben, George M., and Maurice Liebenberg, "Inventories in Postwar Business Cycles," *Survey of Current Business* (April 1959), pp. 187–214.

Coppock, D. J., "Periodicity and Stability of Inventory Cycles in the U.S.A.," Manchester, School of Economics and Social Studies (May and September 1959).

Daly, James P., "A Review of Existing Estimates of Business Investment in Inventories," *Conference on Research in Income and Wealth*, Vol. 19. New York: National Bureau of Economic Research, 1957.

———, "LIFO Inventories and National Income Accounting," *Survey of Current Business* (May 1953), pp. 16–22.

Darling, Paul G., "Manufacturers' Inventory Investment 1947–1958: An Application of Acceleration Analysis," *American Economic Review* (December 1959), pp. 1161–1190.

Duesenberry, J. S., Otto Eckstein, and Gary Froman, "A Simulation of the United States Economy in Recession," *Econometrica* (October 1960), pp. 416–428.

Eisemann, Doris M., "Manufacturers' Inventory Cycles and Monetary Policy," *Journal of the American Statistical Association* (September 1958), pp. 623–633.

Fujino, Shoyaburo, "Some Aspects of Inventory Cycles," *Review of Economics and Statistics* (May 1960), pp. 218–226.

Hickman, Bert G., "Diffusion, Acceleration, and Business Cycles," *American Economic Review* (September 1959), especially pp. 551–558, 823–833.

Hill, Richard M., "Inventory Cycles and Their Relationship to Distribution," *Current Economic Comment*, University of Illinois, Vol. 19 (August 1957).

———, "Retail Inventories as a Factor in Business Cycles," *Current Economic Comment*, University of Illinois, Vol. 21 (November 1959).

Klein, Lawrence, "Economic Fluctuations in the U.S., 1921–1941," *Cowles Commission Monograph No. 11*. New York: John Wiley & Sons, Inc., 1950.

Kuznets, Simon, "Changing Inventory Valuations and Their Effect on Business Savings and on National Income Produced," *Conference on Research in Income and Wealth*, Vol. 1. New York: National Bureau of Economic Research, 1937.

Lovell, Michael, "Manufacturers' Inventories, Sales Expectations, and the Acceleration Principle," *Econometrica*, 29, No. 3 (July 1961), pp. 323–328.

Mack, R. P., *Characteristics of Inventory Investment: The Aggregate and its Parts*, National Bureau of Economic Research: Studies in Income and Wealth, Vol. 19. Princeton: Princeton University Press.

Metzler, L. A., "Comments on the Influence of Inventory Investment on Business Cycles," *Conference on Business Cycles*, New York: National Bureau of Economic Research, 1951.

———, "The Nature and Stability of Inventory Cycles," *Review of Economics and Statistics* (August 1941), pp. 113–29.

Mills, Edwin S., "Expectations and Undesired Inventory," *Management Science*, 4 (October 1957), pp. 105–9.

—————, "Expectations, Uncertainty, and Inventory Fluctuations," *Review of Economic Studies*, Vol. 22, 1954–55, pp. 15–22.

—————, "The Theory of Inventory Decisions," *Econometrica*, 25, No. 2 (April 1957), pp. 222–38.

Modigliani, Franco, *Business Reasons for Holding Inventories and Their Macro-Economic Implications*, National Bureau of Economic Research, Studies in Income and Wealth, Vol. 19. Princeton: Princeton University Press, 1957.

—————, and Owen H. Sauerlender, *Economic Expectations and Plans of Firms in Relation to Short-Term Forecasting*, Conference on Research in Income and Wealth, Vol. 17. New York: National Bureau of Economic Research, 1957.

Moore, Geoffrey H., ed., *Business Cycle Indicators,* Vol. 2, National Bureau of Economic Research, Studies in Business Cycles 10, Princeton: Princeton University Press, 1961.

Nurkse, R., "The Cyclical Pattern of Inventory Investment," *Quarterly Journal of Economics* (April 1952), pp. 385–408.

Robinson, Newton Y., "The Acceleration Principle: Department Store Inventories, 1920–56," *American Economic Review* (June 1959), pp. 707–719.

Stanback, Thomas M., Jr., "A Critique of Inventory Forecasting Approaches," American Statistical Association, Business and Economic Statistics Section, 1960 Proceedings.

—————, "Cyclical Behavior of Manufacturers' Inventories Since 1945." American Statistical Association, Business and Economics Section, 1957 Proceedings.

Terleckyj, Nestor E., "Measures of Inventory Conditions," Technical Paper No. 5, NICD, 1960. Reprinted in Part II, Joint Economic Committee 1961 Study.

Tinbergen, Jan, and J. J. Polak, *The Dynamics of Business Cycles*. Chicago: University of Chicago Press, 1950.

U.S. Congress, Joint Economic Committee. "Inventory Fluctuations and Economic Stabilization." 87th Cong., 1st sess., 4 parts. Washington: Government Printing Office, 1961. Bibliography in Part III, pp. 205–18.

White, William H., "Inventory Investment and the Rate of Interest," *Banca Nationale del Lavoro, Quarterly Review*, No. 57 (June 1961).

JAMES BURTLE

Financial Planning
in Overseas Businesses

Very often U.S. companies have made substantial foreign operating profits, only to lose most of these earnings in foreign exchange fluctuations.

Companies operating abroad can lose from either devaluation or revaluation. In the case of devaluation, unremitted foreign currency earnings will be worth less in U.S. dollars. Also, a company will lose if it has credits outstanding or accounts receivable to be repaid in depreciated currency. A case in point is the selling abroad of consumer durables on installment credit. On the other hand, a company that is in a net debtor position abroad will lose if there is a revaluation; in effect, a larger debt than was originally borrowed will have to be repaid in upvalued currencies.

Some companies have managed to avoid currency losses by squaring off "long" (devaluation vulnerable) and "short" (revaluation vulnerable) positions against each other. Potential devaluation losses on cash holdings and accounts receivable are offset by potential gains on accounts payable. For revaluation, the losses on accounts payable are offset by gains on accounts receivable. Where it is not feasible to square off long and short positions, it may nevertheless be

The author is grateful to Dr. Edward Marcus, professor of economics at Brooklyn College and Dr. Alan Teck of the Chemical Bank for valuable suggested revisions in content and presentation.

possible, particularly for major European currencies, to use forward currency markets as insurance against currency losses. A U.S. company can enter into a contract to sell the vulnerable currency at the current non-devalued exchange rate at some specific date in the future. Then, if there is a devaluation before the contract date, the U.S. company would not lose from devaluation. Likewise for revaluation, a vulnerable position can be protected by a contract to buy the currency forward.

Thus, especially in countries with better developed financial markets, it is often possible to arrange some form of "cover" against losses from currency adjustments. It is usually a mistake, however, for a company to attempt to protect itself from every conceivable currency loss. Covering foreign exchange risks on forward currency markets often requires paying discounts (on contracts to sell forward as insurance against devaluation) or premiums (on contracts to buy forward as insurance against revaluation). Likewise, a policy of borrowing to avoid devaluation risks may involve high interest charges. These costs will be a waste of money if currency adjustments are unlikely to occur. Hence the rationale for a program to forecast currency risks.

An adviser on company foreign currency policy thus acts as a kind of insurance broker. Besides evaluating risks in foreign exchange exposure, he has the equally seri-

321

TABLE 1.   CURRENCY RISK STATEMENT, APRIL 1971

Countries with a 25%–50% probability of revalution within the next 12 months

---

Germany (Deutsche mark)
Japan (yen)
Switzerland (franc)
Netherlands (guilder)
Belgium (franc)

Countries with a 25%–50% probability of devaluation within the next 12 months

---

United Kingdom (pound)
Sweden (krona)
Norway (krone)
Denmark (krone)

Countries with a low probability (less than 25%) of currency change within the next 12 months

---

Italy (lira)
France (franc)
Spain (Peseta)

---

ous responsibility of recommending whether or not foreign exchange cover will be worth its cost. Sometimes there may be a risk of revaluation or devaluation but the costs of cover may be greater than a reasonable expectation of losses from a currency change. For example, in the summer of 1970 there was perhaps a 25% probability that the Italian lira would be devalued by 10%, but this would not have justified a "cover" operation of selling lira forward at the then prevailing discount of 6.0% on one-year contracts (25% of 10%—the expectation of loss from devaluation—was less than 6%). Likewise, through most of the 1960s, Mexican pesos sold forward at discounts often as high as 4.0%. In retrospect, it seems clear that the probabilities of a Mexican peso devaluation were not great enough to justify paying such high "insurance".

On the other hand, there have been numerous cases when there was strong justification for paying the costs of protection against currency losses. As of September 16, 1968, French francs could have been sold forward for one year at a 1.72% discount; On January 5, 1968 German marks could have been bought one year forward at a

2.50% premium. Both of these costs were reasonable insurance rates against the August 1969 devaluation of the French franc by 11.1% and against the October 1969 revaluation of the mark by 9.3%.

An evaluation of currency risks is usually put in probability form with a rough statement of the chances of future devaluations or revaluations. A simple example is shown in table 1. Sometimes the currency outlook statement is prepared in more detail, with probabilities of currency devaluations or revaluations specified for each of several dates in the future. Based on this evaluation plus its own financial position abroad, a company can devise a strategy for optimal insurance against currency risks. For multinational corporations operating large numbers of subsidiaries abroad in multiproduct, multicurrency businesses, this management strategy may be complicated; according to some experts it requires the use of computers and operations research techniques.[1] But it should be emphasized that, regardless of financial and operations

---

[1] See, for example, Bernard Lietaer, *Financial Management of Foreign Exchange* (Cambridge, Mass.: MIT Press, 1971).

TABLE 2. INDICATORS OF DEVALUTION VULNERABILITY, APRIL 1971

Country	(1) Gold and Foreign Exchange Reserve and Latest Month Available *(Millions)*	(2) Average of Latest Three Months C.I.F. Imports *(Millions)*	(3) Ratio of Reserves to Imports[a]	(4) Months of Import Cover[b]	(5) April 16, 1971 % (Discount)/ Premium on One-Year Forward Contract
Switzerland	$ 3,810 Mar	$ 542 Dec–Feb	58.6%	7.0	1.42%
Germany	15,519 Mar	2,583 Dec–Feb	50.1	6.0	0.47
Spain	2,009 Feb	387 Dec–Feb	43.3	5.2	(1.15)
Italy	5,880 Feb	1,252 Dec–Feb	39.1	4.7	(0.50)
France	5,490 Mar	1,599 Dec–Feb	28.6	3.4	(0.32)
Japan	5,458 Mar	1,637 Nov–Jan	27.8	3.3	1.86
Belgium	3,113 Feb	1,033 Oct–Dec	25.1	3.0	0.30
Netherlands	3,528 Feb	1,230 Oct–Dec	23.9	2.9	0.94
Norway	743 Feb	341 Nov–Jan	18.1	2.2	(0.13)
United Kingdom	3,317 Mar	1,951 Jan–Mar	14.2	1.7	(1.92)
Denmark	596 Mar	404 Oct–Dec	12.3	1.5	(2.70)
Sweden	850 Feb	617 Nov–Jan	11.5	1.4	(1.25)

[a] Column 1 divided by 12 times column 2.
[b] Column 3 multiplied 12 times.

research sophistication, success in foreign exchange managements depends primarily on an adequate forecast of exchange rates.

The next section considers crude lead indicators of the exchange rate outlook. It is pointed out that these indicators, while useful, do not in many cases provide enough lead time for a company to react soon enough to protect itself at minimum cost from the effects of currency changes. Balance of payments analysis, as discussed further on, while more lengthy, tedious, and costly in research time, is likely to give an earlier advance warning of currency changes. Finally, this chapter considers the less quantitative but nevertheless very important political elements in an exchange rate forecast.

LEAD INDICATORS OF EXCHANGE RATE CHANGES

Situations requiring currency devaluations are not symmetrical to those requiring currency revaluations. In the typical case, a country devalues when it foresees a shortage of foreign exchange far below import requirements. On the other hand, a country revalues when the inflow of foreign exchange becomes large enough to be an inflationary danger. Thus, a quite different set of lead indicators is required for devaluation vulnerability as compared to revaluation vulnerability.

For devaluation vulnerability, a rough-and-ready lead indicator is the ratio of exchange reserves to the latest reported level of imports (usually annualized). Exchange reserves are a country's central bank holdings of gold and foreign currencies.[2] In order to smooth out random variations, imports are often taken as an average of the past three months. Sometimes the reserves/imports ratio is multiplied by 12. The resulting figure shows the number of months of the current level of imports that could

[2] Exchange reserves also include International Monetary Fund gold tranch positions and special drawing rights (SDRs).

be paid with the current level of exchange reserves. Table 2 shows the calculation of these ratios for major countries.

There are no hard-and-fast rules indicating when the reserve/imports ratio points to devaluation vulnerability. But table 2 does show that, as of April 1971, the countries with the lowest reserves relative to imports—the United Kingdom, Denmark, and Sweden—were also the countries for which the foreign exchange markets required the greatest discounts for selling their currencies forward.

For revaluation vulnerability, we have less past experience on which to justify the use of a lead indicator. Nevertheless, it is clear that anti-inflation policy is one of the main elements in a decision to revalue. A country has a large inflow of foreign currency that is converted into the national currency. Too much national currency creation is so inflationary that a revaluation is adopted to stop further inflows of foreign currency on a massive scale. Whether or not a currency inflow is large enough to be an inflationary danger can sometimes be appraised by taking the ratio of the change in a country's reserves in a particular quarter (i.e., the amount of foreign currency taken in by a country's central bank) with the money supply at the beginning of the same quarter. For comparability, both amounts should be converted into the same currency. An example of calculations of this ratio for the fourth quarter of 1970 is shown in table 3.

Central banks can to some extent "sterilize" the money supply effects of the reserve inflow by such methods as raising reserve requirements for the banks, selling bonds to the banks or to the public, and raising taxes. Nevertheless, a high reserve inflow/money supply ratio does indicate revaluation vulnerability. In table 3, three of the four countries with the highest reserve inflow/money supply ratios revalued (Switzerland) or allowed their currencies to float upward (Germany and the Netherlands).

But while the methods used in tables 2 and 3 give some forewarnings of proneness to devaluations or revaluations, these indicators should be used with caution and judgment. For example, the relatively high 17.8% annualized reserve inflow/money supply figure for Norway should not be interpreted as a lead indicator of revaluation. Table 2 shows Norway's reserve/import ratio at 2.2 months, which is not high enough to justify revaluation. Also, Norway's close ties with Denmark and Sweden (which have devaluation vulnerable currencies) are a decisive deterrent to its going "out on a limb" with a revaluation.

BALANCE OF PAYMENTS ANALYSIS

The ratios discussed above appear to be the most quickly available lead indicators of vulnerabilities to devaluations or revaluations. But obviously these indicators must be used with extreme care. Sometimes governments, by short-term borrowing or doubtful accounting methods, are able to raise artificially their reserves and thus distort the reserve/import ratio. Inflows of speculative money can temporarily raise the reserve inflow/money supply ratio and thus give a false signal of impending revaluation.

Moreover, the reserve/import ratio and the reserve inflow/money supply ratio may fail to give early enough warning signals of dangers of currency changes before costs of hedging foreign exchange risks become prohibitively expensive. Balance of payments analysis (which is a step-by-step rundown of a country's main sources and uses of foreign exchange) provides, with more lead time, a more dependable but also more costly and time-consuming method for anticipating currency vulnerabilities. Balance of payments items arising from transactions in goods and services are mainly the trade balance (exports minus imports), ship-

TABLE 3.   RESERVES AND MONEY SUPPLIES, MAJOR COUNTRIES AND AREAS

	(1) Reserves	(2) Reserves	(3)	(4)	(5)	(6)	(7)
	End of Third Quarter, 1970	End of Fourth Quarter, 1970	Increase/ (Decrease) in Reserves Third-Fourth Quarter, 1970	Money Supply, End of Sept. 1970 (Seasonally adjusted)	Change in Reserves as a % of Money Supply, End of Sept. 1970 Actual	Annualized[a]	Average Annual Rate of Growth in Money Supply. 1961–69
	(Millions)	(Millions)		(Millions)			
United States	$15,527	$14,487	$(1,040)	$199,700	(0.5)%	(2.1)%	4.1%
United Kingdom	2,666	2,827	161	40,068	0.4	1.6	4.6
France	4,743	4,960	217	38,201	0.6	2.2	8.9
Belgium	2,790	2,847	57	8,002	0.7	2.8	6.3
Canada	4,553	4,679	126	13,070	1.0	4.1	8.4
Japan	3,996	4,839	843	52,386	1.6	6.4	16.7
Italy	4,515	5,299	780	43,878	1.8	7.1	14.0
Denmark	392	484	92	3,747	2.5	9.8	12.3
Austria	1,672	1,757	85	2,720	3.1	12.5	7.7
Sweden	671	762	91	2,785	3.3	13.0	7.4
Netherlands	2,989	3,234	245	7,055	3.5	13.9	8.7
Norway	710	807	97	2,179	4.5	17.8	6.5
Switzerland	4,080	4,701	621	9,497	6.5	26.1	7.8
Germany	11,301	13,610	2,309	25,984	8.9	35.5	7.2
Total of 13 developed countries, excluding United States	$45,082	$50,806	$5,724	$249,572	2.3%	9.2%	9.7%

[a] Actual multiplied four times.

TABLE 4.   U.S. BALANCE OF PAYMENTS, 1970

	Receipts		Payments		Balance
	(In billions of dollars)				
Merchandise trade (goods)	$42.0		$39.9		$2.1
Services	20.9		19.4		1.5
Military		1.5		4.9	−3.4
Investment income		11.4		5.2	6.2
Travel		2.3		4.0	−1.7
Other		5.7		5.3	0.4
Balance on goods and services	62.9		59.3		3.6
Remittances, pensions, and other transfers	...		1.4		−1.4
Balance on goods, services, and remittances	62.9		60.7		2.2
U.S. government grants, excluding military	...		1.7		−1.7
Balance on current account	62.9		62.4		0.4
Long-term government capital	1.5		3.3		−1.8
Long-term private capital	4.6		5.9		−1.5
Direct investment		1.0		4.4	−3.5
Portfolio investment		2.2		0.9	1.2
Bank and other loans (net)		1.4		0.6	0.8
Balance on current account and long-term capital	69.0		71.6		−3.0
Non-liquid short-term capital	0.8		1.4		−0.5
SDR allocations	0.9		...		0.9
Net errors and omissions	...		1.1		−1.1
Net liquidity balance	70.7		74.1		−3.9
Decline in private liquid dollar assets	...		...		−6.0
Balance of payments, official settlements basis,					
including SDRs	...		...		−9.8

Source: U.S. Department of Commerce, *Survey of Current Business,* June 1971, tables 1 and 2.
NOTE: Figures may not add up because of rounding.

ping, travel, and earnings and payments on foreign investment. Also in the balance of payments are one-way payments (called transfer payments) of which the main items are foreign aid and remittances by immigrants. Finally the balance of payments includes capital movements, both short-term and long-term.

Methods of forecasting balance of payments items are not, in principle, different from other types of forecasting. Export and import forecasting, for example, is a special case of forecasting sales. Forecasting foreign aid is a special case of forecasting government policy. International capital, as in domestic economies, will tend to move toward areas of greater return relative to the

risks involved. The main distinction between forecasting on an international level and forecasting in a domestic economy is that controls and restraints on both trade and capital movements are more pervasive in the international economy.

Because it is likely to already be familiar, the U.S. balance of payments will be taken as an example. Special problems relating to the balance of payments of countries other than the United States will be noted. Also we will point out where the U.S. balance has peculiarities not found elsewhere. Table 4 shows a simplified U.S. balance of payments for 1970.

The most well-known item in the balance of payments is, of course, the balance of trade: exports[3] minus imports (at $2.1 billion). The services account in the balance of payments (at $1.5 billion) arises from payments and receipts of investment income, military transactions, travel, and other services items including transportation and royalty payments. The balance on goods and services (at $3.6 billion) combines the merchandise and services accounts.

Remittances (at $1.4 billion outflow) are by immigrants and philanthropic organizations; this item also includes government payments of pensions.

Government grants (at a $1.7 billion outflow) comprise U.S. foreign aid grants excluding military. The other government item in the balance of payments is U.S. official lending (at $3.3 billion) minus repayments (at $1.5 billion), netting a $1.8 billion outflow.

Private capital transactions (at a $1.5 billion net outflow) involve international payments to acquire (or sell) assets abroad. Long-term capital movements—where the investment does not mature within less than a year—are mainly for direct investment (at a net $3.5 billion outflow), portfolio investment (at a net $1.2 billion inflow), and bank loans and miscellaneous transactions (at a net $0.8 billion inflow).

In direct investment, the assets acquired internationally remain under control of the investor. He either acquires a controlling interest in a firm abroad or extends the assets of his own operations abroad as, for example, by building a new plant. In portfolio investment, on the other hand, the funds are used to buy stocks or bonds in a foreign company but do not result in control of the foreign business.

Special drawing rights (SDR) allocations (at $0.9 billion) are a type of "paper gold" issued by the International Monetary Fund and which, subject to relatively minor restrictions, IMF members have agreed to accept in international payments.

Typically nonliquid short-term funds (at a $0.5 billion outflow) go into foreign government obligations or other money market investments. Or short-term money may be deposited in savings accounts in foreign private banks. However, this item excludes changes in liquid short-term assets. These assets in effect arise from balance of payments deficits or surpluses rather than being a component part of the balance of payments. If, for example, foreign banks buy U.S. liquid short-term assets, this is interpreted only as a convenient way of holding the dollars they have gained from a U.S. balance of payments deficit. It is implicitly assumed that, if there were no U.S. balance of payments deficit, foreign banks would not increase their holdings of U.S. liquid short-term assets. (This is the treatment of short-term capital by the Balance of Payments Division of the U.S. Department of Commerce since June 1971. Previously, short-term capital movements—and also some items in the government accounts —had a different interpretation in the officially presented U.S. balance of payments).[4]

The net errors and omissions item in table 4 (at $1.1 billion outflow) arises because, after all balance of payments (liquidity basis) transactions are estimated, the total of transactions should add up to total means of financing—by gold, foreign currency flows, SDR allocations, and changes in foreign private and official short-term claims on the United States. However, statistics of international transactions are never perfect. There is bound to be a discrepancy between the reported items in the balance of payments versus the items financing the balance of payments. This is the errors and omissions item.

---

[3] This analysis (as is the usual practice) excludes U.S. government grants of military hardware. At $0.6 billion in 1970, this credit in the U S. export account is washed out with a debit to foreign aid.

[4] For a technical discussion of these differences, see David T. Devlin, "The U.S. Balance of Payments, Revised Presentation," *Survey of Current Business* (June 1971).

The plus and minus items in (1) goods and services, (2) remittances, (3) long-term capital, (4) short-term capital, (5) SDRs, and (6) errors and omissions, add up to the net liquidity balance (at $3.9 billion deficit including the SDR allocation). However, not all of the balance of payments outflow will necessarily end up in central banks, where at least in principle it would consistitute a claim on the U.S. gold supply. Part of the outflow may remain in private banks. Where the balance of payments includes the change in central bank claims (but not private claims) against the United States, it is called the official settlements balance (at $9.8 billion deficit in 1970). When the official settlements balance rises/falls compared to the net liquidity balance, it means that dollar funds have moved from/to private holdings into/from central banks and thereby raised/lowered claims on the United States by central banks. Thus, the changes in private liquid dollar assets show up in the difference between the official settlements balance and the liquidity balance. For 1970, the $6.0 billion decline in private liquid dollar assets is added to the net liquidity deficit at $3.8 billion to result in a $9.8 official settlements balance. In other words, in addition to the $3.9 billion outflow for specific balance of payments items, $6.0 billion moved from private holdings into central banks.

The sections which follow discuss in detail some of the problems of projecting key balance of payments items.

THE TRADE BALANCE: DEVELOPED COUNTRIES

Forecasting of exports and imports is really a special case of sales forecasting, although a country usually sells a much wider variety of products than would be offered by a single company. As in the case of most individual products, there is a substantial body of econometric evidence indicating that as real incomes rise the volume of imports rises and, though with somewhat less generality, as prices of imports rise the volume of imports tends to fall. On a global basis, exports are the opposite side of the coin from imports. With adjustments for transit time and some technicalities, world imports should equal world exports. But exports of a particular country are determined not only by total world imports but—and here the analogy with sales forecasting is again evident—by its market share of total world imports. For most developed countries, the average of their export prices, compared to export prices of competing exporters, is a key variable affecting market share.

Exports and imports are also affected by strikes, trade restrictions, trade agreements, capacity utilization rates, and a host of other factors. Obviously not all the elements affecting exports and imports can be quantified. But econometric studies of trade balances do "explain" a substantial part of the variations in imports and exports. Among the most recent of these studies are a trade model by the Organization for Economic Cooperation and Development[5] (OECD) and an article by Houthakker and Magee.[6] Table 5 shows some of the Houthakker-Magee regression output. For example, with respect to U.S. imports, a 1.0% rise in U.S. income, on average, matches up with a 1.51% rise in U.S. import volume, a 1.0% rise in foreign prices relative to U.S. prices matches up with a 0.54% decline in U.S. imports. In most cases, especially for income elasticities, these results satisfy the usual criteria for "good" regressions: high R^2, Durban-Watson test values higher than unity, low standard errors, and high t-values

[5] Frans Meyer-zu-Schlochtern and Akira Yajima, "OECD Trade Model: 1970 Version," *OECD Occasional Studies* (December 1970).

[6] H. S. Houthakker and Stephen P. Magee, "Income and Price Elasticities in World Trade," *Review of Economics and Statistics* (May 1969).

TABLE 5. HOUTHAKKER-MAGEE ESTIMATES OF INCOME AND PRICE ELASTICITIES IN WORLD TRADE

Country		Imports Constant	Imports Elasticity Income	Imports Elasticity Price (P_1)	Imports $\bar{R}^2$ (s.e.)	Imports D.W. (d.f.)	Exports Constant	Exports Elasticity Income	Exports Elasticity Price (P_2)	Exports $\bar{R}^2$ (s.e.)	Exports D.W. (d.f.)
United States (F = 10.28)		4.98 (2.40)	1.51 (12.09)	−0.54 (−1.59)	0.976 (0.0421)	1.11 (13)	12.18 (6.85)	0.99 (10.46)	−1.51 (−3.24)	0.933 (0.0480)	1.82 (13)
Canada (F = 4.87)		6.53 (5.89)	1.20 (16.31)	−1.46 (−2.67)	0.956 (0.0472)	1.25 (13)	4.79 (5.48)	1.41 (22.31)	−0.59 (−2.85)	0.973 (0.0396)	1.76 (13)
United Kingdom (F = 20.73)	(a)	1.14 (0.97)	1.66 (10.54)	0.22 (1.07)	0.975 (0.0314)	1.20 (13)	7.26 (7.17)	0.86 (9.38)	−0.44 (−1.45)	0.976 (0.0238)	1.29 (13)
	(b)	2.36 (8.07)	1.51 (23.93)		0.974 (0.0316)	1.29 (14)					
Japan (F = 89.88)		4.12 (3.70)	1.23 (13.06)	−0.72 (−2.40)	0.985 (0.0777)	2.40 (13)	−4.78 (−1.53)	3.55 (14.82)	−0.80 (−1.78)	0.984 (0.0925)	1.04 (13)
W. Germany (F = 1.35)	(a)	1.15 (1.07)	1.80 (17.25)	−0.24 (−0.91)	0.995 (0.0424)	1.17 (13)	−8.45 (−2.66)	2.08 (9.56)	1.70 (1.97)	0.967 (0.0922)	0.55 (13)
	(b)	0.18 (1.12)	1.89 (55.21)		0.995 (0.0422)	1.21 (14)	−2.29 (−3.86)	2.44 (19.18)		0.961 (0.1013)	0.24 (14)
Italy (F = 2.96)	(a)	−1.57 (−0.50)	2.19 (6.48)	−0.13 (−0.18)	0.979 (0.0808)	1.21 (13)	−5.58 (−1.24)	2.95 (10.45)	−0.03 (−0.04)	0.988 (0.0703)	1.13 (13)
	(b)	−2.15 (−5.65)	2.25 (27.48)		0.980 (0.0780)	1.17 (14)	−5.74 (−15.47)	2.96		0.989 (0.0678)	1.13 (14)
Netherlands (F = 0.00)	(a)	−1.00 (−0.51)	1.89 (11.37)	0.23 (0.44)	0.989 (0.0432)	2.04 (13)	3.14 (1.41)	1.88 (37.10)	−0.82 (−1.63)	0.994 (0.0306)	0.97 (13)
	(b)	−0.16 (−0.70)	1.82 (38.14)		0.990 (0.0419)	1.89 (14)		1.88 (43.88)			
France (F = 0.68)	(a)	0.64 (0.28)	1.66 (9.31)	0.17 (0.26)	0.961 (0.0759)	1.42 (13)	11.98 (6.23)	1.53 (31.21)	−2.27 (−5.63)	0.987 (0.0399)	2.35 (13)
	(b)	1.22 (3.24)	1.62 (20.00)		0.964 (0.0734)	1.46 (14)					

NOTE: The number in parenthesis below each coefficient is a t-ratio.

TABLE 5.   (CONT'D)

Imports Constant	Imports Income	Imports Price (P_1)	Imports $\bar{R}^2$ (s.e.)	Imports D.W. (d.f.)	Country		Exports Constant	Exports Income	Exports Price (P_2)	Exports $\bar{R}^2$ (s.e.)	Exports D.W. (d.f.)
1.49 (0.89)	1.94 (13.10)	−1.02 (−2.33)	0.995 (0.0284)	1.27 (13)	Belgium– Luxemburg (F = 0.22)	(a)	−2.33 (−1.25)	1.83 (19.58)	0.42 (1.31)	0.985 (0.0471)	1.17 (13)
						(b)	0.09 (0.35)	1.74 (30.73)		0.984 (0.0483)	0.92 (14)
−0.21 (−0.09)	1.13 (5.42)	1.04 (1.60)	0.796 (0.0954)	1.42 (13)	South Africa (F = 0.84)	(a)	14.10 (3.84)	0.88 (4.93)	−2.41 (−3.76)	0.930 (0.0744)	1.25 (13)
3.49 (6.37)	0.85 (7.21)		0.773 (0.1005)	1.26 (14)		(b)					
3.03 (0.91)	1.42 (4.12)	−0.79 (−1.02)	0.978 (0.0502)	1.50 (13)	Sweden (F = 1.14)	(a)	−3.52 (−1.56)	1.76 (25.33)	0.67 (1.52)	0.987 (0.0406)	2.01 (13)
−0.36 (−1.14)	1.76 (25.57)		0.978 (0.0503)	1.43 (14)		(b)	−0.11 (−0.47)	1.69 (32.25)		0.986 (0.0425)	1.31 (14)
1.72 (0.75)	0.90 (5.06)	0.83 (0.86)	0.620 (0.1348)	1.01 (13)	Australia (F = 1.75)	(a)	2.79 (3.29)	1.18 (15.90)	−0.17 (−1.37)	0.972 (0.0468)	2.74 (13)
3.59 (4.40)	0.90 (5.12)		0.627 (0.1336)	1.10 (14)		(b)					
1.10 (0.21)	1.81 (7.82)	−0.84 (−0.45)	0.974 (0.0679)	0.92 (13)	Switzerland (F = 3.12)	(a)	3.27 (4.75)	1.47 (46.54)	−0.58 (−3.36)	0.997 (0.0176)	2.81 (13)
−1.27 (−3.47)	1.90 (24.31)		0.975 (0.0659)	0.91 (14)		(b)					
5.00 (1.71)	1.31 (4.54)	−1.66 (−2.40)	0.987 (0.0463)	1.54 (13)	Denmark (F = 2.21)	(a)	1.88 (1.30)	1.69 (39.49)	−0.56 (−1.69)	0.992 (0.0312)	1.60 (13)
2.49 (2.25)	1.40 (10.74)	−0.78 (−3.50)	0.992 (0.0309)	1.90 (13)	Norway (F = 0.79)	(a)	−1.57 (−0.64)	1.59 (20.45)	0.20 (0.40)	0.967 (0.0588)	1.05 (13)
						(b)	−0.61 (−1.79)	1.58 (21.60)		0.969 (0.057)	1.06 (14)

of regression coefficients. [Where price regression coefficients were insignificant or illogical in sign (plus instead of minus) the regressions were repeated without including the price variable. Regressions without prices are indicated by (*b*) under country.] But in spite of the relatively good results by regression studies of international trade, it cannot be repeated too often that regressions are nothing more than a formal way of assuming that history repeats itself. The best of regressions will go wrong when there is a change in structure. Structural changes could affect international trade if, for example, the United Kingdom and some other European countries joined the European Economic Community. Abolishing Japanese import restrictions could result in another important structural change. Sometimes regression analysis can be supplemented by survey data in which major importers and exporters are asked their opinions on the likely outlook. For the United States, such surveys are carried out annually by the National Foreign Trade Council. Replies to questions can be a useful check on regression results and may give advance warning of an impending breakdown of an apparently "old reliable" regression.

An alternative to the aggregative regression analyses of the OECD and Houthakker-Magee studies is to attempt a breakdown of exports and imports according to classification by commodities and/or destinations. Then, it can be argued, regressions will reflect more "pure" structural relationships. Such a breakdown may be useful for a basic research project but seems impractical for business economists who, especially in the international area, usually have limited resources. Moreover, there is little evidence that for developed countries such disaggregation does improve the already technically adequate aggregative regressions explaining exports and imports. Finally, for some countries detailed export and import data become available too late to be useful for many forecast end purposes, notably exchange rate projections.

There is a possible compromise between the "splitters" who want endless breakdowns of trade data and the "lumpers" who are generally inclined, for most developed areas, to aggregate all imports and exports for each country. One can exclude from total export and import data certain products for which the demand has a significantly different structure. Obviously this list should be kept small; otherwise there will be a resurgence of the problem of unmanageable data. The OECD regression analysis excludes "Car trade between the U.S. and Canada, German imports of weapons, Canadian exports to Communist countries, and U.K. imports of aircraft from the U.S." There is also a strong argument for special treatment of U.S. agricultural exports.

Another difficulty in a regression-based forecast is that the buck is passed to forecasting independent variables. As indicated in table 5, imports and exports depend on future prices and incomes. In a complete model, as is done for major macroeconomic variables in some countries, unknown parameters in a whole set of equations are estimated simultaneously. Such has not been achieved for the international economy[7] and it is not usually possible for an international business economist to attempt his own forecasts of major macro variables in all foreign countries. He has to make a discriminating choice among forecasts made in other countries. Major sources of forecasts abroad are the Organization for Economic Cooperation and Development (Paris), National Institute for Economic & Social Research (London), Business International (New York), and the United Nations Economic Commission for Europe

[7] But there are some beginnings. See B. Hickman, L. R. Klein, and R. R. Thomberg, "Background, Organization and Preliminary Results of Project LINK," and J. Waelbroeck, "The Methodology of Linkage," papers presented to the Second World Congress of the Econometric Society, September 1970.

(Geneva). The OECD forecasts cover the broadest range including GNP components, prices, balance of payments data, and industrial production. OECD forecasts are probably backed up by the most staff work compared to other forecasting groups. Some observers believe, however, that the OECD can be politically influenced against forecasts that are too gloomy.

It should be emphasized that the accuracy required of independent variables for analysis of exports and imports may be less than what might be required for purposes of domestic policy. A forecast that would be inadequate for fiscal-monetary management of a country might be adequate for projecting exports and imports. This is especially true of price trends where a crude extrapolation of year-end prices into the next year may suffice unless there is clear evidence that some structural changes (such as the French upheaval of 1968) will result in a rapid buildup of inflation.

THE TRADE BALANCE: LESS DEVELOPED COUNTRIES

Thus far we have mainly considered the trade balance of developed countries. For these countries, as already noted, imports tend to tie in with incomes and relative prices. For less developed countries, however, there is a tendency for demands for imports—if simply related to incomes—to rise so rapidly that foreign exchange reserves would be exhausted. Usually, by a wide variety of controls, imports are restricted to availabilities of foreign exchange. The OECD study[8] found that imports of non-OECD countries were "explained" with a highly significant relationship, as follows:[9]

[8] *Ibid.*

[9] $R^2 = 0.984$, $D.W. = 1.50$. $t =$ values of regression coefficients are: 6.6 for lagged exports, 2.9 for capital, and 5.8 for reserves.

Log deflated imports
$$= +0.527 \text{ log export volume of} \\ \text{previous year} \\ +0.310 \text{ log deflated capital inflow} \\ +0.313 \text{ log deflated reserves}$$

This means that aggregate imports of less developed countries could arise from spending part of the proceeds of exports plus part of the net capital inflow plus part of reserves. The formula is not necessarily accurate for each less developed country when considered separately, but it may be indicative of some overall tendencies.

An alternative way of projecting imports of less developed countries is to project all balance of payments credit and debit items except imports, make a judgment about how much reserves will be drawn down (or built up) and thus come out with imports as a residual. The main difficulty in this method is that it requires projecting each balance of payments item separately; for many of these, there are neither adequate data nor adequate methods for projecting.

It is clear, however, that whatever forecasting method is used for less developed countries, the tie-in between imports and exports becomes more direct. Thus a projection of exports aside from its direct interest is usually a *sine qua non* for projecting imports. In the typical less developed country, a large proportion of export earnings are derived from primary products such as coffee, sugar, copper, and petroleum. Thus the projection of imports of a particular less developed country usually leads to a projection of prices and volumes of primary products.

A substantial literature is beginning to develop on projecting primary product output and prices. Demand for most primary products is insensitive to prices but sensitive to incomes. Thus the revenues from most of these commodities fluctuate widely. In special cases such as petroleum and aluminum, however, the world market is oligopolistic without violent price swings. For petroleum, copper, and some other industries, often foreign owned, an estimate of future profit remittances should of course be deducted from export earnings in estimating import capabilities.

Guidance in formulating models of trade and prices of agricultural products can be obtained from the economic advisory services of the U.S. Department of Agriculture and from the Economic and Social Department of the Food and Agricultural Organization (Rome). Models of production and prices of primary metals are being pioneered in the Clearinghouse for Federal Scientific and Technical Information at the U.S. National Bureau of Standards.

SERVICES ITEMS IN THE BALANCE OF PAYMENTS

Aside from the merchandise account, the current account balance, as shown in table 4, includes military grants, investment income, travel, and a wide range of other noncapital items which will not be considered separately. Most of the latter items are not practical to project individually with much degree of precision, but are likely to show a rising trend or (as may be the case of transportation expenditures) some simple correlation with trade data. However, the three items noted require further comment.

Projection of military expenditures[10] is to a great extent a matter of political judgment of how much is likely to be appropriated for this purpose. There is, how-

---

[10] This item includes U.S. military spending abroad under grants but not shipments of military hardware. As noted earlier, shipments of military grants are included in exports broadly defined; then this item is offset by an entry in the foreign aid account. In our balance of payments statement we have netted out both of these figures.

ever, usually a substantial amount of foreign military expenditure in the pipeline between appropriations and expenditures so that, even if the military budget is cut, there may be a lag before the curtailment shows up in the balance of payments. Projecting the debit military item in the balance of payments is also a political judgment—usually to what extent foreign governments will be persuaded to pay part of the military bill.

Investment income depends on the amount of assets and liabilities abroad and the rate of remittances on these investments. For the United States, a detailed breakdown in assets and liabilities is presented in the latter part of each year in the *Survey of Current Business*. Other countries present much less data, although some rough indications of assets and liabilities abroad can be gained from statements of the foreign official debt and by adding up previous net capital outflows. Applying expected interest rates to various government securities can give a rough indication of the extent of government remittances. For private capital, the problem is more complicated because of great uncertainties of (1) rates of return on these investments and (2) the amount of earnings that are retained overseas. The *Survey of Current Business* annually shows the book value of U.S. investments abroad and the net income on these investments. From these data a rate of return can be derived, but its exact meaning may be deceiving inter alia because of lack of uniformity of accounting methods and write-ups of foreign businesses acquired by U.S. companies. We are working on a model for rates of return on U.S. investment abroad in manufacturing. A key element here is to develop rough indicators of profit margin changes abroad from data on productivity, wages, and prices. Forecasts from such a model will have a wide range of error but may point to extreme profit squeezes such as occurred in Germany in 1967 or Italy in 1969.

The travel item in the balance of payments is important as a debit for a number of developed countries, including the United States and Germany. On the other hand, it is a big plus item for such tourist areas as Switzerland, Italy, Spain, Mexico, and Greece. In principle, travel can be treated as a consumer good. With higher income, consumers spend more for travel. They also tend, *ceteris paribus*, to prefer cheaper countries to more expensive countries. Both of these elements account for France swinging away from a highly favorable travel balance of payments up to 1964, to a minor or negative balance in more recent years. With higher French national income, more French nationals traveled abroad and, with higher French prices, France became relatively more expensive for incoming tourists.

Tourism is also affected by political disturbances, by government restrictions on spending abroad, and by air fares. Political tension in a particular area is an obvious deterrent to tourism. Governments under balance of payments pressure severely limit the amount of foreign exchange that travelers may take abroad. World tourism has obviously benefited from the long-term downward trend in air fares. (It should be noted, however, that passenger fares per se are included in the transportation account, not in the tourist expenditure account.)

In table 4 private (nonbusiness) remittances are, in line with standard balance of payments practice, considered separately from the goods and services account. This, along with government grants mainly for foreign aid, is dubbed a transfer since it is neither a payment for goods and services nor a movement of capital. Private remittances arise mainly from payments sent to their original homes (usually to relatives) by persons working abroad. Countries for which remittances are a significant credit item include Italy, Spain, Ireland, Greece, and Portugal. This item tends to follow a rather smoothly rising trend except in cases where the country receiving immigrant

workers has a recession (as in Germany in 1967) or restricts immigration (as the United States in the 1920s or Switzerland in 1970). Donations abroad by philanthropic organizations are also included in this item. These are especially important to Israel's balance of payments.

THE GOVERNMENT ACCOUNTS

As shown in table 4 the government account comprises loans, which are a capital transaction, and grants, which are a transfer.[11] There are of course loans among developed countries, such as the loans to the United Kingdom in the 1960s in an effort to support sterling, the loans to France after the disturbances of 1968, and purchases of so-called Roosa bonds by other developed countries from the United States in an effort to support the dollar. Most of these loans follow a balance of payments crisis in a major country and thus should be forecast on an ad hoc basis. The other major part of official lending is from developed countries to less developed countries.

Since loans to less developed countries are usually soft in that they are long-term and low interest, it is convenient to group these with government grants and label the total as foreign aid. Projecting foreign aid is mainly an exercise in political judgment. There has been a tendency for U.S. foreign aid to decline. It dropped from $3.6 billion in 1964 to $3.1 billion in 1970 (OECD basis).[12] There is a lag, however, between foreign aid appropriations and actual balance of payments results. Some types of aid such as Export-Import Bank loans and farm

[11] Government transfer payments also include reparation payments of substantial importance between Germany (debit) and Israel (credit), and between Japan (debit) and the Philippines and Indonesia (credits).
[12] Development Assistance Committee, Organization for Economic Cooperation and Development, *1971 Development Assistance Review*. This is the so-called DAC report which is produced annually.

TABLE 6.   OFFICIAL DEVELOPMENT ASSISTANCE AND NATIONAL PRODUCT

Country	1964	1965	1966	1967	1968	1969	1970
Net Flow of Official Assistance in Relation to Gross National Product, 1964–70[a]							
France	0.89%	0.75%	0.69%	0.71%	0.69%	0.69%	0.65%
Netherlands	0.28	0.36	0.45	0.49	0.49	0.53	0.63
Australia	0.48	0.52	0.53	0.60	0.57	0.56	0.59
Belgium	0.45	0.59	0.42	0.45	0.42	0.51	0.48
Portugal	1.83	0.57	0.59	1.02	0.68	1.04	0.48
Canada	0.17	0.19	0.33	0.32	0.26	0.34	0.43
Denmark	0.11	0.13	0.19	0.21	0.23	0.41	0.38
Sweden	0.18	0.19	0.26	0.25	0.28	0.44	0.37
United Kingdom	0.53	0.47	0.46	0.44	0.40	0.39	0.37
Norway	0.15	0.16	0.18	0.17	0.29	0.31	0.33
Germany	0.44	0.38	0.37	0.43	0.41	0.39	0.32
United States	0.57	0.50	0.45	0.44	0.38	0.33	0.31
Japan	0.15	0.28	0.28	0.32	0.25	0.26	0.23
Italy	0.09	0.10	0.12	0.22	0.19	0.16	0.16
Switzerland	0.07	0.08	0.08	0.08	0.14	0.16	0.15
Austria	0.14	0.34	0.31	0.24	0.20	0.12	0.13
Total DAC countries	0.49%	0.45%	0.42%	0.43%	0.38%	0.36%	0.34%

Source: OECD DAC Report, 1971.

[a] At market prices.

product disposal programs are funded for several years ahead. As already noted for military expenses, moneys in the pipeline may be spent even though appropriations may be cut off.

After World War II, the United States was by far the greatest donor of foreign aid. However, its importance relative to Europe began to decline in the 1960s.

Later on in the 1970s, it seems unlikely that U.S. foreign aid will continue to decline. Table 6 shows percentages of foreign aid to GNP of OECD countries. The United States now ranks twelfth among the sixteen countries considered. There is some reason to suggest, however, that the OECD definitions of foreign aid are prejudicial to the United States, which does not have nationals in formerly dependent territories benefiting from foreign aid. Nevertheless, there is a strong possibility that, if its proportion of aid to GNP declines much more, the United States will come under international pressures to raise its foreign aid. Looking ahead, another possibility is that foreign aid may not grow much in the future but the developed countries will adopt a "trade, not aid" policy of giving preferences to imports, especially of manufactures, from less developed countries. A straw in the wind is the proposal of the European Economic Community Commission (the executive body of the EEC) to permit, subject to some limitations, duty-free entry from less developed countries of up to 5% of total EEC 1968 imports of each manufactured product.

THE PRIVATE CAPITAL ACCOUNT[13]

As shown in table 4, the private capi-

[13] An econometric analysis of international capital movements using relatively up-to-date statistical information is found in William H. Branson and Raymond D. Hill, Jr., "Capital Movements Among Major OECD Countries: Some Preliminary Results," *Journal of Finance* (May 1970), Papers and proceedings of the American Finance Association.

tal account is broken down between long-term and short-term capital. Long-term capital comprises direct investment, portfolio investment, and bank and miscellaneous lending. Private international short-term capital includes capital transactions of less than one-year maturity. However, as already discussed, increases in liquid deposits, borrowing, or other international assets/liabilities are not included in the U.S. balance of payments. This is because the dollar is a reserve currency. Thus inflows of short-term capital into U.S. banks are not interpreted as an improvement in the U.S. balance of payments, but simply as an improvement in other countries' reserves that are put into liquid dollar assets as a store of value. For most other countries, however, short-term capital inflows/outflows from/to abroad are counted as part of the balance of payments surplus/deficit.

Another important difference between the United States and other countries is in the calculation of the direct investment outflow/inflow. In U.S. balance of payments accounting, the direct investment outflow excludes reinvested earnings of subsidiaries of U.S. companies. However, in some countries the amount of direct investment is swollen to include reinvested earnings. The reinvested earnings are offset, however, in the investment income account. In other words, it is assumed that all earnings are repatriated and then part of these earnings are again remitted abroad for direct investment. For some countries this procedure may be unavoidable because of lack of full data on foreign investment transactions. Otherwise we have a perhaps chauvinistic preference for the apparently simpler U.S. method of direct investment accounting.

DIRECT INVESTMENT

As already noted, the *Survey of Current Business* each year publishes a comprehensive statement of United States direct investment abroad indicating outflows, book values, and earnings. These data might enable an econometric basis for forecasting, but unfortunately the usable part of the series is not long enough. The Department of Commerce data extend back through the 1950s, but only since 1958 has there been nonresident convertibility of European currencies. This sharp change in structure leaves us with about twelve observations in each country—not enough for an econometric analysis of a complex subject. Moreover, outflows of U.S. direct investment have been curtailed since January 1, 1968 by Office of Foreign Direct Investment regulations. Since the regulations were imposed, direct investment has gone up from $3.0 billion in 1968 to $4.4 billion in 1970. This seems to indicate some easing by the administration of OFDI regulations but, as with so many other balance of payments items, a political judgment is required for looking ahead. If the dollar comes under much greater pressure, OFDI regulations could be tightened.

Compared to U.S. direct investment abroad, foreign direct investment in the United States, at $969 million in 1970, is relatively small. But this item is growing rapidly; in 1968 at $319 million it was less than one-third as much as in 1970.

Direct investment to and from countries other than the United States is more difficult to estimate simply because most non-U.S. data on book value, earnings, and rates of return abroad are at best scrappy and indequate. On an a priori basis there will be a tendency for direct investment to move where rates of return are highest. But some countries with relatively high rates of return, notably Japan, restrict foreign direct investment. In other cases, especially in less developed countries, rates of return may be high but so are the political risks. In these areas capital inflows are likely to respond only to relatively high rates of return.

PORTFOLIO INVESTMENT

Portfolio investments into the United

States tend to be sensitive to gyrations in the U.S. stock market. A bull market attracts portfolio investment. A bear market, as in 1970, repels it. The same tends to be true of foreign stock markets but for some countries, notably France and Italy, lack of complete or accurate information is a deterrent to security purchases. Many foreign stock markets are thin and there are no controls comparable to Securities and Exchange Commission regulations. The consequent danger that security prices will be manipulated is an obvious minus for portfolio investment.

If the outlook for the dollar can be stabilized, it seems reasonable to expect that fluctuations in foreign purchases of U.S. securities will be superimposed on a rising secular trend. This conclusion follows from prospects for greater savings in the developed world, more concern with finding inflation hedges, and better organization, compared to other countries, of the U.S. capital market.

Except for Canadian securities, U.S. purchases of most foreign securities were restricted by the September 1963 Interest Equalization Act. This imposed special taxes on purchases by U.S. nationals of foreign stocks and bonds. U.S. security buying abroad is substantially less than foreign purchases of U.S. securities. In 1969 (a more normal year than 1970 for security purchases) U.S. net purchases of foreign securities were $1.5 billion, while foreign purchases of U.S. securities were $3.1 billion.

SHORT-TERM CAPITAL

Private short-term capital movements are usually motivated by either (1) interest arbitrage or (2) capital flight. Capital flight involves a movement away from a weak currency widely expected to devalue (such as the British pound in 1967), or a movement of funds into a strong currency widely expected to revalue (e.g., the German mark

in 1969). As already noted, the forecaster should evaluate a country's balance of payments prospects before capital flight becomes large enough to dominate the balance of payments. At that stage of the game, forward discounts or premiums are likely to become so expensive that there may be little benefit from using forward contracts as protection against currency changes.

Aside from capital flight, interest arbitrage is a major factor in short-term capital movements. In some cases a high interest rate will be sufficient to attract short-term capital into a country. In other cases lenders may fear the danger of devaluation and borrowers may fear revaluation. These risks can be hedged by selling or buying forward contracts in the devaluation or revaluation vulnerable currencies. It turns out that short-term arbitrage capital will tend to move into countries where short-term interest rates plus the premium/discount of a corresponding contract are greater than prevailing rates elsewhere. For example, if the rate of interest on three-month commercial paper in a particular country is 6%, and three-month forward contracts sold at 0.5% discount, the hedged rate will be 5.5%. If this is greater than corresponding short-term rates elsewhere, short-term capital will tend to enter the country. On the other hand, if the hedged rate is less than interest rates elsewhere, arbitraged short-term capital will tend to leave the country. Table 7 shows an example of the calculation of United Kingdom hedged interest rates on three-month sterling. Eurodollar rates are taken as representative of interest rates external to the United Kingdom. Thus, forecasting interest arbitrage movements of short-term capital becomes a problem of:

1. Forecasting short-term interest rates (discussed in the chapter by McKenney and Jones) and
2. Forecasting premiums or discounts on forward exchange rates

In many cases a country in balance of payments difficulty, of which Denmark in 1970

TABLE 7.   COMPARISON OF INVESTMENT YIELDS: POUND STERLING SECURITIES VS.
EURODOLLAR INVESTMENTS, MARCH-JUNE 1971

Date	Current Yields on 90-Day Eurodollar Investments	Current Yields on 90-Day Pound Sterling Investments (Prime hire-purchase paper)	Cost of 90-Day Hedge (Expressed on a % per annum basis)	Net Yield on Pound Sterling Investments After Cost of 90-Day Hedge	Net Yield on Pound Sterling Investments After Cost of 90-Day Hedge Over/(Under) Eurodollar Investments
3/ 5/71	5.00%	8.13%	(3.70)%	4.43%	(0.57)%
3/12/71	5.06	8.50	(3.43)	5.07	0.01
3/19/71	5.06	8.13	(3.21)	4.92	(0.14)
3/26/71	5.31	8.13	(2.94)	5.19	(0.12)
4/ 2/71	5.63	7.25	(2.39)	4.86	(0.77)
4/ 8/71	6.37	7.25	(2.58)	4.67	(1.70)
4/16/71	5.75	7.25	(2.75)	4.50	(1.25)
4/23/71	6.00	7.13	(2.36)	4.77	(1.23)
4/30/71	6.25	6.50	(2.10)	4.40	(1.85)
5/ 7/71	7.25	6.63	(1.31)	5.32	(1.93)
5/14/71	6.87	6.50	(1.17)	5.33	(1.54)
5/21/71	6.56	6.88	(1.17)	5.71	(0.85)
5/28/71	7.88	7.25	(0.93)	6.32	(1.56)
6/ 4/71	7.00	7.00	(1.17)	5.83	(1.17)

was an example, will adopt high interest rates in order to attract short-term capital. However, if this tactic is adopted after a currency's parity is obviously doomed, the balance of payments advantage of a high short-term interest rate may be vitiated by a higher forward discount. Thus the forecaster of exchange rates should be suspicious of balance of payments viability maintained by short-term capital inflow. Such money is fickle and will turn around in a hurry in response to relatively small changes in interest rates or forward discounts.[14]

[14] Sometimes there is a third scene in the drama of a country defending its exchange rate on the short-term capital front. As noted, scene one is higher interest rates, and scene two is an offsetting high discount on forward exchange rates. Scene three is government support of the forward rate by issuing more contracts to buy the currency in the future and thus prevent a large forward discount. However, if the government's holdings of forward contracts become large, as was the case with the United Kingdom in 1967, devaluation can become all the more of an

Aside from covered interest arbitrage money, there is also a certain amount of uncovered interest arbitrage money moving between countries. Thus, for March–June 1971, analysis of the British balance of payments seems to indicate that there was an inflow of short-term capital in spite of the fact that hedged interest yields in the United Kingdom were usually less than for Eurodollars. A substantial part of the money market was willing to take the risk of U.K. devaluation in order to benefit from higher unhedged yields.

SPECIAL DRAWING RIGHTS

Special drawing rights allocations are predetermined by the International Mone-

embarrassment. The government will be obliged to use up much of its surviving reserves to buy back its currency at a predevaluation rate.

tary Fund and should not therefore present a short-run forecasting problem. Looking further ahead, the outlook for SDRs is highly uncertain. SDRs were developed when it was widely believed that there was a shortage of international liquidity. However, the massive United States deficits of 1969 and 1970 and the expansion of the Eurodollar market (a mechanism that unfortunately space does not permit us to discuss here[15]) have led to a situation that many economists consider excessive world liquidity. Hence the doubtful SDR prognosis.

ERRORS AND OMISSIONS

As already noted, the errors and omissions item in a country's balance of payments arises because total *recorded* payments do not add up exactly to its total receipts plus the change in its net short-term assets. Several elements are important in the errors and omissions item:

1. There are often serious recording errors in reporting exports and imports. Particularly when goods are duty-free, valuations may be notoriously careless. Data applicable for one year may be held over until the next year.
2. Many estimates of other current account items, notably tourist expenditures, are at best rough guesses. In some countries, of which Italy and Spain are likely examples, when the currency is endangered "tourist expenditure abroad" rises as it thinly veils a substantial amount of capital flight.
3. Exports and imports are recorded on a value, not payment, basis. But payments are often delayed (especially when devaluation threatens) or speeded up (when revaluation seems likely, as with the yen in 1971). If imports and exports each amount to $10

billion, a 10% rise in payments for imports and a 10% slowdown in payments for exports can swing the balance adversely by $2 billion. This is the so-called leads and lags effect.

4. Finally, the errors and omissions item normally includes a substantial amount of short-term capital moving through unrecorded channels. Usually this item swells when a currency is threatened with devaluation. In some countries there may be evasions of exchange controls or, as in the United States, the workings of a sort of grey money market. Since 1965 the United States has imposed "voluntary" controls on bank lending to foreigners. However, there are no controls on private individuals placing funds abroad.

THE LIQUIDITY AND OFFICIAL SETTLEMENTS BALANCES

By summing up his estimates of all the items just discussed, the intrepid forecaster can project the U.S. balance of payments on a liquidity basis. An even greater challenge is estimating the U.S. balance of payments on an official settlements basis. As already noted, this requires estimating changes in liquid dollar holdings of private individuals and conversely the changes in dollar reserves of central banks. In principle, estimating the official settlements balance thus involves an analysis of the balance sheets of private and central banks in each country. Events remote from U.S. monetary management can cause substantial swings in the official settlements balance. This was true in 1969 when, after the mark revalued, dollars that had entered Germany speculatively moved out of the German central bank and into Eurodollar banks. Thus dollar claims on the United States declined and the official settlements balance improved.

Some clues to future official settlements balances may be provided by interest rate differences. If interest rates on Euro-

[15] See, for example, Dr. Fritz Machlup, "The Magicians and Their Rabbits," *Morgan Guaranty Survey* (May 1971).

dollars (i.e., dollars in private banks abroad) move higher than interest rates on other currencies, there will be a tendency to hold back dollars from central banks and put them into Eurodollar deposits. Such a move can improve the official settlements balance. But this model has in recent years lost its simplicity since central banks have themselves become major depositors in Eurodollar banks. There is, however, now some concern that as central banks have put their own dollars into Eurodollars, these deposits have become boomerang money that speculators or interest arbitragers put back into central banks. Through a process analogous to the textbook story of credit expansion under fractional reserve banking, Eurodollars have expanded at a rate far beyond world liquidity requirements. Against this background, the Bank for International Settlements, which manages much of the placement of central bank reserves, is reviewing the workings of the Eurodollar market. The result, and it may already have started, may be a withdrawal of central bank Eurodollar deposits. This withdrawal may be highly desirable for world liquidity control but, since it will increase central bank dollar holdings, one consequence may be further deterioration in the official settlements balance.

THE POLITICAL SIDE OF CURRENCY FORECASTING

Thus far we have presented some simple lead indicators of currency changes: reserve/import ratios as harbingers of devaluations and reserve inflow/money supply ratios as pointing toward revaluations. However, in order to avoid foreign exchange cover costs, it is desirable not to wait for these indicators to flash the red light. Instead, the indicators should be forecast at least in rough order of magnitude. This is done through balance of payments analysis.

But it is insufficient to evaluate a currency outlook only vis-a-vis the balance of payments and the lead indicators. There have been numerous cases in which governments were able to revive a weak currency. Especially in cases of threatened devaluations, currencies have been protected by austerity policies that had the effect of restraining imports, pushing up exports, and otherwise turning around the balance of payments. Likewise, expansionist policies can prevent revaluations.

Thus the final judgment of a currency outlook is as much political as economic. It depends on whether or not the government of a country with a vulnerable currency has broad enough political support to carry through an austerity program. Also involved is the priority the government gives to currency stability. Countries with currencies that serve as reserve currencies or in widespread international financial operations are likely to have a higher priority for the avoidance of exchange rate changes.

Since austerity programs usually involve slower rates of economic growth, key elements in judging whether a government will decide to devalue are its growth rate (usually in real GNP) and its unemployment rate. A country with slow economic growth, a high unemployment rate, and a beleaguered currency, usually sacrifices the exchange rate. On the other hand, if the real GNP growth rate is high and unemployment is low, it may be relatively easy for a government to restrain the economy without moving under a political cloud.

BIBLIOGRAPHY

Bank for International Settlements (Basle), *Annual Report*.

Branson, William H., and Raymond D. Hill, Jr., "Capital Movements Among Major OECD

Financial Planning in Overseas Businesses 341

Countries: Some Preliminary Results," *Journal of Finance* (May 1970), Papers and proceedings of the American Finance Association.

Commerzbank (Dusseldorf), *Foreign Exchange Market Report* (weekly).

Duprez, C., and E. S. Kirschen, eds., *Megistos, A World Income and Trade Model for 1975*. Amsterdam: North-Holland Publishing Company, 1970.

Financial Times (London), Columns by Samuel Brittan and C. Gordon Tether (Lombard).

Food and Agricultural Organization (Rome), *Yearbook of Agricultural Statistics* and numerous special studies.

Houthakker, H. S., and Stephen P. Magee, "Income and Price Elasticities in World Trade," *Review of Economics and Statistics* (May 1969).

Hudson, Michael, *A Financial Payments-Flow Analysis of U.S. International Transactions: 1960–1968*. New York University Institute of Finance, Bulletin Nos. 61–63, March 1970.

International Monetary Fund, *International Financial Statistics, Balance of Payments Yearbook, Balance of Payments Concepts and Definitions (1969), Balance of Payments Manual (1961)*.

Journal of Commerce (New York), "World Money Front," a daily review of foreign exchange developments.

Kruger, Anne O., "Balance of Payments Theory," *Journal of Economic Literature* (March 1969).

Lietaer, Bernard, *Financial Management of Foreign Exchange*. Cambridge, Mass.: MIT Press, 1971.

Morgan Guaranty Trust Company, *World Financial Markets*.

National Foreign Trade Council, Annual press release on results of their survey of trade expectations. *Breve* (Europe) and *Noticias* (Latin America): digest of leading press articles.

National Institute for Economic & Social Research (London), *National Institute Economic Review*.

Organization for Economic Cooperation and Development (Paris), "OECD Trade Model: 1970 Version" by Frans Meyer-zu-Schlochtern and Akira Yajima in *OECD Occasional Studies* (December 1970), Annual economic surveys of member countries, *Economic Outlook, Main Economic Indicators*, Annual reports of the Development Assistance Committee.

Reimann, Guenter, ed., *International Reports* (weekly). Includes up-to-date data for interest arbitrage analysis.

Rundt, S. J., *Rundt's Weekly Intelligence* (New York). Includes weekly forward rate quotations.

United Nations, *Monthly Bulletin of Statistics, Annual Report of the Economic Commission for Europe, Yearbook of International Trade Statistics*.

U.S. Bureau of Standards, Reports of the Clearinghouse for Federal Scientific and Technical Information.

U.S. Department of Agriculture, Annual Foreign Crop Forecast.

U.S. Department of Commerce, *Overseas Business Reports, Survey of Current Business* (especially the June 1971 issue explaining the new form and concepts in U.S. balance of payments accounting).

Weekly Bond Buyer (New York), Foreign Exchange and Money Market column by Patricia O'Brien and London Arbitrageur's Letter by Sydney Gampell.

RICHARD H. KAUFMAN

Assessing the International Environment for Business

The scope of international business has expanded significantly over the decade of the 1960s. And further expansion is in prospect for the 1970s. Gone are the days when international business only meant exporting, importing, and licensing agreements—and when overseas investment was concentrated in the extractive industries. Gone, too, is the very subordinate role of international departments in overall company policy. Indeed, profits derived from their overseas operations were a major factor in bolstering the overall profit position of many U.S. companies during the 1970 economic recession.

International business increasingly involves the establishment of operating facilities in foreign countries in order to take better advantage of evolving market opportunities. The decision to invest abroad often follows a successful exporting effort, where the market has been tested and a distributorship network has been set up. The growing number of companies with investments abroad—the multinational companies—has been one of the major economic phenomena of the past decade and has had enormous implications for national economic development and international finance. Today, there are few large American companies where some aspect of foreign business isn't under constant review—be it a decision to establish facilities in a particular country or to hedge a foreign currency. And news of

an impending devaluation or revaluation is listened to intently by an increasing number of businessmen around the boardrooms of the world.

As more and more companies become involved in international business, there is a corresponding growth in the need to know more about the future business environment around the world. Unfortunately, many of the techniques used to assess the international environment when it was of little concern to the average businessman are still in use today, despite the growing importance of international business matters for many companies. One of the major problems in forecasting the international environment for business is that it is tied closely to overall economic conditions. But the economic environment, in turn, is heavily influenced by noneconomic factors. An investor in the United States can more or less assume that social and political factors are "given" and thus need not interfere with his forecast of the overall economy and its implications for his particular industry. But once the investor goes beyond his borders, the informational problem begins to magnify. He must take more variables into account, often with less specific information on each variable.

In such a situation, businessmen tend to rely on crude indicators of future developments. For some strange reason, they are more inclined to believe what foreign gov-

342

ernment officials have to say about their countries' prospects than what their own domestic officials say about domestic conditions. The fact is that government officials can later justify any remark by the need to restore confidence in any particular situation. The fires of hell burn brightly with finance ministers who denied even the possibility of a currency devaluation right until the time when the currency was devalued. How many government spokesmen have said that the economy has just turned the corner, when it was really slipping further downhill? And how many leaders of government have downgraded their economic critics as purveyors of gloom and doom, and stubbornly resisted taking necessary corrective action? It is only natural that government leaders, as politicians, try to cast everything in the best possible light. It is also only natural for investors to disregard their statements and reach their own conclusions about business and financial prospects from less biased sources.

DATA PROBLEMS

Considering the heavy financial involvement of companies in international business, there is no reason why this field should resist more scientific determination. This means, first and foremost, taking a hard look at the quantitative information. The problem here, however, is the availability of information and the reliability of what is available. While this problem is general, it is more acute when analyzing a typical less developed country. The economist generally has only a minimum amount of statistical information available to him and much of this is not very current and hence not very useful. Most of the statistical information comes from such sources as central banks, government statistical offices, the U.S. government, the International Monetary Fund and the United Nations. While

substantial improvements have been made in improving the flow of information in recent years, there are still widespread deficiencies that challenge the business forecaster. He must treat basic GNP figures with considerable skepticism, with the real figure within a range of plus or minus 20% from the official data. Even population figures, which are the basis of per capita calculations, are themselves subject to much error. In trying to forecast the situation six months ahead, it is not unusual to be working with data that are six months old or more. Revisions of preliminary data tend to be substantial. All this leads to considerable forecasting uncertainties and a tendency to substitute one's own judgment for more scientific analysis.

In forecasting business conditions in the developed countries, the informational problem is much less serious. A continual stream of statistics flows out of the various government agencies and private institutes. While often not as detailed as in the United States, the information is generally usable for quantitative analysis. Of all the countries, Japan probably ranks on top in terms of speed of reporting and method of presentation. They have developed the knack of getting figures out rapidly—seemingly before the reporting period is over. In the advanced countries, the problem is not so much the adequacy of the data—although there is always room for improvement in any country—as in its interpretation. The fact that a country's foreign exchange reserves are rising does not necessarily indicate a favorable balance of payments trend, because foreign borrowings could mask a basic payments imbalance. And the fact that a country's cost-of-living index is stable does not necessarily mean the absence of inflation, since rising imports could at least for a time absorb the inflationary pressures.

The textbook kind of economic theory still provides the best insights into analyzing current and prospective situations, despite the different institutional arrangements of the various countries. Where wages rise faster than productivity, the result will be higher prices. Where domestic prices rise faster than in other countries, the result will be balance of trade and balance of payments pressures. And where such pressures arise, the result will be foreign exchange controls of one kind or another and/or currency devaluation. The problem is not so much to determine the trend as to gauge the timing and actual extent of future changes. Here is where quantitative information needs to be supplemented by a judgment of the strength of economic factors. But social and political considerations also need to be taken into account.

In assessing a country's business environment, it is essential that the long-term factors which will influence its financial prospects be given high priority. This is especially important where a long-run investment is involved, since there are innumerable short-term situations that go against the underlying long-term trend. While social and political forces are considered to be outside the purview of the economist, it is almost impossible to assess the investment climate without them. In many cases it would be bad judgment—leading to wrong conclusions—to regard such factors as "given." Nowhere is there more a need for the reemergence of the political economist than in the field of international forecasting. The fact is that many of the mistakes in the field of international financial planning came from too little emphasis on political and social factors—or even longer-term economic trends—just because they are so difficult to get a handle on. Yet, these underlying factors are crucial for any long-term investment commitment.

EXTRAPOLATING PAST TRENDS

Another problem is the placing of too great an emphasis on past trends. To be

sure, the past is important, and provides the necessary data inputs for making an informed judgment. Yet, overconcentration on the past can lead to mistaken judgments about the future, especially if only economic variables are considered.

First, take the U.S. balance of payments. We've been living with a payments problem for so long that some of us have gotten accustomed to it. Instead of the cries of the Cassandras, who only a few years ago were warning of impending disaster if the U.S. payments deficits continue unabated, we now hear arguments justifying the even larger deficits of today as part of the normal order of things. The argument goes that the world is really on a dollar standard and that our European creditors have no choice but to accept this fact, unpleasant as it may be to them. In the short run—yes; the Europeans have to continue to accept our dollars. If they tried to cash them in at the treasury, we would close the doors on them; no one expects the treasury to sell our gold to foreign central banks down to the very last ounce that is in the vaults of Fort Knox.

But the currency crisis of May 1970 clearly indicates that the situation is not stable. That crisis saw the floating of the German mark and the Netherlands guilder, and the revaluation of the Swiss franc and the Austrian shilling. As European holdings of dollars continue to increase, pressure builds up on the international monetary structure. The Europeans have already taken the initiative toward forming their own currency, which would in effect become a rival world currency to the dollar. The inability of the United States to get inflation down further from high levels, plus the prospect for more inflationary pressures in the coming years as economic policies turn strongly expansionary, is adding to the jitters of our foreign creditors. Thus, the outlook is for recurrent currency crises in international financial markets and a further questioning of the convertibility of the dollar into gold.

Another example with regard to projecting past trends into the future concerns foreign investment in the less developed countries. Such investment showed a strong uptrend in the 1960s, which was termed the Decade of Development. A projection of prospects this decade, based just on past trends, would show an even more vigorous expansion of private capital to the less developed regions of the world. But this is unlikely to be the case. The inflow of foreign capital is producing a negative reaction to the control which such capital inevitably exerts over foreign economies. The trend is now toward a more virulent form of economic nationalism, where the operations of foreign companies will be more closely scrutinized, especially the amount of capital and profit they seek to repatriate. Borrowings from local financial institutions will also be more restricted in order to insure adequate credit availabilities to nonforeign affiliated companies. Some governments will decide that nothing short of nationalizing important foreign-owned companies will satisfy their aspirations for more control over their own economic destinies—a la Chile and Peru. Economic nationalism is especially strong today in Latin America, but it is spreading rapidly to the other less developed regions of the world. The outlook, then, would be for a trying period ahead for the foreign companies that have large investments at stake in the less developed world.

Current and prospective difficulties will also reduce the net inflow of new capital to these countries, thus impairing their overall development progress and, specifically, their balance of payments positions. This means that, as a group, the less developed nations will be hard pressed to meet their debt servicing obligations. Many of these countries already devote a substantial portion of their export earnings to the payment of interest and amortization. With the donor countries demanding harder terms on foreign aid and private capital in-

flows dropping off, the servicing of foreign debts will weigh heavily on the balance of payments of these countries. In some cases, creditor countries will be forced to agree to a partial postponement, stretching out, or moratorium on debt repayments, in return for commitments on future economic performance. This is hardly a promising financial environment.

Finally, there is another trend that will significantly affect international business and finance this decade—one that could not be detected just by an examination of the past data. During the 1960s, the so-called invasion of U.S. direct investment around the world had received considerable attention. It formed the subject of the book, *The American Challenge*, which was an instantaneous bestseller in Europe. Concern about U.S. investment abroad, however, has tended to obscure the reverse trend, the flow of European and Japanese direct investments to the United States. To be sure, such flows are still relatively small: the $11.8 billion book value of foreign investments here at end-1969 compares with $70.8 billion of U.S. investments overseas. Nevertheless, all indications are that foreign investments in the United States will accelerate this decade. Their yearly growth has already reached $1 billion. The further expansion of this flow of funds could well become a major trend of the 1970s and 1980s. And this should have enormous implications for American business.

ASSESSING THE INVESTMENT CLIMATE

Ask any seasoned corporate manager of international operations what is the most important criterion for investing abroad and the answer will almost invariably be the "investment climate." While there is considerable agreement on the significance of the investment climate, there is little consensus on how best to assess it. To some, this reading is done intuitively—the result of a strong hunch that a given foreign market area is likely to prove profitable. To others, the decision to "go" is the product of past economic trends as well as other companies' experience in the area. Because there is no systematic way to assess how the investment climate affects a particular project, many companies base their foreign investment decisions on inadequate or inaccurate information. This often results in serious losses to them, in terms of both money and missed business opportunities.

The problem is that when the businessman comes to the economist to get "expert" opinion on a country's investment climate, the opinion is generally not very operational. It deals with such basic factors as family formation and labor force growth without assessing their relevance for the particular investment situation being considered. There is a gap between the economists' tools and the businessman's needs, which has proven difficult to bridge. More often than not, the economist's advice revolves essentially around his personal judgment on a particular country: country X is "bad" because the government there cannot deal effectively with the militant labor unions, while country Y is "good" because it just passed a decree welcoming private foreign capital. Since businessmen have their own judgments and biases, they have little need for the judgment and biases of economists—unless these are bolstered by a reasoned and relevant analysis of a situation.

The fact is that the investment climate varies with the particular investment being considered. It could be positive or negative, depending on the size of the investment, the extent of local equity participation, the extent of local personnel in managerial and supervisory capacities, the number of government concessions requested, and many other factors. As such, the investment climate is something more

than can be determined by demographic studies on family formation and the age distribution of the population. It is more than the size of the local labor supply, level of labor productivity and the income distribution of the country. It is more than the availability of raw materials and sources of energy, road and port facilities, communications network, and geographic position. The investment climate is also more than the extent of investment incentives being offered —on taxes, leasing of space, and import of raw materials and equipment.

The investment climate is not a static phenomenon that a foreign investor must accept as "given" as he makes his future plans. Moreover, foreign investors themselves play a significant role in determining what the climate is. Their actions, both real and alleged, contribute to how the local community regards them. In the less developed countries, in particular, the operations of the foreign investors are under close scrutiny. They are being pressured to integrate their operations more closely into the economies of their host countries. This is not merely more than just being good corporate citizens, paying taxes fully and on time, and meeting other legal obligations. It means, especially for large foreign companies such as banks, a willingness to incorporate locally, arrange for an increasing share of local equity participation, employ more local people at all levels of management including the top positions, train local employees in the necessary skills, and purchase as many goods and services as are available from local sources.

Even doing all these things, however, will not guarantee the foreign investors a favorable investment climate, free of expropriation and nationalization. For in those countries where economic growth is barely able to keep pace with the population increase, foreign enterprises have become scapegoats for the resulting frustrations and the inability of government leaders to fulfill past promises. The fact is that a growing economy brings about a healthy investment climate—which is no less important a relationship than the standard economic proposition that investment promotes economic growth. Thus, one of the key factors that the international economic forecaster must determine is the country's prospective rate of economic growth.

ECONOMIC GROWTH PROSPECTS

Here, too, this is not simply a matter of adding up the land, labor, and capital resources of a country. Past experience has amply demonstrated that resources themselves are neither necessary nor sufficient for economic growth. This statement deserves some amplification. In the past, the standard treatment of economic development stressed such magnitudes as the amount of cultivable land, the size of the labor force, and the level of savings available for internal capital generation. Generally ignored was the fact that barren land can be made fruitful given sufficient incentive and knowledge—as shown by how successfully the Israelis have made their Negev desert bloom. Also, fertile land itself may not lead to development if government policies discourage farmers and ranchers from expanding their operations, as shown by Argentina's experience in sacrificing its agricultural potential on the altars of industrialization.

Labor can be either a stimulus or a hindrance to the realization of economic development, depending on such intangibles as whether the people are properly motivated toward achieving material progress and whether they have the necessary training to undertake needed tasks. A few decades ago, Japan was considered an overpopulated country, because of its small geographic size and lack of any significant volume of natural resources. But the motivation and skill of its people have pushed up economic growth to the extent that the concern now is that Japan is an underpopulated nation. There are too few people to enable the country to continue raising output by over 10 percent each year. Efforts are thus being made to economize on labor by transferring people from low productive activities in agriculture and small-scale industry to more productive pursuits in heavy industry.

In many of the less developed countries, the investor is confronted with a labor market which has large numbers of unemployed and unskilled workers, and at the same time a severe shortage of skilled workers. Indeed, this appears to be the typical case. Unless aware of the seriousness of this problem, the business forecaster can lead his company or client seriously astray. Data on labor availabilities and labor force growth are virtually meaningless if the labor that is available is unskilled, and hence necessitates extensive training at the company's expense or else the bidding away of skilled workers from other companies. This does not mean that such an investment should not be made, but rather that the business decision on whether or not to invest should be made with full awareness of the added costs and time involved in getting an operational work force.

The early theories of economic development stressed the key role of capital formation in the growth process. While there is no denying its importance, there is growing realization that capital alone will not bring about the desired results. The current disillusionment with foreign aid programs stems from the fact that too much had been expected from an effort to pump more and more funds into countries whose people were not yet ready for a major development effort. The few cases where foreign aid has been successful—Taiwan, Israel (and, in a similar sense, Western Europe and Japan after World War II)—involve countries whose people had the motivation and ability to make effective use of capital inflows.

The amount of land, labor, and capital is not as significant for determining future economic growth as is the quality of these factors of production, especially the quality of a country's manpower resources. This is what will influence a nation's future economic progress, and determine whether it is able to achieve a rate of economic growth that exceeds its population increase and thus allows for raising personal income levels. In such a country, there is a growing long-run demand for goods and services—the kind of environment best suited to the profit requirements of the foreign investor.

In the developed countries, the business forecaster need not be so concerned about the quality of a country's resources. While quality considerations are by no means unimportant, the fact that these countries, by definition, have reached a certain level of economic activity does mean that such basic qualities as motivation and skill which are prerequisite to sustained growth have been attained to an acceptable extent. In such countries, future economic growth is dependent on increasing both the quantity and the quality of available resources. To be sure, some countries have more catching up to do than others in terms of individual standards of living, and hence may be expected to devote a greater national effort toward achieving economic goals as opposed to social and political objectives. But not always.

From a practical point of view, investors in the developed countries are more concerned about market factors than about factors of production. Many of them got involved in overseas investment in the first place in an effort to protect a market that had been penetrated and cultivated by means of exporting. For a number of reasons, their market position became threatened by the development of strong local competition or the imposition of a higher tariff on imports of their product. The growing trend toward regionalism in Europe, starting with the Treaty of Rome in 1958,

has provided a major stimulus to the direct establishment there of productive facilities by U.S. companies. Based on their U.S. experience, these investors were well aware of the market opportunities presented by an economically unified Europe. They wanted to get in on the ground floor of what they considered to be, and what in fact turned out to be, a period of substantial economic growth.

The key question faced by these companies was not whether to invest in Europe, but rather where to invest. Since market considerations generally dominated over concern for the availability of raw materials and skilled labor, location was generally determined by ease of penetrating national and regional markets. This involved such other considerations as nearness to major market centers and availability of transportation facilities for moving goods into and out of the region. Adequacy and dependability of energy sources were factors of key importance for those companies heavily dependent on power supplies.

But market considerations involve much more than physical availabilities. They are also heavily influenced by the overall growth of the country in which they are located and the growth of those neighboring countries which are also consumers of their products. Here is where the business forecaster is put to the test—or to the wall, if he fails. The problem is not so much to determine the prospective gyrations in economic activity over the coming six to twelve months, which tend to be the focus of concern for the U.S. economic forecaster. Rather, business tends to be more concerned about likely developments over the next two to five years, unless of course a major economic or financial crisis is a prospect during the coming two years.

It is difficult enough trying to forecast the progress of the U.S. economy over such a relatively long period as two to five years. To tackle the European economies is far more difficult, due to less quantifiable information available and the different institutional setting. And to attempt to forecast demand for any particular industry without first estimating the course of the economy is a prescription for major error.

Faced with such a situation, the business forecaster must assume away short-run cyclical problems and concentrate instead on long-term influences. He resorts to standard economic forecasting techniques as regards long-run projections. He bases estimates of future GNP growth on such magnitudes as growth in labor force and increase in labor productivity. Demographic projections may give some clues as to whether the demand for the product or services of the industry he is concerned with will rise faster or slower than the overall economy. Use of industry data and knowledge of the market and the prospective state of the competition will enable the forecaster to estimate the share of the market which his company may obtain and hence its overall sales level. If the company is already in operation, this estimate will prove useful in deciding whether or not to expand facilities; if not in operation, the estimate will be an important input into the discussion of whether or not a new investment would be profitable.

ASSESSING THE ROLE OF GOVERNMENT

One of the most difficult tasks facing the business forecaster is to determine the likely course of government policy. And this means much more than compiling a checklist of concessions which are available to qualifying foreign investors. To be sure, such concessions can be important and the investor should be aware of what is being offered: tax benefits, financing assistance, help in training personnel, and free trade zones. But investment incentives are not the

only way or even the prime way in which government action affects the investor.

Of key concern should be the overall direction of the government's economic policy. Official attitudes toward inflation, for instance, play a part in forecasting market growth. While most multinational companies have learned to live with worldwide inflation, an excessive rate of inflation in a particular area is likely to create severe distortions. For one thing, persistent inflation tends to have a deleterious effect on local money and capital markets by preventing a rational allocation of funds. Also, faced with an inflationary spiral, governments are likely to initiate two kinds of policy response. On the one hand, restrictive economic policies may be implemented to slow down the rate of economic growth, and thus curb the price rise; this is bound to affect the company's sales operations. The government control may, on the other hand, develop a complacent attitude toward inflation on the grounds that restrictive economic policies are politically acceptable since they raise the level of unemployment. Such a deliberate policy of inflation has in the past been used as a means to promote economic growth. The result, inevitably, is economic recession and/or stringent exchange controls, which affect the repatriation of capital and profits.

The state of the balance of payments and its priority in overall government policy is another area that the international business forecaster must examine. Trade data are sufficiently well developed so that reasonably good projections can be made of future export and import levels. Imports are generally related to the state of local economic activity and so can be derived from projections of the latter. Exports are more complicated. They are related both to overseas demand and to local output. Where a country's exports consist principally of one or two agricultural products, its foreign exchange earnings are subject to wide fluctuations due to varying weather conditions.

Even if output holds up well, good crops in other countries may push down world prices substantially and in this way reduce export earnings. And since exports are used to purchase imports, total economic activity can be affected by such changes. Government efforts to diversify exports and strengthen the nation's balance of payments thus tend to improve the climate for foreign investment. At the same time, the foreign investor can contribute to such an improvement by actively seeking ways in which his own operations can add to his host country's foreign exchange receipts—via export, substituting for imports, and bringing in new capital from abroad.

The risk of investing in a country is considerably heightened if its balance of payments position is weak and its supply of foreign exchange reserves is low. In such circumstances there is not only the possibility of restrictions being imposed on the remittance of profits and the repatriation of capital to the home country; there is also the possibility that needed imports of raw materials, spare parts, and machinery may become restricted by licensing requirements. In addition, the threat of currency loss through devaluation is ever present.

In assessing government policy, it is essential to investigate all the influences pressing upon the government leaders. Personalities are as important in determining policies as any other single factor. Government actions which seem to be irrational on economic grounds (such as nationalizing the country's largest foreign exchange earner, as Forbes Burnham of Guyana did with the Demerara Bauxite Company) become understandable and even to some extent predictable in the context of such social conditions as growing pressures on the government from militant black power advocates. The attempt to remain in power, even by becoming more radical than one's critics, has led many political leaders to adopt economic policies which not only do not work but are also not in the long-term economic interest of their countries. Admonitions by foreign economists won't really help when power positions are at stake.

QUANTIFYING THE INVESTMENT DECISION

U.S. companies investing abroad generally anticipate a high rate of return on their investment. But this is not the driving reason for going multinational. As mentioned earlier, the desire to protect a market position or take advantage of a perceived market opportunity is the main factor. Business forecasters generally use three steps in forecasting the overseas sales prospects of their company. First, they assess the outlook for the general economy. Next, the industry's prospects are analyzed on the basis of the overall economic outlook. Finally, the industry prospects are used to evaluate the market position of the particular company under investigation.

In trying to quantify factors relating to investment decisions, most companies tend to rely on one of two approaches—although there is a third method that is being increasingly resorted to. These approaches are the use of:

1. Past experience
2. Cutoff points
3. Probability analysis

Past Experience as A Guide to Future Decisions

In this approach, a company accepts or rejects an overseas investment decision on the basis of specific characteristics—often with little regard for the general investment climate. For instance, past foreign exchange losses incurred by the company may be the deciding criterion against investing further in a particular country. Although this approach has the advantage of reducing the amount of investigation to be done in looking for foreign investment opportunities, some good investment opportunities may be passed over because a particular country was rejected on the initial screening.

Cutoff Points

The company using a specific cutoff point demands a higher rate of return on investment in countries with poor investment climates. For instance, some companies use a 15 percent rate of return as a minimum in industrial countries, while a 25 percent return is required in developing countries. A rating scale is often used in screening countries as part of a search process. The major problem in this method is that the assignment of a risk premium for a country assumes that the degree of risk is uniform over the life of the project. This, however, is unlikely since the risks differ for various years of a project's life. An unwelcome event occurring in the first year of the project has a much more serious effect on the net present value of the project than does a similar event occurring five years later.

Probability Analysis

This is a technique which is growing in popularity, especially among the petroleum companies. It attempts to put judgmental factors regarding specific investment decisions into a quantitative framework. Using this framework, it is possible to determine what effects different judgments on the future would have on the decision to invest abroad. The probability analysis technique requires close coordination between the economic forecaster and business management. Together they estimate the range within which the rate of return of the investment is likely to fall. The probability

of the actual rate of return reaching the various values specified within the range is then determined. This probability distribution is based on the economist's view of the country's economic growth and the overall investment climate, and the businessman's judgment based on his past experience with similar investment situations. This distribution is then used as the basis for determining whether the possible gain of undertaking the investment is more or less than the opportunity loss of not investing. Such a calculation would determine the advisability of going ahead with the project.

The following example may serve to highlight the basic workings of this technique.

Assume that a company is considering a $10 million investment in a foreign country. Company managers believe that they need a rate of return on their investment of at least 20 percent for the project to be worthwhile. The firm will invest if its analysts estimate that the rate of return P will be over 20%. They will abandon the project if the expected return is thought to be less than 20%. At a projected 20% rate of return, the company is indifferent between investing and not investing.

Since the actual rate of return is of course unknown to the company, the decision-makers may fall into two kinds of judgment errors in deciding for or against the project. They may reject the program when actually it is profitable (P is projected to be smaller than 20%, when it is actually greater than 20%) or go ahead with the project when it is in fact unprofitable (P is projected to be greater than 20%, when actually it is smaller than 20%). In dollar terms, the farther the actual P is away from the indifference point ($P=20\%$), the greater are the losses when an error of judgment is made. This is why the decision-makers have to consider the probability of the different values of P, the actual rate of return.

To be sure, no one knows what the rate of return on the $10 million project

TABLE 1.   PROBABILITY DISTRIBUTION

P = Actual Rate of Return	Probability of P
0%	35%
10	10
20	10
30	20
40	20
50	5
	100%

TABLE 2.   SCHEDULE OF GAINS AND LOSSES

P = Actual Rate of Return	Invest (shortfall)	Not Invest (opportunity loss)
0%	$-2,000,000	$+2,000,000
10	-1,000,000	1,000,000
20	0	0
30	1,000,000	-1,000,000
40	2,000,000	-2,000,000
50	3,000,000	-3,000,000

will turn out to be. But the company has some feeling that certain values attributed to P are more likely than others. It is this feeling—a composite of the firm's past experience in the country; knowledge of social, political, and economic trends in the region; and intuition—that can be captured in the form of "subjective probability." This information is then formalized in the form of a probability distribution as indicated in table 1.

Based on past experience and on economic analysis of the current investment situation, the company's managers believe that there is a 35% probability that P will turn out to be 0%, and a 5% probability that it will be 50%.

Not knowing the true value of P, the company of course runs the risk of making the wrong choice. If it believes that P will be greater than 20%, it will undertake the investment. But if P turns out to be smaller than 20%, the company gets less of a return than what it considers worthwhile. If P is

10%, the shortfall is $1,000,000: $10,000,000 × (.20-P). By the same token, if the company's judgment is correct and P actually is over 20%, the company gains a more than minimal rate of return. If P is 40%, the gain is $2,000,000: $10,000,000 × (P-.20).

Similarly, there is an opportunity loss if the company abandons the investment because it believes P is less than 20%, when actually it is greater than 20%. This opportunity loss is equal to $10,000,000 × (P-.20). Thus, if the actual rate of return is 40%, the opportunity loss is $2,000,000. But if the company is right and P is only 10%, the company's decision not to invest will save it from a loss of $1,000,000.

Now it is possible to compute a schedule of gains and losses based on the value range of P, as shown in table 2.

This table shows in quantitative terms the various possible gains and losses based on different values of P. Of course, if the actual rate of return turned out to be negative and a decision were made to invest, the

TABLE 3.   WEIGHTED EXPECTED GAINS AND LOSSES

P = Actual Rate of Return	Probability of P	From Investing	From Not Investing
0%	35%	$ −700,000	$ 700,000
10	10	−100,000	100,000
20	10	0	0
30	20	200,000	−200,000
40	20	400,000	−400,000
50	5	150,000	−150,000
	100%	$ −50,000	$ +50,000

loss would not only represent a shortfall from the 20% minimum rate of return but also a real loss of capital.

Using the probability distribution assigned to the unknown parameter P, we multiply the schedule of gains and losses (table 2) by the probabilities of occurrence of P (table 1).

Table 3 weighs the gains and losses of investing and not investing by the probability distribution of P, the actual but unknown rate of return. The sum of the possible gains and losses from investing and not investing provides quantifiable criteria for a management decision on whether or not to invest. In the above example, there is a net gain to the company by not investing, and so the decision should be made to scrap the project. Using a different judgment as to the probability of P, a different decision might be made. Were a 20% probability assigned to P being 0 percent, and a 35% probability to P being 40%, there would be a net expected gain of $550,000 from undertaking the investment.

CONCLUSIONS

The time when judgment no longer plays an important role in overseas investment decision is not even on the horizon, nor is it likely ever to be. Even so, this does not at all mean that judgments should not be incorporated into a framework, such as probability analysis, where the results of different judgments can be quantified and alternative investment strategies mapped out. In so doing, personal judgments are separated from objective analysis and yet both are incorporated into the final investment decision.

A number of large U.S. companies with extensive international operations, such as commercial banks, are beginning to develop econometric models of various aspects of the international scene. These include models of U.S. commodity trade, world trade aggregates, overall economic activity of major developed countries, the Eurodollar market, and the U.S. balance of payments. While it is still much too early to determine the success of these models in predicting future magnitudes and while many more years of hard work may be required to make them reasonably reliable, they could eventually be an important input for helping to make investment decisions.

In the international field, it is clear that business forecasting is both an art and a science. While judgmental factors predominated in past years, current efforts are giving more attention to putting such forecasting into a more rigorous, quantitative framework. What additionally is needed is recognition and then analysis of the non-economic factors that heavily influence business activity and the investment climate. The forecaster who ignores these factors is doing only half the job required.

HERBERT BIENSTOCK

Forecasting Manpower and Employment Trends

The ultimate success of a program for economic development at the macro or micro level will depend in large measure on the availability of manpower possessing specific skills and training. Moreover, the development and training of skilled manpower must be an integral part of any overall development plan if that plan is to succeed.

Manpower is an economic resource just as material, equipment, electrical energy, and money are economic resources. Manpower in the economic sense is the managerial, scientific, engineering, technical, skilled, and other personnel employed in creating, designing, developing, managing, and operating productive and service enterprises and economic institutions.

The manpower component forms a meaningful element in the wide range of economic activity and consequently, economic forecasting. The demographic configurations, both short- and long-term, have significant influence on projections of sales volume, housing and construction, and financial patterns, as well as on the demand pressures in specific fields.

Population patterns will often exert influences which are fundamental as a frame for forecasting both the short and the long term. For example, as soon as the returns were in on the birth crop of 1947 it was clear that six years later, in 1953, the educational system in America was due to come

under substantial pressure as it moved to accommodate this large number of young people.

Further, it was clear that by 1963, the 1947 crop of babies would reach age 16, the modal age of school dropouts, and at that point the American labor market would feel the brunt. Unfortunately, our ability to respond to these trends did not equal the amount of lead time which the projections offered. By 1965 the postwar (World War II) baby crop had reached age 18 and began to move in two important directions of impact.

Firstly, at age 18 a large component moved directly into the labor market. A second group moved on to the college campus where they ran into a shortage of prime faculty-age people in their mid-thirties. The latter, products of the depression-year birth patterns of the 1930's, were around in fewer numbers than would otherwise have been the case. The generation gap was as much a numbers gap as an attitudinal one!

By 1970 the 1947 baby crop had reached the modal age of male first marriage in America, age 23, and the impact on catering and related services was soon evident. Throughout the 1970s impacts will continue as the decade of family formation proceeds apace. First the baby goods manufacturers and suppliers and then the housing pressure on family expansion begins to impact in this connection. Indeed, it is not very bold to forecast the retirement wave which may be upon us as we go past the year 2000, at which point the 1947 baby crop will have reached the ripe old age of 53. By the year 2010 the emphasis may very well be shifting to geriatrics!

The thrust of all this is to point out the enormous significance of the basic patterns and trends which underlie shifts in the economic winds (see chart 1). Other influences are more difficult to deal with. For example, changes in styles and attitudes, women's "lib," and youngsters' attitudes toward work will clearly impact on labor force participation, as will changing patterns of educational attainment.

AGE GROUP	Percent change in the labor force	
	1960–1970	1970–1980
16–24	53	19
25–34	16	49
35–44	−1	13
45–54	15	−4
55–64	21	14
65 and over	−8	6
TOTAL LABOR FORCE	18	18.3

The largest labor force growth in the '60's was among those workers 16–24 years old. The dramatic increase in the '70's will be among young adults—age 25–34—those entering their prime working years.

Chart 1   The Number of Workers in the Prime 25–34 Year Old Group Will Increase Dramatically

Economic decisions by policymakers to trade off or at least attempt to modulate relationships between unemployment and prices will also clearly impact on employment levels, as will forces such as policy postures on national defense and environmental control, among other things.

All of these factors and many others are a vital part of the considerations which enter into the calculus of manpower and employment projections.

The method followed by the Bureau of Labor Statistics in projecting manpower requirements is often referred to as the "Industry-occupational matrix approach." It is an analytical approach and a composite of several different methods. This research has been carried on for two decades and serves as the basis for the *Occupational Outlook Handbook,* which has been published almost every two years since 1949, and other studies of the Bureau of Labor Statistics.

Manpower projections are inextricably interwoven with the changing nature of the economy: Will it be growing? How many workers will want jobs? What will be our manpower requirements? Will advancing technology affect the nature of jobs? How will productivity changes affect job requirements? (see chart 2)

The Bureau of Labor Statistics has developed and refined its projections so that they now encompass several integrated components that permit a comprehensive view of tomorrow's economy and its manpower needs. Specifically, the projections cover labor force; hours of employment; output per man-hour; potential demand (gross national product or GNP); the composition of demand, output, and productivity by 82 detailed industry groups; and employment in over 250 industries and in detailed occupations. The projections are interrelated; the growth of GNP, a foundation of the projections, is conditioned upon labor supply, productivity changes, and hours of work. The rate and direction of changes in the major demand components of GNP in turn yield changing requirements for labor by industry and occupation.

One thing must be clearly understood about any projections of future requirements. That is that such forecasts must be based on a set of agreed upon assumptions by the forecaster. Changes in the basic as-

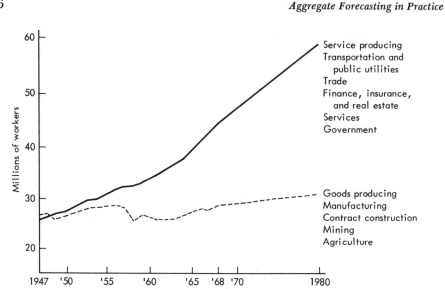

Chart 2   Employment Trends in Goods-Producing and Services-Producing Industries, 1947–1968 (Actual) and 1968–1980 (Projected for a Services Economy with 3-Percent unemployment)

sumptions will of course alter the configurations of the projections.

The current BLS projections about the world of 1980 are based on the following specific assumptions:

The international climate will improve. The United States will no longer be fighting a war but, on the other hand, a still guarded relationship between the major powers will permit no major reductions in armaments. This would still permit some reduction from the peak levels of defense expenditures during the Viet Nam conflict.

Armed forces strength will drop back to about the same level that prevailed in the pre-Viet Nam escalation period.

The institutional framework of the American economy will not change radically.

Economic, social, technological, and scientific trends will continue, including values placed on work, education, income, and leisure.

Fiscal and monetary policies will be able to achieve a satisfactory balance between low unemployment rates and relative price stability without reducing the long-term economic growth rate.

All levels of government will join efforts to meet a wide variety of domestic requirements, but Congress will channel more funds to state and local governments.

Efforts to solve the problems posed by air and water pollution and solid waste disposal, although they may preempt an increasing amount of the nation's productive resources, will not lead to a significant dampening of our long-run potential rate of growth.

Fertility rates will be lower than in the recent past.

One of the most important assumptions underlying manpower projections describes the labor force in the target year (see chart 3).

Another important assumption under-

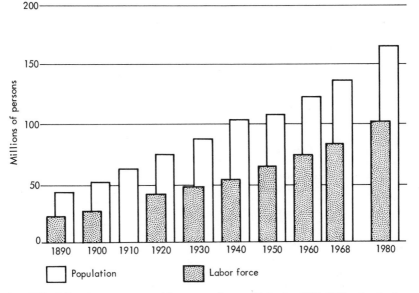

Data for 1890–1940 refers to persons 14 years and over. Data for 1950–1980 refer to persons 16 years and over. Comparable labor force data not available for 1910.

Sources: U.S. Department of Commerce, Bureau of the Census; U.S. Department of Labor, Bureau of Labor Statistics; John D. Durand, the Labor Force of the United States, 1890–1960 (New York: Gordon & Breach, 1968); Gertrude Bancroft, The American Labor Force (New York: John Wiley and Sons, 1958).

The labor force—those who are working and those seeking work—is expected to number more than 100 million workers by 1980, growing by 15 million in the '70's.

Chart 3   Labor Force and Population, 1890 to 1980

lying the employment projections focuses on the expected unemployment rate in the target year. An unemployment rate of three percent was selected for 1975 after considering the unemployment experience of the 1960s and current emphasis on manpower utilization and training programs.

Although a variety of techniques were used in the methodology behind the current BLS estimate, two steps generally were followed in projecting the growth of occupations. The first step was to project total manpower requirements in each detailed industry. Secondly, the trends in the use of each occupation in each detailed industry were projected. The projected proportion (ratio) of each occupation in each industry was then multiplied by projected total man-

power requirements in the industry, resulting in an estimate of occupational requirements in each industry. Requirements in each occupation were then summed across all industries resulting in projected total employment requirements by occupation. Employment requirements in some occupations were also projected independently of the occupation's relationship to particular industries. This technique was particularly useful for occupations that are affected by a limited number of variables or are located primarily in one industry or group of industries. When both major techniques were used, the differences in the results were analyzed and reconciled, based on the judgments of the analysts.

The first step in developing projec-

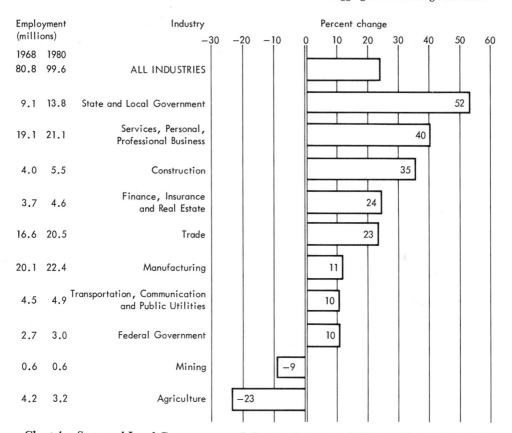

Chart 4   State and Local Government and Service Industries Will have Especially Rapid Employment Gains

tions of detailed industry employment was to estimate the level of economic activity (real GNP). If a 3 percent unemployment rate is to be achieved, real GNP must be high enough to provide employment for 97 percent of the civilian labor force. In estimating real GNP, *preliminary* projections of total employment as well as projections of output per worker were made for each of the nine major industry divisions. The sum of the product of output per worker (in constant dollars) and total employment in each of the nine major industry divisions was the level of economic activity required to achieve the civilian employment goal for the target year.

In making the preliminary projections

of total employment by major industry division, no single source provided historical employment data for all classes of workers for the eight nonagriculture major industry divisions. However, historical data for the great bulk of employment—private wage and salary workers—were available from the BLS establishment employment statistics series as published in Bulletin 1312.5, *Employment and Earnings Statistics for the United States, 1909–1967*. In addition, the decennial population censuses and the current population survey (CPS) provided historical data on self-employed workers, unpaid family workers, and domestic workers. Using projections of wage and salary employment in each of the nonagricultural major industry divisions as a base, employment projections for the other classes of workers were developed and distributed among the eight nonagricultural major industry divisions (and an estimate of the number of dual jobholders subtracted), and the sum of the totals for the major industry divisions were adjusted to agree with the estimate of total civilian employment (see chart 4).

To the extent that subsequent detailed industry wage and salary employment projections did not add to the *preliminary* employment projection for a major industry division (after adding in the projection of employment for the other classes of workers), adjustments were made in employment either at the detailed or major industry division levels and/or in GNP, so that the system in the target year was in balance in terms of expected productivity changes, civilian employment, and real GNP.

Three approaches were used in developing projections of detailed industry wage and salary employment requirements. The first approach involved the use of regression analysis to estimate employment in each industry consistent with the assumption underlying the overall model. Equations were developed which related industry wage and salary employment in the 1947–66 period with different combinations of the following variables: real GNP, national rate of unemployment, number of personnel in the armed forces, civilian noninstitutional population fourteen years old and over, and time. These variables were selected because they were considered strategic in determining long-run changes in aggregate employment, and because they allowed cyclical and other factors to be separated from secular trends. Detailed industry wage and salary employment projections derived from the combination of variables providing the best statistical tests were tentatively selected as final estimates.

A second approach to projecting industry employment requirements involved

the use of input-output analysis. Essentially, this technique requires that final demand (GNP divided into its components: investment, consumption, etc.) be specified by producing industry. The demand is then traced back through the chain of production to determine the output required from each industry supplying materials or services to produce the end product. For example, the final demand for automobiles creates an intermediate demand for steel, rubber, etc. The intermediate demand for steel will then create a demand for iron ore, coal, etc. By computing total output requirements for each industry (the sum of final and intermediate demand) in the target year, and relating it to expected output per man-hour in each industry, a projection of industry employment is obtained. A complete set of projections was developed for 1970 and 1980 using this approach; 1975 projections were developed by interpolating the 1970 and 1980 data.

The third approach was to study industries individually and examine the factors expected to influence their future growth. This approach was used for industries in which past trends in employment were not considered indicative of future trends and for those industries for which the model provided unacceptable results (poor statistical tests or unreasonable employment projections). In this approach, a variety of regression equations were developed and tested. For example, in the motor vehicle manufacturing industry the variables which were tested in different combinations included personal disposable income, expenditures for producers' durable equipment, driving, age population, number of households, number of motor vehicle registrations, and number of families with more than $10,000 annual income. Where important, interindustry relationships were taken into account using this technique.

The equations for which the combination of variables provided the best statistical results were used to project employment in 1975. Considering the results obtained from the regression equations, the input-output analysis, the individual industry studies, and qualitative information concerning technology and the structure of the industry, employment projections were made for each detailed industry based on the best judgment of the analysts. Before these projections were considered final, they were reviewed for the following reasons:

1. To reconcile detailed industry employment projections with the preliminary broad industry employment projections previously made, and broad industry employment projections with the civilian labor force estimate.
2. To insure that productivity expectations, real GNP, and civilian labor force estimates were in balance.

3. To make certain that the projections were consistent with the overall assumptions.

Each industry in the economy requires a specific mix of occupations. The relative importance of particular occupations changes over time, however, in response to technological advancement and changes in scale of production mix, and organization of industries, among other factors. To reflect these circumstances, occupational patterns for each industry in the economy were developed for 1960 and projected to 1975. These patterns were developed on the basis of occupational trends between 1950 and 1966 as interpreted from available data.

The main source of detailed and complete information for the national matrix for 1960 was the Census Bureau's *Occupa-*

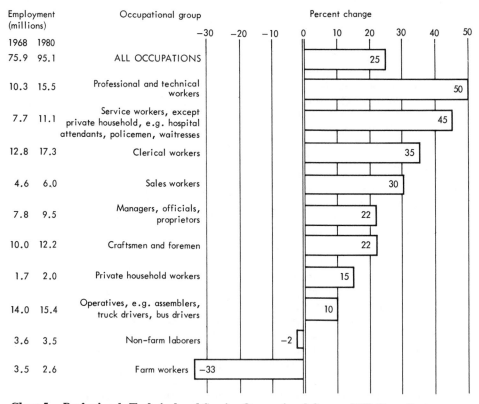

Chart 5   Professional, Technical and Service Occupational Groups Will Grow Fastest

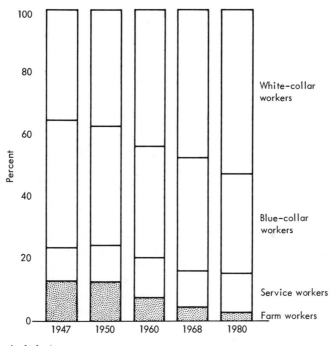

Farm workers include farm managers.

Chart 6   Employment Trends Among Major Occupational Categories, 1947–68 (Actual) and 1980 (Projected for a Services Economy with 3% Unemployment)

tions by Industry report based on the 1960 census. The BLS occupation by industry matrix, however, differs from the census report in two major ways: (1) the BLS matrix was made consistent with other sources of data and (2) the BLS table makes use of occupational data from a number of sources considered preferable to decennial census data. It was desirable to make the matrix consistent with broad industry and occupational group employment estimates available from the monthly household survey (CPS) so that full advantage could be taken of data available between decennial census years. The following occupational data were used in the BLS matrix in addition to the broad occupational group estimates from the CPS: employment of scientists and engineers by industry based on BLS surveys of employers; employment of teachers and

librarians based on data collected by the Office of Education; employment by occupation data collected by regulatory agencies for interstate industries including railroads, airlines, telephone and telegraph communications, and pipelines; employment data collected by professional societies, especially for medical and health occupations; selected data from BLS industry and community wage surveys; information from the Post Office Department on postal employment by occupation; and federal Civil Service Commission statistics on employment by occupation in other federal government agencies.

The projection of the occupational structure of each industry was based on examination of historical statistics and evaluation of other factors that might influence occupational structure, such as expected new technology, changes in the product mix, and general organization of industries (see charts 5 and 6).

First, historical statistics on the changing occupational composition of detailed industries were projected by simple time-trend. The trend for each industry-occupational ratio derived from census data was extended to 1975, and the indicated change from the 1960 level was added to the appropriate ratio in the base period (1960) industry-occupational employment table. A variety of other statistics covering varying spans of time between 1950 and 1965 was gathered and arranged to reveal evidence of trends in employment by occupation for particular industries or for the entire economy. Analysis was directed to finding the causes of past changes in occupational structure. An attempt was made to determine whether these factors were likely to continue to affect occupational structure in the period ahead to a similar, greater, or lesser extent. In developing the 1975 matrix, efforts were also made to uncover emerging technological and other factors which may have a significant impact on manpower requirements in the years ahead.

For many occupations an analysis of the factors affecting employment was the basis for direct estimates of future employment requirements. The growth of each occupation is affected by its own complex set of social and economic variables. The number of teachers required, for example, is affected by the number of pupils (which in turn is affected by birthrates and trends in the proportion of children who attend school) and by trends in the ratio of teachers to pupils (which depend upon educational practices and financing). The number of automobile mechanics required depends on the number of vehicles in use (which in turn reflects population growth, and levels of consumer income and business activity), the frequency with which they need repair, the relative costs of repair and of replacement of defective parts, and a variety of other factors. The requirements for physicians are

related to the size of the population, the age distribution of the population, technological developments, and expenditures for health care. Other occupations that were projected directly include engineers and scientists, dentists, registered nurses, television and radio repairmen, and business machine repairmen. For occupations in which the direct projection technique as well as the industry-occupational matrix approach were used, the differences in the employment projections were analyzed and reconciled.

Unless bases were found for modification, the effect on industry employment and occupational composition of social and technological trends in the post-World War II period were assumed to persist in the period to 1975. Thus for many occupations, particularly those of small size, the initial projections—a continuation of past trends—were accepted. On the other hand, projection of ratios of large size were often modified from past trends on the basis of the analysis of underlying factors. As an increase or decrease in proportionate employment for one occupation in a particular industry requires offsetting changes in other occupations in the industry, few of the final occupational ratios that were as large as one percent were exact extensions of past trends.

The industry-occupational ratios for 1975 reflect the skill patterns that will be required by the technology of production in each industry in 1975. In developing these ratios, no specific consideration was given to the availability of workers with the required skills. Yet many of the industry-occupational ratios for 1975 (particularly those of small size) are extensions of the changes in ratios reported for the period 1947–65. These ratios, therefore, embody a continuation of unidentified past adjustments to shortages (or increasing relative costs) for some of the occupations. Moreover, the occupational ratios were developed in relation to particular levels of national industry employment. Estimates of industry employment which differ appreciably from these may imply a difference in scale of operations or production methods and therefore a difference in the occupational structure of the industry.

The above describes the basic approaches to macro employment projections of the national labor market. The projections provide basic insight into the prevailing approach to forecasting national employment trends and patterns.

Manpower planning carried out by the employing organization for its own purposes, or micro planning, resembles that initiated by the federal government on an economywide base, or macro planning, in many respects. This similarity results partly from the complex framework of the free enterprise, highly industrialized, decentralized, and democratic society in which planning is done, and the consequent need to provide linkages between and among individual employees, employers, unions, and governmental, educational, and social agencies. In manpower planning, one such linkage is provided by the interchange of data, whereby firms may use national or regional labor force data in drawing up their plans, and government agencies may collect data from firms to provide aggregate manpower measures (as on job vacancies). Moreover, both micro planning and macro planning reflect a basic concern to insure that manpower resources are committed, developed, applied, utilized, and conserved. In both cases, also, planning is highly complicated by the need for much more knowledge about human behavior in general and employment behavior in particular.

Many of the concepts, problems, and methodologies of macro planning are not only similar to, but may prove useful in, micro manpower planning. Obviously, a major aim of macro manpower planning is to provide guidelines for national manpower policies and programs.

General micro manpower planning is, however, concerned with proposed designs and methods of action or procedure in using manpower resources to attain organizational objectives. It is a very broad concept concerned with the totality of manpower management in the employing organization; that is, personnel administration and labor relations. Yet most current efforts at micro manpower planning seem directed toward only the portion of planning called manpower forecasting. A forecast is a tool—a necessary and indispensable step in planning. It is an attempt to appraise the future. But a plan also includes goals and targets, and objectives and programs for achieving them.

Even the limited development of private manpower planning is very uneven from industry to industry. In some industries, planning is used essentially to insure supplies of top professional and managerial talent. In others, it may be used to anticipate and meet a variety of manpower problems peculiar to a particular organization.

Manpower planning at the company level requires answers to more detailed, more specific questions than at the macro level. Nevertheless, overall patterns and trends form a very significant part of any micro manpower planning function.

The basic data on population, labor force, industrial, and occupational employment, which are readily available from the Bureau of the Census and the Bureau of Labor Statistics, are the basic source of raw materials used in forecasting manpower and employment trends.

BIBLIOGRAPHY

Department of Labor, *The Forecasting of Manpower Requirements.* BLS Report No. 248. 1963.

Department of Labor, *Symposium on Forecasting Manpower Requirements*. Manpower Administration: International Manpower Institute. 1966.

Department of Labor, *Tomorrow's Manpower Needs*, Vols. I–IV. BLS Bulletin 1606. 1969.

Department of Labor, *Employer Manpower Planning and Forecasting*. Manpower Administration Monograph No. 19. 1970.

Department of Labor, *The U.S. Economy in 1980*, a summary of BLS projections. BLS Bulletin 1672. 1970.

Department of Labor, *U.S. Manpower in the 1970's—Opportunity and Challenge*. 1970.

LAWRENCE A. MAYER

Long-Term Economic Projections

The other portions of this book are about short-term forecasting, but the title of this chapter contains the phrase "long-term *projections*." The distinction between a forecast and a projection is not trivial. An economic forecast is a statement of what its author expects will actually happen—usually within a relatively brief period, most often from three months to perhaps eighteen months ahead. An economic projection is a statement of what its author expects will happen if normal conditions prevail— usually five years, and quite often ten years ahead. A projection, in other words, a- mounts to a description of the economy's likely dimensions in the longer term, pro- viding the factors that determine economic growth act much as they did in the past.

To put the matter somewhat different- ly, a short-term forecast starts from where the economy stands at some given moment —be it in recession, reasonably full employ- ment, or in a superboom—and tries to trace and time the next upward or downward fluctuation. A long-term projection, how- ever, attempts to determine the size and the contours of the economy a decade or so in the future, most commonly on the assump- tion that full employment will then prevail. It might be asked what the use of such a long-term projection is; after all, the econo- my could be smack in the middle of either a recession or an inflationary boom ten years from now. The answer is that many busi-

nesses and government agencies must plan their activities for ten or more years ahead, and for this purpose they need to know the normal size of demand (or of supply) that might confront them.

Since the declared policy of the U.S. government is to try to maintain full em- ployment, it is really not important whether the tenth year from now actually turns out to be a full employment year. If it is not, for at least 25 years it has been safe to as- sume that some period shortly before or shortly after that tenth year will be char- acterized by full employment. And of course, as that tenth year gets nearer and nearer, most managements (be they running busi- nesses, governments, or nonprofit organiza- tions) remain free to exercise considerable options as to how closely they adhere to plans started on the basis of projections made a good many years earlier. Moreover, by then the original target date will also be moving into the range of the short-term forecast.

The fairly rigid distinction that has so far been made between the short-term forecast and the long-term projection has certainly been true of the past history of eco- nomic forecasting. Now, however, through the use of econometric techniques, attempts are being made to produce what amounts to genuine long-term forecasts rather than just projections. One such example is the ten-year forecast of Chase Econometric Associates (an economic consulting arm of the Chase Manhattan Bank). The first version of this *forecast* (dated July 1971, before the wage-price-freeze instituted on August 15) hypothesized a slowdown or recession in 1974. The accompanying written analysis suggested that it might take two recessions to reduce the rate of inflation to what was deemed a "manageable" level of below three percent by 1980. The analysis also put forward an unemployment rate of 4.4 percent in 1980, thereby implying a GNP as much as 10 percent smaller than would reign in an economy of full employment (usually taken to allow for only 4 percent unemployment).

It is likely that an increasing number of long-term projections will start to exhibit the more ambitious forecasting characteristics of the Chase model. Of course, it remains to be seen how accurate or useful such attempts turn out to be. It may be that they will prove more instructive as guides to thinking about long-term economic policies (such as the consequences of containing inflation), rather than as unusually accurate guides to all the economic ups and downs that may occur in a subsequent decade.

It is also probable that an increasing number of long-term projections or forecasts will be based on more rigorous, or at least more detailed, mathematical procedures than has so far generally been the case. For example, the National Planning Association, which has for many years been doing detailed long-term economic projections, is switching to an econometric method.[1] And Professor Clopper Almon of the University of Maryland has pioneered in adapting input-output techniques to long-

term forecasting,[2] as has the Bureau of Labor Statistics.

MAKING THE PROJECTION

Although more sophisticated—or at least more complicated—methods of projecting GNP are coming into practice, the conventional methods are still bound to prove useful. For one thing, they can be performed as elaborately or as simply as one wishes; therefore, they can be employed by an economic research group big enough to pin down every detail, or by a single economist who needs to obtain only broad outlines. For another, they allow one to make rather simple checks of the plausibility of the projections of other economists.

To begin with, it is important to establish a proper starting point when one calculates aggregate GNP at full employment for a decade hence. On the one hand, if the year from which the calculation is started is a recession year, then the GNP ten years hence will be too low unless the growth rate used is correspondingly greater than the normal long-term rate. On the other hand, if the base year is one in which there is overemployment and an abnormally high number of hours worked per week, the resulting future GNP—using a long-term normal growth rate—will be too high. If the base year is quite abnormal in either respect, the economist can avoid the difficulty by using an artificially constructed normal full-employment GNP as his starting point. Such a GNP is conveniently available in the Department of Commerce's monthly publication, *Business Conditions Digest.*

---

[1] See Ahmad Al-Samarrie and Graham C. Scott, "An Econometric Model for Long-Range Projections of the United States Economy," American Statistical Association, *1970 Proceedings of the Business and Economic Statistics Section*, p. 60 ff.

[2] Clopper Almon, Jr., *The American Economy to 1975, An Interindustry Forecast* (New York: Harper & Row, 1966). A revised and expanded version of this book, which will contain forecasts to 1980, was in preparation as the present chapter was being written.

That publication contrasts the GNP as actually reported with a calculated "potential" (or normal) GNP, and this normalized GNP can be used as a base to extrapolate into the future.[3]

TWO RELATED METHODS

It may often prove simplest to take a "normal" base period GNP and multiply it by the presumed normal rate of future annual economic growth for the required number of years, compounded. That growth rate is made up of three elements. One is the increase in the labor force. Projections of this increase are made from time to time by the Bureau of Labor Statistics, and these are quite commonly used.[4]

The most recent BLS projection calls for an average rate of increase in the labor force of 1.7 percent per year until 1980. This figure is generally reduced somewhat by the second element used in projecting. That element is the historical trend to fewer hours of work per man-year (because of shorter work weeks, longer vacations, or an increase in the proportion of part-time jobs). In its economic growth projections, BLS allows for a 0.1 percent per year decline in the average workweek.[5] The Con-

ference Board,[6] however, allows for about a 0.3 percent annual decline in the workweek. The third element is the rise in productivity, or output per man-hour. Total productivity in the private sector of the economy is generally estimated to increase something more than 3 percent a year over the long term.[7] But productivity in the government sector is assumed not to increase at all—not because this is known to be the case, but because the GNP accounts are at present so constructed that they imply no change in the productivity of government workers, and it is the official version of GNP that one tries to project. So, total productivity is generally assumed to increase about 2.7 percent a year.[8]

Allowing for some few tenths of difference as to what various projectors think is normal on the foregoing counts, it can be seen why most projections of long-term GNP growth have arrived at a figure of between 4.1 percent and 4.3 percent a year between 1970 and 1980. To review: a 1.7 percent or so per year increase in the labor force; a 0.1 percent or slightly greater decline in man-hours; plus about a 2.7 percent a year increase in output per man-hour adds

---

[3] The potential GNP is at present given in dollars of 1958 purchasing power. This data can, of course, be converted into purchasing power of a later year by suitable conversion of the price deflator for the GNP.

[4] Since the number of people who will be of working age in the next ten or fifteen years has already been born, and net immigration is reasonably small and predictable, what BLS does is to project the proportion (and thereby the number) of people by sex and by age who might actually be in the labor market in the future.

[5] This is part of the detailed BLS projection, *Patterns of U.S. Economic Growth.* BLS Bulletin 1672, like The Conference

Board's publication (see footnote 6), contains much useful information on specific-long term projections and methods. The latest BLS labor force projection appears in *The U.S. Labor Force: Projections to 1985*, Special Labor Force Report 119. A handy short version of all this BLS research appears in *The U.S. Economy in 1980, A Summary of BLS Projections*, Bulletin 1673. (Revisions are due in late 1973.)

[6] See The Conference Board's pamphlet *Economic Growth in the Seventies*, by M. F. Elliott-Jones, issued in 1970.

[7] For the derivation, see, for example, the table on "Indexes of output per man-hour" in the statistical appendix to the most recent *Economic Report of the President.*

[8] In *The U.S. Economy in 1980*, table A-10, p. 44, BLS gives a median figure of 2.6 percent.

up to a bit over 4 percent. Calculated in dollars of 1970 purchasing power, a rise of 4.3 percent a year compounded puts the 1980 GNP at almost $1.5 trillion, compared to the actual 1970 figure of about $975 billion.

A related method of projecting makes use of the same calculations. The man-hours worked in the base year can be calculated, and the answer divided into the GNP for that year.[9] This results in a dollar value of output per man-hour. Multiplying that figure by a presumed average annual increase in output per man-hour (productivity), one compounded over a decade ahead (or for any other desired period), produces a new —and higher—dollar output per man-hour in the projected year. That figure must, in turn, be multiplied by the projected number of man-hours worked in the future— that is, total man-hours worked in the base year multiplied by the projected rate of increase in the labor force less any assumed rate of decline in hours worked. The product is a projection of GNP the desired number of years ahead in dollars of the base period's purchasing power.

This last method is well described in The Conference Board's *Economic Growth in the Seventies.* The Conference Board study, however, performs the calculation separately for farm, private nonfarm, and government sectors of the GNP, and then sums the results. The difficulty with the procedure just outlined above is that it presents some problems if "potential" rather than actual GNP is employed for the base period. If something other than actual GNP is used, then the projected change in man-hours or in productivity must be adjusted accordingly. The Conference Board, in fact, started from 1968, a year when unemployment was only 3.6 percent. It then projected to both 1975 and 1980, but by 1975 its projected unemployment rate was 4 percent. The study does not make precisely clear exactly how its projections were shaped to move from the 3.6 percent rate to the 4 percent rate (see page 6 of the study).

[9] Total man-hours worked in the base year are calculated as follows. Average hours actually worked per week (not hours paid for) during the year are multiplied by 50 (or whatever number of weeks are assumed to constitute the average work year after vacation time is allowed for). The result is in turn multiplied by the average number of people at work during that year. The necessary data appear in the "Monthly Report on the Labor Force," which is published by the U.S. Bureau of Labor Statistics in the opening pages of *Employment and Earnings.* The data can be compiled from single issues, from one of the issues during the first quarter that summarize the previous year's figures, and easiest of all, from one of the "Special Labor Force Reports" published later during the year in the BLS *Monthly Labor Review.* One "Special Labor Force Report" always gives a convenient summary of the previous year's employment, unemployment, and hours data, and the subsequent reprint from the *Monthly Labor Review* usually provides additional or more conveniently accessible statistics.

THE DEMAND SIDE

Either of the foregoing methods gives a projection of GNP from the *supply* side— an estimate of the amount of goods and services potentially available at some future date. Often, however, the user of a projection also wants to know what the *demand* side will look like. This requires a look at the possible future composition of GNP, that is, a breakdown of purchases of goods and services in the future. Demand analysis is also independently useful as a check on whether there are any prospective imbalances between demand and supply, or whether the projection of the size of total future GNP makes sense.

Demand projection can be as simple or as detailed an exercise as one desires. The National Planning Association, for example, calculates virtually the entire voluminous set of GNP tables plus some related statistics. The Conference Board's study is less detailed, but still reasonably comprehensive. The Bureau of Labor Statistics, while taking a good look at demand for future GNP, quite naturally focuses most heavily on the array of jobs and skills that are likely to be needed to produce that GNP. Some elaborations of the basic forecast may include estimates of the income generated at a future level of GNP by type of income (e.g., profits, government revenues, disposable personal income) as well as by the possible shape of the distribution of income among families and individuals.

Demand projections are commonly of three kinds, all of which are usually modified by the projector's generalized knowledge about the future, or specialized information available from other sources. For example, as this is being written in late 1971, it seems reasonable to expect (1) that the share of government expenditures going to the war in Vietnam will go down further (though perhaps expenditures to support the economy of southeast Asia might increase), (2) that spending on highways will peak before the decade is out, and (3) that an increasing share of government spending will be directed toward the alleviation of social and environmental problems afflicting the United States. It also seems reasonable to expect that the coming decade will be a strong one for home building. Consumers will probably allocate an increasing portion of their income to travel and leisure time pursuits. A large market may develop for devices that will enable owners of television sets to project entertainment or instructional materials of their individual choice on their own sets. And so on.

Considerations of this type can easily be introduced into even the simplest procedure for allocating demand for GNP. The simplest way is to calculate the historical percentage relationships of various expenditures to total GNP. This calculation, of course, can be made by large sectors of

GNP, or in as much detail as one desires.[10] Percentages used in the projection can then accord with past trends as well as be modified by the sorts of considerations mentioned in the preceding paragraph. (Some of the techniques of short-term forecasting described in the other chapters of this book that deal with specific sectors of the GNP may also provide insights and guides for determining the composition of GNP in the longer-term future.)[11]

Econometric techniques can also be used to project the GNP by sector. The most elaborate developed thus far are for the consumer sector. They were published in 1966 by Hendrik S. Houthakker and Lester D. Taylor in their book, *Consumer Demand in the United States: Analysis and Projections.* (Harvard University Press issued a second and enlarged edition in 1970.) Clopper Almon used the Houthakker-Taylor equations for consumer spending when he began his work, but then substituted equations that he developed himself.[12] The consumer section of The Conference Board's study also made use of the Houthakker-Taylor research.

At the time of this writing, more detailed work appears to have been carried out on consumer than on investment or other expenditures, though research on investment is progressing. Wharton EFA, Inc. (a Philadelphia enterprise that commercial-

[10] There is some virtue in making this calculation in both constant prices and current prices in order to get a feel of how relative price movements may have affected demand in the past. The more detailed long-term projections being made nowadays also take into account possible future shifts in relative prices among the various goods and services, and their effects. In fact, many detailed projections now present their results in both current and constant prices.

[11] For an example of a long-term projection using such sector-by-sector techniques, see *Markets of the Sixties* by the Editors of Fortune (New York: Harper & Brothers, 1960).

[12] For details see chapter 2 of Almon's book, cited in footnote 2 above.

ly markets forecasts that grew out of those produced by the so-called Wharton Model developed at the University of Pennsylvania) is one group doing detailed long-term econometric investigations of investment. So is Data Resources, Inc. of Lexington, Massachusetts.

The third technique of disaggregating projected GNP is through the use of input-output methods. This technique was also used by the Bureau of Labor Statistics[13] as well as by Clopper Almon. The BLS also projected two types of economy—one oriented toward spending on services and one oriented toward spending on durables. BLS presented both versions with an underlying rate of unemployment of 3 percent as well as with an underlying rate of 4 percent. As much of the foregoing suggests, most projectors—even those using the most complex methods—may blend a variety of techniques in order to bolster or cross-check their work.

NEW UNCERTAINTIES IN PROJECTING

Some years ago this chapter would have been ended at this point. But recent developments in American life have raised doubts about the merits of a long-term projection that merely presents a straightforward "normal" growth rate. Some of these developments may change the level of total output, others may change its distribution, and some may do both. *Fortune* raised a number of these uncertainties in a series of

articles published from January through August of 1971.[14] Uncertainty begins with the fundamentals of a projection. For example, productivity grew at a subpar rate from 1966 to 1970. During 1971 productivity started to snap back, but there was some question about whether its rise would be normal over the longer term. For one thing, younger workers, who will be the major source of labor force growth in the 1970s, may be a less disciplined and less zestful work force than their predecessors. For another, some industries which have made large contributions to past increases in national productivity may no longer contribute as heavily. Because the electric power industry has concentrated its generator of energy production in ever larger generating units, a breakdown of a single unit now can mean huge productivity losses. And some of the most important past sources of increased productivity took place in the telephone industry, as it converted to dial telephones and received the benefits of the automation that came with them. Future improvements in the telephone industry might not have as great an effect in increasing productivity.

The labor force increased a third faster during 1966–70 than it was projected to grow, although for the 1960s as a whole growth was very much in line with what BLS expected. This occurred, however, because there were offsetting errors in the BLS projection for the decade. The projected male labor force was too high (partly because of the Vietnam mobilization). Much more important, however, the projected rise in the female labor force was too low. The "labor force participation rates" of women twenty years of age and over continued to increase very rapidly. These days, young

[13] See citations in footnote 5 above, and Jack Alterman, "Input-Output Projections of the U.S. Economy to 1980 and some Implications," American Statistical Association, *1970 Proceedings of the Business and Economic Statistics Section*, p. 73 ff. See also Beatrice N. Vaccara, "An Input-Output Method for Long Range Economic Projections," *Survey of Current Business* (July 1971), p. 47 ff.

[14] These articles were collected in a book titled *The U.S. Economy in an Age of Uncertainty* (New York: Little, Brown and Company, 1972).

women tend to get married later than their predecessors did, and after they do get married they tend to delay having children. Consequently, a larger proportion of young women enter or remain in the labor force than previously. Moreover, an increasing proportion of women with young children take jobs—often part-time jobs—and more and more women whose children have grown reenter the labor force. If the philosophy of "women's lib" spreads more widely the tendency of women to form a larger part of the labor force will, of course, be further enhanced.

There are signs, however, that a trend in the opposite direction—toward less labor force participation—might take place simultaneously. This would certainly be the case if a new antiwork or anticonsumption ethic takes widespread root among young people. Among others, Charles Reich has written about these tendencies in *The Greening of America,* and Theodore Roszak in *The Making of a Counter Culture.*

Some of the uncertainties that have begun to affect long-term projections in the United States stem from broad new social concerns or problems that have come to public attention. Most have to do with the preservation of natural surroundings, the control of pollution, or the prevention of overcrowding. Consequently, citizens in some urban centers mobilize against the construction of new airports. And opposition to continued rapid inflows of population and to indiscriminate economic growth has begun to occur not only in such conservation-conscious states as Oregon, but also in Florida, a state with a long history of boom psychology. Utilities are finding it difficult to get permission to build new or larger plants, particularly if they are to be plants using nuclear fuel. Automobiles, by law, will have to stop creating air polluting exhausts by the mid-1970s, and this could conceivably reshape the auto market, as could the development of greatly improved mass

transit systems. The whole movement—both in law and in public opinion—to restrict or eliminate pollution may considerably change the relative prices (and consequently the demand) among important classes of goods and services.

The capital/output ratio (the amount of capital equipment needed to produce a given unit of output) could well rise in the future for reasons that would, in effect, make a given unit of capital equipment less efficient in the conventional sense. Factories will need to install many more or more effective antipollution devices than they now possess. Government policies may actively foster changes in the distribution of population in order to curb overcrowding in present urbanized areas, as well as to build up ruralized areas that are declining. This would increase the relative need for capital not only in the form of new factories, stores, and utilities, but also of schools, hospitals, churches, and such installations as waste disposal facilities.

SOME SCENARIOS

It is evident that anyone who makes long-term projections today must at least begin to think about possible departures from the conventional 4.3 percent or so growth rate. By way of illustration, *Fortune* hypothesized a low rate of increase in productivity and a low rate of increase in the labor force that would together produce an annual growth rate of 2.5 percent in GNP. It contrasted this situation with one in which there was a high rate of increase in productivity and in the labor force, thereby causing GNP to rise at about a 5.75 percent rate. Starting in 1970, the higher growth rate would produce about $500 billion more in GNP (measured in 1970 prices) by 1980 than would the lower.

In 1971 the General Electric Company's MAPCAST forecasting service[15] set forth more realistic alternatives for economic growth from 1970 to 1980. These were its Scenario I, the bench mark or more probable projection of 4.3 percent annual growth; Scenario II, with a reduced level of real growth (3.2 percent), but with higher inflation and greater unemployment; and Scenario III, the most optimistic projection with respect to growth (5.1 percent), with low inflation and low unemployment.

The new uncertainties about the economic future obviously raise new problems for those who furnish long-term projections as well as for those who use them. It is clear that long-term economic projections need to be produced with a higher degree of sophistication than ever before. Consequently, in order for projections to be of maximum use as guides for decision-makers, the producers of those projections will have to work harder and more ingeniously than ever at their craft.

[15] The General Electric projections, like those of the Chase, National Planning Association, Wharton EFA, and Data Resources mentioned earlier, are generally available only on a subscription basis. The Bureau of Labor Statistics and The Conference Board studies may be purchased at relatively moderate prices (the Board has a special rate for teachers and students). Clopper Almon's ongoing research is available on a current basis to industrial sponsors of the research.

KAREN GERARD

Regional and Urban Forecasting

INTRODUCTION

Interest in regional and urban forecasting is expanding rapidly. Until fairly recently, the business economist, considering the task secondary to his primary responsibilities in macroeconomic forecasting, traditionally prepared local or regional forecasts only in conjunction with marketing forecasts and with plant location decisions.

Today, the scope of interest is much broader. The social, environmental, and economic problems associated with the urbanization of the United States require an understanding of trends and their implications across a wide range of topics. Though the business economist may feel at times that the tools of his trade are inadequate, he is in a position, through the disciplines of economics with which he is familiar, to contribute to his company's understanding of these problems. His work may encompass an examination of the economic implications for the corporation or its clients of projected social and environmental conditions in given metropolitan areas. Or, his responsibilities can be considerably wider, with the economist advising senior management on questions of public policy such as welfare, metropolitan transportation, low-income housing, and city finances.

With the spreading out of his con-

cerns, the urban economist may find that his specialized field is no longer sharply defined. Rather, he may think of himself as part economist, part sociologist, and part philosopher, with the proportions varying according to the problem with which he is dealing. For some economists this mixture of strictly mathematical economics with social theorizing is alien to their nature. Data limitations, the problems of translating social phenomena into economic terms, and, perhaps most challenging, the need to understand complex interrelationships and feedback effects—all can present serious difficulties for economists. However, for those who are actively involved, urban economics presents an opportunity to make a meaningful contribution to their corporation as well as toward broader social goals.

I. GEOGRAPHIC SCOPE OF THE FIELD

Defining regional or urban economics simply in terms of its geography can in itself present a problem. In the early days of the discipline, the state or the metropolitan area was usually the unit considered. Of the two, the metropolitan area tends to be favored in forecasting models since it typically qualifies more as an economic unit than does the state (which is predominantly a political entity). However, this classification is only the beginning of possible geographic choices.

Accepting the metropolitan area as a basic unit, the forecaster must arrive at an acceptable definition of the geographic scope of the area. He usually starts with the Bureau of the Census classification for Standard Metropolitan Statistical Areas. (There are presently 247 SMSAs. Each SMSA is comprised of at least one *central city* having a population of 50,000 or more, plus a variable number of surrounding counties). Still, if he is forecasting, he must decide whether his mission is to forecast for the SMSA as its boundaries are presently defined, or if his forecasting job entails a projection of the geographic expansion of the metropolitan area itself. In the former case, if the geographic boundaries have changed over time (for example, the Rochester SMSA contained four counties in the 1970 census against one in 1960), he may have to adjust historical data to meet the 1970 census definition. On the other hand, if he prefers a technique encompassing expansion of geographic boundaries, he will have to project the rate at which further urbanization and suburbanization will occur. The National Planning Association, which has prepared population, employment, and personal income projections for 230 metropolitan areas, uses variable SMSA boundaries for historical years; this implicitly allows for boundary extension in their projections.[1]

For many forecasting purposes neither the state nor the SMSA serves as the appropriate geographic unit. Those interested in regional economics, particularly when their viewpoint is long-run, may see the region as spilling across state boundaries and with a sphere of economic influence that is more extended than the metropolitan area as pre-

sently defined. Thus the Department of Commerce in a joint program with the Water Resources Council has prepared projections of population, employment, personal income and earnings for 173 economic areas, many of which cross state lines. Some of the economic areas include no SMSA while several contain more than one. The Regional Plan Association includes 31 counties with 20 million residents in the tri-state area of New York, Connecticut, and New Jersey as the economic region which has its core in New York City. In contrast, the New York SMSA contains 9 counties with 11.8 million persons and the New York-Northeastern New Jersey Consolidated SMSA comprises 17 counties with 16.4 million residents. The nature of the economist's interests as well as the time and financial resources he has at his command will influence which approach he follows.

At the same time, the geographic area to be treated may be broken down into units smaller than the SMSA. The most common division of the SMSA is into *central city* and *outside central city* (often referred to as the suburbs even though outside central city may contain heavily urbanized areas). When projections are made solely in terms of the SMSA, the conglomerate figures can give an accurate picture of the area's overall growth, but they may woefully conceal the sharp disparity between the performance of the central city and the outlying areas. Economic measures for the SMSA as a whole generally mask the economic and social deterioration which is occurring in the central city and the spillover which may be taking place in the close-lying suburbs. A composite SMSA analysis cannot provide insight into the dynamics of change within the metropolitan area: it does not tell us where, within the area, growth or contraction will take place.

The smaller the geographic unit considered, the greater are the problems of obtaining adequate data and the larger is the probability of error. Units below city size

---

[1] See National Planning Association, Regional Economic Projection Series, Report No. 71-R-1, *Income, Saving and Consumption Patterns for Regions, States and Metropolitan Areas, 1960–1980*, October 1971.

rarely can be thought of as economic entities. Still, with the multiplicity of community development programs and the concerns for rebuilding decaying neighborhoods, there is a crying need for economic analysis at the small area level. Thus, city block, census tract, zip code, neighborhood, county, and central city are all legitimate geographic entities for which forecasts are made.

The business economist may find himself in unfamiliar territory when he first attempts to perform small area forecasts. The most important handicap is the lack of reliable timely data on most basic economic measures. For small area analysis, the primary data source is the decennial Census of Population and Housing. Typically the census is used by building up census tract data into the desired geographic unit. The 1970 census for the first time contains summary tapes by zip code. Fragmentary income distribution data is now published on a zip code basis by the Internal Revenue Service from income tax returns (with 1966 the first year). After 1973, another valuable small area data source will be added when the Census of Business becomes available by zip code.

In order to supplement the limited federal government data, the business economist may look to independent surveys or to data collected by the locality itself. However, before he starts his analysis, the business economist must recognize the problems involved in developing data on a uniform geographic basis. A community may keep vital statistics by health districts, educational data by school districts, crime reporting by police precincts—each area with a different geographic boundary. Furthermore, the data may be difficult for the economist to work with since it is usually recorded by local government for operating purposes rather than for economic analysis. With more sophisticated recordkeeping and computer capabilities, these problems should be reduced, although they can still form major

roadblocks even for the analyst well versed in the statistical sources of a particular community.

As the economist moves to forecasting of units of county size and larger, more reliable data sources are available. For example, County Business Patterns provides an annual bench mark for employment by county, although the coverage is incomplete. The various federal censuses of business at four and five year intervals provide some historical continuity. For major SMSAs, the federal government, principally through the departments of commerce and labor, publishes a considerable amount of data such as monthly payroll employment, cost of living indexes, and annual labor force and personal income estimates.

To a large degree, before a business economist can forecast for a local area, he must start by first estimating where statistically the local area is at the base date for the forecast. Such basic information as population, labor force, and unemployment is not even available annually for most cities, much less for units of smaller size. Professional demographers did not know whether the population of New York City was rising, falling or remaining unchanged between the 1960 and 1970 census dates. The economist could choose from at least six separate government reports (two city, two state, and two federal) as well as numerous private studies and select the number he liked best. Even when the final 1970 census figure was released, showing an increase of 113,579, experts did not agree on how accurate the count was. Suspicions remained that a sizable number of blacks and Puerto Ricans had been missed in the census count.

Such data problems can be more pronounced when geographic areas below city size are analyzed. The challenge to the business economist is, of course, to go ahead with what he has and to improvise where necessary. He should, however, be aware of the limitations of his data and how they affect the degree of confidence he has in his forecasts. Generally speaking, the smaller the geographic unit and the poorer the data, the less the economist should employ rigid forecasting models and the more he should be prepared to modify his findings by judgment. In many cases that judgment can best be sharpened by moving out of the office and into the field to physically inspect the area under consideration. (East Coast economists may have trouble convincing their employers that they can conduct a thorough analysis of West Cost cities only by visiting, but there is some truth to the assertion.)

II. WHAT THE BUSINESS ECONOMIST FORECASTS

Not many years ago, the business economist's interest in regional or local area forecasting was mainly market-oriented. He would attempt to project those variables which he considered closely related to sales of his company's products. Sometimes, less frequently, he would be called upon to assist in plant location decisions with forecasts of labor supply and analyses of comparative costs. Today with the broader scope of urban economics, the business economist may find himself projecting local crime rates, public assistance case loads, the impact of alternative forms of solid waste disposal, or the potentials for developing a new town. The forecast may be prepared to assist his own company which may be actively increasing its social involvement, or it might be for the benefit of a corporate or government client as part of the growing market for consultants in the environmental problem field.

In preparing such forecasts a variety of techniques can be employed depending on the complexity of the question, the availability of data, and the time and resources open to the analyst. However, some common elements form the base for most pro-jections, regardless of the end product to be forecasted. The fundamentals to be projected are similar to those the macroeconomist is accustomed to forecasting. The main difference is that the regional or urban economist does not have available a consistent set of historical data comparable to the national income and product accounts or input-output tables. He must first either construct such accounts from fragmentary data or use proxies instead. Several state product accounts have been constructed (such as those for California, Oregon, and Washington appearing in the Bank of California's *Pacific Coast Market and Business* letter). Several regional input-output tables have also been developed, usually in conjunction with university studies (such as at the University of Pennsylvania, i.e., Wharton School's model for the Philadelphia region). However, most business economists do not construct a full set of regional income and product accounts unless large resources are available for an extended study. Given the gaps in data (particularly on the export and investment side), the potential for error may be greater than the additional knowledge to be gained. Of course, as interest in urban and regional economics spreads, it is hoped that these data gaps will be reduced, and it will become more feasible to replicate national accounts at the state and local level.

In the present circumstances, the business economist tries to work, as far as possible, from existing data sources. This means that for states and SMSAs, the principal series forecasted will be population, employment, and personal income. Other series that typically form the basis for forecasts are payroll employment and wage rates by industry, retail sales, selected service industry receipts, construction permits (or contract awards), and value added in manufacturing. In areas smaller than the SMSA, with less usable data, primary reliance is placed on population, employment, and income projections as proxies for more sophisticated economic measures. These projections in turn provide the framework for analyzing the particular problem with which the economist is concerned. Developing linkages between the basic series and the ultimate area of interest (whether it be low-income housing needs or welfare case loads) is one of the economist's most important challenges.

III. THE THEORETICAL FRAMEWORK FOR FORECASTING

All regional forecasting is prepared within the framework of the national economy. States and localities do not exist in a vacuum. Either explicitly or implicitly, assumptions must be made about the future course of the national economy. The smaller the geographic area under study the less direct the linkage to the national economy may seem, but it will still exist. Sometimes the economist develops his projections in a formal stepped progression, forecasting first the U.S. economy, then the region (a group of states), then the state, then the SMSA, and finally individual parts of the metropolitan area. Frequently, some of the linkages are skipped in the formal projecting procedure. And a "build up" technique from smaller units as well as a "breakdown" from larger units can be helpful in developing a set of consistent projections. However, no matter what the specific technique, a national backdrop is essential.

In a short-run forecast, the economic structure of the region is given. The economist's job is essentialy to estimate how the local economy, given its structure, will respond to national economic forces. If defense expenditures are cut, what will the local impact be? If the national unemployment rate moves from four percent to six percent, how will the local unemployment rate change? If housing starts increase twenty percent nationally, what will the local

trend be? In all these cases, national trends are dominant, and the locality will respond more or less than national averages, according to its own characteristics.

In a long-run forecast, national economic trends still provide the framework for regional analysis. However, another element is added to the picture. A locality's economic structure cannot assume to be given for all time. Rather, the forecasting problem becomes: Given the locality's present structure, and given national economic trends for the future, how will the local economy's structure change over time? Recognizing shifts in trend, and determining how the historical relationship between the region and the nation is going to change— this is the core of the regional or urban forecaster's job.

Trying to arrive at a judgment as to the timing and extent of a major shift (At what point will a declining region resume growth? When will a rapidly expanding area reduce its growth rate?) requires an understanding not only of national economic forces but of technological, political and social change as well.

Technological change, with improved transportation and communications, has altered the geographic determinants of plant location. Closeness to a rail center, a seaport, or primary natural resources no longer has the same locational force for manufacturing as formerly. Furthermore, the shift in the national economy from goods production to services means that a different set of forces is gaining dominance. Perhaps industry is no longer so closely tied to specific geographic locations. It is not entirely clear how those locational forces operate. At what point in growth can a local bank begin to perform national banking services? How much face-to-face contact do business services such as legal, advertising, and management consulting, in fact require? Do improved communications and transportation negate the economic rationale for central cities? When do the economies of scale offered by a large central city turn into diseconomies of size? Jane Jacobs in *The Economy of Cities* suggests that the relative growth rates of cities are influenced by their ability to innovate, to replace stagnant or dying industries with new industries. To the extent that this is true, successful forecasting requires an ability to evaluate when and where new industry will develop.

Along with the changing role of technology, powerful political and social forces influence the relative growth rates of geographic regions in ways that are not readily predictable. This, of course, is not a new phenomenon. Much of the immigration to the United States reflected not simply the pull of economic opportunities, but the push of specific political occurrences taking place at a particular point in history in the nations from which the new arrivals came. Within the United States, political and social forces also play a powerful distributive role. Frequently, the full impact of such forces is not understood until well after the fact. The political decision to support highways rather than railroads shaped the pace and pattern of suburban growth. Agricultural policies speeded the degree and direction of rural-urban migration. Federal public assistance policies did much to insure that a large proportion of that migration ultimately became a welfare burden concentrated in central cities. Long-standing traditions of racial discrimination resulted in patterns of housing segregation which have had far-reaching effects on the health, education, and economic opportunities of blacks and other minority groups.

Although the economist engaged in macroeconomics knows that he cannot forecast exogenous events with certainty, he builds certain basic noneconomic assumptions into his model. He generally assumes that the United States will not be engaged in a full-scale war during his forecast period; he assumes that a radical change will not occur in the work ethic of society; he assumes that a certain rate of technological change will take place. Likewise, the urban or regional economist must also make assumptions such as these, based on less than perfect knowledge of the future. However, because technological, political, and social forces—which form an implicit underpinning to national economic projections—can have far more than an "average" impact on a particular geographic area, it becomes extremely important for the urban or regional economist to be aware of the complex interrelationships between factors such as these and the economic prospects of an individual locality.

IV. FORECASTING METHODOLOGY

Given the difficulties in local area forecasting, the job still must be done. Experience has been building up in recent years with several forecasting techniques, so that the business economist new to the field does not have to start from scratch. Such sources as Wilbur R. Thompson, *A Preface to Urban Economics*; Charles M. Tiebout, *The Community Economic Base Study*; Regional Plan Association, *New York Metropolitan Regional Study*; U.S. Department of Labor, *Tomorrow's Manpower Needs, Developing Manpower Projections*; Walter Isard et al., *Philadelphia Regional Input-Output Study*; National Planning Association, *Regional Economic Projections Series*; and New York State Department of Labor, *Manpower Directions, New York State 1965–75* can provide working guides for the business economist interested in practical methodology. The list, of course, is illustrative and by no means a complete documentation of the sources currently available. Some of the techniques most commonly employed are summarized in the following sections.

A. Population

A population projection is basic to almost all local area forecasting. Product markets, housing requirements, school needs, labor force characteristics—all are related to the size and age distribution of the area's population. Two approaches can be used in making population projections. One method assumes that the population of an area reflects job opportunities. Employment is projected first, and then population is projected as a function of employment. The second approach assumes that population change for the most part is independent of job opportunities, and that the age and ethnic distribution of the locality along with national trends in birth and death rates are major determinants of regional population growth. In the real world, population trends and employment opportunities interact, and a fully consistent set of forecasts will work both from the top down and the bottom up.

A forecast from the "bottom up" stresses the role of employment opportunities in producing local deviations from national population trends. For example, the National Planning Association projects metropolitan area population by linkages to employment changes in the area. Their projections assume that migration adjusts to employment opportunities. Changing demographic structure is reflected in a projection of the local population/employment ratio, which in turn is linked to a projection of this ratio for the larger analytical region (a state or group of states), of which the metropolitan area is a part. The following formula is used:[2]

$$H_z = m_z \cdot E_z \left(\frac{H_z'}{E_z'} \right)$$

[2] National Planning Association, *Regional Economic Projectors Series*, Report No. 70-R-2, *Metropolitan Area Growth Patterns for the Coming Decade*, December 1970.

where H_z = population in the metropolitan area in year$_z$

m_z = ratio of the metropolitan area's population/employment ratio to its larger analytical region's population/employment ratio in year$_z$

E_z = employment in the metropolitan area in year$_z$

$\frac{H_z'}{E_z'}$ = ratio of population to employment in the larger analytical region of which the metropolitan area is a part, in the year$_z$

Forecasting population mechanically from a projection of job opportunities can produce unrealistic results if the age and skills structure of the resident population is ignored, if the migratory response is not as rapid as purely economic considerations would suggest, or if commuting plays a large role in the region's economy. Because employment-derived population forecasts do have limitations, independent forecasts of population are also made. First, they serve as a check on projections of employment that have been made without regard to demographic trends or to trends in labor force participation rates. Second, independent population forecasts often act as variables in employment forecasts for those industries which are tied to local markets. Third, independent population forecasts provide information on age distribution, labor force skills, and migration that cannot easily be derived from employment projections alone. Frequently this type of information is of primary importance for public planning needs, while the industry employment data is secondary.

The methodology for independent population forecasts can be relatively complex or straightforward, depending, as in so much of local area forecasting, on the resources and time available. Basically, the forecast involves relating local population changes to trends at the national level. On the crudest level, one could simply project trends in the ratio of the area's population to the nation's and then apply the ratio to national population projections to arrive at total area population for any given year.

With a slightly more complex methodology, the analyst can project the regional/national population ratio for each age group, and then sum the totals. Since state population projections are available from the Department of Commerce for five-year periods up to 1985, state population figures can be substituted for national totals in this procedure.

There is second approach which goes further into forces behind differential growth rates. It projects birth rates and death rates per thousand of population, basing the projection on the relationship of the area's birth and mortality rates to those in the nation (or state) as a whole. Again, this procedure can be carried out in considerable detail by projecting survival rates by age-cohorts. No matter what the complexity of the methodology, the forecast involves relating the locality to national population trends. Using these procedures, the rate of natural increase in a locality will deviate from the national picture because of differences in the age structure of the area (for example, a retirement community versus a bedroom suburb), as well as differences in birth and death rates for comparable age groups. (A low-income community will tend to have higher birth and death rates than a high-income community.)

Given the rate of *natural increase*, which can be arrived at by fairly mechanical means, the crucial factor in the local area population forecast is the estimate of net migration. The net flow of migrants to or from an area is a major determinant of local population growth. Even with high birth rates and low death rates, a community that shifts from net in-migration to net out-

migration can lose population on balance. Empirical investigation suggests that out-migration is related to the life cycle, while in-migration is a function of job opportunities. Arriving at a judgment on net migration can be one of the thorniest problems of population forecasting, even though the procedures for developing a first estimate may be relatively uncomplex. The analyst can look at past trends in net migration and project them forward, usually with an underlying assumption that interarea migration will gradually diminish (as economic differentials among regions are reduced). Or, the analyst can build up employment projections. The difference between the labor force required to meet employment projections and the labor force derived from natural increase population projections is assumed to be filled by migration. Then, applying the appropriate labor force participation rates, a total migration figure is attained which is added to (or subtracted from) the local population base. Judgment must come into the process at some point. If the first procedure produces total population estimates that seem inconsistent with trends in job opportunities, then migration estimates should be revised. If the second procedure working bottom up from job opportunities produces a migration estimate that is totally out of keeping with past experience, then the job forecasts should be reevaluated. In both cases, adjustment for commutation should be made for local areas where commuters hold a substantial role.

In making judgments about migration, one must keep in mind that other factors besides job opportunities can be important in the migratory push or pull. The migration of the black population from southern farms to central cities is only partially a reflection of relative job opportunities. Life in the city compared to life on the farm (even when both are lived at near poverty levels) seems to have held an independent attraction. Public assistance payments and policies have also had an impact. Even if people migrate initially because of relative job opportunities, they may not leave an area when satisfactory jobs fail to appear, if public assistance levels permit a standard of living that is high compared to elsewhere. Certainly, housing discrimination has played a role in determining patterns of migration.

In another context, the attraction of a life-style can in itself influence where job opportunities will evolve. Disillusionment with one city as a place in which to live and work (perhaps because of crime, schooling, the pace of business life), not the lack of job opportunities, can cause some professionals and executives to migrate to other cities. A desire of businessmen to eliminate commuting and to work near their homes in a relaxed setting has been a factor in corporate relocation from the central city to the suburbs. Economic forces certainly are important in these decisions, but the attraction of a life-style, whether it be for a corporate executive, the members of a commune, or a welfare family, should not be ignored in assessing migration trends.

B. Employment

For the business economist, a population projection provides a necessary input to area analysis, but an employment projection is the key to understanding the economics of the region. A fairly large body of theory has evolved which is useful in developing employment projections. Again, the national economy provides the framework within which the regional forecast is made. The question is, given national trends, what route will the local economy follow? To be able to answer this question, regional forecasting requires an understanding of the area's economic base.

One analytical approach entails examining the local area's *industry mix*. Through a fairly simple mathematical pro-

cess the region's industrial structure and industry growth rates can be compared to that of the nation (or an appropriate analytical region). By looking at the *proportion* of the labor force engaged in each industry, the analyst can determine whether the region is favored with relatively rapid growth industries or whether it is saddled with slow growth industries in terms of national economic averages. Then by examining the growth rate of each local industry, the analyst can conclude whether the region he is studying has a *competitive* advantage for each industry compared to other regions in the nation. Thus, New York is favored by its heavy concentration of rapid growth service industries, but this tends to be offset by the fact that these industries are expanding less rapidly in New York than in the nation as a whole. On the other hand, Texas has a high share of relatively slow growth industries, but its rate of growth in these industries is above national averages.[3]

The forecaster using the industry/mix method can simply extrapolate the ratio of area employment to national employment and apply the projected ratio to the national employment estimate for the desired year. Or, for more complete trend analysis, regression estimates can be made in the form of

$$Z = a + bt$$

or

$$\log Z = a + bt$$

where Z = regional employment as a percent of U.S. employment
t = time

New York State used this methodology in developing industry employment projections for the state as a whole (see table 1). Then for metropolitan area projections within the state, a combination of extra-

[3] See *Survey of Current Business*, Department of Commerce, May and August 1970, for an analysis of past growth on an industry mix and competitive advantage basis.

TABLE 1.   **REGRESSION ESTIMATES FOR EMPLOYMENT, BY INDUSTRY, NEW YORK STATE, 1970 IN THOUSANDS**

Industry	New York State employment			State as percent of U.S.	
	Log-log A	Linear B	Loga-rithmic C	Linear D	Loga-rithmic E
All industries (nonagricultural)	6,349.8	6,679.7	6,864.6	7,066.6	7,142.1
Manufacturing	1,887.3	1,780.3	1,824.7	1,853.2	1,900.5
Durable goods	854.3	858.4	872.7	884.5	895.5
Lumber and wood products	15.8	12.1	13.0	14.9	14.9
Furniture and fixtures	34.9	31.5	31.9	32.4	33.4
Stone, clay, and glass products	48.9	49.3	49.5	51.4	51.1
Primary metal industries	76.5	67.3	68.3	69.2	70.3
Fabricated metal products, including ordnance	116.7	110.5	110.5	98.9	102.9
Machinery, except electrical	161.5	168.0	169.3	182.6	183.0
Electrical machinery, equipment, and supplies	175.3	194.6	202.7	216.8	218.0
Transportation equipment	115.8	113.8	115.5	98.4	99.2
Instruments and related products	108.9	111.3	112.1	119.9	122·7
Nondurable goods	1,033.0	921.9	951.9	968.7	1,005.0
Food and kindred products	151.2	134.1	136.2	135.8	136.6
Tobacco manufactures	2.9	1.9	2.2	2.4	2.4
Textile mill products	57.1	34.8	43.5	51.2	51.9
Apparel and other finished fabric products	305.5	239.8	254.7	252.7	277.5
Paper and allied products	68.3	69.3	69.3	65.2	68.3
Printing, publishing, and allied industries	175.4	183.6	184.5	185.5	187.7
Chemicals and allied products	89.8	92.4	92.7	87.8	91.3
Petroleum refining and related industries	11.6	9.5	9.7	8.3	8.5
Rubber and misc. plastic products	20.6	20.7	20.7	23.3	23.5
Leather and leather products	57.4	47.2	46.9	50.7	51.8
Misc. manufacturing industries	93.2	88.6	88.8	105.8	105.6
Nonmanufacturing	4,462.5	4,899.4	5,039.9	5,213.4	5,241.6
Mining	9.0	8.2	8.2	9.1	8.9
Contract construction	273.6	298.7	306.0	326.8	327.9
Transportation, public utilities	473.5	445.7	448.4	455.1	460.9
Wholesale and retail trade	1,280.1	1,360.0	1,369.6	1,379.7	1,388.7
Finance, insurance, and real estate	504.9	564.9	581.7	542.1	547.6
Services and miscellaneous	1,023.4	1,200.1	1,258.4	1,351.3	1,354.8
Government	898.0	1,021.9	1,067.6	1,149.3	1,152.8

Source: New York State Department of Labor, *Manpower Directions, New York State 1965-75,* Technical Supplement, 1968, p. 45.
A. $\log Y = a + b \log t$ B. $Y = a + bt$ C. $\log Y = a + bt$ D. $Z = a + bt$ E. $\log Z = a + bt$
where $Y =$ state employment
      $Z =$ state employment as percent of U.S. employment
      $t =$ time

polation and regression analysis was used, with the statewide projections acting as a reference base.[4]

One major weakness of a strict application of industry mix projections is that the broad SIC categories used for analysis may conceal important underlying differences in industrial structure. Local area data may be available, for example, only for a composite "transportation equipment" group, but this industry may be highly specialized in the area under study rather than diversified as in the nation as a whole. A second problem is that the growth process is more complex than suggested by industry/mix analysis. Some local industries are far more closely tied to national trends than others and play a more important role in determining the rate of growth of the local area.

A body of theory has been developed which views a region within a country much as it would look at a nation in the world of trade. The area's export base is considered the main element that supplies dynamism to the region, while purely local industry is viewed as expanding or contracting in response to developments in the export structure. The export of basic industry sector sells a substantial proportion of its output in national markets or outside of its own geographic region. It is influenced primarily by broad economic developments. Agriculture, mining, and manufacturing are the major basic industries. Construction is considered a local industry by some analysts since the product is not "exported," but other economists treat it as a basic industry because its performance is so strongly conditioned by broad economic conditions. Local industries such as trade, transportation, communications, services, and finance are

dependent essentially on economic activity within the area under consideration. However, a proportion of their output is affected by supply and demand conditions outside the area and can be treated as a part of the export sector. In some regions, industries that have traditionally been thought of as local in nature are actually the area's most important export sectors (e.g., finance in New York or medicine in Boston).

The National Planning Association's Regional Projection Projections Series[5] provides a model for metropolitan area export base projections. First, employment is projected in each basic industry by extrapolating the metropolitan area's share of projected employment in its larger analytical region (usually a state or group of states). Then the export component of local industry employment is calculated. The export component is assumed to be represented by the difference between the metropolitan area and its larger region in the ratio of each local industry's employment to total population of the area. It can be projected by examining the trend in the export component over time.

$$P_{jt} = \left(\frac{Y_{jt}}{H_t} - \frac{Y'_{jt}}{H'_{jt}} \right) \cdot H_t$$

where P_{jt} = export component employment in the metropolitan area in industry j

$\dfrac{Y_{jt}}{H_t}$ = ratio of local industry employment to total population in the metropolitan area

$\dfrac{Y'_{jt}}{H'_t}$ = ratio of local industry employment to total population in the larger analytical region

Basic industry employment and the export component of local industries are

[4] New York State Department of Labor, *Manpower Directions, New York State 1965–75*, Technical Supplement, 1968 and *Manpower Requirements, Interim Projections, New York State 1968–1980*, July 1971.

[5] Report No. 70-R-2 and No. 71-R-1.

considered growth generating employment. It is assumed that the rest of local employment is a function of growth generating employment. In other words, export industries have a multiplier impact; local employment is projected by extrapolating the trend in the ratio of local industry employment to export employment. As part of this analysis a location quotient may be calculated for local (i.e. residentiary) industries. The location quotient is the ratio of an industry's share of total employment in the geographic area to that industry's share of total employment in the nation. In other words, if .16 of Denver's employment is in services while the comparable ratio is .15 for the United States, then the location quotient for services in Denver is 1.07. Working from projected location quotients and projected employment in export industries, employment for each local or residentiary industry can be derived.[6]

In some models a direct link between the export and local industry sectors is not used. Rather, exports are analyzed first, and then local industry employment in sectors such as trade and services is projected through analysis of trends in the ratio of employment in these industries to local area population.

After the business economist devotes a certain amount of time to perfecting either export base or industry/mix projection techniques, it generally becomes apparent that these tools provide only a first approximation of the dynamics of the growth process. Many factors are left unexplained and not fully understood. A simple multiplier analysis leaves much to be desired for uncovering information about shifts in the export multiplier; it certainly fails to throw much light on how local industries, if they become large or diversified, have a multiplier impact

themselves on export industries. Input-output analysis is being employed in some regions to further refine knowledge of the linkages between industries. Unfortunately, national input-output tables cannot simply be applied to the local industrial structure without grave danger of distortion. (The coefficients can be radically different at the local level. For example, New York's manufacturing headquarters firms obviously do not have the same coefficients as manufacturing production firms which form the basis for the national input-output tables.) Input-output tables can be developed at the local level, but it is a time-consuming, costly process requiring a piecing together of published data, sample interviews, and judgmental conclusions.[7]

Far more fundamental, and this problem bedevils any kind of trend *analysis, is the fact that* neither industry/mix nor export base analysis can provide the key to understanding what will bring about a change in the underlying industrial structure. Over the short run, the industrial structure of a region is relatively fixed, and the area's growth is strongly influenced by national trends. But much of the dynamics of change in a local area is determined by its ability to replace slow growth industries in its export sectors with more rapidly growing functions. If a metropolitan area loses a competitive advantage in a major export industry, will the local economy go steadily downhill or will another industry move in to more than take its place? Trend analysis in the Boston area might well have predicted the loss of the textile industry in the late 1940s and 1950s; it would not automatically have forecast the new role of research and development in the area, even given accurate national projections of the growing importance of R & D.

---

[6] See, for example, U.S. Department of Commerce, "State Projections of Income, Employment, and Population," *Survey of Current Business*, April 1972.

[7] See, for example, Walter Isard et al., *Philadelphia Region Input-Output Study*, Preliminary Working Paper, Regional Science Research Institute, Philadelphia, March 1966.

Long-run trend analysis provides a picture of increasing concentration and expansion of the office worker sector in New York City. However, 1970–71 saw a large number of corporations moving their headquarters out of the central city into the suburbs. The analytic tools are not at hand to determine from strictly mechanical projections whether the 1970–71 phenomenon reflects a short-run aberration or a marked permanent shift in trend. What these caveats are meant to suggest is not that trend analysis is useless, but that it is only a starting point for providing a framework for further judgmental analysis.

C. Income

Much of what has already been said about employment projections is true for income projections and need not be repeated. The shortcomings naturally follow since one of the primary methods of forecasting personal income is to apply average earnings data to industry employment projections. For example, it may be assumed that wage rates in an industry will rise at a certain rate (probably determined by the relationship between national and local area wages). Then the projected wage level is multiplied by the projected employment level to give average and annual salary estimates by industry. Other elements of personal income such as property income and transfer payments are projected to change in line with their relationship to national trends or according to their historical proportion of local area personal income. A somewhat cruder shorthand method would skip the employment/wage rate step and simply project industry wages and salaries by their relationship to national (or state) trends.

As one moves from projections of total personal income to estimates of median income levels and family income distribution, time-series analysis often proves inadequate. In many cases, data are simply not available to provide a meaningful historical picture. Local area family income data, for example, are obtained only decennially from the Census of Population. To overcome this problem, cross-sectional analysis can provide another useful forecasting tool. Relationships between variables in many different localities at one point in time (or over two or three census periods) provide the basis for cross-sectional analysis. Thus, Wilbur R. Thompson[8] outlines the findings of a cross section multiple correlation and regression analysis of 135 SMSAs. Median income is expressed as the function of nine variables with education, labor force participation, manufacturing specialization, and population all playing a role as in the equation below.

$$Y_M = 1155 - 58E_L + 55F + 41L_M \\ + 96M_{C/L} + 81E_{H4} + 272P_{60} \\ - 42L_S + 10M_D$$

where $Y_M =$ Median income of families, 1959

     $E_L =$ Percent with six years school or less, 1960

     $F =$ Percent foreign, born, 1950

     $L_M =$ Male, percent in labor force, 1960

     $M_{C/L} =$ Capital/labor ratio, 1960

     $E_{H4} =$ Percent with four or more years college, 1960

     $P_{60} =$ Logarithm of 1960 population

     $L_S =$ Male, self-employed as percent of employment, 1960

     $M_D =$ Percent employed in durable goods, 1960

[8] "Internal and External Factors in the Development of Urban Economics," in *Issues in Urban Economics,* by Harvey Perloff et al. (Resources for the Future, Inc., Johns Hopkins Press, 1968).

The median income equation is tied in with a full set of associated regression equations which relate population growth, income growth, and educational change (see figure 1).

Cross-sectional analysis can provide insights for a wide range of variables for which adequate time series are not avail-able. Housing values, residential racial segregation patterns, commutation distances, airport travel, and population densities are all examples for which local area studies can be aided by cross-sectional analyses. The major cautionary note that must be sounded is an elaboration of the usual caveats sounded about the "explanatory" nature of variables

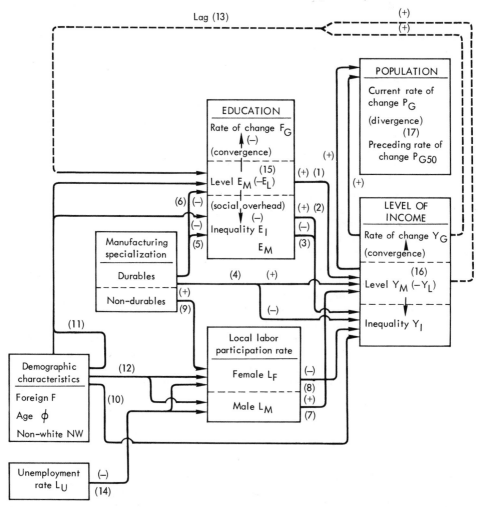

Source: Thompson, Wilbur R., "Internal and External Factors in the Development of Urban Economics," Issues in Urban Economics, *Resources for the Future, 1968, page 76.*

Figure 1   Schematic Simplification of the Principle Associations Between Population, Income Level, and Education.

in regression equations. The analyst is projecting into the future for a particular geographic area on the basis of observed relationships at a specific point in time for many different places. It should be quite obvious that differences among variables at one point in time may not in fact "explain" variations that will occur over time in any one given locality. However, the inherent limitations of the methodology do not negate judicial use of the analytical procedure. Full knowledge of causal relationships may not be obtainable, but the analytical tools can begin providing insights into the processes of change.

D. Beyond the Basics

Population, employment, and income projections provide only the beginnings, the basics from which other variables of interest to the urban economist will be forecast. In many situations simple or multiple regression analysis can be used. Telephone calls may be a function of population and median income; electricity usage may be a function of industrial employment and households; property tax receipts may be a function of total personal income and new construction. These examples are typical of forecasting relationships with which business economists are accustomed to deal. However, as the problems of our cities continue to loom larger on the American scene, it is becoming apparent that far more complex interrelationships must be unraveled if we are to understand the processes of change and be able to responsibly formulate policy recommendations to influence society.

It is clear that we still do not understand the dynamics of central city versus suburban growth. We have not developed a methodology to determine the optimum size for an urban area or to evaluate where within an area, given overall size, population and industry should locate. Emotional outpourings flow forth on the impending death of central cities. According to some views the phenomenon would be a good thing for society; according to others, it would be a harbinger for the doom of civilization. We have not, in truth, developed the theoretical framework to enable us to make objective judgments on such problems. One reason for our inability is that we are accustomed to examine problem areas discretely, that is, solely in terms of the immediate objective at hand. If a highway program is to be developed: How many automobiles must be provided for and at what dollar cost? If low-income housing is to be built: What is the size of the poor population? If a subsidized industrial park is to be built: What incentives must the community provide to attract the necessary tenants? Typically, each problem area is analyzed in isolation, without considering the repercussions on other areas.

Today, serious analysts have arrived at the point where they know they must include feedbacks as an integral part of their analytical systems. Too often we have been surprised by unforeseen results which might have been anticipated if the original analysis were more complete. Thus, the construction of highways affects housing patterns; the provision of low-cost housing in central cities creates additional social costs for local government; an industrial park often requires community investment in transportation or housing or both. The national tragedy of welfare, the physical blight of our cities, and the environmental destruction of pollution are all related to (if not necessarily directly caused by) failures to understand and take into account complex economic, political, and social interrelationships.

With the increasing ability of economists, psychologists, and political scientists to harness the computer to test their hypotheses, the capability to analyze complex interrelationships among countless variables is increasing. Elaborate models can be constructed with the multitude of feed-

STD.

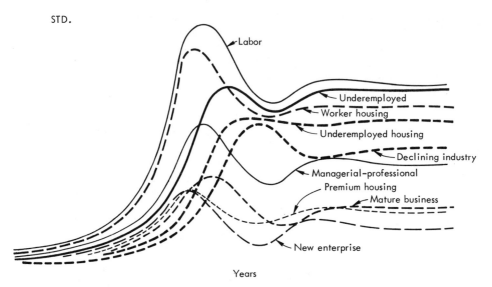

Years

Source: Forrester, Jay W., Urban Dynamics, *p. 4, the M.I.T. Press, 1969.*

Figure 2   Life Cycle of an Urban Area—250 Years of Internal Development Maturity and Stagnation

backs as an integral part of the system. The most serious drawback, of course, is that adequate data frequently do not exist with which to scientifically test a model which may have the appearance of being conceptually sound.

One of the most important examples of this type of systems modeling was developed by Professor Jay W. Forrester at Massachusetts Institute of Technology and outlined in his book, *Urban Dynamics.* Professor Forrester analyzes the city as a closed system in which all the important cause and effect relationships are accounted for and linked together, so that a change in any one part can be measured in any other part of the system. The system includes 156 equations for which statistical relationships have been estimated to simulate the growth, decline, and stagnation of a city over 250 years. Job opportunities and housing availability hold major roles in the system (see figure 2).

The kinds of public policy conclu-

sions which flow from Forrester's model suggest, for example, that providing low-income housing in an urban area only increases the inflow of the poor. In the short run, housing and jobs may increase, but in the long run congestion will be worse than before and job opportunities will decline. The Forrester model by no means yields all the heretofore hidden secrets of urban dynamics. Because the model is constructed on the basis of what urban experts themselves conceive of as the major interrelationships rather than on the basis of hard data, which simply do not exist, the system tends by its very nature to reflect the thinking of those who constructed it. Furthermore, since the model is conceived of as a closed system, it fails to take sufficient account of the influences of "outside" factors. In-migration responds not only to housing availability and job opportunities within the urban area under consideration; it also reflects welfare and farm policies, as well as competing job opportunities in the "outside" world. Also, an urban area, as should be obvious, is not a homogeneous economic unit; the interactions between central city and suburb are not sufficiently dealt with in the system.

Nevertheless, *Urban Dynamics* represents a breakthrough in the field of urban economics. The concept of computer modeling of urban systems is a major step forward from two points of view. First, it forces a methodical thinking through of urban problems. Second, it provides the mechanical hardware with which to test the hypotheses. All of the usual caveats concerning simulation models must of course be heeded. But experience with simulation models is being accumulated as economists construct such models for individual metropolitan areas and learn to what degree historical data must be used for parameter estimates and when judgment and reasonable hypotheses can serve as proxies, at least on a trial basis. At the time of writing, economists at the

National Bureau of Economic Research, Harvard Business School, Joint Center for Urban Studies of MIT and Harvard University, the Urban Institute and at many other institutions were experimenting with simulation models. Some of the models emphasize a particular sector such as housing; some are geared to public policy implications; some are structured for analysis at the census tract as well as at the city or metropolitan area level. As experience is gained, simulation models, now built up painstakingly and often at considerable cost for specific locations, will no doubt become "generalized" so that the business economist will in time turn to them as a matter of course. Without question, further strides will be made in the emerging field of urban economics as we learn to combine the traditional tools of the trade with the more complex capabilities that can be achieved with the judicious use of computer art.

BIBLIOGRAPHY

Berman, Barbara et al., *Projection of a Metropolis, Technical Supplement to the New York Metropolitan Region Study*. Cambridge, Mass.: Harvard University Press, 1960.

Forrester, Jay W., *Urban Dynamics*. Cambridge, Mass.: M.I.T. Press, 1969.

Haig, Robert M., *Major Economic Factors in Metropolitan Growth and Arrangement*, Vol. I, Regional Survey of New York and Environs. New York: The New York Metropolitan Area Regional Study, 1928.

Isard, Walter et al., *Methods of Regional Analysis: An Introduction to Regional Science*. New York: John Wiley & Sons, Inc., 1960.

Isard, Walter et al., *Philadelphia Region Input-Output Study*, Preliminary Working Paper, Regional Science Research Institute, Philadelphia, March 1966.

Muth, Richard, *Cities and Housing, Spatial Patterns of Urban Land Use*. Chicago: University of Chicago Press, 1969.

National Planning Association, Regional Economic Projections Series, *Metropolitan Area Growth Patterns for the Coming Decade*, Report No. 70-R-2, December 1970.

National Planning Association, Regional Economic Projections Series, *Income, Saving and Consumption Patterns for Regions, States, and Metropolitan Areas*, 1960–1980, Report No. 71-R-1, October 1971.

New York State Department of Labor, *Manpower Directions, New York State 1965–75*, Technical Supplement, 1968.

New York State Department of Labor, *Manpower Requirements, Interim Projections New York State 1968–1980*, July 1971.

Perloff, Harvey et al., *Issues in Urban Economics.* Resources for the Future, Inc., Johns Hopkins Press, 1968.

Perloff, Harvey et al., *Regions, Resources and Economic Growth.* Resources for the Future, Inc., Johns Hopkins Press, 1960.

Thompson, Wilbur R., *A Preface to Urban Economics.* Resources for the Future, Inc., Johns Hopkins Press, 1968.

Tiebout, Charles M., *The Community Economic Base Study,* Supplementary Paper No. 16. New York: Community for Economic Development, 1960.

U.S. Department of Commerce, *Survey of Current Business,* various issues, especially May 1970, August 1970, April 1972, and May 1972.

U.S. Department of Labor, *Tomorrow's Manpower Needs,* Vol. I, Developing Area Manpower Projections, Bulletin No. 1606. Washington: Government Printing Office, 1969.

Part Four

INDUSTRY AND SALES FORECASTING

Parts II and III presented a series of chapters on the techniques for forecasting GNP and its components. While this concept is extremely useful for gaining insight into the over-all tone of the economy, it does not, in its usual form, present details on the individual industries comprising the fabric of our system. To be sure, when business in general is good most industries share in the advance, and vice-versa. But this is hardly an adequate way to estimate the outlook for specific industries. One approach to this problem was already described in the chapter on Input-Output. However, other procedures are often used which vary from industry to industry. Part IV describes how forecasts are prepared for some industries.

At this level of forecasting, the sequence proceeds from the national economy to the industry involved—and finally to the specific firm and its own outlook. And paradoxically, the closer one gets to home, the greater the amount of disaggregation, the more difficult it becomes to achieve an accurate forecast. Competitive aspects, managerial factors, governmental policies—all must be carefully appraised in deriving a given firm's sales picture.

The section opens with a chapter describing in general the techniques and hurdles involved in the preparation of sales forecasts at the firm level. These techniques are illustrated in the following chapters on automobiles, steel and advertising.

ROBERT S. SCHULTZ

Sales Forecasting

In all the field of business economics, probably no area is more challenging than sales forecasting for the individual company, nor of more direct relevance to policy formation. The challenge arises from the discreteness of the unit involved. It is more difficult to predict the responses of an individual than of a universe; the possibility of salvation through compensating errors declines as the size of the sample is reduced.

The relevance arises from the direct use of the sales forecast in formulating company policy. The direct use of an economic forecast is rare. Government economists may forecast, say, the gross national product with great accuracy, but it is not possible to base government economic policy upon this forecast. Policy must also consider a host of noneconomic factors, special interests, and sensitivities on both the foreign and domestic scene, including the slowness with which a representative government changes its laws. The forecast itself can serve as a guide to policy to only a limited extent.

Similarly, an industry forecast can rarely be used directly for policy formation. For example, the ceremonial forecasts of strong automobile demand with which Detroit commentators inaugurate each model-year, however accurate they may be, deal only with an abstraction—the industry—and ignore the specific points which a company must consider, such as the appropriate pesticide for the beetle menace. A further

characteristic of public forecasts by government and industry spokesmen is that they tend to keep in mind the feedback effect on others, and are often designed not to guide policy which the forecaster may be able to control, but to influence the actions of others (for example, customers—over whom the forecaster has no control). In the writer's opinion the potential significance of feedback is exaggerated, but a distinguished econometrician has cited this as one area requiring careful analysis in the future development of econometrics.[1]

In contrast to the published forecasts —which are abstract, which cannot be used directly to formulate policy, and which aspire to influence events as well as to predict them—the sales forecast of a modern business corporation can and should be a complete expression of the outlook for the particular company; it can constitute the complete frame of reference within which company policy is formulated. In view of the difficulties of exact prediction, of course, the forecast should be only a framework for policy, not a straitjacket, and should be subject to review in the light of changing circumstances.

The question of continuing review is extremely important. Economic conditions

[1] Lawrence R. Klein, "Whither Econometrics?" *Journal of the American Statistical Association* (June 1971).

usually change slowly and gradually, but they are sometimes susceptible to extreme shifts, and a company should not be locked in by a sales forecast outmoded by the swift pace of events. In addition there is the possibility, however remote, that the forecast, by warning of potential dangers, may be invalidated by a "feedback" of corrective action. For example, a sales manager, warned by an otherwise valid forecast that sales will decline, may adopt some new and effective policies (which he should have been following all along). In this way he may cover himself with glory and make the poor forecaster look like a pessimistic idiot.

Such a development, of course, is not actually an instance of feedback invalidating the forecast, but of a failure in effective communication, and an example of the need for continuing review of forecasts. With new policies in effect, the forecast should be modified to reflect them, so that company planning generally can be adapted to the new program. An unexpectedly good sales record can pose problems for the manufacturing department, for example. And while these are the kinds of problems business likes to face, the effects of such problems can be reduced and profits increased, if manufacturing is allowed to know the plans of the sales department, if the sales forecast is adjusted to reflect all significant known factors, and if company planning at all levels is based upon one cohesive, consistent plan.

A further instance of "feedback thinking" in corporate policy is the practice reportedly followed by some companies of having three sets of sales forecasts: a coldly realistic forecast for top management; a more favorable one for supervisory personnel; and a highly optimistic one for salesmen.[2]

Admittedly, there is wide skepticism

on the entire question of forecasting. Many individuals are so keenly aware of the importance of the unpredictable in human events that they suggest that the forecasting effort should be abandoned. This viewpoint has been eloquently expressed by E. B. Weiss, of Doyle, Dane, Bernbach, Inc., whose annual "Pox on Prognosticators" was long a feature of *Advertising Age*.

> The professional economist is no more able to forecast the economic future than is the businessman or, for that matter the man on the street . . . because:
> 1. The course of business is dictated, in large measure, by events that cannot be anticipated. (Cuba would be an example; the Kennedy-Blough fracas would be another.) . . .
> 2. Our business indices, including especially Gross National Product, are statistical monstrosities. . . .
> 3. The professional economist is today unable to assign a statistical weight to each of the indices he employs in his folderol. . . .
> 4. There is no scientifically valid formula for evaluating the significance of the available statistics. . . . So—a pox on prognosticators. May their tribe decrease and may their followers return to tea leaves, to the lunar tides . . . and may business recover from its case of economic hypochondriacism.[3]

Now there is, of course, much merit in this saying. The unpredictable is frequently important—perhaps of overriding importance. Our economic measures, even if not statistical monstrosities, have many serious inadequacies, and are sometimes used in inadequate, if not monstrous, ways.[4] Problems of statistical discrepancies and intercorrelation of variables, along with serious gaps in our basic theories, make it easy

---

[2] Cf. George Cline Smith, "The Law of Forecast Feedback," *American Statistician* (December 1964).

[3] E. B. Weiss, "E. B. Puts His Annual Pox on Prognosticators," *Advertising Age* (December 17, 1962).

[4] Cf. Oskar Morgenstern, *On the Accuracy of Economic Observations*, 2nd ed. (Princeton, N.J.: Princeton University Press, 1963).

to obtain fallacious parameters in econometric analysis and modelbuilding. But all these points simply illustrate the difficulty of developing accurate forecasts, and the necessity to review past projections against current developments to check on the desirability of modifying future forecasts.

Despite all these difficulties, you have to forecast. Every action taken, every policy formed, is based on some implicit forecast of future results. The basic purpose of making the forecast explicit is simply to test the reasonableness of the fundamental assumptions and to quantify the hypotheses on which decisions are made. It is desirable to have an economist do the job, instead of having the businessman do it himself, partly to free the businessman for other activities and partly to assure the systematic, objective allowance for known factors for which the businessman—whose skills incline to more profitable directions—is rarely equipped by either training or temperament.

The business economist is not a shaman who can "look into the seeds of time and say which grain will grow and which will not," but simply a student attempting through the systematic analysis of inadequate data to determine probable outcomes. The function of the sales forecast is not to eliminate all odds so that gamblers can wager on sure things. It has the more realistic, if less ambitious, goal of narrowing the frame of reference within which management must decide. Business genius—an amalgam of instincts in buying, selling, producing, and investing—is the essential hallmark of management. And sales forecasting, like any other staff function, is only a supplement or support to managerial genius, not a substitute for it.

The future is necessarily uncertain, but its uncertainties transpire within a framework given by the certainties of the past (however uncertainly measured). By a careful review of the record of the past, we can indicate a reasonable course of future developments and perhaps provide a standard for gauging the significance of the unexpected.

In any company sales forecast there are three basic factors which may be considered explicitly, but which are necessarily implicit, even where no specific, systematic allowance is made for them. First, the outlook for the general economy, which determines the general environment within which operations will take place. Second, the outlook for the particular industry (or industries), which is conditioned by the general economic environment and which in turn determines the basic environment for the individual company. Third, the industry position or market share of the individual company, which is the part of the total demand for the particular industry which can be obtained by the specific company.

The extent to which these three separate factors are considered explicitly will depend upon many variables: the purpose of the forecast; the availability of data; the importance of general economic developments in the demand for the particular product (in technical terms, the elasticity of demand with respect to income); the nature of the company's particular market and the importance of forces other than the general economic situation in the demand for the products of the particular company; and a host of other factors. But implicitly or explicitly, there must be either (1) an allowance for these three separate values or (2) an assumption that the demand for the company's product is independent of general economic developments, or independent of industry developments, or both.

An additional point should be made on the basic nature of sales forecasting, only implied above. *All sales forecasting is demand forecasting.* If demand exceeds supply, if the market for a product is greater than the amount which can be produced, the sales forecast becomes an engineering estimate of maximum output, and "sales" become simply the optimum allocation of the maximum output to the more profitable customers. In such a case the engineer and the cost accountant allot output to the salesman, who has become an order taker. The "sales" forecast, as an analysis of potential demand, becomes only a statement of what might have been, and the business economist is left with the invidious assignment of warning that this delightful euphoria does not represent a permanent way of life.

In the usual course of events, however, capacity equals or exceeds demand, and can, at least in the long run, always be expanded to exceed demand, and so usually the forecast of what can be sold is an essential and integral part of company policy; it is, in fact, the very basis of company policy.

Basically, we can distinguish three distinct purposes of sales forecasts, each of which requires a separate type of forecast. First is the *short-term forecast,* which is used for planning current policy and assessing current developments. The concern of this forecast is limited; it covers a period of perhaps two to six months. Its use is for planning current policy on inventory, hiring, shutdowns, and similar day-to-day concerns of management.

Second, the *budget forecast* usually covers an entire fiscal year. It is used for setting standard costs and prices, for determining cash flow, and generally for establishing basic policies for the coming year— policies which, of course, will require adjustment over the year to such extent as actual developments differ from the forecast. Both of these first two types of forecast are basically concerned with the most efficient use of a company's existing capital equipment and financial structure.

The third type of forecast is concerned with changes in these factors. This third type, the *long-term forecast,* covers any period from five to fifty years. It is used primarily for planning capacity changes and other capital expenditures, for considering entry into new markets, for long-term financial planning, and for any other purposes

involving a change in the company's capital equipment, financial structure, market areas, product mix, and so on. By and large, the long-term forecast represents projections of secular trends, with no allowance for cyclical or other nontrend forces. The short-term and budget forecasts, however, attempt to predict actual sales, and to allow for all factors.[5]

BASIC FORECASTING METHODS

Along with these three basic types of forecasts we may distinguish three essentially different methods or techniques of sales forecasting. First, the informed estimates (or guesses) of line personnel. These are usually sales managers, occasionally corporate executives or customers. Second, the internal analysis of individual company data. Third, analysis of company data in relation to external standards of performance by the industry or the economy: correlation analysis, econometric analysis, the sophisticated use of statistical techniques to focus the insight of line personnel and to narrow the area of managerial judgment.[6]

[5] A fourth type of forecast, which may be called the *interim forecast,* midway between the *budget* and the *long-term,* may also be found occasionally. This type of forecast attempts to allow for cyclical and other nontrend factors, as well as for secular trends, for two or three or more years ahead. Arthur Dahlberg at U.S. Economics Corporation and Frank Murphy at General Electric Company have done exploratory work along these lines. Some models now available incorporate cyclical forecasts three years in advance.

[6] An excellent review of sales forecasting techniques is found in Robert S. Reichard, *Practical Techniques of Sales Forecasting* (New York: McGraw-Hill Book Company, 1966). See also National Industrial Conference Board, *Forecasting Sales,* Studies in Business Policy No. 106, New York 1963; and National Industrial Conference Board, *Sales Forecasting, an Appraisal,* Experiences in

Each of these methods has its strengths and weaknesses. Ideally, all three methods will be used to the extent permitted by the availability of time and of data, for each approach supplements the others.

Before considering the use of these various methods, it is necessary to consider the question of availability of data, particularly on the company level.

The Need for Comparable Data

Regardless of the techniques employed, the first need in sales forecasting is to have statistics on sales, statistics which are comparable and consistent over a goodly period of years—preferably a full decade or more. In all the problems of sales forecasting, this is probably the one most easily overlooked. There is no lack of statistics in most companies. Flowing across every manager's desk is a constant stream of statistics: sales reports, production reports, company reports to trade associations, trade association reports to the company, and many others—more statistics than the mind can grasp, let alone analyze. The difficulty with all this wealth of data is that none of the figures have been compiled for forecasting purposes, and so the figures as they stand may need adjustment for this purpose. The major categories of internal data are compiled for cost accounting, sales records, production statistics, and so on. Usually there

Marketing Management No. 25, by Stanley J. Pokempner and Earl L. Bailey, New York, 1970. Also, American Management Association, *Materials and Methods of Sales Forecasting*, Special Report No. 27, New York, 1957; American Management Association, *Guidelines for Marketing Research and Economic Forecasting*, Research Study No. 73, New York, 1966; and American Management Association, *Practical Sales Forecasting*, New York, 1970. Also, Stanford Research Institute, *Projections in Planning*, Long-Range Planning Report No. 208, Menlo Park, Calif., April 1964.

will have been many changes over time in the categories the various departments have found appropriate: perhaps because of changes in departmental cognizance; perhaps because of growth in some particular line, justifying a split into two categories; perhaps because of changes in manufacturing techniques. Or the company may have acquired another company or companies in recent years, and the records of the acquired company may have been kept differently (different bases, different categories) than those used by the acquiring company. Or there may have been changes in product specifications which make comparison difficult. For example, the *basis weight* of containerboard in corrugated boxes may have changed, or the weight of steel in a "tin" can, so that figures based on units show a different trend from figures based on weight. Or, there may have been a change in the size of the package (for example, a growth in the use of 50-pound bags of fertilizer, a decline in the use of 100-pound bags; a growth in the use of the giant cola drink bottle, a decline in the traditional size).

Factors such as these make it extremely difficult to use existing company records as they stand for forecasting purposes, because the essential requirement for such statistics is that they reveal the changes which have taken place in the past, as a guide to the changes which may take place in the future.

If responsibility for sales of a particular product has been transferred from one department to another, the past record of neither offers any useful guide to the future unless the records are adjusted to reflect the transfer. If there has been an acquisition of a company in a related field, it is necessary to combine the sales records to get meaningful data. If there has been a shift in weight per unit, figures kept on a weight basis will follow different trends from those kept on a unit basis.

Wholly aside from the question of the incomparability of the figures over time, there is a question of what figures to use. From different points in the organization there may well be four entirely different sets of figures: (1) new orders; (2) production; (3) shipments from the plant, including shipments to warehouses; and (4) shipments to customers, including mill shipments to customers and shipments to customers out of inventory, but excluding plant shipments to warehouses.

In addition, trade association or government data, if available, may well be compiled according to different categories and in different units, than are the figures of the individual reporting companies. Any one set of figures may be entirely adequate, but it is necessary to decide on one set, and to have this set used consistently at all stages of the forecasting process. The alternative can be a chaotic talking at cross-purposes, with different individuals or departments reaching different conclusions from different figures.

Much time and effort may be required to develop consistent statistics, comparable over time, and perferably comparable with other data (for example, company and industry). But this is time well spent. Without such data, systematic analysis is difficult and erroneous interpretation is easy. With such figures, it is possible to assess the significance of past developments with increased precision, and to narrow the range of future probabilities.

Needless to say, too much nit-picking must be avoided. The vagaries of the calendar and the diversity of business organizations, in addition to the normal problems of obtaining accuracy in measurement, all combine to introduce a certain degree of inaccuracy into business data. The quest for complete accuracy is futile. But at the very least, past figures should be reviewed carefully. Even where no precise adjustment may be feasible, some "horseback guesstimate" of the probable margin of error in comparability should be developed.

Once a set of comparable data has been developed—say, sales by major product lines, by months, for the past ten years —where do we go from there? How do we handle the three concepts of U.S. economy, industry relation to economy, and company relation to industry, according to the techniques of informed opinion, internal analysis, or correlation, to develop short-term, medium-term, and long-term forecasts? Sales forecasting, like forecasting generally, is more an art than a science; different individuals use different methods and approaches to the same problem. The present discussion, while attempting a broad view of the general problem of sales forecasting, is necessarily heavily weighted by the experience and opinions of the writer, based on some 25 years in the field of sales forecasting and business economics generally. The discussion attempts to deal both with the formal and generalized concepts and techniques of sales forecasting, and also with the kind of practical problems faced by the practitioner—problems of little or no theoretical significance but of great operating importance.

Informed Estimate

The informed-opinion forecast is the oldest and least sophisticated method of sales forecasting. It has great advantages of ease of operation, and—at least ostensibly— of inexpensiveness, and of drawing upon the immediate knowledge of men in the field, men in direct contact with the sales effort.

In its simplest form, this method of sales forecasting consists simply of asking salesmen or sales managers how many units of a commodity they expect to be able to sell in the next month or two, or year or two, or decade or two. Replies may be simply on a divisional basis or in more detail, with individual product lines specified. The forecasts may be on a total sales basis or may specify anticipated sales to individual customers. On whatever basis the forecasts are presented, it is desirable that they should be submitted on a *form* centrally prepared, to insure consistency and completeness in coverage. This form should include actual figures for previous periods comparable to the categories covered in the forecast. (Lacking these figures, a salesman who may be operating on a different set of figures compiled for different purposes according to some different set of categories, may easily present a forecast on an entirely different basis, adding unnecessary confusion to the entire process.)

There are many advantages to the use of this forecasting technique. It draws directly on the knowledge of the men directly concerned with sales, men in a line activity with an immediate awareness of the many specific factors influencing sales which may well be unavailable to a staff analyst. Customer A may be putting up a new plant right next door to one of your plants. Customer B may be so pleased with your service and so annoyed with Competitor X that he plans to double the business he places with you. Customer C may be about to double his output in a particular line for which he buys your product. Or, since news is not always good, Customer D may be merging with Competitor Y and the president of Customer E may be engaged to marry the daughter of the president of Competitor Z.

There are an infinite number of possible changes which may be in the nature of "offsetting errors" so far as the industry is concerned, but may have strong significance in one particular direction for an individual company. Knowledge of such changes, obtained by line personnel in the normal course of business operations, is not so readily obtained by a staff forecaster whose concentration on the broad picture necessarily renders it difficult to obtain specific individual details. Offsetting these advantages are several definite drawbacks to the use of informed sales opinion as a forecasting technique. In the first place, the

salesman is simply not equipped by training or temperament for the objective analysis of data. Recent experience gets a disproportionate weight in his calculus of future probabilities. (The salesman is not alone in this. Even supposedly objective business economists have been known to succumb to the lure of forecasting through projecting the recent past—a method which admittedly may often give satisfactory results.) If times are good, with sales high, there tends to be an assumption that times will remain good or get better. If times are hard, there tends to be an assumption that they will stay bad or get worse or—equally subjective—an uncritical assumption that things must soon improve. Even should he have the inclination and background, the salesman does not have the time to undertake the systematic analysis of sales statistics. Adjustment for seasonal variation he can handle only intuitively; the effects of changes in general business activity tend to be considered in only the most general fashion; the distinction between a change in the company's market share and a change in the overall market can be handled only approximately.

The strength of detailed knowledge of the marketplace which is brought to bear in sales forecasts based on informed opinion is reduced by the lack of ability to organize this knowledge, and by the failure to make systematic allowance for more general factors.

The significance of these strengths and weaknesses of this technique of sales forecasting varies from industry to industry (or company to company), and according to the type of forecast wanted.

In any industry where demand responds only moderately, if at all, to changes in the level of general business activity, the informed opinion approach can be appropriate and successful, particularly for short-term and intermediate-term forecasts. Various beverages and food items fall in this category; also tissue and sanitary papers, and many items in the nondurable goods category. In such instances, the particular, almost random, factors which sales personnel know directly can acquire prime importance, and sales forecasting through informed opinion can be wholly adequate. Yet even here, something more seems to be needed. Some of the most detailed, analytic, and objective staff forecasting is done by firms in these very fields.

Again it might seem that companies whose products have long lead times (for example, machine tools) could operate with no real need for sales forecasting. Ostensibly, they could operate entirely from their order book, using production schedules based on orders-in-hand as a sales forecast. Yet this too seems inadequate—some of the nation's outstanding business economists are found in the machine tool industry.

Where seasonal variation is important, the informed opinion approach becomes difficult to use on a short-range basis. The techniques of determining the significance of seasonal factors, discussed in the following section, are not difficult. However, the process is time-consuming. Once the factors have been determined, incorporating them in an opinion forecast constitutes one additional step in a process basically outside the recognized sales responsibilities. The salesman may consider seasonal variation, in an off-the-cuff way, in any forecast he prepares on a monthly basis, but this allowance will fall short of the precision which is possible through statistical analysis of seasonal patterns.

Inventory change is a second factor which it is particularly difficult to allow for through the informed-opinion approach. (This question is discussed below in the section on correlation analysis.) Current takings of any customer, except perhaps the ultimate consumer, have two aspects: consumption needs and inventory change. When consumption is rising, it is generally necessary to add to inventory; there is at least some tendency for inventory targets, in

relation to consumption needs, to rise as consumption rises. (The reverse relationships tend to prevail as consumption declines.)

The tendency of informed-opinion forecasts to place greatest weight on recent developments makes this type of forecast particularly vulnerable to the danger of confusing inventory changes with basic shifts in demand, of overestimating potentials when sales have been increasing for some time, and conversely.

When it comes to long-term forecasts, covering five years to five decades, the informed-opinion approach is least suitable. The significance of the specific factors which the salesman knows best may be of prime importance in the short and intermediate range of, say, two months to two years; however, over the longer term, the significance of the "random" factors tends to be canceled out, and basic trends acquire more significance. The identification of the basic trends is essentially a statistical process, and while it may pose fewer problems than cyclical forecasting, it is one where the intuitive allowance, seat-of-the-pants approach becomes particularly unsatisfactory. In any long-term forecasting it is essential to avoid the temptation to give greater weight to more recent observations. This temptation is more easily avoided through objective statistical analysis than through the informed opinion of line personnel.

In addition to these fundamental drawbacks to the informed-opinion approach, arising out of its lack of systematic allowance for basic factors, there is the further difficulty that a sales-originated forecast—whether consciously or not—may tend to be a self-serving document. In poor times, the salesman has a definite incentive to understate his potential. Then, if he exceeds the target—that is, achieves only what he believes he can do—he is a hero. Conversely, in good times—at least in times good enough for demand to press close to capacity—the salesman has an incentive to overstate his potential, so that he will not be subject to some quota holding his sales below potential.

Despite all its drawbacks, however, there is one very strong advantage to the method of basing a sales forecast on the informed opinion of line personnel: the forecast is prepared by the men who have the responsibility for carrying it out. The forecast is not an ironbound order imposed by superior authority, but is rather a quantified statement of what the sales department believes can be achieved.

The two strong advantages of forecasting through informed sales opinion are thus the immediate and detailed market knowledge reflected in the forecast and the personal involvement of the salesman in the forecast. The basic drawback is the substantially unsystematic nature of the forecast.

It is sometimes possible to combine the systematic methodology of a staff forecast with the detailed market knowledge of the sales force. This possibility is discussed in a subsequent section.

This discussion to date has considered the use of the informed-opinion method entirely in terms of sales opinion. The opinion survey method may also be used with other groups. Some companies reportedly base sales forecasts on the opinions of top management, instead of simply having top management review the forecasts, which must of course be the final stage in the formation of any policy. Some concerns ask customers about purchasing intentions. The basic pattern is identical, however. Sales forecasts are based upon the opinions of individuals whose opinion merits attention because of direct involvement in and knowledge of the market, not because of any systematic analysis of the underlying trends in the market.

Internal Analysis

Internal analysis of data may be regarded as the beginning of statistical wisdom. It is not necessarily of itself a complete technique for sales forecasting, but it constitutes an essential starting point for many purposes, and may sometimes be useful by itself for forecasting purposes.

By *internal analysis* we mean the study of a time series—in this case, of figures on sales by an individual company—to resolve it into its component parts in order to evaluate the significance of the various factors resulting in changes in sales levels over time. Sales, on a monthly basis, reflect the impact of several different factors. First, and most important for many purposes, are the seasonal factors, the influence of the calendar per se (that is, differences in sales from one month to the next resulting from differences in the number of operating days per month), and also the influence of seasonal changes as such. These may be institutional factors, such as the tendency of retail sales generally to cluster around gift-giving holidays, particularly Christmas; or more strictly seasonal factors, such as the tendency of sales of air-conditioners to cluster in the hot months, or sales of ski equipment to cluster in the wintertime.

A second basic factor in sales is the cyclical factor. This is the tendency for sales to rise or fall in line with the business cycle, with the increases and decreases in the level of general business activity or some more or less independent cycle such as that of the construction industry. The cyclical factor should properly be regarded as having two parts: (1) cyclical changes in *consumption* and (2) cyclical changes in *inventory*.

A third basic factor is that of secular change, the growth (or sometimes decline) in the demand for a product in line with basic, long-term trends in consumer taste, industrial practice, and so on. Examples include the growth in acceptance of synthetic fibres and frozen foods, the growing use of electronic computers, and the decline in demand for paper dry-cleaning bags as this market was suddenly preempted by polyethylene bags.

In addition to these three basic factors there are the random factors: the chance bunching of sales in a particular month; the chance decline in sales reflecting overordering or underordering; minor strikes; freak weather; sudden shifts in taste; or any of the thousand random forces which may result in temporary shifts in sales about the general level given by the three basic factors of seasonal, cyclical, and secular forces.

In addition to these factors, which influence overall industry sales levels, the individual company has the factor of shifts in its own industry position, its own share of the total market.

Internal analysis of data represents a device for measuring the significance of various factors, decomposing the series into the component parts of seasonal, cyclical, secular, and random deviations. Internal analysis does not provide any automatic device for distinguishing between the consumption and the inventory aspects of cyclical change, nor is it immediately suitable for indicating the significance of changes in market shares. But it is still a very powerful analytical tool and can constitute at least the first step in any statistical approach to sales forecasting.

The first step in this process is analysis of the data to remove the effects of seasonal variation. The techniques for this are well known and need not be discussed here, although it may be worth pointing out that whenever calendar variations as such are significant (for example, changes in the number of working days from one month to the next) the sales data should be adjusted for this factor before analyzing the figures for seasonal variation in the more technical sense. A variation on this device is to analyze the raw data for seasonal variation, and then to determine the significance of the workday adjustment factor by correlating the residuals—the ratio of the actual observation to the seasonally adjusted observation—with the number of workdays in the month.

In many cases, if not most, this refinement is quite unnecessary. The significance of one workday is the same as another. But at least in certain lines this is definitely not the case. In retail sales, for example, different days of the week tend to account for different proportions of a week's business (even if there is no difference in operating hours). A January with 27 selling days, of which 5 are Saturdays, may very well have a different "seasonal" value than a January with 27 selling days but only 4 Saturdays.

In addition to the workday factors there are other quasi-seasonal forces whose effects can be analyzed. For example, air-conditioner sales and beer consumption tend to be lower in a cold summer than in a warm summer. Accordingly, if residuals are correlated with temperature, it may be possible to explain some additional part of the total pattern of sales fluctuations, particularly with data on a regional basis. Removing the effects of factors such as this may permit a more nearly accurate determination of the strictly seasonal factors themselves, if the seasonal analysis is repeated with data adjusted for any measurable effects of workday variations, temperature changes, and so on. It should be added that these various refinements may frequently be quite inappropriate. Almost all sales figures contain a high degree of random variation, and elaborate study may offer little or no improvement over the most elementary type of seasonal analysis. Common sense must be employed in determining the extent to which a highly refined analysis is justified.

Once the effects of seasonal and quasi-seasonal factors are removed from the data, there remains a series showing random fluctuations about a composite trend of cyclical and secular variation. By the use of moving averages, or perhaps by simply drawing a curve through the seasonally adjusted observations, it is possible to eliminate the random factors and develop a trend which may be regarded as representing the basic long-term movement of sales, modified by short-term cyclical fluctuations.

The basic problem of sales forecasting is to project this trend for the requisite distance into the future. If annual forecasts are called for, this projection constitutes the forecasts (and such projections can be made from annual data, without seasonal analysis). If monthly forecasts are desired, the monthly projected-trend values can be multiplied by the seasonal factors to give a forecast of sales on a monthly basis.

There are many techniques of trend projections, of varying degrees of statistical complexity. The easiest of course is simply to chart the data and draw a freehand curve through them. Or curves may be fitted by various mathematical formulas: least squares, Gompertz and Pearl-Reed growth curves, and so on. Moving averages can be used; or the more complex exponential smoothing which gives heavier weight to more recent observations;[7] or the highly mathematical Box-Jenkins approach.[8]

The basic dilemma in sales forecasting through trend projection is that it allows only for trend, and makes no allowance for the cyclical changes in sales reflecting the general ups and downs of the business cycle. As mentioned earlier, some industries have a relatively slight elasticity of demand with respect to changes in the general level of business. This may reflect either a generally stable demand, as in staple food items (where fluctuations are related more to crop changes than to income changes); or an industry such as electronic computers, where a rapidly growing demand hides the cyclical impact.

For most industries and companies, however, the business cycle represents a factor of definite importance to be considered in preparing sales forecasts. This is best handled through the correlation techniques discussed below.

An alternative technique for cyclical study, staying within the confines of each particular series, is offered by *harmonic analysis*. This approach assumes that the periodicity found in many natural cycles is similarly to be found in economic data, and that the fluctuations in the observed data represent the combined effect of different cycles of varying amplitude and duration. Through a process, substantially that of trial and error, harmonic analysis attempts to identify these individual cycles. Since each individual cycle is assumed to continue indefinitely, forecasts are automatically derived through projecting each cycle as far as desired, and combining them.

Most students of the subject are extremely skeptical of the concept of periodicity in economic affairs. After exhaustive analysis, the National Bureau of Economic Research concluded that there is no regular periodicity in the business cycle.[9] The concept of harmonic analysis received wide attention in 1947 with the publication of Dewey and Dakin's *Cycles—The Science of Prediction*.[10] Since the 1946–47 peak predicted in that volume ("working downward to the bottom of the trough in perhaps 1951 or 1952") failed to materialize, general interest in harmonic analysis has apparently evaporated.

But like old soldiers, old ideas do not die; they merely fade away. Sometimes, again like old soldiers, they may return. (Witness the flaming recrudescence of monetary theory in recent years.) Mr. Dewey has

---

[7] See, for example, American Institute of Certified Public Accountants, *Techniques for Forecasting Product Demand* (New York, 1966); and Robert G. Murdick, *Sales Forecasting for Lower Costs and Higher Profits* (Englewood Cliffs, N.J.: Prentice-Hall, Inc., 1967).

[8] George E. P. Box and Gwidym M. Jenkins, *Time Series Analysis, Forecasting and Control* (San Francisco: Holden-Day, Inc., 1970).

[9] See, for example, Arthur F. Burns and Wesley C. Mitchell, *Measuring Business Cycles* (Princeton, N.J.: National Bureau of Economic Research, 1946).

[10] Edward R. Dewey and Edwin F. Dakin, *Cycles—The Science of Prediction* (New York: Holt, Rinehart & Winston, 1947).

published another book,[11] and it is possible that interest in harmonic analysis—which is now armed with the tremendous power of the computer—may again revive.

Despite lack of periodicity in aggregates the possibility of independent periodic cycles cannot be completely ruled out. There have been instances in the textile industry of a fairly regular two-year cycle about a pattern of cyclical change given by the industry's response to the general business cycle.[12] Other industries may show similar patterns. While we may doubt their possibility, they would certainly be useful for forecasting purposes.

While internal analysis may rarely find useful instances of independent periodic cycles, it is frequently possible, on an ad hoc basis at least, to adjust for the effects of specific known forces, sporadic rather than random, whose timing may be anticipated and whose effect can be predicted, at least in part. For example, it has been possible in recent years, in analyzing or forecasting data on steel production, to make a specific allowance for the effects of inventory-building in anticipation of a steel strike. Precise values may not be determinate, but an approximate allowance can be made for such factors. A somewhat similar example is offered by the NBER's experience in developing seasonal adjustment factors for the coal industry in the years 1904–14. The bureau found that the pattern of a two-year contract with a strike at the termination of each, and attendant variations in coal-stocking, necessitated two sets of seasonal factors, one for the odd (peace) years and one for the even (strike) years.[13]

[11] Edward R. Dewey with Og Mandino, *Cycles, the Mysterious Forces that Trigger Events* (New York: Hawthorn Books, Inc., 1971).

[12] Thomas Jeff Davis, *Cycles and Trends in Textiles* (Washington: Business and Defense Services Administration, Department of Commerce, 1958).

[13] Burns and Mitchell, *op. cit.*, p. 61.

Against this background, how can we assess the effectiveness of internal analysis as a technique for sales forecasting for the individual company?

The technique is probably best suited for short-term forecasts, particularly where seasonal variations are highly important. Within limits, it is useful for long-term forecasts, and may be the only systematic technique available. It is probably least satisfactory for medium-term "budget" forecasts.

In the short period of six months or less, sharp changes in composite cyclical-secular trends are rare. Accordingly, it is usually feasible to develop a reasonably accurate short-term forecast by some kind of projection, using any of the techniques discussed earlier. It may even be feasible simply to take the most recent trend value, or an average of recent values if inspection suggests this is more reasonable, and to assume that this value will hold for the next few months. Forecasts made by this approach are virtually guaranteed to contain some error, and to miss all turning points. However, the margin of error should usually not be great, particularly if the forecasts are recomputed at reasonably frequent intervals. If the cyclical-secular trend has been rising or falling for some time, and if there seems to be little likelihood of a reversal of this pattern in the near future, a more accurate forecast may be obtained through some kind of extrapolation of the recent trend. This approach of course runs the risk that the trend may reverse immediately, in which case the forecasts will be wider of the mark than if the projection had been based upon the most recent observation, or some recent average. Sometimes, the forecaster may actually decide, on the basis of a hunch if nothing else, that some sort of trend reversal is likely, and project a trend which diverges from the record of the recent past. This approach offers the greatest danger of inaccurate forecasts, although of course when the trend evaluation is correct it will be most dramatically accurate, in contrast to the safer methods of extrapolating the current situation or extrapolating the trend of the recent past. The forecaster must use good judgment, based on experience and feel, in deciding which type of projection to use.

But in any case, particularly where seasonal or other measurable short-term factors are involved (for example, strike-threat induced inventory-building or depletion), projections deriving from the techniques of internal analysis of company sales data generally offer a reasonably accurate device for short-term forecasts of company sales. And reasonable accuracy, it should be emphasized, is the proper goal of sales-forecasting. As mentioned earlier, its function is to narrow the area of managerial decision, not to eliminate all odds.

The discussion above has no specific reference to the problem of changes in an individual company's industry position or share of the total market. This is a complicating factor. In most cases a sudden, sharp shift in a company's market share represents a random, nonrecurring factor, and can be ignored in forecasting. Trends of either growth or decline in position are generally slow-moving, and adequately subsumed in the basic cyclical-secular trend. Sometimes, of course, a sharp shift in industry position may represent not a random deviation but a basic change—a permanent gain or loss of an important customer, the introduction of some new wrinkle in a product giving the particular company's line a sharply increased consumer acceptance, and so on. This kind of development, which can be handled adequately, if not systematically through the informed-opinion technique, can be allowed for by the staff forecaster only where close liaison with line personnel keeps him informed of the significant market developments which may produce permanent shifts in relationships.

For long-term forecasts, internal analysis may often offer an adequate approach. If comparable industry data are not available it may indeed be the only systematic approach possible. If a company is well established in an industry, a projection of the past sales record into the future may provide a reasonably accurate estimate of future potential. The number of years for which earlier data are available will affect the number of years which can be safely handled in a projection. If figures are available for, say, only 5 previous years, it is scarcely wise to use these data, without qualification, for a 50-year projection. Some other cross-check—if only a judgment as to whether the results appear reasonable in the light of general knowledge—is called for (in other words, relying on the informed opinion approach).

Determining the correct type of projection to use is a matter of judgment, based on the general pattern of the figures to be projected, on the time period covered, and, again, on what appears reasonable. If, for example, demand for a product has been growing very rapidly, a 50-year projection which assumed a continuation of this rapid growth rate would probably give ridiculous results. A 5-year forecast, on the other hand, could use the current growth rate with greater safety. Generally speaking, the greater the rate of increase, and the farther into the future one wishes to peer, the more it is desirable to use some mathematical trend-fitting technique which will dampen the rate of increase in the distant future. An excellent illustration of this approach, using the Gompertz curve, is given in the Conference Board study, *Growth Patterns in Industry*.[14]

For medium-term "budget" forecasts, internal analysis offers a somewhat unsatisfactory approach, because it is within this range that cyclical changes tend to be most significant and that it becomes most important not to miss the turning point. A particular danger of the internal analysis approach is that it offers no device to distinguish between consumption demand and in-

[14] National Industrial Conference Board, *Growth Patterns in Industry: A Reexamination*, Studies in Business Economics No. 75 (New York, 1961).

ventory demand so that there is some tendency for this approach not only to miss turning points but also to estimate basic demand at too high a level when customers are adding to stocks and at too low a level during periods of inventory liquidation. Considerations of operating simplicity, particularly where sales forecasts must be made for a great many products, may often dictate reliance upon techniques of internal analysis for budget forecasts, but wherever this is necessary some kind of general watch should be kept on the state of the overall economy and of such specific markets as may be feasible, to avoid being hog-tied by a forecasting technique which tends to produce serious divergences at turning points.

Correlation Analysis

Correlation analysis, a logical extension of internal analysis, represents the most systematic approach for analyzing and forecasting sales. (The analysis as such is usually conducted in terms of annual data, although subsequent stages can handle figures on a monthly basis.) The basic weakness of internal analysis is that it cannot handle in any organized way the problem of the impact on sales of external factors. We have already discussed the possibility of strengthening internal analysis through allowing for the significance of such external factors as temperature changes, strikes, etc.

The basic emphasis in correlation analysis, however, is to measure the impact on sales of changes in general business activity. Having determined a relation between sales and business activity, it is then possible to forecast sales through a forecast of business activity. (Such a statement usually raises the question: How do you forecast general business activity? Since this is the major topic of this entire volume it is possible to ignore the question in this particular section.)

The techniques of correlation analysis

are many and varied, ranging from simple graphic methods through elaborate econometric models.

Any detailed technical discussion of the techniques of correlation analysis is beyond the scope of this brief review. An extremely useful introduction to methods can be found in Spencer, Clark, and Hoguet, *Business and Economic Forecasting.*[15]

An excellent practical summary of correlation analysis and other statistical techniques is given in a brief Department of Agriculture volume, *Graphic Analysis in Agricultural Economics.*[16] This work indicates simple graphic methods as substitutes for more elaborate machine computations. Most statistics textbooks have effective discussions of the question, and the topic is covered exhaustively in Ezekiel and Fox's classic on correlation and regression analysis.[17] Some illustrations of the effective use of the graphic approach (covering the stock market, elections, and crops and weather as well as business conditions) are presented in Louis H. Bean's *The Art of Forecasting.*[18] For analysis of econometric techniques, see, for instance, Lawrence R. Klein's *Introduction to Econometrics,*[19] or the Wonnacotts' *Econometrics.*[20]

[15] Milton H. Spencer, Colin G. Clark, and Peter W. Hoguet, *Business and Economic Forecasting* (Homewood, Ill.: Richard D. Irwin, Inc., 1961).

[16] Frederick V. Waugh, *Graphic Analysis in Agricultural Economics,* Agriculture Handbook No. 128 (Washington: Agricultural Marketing Service, Department of Agriculture, 1957).

[17] Mordecai Ezekiel and Karl A. Fox, *Methods of Correlation and Regression Analysis,* 3rd ed. (New York: John Wiley & Sons, Inc., 1959).

[18] Louis H. Bean, *The Art of Forecasting* (New York: Handom House, Inc., 1969).

[19] Lawrence R. Klein, *An Introduction to Econometrics* (Englewood Cliffs, N.J.: Prentice-Hall, Inc., 1969).

[20] Ronald J. Wonnacott and Thomas H. Wonnacott, *Econometrics* (New York: John Wiley & Sons, Inc., 1971).

The concern of this particular study is more with application than with methodology. However, some methodological questions necessarily arise, because the basic concepts and methods of correlation analysis, arising out of the physical sciences and generally dealing conceptually with relations at a given point in time, pose certain problems when borrowed for the analysis of economic time series.

The initial concept behind the correlation approach to sales forecasting is that changes in the level of demand for a product tend to be associated with changes in the general level of business activity. As income rises and consumers have more money, the demand for most products tends to rise. Conversely, as income falls and consumers must reduce spending, the demand for most products tends to fall. Similar considerations apply to business demand for inventory, and to some extent for capital goods. With the entire structure of demand closely related to the level of business activity, it is obviously desirable to make some allowance for changes in the level of business activity in forecasting sales of (i.e., demand for) any particular product.

The usual approach in sales forecasting, where industry data are available, is to analyze and forecast industry demand related to general business activity, and then to forecast the share of the market which the particular company may expect to fill. Where industry data are not available, individual company sales figures may be studied directly in relation to business activity. This, of course, is less satisfying since there is always the danger that sales shifts may simply reflect changes in the market share of the particular company.

The nature of the relationship to general business activity (in technical terms, the elasticity of demand with respect to income) varies from product to product. It is generally recognized that the more durable a good the easier it is to make do with the old one, so that the more durable the good the

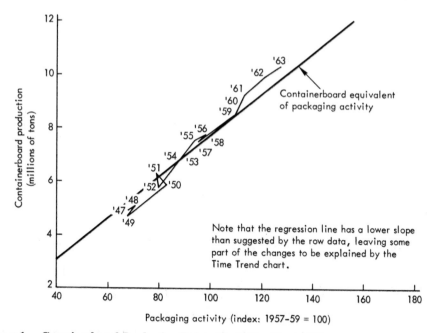

Chart 1   Containerboard Production Related to Packaging Activity

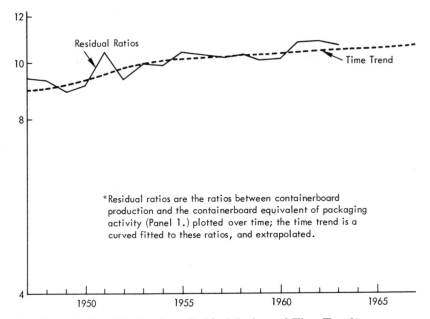

Chart 2   Containerboard Production—Residual Ratios and Time Trend*

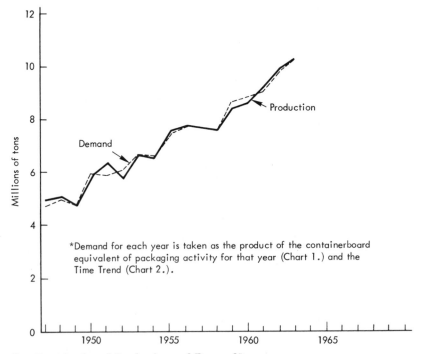

Chart 3   Containerboard Production and Demand*

408

greater the tendency for sales to fall as consumer income falls and to rise as income rises. Income elasticity also tends to depend upon price: sales of big-ticket items tend to fluctuate more sharply than sales of lower priced goods. Presumably this reflects not only durability but also visibility of the higher priced goods. Only the most budget-conscious can see the saving through reduced spending on low-priced items.[21]

A simple example of correlation analysis is given in the accompanying charts showing the relation between the production of containerboard (the raw material for corrugated and solid fibre shipping containers) and an index of packaging activity, developed by the writer. This index consists of the FRB index of nondurables, with a weight of 60; and the FRB index of home goods, with a weight of 40. Chart 1 shows production of containerboard plotted against the index of packaging activity, by years, and the chosen regression line between the two variables. Chart 2 shows the residual variations of actual board production and the level warranted by the regression line, with a trend drawn through them, reflecting the growing use of containerboard in the total packaging mix. Chart 3 compares actual production of containerboard with demand for containerboard calculated from the two factors of packaging activity and time-trend.

The time-trend represents an important concept which is sometimes overlooked in the use of correlation analysis. For many if not for most products, demand is affected both (1) by changes in business activity, consumer income, or other aggregates and (2) by changes occurring over time, independent of

changes in general business activity, reflecting changes in consumer taste, in business practice, in technology, and in other factors. The effect of cyclical changes may be the same (for example, a 10 percent rise or fall in packaging activity is associated with a 10 percent rise or fall in the demand for containerboard), but these cyclical shifts occur about changing levels, over time, reflecting fundamental noncyclical changes.

For example, the proportions of income allocated to European travel, to hi-fi equipment, and to frozen foods have all increased over the postwar years. While this change partly reflects rising incomes, it also reflects changes in taste; spending habits, and life styles. The change may be associated with a rise in income, but there has also been a change in consumption patterns: a reduction in income to former levels would not be associated with a reduction in demand for these new products to former levels. Similarly, continued growth in income would not necessarily result in a continued growth in demand at the recent rate. Tastes are continually changing over time. In the future some new goods and services will come along, to grow more rapidly, while the demand for today's sharp-growth items grows less rapidly or even stabilizes. Failure to distinguish between growth associated with rising income and growth associated with changing taste can result in serious misinterpretation of market levels and prospects.

The problem can be seen most clearly in analysis of the demand for basic materials whose use is gaining or declining in competition with other materials. Relating the demand for aluminum, say, to the index of industrial production, without allowing for the independent growth trend in the demand for aluminum, could indicate that a 10 percent increase in industrial production would be associated with a 22 percent increase in the demand for aluminum.

Changes in growth rates usually occur slowly enough so that this kind of result will

[21] An unpublished paper prepared at the Econometric Institute by Albert C. Neisser, now a fiscal economist with the Office of Satellite Communications, Federal Communications Commission, developed a systematic analysis of this question. See also Louis J. Paradiso, "Classification of Consumer Expenditures by Income-Elasticity," *Survey of Current Business* (January 1945), pp. 7ff.

not give a distorted picture of markets one or two years ahead. But if the projection is carried very far into the future the result can be a serious overstatement of potential. And, of course, the relation seriously overstates the potential decline in demand associated with recession. The effectiveness of an otherwise very useful analysis of paper demand by the Business and Defense Services Administration[22] is seriously weakened by reliance on a single variable, with no allowance for time-trends in the demand formulas.

One solution to this problem is to reverse the stages of correlation suggested above. Instead of correlating, say, production of containerboard with the index of packaging activity, first determine the long-term trend of each variable, by some appropriate method of trend-fitting, and then correlate the deviations of each series from its trend to determine the cyclical relation between the two. This is a somewhat more elaborate method, and has the conceptual drawback of regarding all secular growth in demand for a product as inherent in the product itself, independent of general economic growth. But it is a method which has pronounced advantages in analyzing products with strong growth trends. (It is less satisfactory for the postwar years, when income shifts have been relatively slight, than for the 1929–39 period, where income shifts were extreme.) An amusing example of the dangers of overlooking the time-trend factor in correlation analysis can be seen in the case of steel, correlated with industrial production, for the period 1955–62. In these years demand for steel was particularly hit by competition from other materials and imports, by the growth of the compact car (less steel per car), and other factors. (Some of these problems still remain.) In 1955–58 steel production averaged about 108 million tons per year, and the industrial production

index, 98. In the years 1959–62, steel production averaged 97 million tons per year, and the industrial production index, 111. Taking the relationship between these two sets of observations literally, ignoring the time-trend would indicate that the demand for steel declined as industrial production rose, and that a full-scale depression would get the steel industry operating at capacity levels.

Correlation analysis is a useful technique for all kinds of sales forecasting: short-term, medium-term, and long-term. Lack of or delay in availability of current data may limit the usefulness of the technique for purposes of short-term forecasting, however; conclusions based on preliminary data may have to be revised drastically when revised figures are published.

Further, the time required to review and forecast demand each month, and perhaps to estimate missing data (estimating unavailable data can be more difficult and time-consuming than forecasting itself) may be excessive in relation to available manpower. For these reasons, trend projections derived from internal analysis of the individual company's own sales may offer a more satisfactory systematic approach for short-term forecasting than the more elaborate, and conceptually more satisfactory, approach of correlation analysis. (This is particularly true with a computerized program, as discussed below.)

But for medium-term (budget) forecasts, or long-term (capital planning) forecasts, the more complete approach based on correlation analysis is usually more satisfactory.

In using correlation analysis, it is important to choose a reasonable independent variable. Demand for machine tools, for example, is not directly related to consumer income. Demand for flour or potatoes has little direct relation to corporate profits. It is always necessary to select an independent variable which has some reasonable connection with the dependent variable you are trying to explain and forecast.

[22] Business and Defense Services Administration, Department of Commerce, *Pulp, Paper, and Board Supply-Demand*, Union Calendar No. 292, House Report No. 693. (Washington, 1963).

Care is also required in using population as an independent variable. In the case of goods widely used by most or all sectors of the population, this poses no problem. The per capita demand for food items, for example, is a perfectly reasonable concept. So is the per capita demand for shoes (although this might better be broken down into the three groups of men, women, and children). On the other hand, to consider the per capita demand for mink coats or Cadillacs is to exaggerate the extent of affluence. Similarly, it makes no sense to consider such items as the per capita demand for lumber or steel, because such materials are used in such widely diverse ways, some more or less directly related to population, some completely independent. It is always possible to divide the dependent variable by population and to relate this to some per capita measure of economic activity, but this becomes an exercise in nonsense, unless there is some reason to regard demand for the product as widespread among all population groups and among all income groups. Frequently, for such commodities as tissue and sanitary paper (or cigarettes before the various health scares developed), it will be found that fluctuations in per capita production, usually very slight, are independent of changes in economic activity and can be forecast entirely through trend projection, converted to a total base by multiplying the projected per capita figures by projected population.

Inventory Changes

We have referred earlier to the importance of inventory changes in the total demand for a product. An increase in sales may reflect both an increase in consumption —perhaps sustainable—and also a frequently unsustainable rate of addition to inventories by customers. Conversely, a sales decline may reflect a cyclical decline in consumption, intensified by inventory liquidation. It was pointed out that techniques of internal analysis could not distinguish between these two phenomena. With a demand equation obtained by correlation analysis, however, it is possible to obtain a rough estimate of the significance of inventory-building or depletion. Assume, for example, that a demand equation based on the long-term relation between output of a particular product and real disposable personal income indicates that, at the going income level, demand equals 100,000 tons per month, while output is actually running at 110,000 tons per month. The divergence between production and demand suggests that somewhere in the structure of production, inventories are being accumulated at an excessive rate. If this divergence continues for long, some correction in output must be anticipated, even if consumption, or basis demand, continues firm. Conversely, if output is running well *below* calculated demand levels, an increase in output can be anticipated, even without an increase in consumption, as the process of inventory liquidation ends.

Care must be used in interpreting this evidence, of course. The demand structure for the product may have changed, or there may be some other error in the formula. The production data may be incorrect, and revised figures, when available, may show production quite in line with demand. But by and large, with a demand formula based on a significant number of years, where a dependent variable has a reasonable relationship to the independent, a significant divergence between actual shipments or production and calculated demand or consumption may well be a caution signal—or encouraging sign—that inventory changes are an important and temporary part of the current demand structure.[23]

[23] To the best of the writer's knowledge, this approach was first developed by Charles F. Roos at the Econometric Institute. Many techniques pioneered by Roos have now become standard forecasting procedures, but the inventory significance of divergence between "actual" and "calculated" values has apparently received little attention.

Correlation Analysis: Multiple Correlation

The preceding analysis has discussed correlation analysis entirely in terms of two separate independent variables: a cyclical measure of economic activity and, where necessary, a time-trend to reflect gradual noncylical changes in taste and technology.

Correlation analysis need not be limited to so small a number of independent variables, however; it is possible to use two, three, four, or any number of independent variables, in addition to a time-trend. Through graphic, calculator, or computer methods, it is possible to develop formulas expressing changes in the dependent variable as a function of the combined changes in a host of different independent variables. One might say, for instance, that the demand for steel depends on the production of tin cans, automobiles, machinery, and appliances; on oil field drilling; construction activity, and so forth. One could obtain figures showing activity in these various lines over the past 10 or 15 years, crank all the numbers through a computer, and come out with a formula assigning a specific response in steel demand to a given change in each of these different lines.

There are, however, serious problems involved in this process. In the first place, there is frequently a high degree of intercorrelation, or multicollinearity, between economic time-series, and there is always some degree of inaccuracy in economic data. While it is possible to analyze independent variables to remove the effects of intercorrelation, the final results may produce values showing changes which are inconclusive within the limits of accuracy of the original data. The effect of multicollinearity, along with the effect of other variables not included in the equation, may be to obtain results which are at best potentially nonsensical. The writer was once shown, in confidence, a multivariable sales analysis for one of our great corporations which included

number of outlets among the variables and which indicated that sales were inversely correlated to number of outlets: the greater the number of selling outlets, the smaller the total sales volume. The corporation did not follow the report to its obvious conclusion: maximize sales by closing all outlets.[24]

Despite the drawbacks it may be necessary to use multivariable equations. In a product where demand may be sharply affected by, say, income, housing starts, advertising expenditures, and temperature, it may be necessary to crank everything through a machine and come out with automatically determined answers. But often it is possible to use a modified approach, where judgment can be employed more regularly.

In the case of the demand for steel, for example, where data are available on shipments by end use, it is possible to assign weights directly to individual consuming industries, at least on a rough basis, rather than working out a multivariable least-squares solution. Such a method— which may be called the *bill of materials* approach—has the advantage that weights can be shifted if necessary (for example, where the era of the compact reduced the amount of steel per car), and that the analyst is in full control of his formula at all times. In view of the high degree of inaccuracy in economic data and in view of the frequency of strong intercorrelation, the possibility of greater control is a strong advantage for this type of approach.

In addition to the analytical problems, the use of many variables in forecasting, whether cranked through a machine or handled by a bill of materials approach, poses the additional difficulty of developing meaningful independent forecasts for each

[24] An unusually frank review of some of the problems in econometric models is provided in Charles Richter, "Some Limitations of Regional Econometric Models," a paper presented at the annual meeting of the Western Regional Science Association, February 26, 1971.

variable.

This would not be a conclusive objection if it were not for the analytical problems. It is frequently possible to develop meaningful independent forecasts and in any case correct identification of the significance of individual variables can at least improve the interpretation placed upon whatever variable can be forecast. But the combination of analytical difficulties and forecasting problems requires the greatest care in using the multiple correlation approach in sales forecasting.

The Problem of Market Shares

The discussion thus far has been essentially in terms of forecasting demand for an industry, rather than of forecasting sales for an individual company. Where industry data are not available, the same techniques can be used to forecast company sales directly, but this is less satisfactory. Since the market share of an individual company is not necessarily constant, it is preferable—as indicated earlier in this study—to develop industry forecasts and then to convert these into estimates of the sales potentials for the individual company.

This is not an easy process. Our theoretical understanding of the fluctuations of corporate fortunes is woefully inadequate. There are, however, a few useful relationships. For instance, when new capacity comes into an industry, it will be operated, virtually regardless of market conditions. (New capacity is never excess capacity; it is the old, high-cost capacity which is excess.) If the new capacity represents a new entrant in the industry, he will come in by the "price route" and established firms must be prepared to move over. On the other hand, if the firm with new capacity also has older, higher-cost capacity, this may be shut down, with limited effect on market shares.

Or again, if there is a dominant firm in the industry, its response to bad times will probably be to hold a price umbrella over the industry, surrendering market position to competitors who price more aggressively. (This point is not widely understood. The writer once heard the leading Wall Street analyst of an important durable goods industry forecast conditions for that industry and market shares of a dozen of its major firms. The analyst concluded by pointing out that the forecasts assumed that the dominant firm would continue a passive pricing policy, but "if they start pricing like the rest of you it's a new ball game." At that time the industry had a general reputation for noncompetitive pricing.)

Relative costs can be important in market shares, in location of customer industries and shifts in these locations, in changes in consumer tastes and many other factors.

When the necessary data are available, the analyst may be able to devise some systematic relationships for forecasting a firm's market share. Lacking such data, it may be satisfactory to assume continuation of the existing industry position or some average of recent experience.

An alternative device, and one which should at the very least be used as a supplement, is to consult the sales managers for the various products. This approach is not without its dangers. It is easy for an optimistic, aggressive product director to assume that if his sales this year account for five percent of the market he can give it the old college try and grow to six percent next year. But this putative change of only one percentage point represents an improvement of 20 percent for the individual company—a brilliant achievement, not a foregone conclusion. However, the sales manager has a firing line knowledge of the many factors affecting his market share and some kind of gut feeling for their combined impact. Even though it may be necessary to dampen his natural ebullience with the presumably colder realism of the analytical forecaster, his expertise should certainly be called upon.

Sales Forecasting: A Combined Process

Where industry data on shipments or production are available, this consultation with sales managers can be part of a combined forecasting process which will maintain the objectivity of the ivory tower approach, while at the same time involving sales personnel, and their insight and knowledge, so that the forecasts are essentially forecasts developed by the sales departments rather than schedules imposed upon them by an outside group.

The first step in this process is to develop a forecast of the general economic outlook which receives the approval of top management. This is a necessary step for purposes of consistency. If one department is forecasting on the assumption of great prosperity and a second on the assumption of moderate recession, it is not feasible to develop a coherent overall policy from a combination of the two forecasts. The differences will not reflect differences in sales potentials.

From a management-endorsed view of the general economic outlook, the economics department can develop forecasts of the specific aggregates of most significance to the industry, and forecasts of total industry shipments or production.

These forecasts, together with historical data showing both industry and company sales, and the company as a percent of industry, are given to the sales manager (or whatever line position is involved), and his assignment is then, not to make a sales forecast—in a vacuum, as it were—but to forecast the share of the industry total which he feels his particular organization can achieve. He is also, of course, free to modify the industry forecast, perhaps even—if he dares—to challenge the general economic forecast which management has approved.

But whatever changes or modifications he chooses to make, the ideas influencing the sales forecast must be made explicit. It is no longer a question of "We sold one million pounds last year so I think this year we should be able to sell 1.05 million pounds."

With this more systematic procedure, the sales manager is forced, in the first place, to accept or modify the objectively-made industry forecast, thus supplementing economic analysis with his detailed knowledge of the industry. Once agreement is reached on the industry outlook, the sales manager is asked to forecast not his own level of sales, in a vacuum, but that percentage of the total industry sales which he expects his organization to achieve. Since the past record of market shares is a part of the forecasting work sheet, there is an immediate test of the reasonableness of the forecast. Any anticipated improvement in industry position must be justified in the light of special circumstances or techniques not available to the competition, or on the basis of other special situations or unique factors.

With a forecast of industry shipments or production, and a forecast of the industry position for the particular company, the company sales forecast is obtained automatically, with the major factor underlying this forecast stated explicitly, rather than being implicitly lumped in with other values in a forecast based at best on internal analysis of the company's own sales record.

This combined method is of limited value in short-term sales forecasting, partly because of the time required and partly because random factors may produce strong shifts from one month to the next which make it unprofitable to use this time-consuming approach, calling for frequent reappraisals because of factors not really representative. (For short-term forecasting, trend projection based on internal analysis is probably the most satisfactory approach.)

But for medium-term and long-term forecasting, the combined approach is extremely effective, and while special factors may limit its applicability in particular situations, the possibility of using this approach should always be explored.

Sales Forecasting and the Computer

In the last several years, as computers have become more and more available, particularly through time-sharing, the use of these demon calculators in sales forecasting has grown sharply. Many concerns now have computerized forecasting programs, and if one is in doubt about how to set up such a program, various data processing companies offer instruction on the topic.

The great advantage of the computer over other computational techniques is its ability to handle vast amounts of data quickly. Thus the suitability of the computer for sales forecasting depends basically upon what the individual company demands of its sales forecast, and upon how it is prepared.

For a company satisfied with informed opinion forecasts, the computer offers nothing, unless perhaps so many informed opinions are asked that tabulating and analysis become time-consuming, as in a public opinion survey. On the other hand, if the company wants a forecast showing sales, by months, for a wide range of products, in each of the fifty sovereign states, the District of Columbia, and two dozen foreign nations, the computerized approach is virtually essential.

Probably the first widespread use of computers in sales forecasting developed out of seasonal adjustment techniques. The advantage of the computer in the lengthy and tedious process of developing seasonal adjustment factors is obvious, and programs are available for this purpose, usually with moving seasonals. However, the process need not stop here. Programs can be obtained which offer not only the seasonal factors and the seasonally adjusted data, but which also isolate the effects of cyclical, secular, and random factors, and extrapolate the trends by some form of exponential smoothing. By putting the seasonal factors "back in" it is thus possible to obtain a forecast of sales (or whatever series is studied) for six to twenty-four months in advance, both on a seasonally adjusted basis and without seasonal adjustment.

This is an extremely powerful forecasting tool. It is, of course, subject to the various drawbacks discussed earlier for any internal analysis techniques, but the possibility of a speedy systematic forecast for many product lines may often outweigh the disadvantages. Forecasting is a pragmatic art, at best, and it may well be preferable to accept one approach, out of administrative considerations, even though a logically more complete approach might occasionally give better results.

Correlation analysis, the econometric approach to sales forecasting, is another field where the computer can be extremely valuable, depending upon the amount of data to be presented. If the forecaster is analyzing a limited number of product lines, and using only one or two variables, the desk calculator may be wholly adequate. But where there are many product lines and many separate markets, where there are many different independent variables to be tested, the computer is virtually essential.

Model building is an area of company forecasting where the computer is again virtually essential. In this field the goal is not simply to forecast sales, but also to forecast all company operations: purchasing and inventory needs; costs, profits, cash flow, financing needs, etc.[25] Corporate models can be handled by traditional computational methods, just as econometric models were constructed before the electronic age, but only very crude, limited models are feasible with these techniques. A sophisticated model, involving vast masses of data, requires a computerized operation.

A corporate model is essentially a spe-

[25] For an illustration of the techniques of company model building, including the various tradeoff decisions involved, see George W. Gershefski, "Building a Corporate Financial Model," *Harvard Business Review* (July-August 1969).

cial form of an input-output table. Like an input-output table, the model is not a forecasting device in its own right, but simply a statement of relationships at a given point in time, which can show the implications of any given set of forecasts which may be selected, on the assumptions that the relationships do not change, or that there is enough knowledge of the pattern of these relationships so that the model can be adjusted for future changes. A corporate model, based upon corporate data, is presumably less subject to such problems as allocating secondary products and estimating unavailable data than, say, the OBE tables, but the certainty of changing interrelationships requires great caution in using any program based upon relationships at any single point in time.[26]

An exciting potential use for computers is the development of more detailed analyses of sales by individual customers than is feasible by hand computation. The customer is the immediate reality for any business, and computer review of customer-takings offers the chance of detecting inventory-building or liquidation, switching to new supply sources, and similar invaluable data for forecasting, to an extent not feasible through the more laborious hand operations. Other uses of the computer in simulation techniques and linear programming offer further exciting possibilities for extending the scope of sales forecasting.

But there are problems as well as possibilities in the use of the computer. (These are aside from the inherent complexity of programming, which is one of the more recondite skills of the modern age.) The basic problems already discussed, are three: (1) the inaccuracy of much of the basic data for the independent variables (the aggregates);

(2) the incidence of intercorrelation of the aggregates; and (3) the frequent importance of random forces in the dependent variable.

Programs can be written to cope with the problem of multicollinearity, but when you are attempting to use three or four variables, all highly correlated and each subject to a margin of error which may exceed their differences after adjusting for intercorrelation, it is difficult to know how much confidence to place in any given parameter. This difficulty is compounded by the problem of random deviations in the dependent value, already referred to. The great advantage of the less sophisticated methods—particularly graphic correlation—is that the analyst at all times has complete control of his data. He can disregard the significance of an observation—or of several observations—if his graphic correlation, perhaps supplemented by independent knowledge, suggests that they are atypical or yield nonsense results. He can interpret the significance, and modify its weight accordingly, of any particular observation where his knowledge suggests that special factors distorted the pattern of that observation.

The same possibilities of adjustment can be achieved, at least potentially, in the computer operation, but such adjustments are time-consuming and offset the basic advantage of the computer techniques.

The sales forecaster should fully explore the possibilities and advantages of computer operations, but he must remember that there are inherent limitations in his basic data. He is hampered by the frequent inaccuracy of the figures, by the vagaries of the calendar, by lack of independence of individual observations, by intercorrelation of many economic time series. These problems are not solved by the use of high-speed electronic computers, any more than by any other calculating device. The statistician and the sales forecaster must at all times be prepared to check formulas and results both for inherent reasonableness and for agreement with the record as it unfolds. The elec-

---

[26] For a discussion of some of the generally overlooked problems in input-output analysis see Robert S. Schultz, "The Matrix Discipline of Input-Output: Palomar Lens or Procrustes Bed?" *Business Economics* (Fall 1966).

tronic computer should assist judgment, not substitute for it.

CONCLUSION

All decision-making involves a forecast, implicit or explicit. By making the forecast explicit, we can test its reasonableness and use it as a consistent guide to policy formation in different areas.

A business enterprise needs specific sales forecasts for short-term, medium-term, and long-term planning, from which consistent policies can be formulated in all the various fields of corporate planning and ac-tivity. By the use of statistical techniques, preferably supplemented by or as a supplement to the detailed market knowledge of line personnel, the staff economist can develop systematic, quantified statements of probable future results which can serve as a basis for consistent policy formation in many lines.

The forecast must be regarded as only a statement of the probable outlook, in the light of the currently known information, and must be subject to change in case of unanticipated developments. The sales forecasts must be regarded as a guide to narrow the area of managerial judgment, not as a ukase to paralyze judgment, nor as a magic spell to eliminate the need for judgment.

BIBLIOGRAPHY

Abramson, Adolph G., and Russell H. Mack, *Business Forecasting in Practice*. New York: John Wiley & Sons, Inc., 1956.

American Institute of Certified Public Accountants, *Techniques for Forecasting Product Demand*. New York, 1966.

American Management Association, *Materials and Methods of Sales Forecasting*, Special Report No. 27. New York, 1957.

———, *Guidelines for Marketing Research and Economic Forecasting*, Research Study No. 73. New York, 1966.

———, *Practical Sales Forecasting*. New York, 1970.

Bean, Louis H., *The Art of Forecasting*. New York: Random House, Inc., 1969.

Box, George E. P., and Gwidym M. Jenkins, *Time Series Analysis, Forecasting and Control*. San Francisco: Holden-Day, Inc., 1970

Burns, Arthur F., and Wesley C. Mitchell, *Measuring Business Cycles*. Princeton, N.J.: National Bureau of Economic Research, 1946.

Business and Defense Services Administration, Department of Commerce, *Pulp, Paper, and Board Supply-Demand*, Union Calendar No. 292, House Report No. 693. Washington, 1963.

Buzzell, Robert D., "Predicting Short-term Changes in Market Shares as a Function of Advertising Strategy," *Journal of Marketing Research* (August 1964), pp. 27–31.

Cohen, Morris, "Forecasting Capital Goods: the Eclectic Approach," *Business Economics* (September 1970), pp. 66–72.

Davis, Thomas Jeff, *Cycles and Trends in Textiles*, Business and Defense Services Administration, Department of Commerce. Washington, 1958.

Dewey, Edward R., and Edwin F. Dakin, *Cycles—The Science of Prediction*. New York: Holt, Rinehart & Winston, Inc., 1947.

————, with Og Mandino, *Cycles, the Mysterious Forces that Trigger Events.* New York: Hawthorn Books, Inc., 1971.

Ezekiel, Mordecai, and Karl A. Fox, *Methods of Correlation and Regression Analysis,* 3rd ed. New York: John Wiley & Sons, Inc. 1959.

Foote, Richard J., *Analytical Tools for Studying Demand and Price Structures,* Agriculture Handbook No. 146. Agricultural Marketing Service, Department of Agriculture. Washington, August 1958.

Frazier, George D., "A Corporate Long Range Planning Model," *Business Economics* (September 1969), pp. 62–65.

Friedman, Joan, and Richard J. Foote, *Computational Methods for Handling Systems of Simultaneous Equations with Application to Agriculture,* Agriculture Handbook No. 94. Agricultural Marketing Service, Department of Agriculture. Washington, November 1955.

Gershefski, George W., "Building a Corporate Financial Model," *Harvard Business Review* (July–August 1969), pp. 61–72.

Gibson, Weldon B., "Long Range Forecasting as a Management Tool," *Business Economics,* (September 1969), pp. 36–39.

Gort, Michael, "Stability and Change in Market Shares," *Management Research Summary.* Small Business Administration. Washington, 1963.

Harmon, Paul C., "Long Range Forecasting in the Steel Industry," *Business Economics* (September 1969), pp. 59–61.

Kahle, R. V., "Mathematical Techniques In Corporate Planning," *Business Economics* (Winter 1965–66), pp. 58–61.

Karfunkle, Richard D., "Statistical Indicators of the Textile Cycle," *Business Economics* (May 1969), pp. 13–17.

Klein, Lawrence R., *An Introduction to Econometrics.* Englewood Cliffs, N.J.: Prentice-Hall, Inc., 1969.

————, "Econometric Model Building for Growth Projections," *Business Economics* (September 1969), pp. 45–50.

————, "Whither Econometrics?" *Journal of the American Statistical Association* (June 1971), pp. 415–421.

Mitchell, Walter, Jr., "Corporate Planning Procedures," *Business Economics* (January 1969), pp. 27–33.

Moore, James A., "Long Range Forecasting of Commercial Airline Passengers," *Business Economics* (September 1969), pp. 66–70.

Morgenstern, Oskar, "Qui Numerare Incipit Errare Incipit," *Fortune* (October, 1963), pp. 142–145, 173–174, 178–180. For more extended treatment, *On the Accuracy of Economic Observations,* 2nd ed. Princeton, N.J.: Princeton University Press, 1963.

Murdick, Robert G., *Sales Forecasting for Lower Costs and Higher Profits.* Englewood Cliffs, N.J.: Prentice-Hall, Inc., 1967.

National Industrial Conference Board, *Growth Patterns in Industry: A Reexamination,* Studies in Business Economics No. 75. New York, 1961.

————, *Forecasting Sales,* Studies in Business Policy No. 106. New York, 1963.

————, *Sales Forecasting, An Appraisal,* Experiences in Marketing Management No. 25, by Stanley J. Pokempner and Earl L. Bailey, New York, 1970.

Oxenfeldt, Alfred R., "How to Use Market Share Measurement," *Harvard Business Review* (January–February 1959), pp. 59–68.

Paradiso, Louis J., "Classification of Consumer Expenditures by Income-Elasticity," *Survey of Current Business* (January 1945), pp. 7–10.

Reeder, Charles B., "The Seasonal Adjustment Program: Problems and Applications from the User's Point of View," *Business Economics* (September 1969), pp. 78–79.

Reichard, Robert S., *Practical Techniques of Sales Forecasting*. New York: McGraw-Hill Book Company, 1966.

Richter, Charles, "Some Limitations of Regional Econometric Models," Paper presented at the annual meeting of the Western Regional Science Association, February 26, 1971.

Roos, Charles F., "Survey of Economic Forecasting Techniques," *Econometrica* (October 1955), pp. 363–395.

Rosenblatt, Harry M., "A New Look and Beyond Traditional Methods of Seasonal Adjustment," *Business Economics* (September 1969), pp. 74–77.

Schultz, Robert S., "The Matrix Discipline of Input-Output: Palomar Lens or Procrustes Bed?" *Business Economics* (Fall 1966), pp. 21–24.

Seward, James S., "Systems for Forecasting Markets," *Business Economics* (Spring 1966), pp. 33–36.

Shiskin, Julius, "The Census Bureau Seasonal Adjustment Program," *Business Economics* (September 1969), pp. 71–73.

Smith, George Cline, "The Law of Forecast Feedback," *American Statistician* (December 1964), pp. 11–14.

Sonnenblum, Sidney, "Some Perspectives on Long Range Projects for Business Planning," *Business Economics* (September 1969), pp. 40–44.

Spencer, Milton H., Colin G. Clark, and Peter W. Hoguet, *Business and Economic Forecasting*. Homewood, Ill.: Richard D. Irwin, Inc., 1961.

Stanford Research Institute, *Projections in Planning*, Long-Range Planning Report No. 208. Menlo Park, Calif.: April 1964.

Waugh, Frederick V., *Graphic Analysis in Agricultural Economics*, Agriculture Handbook No. 128. Agricultural Marketing Service, Department of Agriculture. Washington, 1957.

Weiss, E. B. "E. B. Puts His Annual Pox on Prognosticators," *Advertising Age* (December 17, 1962), pp. 76, 78.

White, John R., "The Use of Input-Output Economics in Corporate Planning," *Business Economics* (September 1969), pp. 51–54.

Wonnacott, Ronald J., and Thomas H. Wonnacott, *Econometrics*. New York: John Wiley & Sons, Inc., 1971.

Zymelman, Manuel, *The Cotton Textile Cycle: Its Nature and Trend*. Department of Commerce. Washington, 1963.

Various unpublished papers should also be mentioned. For the past seven years, in its Annual Forecasting Conference, the New York chapter of the American Statistical Association has included talks on sales forecasting, offering useful case studies, methodological examples, or philosophical comments, or combinations thereof. Few if any of these studies have been published elsewhere, but it is possible that copies may still be available from the authors.

1959 Bean, Louis H., No title cited in program.
      Brown, Arthur A., No title cited in program.

1960 Fernald, Robert," A Marketing Analysis Approach to Five-Year Sales Forecasts."
Morris, William, "Mr. Computer Looks at His Crystal Ball."

1961 Burgess, Ralph, "Short-Term Forecasting—Nondurable Goods Sales."
Rich, James, "Short Term Sales Forecasting—The Problem of Durable Goods."

1962 Blank, David, "Forecasting Short-Run Fluctuations in National Advertising."
Brinberg, Herbert, "Derived Demand and Sales Forecasting."

1963 Gross, Alvin D., "Sales Forecasting: Keystone for Profit Planning."
Thek, Robert R., "Sales Forecasting in New Product Development."

1964 Bopp, Eberhard W., "Better Short-Term Planning."
Christopher, William F., "Improving Reliability of Short-Term Forecasts for Industrial Products."
Crook, Gordon J., "Application of Recent Statistical Forecasting Techniques to Operations Research Projects."
Murphy, Francis P., "New Perspectives on Appliance Forecasting."

1965 Gould, Jay, "Input-Output Analysis in Sales Forecasting."
Wood, Homer G., "A Carpetbagger in the Holy Land."

1966 Frechtling, John, "The Outlook for Autos."
Levy, Harold, "Appliance Trends."
Pace, Norma T., "Forecasting Consumer Durable Goods Trends."
Rich, James L., "Forecasting in the Steel Industry."

1967 Feeney, George J., "Multi-Sector Bayesian Forecasting."
Kretschmer, Kenneth S., "Multi-Product Forecasting Models."
Leininger, William J., "Auto Sales Prospects."
McCarty, Daniel, "Forecasting Non-Automotive Durables."

1968 Evans, Michael, K., "Forecasting Consumer Capital Goods for 1968."
Taubman, Paul, "Forecasting Investment in Plant and Equipment for 1968."

1969 Karchere, Alvin J., "Forecasting with Econometric Models."
Lewis, Robert E., "Operating a Cooperative Economic Data Bank."

1970 Hitchings, George P., "What's Ahead for Automobiles?"
Katona, George, "Predictive Value of Changes in Consumer Sentiment."
Morrison, George R., "Forecasting the Demand for Non-Automotive Durables."

ROBERT J. EGGERT & JANE R. LOCKSHIN

Forecasting the Automobile Market

Together with most other segments of the economy, the automobile industry faces various planning problems for which it uses forecasting as an essential element in its decision making. The horizon of each forecast, namely, where it is distant or very close in time, of course depends on the particular problem at hand.

For example, when a company faces the very short-run problem of setting its production schedules for the months ahead, it must use one type of forecast. At the same time, it might use a somewhat longer forecast horizon in order to plan its volume and establish its budgets and expected volume profit plan for the next model year. Finally, it might use forecasts of the normal average volume of the entire industry for ten years ahead in order to develop its strategy for facilities planning, capital budgeting, and longer-range financial programming and control. In sum, most of the forecasting tools and methodology utilized to estimate the size of the basic market for cars in 1980 are

This chapter retains the valuable insights and contributions of Paul W. McCracken, recent chairman of the President's Council of Economic Advisers and now Edmund Ezra Day University Professor of Business Administration University of Michigan, who was a coauthor in the first edition. We would also like to thank Dr. Daniel S. Hirshfield, who assisted in editing and preparing the manuscript.

a good deal different from those used in March to estimate the strength of the market through the summer as a basis for setting the production schedules for the build-out period of a company's waning model year.

Although most companies use each of these forecast horizons, in terms of the man-hours devoted to forecasting it is the relatively short-run shifts in markets that receive the lion's share of attention. This is inevitable. For if production schedules are not reasonably on target, the company will be faced with added labor costs from subsequent downtime or overtime, with obsolescence of parts and materials that often cannot be used in next year's models, and with a shortage or surplus of cars in dealer inventories. And dealers have been known to be articulate in their displeasure with overloaded inventories, or even with missed sales because stocks of new cars are too low.

The short-term forecast also involves complex methodological problems which consume vast amounts of the forecaster's time. For example, any short-run movement in automobile demand is less apt to be a response to changes in basic business conditions than it is to be a result of more volatile factors, such as changes in consumer attitudes, customer acceptance of new models, or other forces involving special incentives within the auto market itself. The forecaster must examine and evaluate these complex factors in order to make even modest headway in accurately evaluating such short-run market changes.

In this chapter, we shall first discuss forecasting in the long run or the "standard-volume" market. We shall then move on to describe forecasting relatively near-term swings in the market, and finally discuss the analytic methodology we use.

THE LONG-RUN PROJECTION

Does projecting the long-run market volume for automobiles require skills much more complex than the ability to hold a ruler steady on a piece of graph paper and push a pencil along the edge? Do we get better results with sophisticated forecasting techniques? These are legitimate and serious questions if for no other reason than that there has been a persistent growth in the demand for automobiles in the past, and most projections for the decade ahead seem to represent little more than an assumption that prevailing trends will continue. During the last decade, for example, the stock of cars in use has been growing quite steadily at the rate of about 3.8 percent per year. Annual sales of new cars have bounced around a good deal more, but few projections of future volume have strayed very far from the path of the historical trend extended into the future.

Even though this is true, a worthwhile long-term projection of future auto volume must proceed from a careful exploration of the basic forces that can be expected to influence the market. For one thing, such an analysis may provide clues about changes in the market, or even entirely new factors which might cause displacements in the major historical trends. Moreover, such a careful appraisal of these forces which we believe are influencing the basic demand for cars can teach us a great deal about the market itself.

1. Basic Importance of a Growing Economy

In this century, the American has been marked by a high and increasing level of consumer purchasing power relative to the cost of basic necessities. This characteristic was highly relevant to the emergence and growth of the automobile on the American industrial landscape.

At the turn of the century in 1900 our gross national product was $75–$80 billion (in 1963 dollars), less than ten percent of the current level. In terms of today's prices, the average American family's income was about $2,000, and the automobile was little more than a capricious horseless carriage for the few interested in far-out novelties, (there was one in use for every 9,500 people compared with one for every 3 persons now). Detroit in 1900 was a city with a population of about 285,000. The Detroit Edison Company had recently lost one of its night engineers (Henry Ford).

Although $2,000 enabled a family of four to purchase a pretty affluent level of living by 1900 standards, if there had been no further economic gains for the American family, it is safe to assume that Detroit would have remained a cozy little interior city and the automobile an exclusive preserve of the carriage trade. But average family incomes in the United States did continue to increase, at the average annual rate of 1.8 percent per year, and by 1970 the average was close to $9,870 (median family income excluding individual households). And this growth (and all that it meant for Detroit and Henry Ford) in real purchasing power made the huge market for automobiles possible.

In light of these past developments, it is clear that any future projection of the automobile market's standard volume for 1980 must begin with an evaluation of growth prospects for the whole economy and for the family units in it. Chart 1 illustrates the projected growth of the upper segments

Changing Profile of Income Distribution

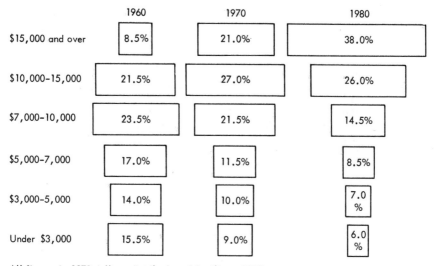

	1960	1970	1980
$15,000 and over	8.5%	21.0%	38.0%
$10,000–15,000	21.5%	27.0%	26.0%
$7,000–10,000	23.5%	21.5%	14.5%
$5,000–7,000	17.0%	11.5%	8.5%
$3,000–5,000	14.0%	10.0%	7.0%
Under $3,000	15.5%	9.0%	6.0%

All figures in 1970 dollars; distribution of families = 100%.

Chart 1   Changing Profile of Income Distribution

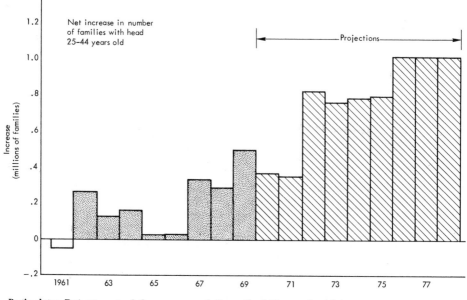

Basic data: Department of Commerce and Council of Economic Advisers.

Chart 2   Growth in Families with Head 25–44 Years Old

423

TABLE 1.   NEW CAR BUYING RATES BY STAGE IN LIFE CYCLE

Life Cycle				Buying Rate	Percent of Total New Cars Sold
Age	Marital Status	Children	Employment		
Under 45	Married	No children	Employed	7%	3%
45 and over	Married	No children	Employed	6	32
Under 45	Married	6 Years +	Employed	10	7
Under 45	Married	5 Years −	Employed	6	14
45 and over	Married	Children	Employed	18	14
Under 45	Single	No children	Employed	17	3
45 and over	Married	No children	Retired	4	6
45 and over	Single	No children	Employed	3	3
45 and over	Single	No children	Retired	3	3
OTHER				5	15
TOTAL				9%	100%

Source: Survey of Consumer Finances, 1970.

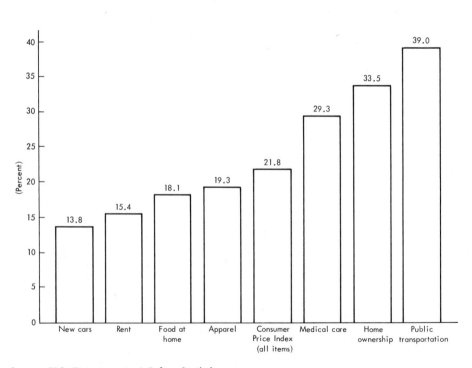

Source: U.S. Department of Labor Statistics.

Chart 3   Percent Change in New Car Prices and Selected Consumer Goods and Services (July 1971 from 1967 Base Period)

of the income distribution. The income classes comprising the $15,000 and over group has grown from 8.5 percent of all families and unrelated individuals in 1960 to 21 percent in 1970, and is projected to contain almost 40 percent of the earning population in 1982. Chart 2 shows the accelerating increases in families with heads 25–44 years old, a trend which is projected to continue through 1978. Table 1 contains new car buying rates by life cycle stage for 1970. Chart 3 illustrates the historical percent increases in new car prices and selected other consumer items. Prices of new cars have historically grown less than other consumption categories, a trend which we believe will continue in the future.

While the prospects for the U.S. economy in the decade ahead is a subject that extends beyond the scope of this chapter, it is clear that a continuation of the sluggish economic pace prevailing in 1970 would give us a markedly different long-run estimate from that we would get if we were to assume a resumption of the reasonably full employment that has characterized most of our history. Anyone making a long-run projection must obviously appraise prospects for doing better in the decade or so ahead than we have during the recession of 1970.

Once we have our assumption (or range of assumptions) about the further growth of the whole economy (in terms projected for a given year, of GNP, for example), how do we translate this number into an estimate of the automobile market in that year? Methodologies here range from the simple to the highly complex, from the mechanistic (which can be highly complex) to the highly flexible and judgmental.[1]

A very conventional approach to this

problem has been simply to compute the number of cars sold per dollar or per million dollars of GNP in each of several years (in constant prices), develop some sort of trend line for this, extend the trend to the target year, and apply the result to our projected GNP for the target year. This is of course easier to state than to execute, since automobile sales data bounce around a great deal and for most of the modern era, market conditions have been disturbed by exogenous circumstances (indeed one could insist that the whole period from 1929 to perhaps 1953 would have to be ruled out of the analysis).

Even so, for a longer-run projection this conventional approach has its uses. From 1961 to 1970, for example, new car registrations per million GNP (constant prices) averaged 13.2, ranging from 11.6 in 1970 to 15.1 in 1965. If our objectives were to project the standard volume for 1976, we could plausibly use such an average. It is a fairly long period, still escaping the abnormal influences that prevailed for the first decade of the postwar period. While it contains some exceptionally good years (1965 and 1968), it also contains some poor years (1967 and 1970). Such an approach would give us an estimate of the normal volume for 1976 of about 12.2 million new car sales, at reasonably full employment. This quick figure seems to be quite reasonable.

A variant of this economic approach to forecasting car sales is to work via the stock of cars (numbers of existing serviceable cars) rather than only with new car sales. This gives the forecaster the advantage of data which inevitably move slowly and (under normal conditions) in step with the secular growth of the economy. In the last decade (1960–70), for example, the number of cars in use (as estimated by R. L. Polk & Co.) per million of constant dollar GNP ranged from a low of 104.5 in 1966 to a high of 115.5 in 1961. The average was 108.7. During 1966–69, however, it has been stable at around 105. If we apply the average to

---

[1] For a very thorough survey of factors associated with the secular growth of the demand for automobiles cf. John A. Frechtling, "A Longer Run Look at Automobile Demand," *Proceedings of the University of Michigan Conference on the Economic Outlook* (October 31, 1963), pp. 42–70.

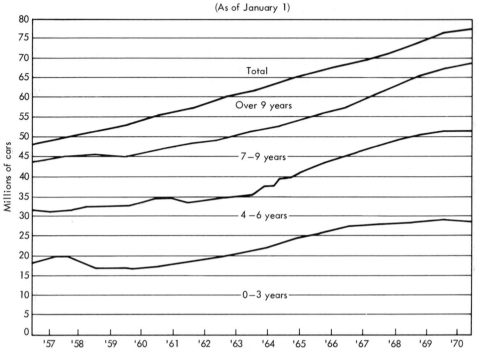

1957–1971
(As of January 1)

Source: *CIT Financial Corporation, George Hitchings.*

Chart 4   Autos in Use by Age Group

our estimated real GNP for 1976, this would give us a projected car population for that year of 100.6 million. Since in 1970 there were 89.3 million cars in use, the car population would have to grow at the average rate of 2.1 percent per year to reach 100.6 million by 1976. Thus, 2 million new cars (100.6 million times 2.1 percent) would be required just to take care of this growth demand.

One problem with this "stock of cars" approach is that it does not include an estimate of replacement requirements (how many new cars will be required to replace those which, on the average, could be expected to fall by the wayside in that year). This is a useful analytical tool, but one which is based on a slippery concept. As Dr.

Godfrey Briefs has pointed out, "Theoretically car life may be extended indefinitely, as the entries in the annual Glidden tour from Cleveland to Detroit prove."[2]

The statistical problems of estimating replacement requirements would be simpler if the automobile, like the famous shay, would just collapse at some predictable point to the day. But since the phenomenon is one of economic obsolescence rather than physical failure, replacement demand has bounced around a great deal and has been related to larger national economic forces.

[2] Godfrey Briefs, "Developing Auto Customer Profiles," in *Dynamic Aspects of Consumer Behavior* (Ann Arbor, Michigan: Foundation for Research on Human Behavior, 1963), p. 28.

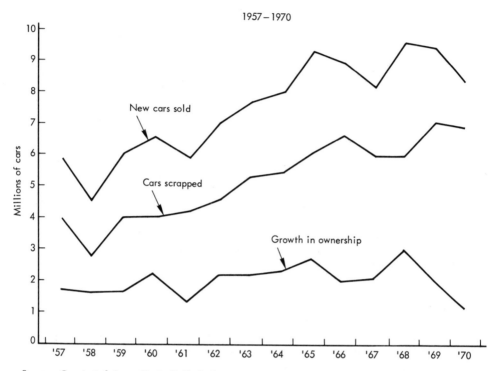

1957–1970

Chart 5   New Cars Sold, Cars Scrapped and Growth in Ownership (Including Imports)

Source: Computed from R. L. Polk & Co., passenger car registrations, new car production and change in dealer stocks. Scrappage measured by cars failing to re-register in following license year up to July 1. Growth measured by change in July 1 car counts, adjusted to January 1 by deducting January–June new car registrations. Mackay-Shields Economics, Inc. George Hitchings.

However, since our interest is in some sort of normal-volume forecast, even this is not too troublesome. As we look at the data (see charts 4 and 5, for example) we find that the proportion of cars scrapped each year has averaged about 8.9 percent of the stock of cars in existence at the beginning of the year (with no clear trend). The high was in 1966 at 10.4 percent; the low in 1970 at 7.8 percent. For a standard-volume forecast we might simply use the average (giving us a replacement demand of about 10.1 million for 1976), add the growth in demand (2), and get an alternative standard-volume estimate for 1976 of 12.2 million cars.

Each of these broad, economy-based tools (GNP, stock of cars, and replacement requirements) is useful in making long-range market forecasts. The results they yield are not intended to be used as a polished standard-volume forecast, but they do indicate, in a bare-bones way, how longer-run prospects for the economy are translated into projections of the automobile market.

2. Extensions of the Analysis

There are, of course, several modifications and extensions of these economy-based approaches, each of which has different degrees of refinement in its variables and in its utility as analytical tools. For example, we could use constant dollar consumer spending as a more refined indicator than aggregate GNP. In a similar fashion, business income could be used to estimate business purchases of cars, and constant dollar disposable personal income could be used to project purchases by consumers. Or the latter variable could be refined still further by using some measure of "discretionary income"—income left over after necessities have been purchased. (This is subject to the obvious difficulty that "necessities" is a changeable concept.) Or we might eliminate imputed services from disposable personal income on the ground that this is not income available for generalized expenditures.

A series of these more sophisticated variables were used in a perceptive paper primarily concerned with exploring the disappointing performance of the automobile market in the 1950s. In it Godfrey Briefs develops a measure of purchasing power or receipts available to consumers which includes gross borrowings plus personal income.[3] (This makes sense in that automobiles represent a consumer investment involving substantial use of borrowed funds.) In the same paper, Dr. Briefs works with total consumer automobile expenditures, (not just new car purchases) and defines it to include outlays for new cars and net purchases of used cars; purchases of tires, tubes, accessories, and parts; outlays for gas, oil, and other services (tolls, insurance, washing, interest on auto debt); and repayments on automobile debt. In short, Dr. Briefs included in his estimates of automobile outlays all amounts spent to buy new and used cars plus car operating costs, and debt service and repayments.

The logic of Dr. Briefs' concept is that consumers may be inclined to allocate a certain proportion of their financial resources to automobiling and if one component of their household budget starts to absorb more of their income, another (perhaps pur-

chases of new cars) will get less. This approach is apparently confirmed by the fact that the ratio of total consumer automobile expenditures to consumer receipts as defined in the study was relatively steady in the decade of the 1950s.

Another way of extending our analysis of projected automobile demand (particularly the replacement component) is to take cognizance of the car age distribution as well as the size of the stock of cars in making our projection for scrappage and, therefore, replacement demand. The existing car population has not been built up smoothly by equal additions in all years. Indeed, during the 1950s the stock of cars in use consisted only of vehicles either quite old (prewar models) or quite young (postwar models). The peculiarities in the age distribution of the stock of cars in use, introduced by this irregular pattern of sales, make a difference in projections of basic demands from year to year, and any refined estimating procedure must take cognizance of this problem.

There are, in principle, at least two ways to do this. One is to estimate, from normal survival tables, the probable scrappage of cars for each model year in the total automobile population. Substantial statistical analysis along this line dates back to the 1920s.[4] The alternative approach is to work with the value of the stock of cars in use. The logic of this approach is that the demand for automobiling services is a function of income, relative prices, and other variables, but the supply of these automobiling services is a function of the value of the total car population. If the net investment in the car stock declines because of average age or other factors, even though the number reaching the scrappage point has not increased, the demand for new cars tends to be stimulated. Gregory C. Chow uses this concept. And John A. Frechtling, in his

[3] Briefs, *ibid.*, pp. 23–41.

[4] Cf. Clare E. Griffin, *The Life History of Automobiles* (Ann Arbor, Michigan: University of Michigan School of Business Administration, 1926).

TABLE 2.   RATIO OF NEW AND USED CARS PURCHASED TO NUMBER OF SPENDING UNITS IN EACH INCOME BRACKET, 1970

Income	New Cars	Used Cars
Under $ 3,000	*%	7%
$ 3,000–$ 4,999	4	17
$ 5,000–$ 7,499	5	22
$ 7,500–$ 9,999	6	20
$10,000–$14,999	10	24
$15,000 and over	21	19

Source: Survey of Consumer Finances, 1971.

analysis of the longer-run demand for automobiles, works with this concept of net investment in car stocks, and also with an alternative index of newness.[5]

The long-run projected demand for automobiles can also be estimated by using cross-section data on income distribution by size. The ratio of the number of cars purchased (or owned) to the number of recipients changes sharply as we move across the income scale. For example, less than 0.5 percent of the spending units in the lowest income group bought new cars in 1970, while 21 percent of those with incomes over $15,000 purchased new cars.

Use of cross-section data has certain obvious advantages for market analysis. It has the inherent advantage of taking explicit cognizance of the pattern of distribution of income.[6] For example, if this pattern is expected to change, this estimate is automatically reflected in our forecast. Or if characteristics of automobile demand or

[5] Cf. Gregory C. Chow, "Statistical Demand Functions for Automobiles and Their Use for Forecasting," in *The Demand for Durable Goods*, ed. Arnold C. Harberger (Chicago: University of Chicago Press, 1960), pp. 149–78. Cf. also his *Demand for Automobiles in the United States: A Study in Consumer Durables* (Amsterdam: North-Holland Publishing Company, 1957). Frechtling, *loc. cit.*, 51.

[6] The phrase *distribution of income* is used here in the technical sense of the degree of inequality in income distribution as measured by, for example, the Lorenz curve.

ownership change in some complex way as we move along the income scale we could also reflect this in our forecasts. (If the demand for autos was found to increase as we moved up the income scale but to taper off again after a certain point, a rise in national income would not necessarily mean a corresponding rise in car sales. A rise in national income that would significantly enlarge the proportion of income recipients having incomes above $15,000 would not, if the pattern in table 2 remained fixed, necessarily be good news for the used car market.)

3. Toward More Dynamic Considerations

In our discussion of how we analyze the longer-run demand for cars, only two variables have received any real attention up to this point. These are consumer income data, and the age distribution and size of the car population. But we also know that other forces which are not so directly related to the economy have a significant effect on the basic demand for cars. These must be taken into account in any evaluation of long-run prospects.

The incidence of ownership or purchase of automobiles has been found to depend on the stage of the family's life cycle. For example, chart 6 illustrates that the pressure of older children in the family seems to increase somewhat the incidence of new car

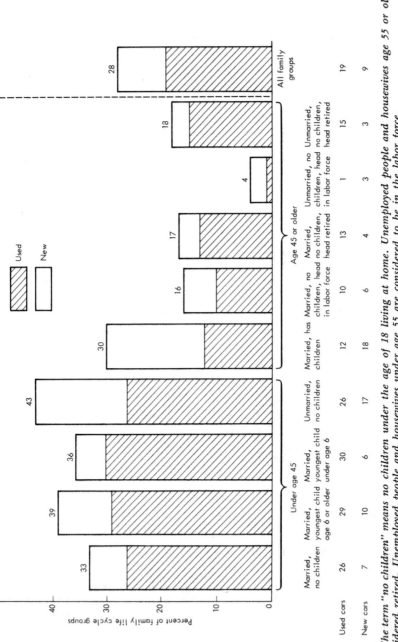

Note: The term "no children" means no children under the age of 18 living at home. Unemployed people and housewives age 55 or older are considered retired. Unemployed people and housewives under age 55 are considered to be in the labor force.

Basic data: Survey Research Center, University of Michigan.

Chart 6   New and Used Car Annual Buying Rates by Family Life Cycle Groups

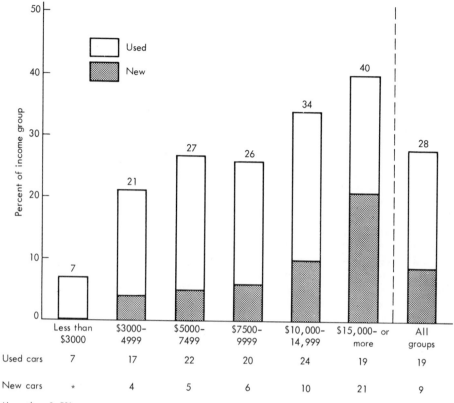

	Less than $3000	$3000- 4999	$5000- 7499	$7500- 9999	$10,000- 14,999	$15,000- or more	All groups
Used cars	7	17	22	20	24	19	19
New cars	*	4	5	6	10	21	9

*Less than 0.5%

Basic data: Survey Research Center, University of Michigan, 1971.

Chart 7   New and Used Car Annual Buying Rates by Income Groups

purchase. Also, as demonstrated in chart 7, the under-45 single group has a high new car purchase rate (17 percent in 1970).

There is also evidence that the location of a family's residence exerts a substantial influence on its demand for a car. At each level of income (except at the very top) a family living in the open country is more apt to own an automobile than one in the city. The next highest incidence of ownership, with incomes held constant, is found among families in smaller cities, followed by those living in the suburbs of metropolitan areas, with the lowest incidence of automobile ownership to be found among families in the central cities of metropolitan areas.

Data on the incidence of car ownership with families arrayed by distance from the central city, with incomes held constant, confirm this factor of location. At all income levels the number of cars owned per thousand families rises as the distance of the home from the central city increases. As even more families move to the suburbs in the decade of the seventies, this factor can be expected to exert added influence.

Finally, forecasters in the automobile industry also must be on the alert for technological, social, and product developments that might alter its penetration in the economy. The industry developed and prospered by making automobile ownership ubiquitous and by increasing turnover rates. All attempts to appraise its long-run prospects must evaluate any forces which may alter its capability to continue this performance. Such factors as costly safety and anti-pollution requirements; the possible revival of rapid transit in metropolitan areas (with the aid of federal subsidies); the rapidity and direction of the shift of people between suburbs and the central city; the current decline in birthrates; the sharp upward trend in leasing (including daily rentals); the further adaptation of cars to meet specialized consumer markets; and the continued improvement of roads, traffic control systems, and parking facilities—these are all important considerations in any final evaluation of long-range automotive volumes.

A brief list of such factors (both pro and con) would include:

Favorable Factors

1. Bulge in real incomes should help increase demand for newness.
2. Big expansion in households under 41 years of age (higher new car buying rates).
3. Continued move of higher-income people to the suburbs.
4. More working wives away from public transportation makes second car essential.
5. Driver licenses continue to expand, suggesting a car per each potential "able" driver over age 16.
6. Lower-priced, easier to drive, easier to park, smaller cars should further stimulate car ownership.
7. Elimination of the seven percent excise tax.

Unfavorable Factors

1. Continued rising cost of repairs, insurance, licenses, and upkeep.

2. Added pollution-, safety-, and damage-resistance devices which make new cars more expensive.
3. Increased mass transit (both local and distance) *may* be forthcoming.
4. Status and emotion are becoming less important as buying motives. Economy, durability, and good value are becoming more important.
5. Industry spokesmen report that future styling changes will be minimized.

SHORT-RUN FORECASTING

The job of the short-run forecaster is different in many ways than that of his colleague making longer-range forecasts. It relies on an added set of tools. These tools are complex and difficult to work with, but the short-run forecast is so important for corporate success that it must receive great emphasis.

The modern large automobile company is an interlaced web of complex operations integrated with those of thousands of external suppliers. The Ford Motor Company, for example, buys from approximately 26,000 independent supplier companies. It is a complex planning problem to keep these flows of parts orderly and in balance. The kingpin of this planning and control operation is a set of decisions about production schedules. Fundamental to these decisions are factors such as: an appraisal of market strength in the near term; a realistic estimate of the company's expected penetration; projected sales of imported cars; and planned levels of dealer stock. Major errors in this forecasting process can create massive profit problems for both manufacturer and dealers.

1. Business Conditions

As in long-range forecasting, short-run analysis evaluates changes in business condi-

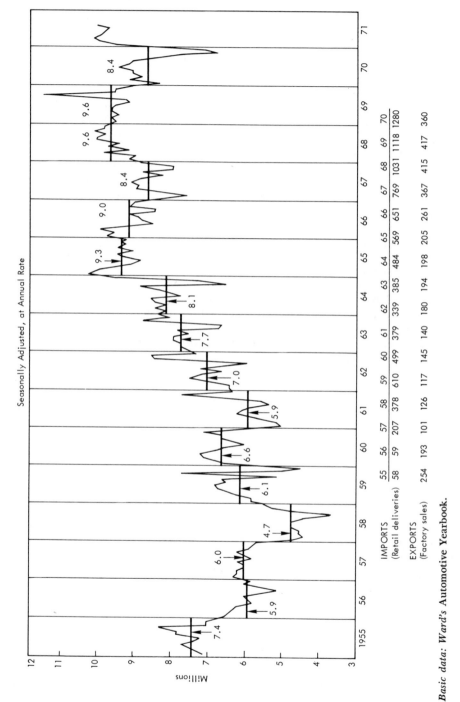

Seasonally Adjusted, at Annual Rate

	55	56	57	58	59	60	61	62	63	64	65	66	67	68	69	70
IMPORTS (Retail deliveries)	58	59	207	378	610	499	379	339	385	484	569	651	769	1031	1118	1280
EXPORTS (Factory sales)	254	193	101	126	117	145	140	180	194	198	205	261	367	415	417	360

Basic data: Ward's Automotive Yearbook.

Chart 8   Auto Sales (Including Imports)

433

tions and prospects. There are strong logical reasons for expecting automobile sales
to be sensitive to changes in the general
credit and business situation. For one thing,
the purchase of a new car (even with a trade-
in) is a substantial item in the average customer's budget and about two-thirds of these
purchases must be financed. The monthly
payment on these often approaches the
weekly paycheck. Future income is committed for periods up to three years ahead,
for about two-thirds of all new cars sold.
Moreover, the timing of the purchase of a
new car can be varied in most cases without
loss of basic transportation, since the great
bulk of new car sales are made with a trade-
in, thus involving the replacement of a serviceable used car.

As a result of the above characteristics,
business recessions tend to induce a sharp
postponement of trading for newer cars.
The buying power of some customers is curtailed. Other potential customers then become concerned about the possibility that
their buying power *might* be affected adversely in the future—there is a loss of con-

fidence. Finally, these developments are apt
to reduce the price of used car trade-ins, and
this can have important adverse "price effects" on the new car market.

Changing business conditions are
transmitted to the automobile market in
complex ways. In both prewar and postwar
periods, for example, there was some tendency for changes in automobile sales to *lag*
behind major turns in business activity. The
1957–58 downturn in the general economic
situation began in the third quarter of 1957.
Automobile sales even in the final quarter
of 1957 were just under the six million rate,
but in the first quarter of 1958 the rate
dropped almost 25 percent. The business
situation exhibited strong improvement
after April 1958, but the automobile market
seemed to recover little of its courage until
the introduction of the new models in the
latter part of 1958. Again in 1960, sales held
up well in the fall even after clear signs that
general business conditions were deteriorating. Sales then fell sharply early in 1961 and
once again did not recover substantial
strength until late in the year, well after the

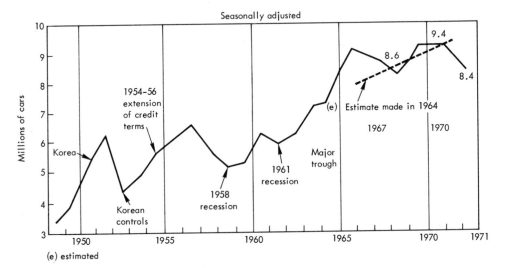

Source: Ford Division projections, January 1964.

Chart 9   New Car Registrations (Including Imports)

upturn in business activity began. (See chart 8).

In spite of the complex lead-lag relationship, often simple trend extrapolation works surprising well. Chart 9 shows a trend line which was originally estimated in 1964,[7] and extended for the last half of the sixties against the actual for the period. It tracks quite well.

These comments are not, of course, meant to suggest that swings in the general economy no longer influence the automobile market. In fact, even the minirecession had an impact on auto sales in 1967 and the recession of 1970 resulted in a decline in consumer expenditures for new cars prior to the General Motors strike. It is, however, clear that increasingly in the postwar period, analytical techniques which relate automobile sales in this month to real disposable personal income in this month in some simple and mechanistic way do not identify the major reason for variability in the market. The relationships are complex, and how the short-term automobile market responds to changes in business conditions depends on the concatenation of other circumstances also affecting the customers' inclination to buy. It is to these matters that we now turn.

2. Attitudes

The spending attitude of consumers is now recognized as a major factor in short-term forecasting. For example, in a study of the role of changes in attitudes on spending, Professor Eva Mueller found no significant correlation between disposable personal income and consumer expenditures on cars a half year later.[8] The simple correlation, in fact, produced a small negative coefficient of

[7] Robert J. Eggert and Paul W. McCracken, "Forecasting the Automobile Market," in *How Business Economists Forecast* (1st ed.), ed. William F. Butler and Robert A. Kavesh (Englewood Cliffs, N.J.: Prentice-Hall, Inc., 1964).

regression, though it was not statistically significant.[9] A multiple correlation, with the Survey Research Center's (University of Michigan) index of consumer attitudes included as an independent variable, worked much better and was an improvement over the results obtained by an equation which substituted an index of buying plans for the Center's index of attitudes.[10]

What then is the forecasting strategy for analysts who try to anticipate those short-range fluctuations that arise from the complex of factors not closely associated with changes in the economy?

The first requirement is to follow as closely as possible what is happening to sales at the consumer level. This intensive, continuing examination of current developments can help to develop a sixth sense about what seems to be shaping up in the market.

In some respects, the information network for the automobile market is well designed to facilitate this process. Sales data are available for each ten-day period (See chart 10) about four working days after the end of the period (major companies have intramural procedures for following their own sales data even more closely). By putting these ten-day sales data on some kind of seasonally adjusted basis, the problem of closely following current development

[8] Eva Mueller, "Ten Years of Consumer Attitudes Surveys: Their Forecasting Record," *Journal of American Statistical Association* (December 1963), pp. 899–917.

[9] The equation was $D_A = -0.01Y_{-1} + 15.91$.

[10] The two equations that Professoor Mueller derived were

(1) $D_A = 0.03Y_{-1} + 0.30A - 23.23$
$$R^2 = 0.70$$

(2) $D_A = -0.05Y_{-1} + 0.09B_c + 16.68$
$$R^2 = 0.23$$

In these equations D_A is automobile sales, Y_{-1} is disposable personal income six months prior to the sales period. A is the Survey Research Center's index of anticipations, and B_c is an index of intensions to buy autos as derived from the surveys.

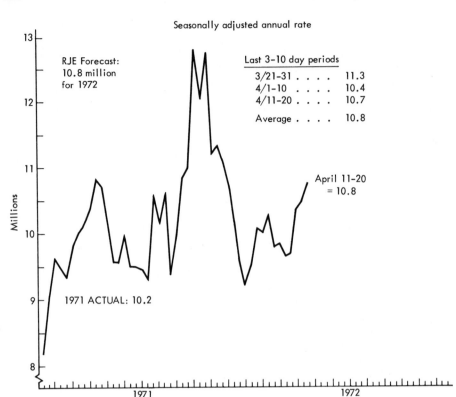

Seasonally adjusted annual rate

RJE Forecast:
10.8 million
for 1972

Last 3–10 day periods

3/21-31	11.3
4/1-10	10.4
4/11-20	10.7
Average	10.8

April 11–20
= 10.8

1971 ACTUAL: 10.2

This chart has been updated almost one year after the chapter was written in order to give the reader as current information as possible. All other charts, tables, and results are based on the data that were availble as of July 1971.

Source: Automotive Manufacturer's Association, seasonally adjusted by Lionel D. Edie & Co.

Chart 10   Auto Sales (3–10 Day Mvg. Avg.)

would seem to be solved. Unfortunately, some formidable problems arise at this point. The seasonal pattern for automobile sales reflects not only the orthodox forces producing an intrayear pattern, but also such things as the timing of model introductions or sales contests by one or more companies. Even so, analysts put much effort into producing a clean seasonally adjusted sales figure for the ten-day data.

The first step then, in the process of putting the "moistened finger in the air" is to determine accurately the realistic level of car sales at the time of the forecast. Variables

such as incoming new car orders, dealer trading practices, installment contract delinquencies, anticipated strike effects, sales contests, supply conditions including expected new model price changes all affect the forecaster's short term outlook. Given these *current conditions*, how many cars are customers taking off the dealer's lot? This involves using the industry daily sales rate for the month (or even for the latest ten-day period) and adjusting it for the normal seasonal factor to arrive at a seasonally adjusted *annual* rate of sales. A good deal of caution and judgment must be exercised here—especially during certain months of the year when these short run factors have a significant influence on the available statistics.

The month of September has the highest variation—influenced by new model introductions and year-end sales contest windups. Also, the month of February seems to be joining the high variation category.

After agreement is reached on the current strength of the demand for cars, attention should then be directed to the changing pattern of used car prices. There is evidence that used car values tend to be a lead indicator for new car sales, although there are often other variables that modify the relationship. The logic behind this observation is that the cost of the new car to the majority of customers is not only determined by the discounted price of the new vehicle, but also by the trade-in value of the vehicle that he is swapping through the dealer or through a private sale. Since it takes a while for a potential new car buyer to find out about the changing value of the car he has on hand, it seems probable that changes in resale value have a forward influence on the new car buying decision.[11]

In view of the importance of this used car price factor, attention is also placed by the analyst on the level of used car stocks. If stocks are high relative to sales, it suggests that used car prices may be vulnerable. Conversely, if used car stocks are low, there is not apt to be a sharp downward adjustment in used car prices.

Another important short-range forecasting tool used in the automobile industry

---

[11] The complexities of the market response reflect in part supply factors. Sales may not respond to an improvement in business conditions if earlier stocks were reduced sharply and cars are not then available to meet rising demand.

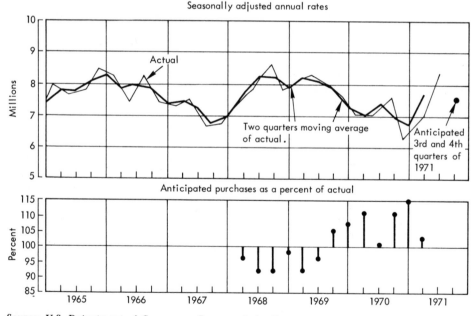

Chart 11   Actual Household Purchases of New Cars

Source: U.S. Department of Commerce, Bureau of the Census.

is the indications of plans to buy as measured through the results of the surveys made by the Survey Research Center at the University of Michigan, the Quarterly Buying-Intentions Survey made by the Bureau of Census and the Conference Board, and the more frequent "weekly buying-plans with confidence" available through Sindlinger and Company. These surveys of what consumers plan to do can be especially helpful during periods when supply shortages interrupt the accuracy of the actual marketplace measurement. The ability of such consumer surveys to *forecast* still remains to be proven (see chart 11 on anticipated purchases as a percent of actual). The consumer seems to underpredict his purchases during economy expansion and overpredict during contraction. It may be that the same forces that cause change in current sales also cause a proportional change in buying plans.[12]

Changes in consumer confidence (as distinct from plans to buy) have also been used as a short range forecasting tool. The results, using the Survey Research Center's index of consumer sentiment, are not yet conclusive. Burch and Stekler have found that "while the sentiment index does have some forecasting value, the results are decidedly mixed."[13] They concluded that while the index provided forecasts of every major turning point in durable goods consumption, it also indicated a number of *false* turning points. On the other hand, Saul Hyman concluded that "changes in consumer sentiment—if properly filtered—do improve the forecasting accuracy of a stock-adjustment model of automobile expenditures. It is apparently possible to forecast ahead at least one quarter (and perhaps further investiga-

tion will suggest still longer) on the basis of the current quarter's sentiment index."[14]

3. Other Factors

One of the dynamic factors the short-term forecaster must consider at model changeover time is the *new model stimulus* factor. In years when a high proportion of the industry has both dramatic and highly acceptable product styling changes, this factor has important forward-volume implications (for example, 1955). On the other hand, when the model styling changes are less pronounced, this factor tends to dampen sales for the upcoming model year. In view of the importance of this influence, a major car manufacturer has been making introduction-day studies of its own and competitive products over the past twelve years. These surveys are conducted on introduction day and the results are available to management by the early part of the week that follows the new car announcement. Such studies conducted on a comparable basis year after year also provide a rough index of the relative level of satisfaction with the manufacturer's products in themselves and as compared with competition.

Another area that is given attention by the short-range forecaster is trends in fleet purchasing, leasing, and government sales. In 1970 such sales on an annual basis amount to about 13.5 percent of the year's total. This is more than double the level of ten years ago. However, during certain seasons of the year, these sales account for nearly two out of ten cars sold. Often these purchases are influenced by forces that are not parallel to those influencing the individual customer.

A final consideration of the short-term

[12] Saul H. Hymans, "Consumer Durable Spending: Exploration and Prediction," in *Brookings Papers on Economic Activity*, 2, 1970, Washington, D.C., p. 195.

[13] S. W. Burch and H. O. Stekler, "The Forecasting Accuracy of Consumer Attitude Data," *Journal of the American Statistical Association* (December, 1969), p. 1233.

[14]Saul H. Hymans, "Consumer Durable Spending: Exploration and Prediction," *Brookings Papers on Economic Activity*, 2, 1970, p. 195.

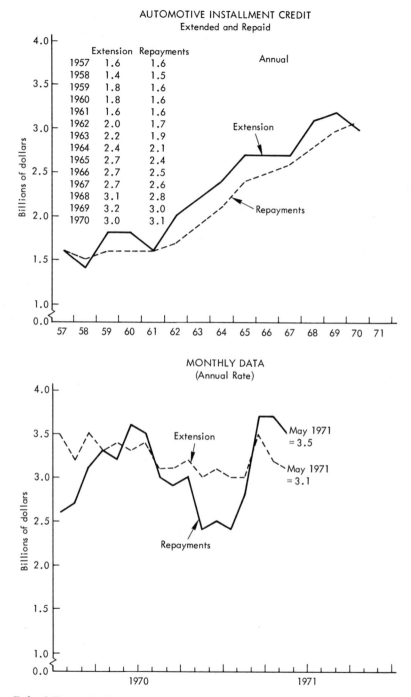

AUTOMOTIVE INSTALLMENT CREDIT
Extended and Repaid

	Extension	Repayments
1957	1.6	1.6
1958	1.4	1.5
1959	1.8	1.6
1960	1.8	1.6
1961	1.6	1.6
1962	2.0	1.7
1963	2.2	1.9
1964	2.4	2.1
1965	2.7	2.4
1966	2.7	2.5
1967	2.7	2.6
1968	3.1	2.8
1969	3.2	3.0
1970	3.0	3.1

Annual

Extension

Repayments

MONTHLY DATA
(Annual Rate)

Extension

May 1971
= 3.5

May 1971
= 3.1

Repayments

Source: Federal Reserve Bulletin, *Federal Reserve System.*

Chart 12

439

forecaster is the changing pattern of cash and credit sales. The easing of credit terms often brings on sales that cannot be sustained when the credit terms level off. For example, an easing of credit in 1955 resulted in a condition which prevented sales from being maintained after the terms stabilized. Furthermore, during periods when extensions of credit have consistently been ahead of repayments, there is a certain vulnerability to other forces. This results in extensions dropping sharply in the near term and often crossing the repayment line. Conversely, a period of months where repayments exceeded extensions tends to set the stage for future recovery. Chart 12 illustrates this pattern during both the recession of 1970 and the weakness of late 1967.

METHODOLOGY BEHIND THE AUTOMOTIVE FORECAST

It may be useful to say a few words about analytical methodology. The strength of the automobile market depends on complex and numerous forces, ranging from business conditions in general to the styling of a specific car. Assembling information on these diverse influences occupies a good deal of the time, resources and man-hours available for market analysis and forecasting. But, even when this information is assembled, there still remains a major analytical problem: How does one add it all up to derive a forecast of automobile sales within the short- and long-term planning horizons? How does one weight the numerous pieces of statistical evidence? Methodology here can range from the intuitive, judgmental evaluation of the facts to a statistical demand function or econometric model of the automobile market, or a combination of the two.

One of the early statistical models of the automobile market was developed by Charles F. Roos and Victor von Szeliski in 1937. In this remarkable pioneering study

the authors developed demand functions with such independent variables as supernumerary income (total income minus necessitous living expenses), prices, and car stocks relative to a measure of optimum stocks. More recently work has been done by many other scholars, e.g., Atkinson, Chow, Dyckman, Suits, and Hymans.[15]

In common with all other present-day forecasting tools, statistical demand functions have their limitations. If a model can be built which is complex enough to describe completely the demand for automobiles, it is certain to contain explanatory variables which are themselves as difficult to forecast as auto sales. On the other hand, if a model is used which ignores many of these difficult-to-forecast variables, its projections might not be accurate enough for practical use.

Despite these limitations, analytical models possess the advantages of consistency and lack of emotion. The statistical method has some persuasive analytical advantages. Quantitative estimates are derived by rigorous analysis of the importance, in terms of coefficients, of the various factors included in the analysis, and the extent to which the coefficients have been statistically significant in the past can be measured. Moreover, the

[15] Cf. Jay Atkinson, "The Demand for Durable Goods," *Survey of Current Business* (June 1950), pp. 5–10; Thomas R. Dyckman, "An Investigation Into the 1955 Automobile Sales Year" (University of Michigan Graduate School of Business Administration, Ph.D. Thesis, 1961); Gregory C. Chow, *Demand for Automobiles in the United States: A Study in Consumer Durables* (Amsterdam: North-Holland Publishing Company: 1957), and his "Statistical Demand Functions for Automobiles and Their Use For Forecasting," in *The Demand for Durable Goods*, ed. Arnold C. Harberger (Chicago: University of Chicago Press, 1960), pp. 149–78; Daniel B. Suits, "The Demand for New Automobiles in the United States, 1929–1956," *Review of Economics and Statistics* (August 1958), pp. 273–80, and his "Exploring Alternative Formulations of Automobile Demand," *Review of Economics and Statistics* (February 1961), pp. 66–69; Hymans, *ibid.*, p. 195.

amount of basic statistical information available is growing rapidly, and the computer has enormously expanded our ability to process large quantities of complicated information. Analysts do use considerable judgment —in deciding which variables are important, what values variables exogenous to the model should assume, and whether the model forecasts are reasonable in the light of other economic and noneconomic variables not explicitly included in the model. But these judgments are for the most part based on experience and scientific study, and are subject to experimental validation.

We present below a sample quarterly regression model designed to forecast the demand for automobiles, will compare this model with other models and will present tests of the model's predictive power. Finally, we will briefly describe a quarterly forecasting model of the economy and use this model to make predictions of automobile sales for the next six years.

The Model: Retail Sales

The regression model explains movements in automobile retail sales by changes in real income, consumer liquidity, the unemployment rate, a dummy variable to account for auto strikes, and lagged automobile retail sales.[16]

Alternative Variables Tested

In order to select the best variables,

[16] All the variables are transformed to the first difference of their natural logarithm except for the unemployment rate which is first differenced only. This transformation has the effect of reducing serial dependence in the error terms and multicollinearity among the independent variables. Real income is measured by GNP in 1958 dollars. Consumer liquidity is measured by real cash balances which are set equal to currency plus demand and time deposits less large CDs deflated by the GNP implicit price deflator.

we tested real disposable income in place of real GNP and a relative price variable, (measured by the ratio of the price deflator for consumer durable expenditures on autos and parts to the GNP implicit price deflator). Neither of these improved the relationship—real disposable income did not explain as much of the variation in actual automobile sales as did real GNP.[17] Our relative price variable was found to be either insignificant or to enter the equation with the wrong sign.[18]

Lagged values for up to as many as seven quarters of each of the independent variables were introduced into the regression model. The final equation was chosen primarily on the basis of goodness of fit, measured by the adjusted R *square* (over the period 1955 I to 1970 III).

The final regression equation selected is:

$$\Delta \ln AUTOSALES = 0.056$$
$$+ \underset{(4.0)}{2.9 \Delta_0^2 \ln RGNP} - \underset{(6.2)}{2.4 \Delta_2^6 \ln RGNP}$$
$$+ \underset{(1.7)}{1.1 \Delta \ln RGNP_{-6}}$$
$$+ \underset{(1.6)}{1.8 \Delta (\Delta \ln M15 / PGNP)}$$
$$- \underset{(5.7)}{0.061 \Delta_0^4 U} - \underset{(4.8)}{0.0096 D37}$$
$$- \underset{(4.5)}{0.36 \Delta \ln AUTOSALES_{-1}}$$
$$\bar{R}^2 = 0.74$$

Standard error of estimate = .051
Durbin-Watson statistic = 2.1
Regression period: 1955 I–1971 II

where

$AUTOSALES$ = Seasonally adjusted automobile retail sales, domestic plus imports.

[17] This result may indicate that real GNP contains a larger transitory income component than does real disposable income.
[18] This result may be explained by the fact that the ratio used is not an adequate measure of relative price. A better measure of relative price might be more difficult to predict than automobile retail sales itself.

$RGNP$ = Gross national product, 1958 dollars.

$M15$ = Currency plus demand and time deposits less large denomination certificates of deposit.

$PGNP$ = Implicit price deflator, gross national product, 1958 = 100.

U = Unemployment, percentage of the labor force.

$D37$ = Strike dummy to account for the 1964 and 1970 General Motors strikes and the 1967 Ford strike. Equals the change in the index of aggregate weekly man-hours of workers in the transportation industry (SIC 37) for 1964 IV; 1965 I; 1968 I, III; 1970 IV; 1971 I, IV; zero elsewhere.

$\Delta_N^M X$ = change in X from $t - N$ to $t - M$.

t = statistics are shown in parenthesis underneath each coefficient and $\bar{R}^2$ is adjusted for degrees of freedom.

This equation indicates that an increase in real income leads to an immediate increase in automobile sales but that this initial effect wears off after two quarters. The negative coefficients of lagged real income and lagged retail sales are part of what we call the *negative stock adjustment,* an adjustment which occurs *after* an initial increase in income and sales has caused an increase in the stock of autos and a narrowing of the gap between desired and actual stock. The real balance term (deflated money supply plus net time deposits), a generalized indication of financial influence, exerts a short-term positive influence. The form of acceleration indicates that changes in the rate of growth of real cash balances is the determining influence in auto sales.[19] Changes in unemployment exert a strong negative influence on auto sales: increasing unemployment lowers the number of potential auto buyers and engenders uncertainty and lack of confidence in those still employed.

Comparisons With Other Models

Our use of logarithmic first differences, while reducing multicollinearity and serial dependence, also increases the amount of noise we find in the dependent variable especially *in a quarterly model.* At first glance, our adjusted R *squares* of 0.74 for automobile retail sales seems low, in comparison to other models.

For example, Dyckman is able to explain 94 percent of the logarithmic first difference of *yearly* new car sales, measured by new car registrations as reported by R. L. Polk & Company. Suits explains 93 percent of annual changes in new auto retail sales.[20] But if we convert our results to compatible

---

[19] The form of some of the independent variables was determined experimentally. Real cash balances appears in the equation as an acceleration, resulting from a former version of the model which contained both $\Delta\ln(M15/PGNP)$ and $\Delta\ln(M15/PGNP)_{-1}$ with coefficients which were of approximately equal magnitude and opposite in sign. The variables were subtracted and an acceleration was used. In a similiar manner, $\Delta_0^2\ln RGNP$, $\Delta_2^6\ln RGNP$, and $\Delta_0^4 U$ resulted from the sum of variables with equal coefficients of the same sign.

[20] Thomas R. Dyckman, "An Aggregate Demand Model for Automobiles," *Journal of Business* (July 1965), pp. 252–66; Suits (Aug. 1958), *loc cit.*

annual terms (by calculating the estimated annual logarithmic first differences from the quarterly estimates), we are able to explain 99 percent of the variation in the annual logarithmic first difference of retail sales.

Test of Predictive Power

The explanatory power of a regression equation may be acceptable by conventional standards (for example high R *square*), but conventional statistics are no guarantee of forecasting ability, a weakness of many early efforts.

To test its accuracy as a forecasting tool, an equation may be evaluated by ex- amining the dependent variable when only an initial set of values is known for it. Values for the equation's independent variables are assumed known. In each quarter after the simulation starts, the model is given no information about the previous quarter's value of the dependent variable; the only information is the previous quarter's predic- tion. Simulations conducted in this manner are called dynamic simulations. By contrast, static simulations are produced by using acual values of all determining variables, in- cluding the lagged dependent variable.

In testing a model's forecasting accu- racy, it is also necessary to consider the inter- val over which a simulation is performed. An ex post dynamic simulation is confined

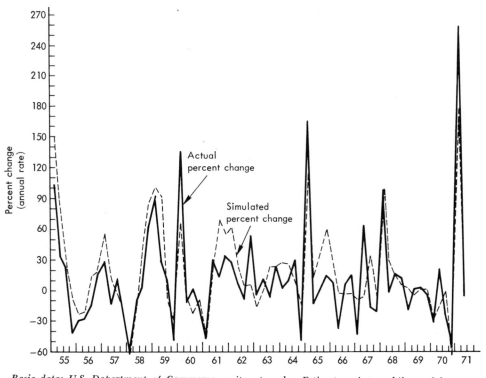

Basic data: *U.S. Department of Commerce, unit auto sales. Estimates: Automobile model.*

Chart 13   Ex Post Dynamic Simulation, Automobile Retail Sales—Percent Change from Previous Quarter (Domestics and Imports)

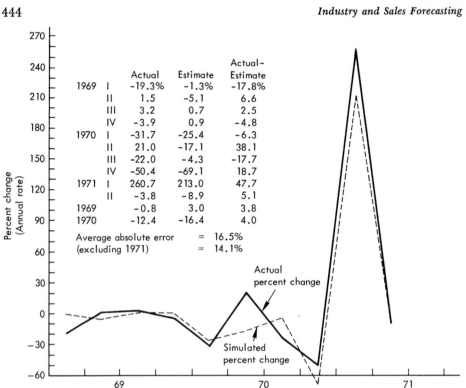

		Actual	Estimate	Actual–Estimate
1969	I	-19.3%	-1.3%	-17.8%
	II	1.5	-5.1	6.6
	III	3.2	0.7	2.5
	IV	-3.9	0.9	-4.8
1970	I	-31.7	-25.4	-6.3
	II	21.0	-17.1	38.1
	III	-22.0	-4.3	-17.7
	IV	-50.4	-69.1	18.7
1971	I	260.7	213.0	47.7
	II	-3.8	-8.9	5.1
1969		-0.8	3.0	3.8
1970		-12.4	-16.4	4.0

Average absolute error = 16.5%
(excluding 1971) = 14.1%

Actual percent change

Simulated percent change

Source: Basic Data: U.S. Department of Commerce, unit auto sales. Estimates: Automobile model (equation reestimated through 68 IV).

Chart 14   Ex Ante Dynamic Simulation, Automobile Retail Sales, Percent Change from Previous Quarter (Domestic and Imports).

to the sample period of the regression; an ex ante simulation extends projections beyond the sample period. Thus, an ex ante dynamic simulation in which actual values of only the independent variables are used is most useful for evaluating the forecasting performance of a particular regression equation.

Chart 13 shows the actual series and ex post dynamic simulation over the sample period for quarterly percent changes (annual rate) for retail auto sales. The equation tracks reasonably well. It does not drift very far from the actual series even when simulated dynamically over a sixteen-year period.

The equation was refitted over the sample period (1955 I to 1968 IV) and extra-polated dynamically beyond the sample period for ten quarters. Chart 14 shows actual and simulated quarterly percent changes (annual rate) for that period. The results are encouraging: the equation picks up the sideways movements in the change in automobile sales during 1969 and the downward movements during 1970, although it called the 1970 II peak one quarter late.

The projected levels from this ex ante dynamic run are pictured in chart 15. The average absolute error is 0.5 million cars (annual rate) for the ten-quarter simulation. The equation missed the 1971 first- and second-quarter levels by over one million cars (annual rate), although it predicted the change in auto sales quite well (1971 I actual

TABLE 4. RCA ECONOMIC FORECASTING MODEL

Gross National Product

$$\Delta GNP = 2.0 + \underset{(5.1)}{2.1}\,\Delta M1 + \underset{(3.2)}{1.8}\,\Delta M1_{-2} + \underset{(1.1)}{0.20}\,\Delta EXPFH + \underset{(1.2)}{0.23}\,\Delta EXPFH_{-1}$$
$$+ \underset{(5.7)}{0.70}\,D37 + \underset{(4.8)}{0.41}\,D33 + \underset{(3.5)}{0.36}\,\Delta GNP_{-1} - \underset{(2.0)}{0.19}\,\Delta GNP_{-2}$$

$$\bar{R}^2 = 0.76$$

Standard error of estimate = 3.4

Durbin-Watson statistic = 1.9

Regression period = 1953 I–1971 I

GNP Implicit Price Deflator

$$\Delta \ln PGNP = 1.0 \underset{(3.8)}{\sum_{i=1}^{7}} \underset{(1.9)}{0.22}(1{-}0.22)^{i-1} \Delta \ln PGNP_{-i} + \underset{(1.2)}{0.028}\,\Delta \ln GNP$$
$$+ \underset{(2.7)}{0.21}\,\Delta \ln RGNPP - \underset{(4.4)}{0.035} \ln\!\left(\frac{RGNPP}{RGNP}\right)_{-1} + \underset{(5.2)}{1.6}\,FPGNP$$

$$\bar{R}^2 = 0.75$$

Standard error of estimate = 0.0020

Durbin-Watson statistic = 2.0

Regression period = 1953 III–1971 II

Gross National Product-1958 $

$$RGNP = 100 * \frac{GNP}{PGNP}$$

Unemployment Rate

$$\Delta U = -0.011 + \underset{(8.0)}{0.21}\,\Delta \ln\!\left(\frac{RGNPP}{RGNP}\right) + \underset{(3.2)}{12.0}\,\Delta \ln\!\left(\frac{RGNPP}{RGNP}\right)_{-1} + \underset{(2.0)}{0.19}\,\Delta U_{-1} - \underset{(1.9)}{0.11}\,\Delta U_{-3}$$

$$\bar{R}^2 = 0.78$$

Standard error of estimate = 0.19

Durbin-Watson statistic = 2.0

Regression period = 1954 IV–1971 I

$D33$ = Variable to account for the 1959 steel strike and for steel inventory movements during years of contract negotiations; equals the change in the index of aggregate weekly man-hours of workers in tne primary metals industry (SIC 33) for strike and contract negotiation related quarters, zero elsewhere.

$D37$ = Variable to account for 1964 General Motors strike, 1967 Ford strike, and 1970 GM strike, equals the change in the index of aggregate weekly man-hours of workers in the transportation industry (SIC 37) for strike related quarters, zero elsewhere.

$EXPFH$ = Expenditures of federal government, high employment budgest, $ billions.

$FPGNP$ = Variable to account for seasonal movements in the rate of inflation.

GNP = Gross national product, $ billions.

$M1$ = Currency plus demand deposits, commercial banks, $ billions.

$PGNP$ = GNP implicit price deflator, 1958 = 100.

$RGNP$ = Gross national product, 1959 $, $ billions.

$RGNPP$ = Council of Economic Advisors potential full employment GNP, 1958 $, $ billions.

U = Unemployment rate, percentage of labor force.

change at an annual rate of 2.7 million versus predicted 2.1; 1971 II actual change of −0.1 million compared to the predicted −0.2 million). Also, the equation did well on the annual projections, missing 1969 by 0.3 million cars and 1970 by only 0.1 million. The superior performance of the model in predicting changes is not surprising since the equation is estimated in percent change form.

Forecasts

The equation may now be used to generate forecasts for automobile retail sales over both the short (through 1972 IV) and the long range (through 1976).

Forecast values for GNP in 1958 dollars, for the GNP implicit price deflator, and for the rate of unemployment are generated using an econometric model currently being used at RCA. The model is based largely on monetarist principles but includes fiscal influences. It is an "outside-in" model in that it starts with an equation for the whole of GNP as affected by exogenous monetary and fiscal policies and then works in to the components of GNP such as consumption.

The equation for GNP is an adaptation of the Andersen-Jordan model[21] relating dollar changes in GNP to dollar change in money stock (demand deposits plus currency) and dollar changes in federal high employment budget expenditures. The GNP price deflator is then predicted using an equation which relates price changes to the expected inflation rate, to the change in GNP, to the change in potential real GNP, to the gap between potential and actual real GNP, and to a variable which reflects seasonal movements in the rate of inflation. The rate of unemployment is then determined by a version of Okun's law which relates changes in unemployment to changes in the gap between potential and real GNP. The equations are summarized in table 4.[22]

Forecast Assumptions

The model forecasts are being made

[21] Leonall C. Andersen and Keith M. Carlson, "A Monetarist Model for Economic Stabilization," *Review, Federal Reserve Bank of St. Louis* (April 1970), pp. 7–25.

[22] Arthur Okun, "Potential GNP: Its Measurement and Significance," American Statistical Association, *1962 Proceedings of the Business and Economic Statistics Section*.

at a time when even more than usual uncertainty surrounds government economic policy actions. This uncertainty provides an opportunity to illustrate how a model's forecasts may be adjusted to reflect events not included in the historical sample period. The United States is in the midst of a 90-day wage-price freeze and so far no decision has been made concerning what government actions will be when the freeze is lifted. Administration comments indicate that some sort of incomes policy is likely, one that falls somewhere between jawboning and a continued freeze, most likely a wage-price review board similar in scope to the construction review board set up during 1971. Such a review board would set guidelines for both wages and prices and would have mandatory authority for review and enforcement. A five percent upper limit for wage increases which allows for basic productivity gains would appear to be realistic. Price increases might be limited to the two to three percent level, which should be governed by productivity considerations for the individual industry under review.

Even if circumstances are better and the forecaster is fully confident of his knowledge of future government actions, he may not be as confident of their effect. The case of a formal incomes policy during peacetime is a good example. A wage-price review board (or something similar) could have a considerable effect on the future rate of inflation, a moderate effect, or even no effect at all.

A great deal of its effect depends upon the way the incomes policy affects the anticipation in the public's mind of future inflation: so-called inflationary expectations. For example, if labor and management expect the rate of inflation to remain high in the future, these inflationary expectations will be built into contracts in the form of inflation escalators or higher rates of wage increases. If investors expect inflation to continue, they will demand an inflation premium for the money they lend in the form

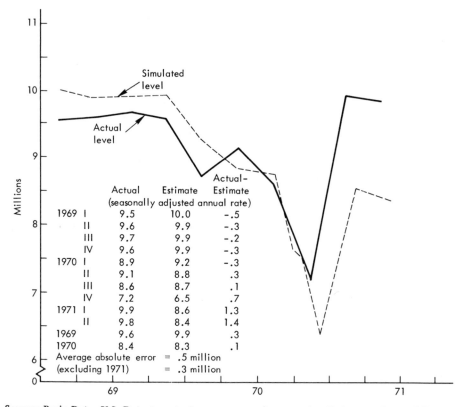

The table within the chart:

	Actual	Estimate	Actual– Estimate
	(seasonally adjusted annual rate)		
1969 I	9.5	10.0	–.5
II	9.6	9.9	–.3
III	9.7	9.9	–.2
IV	9.6	9.9	–.3
1970 I	8.9	9.2	–.3
II	9.1	8.8	.3
III	8.6	8.7	.1
IV	7.2	6.5	.7
1971 I	9.9	8.6	1.3
II	9.8	8.4	1.4
1969	9.6	9.9	.3
1970	8.4	8.3	.1
Average absolute error	= .5 million		
(excluding 1971)	= .3 million		

Source: Basic Data: U.S. Department of commerce, unit auto sales. Estimates: Automobile model (equation reestimated through 68 IV).

Chart 15   Ex Ante Dynamic Simulation, Automobile Retail Sales (Domestics and Imports)

of higher interest rates. So the anticipation of high future inflation in itself contributes to continued price increases.

The model presented above readily lends itself to analysis of the change in inflationary expectations brought about by future federal government policy actions. Inflationary expectations are measured by a weighted sum of past rates of inflation, with the largest weight placed on the most recent price change and the weights declining exponentially over seven quarters.

If the incomes policy initiated by the federal government is effective in moderating the expectation of continued future inflation, the weight placed on past price changes by the public should be reduced; if there is no change in inflationary expectations, the weight will remain as estimated in the regression equation.

This is a question which can only be answered *after* the event but there is nothing to stop the forecaster from speculating about the future and incorporating this speculation into the model forecasts! And the computer certainly aids in this task.

The model is solved under three different assumptions about government policy actions and the way these actions affect inflationary expectations.

The "optimistic" solution assumes that the Federal Reserve is expansive in its

TABLE 5.   ASSUMPTIONS

	Federal Government High Employment Expenditures $ Billions	Optimistic		Most Likely		Pessimistic	
		Money Supply	Money Supply Plus Net Time Deposits	Money Supply	Money Supply Plus Net Time Deposits	Money Supply	Money Supply Plus Net Time Deposits
		Quarterly Percent Change Annual Rate					
1971–I[a]	210.4	6.7%	15.6%	6.7%	15.6%	6.7%	15.6%
II[a]	217.0	12.1	16.1	12.1	16.1	12.1	16.1
III	222.6	7.0	11.0	7.0	11.0	7.0	11.0
IV	228.6	6.5	9.0	6.5	9.0	6.5	9.0
1972–I	234.9	8.0	10.0	6.0	8.0	4.0	6.0
II	239.5	8.0	10.0	6.0	8.0	4.0	6.0
III	244.2	8.0	10.0	6.0	8.0	4.0	6.0
IV	248.9	8.0	10.0	6.0	8.0	4.0	6.0
1973–I	253.7	8.0	10.0	6.0	8.0	4.0	6.0
II	258.7	8.0	10.0	6.0	8.0	4.0	6.0
		Annual Percent Change					
1970	203.5	4.1%	4.2%	4.1%	4.2%	4.1%	4.2%
1971	219.7	7.0	12.4	7.0	12.4	7.0	12.4
1972	241.9	7.8	10.3	6.6	9.0	5.3	7.8
1973	261.2	8.0	10.0	6.0	8.0	4.0	6.0
1974	282.1	6.7	8.7	6.0	8.0	5.3	7.3
1975	304.7	6.0	8.0	6.0	8.0	6.0	8.0
1976	329.1	6.0	8.0	6.0	8.0	6.0	8.0

Basic Data: Federal Reserve Bank of St. Louis and Federal Reserve Board.
NOTE: The high employment budget expenditures are assumed the same in all three projection sets.
[a] Actual.

policy actions (eight percent quarterly increases at an annual rate in the money supply from 1972 I forward, moderating to six percent increases starting in 1974 I) and that the administration's incomes policy is quite effective, reducing the weight placed on past price changes by one-half starting in 1971 IV. This change in the weight is projected to last throughout 1973, after which it is reasonable to assume that expectations will be formed as they had been in the past.

The "most likely" set of assumptions combines six percent quarterly increases in the money supply from 1972 I forward with a reduction by one-fourth during 1971 IV in the weight placed on past price changes. As in the "optimistic" solution, the forming of price expectations reverts to normal by 1974.

The "pessimistic" solution assumes that the Federal Reserve is moderately restrictive (four percent quarterly increases in the money supply from 1972 I forward, graduating to six percent increases starting in 1974 I) and that the administration's incomes policy is completely ineffective in moderating price expectations.

The control solution has been labeled "most likely" because it seems reasonable to expect that an incomes policy will have at least some effect in moderating inflationary expectations. It also seems reasonable to assume the fear of renewing inflation's acceleration will keep the administration from being too expansive in its short-range policy

TABLE 6. GENERAL ECONOMIC PROJECTIONS

	Optimistic				Most Likely				Pessimistic			
	GNP $ Billions	GNP-58 % Change	Inflation[b] Rate	Unemployment Rate	GNP $ Billions	GNP-58 % Change	Inflation[b] Rate	Unemployment Rate	GNP $ Billions	GNP-58 % Change	Inflation[b] Rate	Unemployment Rate
1971-I[a]	$1020.8	7.9%	5.4%	5.9%	$1020.8	7.9%	5.4%	5.9%	$1020.8	7.9%	5.4%	5.9%
II[a]	1041.3	4.1	4.1	6.0	1041.3	4.1	4.1	6.0	1041.3	4.1	4.1	6.0
III	1059.4	2.4	4.6	6.0	1059.4	2.4	4.6	6.0	1059.4	2.4	4.6	6.0
IV	1090.9	9.0	3.2	5.8	1090.9	8.2	3.9	5.9	1090.9	7.5	4.6	5.9
1972-I	1119.5	8.2	2.5	5.5	1117.1	6.6	3.1	5.6	1114.8	5.0	3.9	5.7
II	1143.9	6.4	2.5	5.1	1138.4	4.6	3.1	5.4	1132.8	2.7	3.8	5.7
III	1168.9	5.7	3.2	4.9	1158.2	3.3	3.7	5.4	1147.5	0.9	4.4	6.0
IV	1195.1	6.1	3.1	4.8	1178.7	3.6	3.6	5.5	1162.3	1.0	4.2	6.3
1973-I	1222.1	7.3	1.9	4.6	1200.0	5.0	2.3	5.5	1177.8	2.4	3.0	6.5
II	1249.6	7.2	2.0	4.3	1221.6	5.0	2.3	5.4	1193.8	2.6	2.8	6.6
1970[a]	974.1	−0.6	5.5	5.0	974.1	−0.6	5.5	5.0	974.1	−0.6	5.5	5.0
1971	1053.1	3.0	5.0	5.9	1053.1	2.9	5.0	6.0	1053.1	2.9	5.1	6.0
1972	1156.8	6.6	3.1	5.1	1148.1	5.2	3.6	5.5	1139.3	3.9	4.2	5.9
1973	1263.7	6.6	2.5	4.2	1232.7	4.4	2.9	5.4	1201.9	2.0	3.5	6.7
1974	1369.0	5.3	2.9	3.7	1322.5	4.5	2.6	5.3	1276.8	3.6	2.5	6.9
1975	1466.9	3.4	3.6	4.0	1417.3	4.4	2.7	5.1	1368.6	5.3	1.8	6.5
1976	1570.0	3.0	3.9	4.3	1517.4	4.3	2.7	5.1	1465.8	5.7	1.4	5.9

Basic Data: U.S. Department of Commerce and U.S. Department of Labor.
Projections: RCA Economic Forecasting Model.
[a] Actual.
[b] Inflation rate is the percent change in tne GNP implicit price deflator. All quarterly percent changes are at an annual rate.

449

and, at the same time, the fear of continued high unemployment will keep policy actions from being too restrictive.

The short- and long-range assumptions are presented in table 5.

The model forecasts exemplify the great uncertainty that can exist about the future! For 1972, the numbers cover a wide gamut (see table 6), from an economy in which the rate of price advance exceeds the rate of real growth ("pessimistic" solution, 4.2 percent inflation, 3.9 percent real growth) to one in which real growth, for the first time in three years, outstrips the rate of inflation ("optimistic" solution, 3.1 percent inflation, 6.6 percent real growth). Under these diverse circumstances the rate of unemployment could range from the "pessimistic" 5.9 percent to the "optimistic" 5.1 percent.

The "optimistic" solution, with healthy growth in real GNP, with significantly declining unemployment, and with low inflation resulting in increasing real buying power, projects an extremely healthy increase in auto sales during 1972 (24 percent) to reach the 12.3 million level for the year. The relatively sluggish real growth, the flat unemployment rate, and the continued high (about 4 percent) inflation combine to give the "pessimistic" auto sales forecast of 10.3 million, only 4 percent above 1971 levels. The "most likely" prediction is 11.3 million, quite close to the judgmental forecast presented earlier (see chart 8).

Long-Range Outlook

The long-range model projections presented below fall somewhere between long-term *trend* forecasts and true *business cycle* forecasts. We have tried to project realistic government actions, expressed as smooth growth rates of exogenous policy variables (money supply and high employment budget expenditures). The smooth growth of these policy variables are trend projections; however, the changes in these growth rates over time and the way in which the variables interact in the model setting are cycle projections.

For example, we have assumed that the moderately restrictive money supply growth in the "pessimistic" solution is eased starting in 1974, as the unemployment rate reaches unacceptable levels (6.7 percent) during 1973, and as inflation shows definite signs of moderation (down to 3.5 percent by 1973). We have also assumed that monetary policy (very expansive by historical standards) in the "optimistic" solution tightens starting in 1974 as the rate of inflation remains in the 3 percent range during 1972–73 and as unemployment reaches the acceptable 4 percent during 1973.

These assumptions are realistic in that government *does* react to current economic conditions in making policy actions, but they are also trend projections in that "normal" growth rates move about considerably more than the smooth ones we have assumed.

The spread between the three forecast sets (table 6) widens through 1973 and then narrows as the policy assumptions narrow. The forecasts for nominal GNP range from $1,570 billion for the "optimistic" solution to $1,466 billion in the "pessimistic" run with our "most likely" forecast pegged at $1,517 billion. The major difference in these forecasts appears in the predicted mix between real and price growth. The projected compound annual growth from 1970 to 1976 for real GNP ranges from the "optimistic" 4.6 percent to the "pessimistic" 3.9 percent with price growth over the six-year period projected to vary between a compound annual rate of 3.5 percent ("optimistic") and 3.0 percent ("pessimistic").

In the "optimistic" solution, the rate of inflation stays above 2.5 percent during 1973–74 and is close to 4 percent and accelerating during 1975–76. The unemployment rate remains in the 4 percent range during that period.

By contrast, the "pessimistic" inflation rate falls to 1.4 percent by 1976 while the

TABLE 7.   **AUTOMOBILE SALES FORECASTS**

	Optimistic		Most Likely		Pessimistic	
	SAAR	Unadjusted	SAAR	Unadjusted	SAAR	Unadjusted
	(Millions)	*(000)*	*(Millions)*	*(000)*	*(Millions)*	*(000)*
1971–I[a]	9.911	2339	9.911	2339	9.911	2339
II[a]	9.817	2729	9.817	2729	9.817	2729
III	9.498	2201	9.498	2201	9.498	2201
IV	10.491	2662	10.384	2635	10.283	2609
1972–I	11.554	2727	11.110	2622	10.677	2520
II	12.138	3374	11.357	3157	10.604	2948
III	12.585	2917	11.352	2631	10.194	2363
IV	12.954	3287	11.237	2851	9.669	2453
1973–I	13.122	3097	11.032	2604	9.162	2162
II	13.813	3840	11.315	3145	9.126	2537
	Annual Levels	Annual % Change	Annual Levels	Annual % Change	Annual Levels	Annual % Change
	(Millions)		*(Millions)*		*(Millions)*	
1970	8.396	−12.4%	8.396	−12.4%	8.396	−12.4%
1971	9.931	18.3	9.904	18.0	9.879	17.7
1972	12.305	23.9	11.261	13.7	10.284	4.1
1973	13.984	13.7	11.342	0.7	9.052	−12.0
1974	14.718	5.2	11.882	4.8	9.390	3.7
1975	13.994	−4.9	12.251	3.1	10.512	12.0
1976	13.440	−4.0	12.584	2.7	11.595	10.3

Basic Data: U.S. Department of Commerce.
Projections: RCA Economic Forecasting model.
[a] Actual.

unemployment rate stays above 6.5 percent during 1973–75, only falling below 6 percent during 1976. The "most likely" solution projects unemployment to stay below 5.5 percent during 1973–76, falling to 5.1 percent by 1976. Inflation is projected to fall below 3 percent by 1973, but to remain level at 2.7 percent during 1975–76.

Auto Sale Forecasts

The "optimistic" solution projects auto sales to average 13.4 million cars for 1976 after declining from the 14.7 million peak in 1974 (see table 7 and chart 16). Auto sales increase from 1972 through 1974, the result of high growth rates in real GNP, sub-stantial decreases in the rate of unemployment, and continued strong real buying power. Auto sales start to decrease in 1975 as the slightly more restrictive monetary policy combined with more "normal" formation of inflationary expectations takes its toll in smaller rates of real growth and slight increases in the unemployment rate.

The "pessimistic" solution projects auto sales to average 11.6 million cars during 1976, after climbing from the 1973 trough of 9.1 million. Sales of automobiles increase only moderately during 1972 and decline during 1973 because of low real rates of growth and increases in the unemployment rate which result from the assumption of no easing of inflationary expectations and from the more restrictive policies assumed.

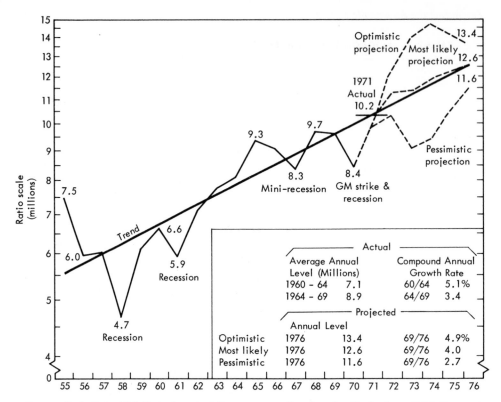

The chart contains the following data table:

	Actual		
	Average Annual Level (Millions)		Compound Annual Growth Rate
1960 – 64	7.1	60/64	5.1%
1964 – 69	8.9	64/69	3.4
	Projected		
	Annual Level		
Optimistic	1976	13.4	69/76 4.9%
Most likely	1976	12.6	69/76 4.0
Pessimistic	1976	11.6	69/76 2.7

Source: Basic Data: U.S. Department of Commerce, unit auto sales. Projections: RCA Economic Forecasting.

Chart 16   Long-Range Projection, Automobile Retail Sales.

Sales start to increase in 1974 as government policy actions ease slightly, and as the previously restrictive policy shows results in lowered inflation, allowing substantial gains in real GNP and decreases in the rate of unemployment.

The "most likely" solution projects 1976 auto sales to average 12.6 million after healthy increases during 1971 and 1972 and relatively sluggish growth during 1973–76. Real growth registers a healthy 5.2 percent increase during 1972 and then hovers in the 4.5 percent range for the next four years. Unemployment, after declining from the 6 percent average of 1971 to the 5.5 percent level of 1972, moves downward rather slowly over the next four years to 5.1 percent during 1976. Rates of growth of real buying

power remain in the 5 percent range during this period. In total, the forecast is an economy operating at slightly less than full employment in 1976 and a resulting auto sales forecast of 12.6 million differing only little from the standard-volume forecast of 12.2 million obtained earlier.

We have presented above a forecasting model for automobile retail sales and demonstrated its use in predicting auto sales. The range of forecasts presented is a good example of the forecaster's task. He must present his prediction of the future as accurately as possible, without losing sight of the uncertainty involved in making assumptions about future events. It is his job both to present what he considers the most likely set of future events and a set of contingencies around this forecast so that management may be as well prepared as possible to make planning decisions.

This brief discussion about methodology really can be reduced to a simple point. If major decisions are going to be influenced by the specific forecast, the important thing is to be as near on target as possible and to examine reasonable alternatives. The corporate front office is not apt to be impressed by the forecasting effort, no matter how formidably complex the analysis may be, if the answer turns out to be too wide of actual events. The forecasting procedures must, therefore, reflect an open-minded willingness to approach the problem from various directions. Few things are more effective in producing this open-minded attitude about the role of various forecasting tools than being held responsible for a continuing forecast. The ultimate test is a measurement against a *previously recorded unadjusted* track record.

CONCLUSION

This chapter opened with an examination of long-run forecasting problems, and it may be appropriate to close on a longer-run note. Most of the forecaster's tools and efforts will inevitably be concerned with short-run changes in the market. At the same time, in automobiles, as in any other industry, it is essential occasionally to look around and see if fundamental changes are shaping up that will cause a major displacement in the industry's share of consumer's income.

Economic growth, on which the industry counts for a continuing expansion of its market, does not move evenly across the economy. It occurs because new and better ways of using productive resources are uncovered. Old ways and old products inevitably become victims of progress rather than its beneficiaries. The automobile gave the economy an enormous forward thrust (and is still doing so), but this was not good news for the railroads or the harness-makers. There is no natural law that grants immunity from the dangers of this dynamic process to any industry, including the automotive industry. And while it is clear that the transportation needs of consumers are here to stay, the automotive industry must be on the alert that it continue to offer the most desirable method of moving people and goods. For example, recent discussion has centered on a world vehicle suitable for use in underdeveloped countries.

A part of forecasting is to look about occasionally to see if the industry is keeping ahead of the game of progress, or whether it is in danger of being clipped from a wholly unexpected direction by something newer and better. No major setback is expected in the decade ahead.

WILLIAM HOPPE

Economic Forecasting
in the Steel Industry

INTRODUCTION

A review of economic forecasting as it is carried out in a basic industry such as steel provides a number of insights into the breadth of vision required by a business economist. The level of understanding, not just of proper forecasting techniques, but also of the many developments shaping demand for the product both within and without the industry, make forecasting in steel a challenging occupation.

This chapter will describe the tools and techniques of forecasting in the steel industry as well as indicate some of the assumptions required in the forecasting procedure. In an effort to develop a feel for the framework within which this forecasting activity is practiced, the following points should be made:

1. When forecasting in the steel industry, the payoff is in determining steel shipments and raw steel production by the domestic industry. However, because of the sizable impact of imports on demand in recent years, it is dangerous and frequently misleading to relate domestic steel shipments or production with measures of economic activity in the United States. The best approach to forecasting steel activity involves measuring apparent steel consumption in the United States. That is:

Apparent steel consumption
= domestic steel shipments
− exports + imports

The most successful of forecasts determine total steel consumption (which can be related to the domestic economy) and then back out independently developed assumptions on prospects for imports and exports.

2. Particularly in short-term forecasts, changes in customers' inventories of steel mill products must be considered. The primary factors affecting inventory levels are changes in customers' business prospects and possible interruptions in steel supplies due to strikes. In the latter case, the buildup and reduction of strike-hedge inventories can have a powerful effect on monthly steel shipment patterns for five or six months on either side of the industry contract expiration date.

3. The dynamic aspects of the U.S. economy must be recognized. Not only do growth rates of various economic sectors vary from year to year, but rates of growth within these sectors also vary. Steel consumption varies considerably, depending on how well those economic sectors most affecting steel are doing. The prospects for each major steel-consuming market must be evaluated within a detailed economic framework.

4. Technological developments, interrelationships with competitive mate-

rials, and indirect trade of steel mill products (e.g., through expected exports and imports of finished manufactured items such as autos or machinery) all bear watching and evaluation in the development of a thoughtful steel forecast.

Before moving on, it is important to clarify one matter of terminology. The steel industry commonly uses two measures of activity: raw steel production and shipments of steel mill products. The two terms are not interchangeable.

Raw steel production measures the output of steelmaking furnaces (ingots or continuous cast strands) which rarely leave a steel plant in that form. On the other hand, *steel mill product shipments* measure the finished product of steel-rolling mills which convert raw steel into finished products (sheets, tin mill products, bars, and so on). The scrap loss between raw steel and finished products is such that shipments generally average about 70 percent of raw steel production. In the United States, most forecasts are expressed in terms of finished mill shipments. However, reference is frequently made to raw steel production and it is important to understand the relationship between these two ways of expressing industry activity.

STEEL INDUSTRY STATISTICAL DATA

The American Iron and Steel Institute (AISI) collects on a regular basis probably as fine a set of statistics on production, shipments by steel products, and shipments by steel markets as are available for any industry. Particular care is taken to cover the activities of minor as well as major producers in the industry, thus providing a virtually complete population count of all steel activity in the United States. The statistics are available to the public in the *Annual Statistical Report* published each year by the

AISI. Various weekly, monthly and quarterly reports are also prepared which provide a continuing flow of information useful and essential in economic and market forecasting in the steel industry. Many of these series are published regularly in general business as well as metalworking publications. Examples of these statistics are available in various charts throughout this chapter.

The Bureau of the Census provides the statistics measuring imports and exports of steel mill products as well as products fabricated from steel. Reports FT-410 and FT-135 provide this data monthly in considerable detail, although a number of organizations, including the AISI, publish summaries of the most meaningful data in this area. (Much of this appears in the previously mentioned *Annual Statistical Report* published by the AISI.)

Data on world trade of steel products between all countries provides valuable insight into the international crosscurrents in the movements of steel. The International Iron and Steel Institute publishes selected data quarterly, and the United Nations releases annual data in its publication entitled *World Trade in Steel.*

TIME RANGE OF FORECASTS

The period covered by economic forecasts is such that they may usually be regarded as being of short-, medium-, or long-term duration.

Short-Term Forecast

The purpose of the short-term forecast is to establish the framework for operations for the immediate quarter out to eighteen months. Short term sales plans, financial budgets, production schedules, raw material requirements, etc., are drawn up based on these forecasts which examine market trends, seasonal and cyclical factors, and the effect of steel imports, as well as estimated changes in customers' stocks. Typically, these forecasts break down total demand by market, product, and region.

Since accurate short-term forecasts are vital for planning purposes, they are revised and modified to reflect changing market conditions at least quarterly. Such quarterly revisions can more closely anticipate actual business developments than forecasts prepared annually or semiannually.

Medium-Term Forecast

The time range of the medium-term forecast is typically two to five years. Such forecasts are used primarily as the basis for product planning and facility modifications, but also serve in estimating manpower and other resource requirements. Factors affecting such forecasts include cyclical turns in long-term growth trends, the influence of technical innovation (both in steel and competitive materials), changes in international trade patterns for steel products, and regional growth patterns. Medium-term forecasts are generally revised and updated annually.

Long-Term Forecast

The long-term forecast covers the period from five to fifteen years hence. It can only outline the trend over the years ahead and is normally made for a range of three to five years around the target date. Included in it are upper and lower limits between which steel demand is expected to fall. Long-term forecasts serve as a basis for major facility investments as well as other broad issues such as company policy and structure. This forecast, generally developed in considerably less detail than either the short- or medium-term forecast, is updated as conditions require.

The accuracy of medium- and long-term forecasts is particularly important in a basic capital goods industry such as steel. It is not unusual for the installation of a new finishing mill to take three or more years from the signing of a purchase order to the rolling of the first product off the mill. With mills costing from around $30 million for a galvanized sheet line to over $100 million for a hot sheet mill, such facilities represent substantial investments. If, when the facility comes into production, the market demand fails to measure up to the forecast—or exceeds it greatly—the profit potential of the steel producer is obviously affected.

FORECASTING METHODS IN THE STEEL INDUSTRY

Currently there are six primary methods available to forecast steel demand. These six methods cover a broad spectrum of forecasting techniques, but each has its place in the forecaster's bag. The methods are:

1. *Global forecasts*, which correlate steel consumption with some general economic variable such as GNP or the FRB Index of Industrial Production. The future level of steel consumption can then be derived from a forecast of the macroeconomic measure chosen.

2. *Sector forecasts*, which are based on a more detailed analysis of activity within economic sectors. Correlations are developed between estimated steel consumption in each major steel-consuming industry (e.g., automotive, construction, machinery) and the activity implied for these industries within the various sectors of the economic forecast.

3. *Econometric models*, which develop forecasts of economic activity and then translate this activity into steel demand. Their greatest advantage is

their ability to quickly simulate the effects on steel of different economic environments.

4. *Time series analysis,* which is based on past trends of demand and is particularly useful in short-term forecasts.

5. *Trend analysis,* which is also based on past trends of demand. It has validity for some long-term forecasts and provides a check on forecasts derived by other methods.

6. *Field surveys and panel consensus,* which involve surveys of customers, panels of experts, or other appropriate sources by qualified personnel to determine the potential sales volume which the company may expect to obtain for particular products, processes, regions, etc., during the forecast period.

The choice of method depends not only on the purpose the forecast is intended to serve but also on the data available and the degree of reliability desired. Following are discussions of the merits of each.

Global Forecasts

As indicated in exhibit 1, a close relationship exists between steel consumption and the general activity of the economy. This relationship provides the basis for global forecasts. GNP is usually the best macroeconomic variable for use in this method but others, such as the FRB Index of Industrial Production, can also be used.

Once the measure of general economic activity has been selected, the relationship

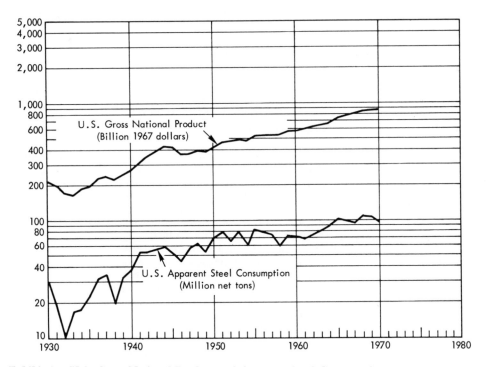

Exhibit 1   U.S. Gross National Product and Apparent Steel Consumption

between it and steel consumption over a period of twenty or more years can be determined through regression analysis. The projection of this relationship, based on the forecast of the single macroeconomic variable, provides the basis for the forecast.

The simplicity of this forecast method makes it ideal for studies by those outside the industry where a ball-park estimate of total steel consumption is desired. If we look again at exhibit 1, careful examination indicates that while a close relationship has existed between steel consumption and GNP, this relationship has not remained constant. In particular, note how steel consumption declined between 1955 and 1962, while growth in the years on either side of this period was quite steady. Ideally, projections should be made from several base periods representing the same stage of economic cycles to provide an idea of the likely range of steel consumption that might be consistent with a future level of the economy.

In the short term, the global method can also be used to provide an indication of the likely change in annual steel consumption. In this case, a formula relating the percentage annual change in steel consumption with the percentage change in industrial production has been used with success.

The global method is primarily used by forecasters in the industry as a check for forecasts developed by other means. Its greatest limitation is its simplicity, forecasting only a total demand figure and not by individual steel product or by consuming industry. The details of product and market demand are most important to steel producers, necessitating the use of more sophisticated forecasting techniques.

Sector Forecasts

Sector forecasts are based on the connection between steel consumption in every

TABLE 1.   PRIMARY FACTORS RELATING STEEL CONSUMPTION TO LEVELS OF ACTIVITY IN MAJOR STEEL-CONSUMING INDUSTRIES

Steel-Consuming Industry	Measure of Consuming Industry Activity (To Be Related to Economy)
Construction (except oil and gas)	New construction value put in place (billions of constant dollars)
Automotive	Domestic production of passenger cars and trucks (millions of units)
	Production of automotive replacement parts (FRB index)
Machinery	Production of nonelectrical, electrical, and farm machinery (composite of FRB indexes)
Railroads	Deliveries of new freight cars (thousands of units)
	Shipments of rails and accessories (thousands of net tons)
Oil and gas construction	Total oil well footage drilled (millions of feet)
	FPC-approved pipeline construction (contracts approved)
Containers	Metal can shipments (thousands of net tons)
	Shipments of barrels, drums, and pails (millions of units)
Appliances	Major appliance shipments (thousands of units)
Furniture	Production of office furniture, fixtures, and home furnishings (composite of FRB indexes)
Shipbuilding	Deliveries of large commercial and naval vessels (thousands of gross tons) and barges (contracts let)
Mining	Production of bituminous coal (millions of net tons)
Ordnance	Department of defense requirements (thousands of net tons)

sector of the economy, and the future rate of activity in these sectors. This method divides total steel demand into a number of major steel-consuming industries as indicated in table 1.

Based on the forecast levels of activity in the principal steel-consuming industries, future steel consumption in terms of product tons for the entire industry is calculated by multiplying the specific levels of consuming industry activity expected by estimated steel unit weights. For example, a million motor vehicles will require X million net tons of steel; 100 million feet of oil well drilling will require Y million net tons of steel; and 100 points of an index of machinery production will require Z million net tons of steel.[1] The sum of steel consumption for each industry, including exports, represents total steel consumption in product tons for the entire economy. Total consumption is then adjusted for imports and changes in steel inventories to determine shipments.

In broadest terms, activity levels in the consuming industries listed in table 1 are examined. A close examination of the table reveals the diversity of industries and economic factors which combine to create demand for steel in the United States.

Basic to the success of sector analysis is the allocation of steel shipments (1) by consuming industry and (2) by product within each consuming industry. Neither of these tasks is easy.

Allocation of Steel Shipments by Consuming Industry. As mentioned earlier, the AISI provides a reliable historical series on steel shipments by consuming market. However, in this data are such categories as ship-

---

[1] Steel unit weights in relation to consuming industry activity change considerably over a period of years as discussed later in the chapter (see the section on Changing Relationships Affecting Steel Forecasts). Most of these changes are gradual and can be anticipated by adjusting steel consumption factors to account for them.

ments to converters, steel service centers, forgings and bolts, nuts, rivets, and screws—categories which do not truly represent consuming industries. These are middlemen in the manufacturing process who, in turn, ship their steel to be made into automobiles, appliances, and other final manufactured products. Shipments to these middlemen must be reallocated to final consuming industries, AISI consuming industry statistics also have a sizable category of nonclassified shipments that must be reallocated.

Once steel shipments by consuming industry have been estimated for a number of years, correlation between economic data and measures of steel-consuming activity reveal a number of reasonably consistent relationships on which forecasts can be based. In all, it is a monumental task, but one which can be accomplished with the proper use of cross-checks and a knowledge of the materials usage patterns of the major steel-consuming industries.

Allocation of Steel Shipments by Product. The share of total steel shipments taken by each product varies in both the short and long term depending primarily on cyclical and secular factors affecting the different markets served by each product. Exhibit 2 indicates the effect of secular change. Sheets and strip, helped by autos and appliances, have enjoyed growth far outpacing other steel products. Rods and wire, while still important, have experienced a decline in share of the total market. Meanwhile, rails and accessories, one of the primary products of the steel industry in its infancy, now represents less than two percent of industry shipments and has been grouped with semifinished steels in exhibit 2.

With the relative strength of each product varying as it does, it is usually important that total demand for steel be translated into demand by product. This is done by analyzing AISI statistics on shipments to consuming industries by product. By studying year-to-year changes as well as those de-

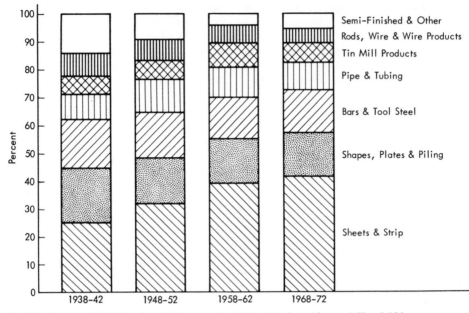

Exhibit 2   Steel Mill Product Shipments in U.S.—Product Share of Total Shipments

veloping over a long period of time, patterns do emerge. Analysis of these trends permits the breakdown of estimates of future steel shipments within each consuming industry into the various products which it consumes. When the future requirements for a specific product (for example, plates or sheets and strip) within each consuming industry are accumulated for all consuming industries, estimates of the total future market for a particular product are obtained.

When building up estimates of individual product requirements from analysis of consuming industries, it is desirable to compare the results with the historical trend of shipments for each product and its share of the total shipments of all steel products. If product shipment forecasts based on sector analysis indicate a marked variation from what is expected on the basis of either the historical growth trend for the product or its historical share of total shipments of all products, then the specific requirements within each consuming industry should be rechecked.

Econometric Models

Econometric model building, as applied in the steel industry, involves (1) taking a series of regression analyses for individual steel industries from the sector method and building a system of independent equations that are estimated simultaneously and (2) linking this system of sector equations to a general economic model as indicated in exhibit 3.

This model involves four components:

1. *Long-term GNP forecasting model,* which provides a general economic framework in terms of final demand and factor payments.

2. *Long-term industry forecasting model,* which converts the general economic framework into levels of activity for a large number of industry sectors.

3. *Steel forecasting model by consuming market,* which relates activity in these industry sectors (together with other economic inputs) to shipments (or con-

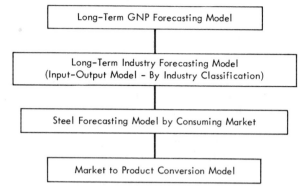

Steel forecasting model

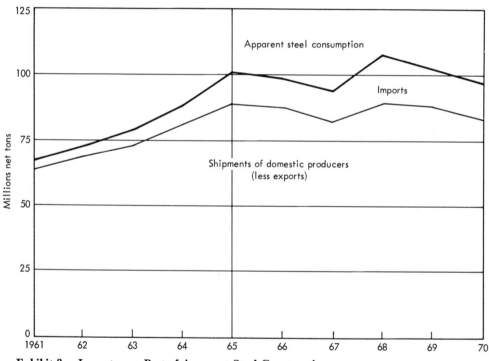

Exhibit 3   Imports as a Part of Apparent Steel Consumption

sumption) in specific consuming markets.

4. *Market-to-product conversion model,* which converts steel shipments (or consumption) by consuming market to shipments (or consumption) by product.

Such an econometric model supplements economic forecasting by other methods, providing a consistent framework within which the interrelationships of various economic factors affecting the steel industry can be studied. The steel industry lends itself to this type of analysis, having a wealth of reliable statistics by consuming market and products, and a reasonably consistent relationship between consuming markets and macroeconomic data.

The advantage of an econometric model is its ability to simulate steel demand under different general economic and industry assumptions in a way which would be impracticable, if not impossible, by the traditional forecasting methods described earlier. This simulation or "sensitivity analysis" provides management with a range of alternatives—steel forecasts under different "what if" assumptions within specified limits.

Time Series Analysis

Time series analysis finds its principal steel industry application in short-term forecasting, where forecasts of shipments for the next three to six months are desired. The purpose of time series analysis is to analyze a series of monthly shipments of individual consuming industries or products and determine when the decomposition of the series into its principal components or smoothing of the data in some fashion can be employed to provide reasonably reliable short-term forecasts. "Data crunching" techniques used by steel analysts include moving average, exponential smoothing, and Census Bureau methods such as X-11.

Short-term forecasts of shipments by such techniques are sometimes supplemented with regression analysis. In view of the importance of short-term forecasts of shipments in profit planning, budgeting, and market planning, the steel industry analyst has to use considerable variety and ingenuity in his choice of methods within the limitations of data availability, time budgets, and the accuracy required. If, in using sound methods, there are still good reasons to question the reliability of forecasts in certain cases, these reservations should be presented as part of the forecast.

Trend Analysis

Trend analysis has a long and respected history in long-range forecasting in the steel industry. A time series, embracing the historical behavior of an economic variable, such as shipments (by market or product) is inspected and various mathematical equations or functions are fitted to the data to develop a method of projecting the series into the future. The confidence with which such forecasts can be employed depends greatly on the use for which the forecast is employed. Trend analysis has two general applications in steel industry forecasting: (1) to forecast long-term demand for specific products and markets and (2) as previously discussed, as a check on forecasts (e.g., of total shipments or consumption) derived by other methods.

To illustrate the first use, annual shipments of metal cans in the United States represents a series with a broad base in a well-established market. The trend projection of such a series can be used with considerable confidence in determining future demand for tin mill products. Here, the trend method provides a reasonably sound approach to forecasting.

Field Surveys and Panel Consensus

Field Surveys. When it is important to have reliable information and there is little product history upon which to base a forecast, a field survey provides the best way to develop necessary data. Fields surveys are particularly helpful in developing background for use in forecasts of new products, new applications of existing products, or improved properties of existing products. Rather than making sweeping inhouse assumptions about the acceptance of a new product (e.g., the potential of steel sheet rolled to foil thicknesses), it is far wiser to get reactions to the product from potential customers.

The sales and metallurgical divisions of major steel companies are usually organized in such a way that selected field surveys can be conducted within the course of normal business at little expense. These efforts are worthwhile since their results help the business economist focus on the primary factors likely to influence demand for the new product. At other times it may be desirable to hire consultants to handle field surveys, particularly when the product is primarily aimed at markets not currently served by the existing sales organization.

Panel Consensus. Apart from strict reliance on historical data and economic factors affecting steel demand, it is important to keep in touch with those actually involved with selling steel products. Particularly for short-term forecasts within the firm, a valid technique involves canvassing sales personnel in various district and product sales offices. These sources can provide estimates of the sales volume which they expect to obtain for particular products and in particular regions in the near term.

Generally before the district and product offices are asked for such estimates, they are provided with some ground rules in the form of a framework of the level of activity expected for the general economy and for specific steel-consuming industries. By this means it is possible to some extent to insure that the various product and regional forecasts prepared by different personnel will be reasonably consistent with one another.

CHANGING RELATIONSHIPS AFFECTING STEEL FORECASTS

If forecasting steel were only a matter of selecting the proper mathematical and analytical tools and applying them to static relationships between steel and the economy, forecasting steel demand would be a simple and almost mechanical task. Such is not the case. To properly forecast steel demand it is important to carefully review and interpret changing steel usage patterns within each consuming market. Following are a few of the major considerations that must be reviewed and quantified in developing a forecast of steel demand:

Changing Activity Patterns Within Consuming Industries

The construction industry provides a good example of this phenomenon. It is not enough to merely measure overall construction activity to determine likely steel demand. The pattern of activity in different construction sectors (industrial, commercial, residential, etc.) varies greatly from year to year, and has great bearing on likely steel demand.

Industrial construction (factories) and commercial construction (office buildings, shopping centers) have relatively high steel consumption rates per construction dollar spent. Farther down the scale, consuming steel at only one-third to one-fourth the rate per construction dollar, are such important sectors as public utilities and other public construction. Even farther down the scale in steel consumption are the dollars spent for residential construction.

The importance of following construction activity by sector is pointed out by developments between 1969 and 1971. During this period, construction expenditures increased in real terms while steel consumption declined. In 1969, industrial and commercial construction had been particularly heavy while residential construction had been depressed. This mix of construction activity was favorable to steel. In 1971, activity in the three construction sectors had reversed. The lower steel consumption by construction in 1971 does not necessarily reflect changing steel usage patterns. Instead it reflects the kind of year-to-year changes in activity by sector that can take place within a major steel-consuming industry.

Product Design Changes by Steel Consumers

Basic to the forecast of steel consumption by a consuming industry is the forecast of that industry's level of activity. Then by multiplying the level of activity by the weight of steel consumption per unit of activity in that industry, one arrives at a forecast of steel consumption. For example, a million automobiles will require X million net tons of steel.

The only problem with the formula described above is that the steel weight of automobiles varies from year to year as does the distribution of steel products going into the automobile. Examples of the product design factors facing steel analysts in the early 1970s included:

1. Changing automotive design. The minicar does not consume nearly as much steel as a standard-sized automobile. How popular will it become?
2. Government regulations on safety and emission controls involve increased usage of steel products. When will they become law and how much steel will the final designs involve?
3. The net loss or gain for steel resulting from competition with other materials (plastics, glass, aluminum).

The factors affecting automotive design, and in turn, steel consumption by the automotive industry, are repeated in most steel-consuming markets. Because of this, it is not sufficient for the steel analyst to merely project past economic relationships to forecast the future. Instead he must attempt to evaluate present and future market developments and then translate these results into changing steel unit weight factors.

Technological Development

Among the most difficult developments to quantify are the many changes in steel usage patterns due to technological advances. Such advances occur on a number of fronts. As an example, a study recently indicated that the costs for steel framing in a twenty-story building actually were slightly lower in 1969 than they had been in 1959, despite the increase in the per pound price of steel.[2] The offsetting economies were achieved through:

1. Improved physical properties in the steel. Although steel costs more per pound ten years later, the strength of the construction grade steel per pound had risen even faster, making the strength/price ratio a favorable one.
2. New design techniques had been developed and approved for buildings at the same time. These techniques allowed designers and builders to capitalize on the improved characteristics of steel construction products.

This same kind of combination has occurred in steel for beer cans, where over the last fifteen years or more steel producers have simultaneously been reducing the amount of tin coating on the steel base metal (until today most beer cans are made of tin-free steel) and reducing the thickness of the base metal as well (can body stock is now about two-thirds the weight it was fifteen years ago). Again, these developments reflect improved products and technology which allow a reduction in the number of tons of steel it takes to do a quantity of work today as compared to ten or fifteen years ago.

Needless to say, technological advances take many other forms. Seeking economies of scale, customers build machinery, ships, and other equipment larger these days than they did in the past. Just as a 300,000 dwt. tanker does not contain ten times as

[2] The study compared steel framing costs for two similar twenty-story buildings actually built ten years apart in the same city, by the same owner/builder, and erected by the same fabricator. Both were designed by well-known architectural firms.

much steel as a 30,000 dwt. one, so it is with most of these moves to larger, more economical equipment. The effects of all of these changes must be considered when comparing measures of activity in steel-consuming industries with actual steel consumption.

Competitive Materials

One of the most important areas for consideration in forecasting steel's potential by consuming industry is an evaluation of its future gains and losses due to competitive materials. Here it is particularly important to understand that in evaluating competitive materials, a materials user is rarely interested in the relative cost per pound—or even cost per cubic inch of the competing materials. Instead, he is interested in the final cost of each material to achieve the desired end result. Such final costs include not only raw materials, but labor, machine time, scrap value, product quality, and a myriad of other factors.

Even factors outside of the control of basic materials suppliers have an effect on the relative economics of competitive materials. An example occurs in the construction industry. Lucrative labor contracts awarded to construction workers in the late sixties and early seventies caused the cost of field labor at the construction site to rise considerably faster than either the cost of basic construction materials or the cost of labor at fabricating works. For many jobs where concrete and steel construction techniques compete, the amount of field labor required for concrete construction is far greater than for steel (where more of the work can be prefabricated in the shop). Thus, in recent years the relative economics of steel versus concrete framing for many construction jobs has shifted in favor of steel—for reasons completely apart from the basic material costs themselves!

As in most other areas of consuming market analysis, it is difficut to make broad statements which cover the future competitive relationships between such basic materials as steel, concrete, aluminum, glass, plastics, and lumber. However, analysts familiar with each of these industries can spot trends and developments and weigh their potential effects in forecasting future developments in steel.

Indirect Steel Shipments

The changing international trade picture affects indirect steel shipments as well as imports and exports of steel mill products. As an example of indirect steel shipments, let us examine the automotive market. While domestic production of automobiles showed disappointing growth in the late 1960s, total new car sales remained reasonably close to trend. The difference? Increased sales of imported cars in the United States. This is considered indirect steel trade, since instead of entering the United States in the form of a mill product, the steel enters as a finished manufactured item. Customs officials do not consider autos as a steel import, but imported autos do take away from steel's potential domestic sales. Indirectly they affect total steel demand in the United States.

Similar patterns of imports growing more rapidly than exports for major appliances, machine tools, and other industrial equipment all indicate shifts in traditional steel consumption patterns within the framework of the U.S. economy.

The quantification of indirect steel shipments due to sales of imported cars is relatively easy because of the availability of data on unit sales and unit weights. It becomes more difficult when measuring shifts in trading patterns for many kinds of machinery where the measure of import and export data is in dollar value and/or shipping weight (shipping weight covers all materials, including crates, not just steel weight). It becomes next to impossible when firms begin shipments of parts produced abroad for assembly as only a part of a finished item (automobile, heavy earthmoving tractor, etc.) here in the United States. The weight of these imported items as a portion of the total steel weight is most difficult to determine—but their importation does have a definite effect on total steel demand in this country.

The measurement and evaluation of the effect of indirect steel shipments is a difficult judgment that must be made in the thoughtful forecast of future steel demand by consuming industry. The displacement of domestic steel demand through this route has been increasing in recent years, making the need for accurate quantification of its effects more pressing.

The changing relationships between economic activity in consuming markets and actual steel consumption which have been mentioned above complicate the preparation of both short-term and long-term forecasts in the steel industry. The preparation of accurate forecasts of steel demand involves not only solid mathematical and statistical techniques but also an in-depth analysis of developments within each major consuming market.

THE IMPORT PROBLEM

The most disruptive factor affecting steel industry growth in recent years has been the rapid growth of steel mill product imports. As indicated in exhibit 4, imports increased rapidly as a part of apparent steel consumption in the 1960s, rising from about five percent in 1961 to almost seventeen percent in 1968 and then declining somewhat in 1969 and 1970.

Prior to 1969 there was almost no basis for anticipating how fast imports would grow or their relative impact by product, grade, or port of entry. Beginning in 1969 a three-year voluntary arrangement limiting

the volume of shipments to the United States was entered into by the major steel producers in Japan and several European nations after consultation with the U.S. government. This arrangement has established some measure of control over imports, but the subject of imports and their impact on both short- and long-range planning remains one of great concern to the steel industry.

Rather than cover the many complexities of a subject significant enough to be a book in itself, a reading of *Steel Imports—A National Concern*[3] is recommended to the student interested in understanding the problem in depth. As mentioned earlier, in taking the impact of imports into account in forecasts, it is best to develop a forecast based on domestic steel consumption first and then use whatever import and export assumptions seem reasonable to convert consumption figures into shipments.

CONCLUSION

A key factor in the enduring strength of the U.S. economy has been its flexibility and ability to respond to the changing needs and capabilities of its inhabitants. In the 1970s, at a time when one might have expected the economy to have become more rigid due to its size, the pace of technological and international developments continues to rapidly alter existing economic patterns.

In attempting to forecast steel within such a dynamic economy, it is essential to have a good understanding of basic forecasting techniques, and where each technique best applies. Beyond this, it is important to have an understanding of the domestic steel industry's position in the world economy. Changing relationships of supply and demand, new applications and designs, and

[3] American Iron and Steel Institute, *Steel Imports—A National Concern*, July 1970. See also the AISI's *The Steel Industry Today*, May 1971.

changes in competitive factors and world trade patterns are only a few of the factors which can have considerable impact on steel industry forecasts. In preparing a forecast, it is important to review and evaluate the effect of anticipated developments regarding these factors.

At all times it is necessary to remember that the basic purpose of a forecast is that of a planning and control tool. It is not an end in itself. A forecast measures the market within a given environment, but is subject to change as the environment changes. Among the many assumptions upon which a forecast is based, some do not come true. One must be willing to alter the assumptions as experience indicates advisable and update one's forecast with enough frequency that it reflects expectations for developments in the industry based on the best judgment currently available.

BIBLIOGRAPHY

American Iron and Steel Institute, *Steel Imports—A National Concern*, Washington, D.C., July 1970.

———, *The Steel Industry Today*, New York, N.Y., May 1971.

Cabinet Committee on Economic Policy, *Report to the President on the Economic Position of the Steel Industry*, Washington, 1971.

Demaree, Allan T., "Steel: Recasting an Industry Under Stress," *Fortune* (March 1971), pp. 74–77, 134–42.

"Forecasting Steel Demand," *Metal Bulletin* (February 20, 1970), pp. 22–32.

Gold, Bela, William S. Pierce, and Gerhard Rosegger, "Diffusion of Major Innovations in U.S. Iron and Steel Manufacturing," *Journal of Industrial Economics*, XVIII, No. 3 (July 1970), pp. 218–41.

Mo, William Y., and Kung-Lee Wong, *A Quantitative Economic Analysis and Long-Run Projections of the Demand for Steel Mill Products*, Information Circular 8451, Department of the Interior, Bureau of Mines, 1970.

"1980 World Steel Production One Billion Net Tons—More? or Less?" *33/The International Magazine of Metals Producing* (September 1970), pp. 68–79.

Skinner, Wickham, and David C. D. Rogers, *Manufacturing Policy in the Steel Industry*. Homewood, Ill.: Richard D. Irwin, Inc., 1970.

"Whither Goest Thou, U.S. Steel Industry?" *33/The International Magazine of Metals Producing* (April 1971), pp. 36–40; (May 1971), pp. 50–53; (June 1971), pp. 38–43; (July 1971), pp. 30–33.

DAVID M. BLANK

Forecasting National Advertising

Expenditures on advertising are usually classified in two ways: First, in terms of the size of the area within which the advertiser sells his products, and second, in terms of the medium employed by the advertiser. The first classification essentially divides all advertisers into *local* and *national* categories, with retailers the dominant local advertisers and national manufacturers the dominant national advertisers. Firms selling over a region larger than a metropolitan area are typically classified as *regional* advertisers and included within the national category.

In 1970, of total advertising expenditures of $19.7 billion, almost three-fifths, or $11.5 billion, was spent by national advertisers. The remaining $8.2 billion was spent by local advertisers.

The second form of classification, relating to medium, categorizes expenditures according to the various vehicles in which the advertising is carried. The major media consist of the print media (newspapers, magazines, businesspapers), broadcasting (radio and television), outdoor advertising, and direct mail. Several of these media carry both local and national advertising (for example, newspapers, radio, and television). Others carry only national advertising (for example, businesspapers).[1] Broadcasting

is usually described as comprising three forms: (1) national advertising placed through networks, (2) national advertising placed directly on local stations (so-called national spot advertising), and (3) local advertising placed on local stations.

Of the $19.7 billion of advertising expenditures in 1970, about 30 percent was accounted for by newspaper advertising, about nineteen percent by television, about thirteen percent by direct mail, about seven percent by magazines, and about seven percent by radio. The remaining media all account for smaller percentages, except for a residual category of miscellaneous advertising expenditures which are arbitrarily estimated at about one-fifth of the total (see table 1).

Both local and national advertising expenditures have increased substantially since the end of World War II, with the last twenty-odd years clearly falling into three discrete periods (see chart 1). The years immediately following the war were characterized by very rapid growth rates in both national and local advertising—ten and eight percent per year respectively. The late 1950s and early 1960s were associated with much lower growth rates—a little less than five percent and three percent for national and local advertising respectively. The last seven

[1] Magazines continue to be treated in the statistics as if they carried only national advertising, but the development of metropolitan editions of national magazines and of local

magazines is beginning to make this an oversimplified view.

468

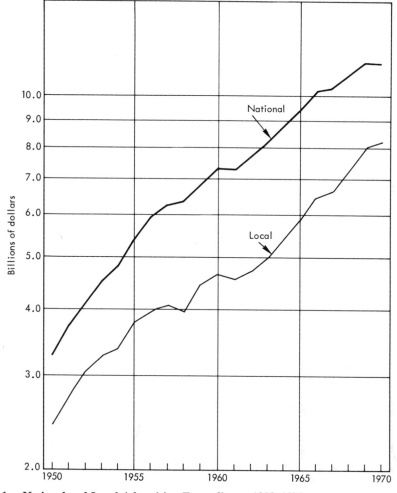

Chart 1   National and Local Advertising Expenditures 1950–1970

or eight years have seen an increase in advertising growth rates, particularly in local advertising. Over this period local advertising was again scoring at almost eight percent a year, while national advertising increased to between five and six percent per year.

It seems highly likely that the relative slowdown in the rate of growth of advertising in the late 1950s and early 1960s is associated with the slowdown in the rate of growth of the economy generally during that period and with the increasing pressure on

corporate profits that prevailed throughout those years. The longer duration and quicker pace of the expansion that predominated throughout most of the 1960s and the improved profit picture during that period led to a substantial revival in the rate of growth of advertising.

The tie between aggregate economic activity and advertising is of course very close. Advertisers represent a very large cross section of the U.S. economy, although with primary emphasis on consumer rather than

TABLE 1. ADVERTISERS' EXPENDITURES:[a] DOLLAR VOLUME BY MEDIA, VARIOUS YEARS 1950–70

	1950	1952	1954	1956	1958	1960	1962	1964	1966	1968	1970
	In Millions of Dollars										
Grand total	$ 5,710	$ 7,156	$ 8,164	$ 9,905	$10,302	$11,932	$12,381	$14,155	$16,670	$18,127	$19,715
Total national	3,257	4,096	4,812	5,926	6,331	7,296	7,683	8,746	10,213	10,883	11,515
Total local	2,453	3,060	3,352	3,979	3,971	4,636	4,697	5,410	6,457	7,244	8,200
Television	171	454	809	1,207	1,354	1,590	1,897[b]	2,289	2,823	3,231	3,613[c]
Network	85	256	422	625	709	783	976[b]	1,132	1,393	1,523	1,658[c]
Spot	31	94	207	329	397	527	629	806	988	1,131	1,248[c]
Local	55	104	180	253	248	281	292	351	442	577	707[c]
Radio	605	624	559	567	619	692	736	846	1,010	1,190	1,301[c]
Network	196	162	114	61	58	43	46	59	64	63	56[c]
Spot	136	142	135	161	190	222	233	256	308	360	375[c]
Local	273	321	309	346	372	428	457	531	639	767	870[c]
Newspapers	2,076	2,473	2,695	3,236	3,193	3,703	3,681	4,148	4,895	5,265	5,830[c]
National	533	562	635	789	769	836	781	848	975	990	1,014[c]
Local	1,542	1,910	2,060	2,447	2,424	2,867	2,900	3,300	3,920	4,275	4,816[c]
Magazines	515	616	668	795	767	941	973	1,108	1,291	1,318	1,321
Direct Mail	803	1,024	1,202	1,419	1,589	1,830	1,933	2,184	2,461	2,612	2,736
Outdoor	143	162	187	201	192	203	171	175	178	208	237
National	96	109	126	136	129	137	115	117	118	137	156
Local	46	53	61	65	62	66	56	58	60	71	81
Businesspapers	251	365	408	496	525	609	597	623	712	714	740[c]
Other media	1,147	1,438	1,636	1,984	2,064	2,363	2,392	2,783	3,301	3,589	3,937
National	610	766	894	1,115	1,194	1,368	1,400	1,613	1,904	2,035	2,211
Local[d]	536	672	742	869	864	995	992	1,170	1,397	1,554	1,726

Source: McCann-Erickson estimates, as given in *Marketing/Communication* (formerly *Printer's Ink*).

a Includes time, space, talent, and production.

b Figures for 1962 and after are not comparable with those for prior years. The network figures for 1962 and after include certain expenditures that were excluded from earlier reports.

c Estimated.

d Includes all expenditures on advertising in local farm publications and local advertisers' expenditures on "miscellaneous."

industrial goods and on goods rather than services. Accordingly, it is not surprising that attempts to relate the volume of advertising to external economic factors almost invariably end up with some measure of total or near-total economic activity as one of the independent variables. Thus, some equations we have developed in our efforts to forecast national advertising use GNP as a variable; others use personal consumption expenditures or consumption expenditures on goods. The best single explanatory variable we have obtained for the quarterly volume of national advertising over the last decade reflects personal consumption expenditures. All such variables are, in a sense, proxies for a weighted corporate sales figure for those corporations that do national advertising.

A second variable is usually included as well. For advertising is not only a response to current sales, it also has some of the characteristics of investment for the future. And, like investment in plant and equipment, the level of corporate profits clearly plays a role in determining advertising volume. As a consequence, corporate profits are the second variable usually found in any estimating equation of national advertising or its major components.

Thus, we obtain some improvement in explaining the quarterly variations in national advertising by adding a corporate-profits-before-tax variable to a personal consumption expenditures variable. And our best equation reflecting data for the decade of the 1960s is based roughly on the same two variables—personal consumption expenditures and corporate profits before taxes.

Finally, because advertising plans are made substantially in advance of actual air or print time, the causal variables tend in general to lead advertising expenditures. We experimented with almost 200 equations in attempting to explain the variation in national advertising expenditures over varying periods dating from the mid-1950s. Of these, the best one-third[2] used 113 independent variables[3] and 89 of these were leading relative to national advertising.

When we turn from an examination of the causal variables related to the changes in national advertising levels to an analysis of short-run fluctuations in national advertising, we find that such fluctuations are directly related to the business cycle. In the postwar period, national advertising, as best we can measure it, has fully conformed to the pattern of general business activity. There is no evidence of major countercyclical activity, nor has national advertising skipped any peaks or troughs in general business. Nor has national advertising varied within cycles of its own timing, as are found in, say, the textile industry or even automobiles. For example, there is nothing to be found in the statistical record of national advertising comparable to the establishment of a peak in retail sales of automobiles in 1955, a year midway up the expansion of 1954–57. In this sense, national advertising must be included among the true cyclical industries. This fact, of course, has important implications for the communications media which depend so heavily on advertising for revenue.

While national advertising conforms closely to the business cycle, it does not conform precisely. Peaks in advertising tend to lag somewhat behind peaks in general business (see table 2). This lag has tended to decline somewhat in recent periods, and for the last two peaks it has averaged around half a quarter. The timing at the troughs has also changed somewhat over recent periods; in the first two postwar troughs, there was some tendency for advertising to lead the

[2] In terms of the levels of the correlation coefficients, as well as the statistical significance of the coefficients of the independent variables and the level of the standard errors.

[3] Many of these variables were the same in a number of equations, of course, so the net number of different variables used in the 61 equations would be much less than 113.

TABLE 2.   TIMING OF CYCLES IN NATIONAL ADVERTISING MEDIA, 1957–70

Medium	No. of Quarters Lag[a] at Business Cycle Peaks			No. of Quarters Lag[a] at Business Cycle Troughs		
	1957 and 1960 Peaks	1966 and 1969 Peaks	All Four Peaks	1958 and 1961 Troughs	1967 Trough	All Three Troughs
Businesspapers	+1.0	+1.0	+1.0	+0.5	+1.0	+0.7
Magazines	−0.5	+0.5	0.0	+2.0	+2.0	+2.0
Newspapers	−1.0	−0.5	−0.8	+2.0	+1.0	+1.7
Radio spot	+1.5	−1.0	+0.2	+1.0	+1.0	+1.0
Radio network	+0.5	−0.5	0.0	+2.0	+1.0	+1.7
Television spot	+0.5	−0.5	0.0	−1.0	0.0	−0.7
Television network	+2.0	+1.5	+1.8	0.0	0.0	0.0
Simple mean of lags:						
Seven media	+0.6	+0.1	+0.4	+0.9	+0.9	+0.9
Three print media	−0.2	+0.3	+0.1	+1.5	+1.3	+1.4
Broadcasting	+1.1	−0.1	+0.6	+0.5	+0.5	+0.5
Television	+1.2	+0.5	+0.8	−0.5	0.0	−0.3
GNP	0.0	0.0	0.0	−0.5	0.0	−0.3
RFB Index of Industrial Production	−0.5	0.0	−0.2	0.0	0.0	0.0

a. From turning points in general business activity.

upturn, but in the last three cyclical troughs this lead has turned into a fairly substantial lag—almost a full quarter.

The duration of expansions and contractions in national advertising are approximately the same magnitude as the expansions and contractions in general business (see table 3). As we know, the postwar expansions in GNP have tended to be somewhat longer than the expansions in industrial output, and the contractions in GNP have tended to be somewhat shorter than those in industrial production. Expansions and contractions in national advertising have tended to be of intermediate length. Thus, the average length of recent expansions in advertising has been somewhat less than thirteen quarters, compared to about fourteen quarters for GNP and thirteen quarters for the FRB index. The average length of recent contractions in national advertising has been almost three quarters, with GNP contractions somewhat shorter than three quarters, and the contractions of

the FRB index, about three quarters long.

The relationships for the amount of rise and fall in national advertising are similar to those for duration (see table 4). In recent expansions, the increases in national advertising have been almost as large in total and about as large per quarter as the increases in GNP, and significantly larger than the increases in industrial production. In recent contractions, the amount of decline in national advertising has fallen somewhere between that of industrial production and the typically milder decline in GNP.

The typically damped cyclical behavior of national advertising, compared with industrial production, is not a reflection primarily of the importance of service firms among national advertisers, nor necessarily of more modest swings in advertising appropriations than in sales for most corporations. Rather it is primarily a function of dominance in national advertising of firms producing or selling goods whose cyclical fluctuations are not great. Thus, about two-

TABLE 3.   DURATION OF CYCLES IN NATIONAL ADVERTISING MEDIA, 1957-70

	Duration of Expansions			Duration of Contractions		
	1958–60 and 1961–66 Expansions	1967–69 Expansion	Three Expansions	1957–58 and 1960–61 Contractions	1966–67 Contraction	Three Contractions
	In Quarters					
Businesspapers	16.0	11.0	14.3	2.5	3.0	2.7
Magazines	14.0	8.0	12.0	5.0	3.0	4.3
Newspapers	13.0	9.0	11.7	5.5	3.0	4.7
Radio spot	15.0	8.0	12.7	2.5	3.0	2.7
Radio network	14.0	9.0	12.3	4.5	2.0	3.7
Television spot	15.0	8.0	12.7	1.5	1.0	1.3
Television network	14.5	12.0	13.7	1.0	1.0	1.0
Simple mean of durations:						
Seven media	14.4	9.3	12.7	3.2	2.3	2.9
Three print media	14.3	9.3	12.6	4.3	3.0	3.9
Broadcasting	14.6	9.2	12.8	2.4	1.8	2.2
Television	14.8	10.0	13.2	1.2	1.0	1.1
GNP	16.0	10.0	14.0	2.5	2.0	2.3
FRB Index of Industrial Production	15.0	9.0	13.0	3.5	2.0	3.0

thirds of the advertising expenditures of advertisers that spend a million dollars or more on advertising are accounted for by firms whose products lie within the consumer nondurable area.[4] Dominant within the consumer nondurable area have been producers of foods, soaps, drugs and toiletries, tobacco products, and beer.

Only about one-fifth of expenditures by million-dollar advertisers are accounted for by consumer durables firms (primarily automobile manufacturers) and only about seven percent by firms dealing in industrial goods. Another six percent of such advertising is accounted for by service firms, primarily transportation companies and utilities.

When we turn to the individual media, we find, as we would expect, more

[4] Million-dollar advertisers themselves account for two-thirds or more of expenditures on measured media.

variation from the patterns determined by general business activity (see chart 2). One or two advertising media are dominated by longer-term movements unique to themselves. Thus, radio networking declined so precipitously during most of the 1950s that it is difficult to see any imprint of general cyclical activity. Conversely, television networking and spot television grew so rapidly during the early 1950s that business cycles had little effect on either.

More importantly, among some media we find short periods of decline that are not caused by business recessions. Some of these are unexplainable. Some are associated with particular events occurring within the specific media in question. A good example of this is the precipitous decline in national television advertising revenues in the first quarter of 1971, associated with the withdrawal of cigarette advertising from the broadcasting media. In any case, the fairly smooth and quite consistent pattern found

TABLE 4.   PERCENT AMPLITUDE OF CYCLES IN NATIONAL ADVERTISING MEDIA, 1957–70

Medium	1967–69 Expansion Total	Per Quarter	Average of 1958–60 and 1961–66 Expansions Total	Per Quarter	Average of All Three Expansions Total	Per Quarter	1966–67 Contraction Total	Per Quarter	Average of 1957–58 and 1960–61 Contractions Total	Per Quarter	Average of All Three Contractions Total	Per Quarter
	Amplitude in Expansions						*Amplitude in Contractions*					
Businesspapers	17.1%	1.6%	25.5%	1.8%	22.7%	1.7%	−5.1%	−1.7%	−6.9%	−2.5%	−6.3%	−2.2%
Magazines	12.2	1.5	35.9	3.0	28.0	2.5	−6.7	−2.2	−6.6	−1.3	−6.6	−1.6
Newspapers	18.0	2.0	21.6	1.8	20.4	1.9	−12.5	−4.2	−8.4	−1.5	−9.7	−2.4
Radio spot	21.8	2.7	38.0	2.8	32.6	2.8	−3.3	−1.1	−8.0	−3.4	−6.4	−2.6
Radio network	3.4	0.4	55.5	5.6	38.1	3.9	−10.8	−5.4	−34.0	−9.0	−26.2	−7.8
Television spot	33.7	4.2	74.3	7.0	60.8	6.1	−7.5	−7.5	−1.2	−0.6	−3.3	−2.9
Television network	22.6	1.9	50.5	3.8	41.2	3.2	−3.8	−3.8	−2.6	−2.6	−3.0	−3.0
Mean amplitude:												
Seven media combined	16.0	1.8	34.3	2.5	28.2	2.1	−4.0	−1.0	−2.7	−0.8	−3.1	−0.8
Three print media combined	12.2	1.4	26.8	2.2	21.9	1.9	−6.3	−1.6	−7.6	−1.9	−7.1	−1.8
Broadcasting	24.1	2.1	81.3[a]	3.3[a]	52.7[b]	2.7[b]	−5.0	−5.0	−0.8[a]	−0.8[a]	−2.9[b]	−2.9[b]
Television	26.1	2.2	89.4[a]	3.6[a]	57.8[b]	2.9[b]	−5.3	−5.3	−2.0[a]	−2.0[a]	−3.6[b]	−3.6[b]
GNP	21.3	2.1	35.2	2.1	30.6	2.1	+1.8	+0.9	−2.1	−1.0	−0.8	−0.4
FRB Index of Industrial Production	11.5	1.3	29.2	1.3	23.3	1.3	−2.8	−1.4	−9.0	−2.8	−7.0	−2.3

[a] 1960–66 only.
[b] Two periods only, 1960–66, 1966–69.

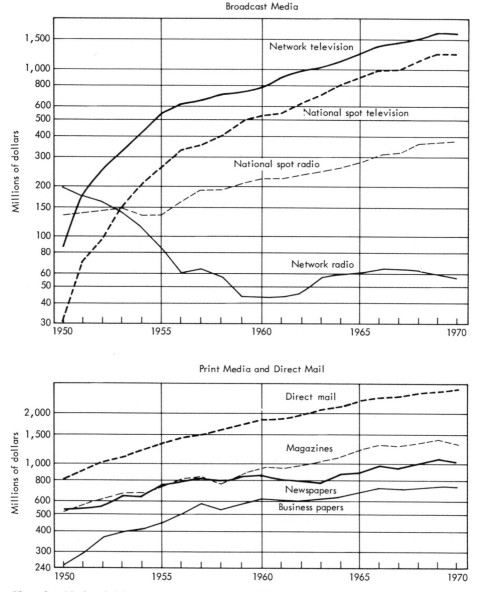

Chart 2   National Advertisers' Expenditures by Media, 1950–1970

in national advertising as a whole is not precisely matched by the performance of the individual media.

The nature of the response to the business cycle varies among the individual media. This variation is usually due to the specific characteristics of the medium in question. First, there are of course substantial differences in growth rates among national advertising media. Television, both network and spot, experienced the largest increases in volume over the last decade—

more than 100 percent in both cases. The next in order of growth was national spot radio; it increased by roughly 70 percent over this period. Then followed the print media (magazines, businesspapers, and newspapers) and network radio, with increases of roughly 20 to 40 percent.

A second difference among media is associated with the kinds of advertiser that tends to use each medium. Television (both network and spot) gets three-quarters or more of its support from firms producing consumer nondurables. Magazines and newspapers get over one-half of their national advertising from consumer nondurables firms, with an additional one-quarter or more of advertising volume coming from consumer durables producers. For newspapers, automobile manufacturers account for the bulk of the consumer durables advertising. Magazines and newspapers receive about one-tenth of their national advertising from service firms: travel and transportation companies, public utilities, and the like. Finally, businesspapers receive about one-third of their advertising from producers of industrial goods such as materials and machinery.

Largely as a result of these variations in trend and in advertiser patronage, the responses of the various media to changes in business activity tend to differ considerably. Thus, television network revenues have very long lags at peaks in business cycle activity and essentially no lags at troughs. Newspapers, conversely, tend to lead at peaks but have long lags at troughs. Magazines have short lags at peaks and fairly long lags at troughs. Spot television reacts quickly at peaks, but tends to lead at troughs. Radio also tends to react quickly at peaks but lags considerably at troughs. And businesspapers lag significantly at both peaks and troughs.

There has been some difference among the various media in the lengths of recent expansions, with network television and businesspapers having somewhat longer than average periods of expansion and the other media, somewhat shorter than average expansions. There has also been some difference in the lengths of contractions, with magazines and newspapers having long contractions and both television media, short contractions.

With regard to amplitudes, television again ranks at one extreme. Both network and spot television have large expansions and small contractions; here we are still seeing the effects of rapid growth rates. The three print media have small expansions and medium-to-large contractions; here the effects of slow growth rates are apparent.

After we summarize the experience of the national advertising media, we are left with the unpleasant fact that there remain some short-term movements that are extremely difficult to explain.

Advertising is a service whose results are neither fully predictable nor, indeed, fully measurable. There is a famous story on this point, variously ascribed to John Wanamaker and Lord Level. Wanamaker (or Lord Level) was once chided for large expenditures on advertising and asked whether he didn't realize that probably half of the money he spent on advertising had no effect and was therefore wasted. Wanamaker replied that, of course, he was perfectly well aware of this but that the trouble was that he didn't know which half of the expenditure was the waste.

Practitioners in the advertising field know much more now than they did in Wanamaker's day. But there is still considerable uncertainty about the relative effectiveness of a dollar spent in alternative forms of advertising. As long as this is so, we must expect some decisions to be made simply because others are making the same decision. As long as this practice prevails, some movements in forms and methods and, indeed, volume of advertising will simply not be forecastable.

Part Five

FINANCIAL FORECASTING

The forecasting of business conditions generally involves the setting down of a whole series of environmental assumptions to provide a framework for the detailed analysis. Yet, if the assumptions are unrealistic or irrelevant, the entire analytical structure will turn out to be faulty. Unfortunately, however, many forecasters merely pay lip service to whole sectors of the economy in zeroing in on more specific areas for their work.

The whole field of finance is a case in point. Blanket statements about the climate of monetary policy are blithely tossed off; whereas, in reality, close attention should be paid to the direction of Federal Reserve actions. Interest rate patterns are far from unimportant in determining both the level and the character of business activity. That is, there is an interdependent relationship between economic and financial changes.

Important changes have taken place in recent years in the thinking of the economics profession with regard to the role of money in the economy and the interpretation of Federal Reserve policy. The issues raised by these developments for business forecasters are the topics covered in the first three chapters of this part.

The reemergence of the corporate treasurer as a power center in American business has led to a considerable concern over the level, composition and quality of corporate profits. Decisions relating to capital spending, expansion, diversification, pricing policies and the like should be carefully appraised in the light of anticipated earnings and cash flow. These issues are discussed in the chapter on forecasting corporate profits.

The final chapter discusses the question most frequently asked of forecasters: What's going to happen to the stock market?

GEORGE W. McKINNEY, JR. & DAVID M. JONES

Forecasting Monetary Policy

INTRODUCTION

Forecasting monetary policy is a common necessity for all economic predictions. The policy course the Federal Reserve follows has an important effect on the cost and availability of money and credit, and ultimately on economic activity. Essentially, two steps are required in predicting monetary policy. First, it is necessary to understand both what the Federal Reserve wants to do (objectives) and how it goes about it (operating tools and targets). Second, there is a need to keep tuned to the Federal Reserve's expectations regarding economic and financial developments and to determine how actual conditions are turning out relative to these expectations.

The forecaster might, in effect, put himself in the place of a monetary official and ask, "How, with my aims for the economy, would I adjust monetary policy in light of current and prospective economic and financial developments?" The important thing to keep in mind is that there is at all times an interplay between Federal Reserve policy and economic activity. Federal Reserve actions both influence and are, in turn, influenced by economic activity.

A significant shift in monetary policy emphasis has occurred in recent years. The monetary authorities have focused more on the monetary aggregates (bank credit, money supply, and time deposits) and less on money market conditions (short-term rates, member bank borrowings, and free reserves). This is not to say that the Federal Reserve would no longer act to stabilize money market conditions when a special shock, such as a major corporate bankruptcy or an international financial crisis, might occur. The point is rather that more attention is being given, under normal circumstances, to steady growth in monetary aggregates over quarterly and longer periods. A major implication of the current emphasis on monetary aggregates may be that unexpected shifts in spending and credit demands will lead to somewhat wider immediate fluctuations in interest rates than previously when stable money market conditions were emphasized.

The recent shift in emphasis is part of a continuing process. Further changes in the focus of monetary policy can be expected in the years ahead as economic and monetary theory continue to evolve, just as evolving theories and new ideas have influenced the development of monetary policies in the past.

POLICY OBJECTIVES

The Federal Reserve is aiming at the broad policy objectives of reasonable price stability, high levels of employment, sus-

479

tained growth, and, on the international front, reasonable balance of payments equilibrium. The desirability of these goals is not in question. They have evolved with practice and interpretation out of the original statement of national economic policy objectives in the Employment Act of 1946. The problem is that these broad goals may be at times in conflict with one another. Something of the nature of the conflict between two of the major policy goals can be seen in charts 1 and 2. Note, for example, that periods of low unemployment are typically associated with accelerating price increases.

The establishment of appropriate priorities among these competing policy objectives, even in the short run, is easier said than done. The Federal Reserve's evalua-

tion of appropriate policy priorities may differ in emphasis from those of the administration. Moreover, inside the Federal Reserve itself, judgment as to appropriate policy priorities may not be the same among various members of the Board of Governors or the Federal Reserve bank officials.

Consumers and businessmen have sometimes based their spending decisions on mistaken assumptions about which broad economic objective was deemed most important by public policymakers or how long the chosen objective might be pursued. Over the extended economic expansion in the 1960s, for example, people seemed to come increasingly to the viewpoint that the risks of doing business had been substantially reduced by a government that was committed first and foremost to full employment. After all, it

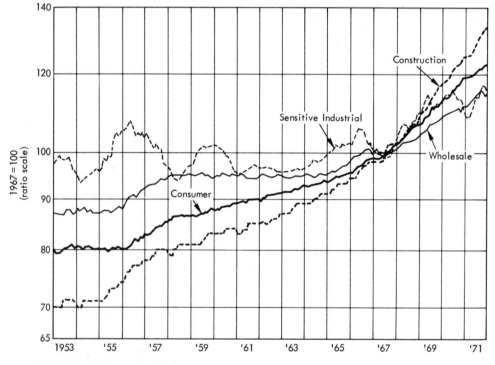

Source: *U.S. Department of Labor.*

Chart 1   Prices

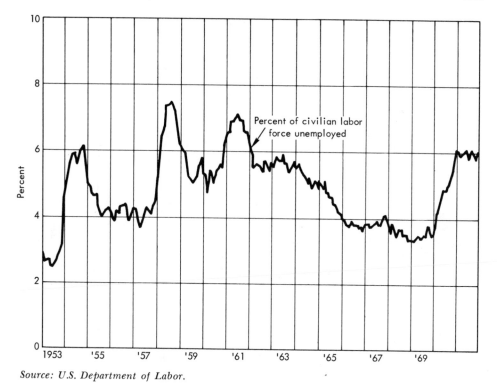

Source: *U.S. Department of Labor.*

Chart 2 Unemployment Rate

was argued, would not any good politician put full employment above everything else? Why not borrow the funds and go ahead with that risky spending decision?

It became clear later on in the 1960s, however, that the government—and the Federal Reserve—would have to deal with accelerating inflationary pressures on a first priority basis. The resulting chain of events included the tax increase in mid-1968, tight money in 1969, an economic slowdown in 1969–70, rising unemployment, the Penn Central bankruptcy, and sharply increased caution on the part of consumers and businessmen. The hard lesson of this experience was that policy priorities must necessarily be changed from time to time as circumstances are altered.

It is not always easy to find out at any given point in time precisely which policy objective is dominating Federal Reserve ac-

tions. In 1970–71, for example, the tone of the statements by Chairman Arthur Burns and other Federal Reserve officials suggested that controlling inflation was probably their foremost aim. But these officials were always careful to add qualifying statements to the effect that the Federal Reserve did not want to be held responsible for allowing "the American economy to stagnate for want of money and credit."[1]

TOOLS OF POLICY

A thorough knowledge of the nature of the tools used by the Federal Reserve in

[1] U.S. Congress, Joint Economic Committee, *Testimony by Arthur Burns*, February 10, 1971.

TABLE 1.   SUMMARY OF FACTORS AFFECTING MEMBER BANK RESERVES

	December[a] 1969	December[a] 1970	Change
	Millions of Dollars		
Starting with:			
Factors supplying reserve funds			
Reserve bank credit outstanding	64,100	66,708	+2,608
U.S. government securities	57,500	61,688	+4,188
Bought outright	57,295	61,310	+4,015
Repurchase agreement	205	378	+ 173
Discounts and advances	1,086	321	− 765
Float	3,235	3,570	+ 335
Other Federal Reserve assets	2,279	1,129	−1,150
Gold stock	10,367	11,105	+ 738
Special drawing rights	...	400	+ 400
Treasury currency outstanding	6,841	7,145	+ 304
less:			
Factors absorbing reserve funds			
Deposits with Federal Reserve banks[b]			
Treasury	1,194	849	− 345
Foreign	146	145	− 1
Other	458	735	+ 277
Other Federal Reserve liabilities and capital	2,192	2,265	+ 73
Currency in circulation	53,591	57,013	+3,422
Treasury cash holdings	656	427	− 229
equals:			
Member bank reserves with Federal Reserve banks	23,071	23,925	+ 854
plus:			
Currency and coin held by member banks	4,960	5,340	+ 380
equals:			
Total member bank reserves	28,031	29,265	+1,234

[a] Average of daily figures.
[b] Other than member bank reserves with Federal Reserve Banks.

implementing monetary policy will aid the forecaster in assessing the significance of policy moves. For example, shadings in policy may be reflected in decisions to inject bank reserves temporarily, through open market operations done under repurchase agreements, in contrast with outright purchases (which have a more permanent effect on reserves). At the other extreme, the Federal Reserve may take actions which should not be interpreted as signaling shifts in policy, but rather represent efforts to modify financial market effects of policy actions previously taken. For example, adjustments in the discount rate frequently are made to confirm market rate movements that occurred in response to earlier policy moves or other influences. Finally, the need for knowledge of tools used by the Federal Reserve extends to selective tools, such as Regulation Q, which are sometimes used as a supplement to or substitute for general policy tools.

Open Market Operations

Federal Reserve open market operations are the primary monetary policy tool. Purchases of U.S. government securities by

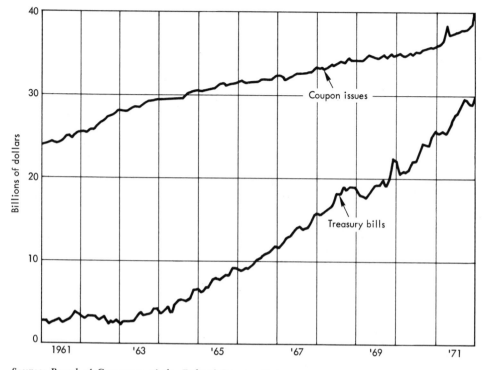

Source: *Board of Governors of the Federal Reserve System.*

Chart 3   Federal Reserve Holdings of U.S. Govt. Securities

the Federal Reserve add to bank reserves, and thus facilitate an expansion in credit and deposits. Conversely, the sale of securities by the Federal Reserve absorbs bank reserves, thereby inhibiting credit and deposit growth. While Federal open market operations in U.S. government securities are by no means the only factor supplying or absorbing reserve funds (see table 1), this policy tool is of critical importance because it gives the monetary authorities general control over the rate of growth in total member bank reserves and other monetary aggregates.

Open market purchases and sales have tended to be concentrated in treasury bills because the bill market is broader and more active and thus less sensitive to large-scale Federal Reserve operations than the market for intermediate and longer-term treasury

coupon issues. Nevertheless, there have been times when the Federal Reserve has engaged in substantial purchases of treasury coupon issues (see chart 3). In the early 1960s, the Federal Reserve sold treasury bills and bought treasury coupon issues in an effort to bolster short-term rates to stem short-term capital outflows and shore up the balance of payments while at the same time attempting to exert downward pressure on longer-term rates to spur domestic growth. The success of this operation "twist" remains a topic of debate, but short-term rates did not, in fact, fall as low in the early 1960s as they had in earlier postwar periods of economic sluggishness and easy money (see chart 4). Long-term rates dropped temporarily lower in the early 1960s, but the decline was no larger than in earlier postwar recession periods.

In early 1971 the Federal Reserve

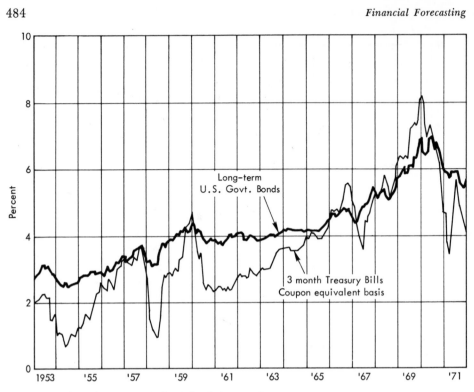

Source: Board of Governors of the Federal Reserve System.

Chart 4   Interest Rates

again purchased a substantial amount of treasury coupon issues. The Federal Reserve sought, in this operation, to supply the reserves required to sustain a moderate rate of monetary growth without exerting further downward pressure on short-term rates. The level of short-term rates had already fallen to the point of triggering substantial international short-term capital flows out of the dollar into short-term German mark investments and other foreign money market instruments carrying more attractive rates of return. As in the early 1960s, the Federal Reserve hoped that a by-product of its purchases of treasury coupon issues would be a general downtrend in longer-term rates which would aid the domestic economic recovery. The Federal Reserve coupon purchases spurred strong temporary drops in note and bond yields, but as soon as the

operations halted, yields rose sharply and unsettled financial conditions emerged. The lesson of this experience was that the Federal Reserve must tread lightly in the generally "thin" market for treasury coupon issues or risk general market instability.

Discount Mechanism

In the early days of the Federal Reserve System, discounts and advances accounted for, at one point, more than 80 percent of total Federal Reserve credit (see chart 5). The share of federal credit extended through the discount window fell sharply in the 1929–1934 depression years when loan demand weakened. During the postwar period, the ratio of discounts and advances to total Federal Reserve credit has

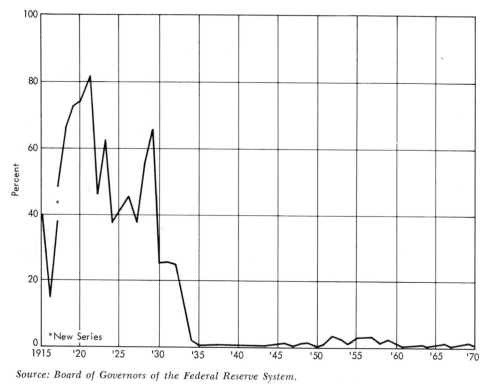

Source: *Board of Governors of the Federal Reserve System.*

Chart 5   Ratio of Member Bank Discounts and Advances to Total Federal Reserve Credit

remained below an almost insignificant 5 percent.

One factor leading to this diminished role of the discount window as a source of Federal Reserve credit has been a growing skepticism on the part of many banks regarding nonprice discounting terms. Many banks worry that the discount window authorities might engage in unusually intensive surveillance of a borrowing bank or that the authorities might arbitrarily limit particular bank loan or funds management operations. The September 1, 1966 Federal Reserve letter to member banks admonishing them to slow down the rate of growth in their business loans or in effect have the discount window slammed on their hands served to heighten bank suspicions concerning the discount mechanism. A rough measure of bank aversion to the discount win-

dow can be seen in the substantial margins by which the federal funds rate on reserves traded among banks exceeded the discount rate in the tight money periods in 1966 and 1969 (see chart 6).

Despite the relatively insignificant role of the discount mechanism as a source of Federal Reserve credit, the monetary policy forecaster will find it helpful to keep in touch with general discounting policies. It is important to keep in mind, for example, that adjustments in the traditionally "sticky" discount rate have frequently been made to confirm previous movements in other money market rates rather than to signal the Federal Reserve's intention to shift policies in one direction or the other.

A special study group under the leadership of Governor George W. Mitchell has recommended that the discount rate be ad-

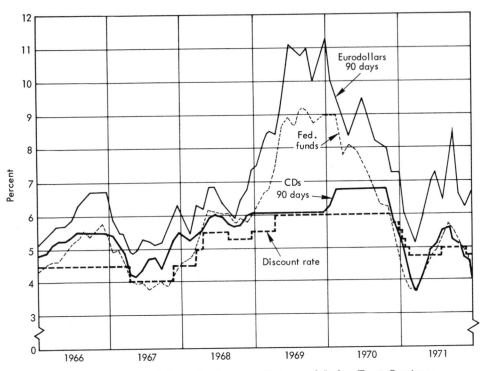

Source: *Board of Governors of the Federal Reserve System and Irving Trust Company.*

Chart 6   Short-Term Interest Rates

justed more frequently and in smaller steps.[2] Other possible reforms which may be put into effect in the coming years include raising the share of Federal Reserve credit extended through the discount window by granting member banks discount credit lines (on a no-questions-asked basis); the standardization of nonprice discounting terms; and the liberalization of collateral eligible for Federal Reserve discounts and advances.

Other Policy Tools

Reserve requirements are another of the major Federal Reserve policy tools, but

[2] Federal Reserve, *Reappraisal of the Federal Reserve Discount Mechanism*, Report of a System Committee (July 1968), pp. 19–20.

they have been adjusted relatively infrequently in the postwar years. Over the decade of the 1960s, for example, there were only four adjustments in the reserve requirements against member bank net demand deposits. There has recently been growing pressure on the Federal Reserve to reduce substantially the 17 to 17½ percent reserve requirement on net demand deposits for Reserve city banks and the 12½ to 13 percent requirement for country banks. It is argued that these reserve requirement ratios put member banks at a serious competitive disadvantage in intermediating deposit funds and discourage the membership of smaller banks in the Federal Reserve. Some critics have asserted that reserve requirements on net demand deposits could be cut in half or more, and that reserve requirements on bank time deposits could be eliminated complete-

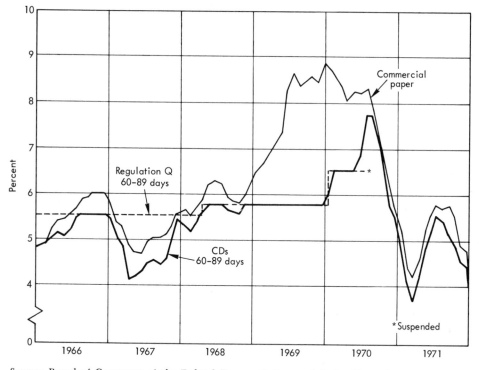

Source: *Board of Governors of the Federal Reserve System and Irving Trust Company.*

Chart 7   Short-Term Interest Rates

ly without impairing the effectiveness of monetary control. (The Federal Reserve proposed in early 1972 to do away with the net demand deposit reserve requirement distinction between Reserve city and country banks. Under the revised plan, reserve requirements of 8 percent were imposed on the first $2 million of net demand deposits for all banks, 10 percent on $2–10 million, 13 percent on $10–400 million, and 17½ percent on net demand deposits over $400 million.)

In 1969–70, the monetary authorities placed increased emphasis on selective reserve requirement schemes. Marginal reserve requirements were imposed on U.S. bank Eurodollar borrowings in October 1969. U.S. banks were required at that time to maintain a 10 percent reserve on Eurodollar borrowings in *excess* of their average level of

such borrowings for May 1969. Subsequently, reserve requirements were applied to funds obtained by member banks through the issuance of commercial paper by their affiliates. Finally, Governor Andrew F. Brimmer of the Federal Reserve has proposed that reserve requirements be applied selectively to bank assets. Under the Brimmer plan, when business spending might be deemed inflationary but greater housing activity is nevertheless desired, the Federal Reserve could attempt to influence where bank credit goes by setting high reserve requirements on business loans, on one hand, and perhaps exempting mortgages completely from these requirements or even applying a reserve credit to mortgages, on the other. A major problem with the bank asset reserve requirement plan is that it would force upon the Federal Reserve the task of establishing

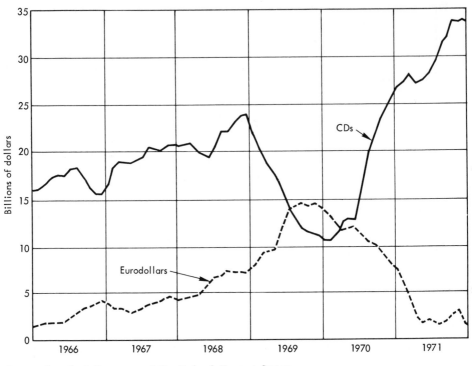

Source: Board of Governors of the Federal Reserve System.

Chart 8   Large Commercial Banks CDs and Eurodollars

social priorities as a basis for determining selectively where credit should be channeled. It might be argued that the Federal Reserve already has its hands full in attempting to control *total* credit and monetary growth. In a recent statement on congressional legislation which would have incorporated the general features of his plan, Governor Brimmer recommended postponing action in view of ". . . a number of questions which should be resolved before the proposal is put into effect."[3]

[3] Andrew F. Brimmer, *Statement Before the Subcommittee on Financial Institutions of the Committee on Banking, Housing, Urban Affairs, United States Senate,* Board of Governors of the Federal Reserve System (April 7, 1971).

Another selective tool relied upon heavily by the Federal Reserve in the 1965–70 period was Regulation Q (ceilings on bank time deposit rates). In tight money periods in the second half of 1966, in early 1968, and in 1969 and 1970, rates on commercial paper as well as on other money market instruments rose above the maximum issuing rates on time certificates of deposit (CDs) permitted by Regulation Q ceilings held rigid by the Federal Reserve (see chart 7). With rates on competing money market instruments more attractive, holders of bank CDs let them mature and placed the proceeds elsewhere.

The intent of the Federal Reserve in deliberately holding Regulation Q rate ceilings rigid in recent periods of monetary restraint was apparently, in part, to selectively

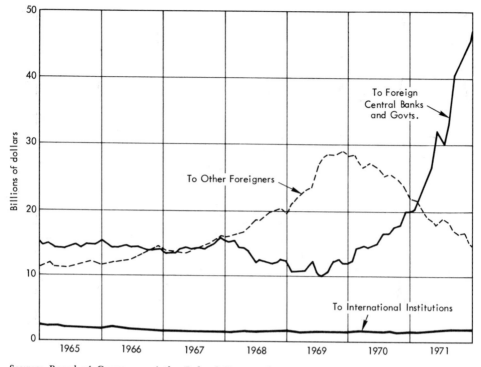

Source: Board of Governors of the Federal Reserve System.

Chart 9   U.S. Liquid Liabilities to Foreigners

limit the flow of bank credit to big business.[4] The same large banks that make the bulk of the loans to big business, it was contended, are the ones most vulnerable to CD runoffs when CD issuing rates are noncompetitive. A reduction in the rate of bank business loan growth was expected to slow inflationary business spending while at the same time enhancing the share of bank credit flowing

[4] Andrew F. Brimmer "Eurodollar Flows and the Efficiency of U.S. Monetary Policy." Paper read at the New School for Social Research, New York, Board of Governors of the Federal Reserve System (March 8, 1969), pp. 4–6; and "Financial Innovation and Monetary Management in the United States." Paper read at the Association of American Banks in England, Board of Governors of the Federal Reserve System (July 9, 1969), pp. 2–3.

into housing and other sectors hit disproportionately hard by tight money.

One flaw in the Federal Reserve's rate ceiling plan was that many businesses were not dissuaded in their efforts to obtain credit even after their bankers said no. There was, after all, the commercial paper market, where many large businesses could borrow funds simply by issuing unsecured IOUs. It was ironic that many of the investors in commercial paper in the recent periods of monetary stress were the same business firms which had allowed bank CDs to mature. The credit flow was merely diverted outside the banking system, where it was beyond Federal Reserve scrutiny and control.

Another by-product of rigid Regulation Q ceilings in tight money periods during the last half of the 1960s was recurring

surges in U.S. bank demand for Eurodollars.[5] The Eurodollar borrowings of U.S.
banks, since they were not encumbered by
rate ceilings, doubled in the second half of
1966, rose strongly again in early 1968, and
surged in 1969 (see chart 8). The Regulation
Q-induced swings in U.S. bank Eurodollar
borrowings over recent years have had a pro-
foundly unsettling effect on international
flows of short-term capital. In 1968–69,
when increasing U.S. bank demand for Eurodollars was pushing Eurodollar rates sharply
higher (see chart 6), private foreigners were
induced to convert their currencies into dollars and place the funds in Eurodollar investments. As a result, the dollar holdings of
foreign central banks fell dramatically (see
chart 9). With the easier monetary conditions that evolved in the U.S. in 1970 and
1971, U.S. banks turned back again to lower
cost domestic CD money and allowed their
Eurodollar borrowings to contract.[6]

Eurodollar rates declined accordingly,
and foreign investors converted their dollars
back into foreign currencies for investment
in foreign money market instruments carrying more attractive yields. Foreign central
bank dollar holdings climbed sharply in
1971, reflecting the combined effects of foreign investor shifts from dollar investments
into higher return foreign currency instruments early in the year, followed by growing

[5] Eurodollars are deposits denominated in
dollars in banks outside the U.S.

[6] An increase from 10 to 20 percent in late
1970 in marginal reserve requirements on
U.S. bank Eurodollar borrowings was apparently intended to limit the drop in these borrowings, but the move proved unsuccessful.
Regulation M provided that U.S. bank home
offices which allowed their Eurodollar borrowings from foreign branches to fall below
a May 1969 reserve free base would have to
hold the higher reserve requirements on all
future borrowings over and above the new
lower level. Apparently banks were not motivated as much by possible future Eurodollar
needs as by the existing reality that domestic
CD money cost less than Eurodollars (see
chart 6).

speculation against the dollar in foreign exchange markets later on in the year. Speculators sought to exchange dollars for stronger
currencies such as the German mark and the
Japanese yen. The unwanted dollars were,
in turn, purchased largely by the German
and Japanese central banks in an effort to
control the climb in their respective currency values relative to the dollar.

To sum up, the Federal Reserve's general policy tools are imperfect but adequate
for the job of overall monetary control.
However, history suggests and more recent
experience confirms, that the operation of
selective policy tools has been by and large
unsuccessful. The forecaster must use caution in interpreting Federal Reserve policy
when selective tools, such as Regulation Q
time deposit rate ceilings, operate to distort
credit and money flows between bank and
nonbank sources. (More discussion on this
point will come later in connection with
monetary aggregates.)

POLICY DECISION PROCESS

A certain mystique has always sur-
rounded Federal Reserve policy decisions.
The underlying view has seemed to be that
the Federal Reserve authorities must possess special financial insights or have access
to substantial amounts of inside information. Actually, central banking is an uncertain art at best, as attested to by many out-
spoken Federal Reserve critics. Moreover,
the economic and financial data used by the
Federal Reserve in diagnosing the health of
the economy are generally available to the
public at large. Awareness of significant economic change is typically not immediate for
observers either inside or outside the Federal Reserve. All Federal Reserve officials
with responsibility for helping formulate
policy are continually reappraising current
and prospective economic developments.
This leads to a continuing discussion—in

Federal Reserve offices, conference rooms, and dining rooms—of the most appropriate set of policies to be followed at any given time.

Personalities

The key decision-making body in the Federal Reserve is the Federal Open Market Committee (FOMC). The FOMC is charged with the legal responsibility for formulating and implementing Federal Reserve open market operations, which, as already noted, lie at the heart of monetary policy. The FOMC, which consists of the seven members of the Federal Reserve Board of Governors plus five voting Federal Reserve bank presidents, usually meets once every four weeks. Supporting staff members are also present at each meeting. The Federal Reserve Bank of New York occupies a permanent voting position on the FOMC, while the remaining four voting spots are filled on a rotating basis by the other eleven Federal Reserve Bank Presidents. Typically, however, all twelve Federal Reserve bank presidents attend each FOMC meeting and enter into discussions.

The backgrounds of the FOMC members are varied. A substantial proportion are economists while others are bankers and businessmen. At the FOMC meetings each member assesses economic and financial conditions, as he sees them from his own viewpoint, and recommends appropriate monetary actions. The chairman of the FOMC (the FOMC chairman and Board of Governors chairman are one and the same) usually attempts to develop a consensus view of the economic and financial health of the country and of the related monetary moves, if any, that should be taken. These wishes are then conveyed in a directive to the manager of the System Open Market Account at the Federal Reserve Bank of New York. Federal Reserve open market operations are carried out in New York because it is the nation's major financial center.

Economic and Financial Information

The basic job of the FOMC is to translate the broad economic objectives relating to prices, employment, growth, and the balance of payments into monetary and financial guides or targets over which the Federal Reserve has direct control.[7] Several times a year the FOMC staff presents to members a detailed analysis and forecast for the coming year of trends in income, output, employment, prices, and the balance of payments. The financial outlook, including credit flows and interest rate movements, is also assessed in these presentations. At each FOMC meeting between these "bench mark" reviews, the staff reappraises current and near-term trends in economic and financial activity. The data examined at these FOMC meetings are generally the same as any business economist might use in diagnosing the health of the economy: GNP and its components, industrial production, new orders, capacity utilization, corporate profits, personal income, liquid asset holdings by the public, the unemployment rate, the Consumer Price Index, the Wholesale Price Index, the Federal budget, money supply growth, bank credit data, total credit flows, interest rates, the U.S. balance of payments, and so on.

In carrying out their important role, FOMC members have two essential tasks. First, they must choose monetary targets that can be directly influenced by the Federal Reserve and that, in turn, have some demonstrable influence on the economy. Unfortunately, not too much is yet known about the specific linkages between financial and real variables in our economy. Secondly, the members of the FOMC must select a relatively few key guides or targets to be used both in conveying orders to the manager of the system Open Market Account and in deter-

---

[7] Federal Reserve, "Monetary Aggregates and Money Market Conditions in Open Market Policy," *Bulletin* (February 1971), p. 84.

mining whether policy wishes have actually been carried out. It is not enough to say that Federal Reserve policymakers look at all relevant financial and economic data. They do, but they must ultimately agree among themselves on a selected few monetary series which will be looked at more closely than others. This is particularly true in the case of FOMC members who may not be monetary or financial experts, but who must nevertheless discharge their public responsibilities in the formulation and execution of policy.

OPERATING TARGETS

The key for the successful policy interpreter is to remain in close touch with the Federal Reserve's operating targets. The movement in these targets provides a real clue to probable future policy moves. For many years the primary operating targets were money market conditions—as measured by short-term rates, member bank borrowings, and free reserves. The Federal Reserve's money market orientation was rooted in large part in its use of open market operations as the primary policy tool. Close Federal Reserve contact with the money market tone followed from the fact that day-to-day open market operations were, as earlier noted, carried out in the nation's major money center. In recent years the Federal Reserve has placed more emphasis on monetary aggregates as operating targets, although money market conditions continue as the primary day-to-day guides for open market operations. Accordingly, free reserves and other money market conditions variables remain good short-term indicators of what the Federal Reserve *is doing* while

monetary aggregates serve as a longer run indicator of what the Federal Reserve *will be doing.*

Money Market Conditions

Conditions in the money market serve as the general day-to-day guides for open market operations by the manager of the System Open Market Account. Instructions relayed from the FOMC typically are worded in terms of maintaining prevailing money market conditions, moving toward firmer money market conditions, or bringing about easier money market conditions. If the operating target happens to be firmer money market conditions, member bank borrowings and short-term rates[8] can be expected to rise and free reserves (excess reserves less borrowings) to fall. The converse is true when easier money market conditions are the target. For this reason, free reserves (or perhaps borrowings) is the single most useful indicator of what the Federal Reserve *is doing* at any point in time. The *best* way, of course, is to keep close tab on all related statistics, including free reserves. Week-to-week fluctuations in free reserves are not significant since they can be wildly volatile. And, as banks utilize their reserves more efficiently, there is a secular decline in the figure, so comparisons over periods of years are not particularly useful. But month-to-month, this one statistic gives important clues to what the Federal Reserve is doing. In contrast, the monetary aggregates discussed below provide a better means of guessing what the Federal Reserve *will be doing*, i.e., they provide a better guideline for *forecasting* monetary policy.

The central role of member bank borrowings and free reserves as money market guides dates back some time.[9] The general

---

[8] The rate target is typically the federal funds rate, usually specified by the FOMC in terms of a desired range of fluctuation. Occasionally, the 90-day treasury bill rate may also serve as a money market conditions target.

[9] For one of the earliest discussions of the relation between borrowings and money market rates see: Winfield Riefler, *Money Rates and Money Markets in the United States* (New York: Harper & Brothers, 1930).

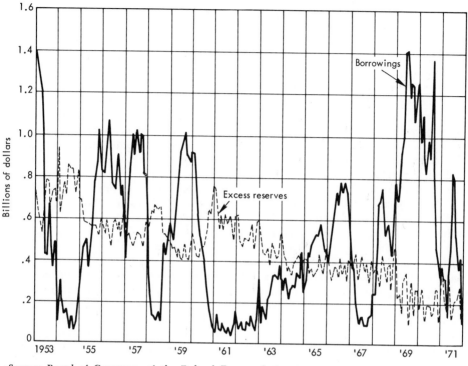

Source: *Board of Governors of the Federal Reserve System.*

Chart 10   Member Bank Borrowings and Excess Reserves

argument has been that Federal Reserve open market sales with accompanying bank reserve pressures lead directly to higher bank borrowings which, in turn, lead to higher short-term rates, at least in the short run. The assertion that high bank borrowings bring about high short-term rates is founded on the view that banks are reluctant to borrow from the Federal Reserve and will therefore act as soon as possible to reduce this indebtedness by restricting loan growth and/or selling investments. The effect in either case will be upward pressures on money market rates. The Federal Reserve is aware, of course, that a continuation of an excessively restrictive policy will ultimately lead to recession and lower rates, and that an excessively expansionary policy, if continued long enough, will lead to inflation and higher rates. In the short run, though, it is assumed that the degree of restraint is

positively correlated with interest rate behavior.

Note in chart 10 that member bank borrowings from the Federal Reserve have fluctuated widely over time. The highest level of borrowing shown in the chart was $1.4 billion during the tight money conditions in 1969. The 1969 borrowings peak was strikingly higher than that reached in the previous monetary squeeze in 1966 when, as noted earlier, the nonprice discounting terms were tightened. Borrowings surged again in mid-1970 when the Federal Reserve opened the discount window to banks facing heavy demands from borrowers unable to roll over their maturing commercial paper debt in the wake of the bankruptcy of the Penn Central, a major commercial paper borrower.

Bank excess reserves (total reserves less required reserves) have trended downward in the postwar years with the decline since 1968 particularly pronounced (see chart 10). Two factors appear to underlie this recent drop in excess reserves. First, in late 1968 country banks, which hold the bulk of the excess reserves, shifted from a two-statement week reserve settlement period to a one week settlement period. This move probably facilitated tighter reserve management. Second, the Federal funds rate rose to unprecedented heights in the tight money conditions in 1969, inducing banks to sell their surplus reserves.

If completely stable money market conditions, as reflected in fixed levels of borrowings, free reserves, and short-term rates, were the one and only operating target, shifts in demands for goods and services and related credit demands would be completely accommodated through increases in reserves and in the supply of new money and credit. A surge in demands for goods and services, and the resultant rise in credit demands, would cause money market conditions to become firmer. The monetary authorities, in an effort to maintain established money market targets, would supply reserves in support of money and credit expansion at a rate fast enough to satisfy additional new credit demands at prevailing money market rates and free reserves levels. The sharper the swings in spending and credit demands, the more pronounced the fluctuations in the supply of money and credit needed to cushion pressures on existing short-term rate and free reserves levels.

In more realistic circumstances, the monetary authorities might dampen the surge in spending and credit demands by setting higher short-term rate and borrowings targets and by cutting down on reserve growth in order to achieve these targets. In fact, this is what the Federal Reserve often did when money market conditions were the primary operating target. In the regular FOMC meetings every three or four weeks close attention was usually paid to sudden shifts in demands for goods and services and

credit. The shifts in spending and credit demands might have been accommodated with new reserve injections to maintain prevailing money market conditions target levels over the periods between two or three FOMC meetings on the presumption that the demand shifts were only temporary and would eventually be reversed. But, if the stronger undesired demands persisted, the Federal Reserve would tighten money market conditions targets and squeeze reserve positions. The presumption was that, with funds more costly and difficult to obtain, demands would eventually subside.

"Proviso Clause"

In May 1966, the FOMC included for the first time a proviso clause in its operating instructions to the manager of the System Open Market Account. The proviso clause took into account explicitly monetary aggregate movements as a conditional or secondary consideration shaping the actions of the manager.[10] The initial choice of required reserves as the monetary aggregate to be used as a target was largely based on the timeliness and availability of this data. Later on in 1966 the FOMC shifted to the bank credit proxy (total member bank deposits subject to reserve requirements) as the target.

The Federal Reserve initially viewed the proviso clause as

---

[10] The May 10, 1966 directive stated in part, "To implement this policy, while taking into account the current Treasury financing, System open market operations until the next meeting of the Committee shall be conducted with a view to attaining some further gradual reduction in net reserve availability [free reserves], and a greater reduction if growth in required reserves does not moderate substantially." The last nine words of this statement beginning with *if* constitute the proviso clause. The monetary aggregate chosen for scrutiny is required reserves. Federal Reserve, *Annual Report* (1966), pp. 147–48.

a means of responding to unexpectedly or undesirably large movements in the banking aggregates, while still allowing open market operations to facilitate a generally smooth day-to-day functioning of the banking system and the overall payments mechanism in the face of sharply fluctuating flows of reserves and deposits in the short run.[11]

This statement seemed to recognize, albeit cautiously, that it was time to introduce a more systematic means of insuring that undesirably wide swings in monetary aggregates do not occur.

The proviso clause, in roughly its original form, was included in FOMC directives through early 1970.[12] In February 1970, however, a subtle but significant change occurred in the wording of the clause. The directive from the February 10, 1970 FOMC meeting stated that

> System open market operations until the next meeting of the committee shall be conducted with a view to moving gradually toward somewhat less firm conditions in the money market; provided, however, that operations shall be modified promptly to resist any tendency for money and credit to deviate significantly from a moderate growth pattern.[13]

Heretofore, the proviso clause had typically been expressed in terms of deviations in actual bank credit growth from rates of increase in bank credit *projected* by the FOMC staff. This projection was high at times, low at other times, and sometimes between. The February directive thus went considerably further than earlier directives in specifying money and credit growth in terms of deviations from a "moderate growth pattern." The implication was that the monetary authorities had in mind a desired rate of growth in monetary aggregates.

Finally, in March 1970 there was a reversal in the thrust of the earlier directives that had given money market conditions primary emphasis and monetary aggregates only secondary emphasis. The directive from the March 10, 1970 FOMC meeting brought monetary aggregates to the fore in stating that

> the Committee desires to see moderate growth in money and bank credit over the months ahead. System open market operations until the next meeting of the Committee shall be conducted with a view to maintaining money market conditions consistent with that objective.[14]

While money market conditions undoubtedly will loom up again temporarily as a primary Federal Reserve concern (as they did in the mid-1970s with unsettling international news and reports of a major corporate bankruptcy) the shift in emphasis favoring monetary aggregates seems to have been of more than passing significance.

Monetary Aggregates

Week-to-week movements in the money supply (demand deposits and currency) are typically quite volatile. Underlying this volatility are wide short-term swings in money needs on the part of corporations and others in connection with dividend and tax payment dates, treasury financings, and a host of other events, some recurring, others unexpected.

---

[11] *Ibid.*, p. 220.

[12] A typical directive from the 1966–69 period stated: "System open market operations until the next meeting of the committee shall be conducted with a view to maintaining about the prevailing conditions in money and short-term credit markets; provided, however, that operations shall be modified if bank credit appears to be deviating significantly from current projections." September 10, 1968 FOMC meeting. Federal Reserve, "Record of Policy Actions," *Bulletin* (December 1968), p. 1011.

[13] "Monetary Aggregates and Money Market Conditions in Open Market Policy," *op. cit.*, p. 97.

[14] *Ibid.*, p. 98.

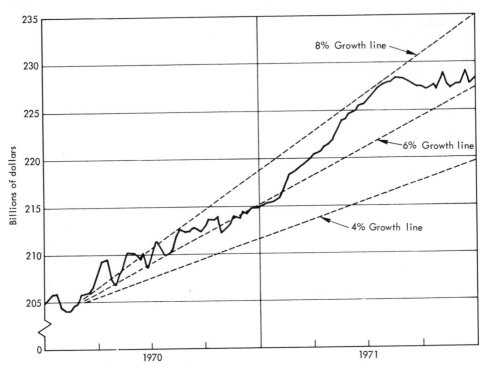

Source: Board of Governors of the Federal Reserve System. Demand deposits and currency. Growth lines originate in February 1970 when monetary policy turned expansive.

Chart 11   Money Supply

Greater Federal Reserve emphasis on a moderate growth rate in money beginning in early 1970 clearly did not iron out wide week-to-week fluctuations in the money supply (see chart 11). Actually, Federal Reserve spokesmen have stated explicitly that it has not been their intent to smooth out wide and often unpredictable week-to-week money supply movements.[15] Note in chart 11 that from mid-1970 through early 1971 weekly money supply movements tended to track roughly along a trend line representing a six percent compound annual rate of growth. In the second quarter of 1971, however, money

[15] See Federal Reserve Bank of New York, "Monetary Aggregates and Federal Reserve Open Market Operations," by Paul Meek and Rudolf Thunberg, *Monthly Review* (April 1971), p. 87.

supply growth climbed sharply above the six percent trend line. Later on in the last part of 1971 a contrasting pattern emerged with money growth slowing to a crawl.

The 1970–71 experience suggests that it isn't easy for the Federal Reserve to maintain a steady rate of money supply growth in line with a desired target growth rate. The monetary policy forecaster must, as a result, be careful not to be led astray by sharp money supply movements in one direction or the other over several weeks. Another caution signal: money supply movements *reflect* Federal Reserve policies, but they also *influence* those policies. In early 1971, for example, the Federal Reserve was trying to stimulate money supply growth, in part *because* money supply growth had been sluggish in late 1970. Thus we had an appar-

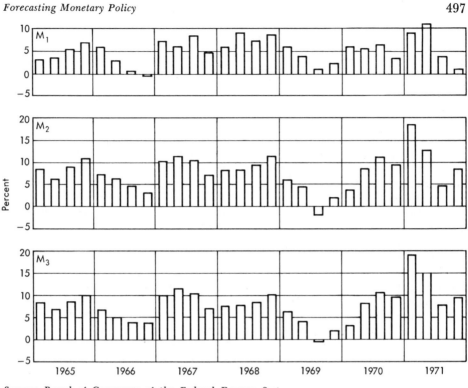

Source: *Board of Governors of the Federal Reserve System.*

Chart 12   Changes in Selected Monetary Aggregates

ent anomaly in early 1971: short-term interest rates were declining rapidly—but the money supply was growing very slowly. The situation completely reversed in the spring of 1971. The money supply began to grow at an alarming rate. To counter that greater-than-desired growth, the monetary authorities slowed reserve growth. Interest rates rose rapidly in response to the emerging monetary restraint—while the money supply grew for a time at a record fast pace. The short-lived surge in money growth apparently reflected in part increased precautionary demands for money on the part of a public that was frustrated and worried over the slow progress in reducing general inflationary pressures despite high nationwide unemployment.

In searching for broader aggregate targets—as opposed to free reserves and other money market targets—the Federal Reserve appears to have settled on two additional measures. One measure (M_2) consists of the money supply plus the bank time deposits excluding large CDs (denominations of $100,000 and more). The other still broader measure (M_3) consists of money supply plus bank time deposits (again excluding large CDs) plus deposits in mutual savings banks and savings and loan associations.

Large bank CDs appear to have been excluded from these measures because of CD volatility, particularly, as discussed above, in periods of tight money when Regulation Q rate ceilings precluded issuance of new CDs. The broader aggregate measures introduced by the Federal Reserve are not, however, purged of all the distorting effects of time and savings deposit rate ceilings. Note in chart 12 that the two broad aggregates performed sluggishly in the second half of 1969 and early 1970 when artificially low deposit rate ceilings induced the small saver to place his funds elsewhere. Subsequently, under easier financial conditions, the rate of growth of the broad aggregates surged as depository institutions were again able to pay attractive rates for savings. These efforts were aided over a good part of 1970 and 1971 by cautious-minded consumers who elected to save an abnormally high proportion of their take-home pay.

Differences in the relative quarterly rates of growth in the money supply and the two broader monetary aggregates have also been related to temporary shifts in the public's preference for demand deposits, as compared with other forms in which funds are held. In the second quarter of 1968, for example, money supply growth spurted when, as a result of a surge in fails (transfers of stock ownership which could not be completed within prescribed periods of time), money and credit needs in the financial sector of the economy increased sharply. At other times, jumps in money supply growth may have reflected increased precautionary money demand by the public, as in the second quarter of 1971. At other times, spurts in money growth have resulted from shifts of funds from treasury deposits (which are not included in the money supply) to private deposits (which are included). Among the influences pushing M_1 growth sharply below growth in broader monetary aggregates in the last half of 1971 were shifts in business demand balances of dollars into foreign currencies in anticipation of the dollar devaluation which eventually occurred in late 1971. These disparities highlight the need for the forecaster to carefully analyze movements in a variety of aggregates rather than focusing irrevocably on one favorite aggregate to the exclusion of all others.

Target Versus Nontarget Indicators

The great advantage to the monetary policy forecaster of following operating targets closely is that he is put on the same wavelength as the Federal Reserve. The operating targets are indeed, as noted in an earlier section, the essential means of communication between the formulators and the executor of Federal Reserve open market operations. If the forecaster can identify and scrutinize the few key financial variables that are being used as operating targets by the Federal Reserve at any given point in time, he is likely to learn something about the intentions of the monetary authorities, and what policy posture in weeks and months ahead is likely to be.

However important Federal Reserve policy targets may be, the forecaster must also take into account other financial indicators. All operating targets are financial indicators, but not all financial indicators are operating targets. Examples of closely watched nontarget financial indicators include the prime bank lending rate, the commercial paper rate, corporate bond rates, mortgage rates, the volume of new corporate bond issues, and bank business loans.

Drawing conclusions about Federal Reserve policy shifts on the basis of sharp movements in general nontarget financial indicators is a risky business. It is extremely important to keep in mind that movements in interest rates generally, for example, reflect the *interaction* of the *supply* of money and credit (which the Federal Reserve can directly influence), and the *demand* for funds which is influenced primarily by the pace of economic activity. Accordingly, a surge in the commercial paper rate resulting from a sudden jump in business spending (due perhaps to a change in expectations) should not be seized upon as evidence of a shift toward restraint in monetary policy. Conversely, sharp declines in the commercial paper rate reflecting efforts by liquidity-conscious businessmen to refinance short-term debt in a generally sluggish business environment should not be taken as a sign of a deliberate Federal Reserve shift toward greater ease. In addition, inflationary expectations may influence corporate bond rates or other longer-term rates levels independently of immediate Federal Reserve policy shifts.

It all boils down to the fact that the forecaster should tie his judgments about recent monetary policy shifts closely to the actual operating targets that the Federal Reserve can and does directly influence. The broader range of nontarget financial variables cannot, however, be overlooked in attempting to *forecast* future Federal Reserve policy shifts. The forecaster must follow many indicators in assessing the financial health of the economy which, in turn, may have an important bearing on future Federal Reserve actions (as will be discussed in the section on the "feedback" forecasting technique below).

Monetarist Viewpoint

The greater emphasis recently placed on monetary aggregates by the Federal Reserve represents a concession but not a conversion to the monetarist view articulated by Professor Milton Friedman of the University of Chicago and others. Professor Friedman has argued for some time that wide swings in the rate of growth in the money supply will have a destabilizing effect on the economy.[16] The solution, according to the monetarist, is for the Federal Reserve to pursue a steady longer-term rate of growth in the money supply. The Federal Reserve has, as discussed above, moved in this direction.

There remain, nevertheless, some basic points of difference between general Federal Reserve pronouncements and the monetarist viewpoint. First, the monetarist asserts that the primary path of causation runs from money to economic activity. The Fed-

eral Reserve, in contrast, leaves the impression that the causation may in the past have run the opposite way in stating that

". . . by placing more emphasis on monetary aggregates in the instructions to the Account Manager, the FOMC has a greater assurance that unexpected and undesired short falls or excesses in the demands for goods and services in the economy, and hence in the demands for credit and money, will not lead more or less automatically to too little or too much expansion in bank reserves, bank credit, and money."[17]

[It should be noted, apart from these possible feedback effects on money and credit growth of short-term volatility in demands for goods and services, that there seems to be *general* agreement, at least among the monetarists and those of a different persuasion within the Federal Reserve, that after a typically long (six months to one year) and often variable time lag, significant shifts in monetary policy do have a significant effect on economic activity.] Secondly, the Federal Reserve has been careful in its general reference to monetary aggregates to place equal weight on money and credit.[18] The monetarist argues, in contrast, that money matters most.

It should be noted further that while the Federal Reserve has placed more emphasis on smoothing out the longer-term movements in monetary aggregates, it has not nor is it likely ever to settle on a hard and fast, inviolable rule for a fixed rate of monetary growth. As a practical matter, the monetary authorities must take into account the potentially destabilizing effect of sudden and unexpectedly sharp interest rate movements on the financial markets and the economy. If, for example, the public's demand for liquidity is increasing sharply, Federal Reserve

[16] Milton Friedman, *A Program for Monetary Stability* (New York: Fordham University Press, 1960); and *The Optimum Quantity of Money* (Chicago: Aldine Publishing Company, 1969).

[17] "Monetary Aggregates and Money Market Conditions in Open Market Policy," *op. cit.*, pp. 86–87.

[18] Federal Reserve, "Record of Policy Actions," *Bulletin* (April 1970), pp. 338–39.

efforts to maintain a steady, modest rate of monetary growth are likely to produce a surge in interest rates. If the economy happens to be in the early stages of recovery and the effects of the sharp interest rate increases include a large diversion of private funds away from socially desirable housing activity, a significant and prolonged slowing in economic activity, and a weakening in employment, the Federal Reserve may be forced to back away from its monetary targets for a time. The policy mix that has evolved in the early 1970s places somewhat greater emphasis on longer-term stability in the money aggregates, but only to the extent that this goal is consistent with smoothly functioning financial markets, both at home and abroad. The selection of operating targets is actually a continuing process, and further changes in target focus are likely. The understanding of the channels through which changes in money policy influence business and consumer spending decisions is bound to be more complete ten years from now than it is today and this knowledge will inevitably influence the choice of future policy targets.

PRACTICAL FORECASTING AIDS

The successful monetary policy forecaster will need to focus in depth on certain key monetary indicators. Certain Federal Reserve publications such as the "Record of Policy Actions" by the FOMC aid in this effort by bringing the monetary authorities' analysis of current and prospective economic and financial developments together with additional information on Federal Reserve aims, intentions, operating targets, and actions. Practical approaches to predicting monetary policy such as the feedback technique (to be discussed below) will also be of assistance in keeping the forecaster's job within manageable limits. Finally, relevant banking data may also help keep the forecasting process on the right track.

Federal Reserve Publications

The Federal Reserve publishes a wealth of economic and financial information, most of which can be found in the tables in the back of the monthly Federal Reserve *Bulletin*. There are, however, certain pieces of Federal Reserve information that deserve special scrutiny:

1. The "Record of Policy Actions" of the FOMC is issued in press release form roughly 90 days following each committee meeting and subsequently published in the Federal Reserve *Bulletin*. The FOMC policy record not only details the directive to the manager of the System Open Market Account, discussed in detail above, but it summarizes the economic and financial basis for FOMC decisions. It also contains economic and financial projections by the FOMC. The "Record of Policy Actions" began appearing in the Federal Reserve *Bulletin* on a regular basis in July 1967. Previously, this policy record had appeared only in the *Annual Report* of the Board of Governors of the Federal Reserve System.

2. Special quarterly articles on financial developments appear in both the Federal Reserve *Bulletin* and the Federal Reserve Bank of New York's *Monthly Review*. These articles typically give an indication of the specific money and credit variables that the Federal Reserve may be watching closely at any point in time. Starting November 1968, informative quarterly reports on financial developments submitted by the Federal Reserve to the Joint Economic Committee have been published on a fairly regular basis in the Federal Reserve *Bulletin*. At other times, articles on capital market developments or time and savings deposit flows may be featured.

3. There are frequent speeches and congressional testimony by Federal Reserve officials, some of which are published in the Federal Reserve *Bulletin* or in the monthly publications of indi-

vidual Federal Reserve banks. These statements often provide valuable insight into Federal Reserve concerns and potential actions. The testimony of Chairman Arthur Burns before the Joint Economic Committee in both 1970 and 1971, for example, was unusually open and lucid with regard to current and prospective economic and financial developments, and current and prospective Federal Reserve policy actions. This may represent a trend toward more of the same.

4. Current information on bank reserves, the money supply, and time deposits as provided by the Federal Reserve Bank of St. Louis. The monthly release on monetary indicators by the St. Louis Reserve Bank is especially helpful in providing current and historical comparative rates of growth in various monetary aggregates. The Federal Reserve Bank of New York, in its weekly Thursday afternoon press conference, also releases up-to-date data on monetary aggregates.

These basic sources of Federal Reserve information should at least put the forecaster on the right track. A close analysis of these sources should provide clues to Federal Reserve thinking, intentions, and potential actions.

"Feedback" Forecasting Technique

The monetary policy forecaster can take advantage of the fact that the policy process is a two-way street. Federal Reserve policies both influence and are influenced by economic activity. The forecaster might determine through the sources cited above what the Federal Reserve expects the economy and financial markets to do and then analyze carefully deviations in actual economic and financial developments from these expectations. If there are significant deviations and they appear to be persisting, the Federal Reserve can be expected to react logically.

Perhaps the best way to illustrate the feedback forecasting technique would be to apply it to a recent situation. How might one have gone about predicting Federal Reserve moves in the brief but unstable May–July 1970 period? The news of the entry of U.S. troops into Cambodia broke on April 30, 1970. In May, financial market conditions deteriorated, interest rates rose, and uncertainty grew. An extremely cautious response by investors to a major treasury refinancing in May 1970 reflected this mood. As these conditions unfolded, the close Federal Reserve "watcher" might well have become increasingly convinced that the monetary authorities would act. The news of the Penn Central bankruptcy later on in June almost clinched the case.

The foreseeable move was not long in coming. The Federal Reserve suspended, effective June 24, 1970, Regulation Q rate ceilings on certain large CDs. In announcing the selected Regulation Q suspension, the Federal Reserve referred to the "current uncertainties in financial markets," which hinted that there had been a shift away from the emphasis earlier in the year on monetary aggregate operating targets, and back to financial market conditions.[19] The Federal Reserve also stated at that time that the discount window would be opened to banks facing heavy loan demands from borrowers unable to roll over their maturing commercial paper debt in the wake of the Penn Central's bankruptcy and the generally unsettled financial market conditions. Finally, open market operations during this period were aimed at providing sufficient reserves to sustain the surge in bank credit and deposits resulting from the renewed ability of banks to raise funds by issuing certain large CDs.

By July the crisis seemed to have passed its peak. The FOMC, at its July 21, 1970 meeting, renewed its earlier emphasis

[19] Federal Reserve, *Press Release*, June 23, 1970.

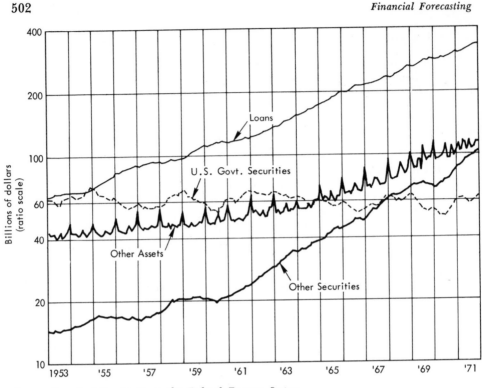

Source: Board of Governors of the Federal Reserve System.

Chart 13   All Commercial Bank Assets

on moderate growth in money and bank credit, but it allowed for a possible continued shift of credit flows from market to banking channels.[20] This return to monetary aggregate targets marked an end to direct Federal Reserve moves in the financially turbulent months in mid-1970.

The alert forecaster who was aware at the time that financial events were deviating sharply from Federal Reserve expectations might well have been able to anticipate at least some of the ensuing monetary policy actions. This is the essence of the feedback forecasting technique. The feedback effect on policy is likely when there are significant and persisting deviations from Federal Re-

[20] "Monetary Aggregates and Money Market Conditions in Open Market Policy," *op. cit.*, p. 100.

serve expectations regarding financial conditions and/or economic conditions.

Banking Data

Banking data are important to the monetary policy forecaster because the banking system is the primary point of contact for Federal Reserve actions. The sensitive guides to the impact of Federal Reserve operations on banks, namely, total reserves, bank borrowings from the Federal Reserve, and free reserves have been introduced in earlier sections of this discussion. Further insight into bank behavior can be provided by examining changes in assets and sources of funds.

Note in chart 13 that bank loans have grown steadily over the past decade. The

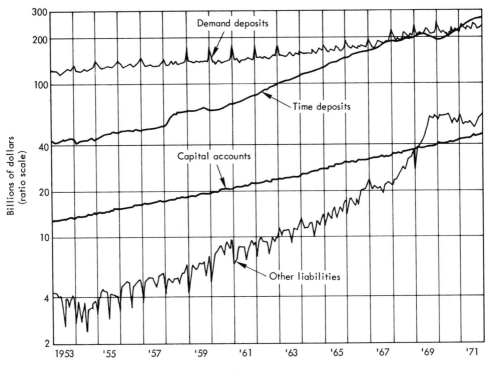

Source: Board of Governors of the Federal Reserve System.

Chart 14   All Commercial Bank Liabilities

growth rate in loans from 1965 to 1970, which included recurring periods of tight money, was not, however, as rapid as during the 1960–65 period of extended monetary ease. The most striking surge in bank investment holdings has occurred in "other" securities (mostly municipals), which increased from slightly more than $20 billion at the end of 1960 to over $100 billion at the end of 1971. At the same time, bank holdings of U.S. government securities have not strayed far from $60 billion. Contributing importantly to these contrasting investment patterns have been sharply increased borrowings by state and local governments as against a much slower rate of growth in federal debt outstanding. Finally, there has been an acceleration over the past decade in the rate of growth in "other" bank assets, including federal funds sold, office equip-

ment, and physical facilities. The revitalization of the federal funds market in the 1960s reflects some significant advances in bank funds management.

A new era in banking was ushered in with the introduction of the negotiable CD in early 1961. Banks which heretofore had accepted deposits more or less passively began to bid aggressively for funds. Bank time deposits have accordingly grown rapidly over the past decade (see chart 14). In the second half of the 1960s banks moved further in stepping up their bidding for nondeposit funds, particularly during the tight money periods when rigid Regulation Q ceilings forced declines in bank time deposits.

It can be seen in chart 14 that bank demand deposit growth in the 1953–71 period has been disappointing at best. The ex-

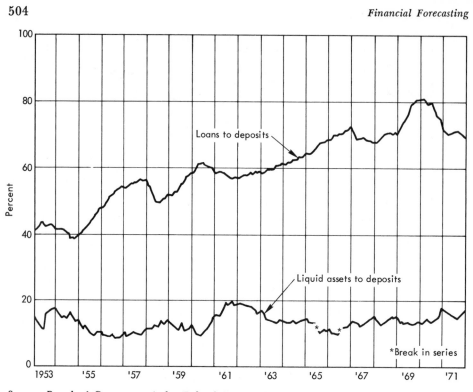

Source: Board of Governors of the Federal Reserve System.

Chart 15   Large Commercial Bank Ratios

tremely slow climb in demand deposits has reflected in large part efforts by bank customers to manage their demand balances more efficiently. Corporate treasurers, in particular, have made every effort to hold down their cash balances and invest their surplus funds in short-term assets carrying attractive interest rates. With customer efforts to conserve demand balances continuing, banks are likely to have to rely increasingly on time deposits and other sources of lendable funds which can only be raised by offering a rate competitive with market rates on alternate investment forms.

The conventional measures of bank portfolio pressures are shown in chart 15. Typically, loan demands intensify and funds become increasingly scarce during periods of economic expansion, pushing up the loan/deposit ratio. With growing pressure on de-

posit sources of loanable funds, liquid assets typically are drawn down and the liquid assets/deposit ratio falls. Conversely, in periods of economic slack, weak loan demand, and easy money, the loan/deposit ratio falls and the liquid assets/deposit ratio rises.

The fact that banks relied increasingly on nondeposit sources of funds in the late 1960s caused the conventional loan/deposit ratio to give a somewhat distorted picture of the true relationship between bank loans and sources of lendable funds. Note in chart 16 that the ratio of loans to total liabilities (both deposit and nondeposit) for large commercial banks rose to a peak of only about 65 percent in the late 1969 monetary squeeze when at the same time the conventional loan/deposit ratio was pushing upward through the 80 percent level.

The greater use of nondeposit sources

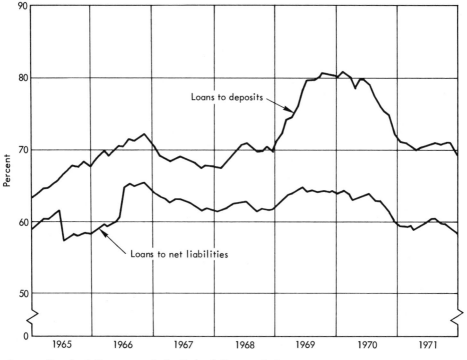

Source: *Board of Governors of the Federal Reserve System.*

Chart 16   Large Commercial Bank Loan Ratios

of funds by banks in 1969 and into 1970 took the form of increased Eurodollar borrowings, the sale of additional commercial paper through bank affiliates (series begins in mid-1969), and gains in "other" liabilities, including federal funds purchases and funds acquired through repurchase agreements (see chart 17). Note that the share of non-deposit funds in total large commercial bank liabilities remained substantial through the second half of 1970 and into early 1971, despite the return flow of deposit funds. Nondeposit liabilities in this period were held up by heavy purchases of federal funds (at attractively low rates) along with additional medium- and longer-term debt issues by banks which operated to partially offset declines in bank Eurodollar borrowings and in bank related commercial paper outstanding.

CONCLUSIONS

The focus of this discussion has been on the practical considerations in forecasting monetary policy. The following conclusions emerge from this analysis:

1. The correct interpretation of the existing monetary posture requires a good understanding of Federal Reserve objectives, tools, and operating targets. The best shorthand statistics for this purpose are "free reserves" of member banks and the federal funds rate. Even these measures are of little value over very short or very long periods of time. Better than any one measure, of course, is a broad continuing knowledge of all relevant data.

2. In order to anticipate policy moves,

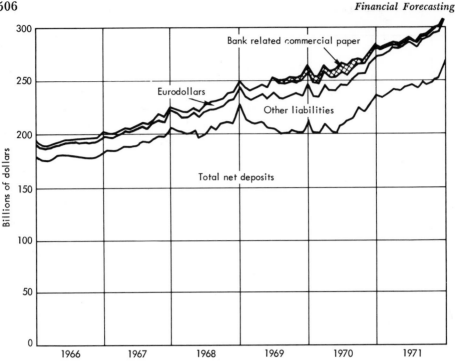

Source: Board of Governors of the Federal Reserve System.

Chart 17   Composition of Large Commercial Bank Liabilities

the forecaster needs to find out what the Federal Reserve has been and is doing, and how the Federal Reserve views business conditions, both now and in the future. On this basis, it is possible to project what the Federal Reserve should be and probably will be doing.

3. The Federal Reserve has in recent years placed increased emphasis on more stable longer-term growth in monetary aggregates. This does not mean, however, that the Federal Reserve will not shift its emphasis temporarily to money market conditions if financial conditions either at home or abroad should become highly unsettled.

4. Care is recommended in using movements in nontarget financial variables as a means of picking up recent monetary policy shifts. These variables cannot be ignored, however, because they may provide important clues to impending Federal Reserve policy moves.

5. The essence of Federal Reserve policy is that it is pragmatic and flexible. Greater emphasis on some particular set of operating targets at any particular point in time is likely to influence the speed and intensity of Federal Reserve reactions to unfolding financial and economic developments. But the Federal Reserve can be expected to "bend" in light of realities, shifting its emphasis temporarily from one set of targets to the other in order to do the "right thing" consistent with its broad price, employment, and balance of payments goals.

6. The Federal Reserve's operating targets can be expected to undergo further refinements and changes in the future in response to advances in economic theory and practice, as they have in the past.

LEONALL C. ANDERSEN

A Monetarist Approach to Forecasting

The St. Louis Federal Reserve Bank has developed a model which differs considerably from the usual forecasting model.[1] To forecast nominal GNP, real GNP, the price level, the unemployment rate, and long-term interest rates, we use five equations and three exogenous variables. The three variables are: changes in money, changes in federal government expenditures, and growth in potential output.

The purpose of developing this model was threefold. First, we desired to develop a model along so-called monetarist lines for the purpose of developing economic stabilization programs. Second, there was the desire to add a monetarist model to the forecasters' kit of models; until recently no such model existed. Third, since monetarists have tended to talk in terms other than an empirically estimated model, we developed ours to fill this void and to challenge other monetarists to produce empirical statements of their economic views.

This discussion covers the following topics. First, the general monetarist view of economic activity is compared with the more prevalent Keynesian view. Next, our general research strategy of model building is discussed. Finally, an assessment of future developments in forecasting with econometric models is given.

MONETARIST VIEW VS. INCOME EXPENDITURE APPROACH

First, consider the contrast between the Federal Reserve Bank of St. Louis view of the economy and the prevailing view. Our approach to these matters has been labeled by some the "monetarist view," inasmuch as we emphasize monetary policy, and more specifically, changes in the money stock as the most important guide to the course of economic activity. Moreover, our theoretical foundation is that of the modern quantity theory of money. Increases in the money stock relative to the demand for money balances induce changes in the rate of spending on goods and services and on financial assets.

In contrast, most economic forecasters work within the Keynesian income-expenditure framework. According to this view, income generates expenditures on goods and services, and these outlays, in turn, generate income receipts. This approach stresses fiscal actions, that is, federal government spending and taxing programs, and other so-called autonomous forces as the major factors which determine the course of production and employment.

[1] Leonall C. Andersen and Keith M. Carlson, "'A Monetarist Model for Economic Stabilization," Federal Reserve Bank of St. Louis Review (April 1970), pp. 7–25.

Monetarist View

The monetarist view holds that monetary actions, measured by changes in the nation's money stock (customarily defined as the general public's holdings of demand deposits and currency), are the major determinant of total spending. Total spending is measured by the gross national product at current prices. This view of how total spending is determined, unlike the Keynesian approach, de-emphasizes the influence of so-called autonomous changes in the components of overall spending such as outlays for new plants, houses, or federal government expenditures. For example, according to our view, a sudden burst of business optimism which results in added spending for new plant and equipment at a time when there is no change in the money stock, operating through the market mechanism, tends to crowd out an approximately equal amount of spending by other parts of the economy.

Changes in the price level, according to our view, are determined mainly by changes in total spending relative to the economy's ability to expand real output of goods and services. When total spending increases greatly, relative to the nation's productive capabilities, as it did in 1968, output increases only insofar as additional resources come into existence, and prices rise rapidly. This is a demand theory of inflation. Past price movements, including wages, may also affect current prices, but such an influence is considered to reflect past demand pressures. Since changes in the money stock are considered to have a great influence on total spending, this view is a monetary theory of inflation.

Finally, we believe that federal government spending and taxing actions have been overemphasized in explaining past economic fluctuations and in forecasting. The influence of these actions, according to the monetarist position, depends on the method of financing a deficit or disposing of a surplus. For example, without monetary expansion the impact on total spending of an increase in government expenditures is little different than the impact of an increase in expenditures for color television sets by consumers. Increased government spending, in the absence of accommodative monetary expansion, must be financed by taxes or borrowing from the public, and as a result, the market mechanism operates to reallocate funds and resources and there will be a corresponding crowding-out of private spending.

Income Expenditure Approach

Let us now focus our attention on the Keynesian income-expenditure view of the economy and how this view is incorporated in forecasting procedures. Most of the large-scale forecasting models have been developed on income-expenditure principles. Furthermore, most present-day forecasters in business and finance usually use this approach to analyze economic developments and to predict the course of economic activity.

The income-expenditure approach to forecasting, in contrast with the monetarist position, usually places little emphasis on the determination of the dollar volume of total spending as represented by nominal GNP. Instead, it generally focuses directly on determinants of real demand for output, and somewhat independently, on the determinants of the price level. Money GNP is considered merely an interesting but not a too important by-product in most other forecasts.

According to the income-expenditure approach, total real output, measured by GNP adjusted for price level changes, consists of individual sector acquisitions of goods and services. Consequently, forecasters using this approach concentrate on forecasting acquisitions of goods and services by households, businesses, and government units. These projected acquisitions are in turn added together to produce an estimate of real output, commonly referred to as real GNP.

This approach holds that changes in the rate of acquisition of goods and services by the various economic sectors are initiated mainly by autonomous forces other than changes in the money stock. Frequently, changes in these autonomous sources of demand are measured by surveys of consumer buying intentions, anticipations of spending on plant and equipment by business firms, and stock market sentiment. Other important autonomous forces, according to the income-expenditure view, are government spending and taxing programs. An increase in government expenditures is considered a direct addition to total demand for real product. A change in tax rates changes disposable income, which in turn exercises a direct influence on total real product.

This view, in its usual application to forecasting, does not in my opinion give adequate consideration to the possibility that an expansion in the rate of purchasing goods and services by one sector may be offset by a like reduction in the purchases of another sector. This is due to the general practice of estimating separately individual sector demands and then adding to achieve an estimate of total demand. Large-scale forecasting models attempt to take into account important interrelationships among markets, but many forecasters who use the judgmental approach do not.

Price level changes are held by the income-expenditure approach to be causes rather than results of changes in total spending. Cost-push, wage markups, the unemployment rate, and monopoly power are considered the main causes of changes in the price level. An example of this view is provided in a paper explaining the main characteristics of the FRB-MIT econometric model presented at the 1967 annual meeting of the American Economic Association. I quote:

... the actual specification of the model reflects the judgment that there have been very few if any periods of demand inflation ... in the United States since the Korean War.
The basic hypothesis on price formation during the period 1953–65 considers "desired" prices as a markup in unit labor costs and costs of raw material inputs, with the markup itself a function of the rate of capacity utilization.[2]

The view I have just cited frequently leads to the conclusion that monetary actions have little direct bearing on price level changes.

ECONOMIC FORECASTING

I believe it is worthwhile to examine briefly the general record of forecasting in recent years. To the extent that there is criticism implied in my remarks, I want to emphasize that it is directed toward the model builders following the Keynesian approach and not necessarily toward the Keynesian theory itself.

Forecasting the course of the economy has proven to be a frustrating undertaking in the inflationary environment of the past six years. Most forecasts for 1967 did not indicate the minirecession of the first half of that year.

Many forecasts for late 1968 and 1969 greatly underestimated the continued strength of total spending on goods and services and the accelerating inflation. These forecasts were based on the assumption that the fiscal package of mid-1968 would have an immediate and significant effect on total spending. Moreover, the usual forecast for 1969 was that real output growth would slow

[2] Robert H. Rasche and Harold T. Shapiro, "The F.R.B.–M.I.T. Econometric Model: Its Special Features," *American Economic Review, Papers and Proceedings* (May 1968), p. 124, 134.

during the first two quarters and be followed by a resumption of rather strong expansion in the last half of the year.

With the benefit of hindsight, we now observe that the actual pattern of real output growth was opposite the one generally projected by income-expenditure models. Output continued to grow at a moderate rate to mid-1969, but then slowed and virtually ceased by the end of the year.

Many early forecasts for 1970 indicated substantial growth in real output accompanied by a considerable moderation in the rate of inflation by the year's end. We now observe that neither of these events occurred. Total spending grew at about the markedly slower rate of the last half of 1969, real output decreased, and the rate of inflation slowed very little.

These errors in forecasting I attribute, in the main, to a prevalent failure to give adequate recognition to the influence on economic activity of monetary actions, as measured by changes in the money stock. The minirecession of 1967 was preceded by no growth in money during the last eight months of 1966. Continued rapid growth in total spending, following the imposition of the income surtax in 1968, occurred against a background of very rapid expansion in the money stock. The slower growth of GNP during 1970 reflected the markedly slower rate of monetary expansion during 1969.

These are not isolated cases. Our studies of the United States economy since 1919, and of the post-World War II experience in eight other industrial countries, support the proposition that monetary actions, measured by changes in the money stock, have been the major cause of business cycle movements.[3]

[3] Michael W. Keran, "Monetary and Fiscal Influences on Economic Activity—The Historical Evidence," Federal Reserve Bank of St. Louis *Review* (November 1969), pp. 5–24; and "Monetary and Fiscal Influences on Economic Activity: The Foreign Experience," Federal Reserve Bank of St. Louis *Review* (February 1970), pp. 16–28.

At the Federal Reserve Bank of St. Louis we have used our model to gain insights into the response of total spending, real output, and the price level to changes in the rate of monetary expansion. Results thus far indicate that a marked change in the growth rate of money is followed about two quarters later by a noticeable change in nominal GNP growth in the same direction. When total spending growth finally slows in response to reduced monetary expansion, growth of output of goods and services slows simultaneously, while at least an additional three quarters are generally required for a marked reduction in the rate of inflation. We estimate that the entire process of curbing inflation normally requires about three years. The process of fully curbing inflation is delayed still longer following a period of prolonged and accelerating price advances.

Our research further indicates that economic conditions prior to a change in monetary actions have an important bearing on the responses of output and the price level to a change in the rate of growth of the money stock. Among such conditions are the level of resource utilization and the rate of increase in prices in the immediate past. In our opinion, the frequently observed variable lag in the economy's response to a marked change in the rate of monetary expansion can be attributed in considerable measure to varying economic circumstances prior to the monetary change. We believe we now have some knowledge of the forces shaping the lag in the response of total spending, real output, and the price level to monetary restraint.

Research Strategy

Let me now present our research strategy for building a forecasting model. One very important point is our view regarding the role of money in economic forecasting. Money is used in our model as a summary measure of the influence of monetary actions—changes in member bank reserve requirements, in the Federal Reserve discount rate, in open market transactions, and in treasury demand deposits—on total spending. The decision to use the narrowly defined money stock is based on our studies which indicate that this definition of money is the best predictor of nominal GNP.

A major part of our research strategy is to start with a few important relationships; therefore, we use a very small model. As I mentioned earlier, we presently use only five equations and three exogenous variables to forecast GNP, real GNP, the deflator, the unemployment rate, and long-term interest rates. Underlying such a strategy is the belief that sectoral detail is not required to produce good forecasts of broad economic aggregates such as GNP.

As the number of specific questions in which we were interested has increased, we have expanded our model. First, we prepared forecasts of total spending and used only one equation.[4] Next, we became interested in forecasting price and output movements, and one equation and an identity were added. Next, we added an unemployment rate equation and a long-term interest rate equation. These equations constitute our basic model, which is a recursive one.

Our strategy of expanding the model further makes use of satellite models. These satellites are connected directly to outputs of the basic model in order to produce forecasts for specific sectors in which we are interested. For example, we have recently experimented with equations which would allow the basic model to produce forecasts of the stock market[5] and the balance of payments. We also have plans to add satellite models for major components of GNP. In

all of these efforts, monetary actions are the main exogenous factors driving the model, since our strategy thus far has been to build a recursive model.

I believe that this strategy has several important advantages over larger-scale models. First, its small size allows one to test it thoroughly with ex post and ex ante dynamic simulations. We have found, as have many others, that good fits of each individual equation in a model does not guarantee good forecasting results when the model is used as a whole. Second, a small model permits one to ascertain quite easily the nature of the model's errors and then to make adjustments in a problem equation. Also, by using a recursive model and extending it by satellite models, changes can more easily be made in one sector without disturbing the reliability of the balance of the model. By limiting the number of exogenous variables to be forecast, the task of forecasting is made easier. Finally, it is much easier to update a smaller model.

How well has our small model performed? We think quite well in these difficult times of both high inflation and unemployment, although our experience in this forecasting game has been of rather short duration. In the fall of 1969, our model indicated that real output would remain little changed throughout 1970, that the rate of inflation would recede very slowly, and that the unemployment rate would rise to the 5½ to 6 percent range. Since the optimistic forecasts of many forecasters, policy makers, and economic commentators have failed to materialize, the view has been expressed that the economy's response to stabilization actions has been a great disappointment. It is our opinion that the response is as our model led us to expect, though we should point out that even our pessimistic forecast underestimated the rise in unemployment.

Since our model does not take into consideration the influence of a major strike, it performed rather badly with regard to changes in output and total spending in late 1970 and early 1971. Nevertheless, it re-

[4] Leonall C. Andersen and Jerry L. Jordan, "Monetary and Fiscal Actions: A Test of Their Relative Importance in Economic Stabilization," Federal Reserve Bank of St. Louis *Review* (November 1968), pp. 11–24.

[5] Michael W. Keran, "Expectations, Money, and the Stock Market," Federal Reserve Bank of St. Louis *Review* (January 1971), pp. 16–31.

flected quite well the movements from the third quarter of 1970 to the first quarter of 1972. Changes over this period bridge over the strike. For instance, assuming actual government expenditures and growth of money, and using coefficients estimated through the third quarter, the model indicated nominal GNP growth at a 5.9 percent annual rate, compared with the 7.1 percent annual rate. A real GNP growth rate of 1.3 percent was predicted compared with the actual rate of 1.5 percent. The rate of inflation indicated was a 4.5 percent rate compared with a 5.2 percent annual rate adjusted for the government pay increase. The unemployment for the first quarter was estimated to average 5.6 percent, while the actual average was 5.9 percent.

I submit that these results are quite good for a five equation–three exogenous variable model. I should also point out that there are no intercept adjustments, add factors, or tender loving care. Furthermore, strike variables are not used; nor, is there any use of autoregression in the residuals. Nevertheless, we are seeking ways to improve the model's forecasting ability.

RESEARCH PLANS

In speculating about the future use of econometric models in forecasting, I believe that there will be four major developments. First, there has been a revival of interest in rather small models, which I believe will continue to gain support. There appears to be some disillusionment with the benefits to be gained from the detail and so-called structural richness of very large and complex models, particularly when the forecaster is primarily interested in broad economic measures.

Second, I believe that the evidence regarding the influence of monetary actions on economic activity is so great that more recognition will be given to these influences in model building. This recognition will be in the form of a shift away from interest rates toward greater use of some monetary aggregate. This has already happened in such large-scale models as the Wharton model and FRB-MIT model.

Third, the federal government sector will be handled differently than I outlined earlier. More explicit handling of the government budget constraint probably will be made, so as to provide a better estimate of the influence of different methods of financing government expenditures.

Finally, I believe that the influence of expectations will take a different form in forecasting than at present. Now, surveys of expectations of such groups as consumers and businessmen are an important input of many forecasts. However, frequently these expectations are not realized and forecasts based on them are wide of the mark. Furthermore, expectations of the future are generally treated as exogenous variables. I believe that important expectations for forecasting are based systematically on longer-run economic developments in the past and are not subject to sharp revisions. Econometric models are beginning to make more explicit recognition of such expectations.

CONCLUSION

In conclusion, it is my opinion that forecasting will come to rely more and more on econometric models. But we are a long way from transforming econometric model building from an art to a science; hence, forecasting will remain an art for some time to come.

TOTAL SPENDING EQUATION

Sample Period: I/1953–III/1970

Constraints: 4th degree polynomial $(m_{-1} = e_{-1} = 0; m_5 = e_5 = 0)$

$$\Delta Y_t = \underset{(3.76)}{2.86} + \sum_{i=0}^{4} m_i \Delta M_{t-i}$$
$$+ \sum_{i=0}^{4} e_i \Delta E_{t-i}$$

$$R^2 = 0.65$$
$$S.E. = 3.83$$
$$D\text{-}W = 1.71$$

$m_0 =$	0.97	(2.36)
$m_1 =$	1.77	(7.50)
$m_2 =$	1.70	(4.75)
$m_3 =$	0.79	(3.48)
$m_4 =$	-0.24	(-0.58)
$\Sigma m_i =$	4.99	(8.02)
$e_0 =$	0.49	(2.61)
$e_1 =$	0.48	(3.68)
$e_2 =$	0.09	(0.51)
$e_3 =$	-0.40	(-3.11)
$e_4 =$	-0.60	(-2.86)
$\Sigma e_i =$	0.06	(0.20)

Symbols are defined as:

$\Delta Y_t =$ dollar change in total spending (GNP in current prices) in quarter t

$\Delta M_{t-i} =$ dollar change in money stock in quarter $t - i$

$\Delta E_{t-i} =$ dollar change in high employment federal expenditures in quater $t - i$

NOTE: t statistics appear with each regression coefficient, enclosed by parentheses. R^2 is the percent of variation in the dependent variable which is explained by variations in the independent variables. S.E. is the standard error of the estimate. $D\text{-}W$ is the Durbin-Watson statistic.

PRICE EQUATION

Sample Period: I/1955–III/1970

Constraints: 2nd degree polynomial $(d_{-1} \neq 0; \; d_6 = 0)$

$$\Delta P_t = \underset{(6.76)}{2.46} + \sum_{i=0}^{5} d_i D_{t-i} + \underset{(10.99)}{0.86 \Delta P_t^A}$$

$$R^2 = 0.89$$
$$S.E. = 1.14$$
$$D\text{-}W = 1.67$$

$d_0 = 0.02$ (2.54)	$d_4 = 0.01$ (1.58)
$d_1 = 0.02$ (6.17)	$d_5 = *$ (1.15)
$d_2 = 0.02$ (5.95)	$\Sigma d_i = 0.08$ (8.63)
$d_3 = 0.01$ (2.54)	

Symbols are defined as:

$\Delta P_t =$ dollar change in total spending (GNP in current prices) due to price change in quarter t

$D_t = \Delta Y_t - (X_t^F - X_{t-1})$

$\Delta Y_t =$ dollar change in total spending (GNP in current prices) in quarter t

$X_t^F =$ potential output in quarter t

$X_{t-1} =$ output (GNP in 1958 prices) in quarter $t - 1$

$\Delta P_t^A =$ anticipated price change (scaled in dollar units) in quarter t

$* =$ less than 0.01

NOTE: t statistics appear with each regression coefficient, enclosed by parentheses. R^2 is the percent of variation in the dependent variable which is explained by variations in the independent variables. S.E. is the standard error of the estimate. $D\text{-}W$ is the Durbin-Watson statistic.

ANTICIPATED PRICE DEFINITION

(p_i from long-term interest rate equation)

$$\Delta P_t^A = Y_{t-1} \left\{ \left[\left(\sum_{i=1}^{17} p_i \frac{\dot{P}_{t-i}}{U_{t-i}} \right) \frac{.01}{4} + 1 \right]^{1/4} - 1 \right\}$$

$p_1 = 0.02$ (1.63) $p_{10} = 0.09$ (11.18)
$p_2 = 0.04$ (3.55) $p_{11} = 0.08$ (10.26)
$p_3 = 0.05$ (6.71) $p_{12} = 0.08$ (9.58)
$p_4 = 0.06$ (12.19) $p_{13} = 0.07$ (9.06)
$p_5 = 0.07$ (19.69) $p_{14} = 0.06$ (8.65)
$p_6 = 0.08$ (21.16) $p_{15} = 0.05$ (8.32)
$p_7 = 0.08$ (17.51) $p_{16} = 0.03$ (8.05)
$p_8 = 0.09$ (14.48) $p_{17} = 0.02$ (7.83)
$p_9 = 0.09$ (12.50) $\Sigma p_i = 1.06$ (20.06)

Symbols are defined as:

ΔP_t^A = anticipated price change (scaled in dollar units) in quarter t

$\dot{P}_{t-i}$ = annual rate of change in GNP deflator (1958 = 100) in quarter $t - i$

$\dfrac{U_{t-i}}{4}$ = index of unemployment as a percent of labor force (base = 4.0) in quarter $t - i$

Y_{t-1} = total spending (GNP in current prices) in quarter $t - 1$

NOTE: t statistics appear with each regression coefficient, enclosed by parentheses. R^2 is the percent of variation in the dependent variable which is explained by variations in the independent variables. S.E. is the standard error of the estimate. D-W is the Durbin-Watson statistic.

UNEMPLOYMENT RATE EQUATION

Sample Period: I/1955–III/1970

$$U_t = 3.89 + 0.03 G_t + 0.29 G_{t-1}$$
$$\quad\; (75.04)\quad (0.88)\qquad (7.47)$$

$$R^2 = 0.92$$
$$S.E. = 0.30$$
$$D\text{-}W = 0.61$$

Symbols are defined as:

U_t = unemployment as a percent of labor force in quarter t

$G_t = \dfrac{X_t^F - X_t}{X_t^F} \times 100$

X_t^F = potential output in quarter t

X_t = output (GNP in 1958 prices) in quarter t

NOTE: t statistics appear with each regression coefficient, enclosed by parentheses. R^2 is the percent of variation in the dependent variable which is explained by variations in the independent variables. S.E. is the standard error of the estimate. D-W is the Durbin-Watson statistic.

SHORT-TERM INTEREST RATE EQUATION

Sample Period: I/1955–III/1970

Constraints: 2nd degree polynomial
($x_{-1} \neq 0$; $p_{-1} \neq 0$; $x_{11} = p_{11} = 0$)

$$R_t^s = -1.31 - 0.17 \dot{M}_t + 1.07 Z_t$$
$$\quad\;\; (-3.21)\quad (-5.42)\qquad (5.16)$$

$$+ \sum_{i=0}^{10} x_i \dot{X}_{t-i} + \sum_{i=0}^{10} \dot{p}_i \left(\frac{\dot{P}_{t-i}}{\dfrac{U_{t-i}}{4}} \right)$$

$$R^2 = 0.90$$
$$S.E. = 0.54$$
$$D\text{-}W = 0.53$$

$x_0 = 0.08$ (6.84)
$x_1 = 0.08$ (7.61)
$x_2 = 0.08$ (7.64)
$x_3 = 0.08$ (7.22)
$x_4 = 0.08$ (6.69)
$x_5 = 0.07$ (6.20)
$x_6 = 0.06$ (5.78)
$x_7 = 0.05$ (5.43)
$x_8 = 0.04$ (5.14)
$x_9 = 0.03$ (4.91)
$x_{10} = 0.02$ (4.71)
$\Sigma x_i = 0.68$ (7.05)
$p_0 = -0.04$ (-0.86)
$p_1 = \;\;\; 0.04$ (1.56)
$p_2 = \;\;\; 0.10$ (8.23)
$p_3 = \;\;\; 0.15$ (18.63)
$p_4 = \;\;\; 0.18$ (13.23)

$$
\begin{aligned}
p_5 &= 0.20 \quad (10.31)\\
p_6 &= 0.20 \quad (8.91)\\
p_7 &= 0.19 \quad (8.12)\\
p_8 &= 0.17 \quad (7.62)\\
p_9 &= 0.13 \quad (7.27)\\
p_{10} &= 0.07 \quad (7.01)\\
\Sigma p_i &= 1.39 \quad (17.01)
\end{aligned}
$$

Symbols are defined as:

$R_t^s =$ four-to six-month commercial paper rate in quarter t

$\dot{M}_t =$ annual rate of change in money stock in quarter t

$Z_t =$ dummy variable in quarter t (0 for I/1955–IV/1960 and 1 for I/1961–III/1970)

$\dot{X}_{t-i} =$ annual rate of change in output (GNP in 1958 prices) in quarter $t - i$

$\dot{P}_{t-i} =$ annual rate of change in GNP deflator (1958 = 100) in quarter $t - i$

$\dfrac{U_{t-i}}{4} =$ index of unemployment as a percent of labor force (base = 4.0) in quarter $t - i$

NOTE: t statistics appear with each regression coefficient, enclosed by parentheses. R^2 is the percent of variation in the dependent variable which is explained by variations in the independent variables. *S.E.* is the standard error of the estimate. *D-W* is the Durbin-Watson statistic.

LONG-TERM INTEREST RATE EQUATION

Sample Period: I/1955–III/1970

Constraints: 2nd degree polynomial $(x_{-1} \neq 0; \; p_{-1} \neq 0; \; x_{17} = p_{17} = 0)$

$$
R_t^L = \underset{(4.75)}{1.28} - \underset{(-3.07)}{0.05\dot{M}_t} + \underset{(12.53)}{1.61 Z_t}
$$

$$
+ \sum_{i=0}^{16} x_i \dot{X}_{t-i} + \sum_{i=0}^{16} \dot{p}_i \left(\frac{\dot{P}_{t-i}}{\dfrac{U_{t-i}}{4}} \right)
$$

$$
\begin{aligned}
R^2 &= 0.94\\
S.E. &= 0.31\\
D\text{-}W &= 0.69
\end{aligned}
$$

$$
\begin{array}{ll}
x_0 = 0.02 \;(3.30) & x_6 = 0.01 \;(1.56)\\
x_1 = 0.02 \;(3.53) & x_7 = 0.01 \;(1.25)\\
x_2 = 0.02 \;(3.44) & x_8 = 0.01 \;(1.01)\\
x_3 = 0.01 \;(3.00) & x_9 = 0.01 \;(0.83)\\
x_4 = 0.01 \;(2.45) & x_{10} = * \quad (0.68)\\
x_5 = 0.01 \;(1.95) & x_{11} = * \quad (0.56)\\
x_{12} = * \quad (0.46) & \\
x_{13} = * \quad (0.38) & \\
x_{14} = * \quad (0.31) & \\
x_{15} = * \quad (0.24) & \\
x_{16} = * \quad (0.19) & \\
\Sigma x_i = 0.13 \;(1.81) & \\
p_0 = 0.02 \;(1.63) & p_6 = 0.08 \;(17.51)\\
p_1 = 0.04 \;(3.55) & p_7 = 0.09 \;(14.48)\\
p_2 = 0.05 \;(6.71) & p_8 = 0.09 \;(12.50)\\
p_3 = 0.06 \;(12.19) & p_9 = 0.09 \;(11.18)\\
p_4 = 0.07 \;(19.69) & p_{10} = 0.08 \;(10.26)\\
p_5 = 0.08 \;(21.16) & p_{11} = 0.08 \;(9.58)\\
p_{12} = 0.07 \;(9.06) & \\
p_{13} = 0.06 \;(8.65) & \\
p_{14} = 0.05 \;(8.32) & \\
p_{15} = 0.03 \;(8.05) & \\
p_{16} = 0.02 \;(7.83) & \\
\Sigma p_i = 1.06 \;(20.06) &
\end{array}
$$

Symbols are defined as:

$R_t^L =$ Moody's seasoned corporate Aaa bond rate in quarter t

$\dot{M}_t =$ annual rate of change in money stock in quarter t

$Z_t =$ dummy variable in quarter t (0 for I/1955–IV/1960 and 1 for I/1961–III/1970)

$\dot{X}_{t-i} =$ annual rate of change in output (GNP in 1958 prices) in quarter $t - i$

$\dot{P}_{t-i} =$ annual rate of change in GNP

deflator $(1958 = 100)$ in quarter $t - i$

U_{t-i} = index of unemployment as a percent of labor force (base = 4.0) in quarter $t - i$

* = less than 0.01

NOTE: t statistics appear with each regression coefficient, enclosed by parentheses. R^2 is the percent of variation in the dependent variable which is explained by variations in the independent variables. *S.E.* is the standard error of the estimate. *D-W* is the Durbin-Watson statistic.

EDMUND A. MENNIS

Forecasting Corporate Profits

In a profit-oriented economy such as that of the United States, knowledge of the trends of and prospects for corporate profits has a vital role in answering the question of how well the economic system is working. Business prospects strongly influence the profit outlook, but often profit forecasts will provide a key to the business climate ahead. The movement of profits is basic to many business decisions. Nevertheless, the statistical tools and techniques in this area are not well known. Therefore, prior to a discussion of profit forecasting, it may be useful to consider the purposes for which such forecasts are made and to differentiate among the various profits series that are available to the analyst.

PURPOSE OF PROFIT FORECASTS

Two of the major users of profit forecasts are the economist and the financial analyst. The economist may be concerned with such forecasts for a number of reasons: to appraise the general health of the economy; to evaluate the incentive for capital investment; to measure dividend disbursements and the savings from retained earnings; to compute the profits on which taxes will be paid, thus providing federal revenue; to appraise the cyclical status of profits, which have been designated by the National Bureau of Economic Research as a leading in-

dicator of business cycle turning points. The needs of the financial analyst are somewhat the same, although his orientation is more toward trends in profits and their evaluation in the securities markets. Consequently, he is seeking some profit series that can be related to security prices. The financial analyst also may wish to compare a particular company's profit performance with that of an industry or with some other aggregate profit measure.

Unfortunately, no one profit measure is available that can meet all of these diverse needs. The appropriate series can be selected after a consideration of the basic types of profit data and the various sources of the time series available.

Basically, three major types of profit measures may be distinguished: (1) profits reported to shareholders; (2) profits reported for tax purposes; and (3) profits as reported in the national income accounts. These three types of profits differ significantly; only the highlights of these differences can be discussed here.[1]

Profits Reported to Shareholders

On an individual company basis, profits reported to shareholders are the most

[1] For a more complete discussion, see Edmund A. Mennis, "Different Measures of Corporate Profits," *Financial Analysts Journal* (September–October 1962), pp. 69–78.

517

familiar and the most widely quoted. This measure of profits reflects management's evaluation of the company's operations, the results of which ordinarily are checked by an annual independent audit. Some problems arise in totaling profits figures from individual company reports because accounting procedures may vary from company to company or even within the same company over a period of time. This difficulty is illustrated by the example of two companies in the same kind of business, each with $10 million in sales, and each using generally accepted accounting methods. The net profit reported for one company was $430,000 and for the second company $1.076 million, the difference arising solely from variations in accounting treatment and not from any factors affecting the operation of the business.[2]

Nevertheless, admitting some reporting differences among companies, profits from shareholder reports have one factor in common: from a shareholder's or a financial analyst's point of view, the audited opinions of management are the final determinants of a company's earnings and, therefore, a major factor in determining dividend policy. Moreover, although not subject to statistical proof, the writer's experience as a financial analyst suggests that these earnings and dividends, as reported, are an important factor in determining stock prices and accordingly the state of business and consumer confidence.

Profits Reported for Tax Purposes

In addition to reporting to shareholders, management is required to submit an annual report of its operations to the Internal Revenue Service. These reports have a far greater uniformity than have reports to shareholders because of the necessity to conform to the requirements of the Internal

Revenue code. However, complete uniformity is not found here either because of the varying accounting treatment permitted under the code for such items as depreciation, depletion, installment sales, and gains and losses on property transactions. Treatment of foreign profits and the degree of consolidation used in reporting for related corporations also affect the profit data.

Individual company tax reports are, of course, not made public, because the Internal Revenue Service is required by law to keep the returns of individual companies confidential. However, the IRS annually publishes a rather detailed compilation of corporate tax returns by industry and in the aggregate in its *Statistics of Income*. The time lag in the availability of these figures is one of their greatest drawbacks; they are generally available about two years after the tax year. Because tax returns may not be filed until a year and a quarter after the close of the calendar year to which the data primarily relate, the delay in preparing these compilations is understandable.

The Internal Revenue Service has made a study of the differences between book and tax profits.[3] In 1964 the overall difference in profits was 34 percent, and the variations are increasing due to changes in the law, the economy, and in accounting practices. Consequently, aggregates of profits reported to shareholders may not be statistically comparable to aggregates of profits reported for tax purposes.

Profits as Reported in the National Income Accounts

The third basic profit series is that reported in the national income accounts issued by the Bureau of Economic Analysis, Department of Commerce. A casual reader

---

[2] T. A. Wise, "The Auditors Have Arrived," *Fortune* (December 1960), p. 145.

[3] Vito Natrella, "Corporate Profits Data: Tax Returns vs. Company Books," *Financial Analysts Journal* (March–April 1969), pp. 37–43.

of this figure in the newspaper might think that it represented the addition of all of the individual company profit figures that are reported and published quarterly. Such is not the case. The Commerce corporate profit figure is rather an attempt to measure the earnings of domestic and foreign corporations which accrue to the account of the residents of the nation. Profits in this context are considered part of the aggregate earnings of labor and properly arising from the nation's current production.

Commerce profit estimates are based, first of all, on profits as reported for income tax purposes. Secondly, certain adjustments are made to this income tax estimate of profits in order to conform to national income definitions. The Commerce Department seeks to measure corporate earnings accruing to U.S. residents without deduction of depletion charges and exclusive of capital gains and losses and inventory profits. Intercorporate dividends also are eliminated, and net receipts of dividends and branch profits from abroad are added. All of these adjustments amount to more than 50 percent of the taxable profit figure.[4]

SOURCES OF INFORMATION

For these basic types of profit data a number of statistical series are available to the analyst. Five of the more commonly used detailed aggregates of profits are summarized in table 1. The sources of these reports are as follows:

1. Internal Revenue Service. This report is the annual compilation of income tax returns of all corporations in the United States compiled by the Internal Revenue Service of the Treasury Department and published in *Statis-*

[4] A reconciliation is published annually in the July *Survey of Current Business* in table 7.5 as part of the updating of the national income data.

tics of Income, Corporate Income Tax Returns.

2. Department of Commerce. This report consists of annual compilations by industry of profits of all corporations prepared for the national income accounts and published by the Bureau of Economic Analysis of the Department of Commerce. The data are published each year in the July issue of the *Survey of Current Business*. Detailed historical data are also found in *U.S. Income and Output*, a supplement to the *Survey of Current Business* published in 1968. In addition, quarterly estimates are published of total profits before and after taxes and inventory valuation adjustments as well as profits before taxes and inventory valuation adjustment for the major sections of (1) durable and nondurable manufacturing; (2) transportation, communications, and public utilities; and (3) all other industries. These series are reported at seasonally adjusted annual rates with a two- to four-month time lag in the *Survey of Current Business* and *Economic Indicators*.

3. FTC-SEC. This report is the *Quarterly Financial Report for Manufacturing Corporations* prepared by the Federal Trade Commission and the Securities and Exchange Commission. Responsibility for this series is being assumed by the Federal Trade Commission, and consideration is being given to broaden the coverage and improve the accuracy of the information currently provided.

4. First National City Bank. This report is compiled quarterly from shareholder reports and presented in the May, August, November, and March issues of the *Monthly Economic Letter* of the First National City Bank of New York. The April issue presents a more detailed tabulation and analysis of annual data.

5. Federal Reserve Board. This quarterly series covers a selected group of manufacturing companies as well as

TABLE 1. COMPARISON OF DETAILED REPORTS OF CORPORATE PROFITS

Basis of Reports	Internal Revenue Service	Department of Commerce	FTC-SEC	First National City Bank	Federal Reserve
	Income tax returns	Income tax returns	Shareholder reports	Shareholder reports	Shareholder reports
Coverage	All companies	All companies	All manufacturing companies	Quarterly (about 900) Annually (about 3,800 leading concerns)	177 large manufacturing concerns; class 1 railroads; utilities; Bell telephone system
Frequency	Annually	Annually +	Quarterly	Quarterly	Quarterly
Time lag	2 years	2 years +	3–4 months	1–2 months	**
Industry classification	Mostly 2-digit SIC basis	2-digit SIC basis	2- to 4-digit SIC basis	Primarily 3-digit SIC basis	6 major manufacturing groups; rails; utilities; telephone
Consistent sample over time	No	No	No	No	Yes
Accounting detail	Income account and balance sheet	Sales, pretax, taxes, net, dividends' depreciation	Income account and balance sheet	Net income, net assets	Sales, pretax, net dividends
Accounting treatment of:					
Capital gains and losses,	Included	Excluded	Excluded	Included	Excluded
special reserve,	Excluded	Excluded	Excluded	Included	Excluded
foreign subsidiary earnings,	Dividends only	Excluded*	Included as reported	Included as reported	Included as reported
intercorporate dividends	Included	Excluded	Included	Included	Excluded if identified

* Although not shown by industry, a "rest of the world" adjustment indicates the net effect of corporate profits and dividends received from abroad by both corporations and individuals in the United States less corporate profits and dividends paid abroad.

* Estimates of seasonally adjusted annual rates of total corporate profits and three of the major components are also available quarterly with a two- to four-month time lag.

** Series has been temporarily suspended; data are available through the fourth quarter of 1969.

class I railroads, class A and B electric utilities, and the Bell telephone system. Data are published in the *Federal Reserve Bulletin*. This series has been temporarily discontinued; data are available through the fourth quarter of 1969.

As indicated in table 1, two of the reports (Internal Revenue Service and Department of Commerce) are based on income tax returns; the other three are based on company reports to shareholders.

Industry Detail

The industry detail in many of the reports is based on the industry classifications given in the *Standard Industrial Classification Manual* published by the Bureau of the Budget. The structure of industrial classification in this manual is in progressively more detailed categories, using two-digit, three-digit, and four-digit numbers as bases. Ordinarily a two-digit classification is so broad it has limited use for financial comparisons of industries. Moreover, definitions of industry classifications have been changed several times in the postwar period, so that comparability over time cannot be made in some instances. Because the industry definitions occasionally differ from those generally used in the financial field, the analyst is well advised to check the definition in the manual before using any series for comparison.

Consistency of Sample

When interpreting changes in the results over time, the analyst must consider whether the sample is composed of the same group of companies or whether changes in the results may be caused by the shifting composition of the sample itself. The Department of Commerce series and the Internal Revenue Service series are so broadly based that, for all practical purposes, they reflect the activities of all corporations, although, of course, not the same corporations from year to year. The FTC-SEC sample changes each quarter, so that, although it represents the entire manufacturing sector, quarterly totals are not strictly additive to obtain annual results. The sample was also revised in 1951 and 1956, but an overlap is provided for these two periods so that the estimates may be spliced for historical analysis. In addition, mergers, especially of large companies in different industrial classifications, may affect the comparability of data from quarter to quarter for particular industries if a major company has been moved from one classification to another.

The First National City Bank series covers companies that publish regular financial reports, and the companies included are only those whose reports are available when the bank's *Monthly Economic Letter* goes to press. Consequently, the series is not consistent from quarter to quarter, although the bank regularly published a seasonally adjusted link-relative index of net income on a quarterly basis. The Federal Reserve series is the only one that contains the same companies over the entire period for which it is available.

Accounting Detail

Variation occurs also in the accounting detail provided; only the FTC-SEC report and the *Statistics of Income* provide balance sheet data. The accounting adjustments vary considerably; only the First National City Bank uses reports to shareholders without adjustments or arbitrary modifications. Treatment of foreign earnings in the *Statistics of Income* and the Department of Commerce series is especially limited, with only remitted dividends included in the *Statistics of Income* report, and the Commerce series excludes foreign dividends entirely from their industry data. In the latter case, foreign dividends and corporate profits from abroad are lumped together in a "rest of the world" sector, and they are netted out against United States corporate dividends paid to foreign stockholders and domestic branch profits of foreign corporations.

PROFITS DATA FOR FINANCIAL ANALYSIS

An additional source of comparative data should be mentioned that is of interest primarily to the financial analyst.

Standard & Poor's

Standard & Poor's Corporation has published annual earnings per share data for its industrial stock average, railroad average, utility average, and composite average from 1926 to date. For these same series, quarterly earnings, unadjusted and seasonally adjusted, are available since 1935. The data are published in Standard & Poor's *Trade and Securities Statistics Manual*. Earnings per share are generally taken as reported by the company and are comparable to the company figures in the Standard & Poor's Corporation Records. Inasmuch as the composition of these per share figures can easily be determined and related directly to the Standard & Poor's stock price indexes, they would seem to afford a most useful comparative tool for analytical purposes.

Standard & Poor's also has a publication, *The S & P Analysts Handbook*, that is of particular value to the analyst. For each industry in the Standard & Poor's industrial stock price index they have made available on a per share basis the following information for the years 1946 to date: sales, operating profit, depreciation, federal income taxes, earnings, dividends, book value, working capital, and capital expenditures. The continuity of the per share figures is main-

tained through adjustments made similar to those in the stock price indexes. The companies in each industry correspond to the companies in Standard & Poor's stock indexes, so that a direct comparison with stock prices can be made. Similar data are available on electric and gas utilities, as well as annual data on railroads and banks. A monthly supplement to the publication provides current data.

SUITABILITY FOR FORECASTING

Having described the profit series generally available, consideration can now be given to their suitability for the various needs of the economist and the financial analyst.

General Analysis

For analysis of savings, capital spending, and other trends in the national economy, the national income series of the Department of Commerce is most useful. Conceptually, this series fits into the framework of the national income accounts and therefore can be used as part of an examination of the U.S. economy. The utility of the series has been considerably enhanced in recent years since the Department of Commerce has provided quarterly detailed data on corporate gross product and its components, which can be used for the analysis of historical profits data and as a base for future projections. A recommended procedure for such analysis and forecasting is described later in this chapter.

For estimating federal government revenues, projections of future income tax receipts are required. Estimates of corporate income tax returns can be made, as will be discussed later, based on the close relationship between the tax returns and the corporate profit figures prepared by the Department of Commerce.

Cyclical Turns

Because of their unusual sensitivity to changing economic conditions, corporate profits have been designated as a leading indicator of cyclical turning points by the National Bureau of Economic Research, and the quarterly Commerce series is ordinarily used by most economists in appraising current profit trends. However, this profits series is subject to the hazard of wide errors in preliminary estimates until the income tax data on which it is based finally become available to the Commerce Department about two years after the year for which profits are reported. A study by the Office of Statistical Standards in February 1960[5] indicated that, for the period 1947–58, the first estimate of corporate profits before taxes missed changes in direction nine times, or 19 percent of the time. Four of these nine times were at cyclical turning points. In addition, if the differences between the first and last estimate for each calendar quarter from 1947 to 1958 are totaled and averaged, this average is 40 percent of the average of the differences between the successive quarterly profit figures finally reported. A further analysis by the writer revealed that of the 48 calendar quarters from 1947 to 1958, in 20 of the calendar quarters revised estimates made subsequent to the first estimate were further away from the final figure than the first estimate. Changes in seasonal corrections are partly responsible for the quarterly revisions.

These errors in early estimates should not be considered the fault of the compilers of this profit series. Considering the nature of the material available, it is remarkable that the compilers do as well as they do. The

Office of Business Economics has frequently stressed the need for better data on which to base estimates for the nonmanufacturing sector, and further exploration of the growing differences between profits reported to shareholders and those reported for tax purposes would seem necessary also. It seems reasonable to say, however, that only the most tentative conclusions regarding corporate-profit movements can be based on the early quarterly estimates of Commerce profits, since their actual movement is not known until two years or more after the fact.

With respect to the suitability of other profit reports as indicators of business cycle turning points, considerable work has been done in exploring the cyclical characteristics of the First National City Bank series.[6] The National Bureau of Economic Research has found that one of the series with fairly consistent leads at cyclical turning points is a computation of the percentage of the total number of companies with profits higher than those of the preceding quarter, the percentage total being seasonally adjusted. The Bureau of the Census publication *Business Conditions Digest* reports this series currently, as does the First National City Bank. For the analysis of current business cycle developments, this series would seem more useful than the somewhat less certain Commerce profit series.

An additional sensitive indicator of profit trends in the manufacturing sector is provided by a time series published monthly in *Business Conditions Digest*. This series, designated as a leading indicator of business cycle turning points by the National Bureau of Economic Research, is called the price-per-unit-of-labor-cost index. It is computed by taking a ratio of an index of wholesale prices of manufactured goods to an index of compensation of employees (sum of wages,

[5] *Revision of First Estimates of Quarter-to-Quarter Movement in Selected National Income Series, 1947–58 (Seasonally Adjusted Data)*, Statistical Evaluation Reports No. 2, Office of Statistical Standards, Bureau of the Budget, Executive Office of the President (Washington, February 1960).

[6] Geoffrey Moore, *Business Cycle Indicators*, Vol. I, Chaps. 11–12 (New York: National Bureau of Economic Research, 1961), especially pp. 345 ff.

salaries, and supplements to wages and salaries) per unit of output. The labor cost per
unit of output takes into account both hourly compensation and output per man-hour.
The series is seasonally adjusted. Inasmuch
as it relates prices to labor costs (one of the
most important elements of cost), the index
is, in effect, an implicit measure of profit
margins. The lead of this series at cyclical
turning points has, on average, been longer
than the lead of corporate profits themselves. The series is also of considerable
value in following profit margin trends.[7]

Industrial and Financial Analysis

For the purpose of comparing a company's profits with those of some industry
aggregate, the First National City Bank
series or the FTC-SEC series in the manufacturing area would seem the most useful
of those considered here. For measuring
broad profit trends, the First National City
Bank series is again the most helpful, and
the bank regularly publishes the seasonally
adjusted link-relative series that indicates
the trends of corporate profits over time.[8]

For the financial analyst, the First National City Bank series, or the FTC-SEC
series, provides useful comparisons for company and industry purposes. The Federal
Reserve Board series provides a measure of
the results of a consistent sample of shareholders' reports for six large manufacturing
groups as well as for three regulated industries. However, the industry detail made

available by Standard & Poor's would seem
to be the most valuable for financial analysis.

One further commonly used compari-
son in the financial analyst's area is the earnings per share of the Dow-Jones Industrial
Average, which is published quarterly in
Barron's. This series is not comparable over
time because of changes in the divisor and
in the composition, but it is widely used
nevertheless. Projections of earnings for this
series can be made by taking the quarterly
or annual earnings estimates for each of the
30 stocks in the Dow-Jones Industrial Average and then totaling the earnings and dividing by the same divisor (published weekly in Monday's *Wall Street Journal*) that is
applied to the stock price series.

HOW TO FORECAST PROFITS

Having considered the various profit
series and their utility for particular purposes, attention can now be turned to forecasting methods for each of these profit
measures.

Forecasting the Commerce Series

In forecasting aggregates of profits, the
estimate most commonly sought by the
economist is the profit series released by the
Department of Commerce. The estimating
technique ordinarily used is to calculate the
correlation between gross national product
(GNP) and profits before taxes, both variables being expressed in terms of quarterly
percentage changes. These equations have
been improved by adding a variable for unit
labor costs.[9]

[7] For a further discussion and description of
this series, see *Tested Knowledge of Business
Cycles*, Forty-Second Annual Report, National Bureau of Economic Research (New
York, June 1962), pp. 9–15.

[8] For an excellent comparison of the First
National City Bank series, the Statistics of
Income series, the Department of Commerce,
and the FTC–SEC series, see "Corporate
Profits Statistics," *Monthly Economic Letter*,
First National City Bank (January 1963), pp.
9–11.

[9] For a discussion of this approach, see Albert
T. Sommers, "Policy and Structure," *The
Conference Board Record* (April 1971) pp.
2–6.

A somewhat different technique uses the detailed information provided by the Department of Commerce that has improved and deepened understanding of the important economic variables affecting corporate profits. With this information, our ability to follow profit performances is enhanced, and our tools for forecasting the implications of changes in the economy on profits are better than they have been heretofore. This information was published originally in the May 1967 *Survey of Current Business* and is updated regularly in each monthly issue as table 9, Corporate Gross Product, in the National Income and Product Tables. The following sections describe and chart some of the new information made available. An analysis of historical profit performance is provided, because this is critical in projecting future profits. Then a method is described for using the data to prepare an estimate of future corporate profits.

Definitions

The data provided by the Commerce Department cover gross corporate product quarterly since 1948 and also gross corporate product originating in the nonfinancial sector of the economy (NFGCP). In addition to NFGCP in current dollars, the series provides a price deflator, which enables NFGCP to be stated in constant 1958 dollars. NFGCP is further divided into its components of costs and profits and also unit costs and unit profits. The most effective way of utilizing this series is to concentrate on the NFGCP sector and treat the financial sector separately.

Most of the terms used are not familiar and require some clarification. The first question, therefore, is what is NFGCP? This series reflects the contribution of the domestic operations of nonfinancial corporations to GNP. Excluded from the nonfinancial area are the results of financial corporations:

commercial banks, mutual savings bank, savings and loan associations, credit unions, financial companies, securities and commodity brokers, regulated investment companies, and insurance carriers.

NFGCP can be considered in two ways. Just as the national income accounts have both an income and product side, NFGCP has both a sales or product side and a balancing income or factor cost side. On one hand it can be looked upon as the sales of nonfinancial firms to other businesses, consumers, government and foreigners, plus inventory change, less purchases from other firms, both domestic and foreign. NFGCP can also be defined as the sum of incomes and charges to this gross product. From this latter viewpoint, it is therefore the sum of (1) capital consumption allowances; (2) indirect business taxes less subsidies plus business transfer payments; (3) compensation of employees; (4) net interest; and (5) corporate profits before taxes and inventory valuation adjustment. Capital consumption allowances in national income terminology include depreciation and accidental damage to fixed capital. Indirect business taxes represent primarily sales, excise, and property taxes. Business transfer payments would include gifts to nonprofit organizations and consumer bad debts. Employee compensation includes monetary remuneration plus supplements such as contributions to social insurance, pension, health, welfare, and unemployment funds as well as compensation for injuries.

In addition to the figures for NFGCP and its factor cost components in current dollars, Commerce also provides data for NFGCP in 1958 prices together with implicit price deflators. The price deflator for NFGCP reflects the current cost per unit of 1958 dollar NFGCP, that is, the costs incurred and the profits earned in producing one 1958 dollar's worth of output in the current period. The current factor costs of capital consumption allowances, indirect business taxes, net interest, employee com-

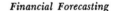

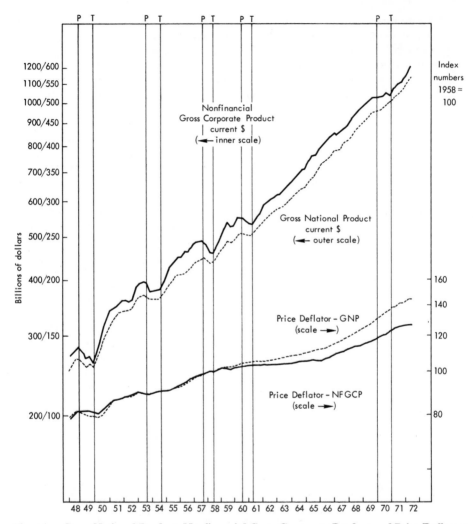

**Chart 1   Gross National Product, Nonfinancial Gross Corporate Product and Price Deflators
1948-72**

pensation, and profits have also been related to NFGCP in 1958 dollars, so that we have not only the dollar costs but also unit labor costs, unit nonlabor costs, and unit profits. This additional information is a significant contribution to the field of profits analysis.

Historical Analysis

Several charts have been prepared that show the historical record of a number of the series described above, arranged in a way that facilitates their use for profit analysis. Chart 1 plots NFGCP in current dollars against GNP and also shows the implicit price deflators for both series. The data are plotted on a semilogarithmic grid, so that rates of change, rather than absolute values, are stressed. In addition, the cyclical peaks and troughs of the postwar period as defined by the National Bureau of Economic Re-

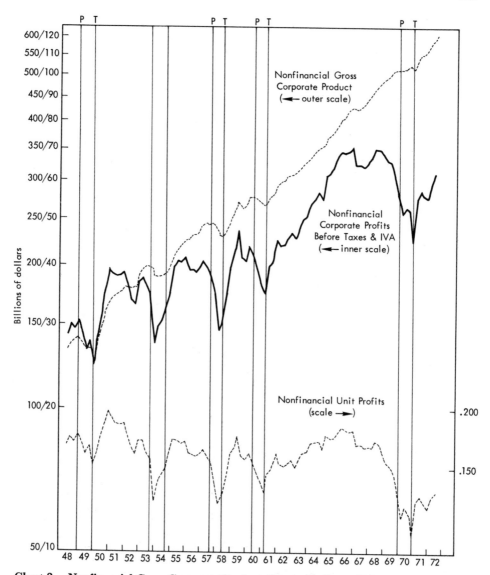

Chart 2   Nonfinancial Gross Corporate Product, Pretax Profits and Unit Profits 1948–72

search are shown on the chart to assist in the analysis.

As the two lines toward the top of the chart indicate, NFGCP, which accounts for about 55 percent of GNP, follows the pattern of GNP fairly closely, although it is more volatile. Its peaks and troughs have in almost all instances coincided with peaks and troughs in GNP. With respect to price changes, the movement of the price deflators of both GNP and NFGCP were quite similar until 1958. Since that time the price deflator for GNP has moved up more rapidly than for NFGCP, presumably reflecting the more rapid price increases in the service component and government sectors of GNP.

Chart 2 plots NFGCP in current dollars and nonfinancial corporate profits be-

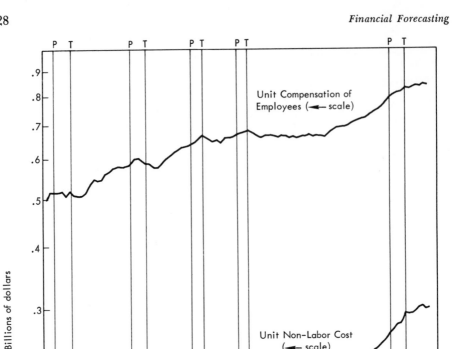

Chart 3   Employee Compensation and Nonlabor Costs Per Unit of 1958 NFGCP 1948-72

fore taxes and inventory valuation adjustment. (The tax factor and the adjustment for inventory profits will be discussed later.) These two series represent the sales and the pretax profits emerging from those sales in the nonfinancial sector of the economy. At the bottom of the chart we have shown profits per unit of real NFGCP, which is a measure of profit margins. However, this measure is not exactly comparable with pre-

tax margins as ordinarily computed by the financial analyst. Pretax margins normally reflect the proportion of pretax dollars to sales dollars. Unit profits represent the percent that current dollar pretax profits are of current output measured in 1958 prices. In other words, unit profits relate to profits per unit of real output rather than current dollar sales.

Examining the lines at the top of the

TABLE 2.   COSTS PER UNIT OF REAL OUTPUT—NONFINANCIAL SECTOR

(1958 = 1.00)

Year	Total Unit Costs and Profits	Capital Consumption Allowances	Indirect Business Taxes	Interest	Total Nonlabor Costs	Labor Costs	Unit Profits
1961	1.029	0.095	0.103	0.013	0.211	0.670	0.149
1962	1.034	0.100	0.101	0.014	0.215	0.670	0.154
1963	1.039	0.100	0.102	0.015	0.217	0.665	0.158
1964	1.050	0.100	0.101	0.016	0.217	0.664	0.168
1965	1.055	0.099	0.100	0.017	0.216	0.665	0.179
% Change 1961–65	+2.5%	+4.2%	−2.9%	+30.8%	+2.4%	−0.7%	+20.1%
1966	1.073	0.100	0.096	0.019	0.215	0.678	0.180
1967	1.104	0.107	0.100	0.023	0.230	0.707	0.167
1968	1.132	0.109	0.105	0.025	0.239	0.727	0.166
1969	1.162	0.115	0.109	0.029	0.253	0.764	0.145
1970	1.208	0.124	0.118	0.035	0.277	0.812	0.119
% Change 1966–70	+12.6%	+24.0%	+22.9%	+84.2%	+28.8%	+19.8%	−33.9%

Source: *Survey of Current Business.*

chart, the strong growth trend in NFGCP is clearly evident. Moreover, from 1961 to 1968 this growth trend accelerated and was much smoother. The impact of this sales pattern on profits is seen in the second line. The cyclical fluctuations in nonfinancial corporate profits are quite pronounced, and the general growth trend from 1958 to 1961 is substantially slower than the growth in NFGCP. From 1961 to early 1966, profits advanced sharply, but profits leveled out thereafter and fell substantially in 1969 and 1970. As shown in the third line on the chart, unit profits were in a declining trend and also had substantial cyclical fluctuations in the period 1948 through 1960. From 1961 to 1966 unit profits had the longest advance in the postwar period, but the ensuing erosion in margins was the longest postwar decline.

The profits performance from 1961 to 1966 and from 1966 to 1970 is most interesting, particularly in view of the sustained rise in sales volume during most of that period. The key to these changes can be found in an analysis of costs that favorably affected unit profits in the earlier period and adversely affected profits since 1966.

Cost Analysis

Chart 3 plots unit nonlabor costs and unit labor costs quarterly from 1948 through mid-1972. In terms of their relative importance, unit labor costs in the postwar period have averaged about 64 percent of total unit costs and profits, while unit nonlabor costs have averaged about 19 percent. The remaining 17 percent, of course, represents unit profits. A substantial portion of the nonlabor costs are relatively inflexible, while other costs vary with sales volume. The shifting patterns of these unit costs have been primarily responsible for the path of profits, especially in the past decade. Therefore, if we can get a better understanding of these components of cost, we will have a deeper insight into the movement of profits.

As indicated on the chart, unit labor costs moved up fairly steadily from 1948 to 1961, although a reduction in unit labor costs was fairly characteristic of the periods shortly after a business cycle peak until early in the recovery after the cyclical trough. The experience after the 1961 cyclical trough was unusual, however, because unit labor

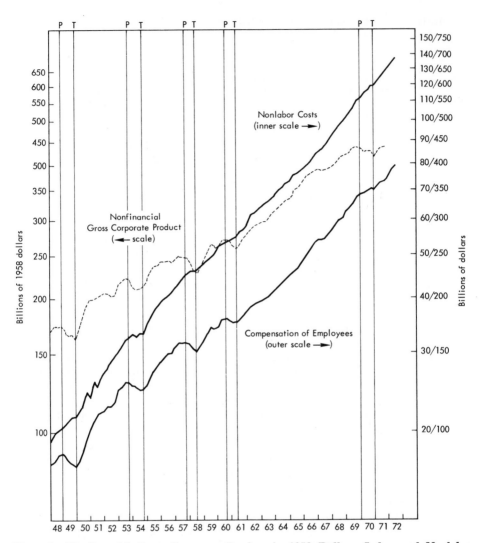

Chart 4   Nonfinancial Gross Corporate Product in 1958 Dollars, Labor and Nonlabor Costs in Current Dollars 1948–72

costs trended downward until 1965. The rise from 1966 to 1971 was quite marked.[10]

[10] This series is similar to the monthly unit labor cost ratio in manufacturing, which is published regularly in the Department of Commerce publication, *Business Conditions Digest*. However, this series covers the entire nonfinancial area and thus includes a broader sector of the corporate universe.

Unit nonlabor costs moved up even more steeply than unit labor costs, reaching a peak in 1962. Thereafter unit nonlabor costs flattened out, actually declined in 1965 and 1966, but rose sharply thereafter. Thus, the rise in unit profits in 1961–66 shown in chart 2 was accounted for by the changed direction of both unit labor costs and unit nonlabor costs beginning in 1961. The 1966–

70 decline was attributable to both types of unit costs increasing again, with the rise in unit nonlabor costs the greater of the two.

A clearer picture of the factors affecting unit costs and profits may be seen in table 2, which shows the yearly figures for unit costs and profits and their components from 1961 to 1965 and then from 1966 to 1970. The percentage change in each factor cost over these two five-year periods is also given. As the table indicates, unit profits increased 20 percent from 1961 to 1965. The increase in unit nonlabor costs was only 2.4 percent and unit labor costs actually declined. An added factor favorably affecting profit margins was a 2.5 percent increase in prices. In sharp contrast, unit profits fell almost 34 percent from 1966 to 1970 to the lowest level in the postwar period. Although prices were up about 13 percent, unit nonlabor costs were up about 29 percent and unit labor costs up almost 20 percent.

Chart 4 takes the analysis one step further by examining both the numerator and the denominator of each unit cost line. NFGCP is plotted in 1958 dollars, which provide a stable unit of measurement for the denominator of each of the two unit cost ratios. Then labor costs and nonlabor costs are plotted in current dollars.

As the chart indicates, nonlabor costs have moved up rather steadily during the entire postwar period, and from 1948 to 1961 the rate of increase was more rapid than NFGCP. Consequently, unit nonlabor costs increased. From 1961 to 1965, the two lines moved in parallel, and the unit nonlabor cost ratio flattened out. A slowing in the gain in NFGCP since 1966, however, has resulted once more in an upward movement of the unit nonlabor cost line.

The relationship of labor costs and NFGCP as shown on chart 4 is similar to that of nonlabor costs and NFGCP. Labor costs moved up more rapidly prior to 1961, paralleled the growth in real output from 1961 to 1965, and moved upward more rapidly since. For a better understanding of

unit labor costs, however, a deeper analysis of its components is necessary.

Labor costs per unit of output are calculated as the ratio of employee compensation (in current dollars) to NFGCP in (constant 1958 dollars). In order to provide a more useful analytical framework, both the numerator and denominator of this ratio can be divided by man-hours, making unit labor costs equal to the ratio of compensation per man-hour and output per man-hour. Thus changes in unit labor costs can be analyzed from the interaction of two key factors: hourly wage rates (including salaries and fringe benefits) and labor productivity. When wages advance more rapidly than output per man-hour, unit labor costs increase. When productivity gains exceed increases in wage rates, unit labor costs decline. Violating arithmetic principles only slightly, the percent change in unit labor costs can be calculated as the difference between the percent changes in hourly compensation and output per man-hour. For example, a four percent increase in wage rates and a three percent advance in productivity result in a rise of one percent in unit labor costs.

Unfortunately, the Commerce data on NFGCP do not provide regular quarterly information on man-hours and compensation per man-hour, and therefore output per man-hour cannot be calculated. However, an acceptable substitute for this information is published quarterly by the Bureau of Labor Statistics in their release "Productivity and Costs in Nonfinancial Corporations." Although not precisely comparable, the movement of unit labor costs in the BLS series and in the Commerce series has been quite similar.[11] Charts 5 and 6 plot the various components of unit labor costs in the BLS series.

[11] For a discussion of the differences between the Bureau of Labor Statistics data and the Department of Commerce data, see "Productivity and Costs—First Quarter 1972," U.S. Department of Labor release 72-242, April 25, 1972.

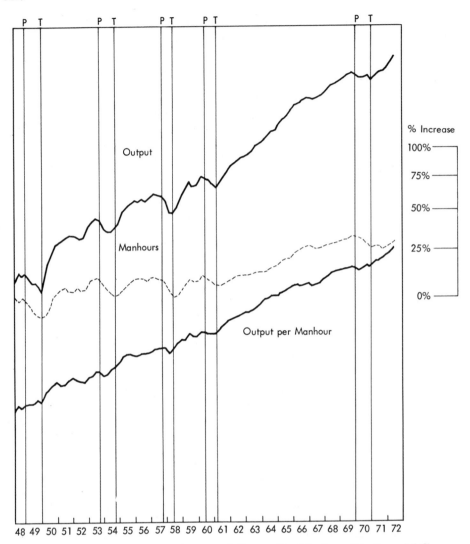

Chart 5   Indexes of Output, Manhours and Output Per Manhour, Nonfinancial Corporations 1948-72 (1967 = 100)

As chart 5 indicates, output has increased faster than man-hours in the postwar period and consequently output per man-hour has moved upward. The gain in output relative to man-hours was particularly pronounced in the 1961–1965 period, partly due to unused resources and available labor supply. From 1966 through mid-1969, the rate of gain in output slowed because the economy had moved to full utilization of its labor force, and demand also slackened. In 1970, output declined. Consequently, productivity gains slowed until man-hours were reduced in 1970. Since then, productivity has picked up considerably as the cyclical rebound in output has exceeded the rise in man-hours.

Chart 6 repeats the line showing out-

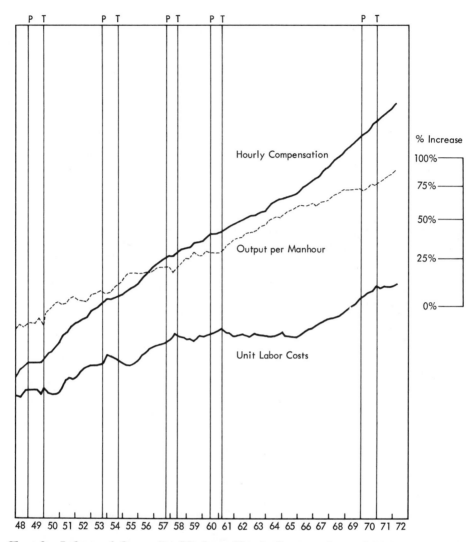

Chart 6 **Indexes of Output Per Manhour, Hourly Compensation and Unit Labor Costs, Nonfinancial Corporations 1948–72 (1967 = 100)**

put per man-hour, shows employee compensation per man-hour, and finally shows the result of those two forces in the unit labor cost line. One interesting fact shown on the chart is the fairly steady increase in employee compensation, with the trend accelerating beginning in 1965. The slower rate of growth in output per man-hour relative to hourly labor costs from 1947 to 1961 ac-

counted for the rising unit labor cost line during that period. The faster rise in productivity, which roughly paralleled hourly compensation from 1961 to 1965, resulted in the leveling of unit labor costs. From 1966 through 1970, the acceleration in employee compensation and the slowing in or lack of productivity gains resulted in one of the sharpest rises in unit labor costs in the post-

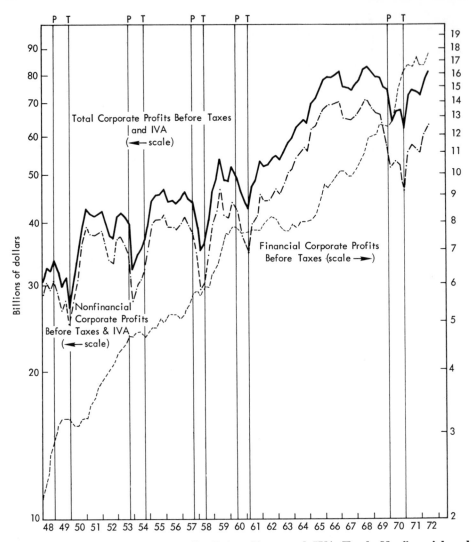

Chart 7   Domestic Corporate Profits Before Taxes and IVA Total, Nonfinancial and Financial 1948-72

war period. More recently, hourly compensation has continued to gain, although the improvement in productivity has slowed the rise in unit labor cost.

Domestic Corporate Profits

Thus far we have examined domestic corporate profits in the nonfinancial sector and the underlying component costs. The profits squeeze from 1966 to 1970 has been identified as caused by some slowing in the growth of output, a rise in unit nonlabor costs, and also a combination of accelerated hourly compensation and slower productivity gains, which together caused unit labor costs to advance. Price increases, which are

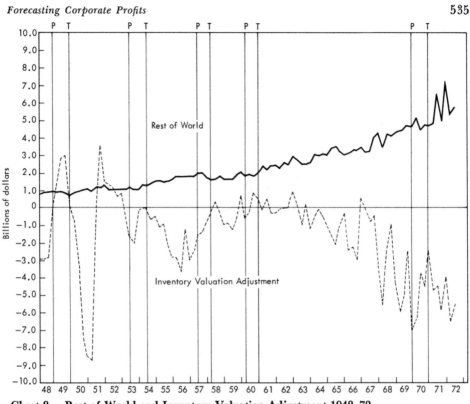

Chart 8   Rest of World and Inventory Valuation Adjustment 1948–72

the offsetting factor to rising costs, did not keep pace with rising costs, so that unit profits declined substantially. The dramatic reversal in the cost components over the past decade presents an unusual challenge to the forecaster and hopefully the analysis and the tools described herein will be helpful to the analyst in assessing the future path of profits.

The last three charts summarize the remaining components that must be included to get a picture of total corporate profits. Chart 7 plots total domestic corporate profits before taxes and inventory valuation adjustment and its two components, nonfinancial and financial profits. Nonfinancial corporate profits have been analyzed in some detail because, as the chart indicates, their path closely parallels the path of total domestic profits. The pattern of financial profits is much different, but it has less influence on the total

because it represents only about 20 percent of total domestic pretax profits.

The financial component of profits is heavily weighted by the banks, which in the past five years have accounted for from 56 percent to 75 percent of total financial profits. Of this total, the private banking system has accounted for from 38 percent to 48 percent of total financial profits, while the share of the Federal Reserve System has ranged from 19 percent to 27 percent. The remainder is accountd for by insurance carriers, security and commodity brokers, credit agencies, and regulated investment companies. The trend in bank earnings has been upward since 1948, although a sharp decline was experienced in 1961 and the growth rate since that time has been slower than the 1948–60 rate due to higher interest charges and a growing proportion of time deposits. Insurance carriers now account for about 25

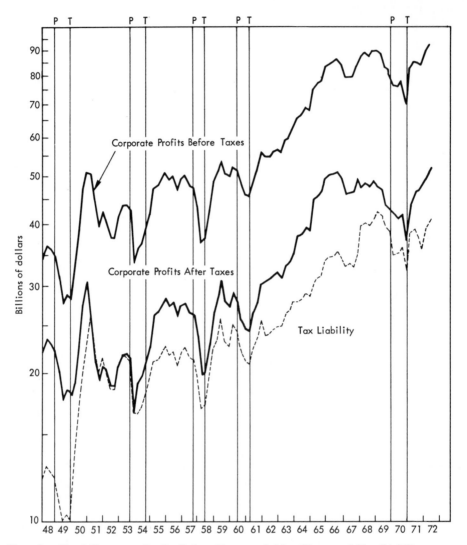

Chart 9   Total Corporate Profits Before Taxes and After Taxes and Tax Liability

percent of financial pretax profits, but their impact on changes in financial profits is significant because of their volatility. The fluctuations are due to the wide swings in the profits of nonlife insurance carriers, accounted for by their insurance operations rather than their investment results.[12] The

leveling of financial profits in 1961–64 was due to the decline in bank profits in 1961 and to the decline in insurance carrier profits in the other years. In 1967 and 1969, the decline was centered in the insurance carriers. The rise since 1970 has been centered in the non-banking area.

[12] I am grateful to John Gorman, associate chief, National Income Division, Office of Business Economics, Department of Commerce for providing unpublished data on the profit trends of financial companies.

Total Corporate Profits

Two other adjustments are necessary to the domestic corporate profit figures in order to obtain the aggregate measures of corporate profits provided by the Commerce Department. These two adjustments reflect the inventory valuation adjustment (IVA) and the adjustment for the rest of the world.

Chart 8 shows the pattern of the IVA and the rest of the world adjustment on a quarterly basis since 1948. The IVA adjustment is necessary because inventory profits are not considered a part of the profits arising from current production and, consequently, are excluded in the national income account profits component. The IVA measures the excess of the change of the physical volume of nonfinancial inventories valued at the average prices during the period over the change in book value as recorded by corporate accountants. As the chart indicates, the inventory valuation adjustment has fluctuated from positive to negative and has ranged from as much as −$9 billion to as much as +$4 billion. (A negative figure means that inventory profits have been included in the book profits for a period.) It is interesting to note that during the period 1958 through 1964 inventory valuation adjustments were rather modest, reflecting the price stability of that period. Inventory valuation adjustments have increased considerably since then and since 1969 they have been running between −$3.0 billion and −$6.5 billion at a seasonally adjusted annual rate. In only two quarters since 1948, during the Korean War, have inventory profits been so large.

The rest of the world adjustment is an allowance for the net receipt of dividends and branch profits from abroad. These receipts may be by either corporations or individuals in the United States. As can be seen, this has been a plus figure since the end of World War II and has been growing fairly significantly, particularly since 1961.

Chart 9 plots the usually reported and most familiar profits figures: corporate profits before taxes (including inventory profits), the tax liability, and corporate profits after taxes. These are the figures regularly reported in the financial press.

Estimating Future Profits

Thus far we have analyzed in some detail the new profit data recently made available, which consider profits as the difference between receipts and costs. Receipts are treated as the product of prices times output, and costs are apportioned among nonlabor costs and labor costs. Costs have been examined on a unit cost basis, with unit labor costs the result of the interaction of hourly wage rate and output per man-hour.[13] It may be helpful now to organize this information in a form that will facilitate either estimating the profit implications of certain economic assumptions or analyzing the quarterly pattern of profits.

The purpose here is to provide a relatively simple and consistent framework for analysis and the preparation of future estimates. Of course, forecasting the future of the economy and of profits is not a simple task. Relatively elaborate and sophisticated econometric models have been constructed for this purpose,[14] and a variety of other

[13] For a further discussion of this analytical approach, an excellent reference is *Profits, Profit Markups and Productivity*, by Edwin Kuh, Study Paper No. 15, Study of Employment, Growth and Price Levels, Joint Economic Committee, Congress of the United States (Washington: Government Printing Office, January 25, 1960). See also "Notes and Numbers on the Profits Squeeze," by Arthur M. Okun and George L. Perry, *Brookings Papers on Economic Activity 3:1970*, (Washington), pp. 466–72.

[14] An excellent example of an econometric model that includes a profits equation has been prepared by the Department of Commerce and is described in the May 1966 *Survey of Current Business*. In the model, pretax corporate profits excluding inventory profits are made to vary positively with corporate sales and negatively with the ratio of

forecasting techniques are also used. However, for the analyst who lacks the time or the desire to engage in the more complex aspects of forecasting, the approach discussed below may be useful. Table 3 provides a quarterly estimate of profits for 1972, with the first two quarters reflecting preliminary estimates by the Department of Commerce and the second two quarters reflecting estimates by the writer.

The starting point in any profits estimate is some assumption about overall economic activity or GNP. Such an estimate can be prepared by the analyst himself or estimates by both private and government economists are often available. From this GNP estimate, an estimate of NFGCP is derived.

We have experimented with linear correlations between GNP and NFGCP, but the results have not been too satisfactory. Although the coefficient of determination, R^2, is very high, the equation characteristically underestimates NFGCP when GNP is expanding rapidly and overestimates NFGCP when GNP is advancing more slowly. Therefore, for near-term profits forecasts, we prefer an equation that uses the percentage changes from quarter to quarter in GNP and correlates these percentage changes with those of NFGCP. The equation, based on quarterly data from 1948 through 1971, is as follows:

$$\%\varDelta NFGCP = -0.747\%$$
$$+ 1.4655\%\varDelta GNP$$
$$R^2 = 0.927; \; Sy = 0.0080$$

The second step in the analysis is to make an assumption about the the movement of prices in the NFGCP area. In this connection the forecaster can be materially helped by either plotting the price deflator on a semilogarithmic grid, as in chart 1, or

money wage rates to the overall price deflator, man-hours per unit of output, and the ratio of capacity to actual output.

alternatively by analyzing the quarter-to-quarter changes in this time series and combining this analysis with a general consideration of the pricing environment.

Line 5 is derived by dividing the current dollar NFGCP figure in line 3 by the price deflator in line 4, thereby obtaining NFGCP in constant 1958 dollars.

The next step in the analysis is to determine unit costs. Lines 6, 7, and 8 reflect the nonlabor costs and are relatively easy to estimate, assuming no changes in either depreciation practices or in excise tax laws. (The change in depreciation allowances adopted in January 1971 is estimated to increase depreciation by about $2.6 billion in 1972, which would reduce profits before taxes by this amount. Repeal of the automobile excise tax on August 15, 1971 is estimated to reduce 1972 indirect business taxes by about $1 billion.) Ordinarily, if capital consumption allowances, indirect business taxes, and interest in current dollars are plotted on a semilogarithmic grid, it will be seen that they fluctuate relatively little. Consequently, the analyst can, with a fair degree of safety, merely extrapolate recent trends over the forecast period. Having derived the dollar amounts for each factor, they can be divided into NFGCP on line 5 in order to derive the respective unit costs.

The unit employee compensation figure is somewhat more difficult to estimate and also is a more critical figure because of its size. The easiest procedure for the analyst is to make his own independent judgment of what increases in productivity and hourly labor costs he anticipates for the forecast period. For example, an increase of 6.5 percent in hourly compensation and 3.5 percent in productivity would result roughly in a 3 percent increase in unit labor costs. As an alternative, the BLS data referred to earlier show quarter-to-quarter increases in output, man-hours, output per man-hour, hourly compensation, and unit labor costs. These data coupled with knowledge of the current labor scene should enable the fore-

TABLE 3. ACTUAL AND ESTIMATES OF CORPORATE PROFITS—DEPARTMENT OF COMMERCE BASIS

	1Q* 1972	2Q* 1972	3Q 1972	4Q 1972	1972 Year
	(Dollars in billions)				
1. Gross national product	$1,109.1	$1,139.4	$1,162.2	$1,190.2	$1,150.2
Gross corporate product, nonfinancial					
2. Actual	582.4	599.3			
3. Computed			612.4	629.4	605.9
4. Price deflator NFGCP	126.7	127.1	127.3	128.3	127.4
5. Gross corporate product, nonfinancial, 1958$	459.6	571.7	581.1	490.6	475.8
Unit costs and profits, nonfinancial:					
6. Capital consumption allowances	0.135	0.138	0.136	0.139	0.137
7. Indirect business taxes, etc.	0.123	0.122	0.122	0.121	0.122
8. Interest	0.037	0.037	0.036	0.036	0.036
9. Employee compensation	0.842	0.841	0.840	0.848	0.843
10. Corporate profits and IVA	0.130	0.133	0.139	0.139	0.135
Total ($= $ line 4 $\div$ 100)	1.267	1.271	1.273	1.283	1.274
12. Corporate profits, nonfinancial and IVA (line 10 $\times$ line 5)	59.9	62.8	66.9	68.2	64.5
13. Inventory valuation adjustment	−6.5	−5.5	−6.1	−5.7	−6.0
14. Corporate profits, nonfinancial	66.4	68.4	73.0	73.9	70.4
15. Corporate profits, financial	16.5	17.5	17.8	18.4	17.6
16. Tax rate- corp. profits, nonfinancial	46.8	46.9	46.9	46.9	46.9
17. Tax rate-corp. profits, financial	46.7	45.7	46.0	46.0	46.0
18. Taxes-corp. profits, nonfinancial	31.1	32.1	34.2	34.7	33.0
19. Taxes-corp. profits, financial	7.7	8.0	8.2	8.5	8.1
20. Taxes-total	38.8	40.1	42.4	43.2	41.1
21. Corp. profits after tax, nonfinancial	35.4	36.3	38.8	39.2	37.4
22. Corp. profits after tax, financial	8.8	9.5	9.6	9.9	9.5
23. Rest of world	5.3	5.7	5.4	5.4	5.5
24. Total corp. profits after tax	49.5	51.5	53.8	54.5	52.3
Recap:					
25. Total corp. profits after tax (line 24)	49.5	51.5	53.8	54.5	52.3
26. Plus tax (line 20)	38.8	40.1	42.4	43.2	41.1
27. Corp. profits before tax	88.2	91.6	96.2	97.7	93.4
28. Plus or minus IVA (line 13)	−6.5	−5.5	−6.1	−5.7	−6.0
29. Corp. profits before tax and IVA	81.8	86.1	90.1	92.0	87.5

NOTE: Totals are subject to rounding error.

* Preliminary estimates by Department of Commerce.

caster to come up with a reasonable estimate of unit labor cost.

When these four computations are completed, corporate profits plus inventory valuation adjustment (line 10) can be derived by subtracting the total of these four unit costs from the price deflator, with the decimal point moved two places to the left. The corporate profits per unit can then be multiplied by real NFGCP (line 5) in order to derive the dollar corporate profits in the nonfinancial sector plus inventory valuation adjustment (line 12).

To this figure must be added an estimate of the inventory valuation adjustment, which can be done most simply by a rough approximation based on recent and expected wholesale price changes and also the recent pattern of the IVA as shown in chart 8. The addition or subtraction of the inventory valuation adjustment produces an estimate of nonfinancial corporate profits (line 14), to which can then be added an estimate of corporate profits in the financial sector (line 15). This figure can be estimated either by a rough approximation of recent profit trends in banks and other major financial institutions, or, alternatively, by extrapolating recent quarter-to-quarter increases in these profits as published by the Commerce Department. Unfortunately, the uncertainty of future underwriting losses in the nonlife insurance carriers referred to earlier introduces an element of unpredictability in this estimate, but the relatively small size of their contribution to total profits minimizes their impact on the total estimate.

With respect to taxes, the tax rate in the nonfinancial and financial areas should be treated separately because the implicit tax rates are different. The usual procedure is to extrapolate the implicit tax rate used by Commerce in the quarterly profits reports, unless a change in tax laws requires some adjustment. Having computed the appropriate taxes for the nonfinancial and financial area, corporate profits after taxes are derived for each of these sectors. To this computation must be added an estimate of rest of the world profits, which then gives the answer of total corporate profits after tax. This rest of the world estimate can best be made by extrapolating recent trends, although consideration must be given to such developments as the impact of government programs to improve the balance of payments and the economic outlook for foreign countries in which American corporations operate.

The last five lines of table 3 indicate a method to derive the usual published estimates of corporate profits. To total corporate profits after tax (line 25) must be added the tax on domestic profits (line 20), which gives total corporate profits before tax; from this total can be added or subtracted the inventory valuation adjustment (line 13). The result will be total corporate profits before taxes and inventory valuation adjustment.

Additional Uses of New Profits Data

The foregoing description indicates a method of forecasting corporate profits that insures the inclusion of all pertinent factors and also simplifies the judgments that must be made. The most critical factors are the estimates for GNP, the price deflator for NFGCP, and the estimate of unit labor costs. Most of the other variables perform in a relatively predictable fashion over the short term and can be readily estimated from a chart plotting their quarterly movements.

A second advantage of the suggested analysis is that it facilitates testing profits results for various assumptions about GNP, price change, or unit labor costs. The nonlabor costs and other profits components would not be materially affected. As a result of the availability of the new data and the procedure outlined in the table, it is relatively easy to experiment with the impact of various economic assumptions on profits.

A third advantage of the suggested analysis is that, using the tabular format provided, an analyst can readily follow the quarterly changes in factors affecting profits.

INTERNAL REVENUE SERIES

Let us now turn our attention to another profit series, the Internal Revenue Service compilation of profits reported for tax purposes, and a suggested method of forecasting this series. As might be expected, this series has a high degree of correlation with the Department of Commerce series, because they are both based on income tax returns and because the differences in the two series have thus far tended to offset each other. For the period 1945–70, we computed the correlation and tested the equation

$$Y = 532.6 + 0.95674X$$

where $Y =$ IRS profits in millions of current dollars and $X =$ Commerce profits in billions of current dollars and before inventory valuation adjustment. The coefficient of determination (R^2) is .992 and the standard error of estimate is $1.68 billion. However, as mentioned previously, only about 50 percent of these two series are identical, and the remaining 50 percent represent adjustments. Some of these adjustments correlate fairly closely with the Commerce series (state income taxes, Federal Reserve profits, and depletion allowances), but some do not (intercorporate dividends and capital gains and losses). Consequently, the analyst should review these adjustments in order to determine if any unexpected deviations are likely to occur that would upset the forecast.

Forecasting for Financial Analysis

For company or industry profit estimates, which are of primary concern to the financial analyst, the usual approach is through a projection of the income account. For most companies or industries, this approach begins with an estimate of physical volume for some future period. Methods of making such projections for some industries have already been considered in other chapters of this book. In some industries (such as autos and steel), market penetration estimates for particular companies can be applied to an industry projection of volume. Ordinarily, historical penetration figures change slowly over time.

After physical volume has been estimated, selling prices can then be applied to arrive at a dollar sales figure. The wholesale price index provides many helpful clues to price trends. In addition, many companies have prepared price indexes that more accurately reflect their own particular product mix; such an index may be known to the analyst, or the company may be willing to discuss it.

Once a dollar-sales estimate is made, cost estimates can be developed. The more important costs are labor and material costs, depreciation, and taxes. Historical patterns of cost can be ascertained from company financial reports. This information can then be combined with current information about labor cost increases, possible depreciation changes, and changes in tax rates. The information made available by companies in their periodic press releases and reports, statements by industry leaders, trade association publications, and interviews with company officials is essential. Many brokerage firms and investment services also prepare estimates of profits for companies and make them available to interested analysts. In the final analysis, however, all estimates depend to a material extent on judgment and experience.

Turning to the problem of profit aggregates for use in financial analysis, care should be taken in using the Commerce profit series as if the level and trend of this series were something that would be reflected in stock prices. The conceptual differences discussed earlier indicate that this profit aggregate does not accurately reflect the profits reported to shareholders of large successful corporations. Consequently, the financial analyst should either use this series with care or use the profit figures reported by Standard & Poor's, which may be directly related to the Standard & Poor's stock price indexes.[15]

[15] An example of the use of economic projections and aggregate profits forecasts to project the near- and long-term outlook for the earnings of stock market indexes is presented in "Corporate Earnings: Long-Term Outlook and Valuation," by Sidney Cottle, Edmund A. Mennis, and Mary Schuelke, and "Corporate Earnings: Short-Term Outlook

SUMMARY

The points made in this paper can be summarized as follows:

1. No one profit series can meet the diverse needs for which profit forecasts are made. The analyst should first determine the series best suited to his requirements.

2. For analysis of trends in the general economy, the Department of Commerce series is the most useful. Forecasts of this series can be made by

---

and Valuation," by Edmund A. Mennis and Sidney Cottle, *Financial Analysts Journal* (July–August 1971).

using a GNP forecast combined with the corporate gross product information provided by the Commerce Department.

3. For estimates of federal revenue, an estimate of profits reported for tax purposes can be made by correlation with estimates of Commerce profits.

4. For measuring current trends in profits and indicators of cyclical turning points in business, the First National City Bank compilations seem the most useful.

5. For the financial analyst, the Standard & Poor's earnings per share series, which can be related to the Standard & Poor's stock price indexes, seem to be the most useful.

BIBLIOGRAPHY

In addition to the material referred to in the footnotes, the following may be of help to those interested in this area.

Cottle, Sidney, and Tate Whitman, *Corporate Earnings Power and Market Valuation.* Durham, N.C.: Duke University Press, 1959.

Ferris, Robert G., and William H. Ferris, Jr., *Profits and Profit Evaluation Sources.* Washington: Econo Trends Publishing Company, 1962.

Hultgren, Thor, *Cyclical Diversities in the Fortunes of Industrial Corporations,* Occasional Paper 32. New York: National Bureau of Economic Research, 1950.

———, *Changes in Labor Cost During Cycles in Production and Business,* Occasional Paper 74. New York: National Bureau of Economic Research, 1960.

———, *Cost, Prices and Profits: Their Cyclical Relations,* Studies in Business Cycles No. 14. New York: National Bureau of Economic Research, 1965.

Paton, William A., *Corporate Profits.* Homewood, Ill.: Richard D. Irwin, Inc., 1965.

Robinson, Claude, *Understanding Profits.* New York: D. Van Nostrand Co., Inc., 1961.

Schultze, Charles L., *Prices, Costs and Output for the Postwar Decade: 1947–1957.* New York: Committee for Economic Development, 1959.

Sherman, Howard J., *Profits in the United States.* Ithaca, New York: Cornell University Press, 1968.

Stevenson, Harold W., and J. Russell Nelson, eds. *Profits in The Modern Economy.* Minneapolis: University of Minnesota Press, 1967.

Stigler, George J., *Capital and Rates of Return in Manufacturing Industries.* New York: National Bureau of Economic Research, 1963.

Terborgh, George, *Corporate Profits in the Decade: 1947–1957.* Washington: Machinery and Allied Products Institute, 1957.

PETER L. BERNSTEIN & DAVID BOSTIAN, JR.

How to Forecast the Stock Market

The presumptuous title to this paper prompts one to begin by posing the question, Is it in fact possible to forecast the stock market? Some people are convinced that you can, so we must explore how they go about it. Some people are certain that you cannot, that you must simply buy and hold, so we must determine what their case is and what the consequences of their policies might be.

In any case, forecasting the stock market is one of the more zestful subjects of business forecasting.

For one thing, the forecaster (and his clients) can track the accuracy of his predictions day by day or even minute by minute. Second, he is pitting himself against an information system that is probably more complete, more sophisticated, more central to more people's thinking, and hence more difficult to outwit than any other in the field of economics and finance. But that is just the point: since stock prices rapidly reflect what most people know and what they think, the forecaster can win only by thinking ahead of the crowd, by having insights and decisiveness that others lack.

In order to avoid cluttering the text with footnotes, I have refrained from providing citations for each statement of fact or reference to the work of others. Instead, I have provided and ample and explanatory bibliography at the end.

Finally, the record of forecasting the stock market is distinguished more by its failures than by its successes. Experience, high position, sophistication, and courage—a combination of qualities rare enough in any field of endeavor—are no guarantee whatsoever that predictions will turn out to be right. Indeed, one can be right about "the market" and still end up with a portfolio of securities that performs far less well than the portfolios of other investors.

Perhaps the most challenging aspect of forecasting the stock market is that, while people should be expected to carry out rational calculations in making an equity investment in a corporation, the decision-making process is occasionally irrational and departs from what normally appear to be the fundamental considerations in deciding whether to invest or to disinvest. While this should come as no great surprise in an area where prices essentially register expectations of future values rather than an estimate of current values, the job of predicting the state of expectations tomorrow or next year or five years from now is a good deal more complex than projecting what earnings, dividends, or interest rates will be at some point in the future.

It was this aspect of the problem, in fact, that prompted John Maynard Keynes, in a famous passage, to compare investing in the stock market to a beauty contest in which:

Each competitor has to pick, not those faces which he himself finds the prettiest, but those which he thinks likeliest to catch the fancy of the other competitors, all of whom are looking at the problem from the same point of view.

This leads, in turn, to the problem of when to sell a security purchased some time in the past. Each investor must believe that he can take his profit and run before the others recognize that a stock is overvalued—which then suggested to Keynes that stock market investing is a game of musical chairs or old maid, and caused others to call it the greater fool theory.

For all these reasons, the use of the old cliche that this is an art rather than a science seems particularly appropriate here. Many people have made fortunes in the stock market, but few of them have been able to teach others how to do it. The approach that the investor chooses will depend more upon his temperment and fundamental philosophical view of life than upon his exposure to economics and finance. In other words, there is no "best" technique, because each will serve some of us better than others. Successful forecasting is not a transferable talent.

Indeed, we would do well to recognize that a wide gap may exist between successful forecasting and successful investing. Although this sounds like a paradox, its meaning is clear. Making a prediction is one thing; acting on it is another. As one experienced and successful portfolio manager once put it, "Investment techniques don't manage money—people do!" For this reason, some people who are very smart are not very rich, while others whose decisiveness is based on instinct rather than analysis have ended up very rich indeed. In short, the investor's prediction and his decision have no consistent relationship to each other.

One further introductory consideration is necessary. While most of us are right in forecasting the stock market some of the time, and while some of us are more frequently right than others, none of us is right all of the time—and even fewer are successful by using only one approach to market forecasting to the exclusion of the others. Consequently, the more consistently successful investors do hedge against the risk of being wrong, recognize that extremes of over- and undervaluation are likely to occur, and still never take their eyes off fundamental trends. *Consistently* good performance, in other words, is more the result of eclecticism and humility than excessively assured specialization.

But this relates to the art of portfolio management, which is a different process from the art of forecasting. What can we say about forecasting as such?

CAN WE FORECAST THE STOCK MARKET?

In early 1955, at some Senate hearings on supposedly excessive activity and speculation in the stock market, each witness was asked what he thought the stock market was going to do. The president of Merrill, Lynch replied, "I don't know." The secretary of the treasury, George Humphrey, said, "I gave up years ago trying to figure out the stock market." Since neither of these gentlemen at that time could be classed as an unsuccessful investor, their responses were significant. If they didn't know, who did?

Yet it seemed ridiculous to abandon hope altogether, even despite the shatteringly wrong forecasts that had been made by people in high places at the time of the Great Crash. Anyone with a sharp eye and some attention to history could see that stock prices did show some sort of consistency in movement patterns and in economic relationship. The trick, therefore, was to develop a set of automatic signals that would tell the investor when to buy and sell and that would relieve him of the necessity of leaning on that frail reed, his own judgment.

Since these patterns and relationships prevailed most of the time, the odds of success would be better by depending upon them than upon the random chance of winning on the basis of judgment.

One of the most popular techniques to come along after the depression was the "formula plan" (today we would call this a "model"). The objective here was to increase the proportion of common stocks in the portfolio by predetermined amounts as prices declined and to sell in the same manner as prices rose. The investor followed the formula and never *anticipated* what the market was going to do. All of these plans operated on one premise: J. P. Morgan's famous phrase, "The market will fluctuate."

But even that simplistic observation implied a forecast, so that the performance of the followers of the formula plans turned out to be very poor when the underlying forecast was proven wrong. The market may fluctuate all right, but, if it fluctuates further than anticipated, or if it fluctuates around a long and powerful uptrend, formula plan investors will find themselves sold out too early in the game. This is precisely what happened to them when the market broke loose from long-established parameters and soared from 23 on the Standard & Poor's 500 stock average in September 1953 (which was already 20 percent above the 1946 high), to 49 in July 1957. It hurt even more when the subsequent bear market low in December was 40, still far above the range that the formula plans considered normal.

On the other hand, Professor Benjamin Graham, distinguished scholar in the field, was convinced that you *could* predict stock prices, because he was able to demonstrate that they bore a consistent relationship to earnings, dividends, and bond yields. This relationship prevailed over such a long period of time that he dubbed it *central value* and stated that stocks would spend most of their time fluctuating within a predictable range around central value. You

sold when they moved to the upper end of that range and bought when they moved to the lower end.

But, like the Morgan forecast, the theory of central value implied a foreknowledge of where that central point was. One of the most successful of published advisory services, the Value Line, was based on the same approach and, like Professor Graham, became increasingly bearish in the mid-1950s, as stock prices broke loose from all the traditional anchors and seemed to be heading for the moon. Both approaches required some doctoring up as we moved into the 1960s.

While this *seemed* like a fundamental approach to forecasting, it was in its own way just as mechanical as the formula plan technique which made no pretense at forecasting. Any forecast based essentially upon an extrapolation of long-term trends will go away when the trends bend. Expectations as to economic growth and inflation in the postwar years were entirely different from what they had been at any time at least since the end of World War I. The levels of liquidity in the personal sector of the economy, the greater stability of employment, the increasing trend toward annual wage increases, and the enormous merchandising job done by the mutual fund industry greatly increased the opportunity for small investors to come into the stock market—most of whom were looking for something better to do with their savings than leave them sitting in the bank or in E bonds while their purchasing power was shrinking. All of these forces—and others—led to an increasing distaste for fixed-income assets and an expanding market for stocks. The fundamentalists simply failed to pay attention to the right fundamentals!

More recently, an effort has been made to apply econometric techniques of model building to the prediction of stock prices, garnished with the model builder's preferences as to the basic motive forces behind economic change. For example, the economists at the Federal Reserve Bank of St. Louis, who are in the vanguard of the use of Friedman-monetarist approaches to the construction of econometric models for projections of business activity, prices, and unemployment, have made an impressive link of their primary model to a projection of stock prices. An examination of the history of their stock market model, however, indicates that it is subject to the same kind of difficulty as any other type of mechanical projection, regardless of the sophistication of the theory that underlies it. In order to make the projections of stock prices fit the actual history from 1952 to 1970, a dummy variable had to be inserted in the years 1952–55 and removed thereafter ("most likely related to a change in attitude about risk"), while a second dummy variable had to be inserted after 1960 ("intended to partially account for an apparent shift in the financial market relationships which distinguished the 1950s from the 1960s"). In short, since only with hindsight can we identify the shifts that necessitated these adjustments in the model, and since we never know when other types of shifts in attitudes or relationships may be occurring (at least, not without the use of *judgment*), even a model based upon an unusually elegant use of economic theory and technique can lead the investor astray.

THE FINAL SKEPTICISM: THE RANDOM WALK

The most powerful attack on the ability of anyone to outperform the market with any degree of consistency has come from the academic world, which has used a combination of probability theory, differentiation of risk, and an analysis of the meaning of efficient markets in an effort to demonstrate that market fluctuations are essentially unpredictable.

This approach rests its case upon three simple observations of what the academics believe is happening in the real world. First, the dissemination of information about a company or even the economy as a whole is extraordinarily rapid in the United States; meaningful inside information is a thing of the past or is "inside" for only a very brief time. Second, stock prices rapidly reflect the judgments and expectations of investors, based on the information available, so that if things look good, the price moves upward so quickly that the recipient of cheerful information has little or no time to act upon it; investors as a group (in contrast to any one investor) know pretty much all there is to know about any one company at any moment in time. Finally, the arrival of new information is itself unpredictable and appears randomly over time. In brief, stock prices move in a manner that we might describe as a random walk.

Many professional practitioners take strong umbrage at the random walk theory. Research directors and technical chartists can provide records of recommendations that outperform the market—but that is different from using these recommendations to make *decisions* that result in outperformance of the market. Consistency in above-average performance is almost impossible to find in available data, if we define consistency as outperforming the averages through both the up and the down periods of a major market swing.

For example, long-term studies of performance ranks among mutual funds show that most funds spend part of the time at the top of the pile and that most funds also spend part of the time at the bottom; good performance in any one year is absolutely no indication that it will be followed by good performance in the next. Furthermore, good stock selection is so overwhelmingly important that even the ability to guess the general market is no guarantee of superior performance. A study that I made of leading mutual funds for the years 1969 and 1970 showed no consistency at all between performance and the percentage of assets invested in common stocks; a high cash position during the bear market and a low cash position during the upswing in the last half of 1970 seemed to produce no better results than being heavily invested on the way down and stuck with a lot of cash on the way up.

Of course, some portfolio managers do seem to outperform the market over meaningful periods. The Wiesenberger Growth Fund Index showed average annual appreciation from December 31, 1962 to December 31, 1970 that was more than double the appreciation of the Dow-Jones Industrial Average (DJIA). But this is a comparison between apples and bananas. The Growth Fund Index showed far greater volatility than the Dow-Jones industrials on both upswings *and* downswings; in other words, it represented investments in stocks with far greater degrees of risk. In the long run, rate of return should be related to degree of risk, and this result only proved the validity of that theoretical postulate. In other words, these fund managers managed to outperform the DJIA, not because they were better forecasters, but rather because they were willing to take a different kind of risk. In view of the nature of the assets they were holding, another six months of bear market in 1970 could have resulted in total disaster for them, even while the Dow-Jones industrials would still have been in business.

Some investors are admittedly outstandingly successful. This result is a consequence primarily of decisiveness and ability to take high risk and live with it. It is also a reflection of the ability, as one writer has put it, to convert "public information into private knowledge." A careful academic substantiation of this viewpoint appears in an article by professors Latane, Tuttle, and Jones, in which they argue that:

> ... lags have existed in the market in the assimilation of at least certain types of information, and investors have not been able to, or did not, adjust instantaneously (or even very quickly) to all financial

information. We argue that it has been possible to use certain published financial information, available to the investor at the time of his investment decisions, to produce superior investment results as compared with other techniques or market indices.

The difficulty with this lies, as we suggested at the outset, in passing the talent for greater insight or boldness or decisiveness on to others—and, in fact, in sustaining them over long periods of time for oneself.

Yet most practitioners would enthusiastically agree with the concept that, while inside information has become increasingly rare, investors respond to available information with varying degrees of speed, rather than simultaneously as argued by random walk theory. Many investors, indeed, are able to overcome uncertainty and inertia only when it is apparent that other investors have begun to take action. That is why a healthy respect for chart patterns of price movements is part of nearly every portfolio manager's kit of tools.

Although we deal with this topic in detail below, we should stress here that such techniques can occasionally promise success for limited periods of time, but that they are unlikely to provide results better than buy-and-hold performance over extended periods of time. The crowd becomes acquainted with them and rushes the gun, or their impact on price patterns becomes apparent to other technicians who see them as another leading indicator and hence also rush the gun. To work, the private knowledge must remain private forever.

Yet the obvious rhythms and the consistent repetition of past patterns in stock prices make this path of study endlessly intriguing. Why, over the last fifteen years, has buying at the end of June and selling the week after the Fourth of July yielded a profit that has averaged 3.8 percent, or an annual rate of some 200 percent? Why, in five out of six times, does the trend of the market for the year follow the lead of January's trend? Or why have the greatest concentrations of market turndowns since 1949 occurred in the first six trading days of January? Why momentum, support zones, trends consistently contained within straight line slopes? Essentially, no doubt, because human beings make prices, and human beings are governed by fundamental rhythms, no matter how complex they may be. The observer who understands this human quality and is objective enough to exploit it can do so with profit for some period of time. No one has yet proved that he can do it all of the time.

Nevertheless, many of those who agree with the random walk adherents that the technical approach is a dead end still insist that the conversion of public information into more accurate earnings estimates will still enable the investor to beat the averages. But even this approach seems to be extraordinarily complicated. Some careful work done by professors Cragg and Malkiel in the United States and professors Little and Rayner in Britain suggests that even the most skilled and professional security analysts have a hard time in coming up with consistently accurate earnings projections, particularly since past patterns seem to be such a tenuous factor on which to base expectations of the future.

Does this discussion then mean that forecasting the stock market is an impossibility, or possible for only very limited periods of time? Not quite. It does indicate that forecasting the market is far from simple, because information does disseminate quickly and prices soon reflect in the present what most people expect to happen tomorrow. It also leads to the conclusion that outperforming the averages is even more difficult than predicting whether prices will go up or down. But it still does leave some room for this essential prediction, particularly for the longer swings.

Let us now, therefore, turn to an examination of some basic relationships that, in the past at least, have been useful in forecasting stock prices.

FUNDAMENTAL FORECASTING TECHNIQUES

As a part owner of a business, the stockholder is obviously concerned with what the business is going to earn over some given time horizon and what sort of a dividend it is going to pay out to him. This is by no means all, however. To the extent that the investor is a rational being, he must engage in opportunity cost calculations. This extends beyond the decision of whether stock A is a superior value to stock B; the wider question is whether, given his assessment of risk differentials, he can earn a higher rate of return on other types of investments. Since the clearest and most logical alternative to equity ownership is debt instruments of various types, or cash, considerations of interest rate expectations and general monetary conditions weigh heavily in investor decisions.

Because of this opportunity cost calculation, stock prices will seldom correlate uniquely or consistently with earnings (or even with lagged earnings to reflect expectations). Thus, investors are sometimes surprised to see stock prices rising during business recessions, but those are periods when interest rates tend downward and money is easy. On the other hand, the myth that stocks are a good hedge against inflation may finally have been buried in the 1969–70 bear market, when, in an extreme but by no means unusual situation, burgeoning interest rates and tight money brought about by the inflationary condition of the economy led to a sharp downward revaluation of corporate earnings.

Leads and lags in these relationships tend to vary, so that hard and fast rules are difficult to establish. Nevertheless, certain relationships are sufficiently clear for us to make the following generalizations:

1. Stock prices usually touch bottom and turn upward within at least three

months of peaks in long-term bond yields.

2. Stocks will continue rising for as long as bond yields are declining (the 1962 stock market break was a conspicuous exception—but the recovery was swift and sharp).

3. Stocks will then continue rising for a while even after bond yields bottom out and turn upward. When the steepness of the rise in bond yields is more apparent, however, as in the late stages of a business boom, stock prices lose their forward momentum, flatten out, and ultimately turn downward until such time as bond yields again reach a peak.

4. Stock prices spend a good deal of time moving in a different direction from earnings, but that is because investors are trying to anticipate changes in earnings trends. This is complicated further by the tendency of earnings to move in an erratic pattern.

5. The troughs in stock prices and earnings come close together in time, with a slight lead—one or two months at the most—in favor of stock prices. The lead appears longer to investors, because earnings are reported at least a month after the end of a calendar quarter, so that stock prices might have turned up as much as six months before investors actually see the higher earnings reported.

6. Since troughs in both profits and stock prices are much more clearly defined than peaks in both series, the sequences at upper turning points are less regular than those at market bottoms, but the tendency is for profits to flatten out or even to peak well in *advance* of the peak in stock prices. The net gain in stock prices following the flattening out of the profits curve is, however, usually modest.

7. Because interest rates both respond to and act upon plant and equipment spending and upon housing starts, (a) stock prices always rise when housing starts are rising; (b) housing starts top out long before stock prices; (c) peaks in plant and equipment spending are associated with troughs in the stock market; and (d) stock prices tend to decline during the late stages of a plant and equipment spending boom.

These relationships, which appear on chart 1, may be summarized in a relatively simple generalization: stock prices rise when the economy has slack, with sufficient idle real and financial resources to make further expansion possible; stock prices decline when slack shrinks to a point where further expansion is likely to be limited and when contraction of business activity and profitability is approaching.[1] The degree to which investors anticipate further expansion or contraction, of course, is a function of the clarity with which they can foresee the future at any particular moment in time.

A PREDICTION OF STOCK PRICES

As an illustrative exercise of how we might use these guidelines in predicting the future level of the stock market, let us consider the situation at this writing in the spring of 1971 and attempt to forecast what the Dow-Jones Industrial Average might sell for in 1974.

In order to do so, we must make assumptions—or forecasts, if you will—as to the level of earnings and the trend of interest rates over this period.

The best estimates for 1971 earnings on the DJIA run around $60, a large jump from the $51 of 1970, but 1970 earnings were depressed both by the business recession and by major strikes in the trucking industry, the rubber industry, General Electric, and General Motors. The $60 estimate for 1971 is only slightly above the previous

[1] This is one of the most useful insights provided by a study of the St. Louis Federal Reserve Bank model referred to earlier.

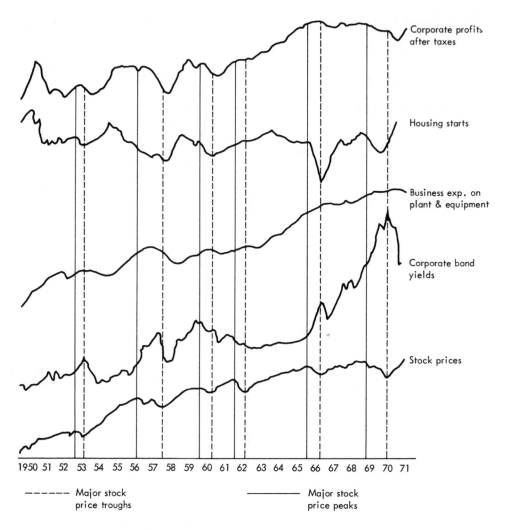

Corporate profits after taxes

Housing starts

Business exp. on plant & equipment

Corporate bond yields

Stock prices

1950 51 52 53 54 55 56 57 58 59 60 61 62 63 64 65 66 67 68 69 70 71

- - - - - - Major stock
price troughs

——————— Major stock
price peaks

peak of $59.60 for the twelve months ended September 30, 1969, and only 4 percent above earnings way back in 1966.

If we extend a line that touches the earnings peaks of 1957 and 1966 out to 1974, that extrapolation would indicate a figure of about $80 for 1974. Earnings of $80 in 1974 would indicate a recovery approximately 50 percent from the 1970 trough, which compares with a recovery of 70 percent in the four years following the 1961 trough. Furthermore, profitability ratios relative to assets and sales in 1970 were at postwar lows; a return to just the low end of what may be considered more normal levels of profitability together with an extension of

the long-term average annual rate of growth in earnings on the DJIA also suggest a total increase in profits on the order of 45–50 percent from the 1970 trough. Let us, therefore, accept $80 as a working estimate for 1974 earnings.

An interest rate prediction is more complicated. If, however, we assume that the rate of inflation will at least be no worse in 1974 than it was in early 1971, that it will probably abate in the meantime, that the rapid growth in the number of people of working age will tend to create unemployment levels that will in turn necessitate a continuation of relatively easy monetary policies, and if, finally, we assume that at least three years will be required before another major upswing in plant and equipment spending gets under way, then we can say with some assurance that high-grade, long-term corporate bond yields will remain below the extraordinary peak they reached in mid-1970. One can probably go further and suggest that the upper limit to long-term rates will be in the area of eight percent and that yields will be below that level at least part of the time under consideration.

Now, under these conditions, what price will investors be willing to pay for $80 in earnings in 1974? At this writing, they are paying about fifteen times estimated 1971 earnings. Except for the period of the 1969–70 bear market, and the bottom of the break in 1966, the DJIA has sold at more than fifteen times earnings without exception since the first calendar quarter of 1958. Since this will presumably be a period of expanding earning power, we should note that during the rapid expansion in earnings from 1961 to 1965, the price/earnings ratio was below eighteen times in only five quarters out of sixteen (three of which included the 1962 break).

Of course, a lot will depend upon exactly where we are in the business cycle. As we have already seen, stock prices depend upon the *rate of change* in earnings and in interest rates as well as upon their *levels*; if the rate of earnings growth in 1974 slackens significantly from that in 1973 and if interest rates are rising sharply rather than moderately, then price/earnings ratios will be lower than if interest rates are stable and the expansionary phase of profit growth is still in existence.

But we can attack the problem from another angle, by running a kind of simulation exercise. For example, if we ask what total rate of return (dividends plus appreciation) on common stocks investors will seek to compensate them for the greater risk in stocks as compared with that in bonds (i.e., the greater degree of uncertainty as to what the rate of return will actually turn out to be), we can then calculate where stocks will have to go to provide that rate of return; the results of that calculation will then tell us whether it produces a reasonable or an unreasonable price expectation.

Let us assume that investors will expect a total rate of return on common stocks 50 percent above the yield on long-term bonds. That implies a total return on the order of 12 percent a year as a maximum. As the dividend yield on the DJIA is currently around 3 percent, we will then require a 9 percent annual rate of appreciation to provide the desired result. A price level of 1170 for the Dow-Jones industrials in 1974 would provide this rate of appreciation from the 900 level prevailing in March, 1971. That would be only 14.5 times earnings of $80. Since we have set 8 percent as the probable maximum for long-term interest rates, since the 50 percent premium rate of return for common stock may be higher than what investors will require in an expanding economy, and since dividend payments in 1974 will probably be higher than they were in 1971, common stocks would seem to be considerably more attractive than long-term bonds at this writing.

THE TECHNICAL APPROACH TO FORECASTING STOCK PRICES

While fundamentalists forecast stock prices on the basis of what they see in economic, monetary, and company statistics, the technical approach uses the past market history of a stock or a market average as the *sole* guide to predicting future price movements. The fundamentalist, in other words, makes a judgment as to whether stocks are overvalued or undervalued relative to earning power and the economic environment, and then believes that other investors will drive prices upward or downward until prices reach what he considers the proper level of valuation. The technician, on the other hand, knows nothing of value in the terms that the fundamentalist uses it; rather, he believes that the *actions* of other investors, as reflected in the price fluctuations of stocks, reveal the true patterns of supply and demand and will thus enable him to predict whether prices are moving higher or lower and even by how much.

Without attempting to refute random walk theory, and in many cases ignorant of it, technical market analysts over the years have developed a vast array of techniques to accomplish their forecasting goals. The spectrum ranges all the way from the relatively simple Dow theory to ultrasophisticated computer models based on the laws of physics. The computer, in fact, has added a new dimension to technical forecasting because of its virtually unlimited memory capacity for previous price patterns and because of its enormous sophistication in detecting patterns more subtle than the human eye could find. These qualities, together with the inability of many investors to have access to or to comprehend the capabilities of the computer, suggest that these methods, at least, will be more effective (and for a longer period of time) than the older technical methods in converting public information into private knowledge.

All technical approaches have one basic premise in common: that a price movement once in force tends to continue for some period of time. In other words, prices move in waves of various shapes and forms —they do not just wiggle. Note that this is the precise opposite of the random walk approach, whose very name denies the existence of consistent patterns of change. The objective of the technical forecaster, therefore, is to identify the trend and to recognize when one trend comes to an end and prices will start moving in the opposite direction. Since movement in any direction is seldom smooth and uninterrupted, the real problem that faces the technician is to distinguish between reversals within the trend and genuine changes of trend. Consequently, most technical approaches give signals only after change has occurred, which leads to risk of whipsaw or profits too small to compensate for taxes and transaction costs.

While the emphasis here is on technical tools for forecasting the direction of the broader market, many of these tools are composites of those used for forecasting price movements of individual stocks. Hence, it would be useful to survey these techniques, which fall into three broad groups: price history only, volume history only, and price and volume history combined.

Price history only is employed by point-and-figure analysis without respect to day-to-day time periods, concentrating only on price movements. Only as a stock's price moves up or down by a given amount (one point, for example, although the practitioner can use any degree of sensitivity he wishes for indicating change) does the point-and-figure chart show any change. A movement of the indicated amount in the same direction as the previous movement is plotted on the vertical scale above or below the previous mark, as appropriate. When the necessary price change is in the opposite direction, the plot moves one column to the right. Thus, a volatile stock might show several plots, vertically and horizontally, during one day, while a less volatile stock might trade for several days without moving enough in price to make any change on its chart.

A point-and-figure chart and a daily basis bar chart on Chrysler are shown in figure 1. The price activity to the right of the arrow on the point-and-figure chart covers about the same period of time as the entire span of the daily basis bar chart shown. Price activity on this point-and-figure chart is based on one-point reversals rather than days. Because a long period of time can be shown in a fairly short space on a point-and-figure chart, this type lends itself to long-term as well as short-term studies. The daily basis bar chart, on the other hand, shows both price and volume on each trading day, and so is suitable for detailed short-term studies (see figure 1).

A more sophisticated employment of price history is found in computations of relative strength in price. This technique, on which significant work has been done by Dr. Robert Levy, is far removed from conventional charting of prices and, by contrast, develops predictive value through relative mathematical weighting of individual security price trends in relation to the market.

Another group of tools employ volume history only. On-balance volume computations attempt to forecast price directions by dealing with conventionally reported trading volume. A more complex approach here involves "tick" volume, whereby each transaction composing the total volume figure is studied to determine the probable direction of future prices.

In the third broad category, we find technical tools that employ some combination of both historic price and volume. Although the most simple form of technical tool using both historic price and volume is the conventional price-volume bar chart, many more sophisticated techniques employing a combination of price and volume are in use today. Most such price-volume tools utilize the absolute or percentage day-to-day price change weighted by volume of trading during the day.

One recently introduced variation on conventional price-volume methodology has been developed by the author of the technical portion of this chapter and is termed the Intraday Intensity Index. This tool utilizes *intraday* price change statistics. This new approach accepts the random walk hypothesis of day-to-day price movement as random in character. It does assume, however, that *intraday* price relationships are *nonrandom*; consequently, it seeks to identify patterns of accumulation and distribution by grouping price and volume statistics for each day, *regardless of the day-to-day*

trend that most technical tools measure. Figure 2 illustrates the different technical indications given by conventional day-to-day analysis and intraday analysis for one stock during the same time period. The conclusion is not that one technical method is always superior, but that these techniques vary widely in concept as well as in forecast.

Whatever weaknesses exist in technical methods aimed at forecasting individual security price movements, the utilization of these tools in combinations covering many stocks and aimed at forecasting the direction of broader market averages inherently filters individual errors by dealing with broad populations.

The most famous of these is, of course, the Dow theory. In its simplest form, the Dow theory identifies a change in trend from up to down when a rally after a downward reaction fails to reach the high point of the previous upswing, and from down to up when the reaction after a rally holds above the previous low. The original Dow theory also stipulated that a change in trend in the rail or industrial average would have no significance unless or until it had been "confirmed" by a similar signal in the other average. Furthermore, many variations on these themes have been developed, including the identification of shoft-, intermediate-, and long-term price trends, with all of them focusing one way or another on a study of the shapes and patterns of price fluctuations around a trend line.

In addition, the technical practitioner uses many of the following tools to determine probable market direction: daily advances and declines; daily new highs and new lows; daily volume on advancing issues (up-volume) and daily volume on declining issues (down-volume); breadth of security group movements; relative volume ratios between the New York and American Stock Exchanges daily trading; the ratio of the average daily NYSE volume to the monthly

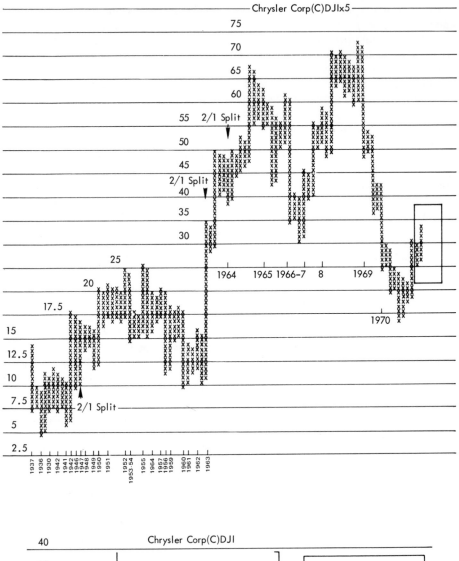

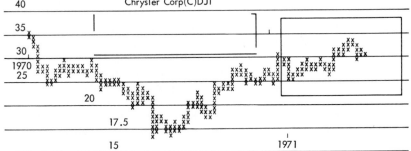

Figure 1   Comparison of Bar and Point and Figure Charts

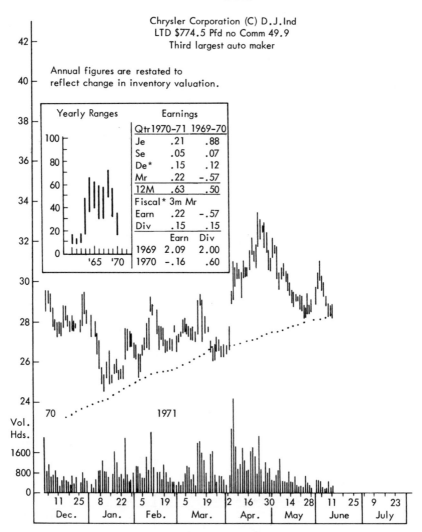

Chrysler Corporation (C) D.J.Ind
LTD $774.5 Pfd no Comm 49.9
Third largest auto maker

Annual figures are restated to
reflect change in inventory valuation.

Qtr	1970-71	1969-70
Je	.21	.88
Se	.05	.07
De*	.15	.12
Mr	.22	-.57
12M	.63	.50

Fiscal* 3m Mr

Earn	.22	-.57
Div	.15	.15

	Earn	Div
1969	2.09	2.00
1970	-.16	.60

Yearly Ranges   Earnings

Vol.
Hds.

Shown at the right is a daily basis bar chart of Chrysler Corporation, covering price ranges and volume for the stock for each trading day over about six months. Below at the right is a long-term point and figure chart of Chrysler covering price movements of five points or more in the stock back to 1937. Many months passed, on occasion, before a new row of x's were made, indicating that prices had made a five point reversal. The small centered chart is a more sensitive point and figure chart of Chrysler showing price changes in whole points back into 1970.

The small rectangle on both the large and small point and figure charts indicates the area covered by the daily basis bar chart. Note the differences. The bar chart is directly related to time on a daily basis, while the point and figure charts have no direct relation to time but respond only to price swings of a certain predetermined amount.

555

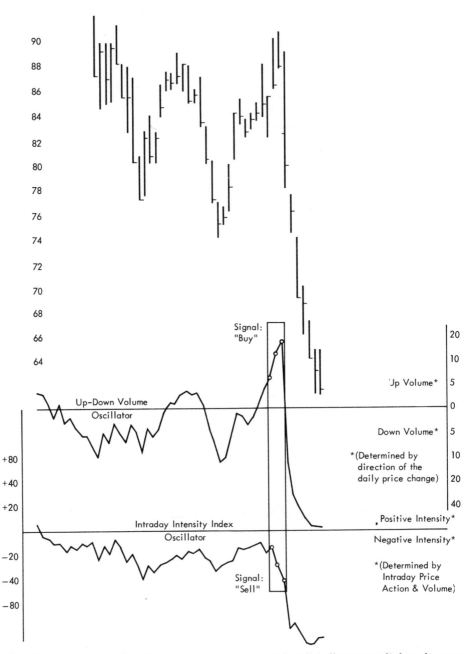

This chart provides an interesting contrast between two technical indicators applied to the same series of market facts. The price action shown is that of an actual stock during 1966. One technical tool suggested that the stock would go up based on a study of price direction and volume and another tool based on intraday price action weighted with volume suggested the stock would go down. The point is that technical approaches can vary significanly in conclusions given the same set of market data.

Figure 2   Technical Tools Do Not Always Agree

Stock Market Indicators

Note the action of the indicators below, at, and following the DJIA's 416 low in 1957, the 525 low in 1962, the 736 low in 1966, and recently, the 627 low in 1970. Study the action to the right of the four dotted lines ANNUAL RATE OF CHANGE OF STOCK MARKET PRICES. This indicator is based on the Dow-Jones Industrial Average and shows that the May 1970 bottom was more oversold than any back to 1957 and also indicates a high degree of upside movement away from this bottom. The rapid upside movement that developed after May 1970 had very bullish long-term implications which intensity data for the DJIA confirmed, ANNUAL RATE OF CHANGE OF STOCK MARKET VOLUME. This indicator based on NYSE volume showed a sharp drop in the volume rate as the May 1970 lows were approached and then a return to a positive rate of change as the rally progressed. Comparison with prior low periods suggests a major bottom. STOCK MARKET GROUP MOMENTUM INDEX. This diffusion index, based on the action of Standard & Poor's 25 groups, developed excellent upside momentum very indicative of the major bull moves following the 1957, 1962, and 1966 lows. A similar picture is shown by charts of advance-decline breadth following these lows. SHORT INTEREST BAROMETER. This indicator showing the NYSE's short interest ratio moved up to the bullish "2 level" following the 1957, 1962, and 1966 market lows. It did so again following the May 1970 low. Widespread skepticism toward the sharp rallies that begin these bull moves seems to nearly always move the short interest ratio into bullish territory.

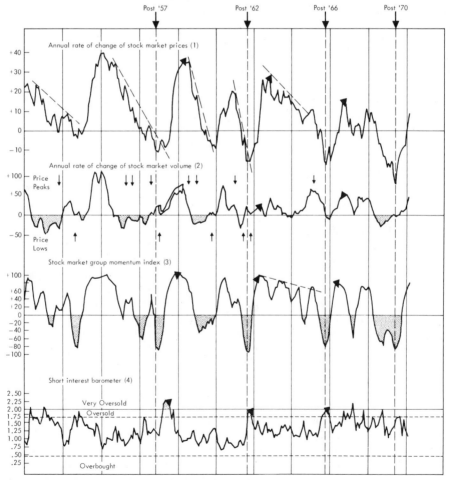

Courtesy of Monetary Research Ltd. Bank Credit Analyst *71*

Figure 3   Technical Forecasting Tools for the Market are Based on Data from Numerous Individual Stocks and Can be of Significant Value

reported short interest; odd lot buying and selling balances; and current price relative to moving averages of earlier prices. The technical forecaster gains both insight into the fundamental judgment of others, as well as psychological conditions in the marketplace, when he uses these tools.

Figure 3 shows four important technical tools which the stock market forecaster employing technical forecasting aids might use. Note how the technical evidence in this figure shows the May 1970 lows to be similar to significant market lows of the past. Using the composite of technical tools in figure 3, the forecaster could well determine that incipient bull market conditions existed at year-end 1970 and, based on historically evident follow-through by the technical series shown, a bullish forecast might be made for 1971. Importantly, the technical forecast for the 1971 market would have had a far greater probability of beging correct than any technical forecast for a specific stock in that market.

THE PRAGMATIC SYNERGISM

At this point the reader should begin to gain perspective. Although purists in both fundamental and technical stock market forecasting do exist, neither approach is wholly exclusive of the other. The fundamentally oriented approach seeks to determine those factors that will be causal in changing the valuation of security prices. Yet, no fundamental forecaster can hope to be so omniscient that his valuation of fundamental factors will always prove to be the same valuation accorded by the marketplace. For example, a given fundamental forecaster might state that the stock market would decline because it was "overvalued" due to bond yields significantly in excess of stock yields. Yet, if the stock market continued to rise despite a forecast based on academically correct parameters, there would be no pragmatic value in the forecast. Specifically, the

fundamental analyst may incorrectly identify those fundamental factors that are meaningful to the market at a given point in market history. Only via a study of the action of the market itself against a given background of fundamental data can the fundamental forecaster gain posible insight into the relevance of his fundamental judgment. The successful fundamental analyst studies market *action* for confirmation of his fundamental analysis, i.e., he uses what in essence is a simple form of technical analysis.

The technically oriented approach to forecasting, on the other hand, would have no value and meaning if numerous fundamental analysts were not continually making market decisions in accord with their considered forecasts. For example, if the majority of fundamentally oriented market participants considered security prices historically low in relation to earning power, *regardless* of low yields in relation to bonds, actions influenced by their forecasts of rising markets would be monitored by the technical analyst. The technical forecaster would project a rising stock market because he had monitored the greater buying power influenced by fundamental analysts viewing prices as low in relation to earning power against the weaker selling pressure of the minority of fundamental analysts viewing the bond/stock yield ratio as the more important factor in forecasting market direction. The sucessful technical analyst makes market judgments based on cumulative market action influenced by numerous fundamental analysts, i.e., the technical analyst's success is contingent upon a degree of correct forecasting within the fundamental camp.

This comparison of fundamental and technical forecasting, while oversimplified, is important in giving the proper perspective: fundamental and technical approaches to the stock market are not diametrically opposed but supplementary techniques for achievement of a successful stock market forecast. Although technical approaches to forecasting of economic statistics may be termed naive extrapolations, technical forecasting of the stock market is a critical part of the overall forecasting strategy whereby skillful technical analysis allows insight into the competitive fundamental judgment of other market participants. This does not automatically mean that conclusions from independent fundamental analysis should be disregarded if technical insights prove contradictory, but given the less than omniscient power of any individual forecaster and the varying valuation criteria emphasized at different periods in market history, contradictory results from fundamental and technical approaches certainly signal a recheck of both types of forecasting tools. On the other hand, when both fundamental and technical forecasting tools produce the same signal, probabilities of success are immeasurably enhanced. The successful market forecast might be termed a unique blend of both art and science.

IS FORECASTING NECESSARY?

Everybody knows that the long-run trend in the stock market has been upward. Why not simply buy and hold, without regard to interim fluctuations?

In view of the dubious success of market predictions, many investors are tempted to avoid forecasting and to let the long run take care of their investments for them. This approach, however, raises some serious problems.

First, although the long-run trend of the market has undoubtedly been upward, it has been sideways or downward for periods long enough to affect the investment success shown by an investor during a large part of his (or his advisor's) business lifetime. The periods 1874–97, 1915–33, and 1925–42 began and ended with common stock prices at identical levels on the average. The investor who bought in 1929 would have been under water for twenty years; forty years

later his appreciation would have averaged out to only about four percent a year.

Second, a really long-run trend line touching the market lows of 1884–1908–1914–1918–1949 and extrapolated out to 1971 would be touching 27 on the Standard & Poor's stock average, compared with its level of about 100 at this writing. Hence, prices could fall 75 percent and still be within the great long-run uptrend of common stock prices.

Third, mechanical extrapolation of the famous 9 percent figure generated by the University of Chicago is also open to question. This figure was based upon the performance of all listed common stocks over the period 1926 to 1960. Although the years covered in this study did include the 90 percent fall from 1929 to 1932, it also included the quadruple from 1949 to 1960. If the distribution of rising and falling prices had been precisely the same, but if the quadruple had come at the beginning and the 90 percent drop had come at the end, the Standard & Poor's 500 stock average would have been at about 20 instead of close to 60 in 1960—which means that stock prices would have risen only 60 percent instead of 400 percent from 1926 to 1960. In addition, the momentum of the postwar bull market stands out as nothing short of extraordinary and probably unique when given historical perspective. Twenty-eight years were required for the market to move up fourfold from the 1898 low. In fact, since 1949, the annual rate of increase in stock prices has been four times as fast as it was during the entire 78 years that preceded 1949.

Furthermore, this great postwar bull market shows distinct signs of slowing down. From 1949 to 1959, prices rose at an annual average of about fifteen percent; the growth rate dropped to seven percent in the next five years; it was less than five percent during the final five years of the 1960s. At its 1970 low, the market had lost just about everything that it had gained over the preceding ten years.

In any case, the sophisticated forecaster recognizes the danger of trend extrapolations when the forces making that trend may be in the process of change. One striking difference emerges in the potential supply of common stocks themselves. Net new common stock offerings during the 1950s and 1960s averaged less than $2 billion a year, while the demand for common stocks was increasing at a dramatic rate. But net new issues averaged over $5 billion even in the bear market years 1969–70. Given the likelihood that American industry will need more external financing in the decades ahead than in the first twenty years after World War II, and that debt creation was extraordinarily

heavy during the 1960s, most projections suggest that the volume of equity financing in the years ahead is going to be much larger than it has been—at a time when bond yields are also much more attractive to investors than they were during most of the postwar period.

In short, no long-term forecast of stock prices can afford to ignore the fundamental forces of demand and supply, forces that show clear signs of following patterns quite different from those established in the 1950s and 1960s. Consequently, blind reliance on long-term price trends would be exceedingly dangerous.

Forecasting *is* necessary!

BIBLIOGRAPHY

The serious student of stock market forecasting must read three classic books on the subject: the fundamental approach exemplified in B. Graham, D. L. Dodd, and S. Cottle, *Security Analysis, Principles, and Techniques* (4th ed.), (New York: McGraw-Hill Book Co. 1962); the technical approach exemplified by R. D. Edwards and J. Magee, *Technical Analysis of Stock Trends* (New York: John Magee, Inc., 1966); and a survey work on random walk theory, P. H. Cootner, ed., *The Random Character of Stock Market Prices* (Cambridge, Mass: M. I. T. Press, 1964). Perhaps we should add a fourth to the "must" list, relating to the monetary approach to stock market forecasting, B. W. Sprinkel, *Money and Stock Prices* (New York: Richard D. Irwin, Inc., 1964).

In addition to the econometric model developed by the Federal Reserve Bank of St. Louis (see "Expectations, Money, and the Stock Market," by M. W. Keran in the January 1971 issue of their *Bulletin*, reissued as Reprint No. 63), mentioned in the text, see also R. S. and D. H. Bower, "Test of a Stock Valuation Model," Reprint No. 16 in the Tuck School Special Series on Computer Applications, Dartmouth College, Hanover, N.H. Another excellent application of monetary statistics to stock market forecasting is to be found in H. Bolton, *Money and Investment Profits* (New York: Dow-Jones Irwin, 1967) and in the monthly publication of the firm Bolton headed, *The Bank Credit Analyst* (1245 Sherbrooke Street West, Montreal). See also M. Palmer, "Money Supply, Portfolio Adjustments, and Stock Prices," *Financial Analysts Journal* (July-August 1970).

The literature on random walk theory is already long and growing constantly. In addition to the Cootner book, the following are recommended (all items mentioned support random walk theory, with the exception of the last four):

Black, F., "Implications of the Random Walk Hypothesis for Portfolio Management," *Financial Analysts Journal* (March–April 1971).

Bostian, D., Jr., *Toward a Synthesis of Random Walk and Technical Trading* (Monograph, New York: CBWL-Hayden, Stone, Inc., 1970).

Fama, E. F., "The Behaviour of Stock Market Prices," *Journal of Business* (January 1965).

———, "Random Walks in Stock Market Prices," *Financial Analysts Journal* (September–October 1965).

Kisor, M., Jr., and V. A. Messner, "The Filter Approach and Earnings Forecasts," *Financial Analysts Journal* (January–February 1969).

Latane, H. A., D. L. Tuttle, and C. P. Jones, "E/P Ratios vs. Changes in Earnings in Forecasting Future Price Changes," *Financial Analysts Journal* (January–February 1969).

Levy, R. A., *On Evaluation of Selected Applications of Stock Market Timing Techniques, Trading Tactics, and Trend Analysis* (Washington D.C.: American University, 1966).

Samuelson, P. A., "Proof That Properly Anticipated Prices Fluctuate Randomly," *Industrial Management Review* (Spring 1965).

Van Horne, J. C., and G. G. C. Parker, "The Random Walk Theory: An Empirical Test," *Financial Analysts Journal* (November–December 1967).

Doubts about the ability of security analysts to predict earnings with any degree of success may be found in J. G. Cragg and B. G. Malkiel, "The Concensus and Accuracy of Some Predictions of the Growth of Corporate Earnings," *Journal of Finance* (March 1968) and in I. M. D. Little, "Higgledy, Piggledy Growth," *Bulletin of Oxford University Institute of Statistics* (November 1962) and also I. M. D. Little and A. C. Raynor, *Higgledy, Piggledy Growth Again* (Oxford: Basil Blackwell, 1966).

The literature on technical analysis is enormous, but, in addition to the Edwards and Magee book already cited, we especially recommend W. L. Jiler, *How Charts Can Help You in the Stock Market* (New York: Trendline, Inc., 1968) and *Encyclopedia of Stock Market Techniques* (New York: Investors Intelligence, 1970). We also suggest:

Chestnutt, G. A., Jr., *Stock Market Analysis: Facts and Principles*. Greenwich, Conn.: Chestnutt Corp., 1971.

Drew, G. A., *New Methods for Profit in the Stock Market*. Boston: The Metcalf Press, 1964.

Gillett, G. H., *Stock Market Timing* (Monograph, Investors Intelligence, Larchmont, N.Y.: 1970).

Granville, J. B., *A Strategy of Daily Stock Market Timing for Maximum Profit*. Englewood Cliffs, N.J.: Prentice-Hall, Inc., 1960.

————, *New Key to Stock Market Profits*. Englewood Cliffs, N.J.: Prentice-Hall, Inc., 1963.

Longer-run projections of the supply of and demand for equities may be found in P. L. Bernstein, "Supply/Demand: Whatever Happened to the 'Shortage of Stocks'?" *Institutional Investor* (May 1970); *The Demand for Corporate Equity: Projections to 1975 and 1980* (Monograph prepared by A. E. Saffer for New York Stock Exchange *Perspectives on Planning* No. 5, January 1970); and W. C. Freund, *Will There Be Enough Stock to Meet Institutional Demands in the 1970s?* (Monograph, New York Stock Exchange, March 1971).

Part Six

THE ACCURACY OF FORECASTS AND THEIR USES BY BUSINESS AND GOVERNMENT

Up to this point the book has centered upon a "how-to-do-it" approach: the methodology and techniques of forecasting as developed and utilized by the business practitioner. But a larger question remains: how accurate have the forecasts been and what use are they? Is forecasting a game—an end in itself? How does the forecaster fit into the broader picture of business and governmental life?

The first two chapters in this section explore the issues associated with the measurement of the accuracy of forecasts. Indeed, methods for determining one's "batting average" are described as part of the attempt to appraise results.

But even the most accurate forecasts may be simply a "five-finger exercise" unless the results are presented to management in a meaningful way and are *used* as part of the decision-making processes. The forecaster cannot expect "management" to be well-versed in the intricacies of econometric methodology; he cannot come into a meeting with dozens of economic scenarios and shrug his shoulders when asked for his best opinion. The client ultimately must be served: simply and directly.

The final chapters deal with these themes. Matters relating to the work of economist-forecasters in industry, government and in general consulting are raised and discussed.

VICTOR ZARNOWITZ

How Accurate Have the Forecasts Been?

There are two major interrelated questions of crucial interest to all serious makers and users of business forecasts: How are the forecasts prepared? and How accurate and useful do they turn out to be? The first question furnishes this volume with its main theme; the second, with a much needed perspective on the state of the forecasters' art and knowledge, the proper use for forecasts, and the possibilities for improvement.

The assignment to evaluate the general quality of forecasts by business economists is so broad that is necessary to select the topics for this chapter and concentrate on what seems most important. The principal limitation of the appraisal here offered is that it covers aggregative forecasts for the economy at large, not forecasts for individual industries and companies. Studies of the macropredictions, though of very recent origin, have been intensive and informative, but regrettably little is known about the micropredictions (which for the most part are made for internal company uses that do not result in research publications). Of course, one of the main functions of the aggregate forecast is to serve as a basic input to the forecast of variables which are of direct concern to business management, such as the company's sales. Major deficiencies of such inputs can cause large errors in the resulting forecasts of sales and related variables, which in turn may lead to costly errors in managerial decisions. Thus business definitely has a stake in efforts to secure more accurate macroforecasts and to learn how to use such information efficiently. The rapid growth of the U.S. forecasting "industry" in recent years suggests that this is increasingly recognized by business executives. (However, it is important to note that other factors also contributed strongly to the increase in volume and diversity of forecasts: the great advances in economics, statistics, econometrics, data collection, and computer technology on the supply side; and the requirements of expanding business, government, and academic activities on the demand side.)

The purpose of this chapter, then, is to summarize what has been learned about the accuracy and related properties of business-oriented forecasts of the nation's economic fortunes. Although liberal use is made of various illustrative materials, these are still of necessity only small excerpts from the extensive documentation now available. The appended bibliography should enable the reader to search out much of the further information that he or she might need.[1]

I wish to thank Mr. Benjamin CuKok and Mrs. Josephine Su for their valuable statistical assistance and Mr. H. Irving Forman for help with the charts.

[1] The bibliography includes primarily general reference texts on business and economic

TABLE 1.   PERCENTAGE DISTRIBUTIONS OF RESPONDENTS BY PRIMARY AFFILIATION,
ASA-NBER QUARTERLY BUSINESS OUTLOOK SURVEYS, 1968–71

| Line | Primary Affiliation | Quarterly Surveys | | | Annual Survey: |
| | | December 1968 | February 1971 | December 1970 | December 1970 |
		(1)	*(2)*	*(3)*	*(4)*
1	Total no. respondents	84	54	47	126
	Percentage in				
2	Manufacturing	39.3	35.1	44.7	27.0
3	Financial institutions[a]	21.4	22.3	21.3	18.3
4	Commercial banking	11.9	9.3	6.4	4.8
5	Other	9.5	13.0	14.9	13.5
6	Consulting or research	11.9	9.3	10.6	11.1
7	Academic	7.1	7.4	4.3	15.9
8	Government	8.3	14.8	8.5	15.9
9	Other[b]	11.9	11.1	10.6	11.9
10	Total[c]	100.0	100.0	100.0	100.0

[a] Includes commercial banking and other financial institutions (see lines 4 and 5).

[b] Includes a very few responses from labor union and trade association economists, but primarily the responses from "others," i.e., those not separately classified by primary affiliation.

[c] Sum of the corresponding entries in lines 2, 3, and 6–9 above, but the component percentages may not add up exactly to 100.0 because of rounding.

I. WHO FORECASTS WHAT, WHEN, AND HOW?

Affiliation and Location of Forecasters

It will be helpful to describe at the outset the forecasts to be examined. This is not difficult to do in general terms as far as

forecasting which can be useful in today's business environments, and more specialized works dealing with the construction and evaluation of forecasts of different types. The emphasis is on general economic forecasts that are of practical interest to business. Sources of data, which are discussed in many of the books and articles cited, are not listed separately. Even within the so limited area, this bibliography, though fairly long, is of course far from exhaustive. The items are numbered for ease of reference in the text and footnotes that follow. Many other references to the literature on economic forecasting will be found in the text listed; see in particular the bibliographies given in [42] and [46].

the *sources* of the forecasts are concerned. Table 1 shows the primary affiliation of participants in the surveys of business outlook organized quarterly and annually by the Business and Economics Statistics Section of the American Statistical Association (ASA) and regularly evaluated by the National Bureau of Economic Research (NBER).[2] The membership in the quarterly surveys is limited to those who quarterly prepare predictions of GNP, its major components, and other key economic indicators for several quarters ahead. It includes many well-known business and economic forecasters and is believed to be reasonably representative of those who are professionally and regularly engaged in the analysis of current

[2] The quarterly surveys were organized in 1968 at the initiative of Geoffrey H. Moore, then president of the ASA. Charlotte Boschan and I share the responsibility for the analysis of these data at the NBER. See [44], [45], and the press releases in successive issues of the *American Statistician* since April 1969.

and future business conditions. The annual surveys attract many more participants, up to two-thirds of whom may perhaps be better described as less regular or only occasional forecasters.

Academic and government economists represent on the average about 15 to 20 percent of the membership in the quarterly surveys and some 30 percent in the annual surveys. All other participants, except for a few labor union and trade association economists, are forecasters from the world of business. This and other evidence from a large collection of data assembled by the NBER for its continuing studies of economic forecasting demonstrates clearly that business economists carry out the great bulk of the forecasting activity, especially when the latter is defined on a regular basis. According to table 1, manufacturing accounts for the largest proportion of business forecasts, followed by financial institutions and consulting or research. Large corporations with nationwide and international activities are particularly well represented, as would be expected. Our samples include members from many states across the nation, but they properly reflect the concentration of corporate headquarters, and hence also of business forecasters, in New York City.

Variables Predicted and Timing Aspects of Forecasts

Most forecasts by business economists use, often loosely, the framework of the U.S. national income accounts. The variables commonly predicted include the gross national product (GNP) and its major expenditure components—consumption, investment, and government outlays—in current dollars. The trend in recent years has been toward forecasting a growing number of interrelated variables. More forecasters report specific numerical predictions for series which, because of their cyclical sensitivity and general volatility, are rightly viewed as

particularly difficult to forecast but also of great interest, e.g., the change in business inventories, corporate profits, and the unemployment rate. Forecasts of industrial production, employment, and the general price level indexes (reflecting the public concern about inflation) also are increasingly available.

In the last 10 to 20 years, forecasts of short-term economic developments have grown ever more abundant and ambitious, not only in terms of extended coverage of various economic processes, but also in terms of disaggregation over time. Most forecasts are still made annually for the next calendar year, but many are now made more frequently for sequences of several shorter (quarterly or semiannual) periods. The spans of the short-term predictions, measured from the time of issue to the midpoint of the target period, vary from one to six quarters (not counting the estimates, really forecasts, of the current or base period). There is a seasonal rhythm to the production of macroeconomic forecasts, with the primary peak season around the end of the year (October–January) and secondary peaks at three more or less quarterly intervals in between.

Forecasting Methods

Predictions by business economists have many particularities corresponding mainly to their distinct purposes, but they vary as much as predictions by economists in academic institutions and government with respect to important structural and methodological characteristics. The forecasting procedures that are most relevant at the present time can be broadly classified as (1) various types of extrapolations of the past values or behavior of economic time series; (2) surveys of intentions or anticipations by units making economic decisions; (3) reading the evidence of series with systematic properties of timing in the business cycle, particularly the leading indicators and diffusion indexes;

and (4) econometric models, that is, equations or systems of equations designed to repsent certain quantitative relationships among the pertinent economic variables and estimated primarily with time series and possibly also with other statistical data. Forecasters may use one or another of these approaches, depending on their purposes and preferences, but there is evidence that they typically use various combinations of them in more or less judgmental fashion. Judgment, of course, necessarily enters the forecasting process at several stages, in the choice of information and analytical methods used as well as in the interpretation and evaluation of the results.

The quarterly ASA–NBER surveys of the economic outlook are used to collect information on the methods and assumptions of the forecasters. In each survey, the participants are asked to rank the items in a short list of general forecasting techniques according to the relative importance of the latter in their own work as forecasters. The replies indicate that large majorities of the participants in each survey use what is called the *informal GNP model*, which includes a variety of procedures whereby the major expenditure components are predicted and the results are combined into an overall forecast, usually after various, perhaps iterative, adjustments for general "reasonableness" and consistency. This is a flexible and eclectic approach which has been labeled intuitive and described elsewhere in this volume.[3] In December 1968, over 80 percent of the survey members reported using it, while about 70 percent reported using leading indicators and anticipation surveys; in addition, approximately one-fifth of the respondents had their own econometric models and more than half referred to models designed by others (see table 2, lines 6 and 7). These pro-

portions, which disregard the ranks assigned to these methods, are also roughly indicative of the corresponding distributions in the later surveys.

About 55 to 65 percent of the participants in each survey ranked the informal GNP model as first; on the average, approximately 13 percent preferred most the leading indicators; 8 percent, the outside models; and 6 percent, their own econometric models (table 2, lines 8–14).

Some General Observations

There is no doubt that forecasting business conditions has of late become increasingly ambitious, as witnessed by the trends towards more specific, numerical predictions of a growing number of interdependent variables. Multispan forecasts that attempt to trace the dynamic developments over a sequence of future periods often replace forecasts consisting merely of single (typically, annual) figures. Forecasting has also become more sophisticated in the sense that the area of purely subjective guesswork is being minimized and that of informed judgment extended, in growing recognition of the hazards of the former and the advantages of the latter. This is indicated by the trends toward the use of macroeconomic models, leading indicators, and anticipations surveys; more concern about the quality of the data, the internal consistency of the forecasts, and the role of policy variables; and more care in keeping the record on the inputs and outputs of forecasting activity.

These developments are generally desirable, and business economists who shared in them are to be commended. However, the advances are still modest and there is some danger that they may lead to exaggerated expectations of the public regarding the potential of economic forecasts and the policies based on them. Business management, too, ought to be aware of the limitations inherent in all forecasting; although the gains

---

[3] See the chapter, "Judgmental Forecasting of the Gross National Product," by William F. Butler and Robert A. Kavesh. In [18], this approach is called "opportunistic."

TABLE 2.   FORECASTING METHODS USED IN THE ASA–NBER QUARTERLY BUSINESS OUTLOOK SURVEYS, 1968–70

Line	Forecasters Who Ranked the Method	Method Used						Total Number of Respondents[a]
		Econometric Model— Own	Econometric Model— Outside	Informal GNP Model	Leading Indicators	Anticipations Survey	Other Methods	
		(1)	(2)	(3)	(4)	(5)	(6)	(7)
		A. December 1968 Survey: Distribution by All Ranks[b]						
1	First[c]	5	11	50	12	2	3	
2	Second	3	7	11	21	23	4	
3	Third	2	7	5	22	20	2	
4	Fourth	5	19	2	1	10	2	
5	Fifth or Sixth[d]	4	1	1	3	2	1	
6	All Users[e]	19	45	69	59	57	12	
7	Nonusers	64	38	14	24	26	71	
		B. Seven Surveys Covered: Distribution by the First Ranks						
	Date of Survey							
8	Dec. 1968	5	11	50	12	2	3	87
9	Feb. 1969	3	6	41	5	0	6	63
10	May 1969	3	4	37	8	0	3	59
11	Aug. 1969	2	2	30	5	0	3	46
12	Dec. 1969	2	2	31	9	0	3	57
13	Feb. 1970	4	2	34	7	1	4	58
14	May 1970	5	3	29	5	1	2	49

[a] Includes, in addition to the forecasters counted in the entries to the left, those not elsewhere classified (who either did not reply to the question on the methods or failed to discriminate between the methods, i.e., tied all ranks).

[b] The total number of forecasters covered by this cross-classification is 83. Of these, 14 forecasters listed one method only; 11, two methods; 19, three methods; 28, four methods; 10, five methods; and 1, six methods.

[c] Most important.

[d] Least important.

[e] Sum of entries in lines 1–5 above.

569

from better forecasts can be substantial, losses from acting on unrealistic expectations concerning the precision of forecasts can easily be greater. Most forecasts now take the form of numerical point predictions, but users should always remember that all forecasts are probabilistic statements. A good practice for the forecasters would be to attach odds to the expected outcomes; if appropriately done, with identification of the most probable value, this would make explicit an important dimension of the forecasts without detracting from their definiteness. However, probabilistic distribution forecasts appear to be regrettably rare in business practice.[4]

II. ACCURACY AND OTHER ASPECTS OF FORECASTS

Criteria for Evaluating the Quality of Forecasts

The main purpose of forecasts by business economists is to help formulate and improve managerial decisions. In principle, therefore, such predictions ought to be assessed according to the degree to which they succeeded in reducing errors in these decisions. Some forecasts may be made for other purposes, e.g., for their public relations value, but such aspects are, or should be, secondary. The rate-of-return criterion of forecast evaluation, an economic concept, requires first, that the forecasts be verifiable; second, that the preferences ("loss functions") of the decision-makers be ascer-

tained; and, third, that the effective costs of producing the forecasts be known or adequately estimated. However, information on the second and third point is typically not available to an outside analyst. Indeed, it is probable that even the forecasters and decision-makers who are directly involved often have but a very incomplete knowledge of these costs and returns, as it is neither cheap nor easy to develop good quantitative data of this sort.

In the absence of firsthand knowledge of loss functions and costs of forecasts, it seems reasonable to measure the quality of the forecasts principally by their accuracy. True, it may not be sufficient to know the *size* of forecasting errors in order to determine the *consequences* of these errors for the decisions based on the forecasts, but in general the decision-maker will rightly prefer forecasts from a source which proved to have a significant advantage in accuracy over others. If a management decision is based on several forecasts combined (with any adjustments that appear desirable), then again the forecasts with a better accuracy record are likely to receive the greater weights.[5]

It might seem that measurement of the accuracy of a forecast after the event, when the data on the corresponding actual values become available, should be a rather simple affair, but several factors must be taken into account.

---

[4] An interesting and promising initiative, however, was taken in the ASA-NBER surveys in which information is collected regularly on the probabilities the forecasters attach to the different possible percent changes in GNP and the implicit price deflator (during the target year) and to a decline in real GNP (in each of several target quarters). See [44].

[5] This presupposes the availability of alternative forecasts derived by different sources and/or methods but comparable in terms of variables and periods covered, the frequency and dates of issue, and perhaps the costs of acquisition and interpretation. The predictions must relate to variables over which none of the forecasters has any appreciable control. (Where such control is present, the forecast shades into a "plan" and its accuracy is no longer an objective quality criterion, since the planner may himself act to invalidate his original expectation of an undesirable development; or he may, conversely, bias his forecast in the desired direction so as to favorably influence the subsequent events.)

1. A single success or even a few successes (or failures) usually lack the power to prove that the given source or type of forecasts is (or is not) accurate with a fair degree of reliability. Such isolated hits or misses could be largely due to chance. To reduce this possibility, it is necessary to study the average performance of a forecaster (or of a forecasting model or method) over a sufficiently long stretch of time including different economic developments. The longer and the more varied the period covered, the more informative is the analysis of the average forecast errors. Unfortunately, the available samples of forecasts are mostly small, since few forecasters have produced long, consistent time series of verifiable predictions.[6]

2. Different types of economic change confront the forecaster with problems of differing nature and degree of difficulty. It is relatively safe and easy to predict the continuation in the months ahead of a business expansion that has already taken hold and is gathering speed, whereas a reasonably accurate forecast of the end of such a movement (represented, say, by a peak in GNP) is usually difficult and rare even over rather short spans.[7] Similarly, such smooth and trend-dominated series as total consumption and state and local government expenditures are much easier to predict accu-

rately than are volatile series such as outlays on consumer durables, change in business inventories, and net exports. It is because of such differences in predictability that it is important for an appraisal of a given set (source, type) of forecasts to include predictions of various economic developments and diverse variables. For much the same reasons, the ability to predict directional changes, and especially the timing of the major turning points in business cycles, is often viewed as a critical attribute of a truly successful forecaster.

3. It is desirable that the mean error of a sufficiently large set of predictions be approximately (i.e., according to tests of sampling significance) zero. Otherwise, there is a suggestion of a bias in the sense of a systematic error of either underestimation or overestimation of the actual values.[8] In principle, bias constitutes an adverse component of predictions that the forecaster who learns from his errors should before long be able to eliminate, but in practice the situation may well be much more complicated. Rather large samples of comparable predictions may be needed to establish the presence of such systematic errors and to evaluate their size and importance, and the available samples are probably often not large enough. Moreover, a successful correction for the bias presupposes that "other things are constant," specifically that the process generating the predicted series remains essentially unchanged, as does the forecasting method used. If these conditions are not met, the series of forecasts may be long but it is not consistent and the apparent bias may be spurious. Finally, an entirely different argument is occasionally raised, namely, that a moderate downward bias may be deliberate—that forecasters often wish to be conservative or cautious and so prefer underestimation to overestima-

[6] The field of the inquiry can be widened by increasing the number and diversity of the forecasts covered, in terms of sources, methods, variables, and predictive time spans. "Cross-sectional" studies of differences among comparable forecasts for a given period can be highly informative and complementary to studies of time series of forecasts. However, even a large number of short series of various predictions, when limited to one relatively short period of time and a somewhat narrow range of developments, cannot very well substitute for long series covering a great many diverse episodes.

[7] For evidence on this and the following point, see [41] and [22]; also, see [13], [25], [27], [36], and [46].

[8] On the concept and measurement of bias, see [36], [37], [22], and [41].

tion (some evidence on this point will be examined later).

4. Ideally, forecasts should be efficient as well as unbiased. This means that the forecast errors must not show a systematic association with the forecast values. For example, the forecaster should not systematically underestimate the high and overestimate the low values of the series, or vice versa. A large dispersion of errors indicates inefficiency. Again, adjustments aiming at elimination of this type of error along with the bias are applicable under assumptions analogous to those discussed in the preceding paragraph. Statistical methods have been worked out to decompose the observed forecast errors into their systematic elements (bias, inefficiency) and the residual variance element. The larger the proportion of the latter, given the size of the total measured errors, the better is the quality of the forecasts, since random errors are preferable to systematic errors. Those forecasting errors that are directly traceable to very short random movements in the economic time series are by and large unavoidable. The measure that lends itself best to the decomposition approach just sketched out here is the mean square error of forecast, computed by squaring the individual forecast errors and averaging the results; it should be noted that large errors are given more than proportionate weight in this measure and small errors, correspondingly, are penalized more lightly.[9]

5. A prediction can be "correct for wrong reasons" (although based on assumptions contrary to fact, it produced but a small error), or the converse. This suggests that a quantitative analysis of forecast errors is not sufficient; a qualitative analysis of how each prediction was derived is needed. However, this argument can be carried too far. Individual predictions can indeed suffer from excusable errors in assumptions about "exogenous," perhaps noneconomic events, but if a forecaster's performance is clearly below par on the average over time, it is hard to accept wrong assumptions as a justification. After all, to be useful, the forecasts must be reasonably accurate much of the time; if they are not, for whatever reasons, they may do more harm than good. Hence the measurement and decomposition of average forecasting errors can be quite informative in their own right, although studies of forecasting methods and assumptions are of course needed as well. One should add that it is generally advisable and prudent for the forecaster to state carefully his basic assumptions. However, surrounding the forecasts with hedges against all kinds of "unforeseeable" events detracts from their usefulness, particularly for business purposes.

6. Forecasting errors are affected by, and include, errors of measurement; yet the former need to be distinguished from the latter. The recent data on which a forecast is based are as a rule provisional estimates which are themselves in part near-term predictions. Errors in these data, which can be estimated from the differences between the preliminary and the revised figures, contribute measurably to the overall forecast errors. Since the highly aggregative data from GNP accounts are subject to frequent and often substantial revisions, measurement errors in this sense present a particular problem for the forecasts of GNP and components (which represent a large majority of all macroeconomic forecasts).[10] Prompter and more accurate information about the conditions prevailing shortly before and at the time the forecast is made could improve the predictions considerably.

7. It should be clear by now that forecast-

[9] For more extensive and technical discussions of the adjustments and decomposition methods introduced in the text above, see [36], [37], and [22].

[10] See [6], [7], and [35, chapter 6], with references to literature.

ing accuracy is a relative and multidimensional concept. Simple error measures show how much the forecasts deviate from the state of perfection (zero errors) which, of course, is unattainable. Aside from this clearly unrealistic criterion, there is no absolute standard by which to judge the quality of economic forecasts. More meaningful criteria are found in comparisons of the forecasts with projections based on some objective bench mark models. An important class of such models includes all the various types of extrapolation of the past history of the series being predicted (and use only the values of the given series). An authentic forecast may contain extrapolative elements as well, but presumably not alone. It is also likely to incorporate at least some of the relations connecting the target series with other variables, external information considered relevant (e.g., from surveys of spending intentions), and, importantly, the judgment of the forecaster on how such data inputs are selected, adjusted, and combined. Thus, comparisons of the errors of forecasts with the errors of the corresponding bench mark extrapolations can provide estimates of the net predictive value (which could be positive, zero, or negative) of the combined nonextrapolative components of the forecast. In other words, since the extrapolations are applied mechanistically, the results of such an analysis indicate the predictive contribution of the forecaster over and above what could be obtained quickly and cheaply from a formula and an electronic computer (indeed, for any of the simple "naive model" projections, by some mental computations or with a desk calculator).

8. The extrapolations that can be used as yardsticks of predictive performance range from the simplest, such as the the last-level or last-change projections, to increasingly sophisticated trend projections, autoregressive mod-

els, and general representations of discrete linear processes which involve moving average as well as autoregressive elements.[11] Some types of extrapolation fit certain series relatively well; others fit series with different properties. In principle, there is an optimal extrapolation for each time series with a known and stable statistical structure, but in practice the economic data of interest may not satisfy the required conditions and it will often be difficult, if not impossible, to find and apply the optimal extrapolation method. However, the formal method of systematic comparisons of average errors of forecasts with average errors of some bench mark model is a general one. Bench marks other than extrapolations could be used in the like manner, e.g., ex post or mechanical ex ante applications of business cycle indicators or regression analysis or larger econometric models; opinion polls or aggregated microexpectations (survey results); and a series of "standard forecasts," i.e., averages of samples of predictions that are viewed as properly representative. This approach can be very helpful, too, in analyzing the relative accuracy of different forecasting techniques and inferring the "structure" of the forecasts (the shares of the informative content that a given set of forecasts has in common with extrapolations or other bench mark models or methods of a certain type).[12]

Summary Measures of Forecasters' Performance

Table 3 illustrates the application of

[11] On the rationale and applications of naive model and autoregressive tests, see the paper by Carl Christ and comment by Milton Friedman in [38, pp. 56–57, 69, 108–11]; also, [26], [41], and [22].

[12] Examples may be found in [22] and other essays in [21], by Jacob Mincer, Stanley Diller, and F. Thomas Juster.

TABLE 3.   SUMMARY MEASURES OF ERROR FOR ANNUAL PREDICTIONS OF GNP, FOUR SETS OF
              PRIVATE JUDGMENTAL FORECASTS AND THREE EXTRAPOLATIVE BENCH MARK
              MODELS, 1953–69

Line	Statistic	Forecast Set			
		B	F	G	M
	Mean Error: $\bar{E} = \dfrac{1}{n} \sum E_t$[a]	(1)	(2) 1953–69	(3)	(4)
1	Base[b] ⎱	−2.8	−3.2	−2.9	−2.5
2	Change ⎬ billions of dollars	−3.2	−4.4	−0.5	−6.8
3	Level ⎰	−6.0	−7.6	−3.4	−9.3
	Mean Absolute Error: $\overline{\lvert E \rvert} = \dfrac{1}{n} \sum \lvert E_t \rvert$				
4	Base[b] ⎱	3.4	3.5	3.4	3.1
5	Change ⎬ billions of dollars	9.2	6.9	7.7	10.4
6	Level ⎰	11.1	9.7	9.6	11.8
	Root Mean Square Error: $M_P = \sqrt{\dfrac{1}{n} \sum (E_t)^2}$				
7	Level billions of dollars	12.5	11.1	11.9	14.0
	Ratios of RMS Error[c]:				
8	$R_1 = \dfrac{M_P}{M_{N1}}$ ⎱	0.328	0.290	0.312	0.374
9	$R_2 = \dfrac{M_P}{M_{N2}}$ ⎬ ratio	0.641	0.570	0.614	0.723
10	$R_2{}^* = \dfrac{M_P}{M_{N2}{}^*}$ ⎰	0.504	0.448	0.481	0.562
			1953–63		
11	M_P billions of dollars	10.7	8.8	7.9	12.8
12	R_1 ⎱	0.435	0.359	0.322	0.531
13	R_2 ⎬ ratio	0.553	0.457	0.410	0.839
14	$R_2{}^*$ ⎰	0.699	0.578	0.518	0.841
			1964–69		
15	M_P billions of dollars	15.2	14.3	17.0	15.8
16	R_1 ⎱	0.276	0.258	0.306	0.294
17	R_2 ⎬ ratio	1.024	0.959	1.140	1.061
18	$R_2{}^*$ ⎰	0.421	0.394	0.467	0.436

[a] A forecast error $E_t = P_t - A_t$, where P_t is the predicted and A_t is the actual value of GNP in the t-th year. $\Sigma \left(= \sum_t^n \right)$ denotes summation over all years in the periods covered. Also see footnote 13.

[b] Errors in the forecaster's own estimate of the value of GNP in the current year (preceding the target year).

[c] The denominators, M_N, are the root mean square (RMS) errors of three types of extrapolation. $N1$ refers to the projection of the last known level, $N2$ to that of the last known change, and $N2^*$ to that of the average historical change (in the post-World War II period). See text and footnote 14.

some of the criteria discussed in the preceding section to four sets of annual end-of-year forecasts of GNP. These are all authentic predictions publicly released ahead of the target period. They are produced by the economic staffs of an insurance company (B), a commercial bank (F), a major business publication (G), and a university school of business administration (M). The authors include business economists and (for the set M) academic economists with business experience who are well-known forecasters with good professional reputation. The forecasts represent the consensus of the teams involved and are based on diverse approaches, but they are all "judgmental" in the sense of being derived mainly by general economic analysis and interpretation of past and current developments; they are not traceable to any specific econometric models of the economy.

The full set of summary measures of error, given for the years 1953–69, consists of averages taken with and without regard to sign and the root mean square errors, all in billions of current dollars. The mean and mean absolute errors are decomposed into the errors of (1) the current-year estimate (base); (2) the predictions of the change from the base to the target year; and (3) the forecasts of the level of GNP in the target year. The base error plus the error of the predicted change equals the error of level, for each forecast and hence also on the average (lines 1–3). As would be expected, the errors of the estimates (partial predictions) of the level of GNP in the current year are on the average much smaller than the errors of the target-year level forecasts, but the base errors are by no means negligible (compare lines 1 and 3, 4 and 6).[13] Furthermore, since the average errors have the same signs, the errors of change tend to be less than the errors of level (lines 2–3 and 5–6). The signs of the mean errors are all negative, which means that both the levels of, and the changes in, GNP have been underestimated most of the time. However, the mean absolute errors are throughout larger than the corresponding mean errors (disregarding sign) and, for the change and level errors, by rather large margins. This indicates that overestimates did occur with sufficient fre-

quency to cause significant variations in the signs of the individual forecast errors. The root mean square (RMS) errors are, of course, still larger than the mean absolute errors, as shown for the level forecasts (see lines 3, 6, and 7).

The accuracy of the forecasts is compared with that of three extrapolative bench mark models: N1, which projects forward the current estimated value of the predicted variable (here, the base-year level of GNP); N2, which adds to that level the last known change; and N2*, which similarly projects the average of past changes.[14] Ratios of the RMS error of the level forecasts to the RMS error of the corresponding extrapolations are shown for each of these three bench marks. (They are labeled R and bear the subscript of the model used in computing the denominator.) The ratios for 1953–69 are all definitely less than one, indicating that the errors of the forecasts have been considerably smaller than those of any of the three extrapolative or naive models, in terms of these summary measures (lines 8–10). This is a general finding that applies to a much larger collection of annual GNP forecasts for the same period, according to a recent National Bureau of Economic Research study [46]. In each case, R_1 is the

---

[13] The errors (E) of the level forecasts (P) are computed for any t-th period as $E_t = P_t - A_t$, where A_t is a preliminary estimate of the actual value [for GNP, the first Commerce Department estimate for the year t, which appears in the February issue of the *Survey of Current Business* in the year $(t + 1)$]. These early figures tend to have more in common with the data used by forecasters than the later revised figures. To use the latter would amount to charging the forecaster with the task of estimating the future revisions of the data; when he revised figures are so used, the culculated errors are on the whole considerably larger. See [7] and [41].

[14] The assumptions underlying these three models may be written as:

$$(N1) \quad A_{t+1} = A_t + u_{1,t+1};$$
$$(N2) \quad A_{t+1} = A_t + \Delta A_t + u_{2,t+1};$$
and
$$(N2^*) \quad A_{t+1} = A_t + \overline{\Delta A} + u_{3,t+1}$$

where A is the actual value, t refers to the base and $(t + 1)$ to the target period, and the u terms are random errors which, in the projection for each model, are taken to equal zero. $\overline{\Delta A}$ is the average value of post changes in A, computed from some starting date (here 1947) up to and including the most recent value known by the time of the forecast. Hence the projections with N1, N2, and N2* are $A_{1,t+1} = A_t$; $A_{2,t+1} = A_t + \Delta A_t$; and $A_{3,t+1} = A_t + \overline{\Delta A}$ respectively. the figures for A_t and ΔA_t are as a rule preliminary estimates, possibily themselves projections.

smallest and R_2 the largest of these ratios, with $R_2{}^*$ ranking in the middle, which means that, of these models, $N1$ gives the weakest and $N2$ the strongest results for the GNP series covered.

As is well known, GNP rose immensely in the seventeen-year period to which our forecasts refer (from \$365 billion to \$932 billion, according to the data here used). Not surprisingly, the average errors of forecasts increased, too, along with the target levels. For a sample of eight forecast sets from the NBER collection, including the four sets shown here, the average of the RMS errors was about \$10 billion in the years 1953–63, \$15 billion in 1964–69, and \$12 billion in the total period 1953–69 (compare the very similar results in table 3, lines 7, 11, and 15). It is important to realize that such an increase in absolute errors does not necessarily denote a worsening of the forecasts: the size of errors tends to vary positively with the size—as well as dispersion—of the values to be predicted. Relative errors derived from the comparisons with the extrapolative bench marks are free of such a dependence on the levels attained by the series and should be more helpful in dealing with the question of whether the forecasts have or have not improved. However, the results of the relative error analysis depend on the periods covered and the bench mark models used; they may not lead to any uniform conclusions when the data are limited to relatively short time intervals marked by very different economic developments.

Thus each of the ratios for 1953–63 is less than unity in table 3, but the R_2 figures for 1964–69 are either close to or greater than 1. Also, ranking the ratios gives $R_1 <$ $R_2 < R_2{}^*$ in the former period and $R_1 <$ $R_2{}^* < R_2$ in the latter period (lines 12–14 and 16–18). The R_1 ratios are smaller for the 1964–69 forecasts than for those in the preceding decade, and the same applies to $R_2{}^*$, but the R_2 ratios are, on the contrary, much larger for the more recent than for the pre-1964 predictions. These measures, then,

show that the GNP forecasts improved relative to $N1$ and $N2{}^*$ (i.e., their errors increased on the average less between the two periods than did the mean annual change in GNP measured either individually in the years covered or cumulatively over the post-World War II period). In contrast, the same forecasts apparently grew much worse relative to $N2$ in the recent years. The reason is that in periods of sustained growth without turning points and major retardations, such as the middle and late 1960s, the extrapolations of last change in GNP are at their very best. Yet such developments are not likely to persist, so that the advantage of such simple projections is transitory; in times of weaker trends and stronger cyclical movements, as during the post-Korean decade, model $N2$ is bound to perform much worse.

When extended to larger numbers of forecast sets and subperiods, measures such as those in table 3 suggest that there is little consistency in the relative performance of forecasters over time. For example, ranking the set with the smallest (largest) RMS error first (last), one finds that some sources have moved upward and others downward in 1964–69 as compared with 1953–63 (set M belongs to the former, G to the latter) but that such reshufflings were usually partial and unsystematic. The correlations between the rankings in the two periods, whether based on averages of the absolute errors or on the R-ratios, are virtually zero [46]. Year-by-year comparisons yield generally similar results [41, chapter 7].

Table 4 presents some measures of absolute and relative accuracy for a few sets of forecasts of GNP and its major expenditure components. The dollar levels of these aggregates differ greatly and no meaningful comparisons can be made between the errors of forecasts relating to these levels or to the corresponding dollar changes. This analysis, therefore, is cast in terms of relative change errors, computed by subtracting the actual from the predicted percentage changes. Set C includes predictions by the

TABLE 4. THREE SETS OF ANNUAL FORECASTS OF RELATIVE CHANGES IN MAJOR COMPONENTS OF GNP, AVERAGE ERRORS AND COMPARISONS WITH TWO EXTRAPOLATIVE MODELS, 1953–69

Line	Statistic[a]		GNP	Personal Consumption Expenditures	Gross Private Domestic Investment	Residential Construction	Total Government Expenditures
			(1)	(2)	(3)	(4)	(5)
			Set B (1953–69)				
1	RMS Error % points		2.00	1.51	10.93	11.92	2.45
2	R_1	ratio	0.320	0.263	0.789	1.032	0.279
3	R_2		0.576	0.583	0.582	0.958	0.464
			Set C (1958–69)				
4	RMS Error % points		1.71	1.44	6.64	7.89	1.79
5	R_1	ratio	0.442	0.236	0.532	0.714	0.219
6	R_2		0.531	0.612	0.637	0.711	0.535
			Set F (1953–69)				
7	RMS Error % points		1.54	1.52	5.95	8.10	3.21
8	R_1	ratio	0.246	0.264	0.430	0.762	0.364
9	R_2		0.443	0.592	0.314	0.757	0.609

[a] All measures are based on percentage change errors. See table 3 and text for the general definitions of the root mean square (RMS) error and tne ratio R_1 and R_2.

economic department of a large manufacturing company, which has in recent years constructed and operated a sizable econometric forecasting model; the other two sets have been described before.

The RMS errors in predicting year-to-year percentage changes in consumption expenditures are similar to, but mostly somewhat lower than, the corresponding errors for GNP. The forecasts of government expenditures show moderately larger, and those of gross private domestic investment (GPDI) show *much* larger average errors. The largest errors in table 4 (see lines 1, 4, and 7) relate to the forecasts of residential construction.

Most of the tabulated R_1 and R_2 ratios are clearly less than unity; there is little doubt that these forecasts are more accurate than the corresponding naive model projections. For consumption and government expenditures, the $N1$ model generally works worse than the $N2$ model ($R_1 < R_2$), whereas for GPDI the contrary is true. (For residential construction, the differences between the ratios R_1 and R_2 are small.) The ratios, particularly R_1, are in most cases larger for GPDI and, even more, for residential construction, than for consumption and government expenditures.

At least in qualitative terms, these results are representative; studies based on larger samples of forecasts for the same variables led to similar findings, both for the total period covered and for subperiods [41], [46].

Variability of Forecasters' Performance

Do forecasters generally do well in some periods and poorly in others, as it is often asserted? Why or why not? Table 5, which reviews the record of eight sets of annual GNP forecasts in each successive year from 1958 through 1970 (and of smaller samples of such forecasts for 1953–57) suggests that some years have indeed been "good" and others "bad" for a rather broad-

TABLE 5.   A YEAR-BY-YEAR RECORD OF ANNUAL FORECASTS OF GNP, AVERAGES, AND STANDARD DEVIATIONS OF ERRORS, 1953–70

| | | | | Errors of Predicted Changes[b] | | | Errors of Predicted Levels[c] | | |
Line	Year	No. of Forecasts	Actual Change[a]	Mean Absolute Error	Mean Error	Standard Deviation	Mean Absolute Error	Mean Error	Standard Deviation
(1)		*(2)*	*(3)*	*(4)*	*(5)*	*(6)*	*(7)*	*(8)*	*(9)*
					Billions of current dollars				
1	1953	4	+19.2	8.1	−8.1	8.2	10.7	−10.7	4.4
2	1954	5	−7.7	6.0	−2.4	7.2	6.4	+0.3	7.0
3	1955	5	+26.7	14.3	−14.3	4.6	18.1	−18.1	5.4
4	1956	6	+21.5	6.3	−6.3	4.0	9.2	−9.2	3.3
5	1957	7	+19.7	2.5	−1.9	2.3	5.5	−5.2	2.9
6	1958	8	−2.6	6.7	+6.7	4.0	3.6	+2.0	4.4
7	1959	8	+37.8	5.4	−3.7	6.4	8.6	−7.7	6.0
8	1960	8	+21.1	11.2	+11.2	2.1	8.7	+8.7	2.2
9	1961	8	+16.9	8.4	−7.6	5.6	8.8	−8.4	5.8
10	1962	8	+35.2	7.9	+6.6	5.3	9.0	+7.6	5.9
11	1963	8	+30.3	10.7	−7.7	8.8	11.5	−8.9	11.9
12	1964	8	+38.7	5.2	−4.4	4.0	5.5	−4.5	4.5
13	1965	8	+47.6	13.3	−13.3	5.7	16.9	−16.9	3.4
14	1966	8	+58.4	12.0	−12.0	4.0	22.4	−22.4	5.3
15	1967	8	+41.7	6.9	+3.9	7.2	3.9	−2.1	5.4
16	1968	8	+70.9	11.3	−11.3	5.9	16.5	−16.5	5.8
17	1969	8	+66.4	8.4	−7.8	4.5	14.3	−14.3	4.9
18	1970	8	+45.1	8.5	+0.4	10.4	7.0	+4.1	7.2
					Averages				
19	1953–70[d]		+32.6	8.5	−4.0	5.5	10.4	−6.5	5.4
20	1958–70[e]		+39.0	8.9	−3.0	5.7	10.5	−6.1	5.6

[a] In the year shown in column 1, from the preceding year. Based on early Commerce Department estimates.

[b] Computed by subtracting the actual change (column 1) from the change predicted by each forecaster.

[c] Computed by subtracting the actual level (preliminary estimate, see footnote 13) from the level predicted by each forecaster.

[d] Weighted by the number of forecasts covered in each year (column 2).

[e] For the eight forecast sets covered since 1958 (see footnote 15).

ly based cross section of forecasters.[15] More-

[15] In addition to the already introduced forecast sets *B*, *C*, *F*, *G*, and *M*, this collection includes: a regular discussion group of well-known economists from several industries, government, and academic institutions (set *A*); an economist associated with a university research center (set *K*); and a business consulting service (set *L*). The groups *A* and *M* are represented by average forecasts. Each of the eight sets covers the years 1958–70 and all but one include some earlier years as well; predictions from four sets (*B*, *F*, *G*, and *M*) are available for each consecutive year since 1953.

over, it appears that the distinction is not random but related to certain differential characteristics of the periods involved.

First, except in their predictions for 1954, 1958, 1960, 1962, 1967, and 1970, the forecasters have on the average underestimated both the rise and the level of GNP in each of the years covered (as indicated by the negative signs of the mean errors in columns 5 and 8). The exceptions clearly do not constitute a random subset: each of the above six years was connected either with a business recession or a subtantial retardation (as in 1962 and 1967). This simply reflects the fact that the forecasters often missed the downturn or the slowdown in GNP; that is, they failed to anticipate an impending, or to recognize an incipient, weakness in the economy at large.

Second, the largest underestimation errors occurred in forecasts for 1955, 1965–66, and 1968–69, all years of booming economic activity and high rates of growth (but also, in the late 1960s, of accelerating inflation). Quarterly and semiannual forecast data, which provide a finer subdivision of time, show similarly that industrial production as well as GNP were underestimated most in those stages of business expansion that saw the largest rates of increase in general economic activity.[16]

Third, the degree of consensus among the forecasters is high at some times and low at others; thus the standard deviations of GNP predictions fall in the range of $2–$3 billion in 1957 and 1960 and of $7–$12 billion in 1954, 1963, and 1970 (table 5, columns 6 and 9). The greater the dispersion of forecasts (and hence also of their errors), the higher is presumably the degree of the always present uncertainty about the future.

Of course, low dispersion need not be associated with greater accuracy of the predictions; forecasters may err strongly in the same direction at the same time. (The forecasts for 1960, with their large overestimation errors, illustrate this; on the other hand, the forecasts for 1957, though likewise not far apart, had relatively small average errors.)[17] Analogously, high dispersion of forecasts and their errors does not necessarily denote low average accuracy, though it does indicate that some of the predictions must be off considerably. (The forecasts for 1954 and 1970, for example, had small and those for 1963 had large average errors.)

Finally, the available data suggest that the variability of GNP predictions from year to year tends to be greater than the variability of predictions by different forecasters in a given period. The standard deviations "across years" are all close to $5.5 billion for both the change and level forecasts (see table 5, lines 19–20, columns 6 and 9). The standard deviations "across forecast sets" (computed, from the same overall collection of individual error figures, as weighted averages of the standard deviations of predictions in each set) are nearly twice as large, varying from $9 billion to $10.8 billion.[18]

That the variability over time of economic forecasts and their errors should

---

[16] Typically, these have been the recovery or early expansion stages. For example, consider the semiannual forecasts of industrial production (1947–49: 100) by a group of about fifty business economists (set *D*). Their mean errors for 1947–62, cross-classified by cyclical stage and predictive span, have been as follows (see [41, pp. 27–29] for further information):

	6-month forecasts	12-month forecasts
Recovery (first year of expansion)	−5.7	−6.9
Upswing (rest of expansion)	−1.2	−4.8
Contraction	+3.6	+4.8

However, not all economic expansions follow the same pattern of acceleration and deceleration; e.g., as this is being written (in mid-1971), the economy is undergoing a rather sluggish recovery from a mild recession that appears to have ended late in 1970.

[17] It is interesting to note that both of these years witnessed business cycle peaks (dated July 1957 and May 1960, according to NBER chronology). But the 1957–58 recession came after a vigorous rise in 1954–55 and many signs of gradual retardation in 1956, whereas the 1960 recession followed more abruptly a short, aborted expansion in 1958–59.

[18] Specifically, these measures of dispersion are, in billions of dollars: 9.0 and 10.2 for the forecasts of changes and levels respectively, in 1953–70; and 9.5 and 10.8 for the corresponding forecasts in 1958–70. Dividing the standard deviations by the overall means of the errors (table 5, lines 19 and 20, columns 6 and 9) one obtains the following coefficients of variations:

often be large, appears plausible. Economic instability has many causes and forms; some types of economic change are more difficult to precast than others and different types prevail at different times. That there are important factors which reduce the variability of predictions from different sources is also easy to perceive. Forecasts for a given macroeconomic variable, issued at the same time for the same target period, frequently do show considerable diversity; yet many are likely to have much in common because competent forecasters draw upon the same body of data, use similar methods, are exposed to the same current events and moods, and to some extent influence each other directly.

Predictions for Different Time Spans

Some forecasters (their number is increasing) regularly predict the course of important economic indicators over several successive time units in the near future; for example, set G includes predictions made semiannually for spans varying from one to four (more recently, to six) quarters and set C provides four times per year chains of forecasts ranging from one to five quarters ahead. Table 6 illustrates some typical properties of such forecasts.

There is abundant evidence that the average absolute errors of short-term forecasts for a variety of economic time series typically increase with each extension of the predictive span. The mean absolute errors and the RMSE errors in table 6 demonstrate this rule for predictions of GNP and three of its major expenditure components. The progression to larger errors for the longer forecasts is uninterrupted in all these cases,

whether the measurement is in terms of levels or relative changes. The results for other forecast sets and variables confirm this strong relationship, with very few exceptions [41], [46].

Although the average errors of prediction increase systematically with the span of forecast, the marginal errors do not. That is, the successive *increments* in the MAE or RMSE measures vary considerably, they are not necessarily larger for the more distant quarters than for the ones in the nearest future and indeed are often smaller.

The forecasts in the set G underestimate the levels of GNP by amounts that increase steadily with the span (table 6, line 1), and they underestimate the changes in GNP in the same manner. Such errors are apparently rather common, e.g., they are typical of the forecasts of GNP and several other variables in sets C and A, but they are by no means universal: thus, forecasts G of GNP and industrial production in 1955–63 show average *overestimation* errors that increase with the span [41, pp. 60–64].

The ratios of forecast errors to naive model errors are generally smaller than one for the periods covered in table 6, but the results for certain subperiods are less favorable; in the late 1960s, as already noted, the last-change projections would have been unusually accurate and the R_2 figures high. The ratios show no general systematic relation to the length of the predictive span: as the latter increases, the relative errors oscillate narrowly in some cases, rise or (more frequently) decline in others. Just like the errors of the economists' forecasts, so also do those of mechanical extrapolations tend to increase with the distance to the target period. The question is, does the accuracy of the former diminish more or less rapidly than that of the latter? When the two naive models are used as bench marks, the answer is frequently that the average errors of forecasts increase less, but the results vary for either model and for different forecasts and variables.

	Across Years		Across Forecasters	
	Changes	*Levels*	*Changes*	*Levels*
1953–70	−1.4	−0.8	−2.7	−1.6
1958–70	−1.9	−0.9	−3.2	−1.8

TABLE 6. FORECASTS OF GNP AND THREE SELECTED COMPONENTS OVER SPANS FROM ONE TO FIVE QUARTERS, SUMMARY MEASURES OF ERROR AND COMPARISONS WITH NAIVE MODELS, 1953–69

			Measures Relating to Forecasts for				
	Error Statistic[a]		One Quarter Ahead	Two Quarters Ahead	Three Quarters Ahead	Four Quarters Ahead	Five Quarters Ahead
Line	Symbol	Unit	(1)	(2)	(3)	(4)	(5)
			Set G: GNP, 1953–69				
1	ME	billions of dollars	−2.6	−3.5	−4.5	−5.8	
2	MAE		7.8	10.3	13.2	15.4	
3	RMSE		9.4	11.8	16.4	18.9	
4	R_1	ratio	0.505	0.431	0.448	0.409	
5	R_2		0.606	0.520	0.566	0.554	
			Set C: GNP, 1958–69				
6	RMSE	% points	1.02	1.96	2.40	2.98	3.31
7	R_1	ratio	0.455	0.522	0.452	0.466	0.459
8	R_2		0.665	0.907	0.764	0.699	0.657
			Set C: Personal Consumption Expenditures, 1958–69				
9	RMSE	% points	0.78	1.02	1.35	1.50	1.77
10	R_1	ratio	0.507	0.348	0.326	0.263	0.234
11	R_2		0.821	0.705	0.585	0.927	0.443
			Set C: Gross Private Domestic Investment, 1958–69				
12	RMSE	% points	5.80	10.20	11.30	13.25	16.01
13	R_1	ratio	0.784	0.903	0.812	0.970	0.848
14	R_2		0.671	0.643	0.454	0.442	0.388
			Set C: Government Expenditures, 1958–69				
15	RMSE	% points	1.35	1.88	2.45	3.62	4.12
16	R_1	ratio	0.570	0.407	0.386	0.421	0.365
17	R_2		0.698	0.683	0.612	0.791	0.754

[a] Measures in lines 1–5 refer to level errors, in billions of current dollars; the forecasts covered number 32, 32, 31, and 31 for the entries in columns 1, 2, 3, and 4 respectively. Measures in lines 6–17 refer to percentage change errors; the forecasts covered number 37, 34, 32, 21, and 13 for the entries in columns 1, 2, 3, 4, and 5 respectively. See table 3 and text for the definitions of the measures used.

More sophisticated extrapolative bench marks such as the trend projections $N2^*$ and predictions from autoregressive equations $N3$[19] are in most cases consider-

ably more accurate than the outputs of the simplest naive models, but many forecasters achieved records superior to any of these mechanical extrapolations over fairly long and varied stretches of time. Thus, the ratios R_2^* are 0.670 for six-month and 0.815 for twelve-month forecasts of industrial production, according to measures for set D, 1947–63 (see footnote 16). For forecasts from set G for GNP 1953–63, relative mean square er-

[19] The assumption underlying $N3$ is $A_{t+1} = a + b_i \sum_{i=0}^{n} A_{t-i} + u_{4,t+1}$, where the u terms are again treated as random errors with expected value zero (see footnote 14). In autoregressions designed to predict more than one quarter ahead, extrapolated values are substituted for the as yet unknown actual values; e.g., if a third-order form is used, the prediction for two quarters ahead would be; $A_{t+2} = a + b_1 A_{t+1} + b_2 A_t + b_3 A_{t-1}$, where A_{t+1}

$= a + b_1 A_t + b_2 A_{t-1} + b_3 A_{t-2}$ (this assumes that A_t is the last known value of the A series). See [41, pp. 102–3] for more detail.

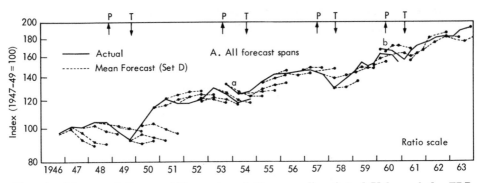

Chart 1   Means and Range of Forecasts and Corresponding Actual Values of the FRB Index of Industrial Production, Three Spans Semiannal 1947–58 and Quarterly 1959–63

rors based on comparisons with the autoregressive ($N3$) predictions yield the ratios 0.700, 0.744, 0.814, and 0.957 for spans of one, two, three, and four quarters respectively.[20]

For several other sets of GNP and industrial production forecasts, as in the above examples, the average errors show a tendency to increase more strongly than the average errors of the $N2*$ and $N3$ projections in consequence of extensions of the predictive span. For the longest spans, of four to six quarters, ratios near or above unity are not uncommon. These conclusions also apply to forecasts of several major GNP components. Apparently, many forecasters fail to use effectively the past records of the series in predicting developments beyond the first two or three quarters ahead. Many ingredients of the forecasts—inputs from leading indicators, anticipation surveys, and other judgmental data—have a relatively short infor-

[20] For more examples, see [41, chapter 6] and [22, pp. 40–43]. It should be noted that these measures relate to level and change forecasts covering at least the late 1950s and early 1960s. In 1964–69, a period of unusually steady growth, the $N2$ extrapolations for GNP had smaller errors than the other bench mark models used and compared favorably with several sets of multispan forecasts (as they did with annual forecasts, see table 3 and text above).

mational "forward reach." They are much more helpful and reliable for the analysis of the present and the very near future than for that of more distant events. Conversely, extrapolations are likely to prove more useful in the intermediate and longer forecasts than in the shorter ones; this may be expected simply because the trend-cycle components of the series grow more important relative to the irregular components over longer time intervals.

Many forecasts appear to be unduly influenced by very recent values of the series which they project into the future, with the result that they turn out to be more accurate when matched with the realizations for the time presently unfolding or immediately ahead than when matched with the realizations for the more distant future periods to which they were in fact meant to apply. This situation is illustrated in chart 1 showing the large group forecasts D of industrial production for 1946–63. It is clear that the mean predictions in this set have systematically underestimated (overestimated) the levels of industrial output when the latter was expanding (contracting). The errors were particularly large in the forecasts made between mid-1946 and mid-1950, a period when most contemporary analysts persistently expected a major economic slump to develop in the wake of World War II. After the outbreak of hostilities in Korea, the out-look shifted in the direction of expansion and the mild decline in output during the second half of 1951 was missed; but the fore-casters scored a significant success by cor-rectly anticipating the contraction of 1953–54. In the second half of the eighteen-year period covered, the forecasts were on the whole substantially more accurate than in the first half, despite relatively large errors in the predictions of the recoveries in 1955 and 1958–59.

Evidently, too, the forecasts for two quarters ahead had most of the time consid-erably smaller errors than those for four quarters, and the latter had much smaller errors than the forecasts for six quarters

ahead, which the group discontinued in 1956. This can be seen in panel A of the chart but even more clearly in panel B, where the predictions for each of the three spans are shown separately and a curve is drawn through the mean points of the dis-tributions of successive forecasts of each span.[21] This second panel shows lags of the

[21] This presentation has an advantage in the present context, but it must not be misinter-preted to mean that the successive forecasts form continuous series. They clearly do not: here, as elsewhere, a forecast made at time t is not based on the previous forecast made at time $(t - i)$ but rather on the data that became available during the ith period up to t.

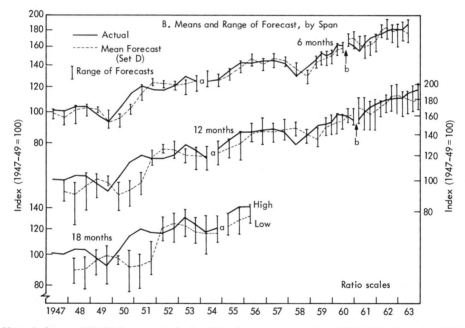

Note: Index on 1935–39 base was revised and the base was changed to 1947–49 in December 1953. The actual values for the second half of 1953 and the first and second half of 1954 (to the left of the break) were raised by the conversion factor 1.756 based on the first ten months in 1953 (i.e., the period of overlap of forecasts and the old index) to make them correspond more closely to the forecasts.

Note: Utilities were added to the index of manufacturing and mining in December 1959. The actual values for the fourth quarter of 1959 and all quarters of 1960 (to the left of the break) exclude utilities to make them correspond more closely to the forecasts.

Chart 1   (Concluded)

mean forecast (broken) curves relative to the actual (solid) curves, lags that are larger for the longer spans. Now suppose that the first forecast curve is shifted back by two quarters, the second by four quarters, and the third (bottom) one by six quarters, relative to the fixed actual curves: this would be equivalent to comparing the predictions in each case with the actual values as of the time the forecasts were made. This experiment results in considerable reductions of errors (the discrepancies between the paired curves are much smaller after than before the shift), which confirms the hypothesis stated at the beginning of the preceding paragraph. The effective horizon of the forecaster is apparently often a good deal shorter than the stated span of his prediction, particularly for the longer forecasts.[22]

Chart 1, panel B, also shows that the range of the two-quarter forecasts is typically smaller than that of the four-quarter ones, which in turn is smaller than the range of the six-quarter forecasts.[23] The group means are generally more accurate than the high forecasts (except for the longest span), and they are in each case much more accurate than the low forecasts which are associated with very large underestimation errors.

Multiperiod forecasts of the type here considered cover overlapping sequences of time units; hence such data lend themselves to an analysis of forecast revisions, that is, changes in predictions for a given target period made at dates successively closer to that period. These revisions reduce the errors in most instances. Consider, for example, the predictions for the first half of 1951 in chart 1, panel A: the lowest of these was made eighteen months earlier, the highest and closest to the actual was the most recent one, of six months ago.

Other forecasts provide similar illustrations. The group mean predictions of GNP from the recent ASA-NBER surveys indicate a systematic learning process. At the time when GNP rose steeply, to a large extent due to inflation, underestimates prevailed and each survey improved upon the previous one by revising the forecasts *upward*: this applies to the predictions of December 1968 and February, May, and August of 1969 (see chart 2). The December 1969 forecasts, failing to recognize a slowdown in GNP, continued the upward adjustment and overshot the actuals. In the next two surveys, however, this error was largely corrected. As overestimates emerged in this period, forecasters revised their predictions *downward*. These results suggest elements of partially successful "adaptive forecasting" or "learning from past errors."

Turning Point Errors

There are two basic types of turning point errors. (1) A turning point did occur but was not predicted. This is a "missed turn." (2) A turning point was predicted but did not occur. This is a "false signal." The tendency for a comprehensive aggregate such as GNP to grow most of the time is well known, so that few declines from one year to the next are predicted for this series and few indeed are recorded. False signals are particularly infrequent. There are only two, that is, less than six percent of all forecasts of reversals in the direction of change in the annual GNP series, according to a count presented in table 7 (column 1).[24]

The record on missed turns appears to be considerably worse: the percentage of turns observed but not predicted is nearly 26 percent for the GNP series. However,

---

[22] Lest these forecasts be judged too harshly, however, let me add that they are, for each span, more accurate than the naive model and simple trend extrapolations.

[23] The range is used here for simplicity, but other measures of dispersion are similarly related to the span of forecasts.

[24] Moreover, these two cases refer to the earliest years covered, 1947 and 1948, when a postwar slump was still widely anticipated (cf. text and chart 1 above).

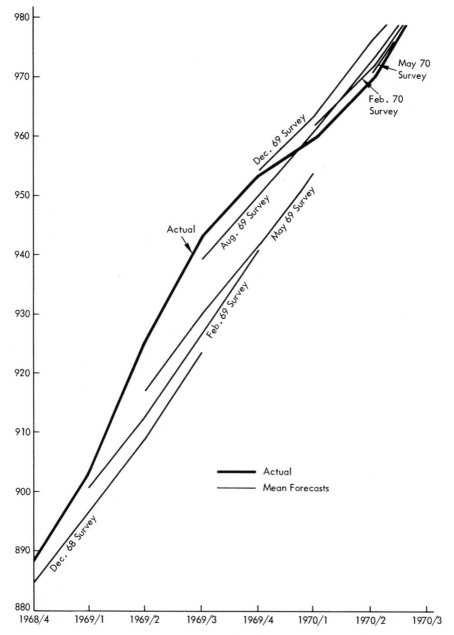

Chart 2 Mean Forecasts of GNP and the Corresponding Actual Values, ASA=NBER Quarterly Business Outlook Surveys (Q4 1968=Q3 1970)

these results must be interpreted with great caution, for they are based on few observations per forecast set and are very sensitive to data errors. All but one of the eleven observations that are here classified as missed turns refer to the 1957–58 decline, which was very small to begin with in the early GNP estimates and was ultimately replaced by a small increase in the current, revised figures.[25]

The turning point errors in the annual GNP forecasts are, virtually without exception, associated with peaks, that is, declines that were posted but not predicted, or vice versa. Not surprisingly, trough-related errors hardly appear at all in these data. Business contractions have been relatively mild and brief ever since World War II and informed people mostly expected them to be so, except in the early postwar years. Moreover, each of the three business cycle peaks in the decade after the Korean War occurred early enough in the spring or summer to be recognized as such by late fall or early winter when the forecasts for the next year were made.[26] Accordingly, the year-end

[25] Thus, had I used the current instead of the early estimates in these comparisons, the same forecasts would have been judged free of directional errors on this occasion. On the other hand, forecasters generally did predict a decline in GNP for 1953–54, which was in agreement with the data for more than a decade. However, according to the revised figures released in July 1965, there was apparently no decrease in the annual GNP series between 1953 and 1954 after all, but rather a minuscule increase. In this case, then, the use of most recent data would reverse my classification in the opposite direction. Clearly, the results of a turning point analysis can be highly uncertain for series subject to small short-term changes and revisions large enough to alter the sign of such changes.

[26] According to NBER chronology, the peaks occurred in July 1953, July 1957, and May 1960. The downturns in GNP are dated II Q 1953, III Q 1957, and II Q 1960; those in industrial production gave much earlier signals.

predictions for 1954, 1958, and 1961 were largely based on the assumption that the economy was already in the midst of a recession that would end before long; and these episodes account for the bulk of the "correctly predicted" turns in the annual forecasts covered in table 7. However, it would be illegitimate to infer that the dates of the expected troughs were well specified in these forecasts. The dates of the turning points implied by the annual predictions cannot be determined with any assurance; a year is simply too long a unit period for that.

Just as generally as for GNP, and for the same reasons, the turning point errors in the annual forecasts of industrial production relate to peaks, but here the proportion of missed declines is smaller and that of falsely predicted declines substantially larger (column 2). For consumption, fewer observations are available, but the percentage frequencies of turning point errors are relatively high (column 3) due to the errors in forecasts of the volatile component of expenditures on consumer durables. The incidence of turning points is particularly high for the investment variables, but the overall percentages of missed and falsely predicted turns in these series are similar to those recorded for the consumption forecasts (column 4). The largest proportions of turning point errors are observed for the most volatile series that can assume negative as well as positive values—net change in inventories and net foreign investment.

Comprehensive indexes of consumer and wholesale prices have tended to rise rather smoothly in the years covered by our data, so the relatively high percentages of turning point errors of both kinds in the forecasts of these variables (column 5) may appear surprising. However, it should be noted that almost all of these errors are in the predictions of the Wholesale Price Index, which encountered many more turning points than did the predictions of the Consumer Price Index. Also, a mitigating circumstance here is the fact that the changes in the Wholesale Price Index were exceedingly small in a number of the years covered.

Annual series conceal not only the short irregular and seasonal variations but also some of the milder and shorter cyclical movements, as exemplified by the recessions of the 1950s; annual forecasts, therefore, can provide only very limited materials for an appraisal of turning point errors. The multiperiod forecasts, which include predictions for several parts of the year ahead, are more relevant for this purpose, although the use of short unit periods may have its own disadvantages.[27]

The second part of table 7 (lines 9–14) shows the absolute and relative frequencies of directional errors in forecasts of sequences of quarterly changes.[28] Forecasters made few errors of predicting decreases instead of increases in GNP and industrial production, but such errors were considerably more frequent in forecasts of business expenditures on plant and equipment (columns 1, 3, and 5). The errors of predicting increases instead of decreases appear with very high frequencies in forecasts of each variable, especially for the more distant quarters (columns 2, 4, and 6). Indeed, approximately 60 to 80 percent of the declines in GNP and industrial production have *not* been anticipated in the forecasts for the first and second quarters ahead, and the frequencies of such errors rose to 90 and 100 percent for the more distant quarters.

These results suggest that the forecasters recognize correctly the predominance of upward movements in comprehensive economic aggregates but are on the whole unable to predict when a decline will occur in terms of quarterly data. Thus, of the 47 forecasts for the nearest quarter ahead, 32 turned out to have the right signs, which amounts to 68 percent or "not much better than one would expect if forecasters knew approximately how often declines would occur, but tossed a coin to decide when they would take place."[29] The corresponding percent-

---

[27] The shorter the unit period of the actual series, the greater, as a rule, the probable frequency of the minor turns that are often both difficult and not very important targets to predict. Reducing the span of forecast will likewise tend to increase the forecaster's exposure to such episodes and the probability of directional errors, particularly for the more volatile variables. But unless unit periods are used that are not too short relative to the business cycle phases, most of the recorded directional changes will be minor turns that would soon be reversed. Moreover, only some of the observed and predicted reversals will be associated with sharp peaks or troughs. An actual turn can be so shallow that a forecast may miss it without involving any large quantitative error, and a falsely predicted turn can be likewise so flat as to be connected with only a small numerical error.

[28] The criterion of identifying turning point errors through cross-comparisons—of the sign of the predicted with that of the preceding actual change—is readily applicable to the single period (here, annual) forecasts, but not to the multiperiod forecasts. This is so because each of the latter comprehends several predictions for increasingly distant future periods, all of which are made at a given date (t), with the aid of only the information then available. The actual change in period $(t + i)$, where $i \geq 1$, is not known to

the forecaster when he predicts the change in $(t + i + 1)$. For this and some other reasons, it is the frequencies of all directional errors that are presented here rather than the frequencies of the turning point errors. To compute the former, it is sufficient to compare the signs of actual and predicted changes for a given interval; it is not necessary to compare *sequences* of signs as must be done in dealing with the latter. See [41, pp. 72–80].

[29] Geoffrey H. Moore [25, p. 7]. The statement is based on a test of significance which, as noted by Moore, assumes that the observations are statistically independent, although they are clearly not (both because of serial correlations in the data and because of correlations across the different forecast sets). These ordinary tests, therefore, are likely to exaggerate the statistical significance of the results.

TABLE 7. FREQUENCIES OF TURNING POINTS AND DIRECTIONAL ERRORS IN FORECASTS OF GNP AND COMPONENTS, INDUSTRIAL PRODUCTION, AND PRICE LEVELS, ANNUAL AND QUARTERLY DATA, 1947–65

	Annual Forecasts of				
	GNP (12 sets)[a]	Industrial Production (11 sets)[b]	Consumption Expenditures (4 sets)[c]	Investment Expenditures (4 sets)[d]	Price Levels (5 sets)[e]
	(1)	(2)	(3)	(4)	(5)
Number of years[f]					
1 Covered	126	127	55	180	78
2 With no TP	81	65	47	65	51
3 With TP observed	43	52	7	99	23
4 Out of which missed	11	8	2	25	9
5 With TP predicted	34	54	6	91	18
6 Out of which falsely	2	10	1	16	4
Percentage of					
7 Observed TP missed[g]	25.6	15.4	28.6	25.3	39.1
8 Predicted TP false[h]	5.9	18.5	16.7	17.6	22.2

Forecasts of Sequences of Quarterly Changes in

Number (Percentage) of Failures to Predict[k]

	GNP (3 sets)[i]		Industrial Production (3 sets)[j]		Expenditures on Plant and Equipment (2 sets)[k]	
	Increases	Decreases	Increases	Decreases	Increases	Decreases
	(1)	(2)	(3)	(4)	(5)	(6)
Interval of Predicted Change (months)[m]						
9 0–3	6 (17.1)	9 (75.0)	1 (4.2)	10 (62.5)	4 (20.0)	3 (33.3)
10 3–6	5 (12.8)	5 (83.3)	3 (11.5)	8 (61.5)	5 (25.0)	1 (14.3)
11 6–9	2 (6.2)	11 (100.0)	2 (7.7)	12 (92.3)	7 (31.8)	3 (100.0)
12 9–12	2 (4.8)	4 (100.0)	3 (13.6)	9 (90.0)	2 (13.3)	3 (100.0)
13 12–15	0 (0)	6 (100.0)	0 (0)	6 (100.0)	2 (33.3)	4 (100.0)
14 15–18	0 (0)	2 (100.0)	0 (0)	5 (100.0)	n.a.	1 (100.0)

TP = turning points.

n.a. = not available.

a Includes, in addition to the forecast sets introduced earlier in this paper, averages of predictions by individuals in a medium-size group (set I), a large opinion poll (set E), and a large collection of diverse annual forecasts (set H).

b Same sources as for the GNP forecasts, except that no industrial production forecasts are available from set B.

c Forecast sets A, B, C, and F. Includes predictions of total personal consumption expenditures and of component expenditures on consumer durables, nondurables, and services.

d Forecast sets A, B, C, and F. Includes predictions of gross private domestic investment, its major components, and net foreign investment.

e Forecast sets A, F, M, K, and L. Includes predictions of the Consumer Price Index and of the Wholesale Price Index.

f Obtained by adding the observations in each specified category across all included sets of annual forecast. The forecast series cover different periods, with a concentration in the years 1953–63 (1947 is the earliest and 1965 the latest year covered).

g Line 4 as percent of line 3.

h Line 6 as percent of line 5.

i Includes sets: C (1985–63); D (1959–63); and G (1955–63, for GNP; 1956–62, for industrial production).

j Includes sets C (1958–63) and D (1959–63).

k The percentages, shown in parentheses, relate the number of failures to predict an increase (decrease) to the total number of increases (decreases) observed in the given quarterly interval.

m 0–3 refers to the change from the current quarter to the one ending 3 months hence; 3–6 refers to the change from the quarter ending 3 months hence to the one ending 6 months hence; etc.

ages are somewhat higher for the quarters that lie farther in the future, but here nearly all correct forecasts refer to increases; declines were seldom predicted at all, and hardly ever with the right timing.

This analysis of multiperiod forecasts poses in effect the requirement of exact dating of turning points in each of the several quarters ahead, which may be considered too demanding. Errors of misdating, particularly when the turns involved are minor or the movements are small, should not be judged very severely.[30] Misdating has not been very important as a source of errors in several forecasts examined [41, pp. 79–80], but there is evidence that the use of longer unit periods (semiannual rather than quarterly changes within the year ahead) does bring about some reductions in the frequencies of directional errors.[31]

Not only business economists but other forecasters as well, including those using econometric models, have yet to demonstrate that they can predict the timing of turning points in the major economic aggregates well in advance of the event.[32] There have been some successes validly claimed, but they are spotty; missed and misdated changes in direction are common, particularly at downturns in economic activity. However, the record does show for a sizable sample of professional forecasters and current business analysts that they were in general able to recognize turning points currently or with short lags, and even occasionally to anticipate the major reversals a few months ahead. This performance, although hardly impressive, is not necessarily poor and it could indeed be viewed as mildly favorable in a proper, relative sense. One must recall here that the lags in the availability of macroeconomic data are substantial; that the lead times of the best indicators of business expansions and contractions vary over time and across the different series and are generally not long; and that it is difficult to distinguish the major, more lasting movements from the minor and brief ones on a current basis. Furthermore, extrapolations of recent levels or changes, or of longer trends, either do not predict any turns at all or merely reproduce the actual turns with lags. Since missed turns are much more numerous than false signals, directional errors in general are considerably less frequent in economists' forecasts than in such mechanical extrapolations.[33]

---

[30] Suppose that a forecaster correctly predicted that a turn would occur the following year but misdated the turn by one quarter. This might be a real achievement under many circumstances, but it would be counted only as another error in such tallies as are presented in the second part of table 7

[31] See [25, table 2 and text]. The record of the annual forecasts was still better than that of the semiannual forecasts in this respect. The longer time unit implies a larger span to be forecast, but also a larger lag in identifying such turns as may have already occurred in the recent past and a smoother course of the series in the target periods.

[32] On forecasts with econometric models, see [38], [29], [33], [36], and [16] for some theoretical considerations and early tests; [11], [14], and other essays in [15], also [12], [25], [35], [46], and [47], for some recent evaluations of the principal U.S. models and related forecasts.

[33] Higher order autoregressive models can produce forecasts of turning points, but there is some evidence that they are poor predictors of the timing of such events [41, chart 5 and text]. Actual changes show much higher correlations with the changes predicted by forecasters than with the changes produced by autoregressive extrapolations [22, table 1-5 and text] To be sure, extrapolative models better than N3 can frequently be constructed, at higher costs in terms of the required information and computational processing [2]. However, it appears that such improvements are more likely to take the form of large reductions in the overall systematic errors than of greater efficiency of the extrapolations as turning point predictors.

III. A CONCLUDING STATEMENT ON TYPES OF ECONOMIC FORECASTS

Predictions by Business Economists and Extrapolations

Forecasts by economists working in the business sector vary greatly in methods used and results achieved, as do forecasts that originate elsewhere in the U.S. economy, but a detailed picture of this diversity is not of primary interest to either practitioner or scientist, and would probably not be worth its high costs. In this chapter, I have rather tried to reduce the variety of forecasting experience and performance so as to highlight the more general and characteristic but also the exceptional. Since the result is, naturally, a summary, there is no need to sum it up much further still. Nevertheless, a few major conclusions may be drawn.

For GNP, 1953–70, the end-of-year forecasts of change in the next year show an average error (without regard to sign) of $10.4 billion. This represents about 1.8 percent of the average level of GNP in that period and about 33 percent of the average annual change in GNP. Our collection of forecasts may be viewed as fairly representative of reputable professional work in this area, and the above results in relative terms appear to be reasonably stable.[34] This, then, is the level of average accuracy one may expect of such forecasts. However, we have observed considerable variability of forecast errors from year to year, which also can be expected to prevail in the future as some types of economic change are more difficult

to predict than others. The annual predictions reviewed, for GNP and other major aggregates, are on the whole substantially more accurate than naive model projections. Most of the comprehensive forecasts are also more accurate, though often by much smaller margins, than the more sophisticated types of mechanical extrapolations (e.g., trend projections and autoregressive models).

Average errors increase steadily with the span of forecasts. Business economists' predictions of GNP and industrial production, for example, are typically more accurate than various types of extrapolation over intervals from one to three quarters ahead. Many longer forecasts, however, are not superior to mechanical extrapolations of recent trends and autoregressive relations. (The evidence that the year-to-year forecasts are superior is consistent with these findings, since such forecasts have effectively average spans of little more than six months and will prove moderately good if they score well in the first two quarters.)

On the average, predicted changes are smaller than the recorded changes for many forecasts in the large and diverse collection under review, as well as in materials examined in other studies.[35] Underestimation of changes (in the sense of the variance of the predicted values being smaller than that of the actual values) is to be expected as a result of nonprediction of the random movements in the actuals; indeed, so defined underestimation is a property of unbiased and efficient forecasts of changes [22, p. 18]. However, biased or incorrect forecasts may also show underestimation, and not just of short irregular variations but of longer movements. There is evidence that the observed underestimates refer mainly to con-

---

[34] For 1958–70, for example, the mean absolute error of forecast represented approximately 1.6 percent of the average level and 29 percent of the average change in annual GNP.

[35] Examples may be found in reports by Modigliani and Sauerlander [8, pp. 288–89], by Theil [36, pp. III–V], and in evaluations of several major econometric models of the U.S. economy (see [15] for references).

servative predictions of growth rates in series dominated by upward trends (as this implies, the levels of such series also are typically underpredicted).[36]

Forecasting Methods and Accuracy

Increasingly complex econometric models of the economy have been constructed and are being used in forecasting, thanks to the rapid development of economic statistics, econometrics, and computer technology, although some economists maintain that relatively simple, small-scale models are preferable so far as macroeconomic forecasting is concerned because they tax less the present inadequate knowledge and data. This is not the place to discuss this issue nor the relative merits of models with different theoretical orientations (Keynesian, Monetarist), but it may be noted that such comparisons raise difficult problems and the evidence bearing on them is as yet skimpy. However, some attention will be given to two topics that are both pertinent and already more clarified: (1) the role of judgment in forecasting with econometric models and (2) the accuracy of the latter as compared with business forecasts.

Most practicing econometric forecasters use their models in a flexible manner, trying to combine them with other information: anticipatory data from surveys, indicators, etc., treated as exogenous variables, and judgment about the probable effects of recent events, exercised by adjustments of constant terms in the equations of the model. The use of anticipatory data has been shown to improve the econometric predictions for the shortest spans.[37] The judgmental adjust-

ments of the constant terms also increase the accuracy of the forecasts and are better in doing so than mechanical adjustments based on the residual errors of the model estimates for the recent periods. This has been well documented for two major U.S. models, Wharton–EFU and OBE.[38] Indeed, the interaction of the econometric forecaster and his model is crucial in these cases, as demonstrated by an analysis which, allowing for the effects of various judgmental and mechanical adjustments, concludes that the ex ante forecasts more often than not compare favorably with the corresponding ex post forecasts. The greater average accuracy of the ex ante forecasts is remarkable because they include the errors in exogenous variables which are absent in the ex post predictions [11], [46], and [47].

The authentic (ex ante) forecasts of the econometricians are therefore often as much a product of their authors' more or less informed judgments as of their formal models. The theoretically sharp distinction between the structured econometric forecasts and the judgmental forecasts not based on explicit, fully specified models is in practice largely a false dichotomy. As a rule, forecasts of future economic developments offered by qualified sources with serious intent (which excepts casual auguries and hunches) include the elements of both "judgment" and "model," in different forms and combinations. Perhaps the main difference between the forecasters who do and those who do not use formal models is that the former disclose to a much greater degree than the latter their assumptions and methods. Dis-

---

[36] See [41, pp. 40–51], [22, pp. 15–20], and [37, in parts, especially pp. 50–53].

[37] See, e.g., [16, pp. 86–89] on the role of consumer attitude and investment intentions data in the Wharton-EFU model. Typically, the lead time of the survey data is short, about six months or less.

[38] The abbreviations refer, respectively, to the Wharton-Econometric Forecasting Unit model [12] and the Office of Business Economics of the U.S. Department of Commerce model [14]. The findings here discussed have been presented first in [11] and extended and updated in a forthcoming National Bureau of Economic Research study by Yoel Haitovsky, George I. Treyz, and Vincent Su. Access to the results of this new study is gratefully acknowledged.

closure is certainly necessary if the forecasting tools and techniques are to be improved, but this, one must note, is true not only for econometric model predictions but also for any other types of forecasts with objective and potentially reproducible ingredients.

Forecasts by business economists, then, may differ in accuracy from the ex ante forecasts by econometric model builders in part because the two groups use different models or techniques and in part because individual judgments diverge. A quantitative analysis of the sources of such differences would be very difficult, and its outcome problematic, in view of the diversity, interdependence, and partly intangible nature of the inputs to the forecasting processes. Still, it is instructive to ask what the differences are. Even this seemingly simple question turns out to be not so easy at all, for it is impossible to match precisely the predictions from these different sources, and the subsamples of forecasts that are at least roughly comparable in terms of dates of issue and target periods are quite small. For what such fragmentary results are worth, the mean absolute errors of the Wharton and OBE ex ante forecasts of GNP in current and constant dollars are, with very few exceptions, smaller than the corresponding measures for the sets A and G but larger than those for set C and the group median forecasts from the ASA–NBER surveys. These comparisons include only those predictions that are similarly dated, for spans varying from one to four quarters; they refer to periods between III-1966 and III-1969 and are based on averages of 2 to 6 forecasts [46, tables 7 and 8 and text]. As for the ex post model forecasts, these are in large past less accurate than the business forecasts.

These findings are somewhat mixed and certainly not very conclusive.[39] However, it seems fair to say that the models, despite their relative complexity and structured character (also higher costs!), do not confer upon the econometric forecasts a clear-cut, general, and consistent advantage over those predictions of business economists which are derived largely by more informal approaches. (This is not at all inconsistent with the view, which I accept, that there are probably very significant gains from the interaction of the econometricians with their models; moreover, it is well to keep in mind that the models provide other than forecasting services, though these are here ignored.)

The ranks attached by the participants in the quarterly ASA–NBER surveys to the forecasting methods they used (see table 2 and text above) have served as a vehicle of another effort to find out how well the different methods work. In separate equations for each survey and predictive span, the errors of individual forecasts of GNP were regressed on dummy variables representing the first-ranked methods (the evidence for other ranks was also used in some tests). This analysis [47] revealed no systematic and consistent dependence of forecasting accuracy on forecasting methods.[40] However, this evidence is not sufficient

---

[39] The comparisons with set C are not so much between econometric and judgmental forecasts as between academic and business forecasts both of which represent the model-cum-judgment approach (recall that the recent predictions in set C are themselves based largely on an econometric model). The averaging of predictions made by members of a group tends to reduce the range of error [41, pp. 123–26], which is a factor that favors the judgmental forecasts A and ASA-NBER. On the other hand, the comparisons may well be biased in favor of the econometric forecasts by the fact that these forecasts have spans that are somewhat shorter than most of the business economists' predictions (the first quarter of the forecasts made with the models is typically half completed at the time the forecast is made). Allowing for this latter factor would eliminate or reduce some of the apparent superiority of the econometric model forecasts.

[40] In the regressions presented in [47, table 5], the constant terms are estimates of the expected values of the errors for those forecasters who ranked the "informal GNP model" first, while the coefficients of the dummy

to justify the strong (and, it would seem, not very plausible) conclusion that it does not matter which methods are being used and how they are combined to produce GNP forecasts. First, the questionnaire used in the surveys refers to general approaches to macroeconomic forecasting rather than to specific models and procedures. Second, it is possible that the general methodological distinctions among practicing economic forecasters are seldom sufficiently large and systematic to produce clear-cut differences in the observed accuracy of aggregative forecasts. If sharper distinctions were available, elements of a stronger relationship between method and accuracy might conceivably be brought to light. However, the fact remains that none of the principal methods enjoyed the general support of regular economic forecasters, and this is significant in that it indicates that none was expected to give consistently more accurate results than the others.

Recent times have witnessed much genuine progress in the development of more and better forecasting tools (economic data) and techniques (time series analysis and extrapolations; indicators of business expansions and contractions; anticipations surveys; econometric models). Further advances on these fronts are to be expected, and they are essential. Yet practical economic forecasting still derives its strength largely from individual skill, experience, and judgment. This is as true in forecasting with econometric models as it is in forecasting based on general economic analysis, the evidence of anticipations surveys, etc. It may well be that the best examples of the private art of predicting aggregate business trends will always outperform the routine results obtained by more explicit and reproducible, scientific methods. But, ultimately, there is no dependable substitute in this area for technical competence in, and intelligent application of, sound economic analysis; and surely it is in the improvement of these abilities that we must mainly place our hope for progress in business forecasting.

---

variables are estimates of the differences between these average errors and those of the groups who ranked the other methods first. Few of these coefficients appear to be statistically significant (about one in six at the five percent level).

BIBLIOGRAPHY

1. Bassie, V. Lewis, *Economic Forecasting.* New York: McGraw-Hill Book Company, 1958.
2. Box, G. E. P., and G. M. Jenkins, *Time Series Analysis, Forecasting and Control.* San Francisco: Holden-Day, Inc., 1970.
3. Bratt, Elmer C., *Business Forecasting.* New York: McGraw-Hill Book Company, 1958.
4. Clark, John J., *The Management of Forecasting.* New York: St. John's University Press, 1969.
5. Chisholm, Roger K., and Gilbert R. Whitaker, Jr., *Forecasting Methods.* Homewood, Ill.: Richard D. Irwin, Inc., 1971.
6. Cole, Rosanne, "Data Errors and Forecasting Accuracy," in [21].
7. ———, *Errors in Provisional Estimates of Gross National Product.* New York: National Bureau of Economic Research, 1969.
8. Conference on Research in Income and Wealth, *Short-Term Economic Forecasting.* Studies in Income and Wealth, Vol. 17. Princeton, N.J.: Princeton University Press for National Bureau of Economic Research, 1955.

9. Cox, Garfield V., *An Appraisal of American Business Forecasts.* Chicago: University of Chicago Press, 1929.

10. Dauten, Carl A., and Lloyd M. Valentine, *Business Cycles and Forecasting* (3rd ed.). Cincinnati: South-Western Publishing Co., 1968.

11. Evans, Michael K., Yoel Haitovsky, and George I. Treyz, assisted by Vincent Su, "An Analysis of the Forecasting Properties of U.S. Econometric Models," in [15].

12. Evans, Michael K., and Lawrence R. Klein, *The Wharton Econometric Model.* Studies in Quantitative Economics, No. 2. Philadelphia: Economics Research Unit, University of Pennsylvania, 1967.

13. Fels, Rendigs, and C. Elton Hinshaw, *Forecasting and Recognizing Business Cycle Turning Points.* New York: National Bureau of Economic Research, 1968.

14. Green, George R., in association with Maurice Liebenberg and Albert A. Hirsch, "Short- and Long-Term Simulations with the OBE Econometric Model," in [15].

15. Hickman, Bert G., ed., *Conference on Econometric Models of Cyclical Behavior.* Studies in Income and Wealth, Vol. 36. New York: National Bureau of Economic Research, 1971.

16. Klein, Lawrence R., *An Essay on the Theory of Economic Prediction.* Helsinki: The Academic Book Store, 1968.

17. Lee, Maurice W., *Macroeconomics: Fluctuations, Growth and Stability* (4th ed.), Homewood, Ill.: Richard D. Irwin, Inc., 1967.

18. Lewis, John P., and Robert C. Turner, *Business Conditions Analysis* (2nd ed.), New York: McGraw-Hill Book Company, 1967.

19. Maisel, Sherman J., *Fluctuations, Growth and Forecasting: The Principles of Dynamic Business Economics.* New York: John Wiley & Sons, Inc., 1957.

20. McKinley, David H., Murray G. Lee, and Helene Duffy, *Forecasting Business Conditions.* New York: American Bankers Association, 1965.

21. Mincer, Jacob, ed., *Economic Forecasts and Expectations: Analysis of Forecasting Behavior and Performance.* New York: National Bureau of Economic Research, 1969.

22. ——, and Victor Zarnowitz, "The Evaluation of Economic Forecasts," in [21].

23. Moore, Geoffrey H., ed., *Business Cycle Indicators*, 2 vols. Princeton, N.J.: Princeton University Press for National Bureau of Economic Research, 1961.

24. ——, "Forecasting Short-Term Economic Change," *Journal of the American Statistical Association* (March 1969), pp. 1–22.

25. ——, and Julius Shiskin, *Indicators of Business Expansions and Contractions.* New York: National Bureau of Economic Research, 1967.

26. Okun, Arthur, "A Review of Some Economic Forecasts for 1955–1957," *Journal of Business* (July 1959), pp. 199–211.

27. ——, "On the Appraisal of Cyclical Turning-point Predictions," *Journal of Business* (April 1960), pp. 101–20.

28. Prochnow, Herbert V., ed., *Determining the Business Outlook.* New York: Harper & Brothers, 1954.

29. Roos, Charles F., "Survey of Economic Forecasting Techniques," *Econometrica* (October 1955), pp. 363–95.

30. Samuelson, Paul A., "Economic Forecasting and Science," *Michigan Quarterly Review* (October 1965), pp. 112–119.

31. Shiskin, Julius, *Signals of Recession and Recovery: An Experiment with Monthly Reporting.* New York: National Bureau of Economic Research, 1961.

32. Silk, Leonard S., and M. Louise Curley, *A Primer on Business Forecasting, with a Guide to Sources of Business Data.* New York: Random House, 1970.

33. Spencer, Milton H., Colin G. Clark, and Peter W. Hoguet, *Business and Economic Forecasting: An Econometric Approach.* Homewood, Ill.: Richard D. Irwin, Inc., 1961.

34. Sprinkel, Beryl Wayne, *Money and Markets: A Monetarist View.* Homewood, Ill.: Richard D. Irwin, Inc., 1971.

35. Stekler, Herman O., *Economic Forecasting.* New York: Frederick A. Praeger, 1970.

36. Theil, Henri, *Economic Forecasts and Policy* (2nd ed.), Amsterdam: North-Holland Publishing Company, 1961.

37. ———, *Applied Economic Forecasting.* Chicago: Rand McNally & Co., 1966.

38. Universities—National Bureau Committee for Economic Research, *Conference on Business Cycles.* New York: National Bureau of Economic Research, 1951.

39. ———, *The Quality and Economic Significance of Anticipations Data* (a conference). Princeton, N.J.: Princeton University Press for National Bureau of Economic Research, 1960.

40. Wolfe, Harry Deane, *Business Forecasting Methods.* New York: Holt, Rinehart and Winston, Inc., 1966.

41. Zarnowitz, Victor, *An Appraisal of Short-Term Economic Forecasts.* New York: National Bureau of Economic Research, 1967.

42. ———, "Prediction and Forecasting, Economic," *International Encyclopedia of the Social Sciences* (1968), Vol. 12, pp. 425–39.

43. ———, "An Evaluation of Price-Level Forecasts," *1968 Proceedings of the Business and Economic Statistics Section.* American Statistical Association, Washington, D.C., 1968, pp. 284–89.

44. ———, "The New ASA-NBER Survey of Forecasts by Economic Statisticians," *American Statistician* (February 1969), pp. 12–16.

45. ———, "The ASA-NBER Quarterly Survey of the Economic Outlook: An Early Appraisal," *1969 Proceedings of the Business and Economic Statistics Section.* American Statistical Association, Washington, D.C., 1969, pp. 241–49.

46. ———, "Forecasting Economic Conditions: The Record and the Prospect," *The Business Cycle Today,* ed. V. Zarnowitz. New York: National Bureau of Economic Research, 1971.

47. ———, "New Plans and Results of Research in Economic Forecasting," *Fifty-first Annual Report.* New York: National Bureau of Economic Research, 1971.

ROBERT B. PLATT

Statistical Measures of Forecast Accuracy

I. INTRODUCTION

All forecasters at one time or another are questioned on the accuracy of their forecasts. The replies are all too frequently a series of broad rationalizations based on the inevitability of forecast errors as a result of data inaccuracies and uncertainties caused by government policies, strikes, and that favorite catchall excuse, changing expectations. But this is not enough. A forecaster's job does not stop with the preparation of a forecast. As a true professional, he knows that much can be learned from his past mistakes, and that buried in his forecast record is a story which not only adequately explains past errors but also can improve his future results.

The purpose of this chapter is to describe a few of the statistical techniques which forecasters use to analyze past forecast errors. The emphasis throughout is on how such an analysis can aid the forecaster in sharpening his performance and in selecting the "best" forecasting procedure. Before beginning the discussion of error analysis, however, a few comments should be made about the data used in measuring forecasts and their realizations, and about the notation which will be used to represent these data.

This chapter is concerned with forecasts of changes in a variable rather than

with forecasts of levels. This is done in part because in most instances the user of the forecast is primarily interested in how much a particular variable will change. But even more important for our purposes, the systematic characteristics of forecast errors are more easily observed when the data are in the form of changes. This will become clearer as the various statistical techniques of error analysis are described.

In regard to notation, P_t is used to denote the predicted change in some arbitrary economic variable from time period $t - 1$ to time period t, where t represents some particular year, quarter, month, etc. A_t is used to represent the actual change, and $e_t = P_t - A_t$ refers to the error of forecast in time period t.

II. GRAPHIC METHODS

A. Introduction

Movements in an economic variable result in part from a number of systematic and recognizable influences. These influences might be identified with specific economic conditions, such as the relationship between business plant and equipment expenditures, and changes in corporate earnings, sales, and the cost of credit. Alternatively, these influences might be recognizable

TABLE 1.   PREDICTED AND ACTUAL CHANGES IN GNP

Year	Predicted	Actual	Error	Cumulative Error
1953	13.0	15.5	− 2.5	− 2.5
1954	− 4.5	− 5.9	1.4	− 1.1
1955	4.4	29.6	−25.2	−26.3
1956	9.0	8.2	0.8	−25.5
1957	9.1	7.7	1.4	−24.1
1958	− 2.9	− 7.3	4.4	−19.7
1959	9.0	27.3	−18.3	−38.0
1960	8.5	11.3	− 2.8	−40.8
1961	7.4	7.8	− 0.4	−41.2
1962	27.5	27.1	0.4	−40.8
1963	14.1	15.9	− 1.8	−42.6
1964	23.9	24.1	− 0.2	−42.8
1965	15.8	30.8	−15.0	−57.8
1966	23.9	35.9	−12.0	−69.8
1967	28.0	16.0	12.0	−57.8
1968	29.0	33.0	− 4.0	−61.8

only as certain types of statistical behavior which can be broadly categorized as trend and periodic occurrences such as those associated with the seasons of the year. In either case, a forecaster uses this information in making his forecast. But there are other influences on economic variables which are not systematic and which can neither be recognized nor predicted. These are the so-called random influences.

In theory, a forecaster captures all of the systematic influences affecting the variable being forecast, but in practice he rarely accomplishes this. The first step in improving his results, however, is to see where he has gone wrong in the past, and for this purpose he should examine his past forecast errors since these incorporate all of the factors he has missed or misjudged in his analysis. This section describes some simple graphic tools useful in highlighting the existence of systematic patterns in forecast errors.

B. The Control Chart

A criterion of forecast accuracy sug-gested by the discussion in the previous paragraph is the absence of systematic patterns in the distribution of forecast errors. Since we are concerned with forecasting changes, this criterion suggests, among other things, that although the forecast errors may be positive in some periods and negative in others, over time their sum should approach zero. If this is not true, then we should be able to improve upon our results by adjusting the forecasts for this persistent tendency to underestimate or overestimate actual changes.

But why might the sum of actual changes differ from the theoretical value of zero? All forecasting approaches with the exception of those which rely on little more than informed guesses use a model, i.e., some simplified representation of the way certain variables are related to one another. This is true even of those methods which do not give the causal relationships in precise mathematical form. It is plausible, therefore, to assume that a nonzero sum of forecast errors results either from the choice of an inappropriate model to represent the systematic variations in the variables or as the result of

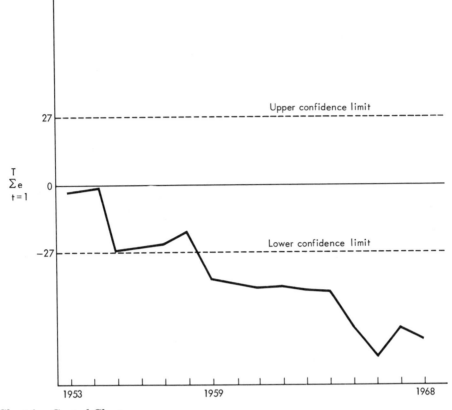

Chart 1   Control Chart

shifts in the way certain variables are related. In either case, a persistent nonzero sum of errors should be a warning to the forecaster that his model is no longer providing an adequate representation of reality. Such a warning is easily obtained in practice through use of the graphic device of the *control chart*.[1]

The preparation of a control chart begins simply with a plot of the cumulative sum of forecast errors. For the purpose of

[1] The expression, "control chart," is borrowed from the literature of statistical quality control. The measure of forecast accuracy used in preparing the control chart, i.e., the sum of forecast errors, is sometimes known as the "tracking signal."

illustration, I will use the data included in table 1, which show actual and predicted changes in GNP for the period 1953 through 1968. All of the predictions were made in November of the year preceding the year forecast. The data are in billions of 1954 dollars through 1965, and are in billions of 1958 dollars for the remainder of the period.

The cumulative errors using these data are plotted on chart 1. In this example, the cumulative sum of forecast errors is always negative. The magnitude of the cumulative error is small up to the year 1955 when it takes a large jump to −26.3. From 1955 through 1958 it fluctuates fairly randomly and in a narrow range. However, in 1959 the cumulative error increases to −38.0, and

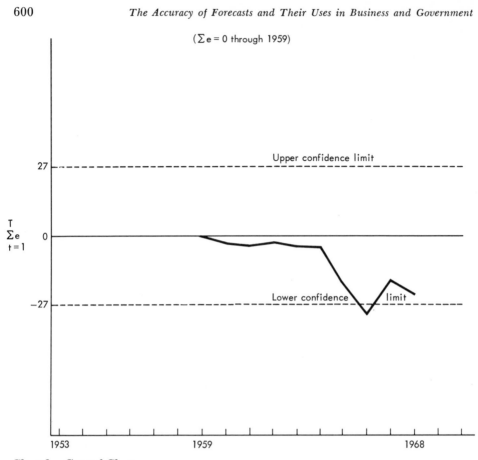

Chart 2   Control Chart

from then on it rises fairly steadily. The data thus suggest that the underlying model has a persistent tendency to underestimate actual changes in GNP.

But can we be sure that this pattern is not just a statistical aberration that will disappear shortly rather than an indication of a fundamental flaw or change in the underlying model? We cannot, of course, be entirely certain which situation is reflected in these results, but our uncertainty can be somewhat reduced by drawing a *confidence band* around the theoretical zero value.

The confidence band is delimited by the two parallel lines, one each drawn above and below the value of zero on chart 1. Its interpretation might be based on the follow-

ing useful rules of thumb. If the cumulative sum of forecast errors is positive or negative but falls within the limits of the confidence band, then one can interpret the results as having arisen by chance. If, on the other hand, the forecast goes out of control, i.e., the cumulative sum is above or below the limits of the confidence band for, say, two successive observations, this should be taken as a clear signal that something is wrong. The forecaster should then search for the cause of his problem. In our example, the cumulative sum of forecast errors remains within the limits of the confidence bands up to 1959. Subsequent to that date it is below the lower limit in all time periods.

It is possible that no matter how extensive the search, the forecaster will be unable to locate the source of the difficulty. Since it is conceivable that the string of negative errors in the example shown resulted from chance, the forecaster should set the sum of the cumulative errors back to zero and see if the next few observations continue the most recent pattern. If the new pattern continues and the forecaster is still unable to locate the source of the problem, he nevertheless might still be able to improve his forecasts by making use of the observed pattern in the forecast errors. For example, this might be done by adjusting future forecasts by the extrapolated trend value of previous forecast errors.

Looking again at our example, it can be seen that if the cumulative sum of forecast errors through 1959 are set equal to zero, the sum of errors subsequent to that date would continue to be negative in each period (see chart 2) and over time it would increase in absolute magnitude. The increase in the sum of errors, however, is fairly moderate up to 1965–66, when once again it breaches the lower confidence limit. The conclusion to be reached from these results, then, is that there is some tendency for the model to underestimate actual changes in GNP. However, the magnitudes of these underestimates were fairly small except in a few particular years, most notably during 1955 and 1959 (which were years immediately following fairly significant recessions in aggregate economic activity), and during the spurt in economic activity in the years 1965–66. Notice, in addition, that the model overestimated changes in GNP during 1954 and 1958, which were periods following cyclical peaks, and during the minirecession of 1967. However, the absolute magnitudes of these overestimates were smaller than the previously discussed underestimates which took place during periods of rapid acceleration in economic activity.

Up to this point nothing has been said about the values above and below zero through which the limits of the confidence band should be drawn. One might take an intuitive approach. For example, the forecaster might calculate the standard error of past forecasts and draw the limits above and below zero at the distance k times the standard error, where k is some integer determined in advance as being "reasonable."

The standard error is calculated using the formula $\sqrt{\dfrac{1}{T} \sum_{t=1}^{T} (e_t - \bar{e})^2}$ where $\bar{e}$ is the average of forecast errors up to time period T. The standard errors and the confidence limits can be recalculated each time a new observation becomes available. In practice, however, the confidence limits are often kept stable from period to period by using the median or mean of past calculations of the standard error.

The choice of k on the other hand may be more scientifically determined from the probability distribution of the forecast errors. Under this condition, the probability of error from interpreting values of the cumulative sum of forecast errors that fall outside the confidence band as representing some persistent tendency of the model to give underestimates or overestimates can be made as small as desired by the selection of an appropriate value of k. The mathematics of this calculation would take us somewhat beyond the scope of this article, but the topic is fairly well covered in the more advanced statistical literature.[2] In practice, a forecaster will most frequently rely on rules of thumb, and values of k of 2 or 3 have been found to work well in the past.

Using our sample data, the standard error of forecast errors for the entire period 1953–68 is approximately 9. The confidence bands on charts 1 and 2 are drawn at a distance above and below the theoretical zero value equal to three times the standard error.

[2] A particularly good reference for the forecaster is Robert Goodell Brown, *Smoothing Forecasting and Prediction of Discrete Time Series* (Englewood Cliffs, N.J.: Prentice-Hall, Inc., 1963), particularly chapters 19 and 20.

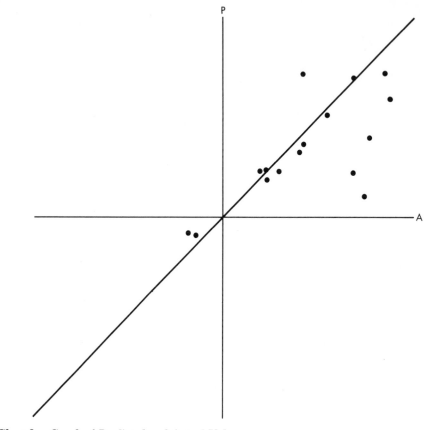

Chart 3   Graph of Predicted and Actual Values

C. The Prediction-Realization Diagram

The control chart is a useful means of keeping a running check on any tendency of a model to give persistent underestimates or overestimates. But this is not the only difficulty the forecaster may encounter in practice, and indeed it may be the least significant of his problems. While a forecasting model may, on average, have forecast errors near zero, it might at the same time have a tendency to miss in its prediction of the direction of change. These *turning point* errors are often symptomatic of basic flaws in the underlying model, and forecasts leading to such errors are not always as easily corrected by using simple mechanical adjust-

ments as are forecasts which correctly predict the direction but not the magnitude of change. The control chart may not capture the effects of turning point errors or even if it does, these errors will not be separated out from those which reflect forecasts in the right direction but the wrong magnitudes. In this section, the analysis of forecast errors is extended to show how it is possible to consider separately both turning point errors and errors in the magnitude of change through use of the simple graphic tool of the prediction-realization diagram.[3]

[3] The prediction-realization diagram is also discussed in Henri Theil, *Applied Economic Forecasting*, (Chicago: Rand-McNally & Co., 1966), chapter 2.

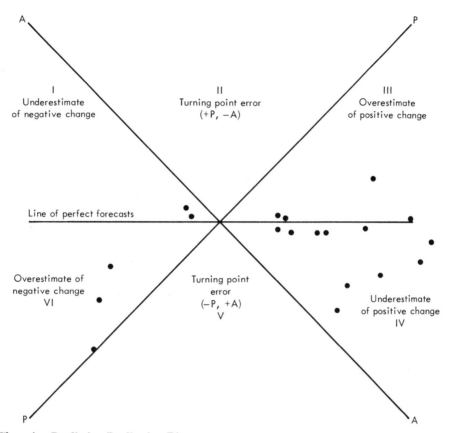

Chart 4   Prediction-Realization Diagram

Suppose, for example, we use the time series of past predicted and actual changes shown earlier in table 1. A simple picture of past forecast performance can be obtained by plotting these points on a two-dimensional diagram, on which the predicted values are indicated on the vertical axis and the actual values on the horizontal axis (see chart 3).

If forecasts were always perfect, these predicted and actual values would be equal in all time periods. This situation is represented on the diagram by the straight line drawn through the origin at a slope of 45 degrees. This is the so-called line of perfect forecasts.

This diagram would be more useful

for analysis, for reasons that will be seen shortly, if it were turned 45 degrees to the right, in order to make the horizontal axis form the line of perfect forecasts. This transformation gives us the prediction-realization diagram (chart 4).

The original axes and the line of perfect forecasts divide the diagram into six sections. Points in the section labeled I, represent forecasts of a negative change, where the realization also turned out to be negative. Note, however, that the actual realization, in all cases falling within the limits of this section, is less than the predicted value. Points in section I, therefore, represent underestimates of a negative change. The further out the point is from the intersection of the various lines delimiting the prediction-realization diagram, and the closer the point is to the A axis, the greater the underestimate.

Similarly, points in section II refer to predictions of a positive change, where, in fact, the change turned out to be negative. Therefore, these points indicate turning point errors. Section III includes positive predictions and realizations, but the magnitudes of the changes in all instances are less than predicted. By similar reasoning, section IV of the diagram includes underestimates of positive changes, section V refers to turning point errors (negative predictions and positive realizations), and section VI includes overestimates of negative changes.

Perfect forecasts, of course, would fall on the horizontal axis. Any point above the horizontal axis (sections I, II, and III) reflect actual changes which are smaller than predicted. Thus, points above the line of perfect forecasts indicate overestimates of the *level* of the series, and by similar reasoning points below the line are underestimates of the *level* of the series.

The prediction-realization diagram can be used, just like the control chart, to keep a running record of the distribution of forecast errors and as a flag to warn the forecaster of the existence of systematic patterns in these errors. It provides more information than the control chart, but includes no device, like confidence bands, to signal automatically to the user that the situation warrants corrective action. But despite this deficiency, its ease of construction and the wealth of information it provides makes the prediction-realization diagram a commonly used tool of the forecaster.

Note that the scatter of points on the prediction-realization diagram (chart 4) tends to confirm the conclusion reached using the control chart. The forecasting model appears to have a moderate but persistent tendency to underestimate actual changes. The prediction-realization diagram, however, also indicates that in no time period did the model fail to forecast accurately

the direction of change in GNP.

The prediction-realization diagram and the control chart have a common deficiency. Neither provides a handy means for obtaining a useful quantitative measure of forecast accuracy. While it is possible with some manipulations to find the magnitude of a particular error using these graphic methods, they do not give us any summary measure of accuracy that would permit a meaningful comparison with errors obtained using alternative forecasting procedures. In the next section some of the more commonly used quantitative measures of forecast accuracy are considered.

III. QUANTITATIVE METHODS

A. The Loss Function

What is the significance of a particular sized error of forecast? There is no universally true answer to this question. For the most part, it depends on the uses to which a forecast is to be put, and the extent to which different types of errors are capable of being corrected. This point was already alluded to in the previous section when it was mentioned that turning point errors, in general, cause a more serious problem to the forecaster than errors of magnitude. But the problem is even more complex than this.

For some uses of forecasts, it may be less serious to err on the side of caution, i.e., underestimates may be less serious than overestimates. In other cases, large errors may be considered more serious than small errors, regardless of their direction. And in some instances, it may not even be important for the analyst to consider errors smaller than some cutoff value. Similar examples can be constructed to fit almost any conceivable forecasting situation.

One of the first tasks facing a forecaster in analyzing past errors, then, is to make some judgment about the seriousness of the consequences of having predictions that miss the actual figures by various amounts in either direction. By assigning some numerical value to different types and magnitudes of errors, the analyst is able to develop a useful quantitative measure of forecast accuracy. The rule that assigns a numerical value to a particular sized forecast error, in either direction, is usually termed a *loss function* in the statistical literature.[4]

There are as many possible loss functions as there are particular situations facing a forecaster. In most instances, however, it is not perfectly clear which loss function is most appropriate to use. Moreover, the use of a large variety of loss functions makes the comparison of the performance of different forecasters and forecasting procedures difficult. As a result, in practice most forecasters have relied on one of a small number of traditional functions to measure the loss incurred by forecast errors. Some of these commonly used loss functions are listed below.

1. A very common approach is to have the loss equal to the absolute difference (i.e., with no special regard to whether it is positive or negative) of the actual and predicted values. If the symbol L is used to represent the numerical loss, and if two vertical lines, one on either side of the error, are used to represent absolute values, this loss function can be written as $L = |P - A|$. Notice that in this function, the loss depends only on the magnitude of the error and is not affected by its direction.

2. Another loss function that is preferred by many forecasters is to have the loss equal to the square of the error, i.e., $L = (P - A)^2$. This function, like the previous one, is symmetrical in the

sense that overestimates and underestimates of the same magnitude are given equal weight. However, since the loss equals the square of the error, this function represents the situation in which large errors are considered by the forecaster as being more serious than small errors.

3. In some situations there may be a threshold involved, in which errors equal to or smaller than some preselected values are considered to be unimportant. Such a situation could be represented, for example, by a loss function in which the loss is set equal to zero if the error is less than the threshold value; when the error is larger than the threshold value the loss is set equal to either the absolute value of the error (as in case 1 above) or the square of the error (as in case 2 above).

As can be seen, then, a large variety of special loss functions can be devised. However, in most situations forecasters use only one of the first two general cases.

A loss function refers to a single error of forecast. To obtain a summary measure of the loss associated with a number of past forecasts, forecasters will typically use the average loss. As an example, the average loss using the absolute difference loss function would be written as:

$$\bar{L} = 1/T \sum_{t=1}^{T} |P_t - A_t|$$

This mathematical expression is usually called the *mean absolute difference*.

For the square loss function, the average loss is given by the expression:

$$\bar{L} = 1/T \sum_{t=1}^{T} (P_t - A_t)^2$$

This average or mean loss is often called the *mean square error*. Sometimes the square root of the mean square error is shown, and this is often called, naturally, the *root mean square error*.

The mean square error has certain

---

[4] For another discussion of the concept of the loss function, see Carl Christ, *Econometric Models and Methods* (New York: John Wiley & Sons, Inc., 1966), chapter 7.

mathematical characteristics that have made it a particular favorite of forecasters. One of these characteristics is briefly discussed in section D below.

B. Comparing Forecast Accuracy

One of the most important advantages derived from the use of a quantitative measure of forecast accuracy is that it facilitates the comparison of the results of different forecasting procedures. Such comparisons, however, must be made with great care. In using forecasts from different methods or prepared by different forecasters, it is a necessary prerequisite of a meaningful comparison that the forecasts were all made under the same conditions. In practice this criterion is often unattainable for a number of reasons. For example, the forecasts might have been prepared with different lead time, and thus the amount of information available at the time of the forecasts would have differed. As another example, one forecast might have been made using one assumption with regard to fiscal or monetary policy, and another forecast might have incorporated an entirely different assumption. Also, the forecasts may have been generated from models using different statistical estimation procedures. In this circumstance it is difficult to distinguish the extent to which the forecasting errors resulted from the models rather than the estimating procedures. Moreover, one forecast might have undergone several ad hoc revisions, while the other might have reflected only the forecaster's initial thoughts.

These and many other conditions of comparability may be lacking in specific instances. It is often difficult, even in cases where two sets of forecasts were prepared by the same individual, to assure that the results provide a meaningful basis for comparison. In most situations, forecasters attempt to get around this problem by relying on comparisons of their forecasts with those produced using only naive mechanical procedures.

These naive procedures utilize little in the way of initial assumptions which might distort their performance, and thus provide the basis for reasonably pure bench marks for measuring the accuracy of the alternative technique. Even more important, they constitute something of an ultimate test. They are often so simple in nature that if the forecasts produced by them are "better" than those obtained from using a more sophisticated approach, then it is a clear indication that the forecasting technique in use is of little practical value.

Some of the naive mechanical forecasting procedures used to provide bench mark forecasts include:

1. Forecasts of no change.
2. Forecasting next period's change by the previous period's change or by the average change over a number of past periods.
3. A more sophisticated version of procedure 2 is to use a so-called autoregressive equation for making the bench mark forecasts. In this approach, current period changes are related to previous changes by a mathematical model. For example, in the simplest case, that of a first-order autoregressive equation, sometimes called a Markov equation,[5] the following simple linear model is used:

$$A_t = \beta A_{t-1} + \mu_t$$

In this model, the current period change is said to equal β (a constant) time, the previous period's change, plus μ_t which is a random error term. The constant β would be estimated from past data using,

[5] The order of an autoregressive equal is determined by the maximum lag used. The title of *Markov equation* for the first-order, or single-period lag, autoregressive equation comes from the name of the Russian mathematician who was first to examine the statistical properties of processes that could be represented by such an equation.

say, the least squares estimating technique. The bench mark forecasts for one time period ahead would then be found by using the estimated value of β times the most recent actual change.[6] More complex autoregressive models could be used as well, if they provide more accurate bench mark forecasts. For example, a second-order autoregressive equation might be used, and this would take the form:

$$A_t = \beta_1 A_{t-1} + \beta_2 A_{t-2} + \mu_t$$

where β_1 and β_1 are constants estimated using multiple regression.

The use of an autoregressive equation may on the surface appear somewhat arbitrary. Actually such equations can often describe the movements of an economic time series remarkably well, since economic processes typically require some time to work themselves out. Thus, current movements in economic variables become inextricably linked to past behavior.

Notice that the naive forecasts of no change and the current period change equal to the past period's change are merely special versions of the first-order autoregressive equation. In the first case, β is assumed equal to zero, and in the second case β is assumed equal to one. Similarly, averages, whether simple or weighted, of past changes are merely special cases of more complex autoregressive processes. Since the autoregressive equations impose fewer initial restictions on the bench mark forecasts, i.e., they let the past data speak for temselves, they are usually to be preferred as a basis for the comparison of forecast accuracy.

C. The Forecaster's Batting Average

A forecaster, like a baseball player, should be judged on his relative performance. One way to accomplish this is to consider the average loss of his forecasts relative to the average loss obtained by other forecasters or by some alternative forecasting technique. For the reasons discussed earlier, forecasts from various naive methods are used most often for this purpose. A forecaster should keep a running record, perhaps on a graph, of his "batting average." If he is doing well, he can proudly display his graph on the wall. If not, he can hide it in the bottom drawer of his desk while at the same time taking corrective actions.

Probably the most commonly used index for measuring a forecaster's batting average is the Theil inequality coefficient.[7] This measure, usually denoted by the symbol U^2, is given by the following formula:

$$U^2 = \frac{1/T \sum_{t=1}^{T} (P_t - A_t)^2}{1/T \sum_{t=1}^{T} A_t^2}$$

The numerator of the Theil inequality coefficient should be recognizable immediately as equal to the mean square error of past forecasts. The denominator is quite simply the mean square error that would have been obtained if, over the same time period, we had used the forecast of no change, i.e., if the forecast in each period was $P_t = 0$.

It should be obvious that it is the numerator that is most important. It measures the actual forecast error obtained. The denominator merely gives us a base measure against which we can compare our results. One of the useful features of the Theil inequality coefficient is that it is a pure number, unaffected by the size of the units being forecast. Thus it makes no difference whether, for example, forecasts are in tons

---

[6] We ignore the error term μ_t in this calculation because it is assumed that on average it is equal to zero.

[7] See Theil, *op. cit.*, chapter 2. The book by Theil includes a number of examples of the use of the inequality coefficient in measuring forecast accuracy. For a number of other examples of its use, see Herman Stekler *Economic Forecasting* (New York: Frederick A. Praeger, 1970).

or billions of dollars. The Theil inequality coefficients of any two sets of forecasts are always comparbale.

The value $U^2 = 1$ is the dividing line. $U^2 < 1$ indicates that the forecasts are "better" than those which would have been obtained using the naive alternative. A value of $U^2 > 1$ indicates the opposite. For perfect forecasts, $U^2 = 0$. Notice, however, that there is no upper limit on the value of U^2, which indicates simply that there is no limit to how bad you can do relative to the no-change prediction.

Using our sample forecasts from table 1, the mean square error of forecast is approximately 95.7. The mean square error of the bench mark forecasts of no change in GNP (i.e., the average of the sum of squares of actual changes over the sample period) is approximately 463.5. The U^2 is the value of the ratio 95.7/463.5, or 0.21. Thus, the conclusion using these data is that the forecasting model used to generate the forecasts shown in table 1 provides significantly better forecasts of changes in GNP than the naive alternative model which would always predict changes in GNP as equal to zero.

Clearly, this good performance of the forecasting model used in generating the results shown in table 1 depends in part on the naive alternative method used for comparison. While the denominator of the Theil inequality coefficient is in most instances the mean square error of forecasts of no-change, it should be obvious that there is no practical limit to which prediction can be used. It would be quite possible, for example, to use in the denominator of the Theil inequality coefficient, the mean square error from the naive model $P_t = A_{t-1}$, or for that matter, the mean square error obtained from using some general autoregressive equation.

D. The Decomposition of the Mean Square Error

This chapter has distinguished between graphic methods useful in recognizing systematic patterns in forecast errors, and quantitative measures useful in obtaining a summary measure of the loss associated with a series of forecasts. One quantitative measure of forecast error, the mean square error, however, has the interesting characteristic that it can be used for both purposes. It is a quantitative summary measure of forecast accuracy, but like the graphic tools, it can also be used to recognize the systematic characteristics of errors of forecast. This second role results from the fact that the mean square error can be mathematically decomposed into three constituent elements, each of which has a very distinct interpretation. In mathematical terms, this decomposition can be written in the following way:[8]

$$(1) \quad 1/T \sum_{t=1}^{T} (P_t - A_t)^2 = (\bar{P} - \bar{A})^2 + (S_P - S_A)^2 + 2(1 - r)S_P S_A$$

$\bar{A}$ and $\bar{P}$ are merely the averages of the past actual and predicted values. S_A and S_P are the standard deviations of actual and predicted values, and r is the simple correlation coefficient between the actual and predicted values.

It is instructive to take a closer look at these three elements of the mean square error. If forecasts were always perfect, the mean square error would be zero. For this to be true, each of the elements on the right-hand side of equation (1) must also be zero, since each of these terms are either zero or positive numbers. The first element $(\bar{P} - \bar{A})^2$ would be zero if, and only if, *on average* the actual and predicted changes were equal. This component, therefore, gives the average tendency of the forecasts to be either underestimates or overestimates. This source of error is sometimes called in the statistical literature the bias in the predictions.

[8] For a proof of this equation, see Theil, *op. cit.*, pp. 29–30.

The second element on the right-hand side of equation (1), $(S_P - S_A)^2$, is similarly useful in pinpointing the source of forecast errors. This element would be equal to zero if, and only if, the standard errors of the actual and predicted changes were equal. While, on average, the forecasting model might predict very well, it is possible that the variations of the predictions around the average might have fluctuated to a greater or lesser degree than the actual changes. This condition would show up as a nonzero value for this second component in the decomposition of the mean square error. The existence of this type of error suggests that the forecasts are either too sensitive (if $S_P > S_A$) or not sensitive enough (if $S_A > S_P$) to changes in the underlying causal variables.

Finally, note that the third element of the mean square error is equal to zero if $r = 1$. But if $r = 1$, then there is a precise and positive mathematical relationship linking the actual and predicted values. If there was no correlation at all between actual and predicted values, r would equal zero, and the third term of the decomposition would be positive and equal to $2S_P S_A$.

Thus, the third term in equation (1) gives the error due to the lack of perfect correlation of actual and predicted values. Unfortunately, this type of error has no simple interpretation. It may exist either because there are random elements in the actual observations that cannot be forecast, or it may exist because the forecasting model is flawed. There is no simple way of judging which is true, or of correcting forecasts for correlation error. As a rule of thumb, a forecaster often continues to "fine tune" his forecasting procedure to the point that he has minimized the bias and variation errors relative to the errors of correlation.

Using the sample data from table 1, $\bar{P} = 13.5$, $\bar{A} = 17.3$, $S_P = 10.2$, $S_A = 12.8$, and $r = 0.7$. Applying the formula shown in equation (1), the decomposition of the mean square error in our example is approximately the following:

$$(2) \quad 95.7 = 14.4 + 6.8 + 74.5$$

Dividing both sides of equation (2) by 95.7, i.e., the total mean square error, we get:

$$(3) \quad 1 = 0.15 + 0.07 + 0.78.$$

Equation (3) indicates that 15 percent of the mean square error results from bias, 7 percent from errors of variation, and 78 percent from less than perfect correlation of actual and predicted values. These results are fairly close to the ideal of having all of the error caused by less than perfect correlation. Nevertheless, a large bias component exists in the forecasts, and this tends to confirm the conclusion reached earlier using the graphic techniques that there is a persistent tendency to incorrectly estimate the magnitude of changes in GNP.

In summary, then, the techniques employed in this paper would suggest the following conclusions with regard to the model used to generate the forecasts shown in table 1:

1. The forecasts are substantially better on average than those of the naive alternative method used to provide bench mark forecasts.

2. The method has correctly predicted the direction of change of GNP in each time period.

3. The forecasting method, however, does provide an area for improvement since it has had in the past a persistent tendency to underestimate actual changes in GNP.

4. While the model has correctly forecast the direction of change at cyclical turning points, it has had a tendency to overestimate changes in GNP following cyclical peaks and to underestimate changes in GNP following cyclical troughs. However, the largest errors in absolute magnitude occur as

the result of underestimates of changes in GNP during periods of acceleration in aggregate economic activity.

Oh yes! About those forecasts. They are actual results obtained by the econometric model developed by Daniel Suits and various colleagues of his, and released at the annual conferences on the economic outlook which are sponsored by the economics department at the University of Michigan.[9]

[9] See *The Economic Outlook for 1969* (Papers presented at the Sixteenth Annual Conference on the Economic Outlook, November 14–15, 1968, at the University of Michigan, Ann Arbor), p. 12.

BIBLIOGRAPHY

Brown, Robert Goodell, *Smoothing Forecasting and Prediction of Discrete Time Series.* Englewood Cliffs, N.J.: Prentice-Hall, Inc., 1963.

Christ, Carl, *Econometric Models and Methods.* New York: John Wiley & Sons, Inc., 1966.

Stekler, Herman, *Economic Forecasting.* New York: Frederick A. Praeger, 1970.

The Economic Outlook for 1969. Papers presented at the Sixteenth Annual Conference on the Economic Outlook, November 14–15, 1968, at the University of Michigan, Ann Arbor.

Theil, Henri, *Applied Economic Forecasting.* Chicago: Rand-McNally & Co., 1966.

WALTER E. HOADLEY

Reporting Forecasts to Management and the Use of Forecasts As a Management Tool

Through forecasting the business economist fills his principal role as a professional aide-advisor to management in the corporate decision-making process. To be fully effective in this important role, the economist must win his acceptance on the business management team as someone who can be helpful in both *what* he has to say and *how* he says it. In other words, the primary skill of the business economist is *selling useful forecasts to management*. A fundamental premise on which this skill is based is that good ideas don't sell themselves: they are sold by competent people.

Since no business economist can hope to make a significant contribution to any management without emphasizing the future, perhaps even a new title is in order: *economist-forecaster*, as a constant reminder to all concerned that his greatest opportunity as well as his never ending challenge lies in forecasting.

Most of the largest United States business organizations now employ one or more professional economists. However, the supply of "suitable" business economists who can demonstrably assist managements in policy decisions always seems to be limited. While many academically well-trained economists are turning to business for employment, especially because of mounting budget stringencies in education, few seem to have the well-rounded skills to forecast for a profit and work effectively with a management

team. In many cases, academic training has not developed skills which allow them to report effectively to management.

This point warrants emphasis, because the success or failure of the economist-forecaster in private business can be traced not only to his basic ability, training, and experience, but also to his personality and related skills in selling himself and his creative ideas to senior executives.

WHY FORECAST?

The truly important management decisions concern the future, thus some degree of forecasting is unavoidable. The forecast may be explicit, but sometimes it is only implied in the dangerous assumption that current economic conditions or trends will remain unchanged.

Some executives still tend to ridicule forecasting as mere crystal gazing, and claim that no human can honestly claim to know precisely what lies ahead. While this may be perfectly true, it still does not provide any basis for rejecting the forecasting process. No management can escape the need to predict. Not to forecast is really to assume indefinite continuation of the status quo. In these dynamic times, to expect no change is very shortsighted and unrealistic.

Thus, the principal question which

management faces is not: Shall we forecast? Rather, it is: How can we improve our forecasting? The services of a competent economist can be one means for such improvement.

FORECASTS MUST BE USEFUL FOR MANAGEMENT POLICY AND ACTION

The economist-forecaster must always remember that for management a forecast is a *means* to an end and never an end in itself. Management is responsible for conducting a successful business and only those individuals, policies, and programs which contribute to this end can be useful and enduring.

Broadly speaking, most management decisions involve some economic considerations. The economist, therefore, can be helpful in guiding many decisions, but few satisfactory decisions are made on economic grounds alone. Political, social, and psychological factors also exert powerful influences upon areas of management responsibility and action; the successful business executive and economist must make appropriate allowance for them. No forecast then can be trustworthy or really useful unless it is economically reasonable, politically possible, socially acceptable, and psychologically probable.

Since competent managements are continually evaluating their activities and plans, they tend to view a forecast primarily as a device for confirming or denying the general validity of what they are now doing or thinking they might do in the future.. For this reason, the positive or negative "tone" of each forecast, particularly at a major decision point, can be infinitely more critical than the forecast details, important as they are.

Each business management seeks to make decisions which will have the highest possible degree of accuracy as to (1) proper scope of activity and (2) direction, timing, and degree of policy actions. Accordingly, almost any forecast which promises to help in these areas will spark some management interest. The forecast must be believed, however, if it is to be used. This is why effective forecasting for management is such a very personal function, with the credibility of the economist-forecaster being much more important than the actual forecast—whether computer printout or handwritten note. Even so, few economic forecasts are accepted in toto by management—simply because of inevitable differences in human judgment.

Inasmuch as forecasting is by no means confined to the economist's office within a major business organization, the work of the economist-forecaster is useful to management as part of an internal forecasting check and balance system. Usually the economist is expected to provide the *general* guidance information and the "basic economic assumptions" for the company. Divisional, departmental, and marketing specialists are expected to provide the more *specific* product and market forecast information. Measuring and reconciling the degree of consistency between internal forecasts can be very useful to management in weighing all variables and uncertainties in the final decision process.

The chief executive officer and each profit center officer are, of course, ultimately concerned with the profit forecast prepared by the financial or budget team. The role of the economist-forecaster can be crucial here, since his work should provide the economic underpinning for the entire profit forecast. Once the profit forecast is completed, however, there is at least one further major step in which management can expect the economist-forecaster to play a part. That is to assist in continually evaluating the probability that the actual profit results will materialize as projected. Furthermore, many managements are now asking their staffs, including the economist, to engage in contingency planning and to prepare a "fail safe" or standby plan B in case the original plan A proves overly optimistic or pessimistic. All this means that probabilities—even more than absolutes—are essential in useful forecasting.

In short, dynamic forecasting will involve the economist on a continuous basis in helping strengthen management decision making. High caliber management is always looking for help, but whether and how intensively it continues to look in the direction of the economist-forecaster clearly depends upon how much real help is actually forthcoming, and upon what can be expected from this source in the future.

WHAT SHOULD BE FORECAST FOR MANAGEMENT?

Policies necessarily must be formulated in the present, but their ultimate wisdom obviously will only be known as the actual results unfold. Consequently, one of the principal objectives of any management in its decision-making process is to determine the key influences which will affect the business over the period ahead. In general, such influences can be divided into (1) those which lie outside the realm or control of management because they are *external* to the firm and (2) those which are more immediately within the control of management because they lie within the *internal* scope and operations of the firm.

The economist is most useful to management in forecasting and in providing information and perspective on the principal *external* influences affecting the company's operations and profits, but to an increasing extent he is able to assist in appraising and projecting *internal* influences as well.

Here are some illustrative economic questions involving external influences which managements often ask:

1. What is the outlook for the national economy? What are the most important local, regional, or worldwide economic trends? Is an upturn or downturn immediately ahead?

2. What is the outlook for inflation? What is ahead for prices of raw materials and finished products, as well as for costs of other goods and services? For wages, salaries, and benefit costs?

3. What is the outlook for government monetary and fiscal policies and regulations? Protectionism?

4. Will the availability and cost of credit tend to expand or depress buying? Are "tight" money or "easy" credit conditions ahead?

5. Where are the best sales prospects in both new and established markets?

6. What is the productivity and profit outlook?

7. Where is domestic and international competition likely to intensify or diminish?

Countless other management problems and questions with economic orientation could be cited, but these seven are sufficient to indicate the broad areas of potential contribution by the effective business economist. Reasonably accurate answers to these and similar inquiries should enable managements to plan more wisely the scope and direction of their strategic programs, as well as the timing of their specific actions.

As suggested, the qualified economist who has achieved full status on his management team can also often be helpful in guiding decisions which concern more immediate internal company policies. A broad economist-forecaster point of view can be relevant in finding answers to questions such as these:

1. What will be a reasonable sales and profit budget for next year? Longer-range sales and profit goal?

2. What level of capital expenditures should be planned over the next few years?

3. What will be the most appropriate production schedules and inventory policies for the next two quarters?
4. What changes in wage and price policies should be made now?
5. How much cash will be available next month and generally how should it be invested?

Management is becoming less and less interested per se in GNP and related numbers, being content to have the technical economist keep them under study. Accordingly, the economist-forecaster must now intensify his efforts to convey what the numbers mean and whether management policies should be changed. Emphasis should be on the key assumptions or uncertainties weighted by a range of probabilities so a Plan B, as well as a Plan A, can be programmed for management action if needed.

FORECASTER CREDIBILITY PREREQUISITE TO MANAGEMENT ACCEPTANCE

Most managements now have considerable sophistication in economics, although many individual executives may deny it. Senior officers are looking primarily for new insights and interpretations, not a rehash of popular economics discussions found readily in the press and business magazines.

Highly important to the economist's contribution is a complete understanding by all concerned that he does not have an infallible method of forecasting. No one does. This should be obvious, but at times professional economists without much practical experience tend either to refuse to concede error or to shy away from accepting responsibility for forecasting. Actually most forecasts will be wrong to some degree, but reasonable accuracy is all that is required in most circumstances.

The successful economist-forecaster usually sets an objective of minimizing surprises for management from general economic and market developments. His analysis of trends and cycles should enable him to alert his management group to those business developments which are foreshadowed in the stream of economic data available on a regular basis. Also, an economist can frequently be as helpful in reassuring management that an important trend will persist as in pointing out the probabilities of a turning point in some activity of importance to the company. While it is too much to expect that anyone can eliminate all surprise, it is reasonable to expect that a competent economist can minimize economic surprises, so that management can pursue a more orderly course of planning than would otherwise be the case.

The professional economist is a technically trained individual. During the past decade in particular, formal economic instruction has become considerably more technical—with heavy emphasis upon mathematics, wide application of electronic computers, and the use of complex quantitative techniques. Traditionally, the field of economics has been noted for its wealth of varying and complex theories relating to such matters as competitive conditions, the role of money and credit, overall influences upon the course of general business and the individual firm, and the most appropriate public and private economic policies to achieve maximum growth and profits. More recently, these considerations have taken on increasingly international dimensions, requiring a greater perspective than ever before.

To these techniques and theories must be added the huge quantities of economic statistics (with their inevitable inadequacies and gaps) which are the raw material for the economist-forecaster. Analysis and synthesis of theory and data provide the means by which the economist can bring a penetrating perspective to management problems. To achieve credibility, however, he must guard against overuse of technical terminology in communicating with his management executives: what management does not understand it will almost automatically reject.

In summary, the economist has a major responsibility (1) to interpret complex economic developments in the business environment, (2) to make his observations relevant to his company's policies and objectives, and (3) to make his observations meaningful to senior personnel in particular.

Traditionally, economics has been labeled "the dismal science" because of the great stress that has been placed upon such historical economic problems as poverty, deflation, stagnation, and overpopulation. Professional economic training emphasizes rigorous analysis and problem detection. While this is really no different from the formal diagnostic approach in other sciences, it does make many economists somewhat cautious and reluctant to express positive opinions unless there is more than ample evidence at hand to support their views. As a result, a conflict may arise between the innate optimism and sharp opinions of some management personnel and what may seem to be a pessimistic or cautious bias on the part of the economist.

The cautious economist may serve a useful purpose in tempering less carefully considered opinions. In most instances, however, chronic pessimism will make the economist ineffective. Accordingly, he can establish credibility and serve management best if his inevitable forecasting errors tend to be distributed on the optimistic as well as the pessimistic side. In particular, he must try to avoid being labeled a chronic pessimist. The economist-forecaster clearly is a professional, and to be truly effective he requires the respect of his professional colleagues in other firms, in universities, and in government. To gain this respect, his forecasts must be credible to a general external audience—not merely to management. He needs to develop contacts throughout the profession, to gain access to new insights

and information not otherwise available. Extensive familiarity with reference source materials is essential, but it is still more important that the economist know individuals who are specialists in particular fields relating to his work. The economist will benefit greatly from mutual understanding and confidence with his professional colleagues and contacts outside the company, and this will take time. One means of determining the caliber and usefulness of an economist is to check his ability to obtain current relevant information and analysis quickly by phone or cable rather than by lengthy research from either readily available or obscure reference sources. His own creativity and knowledge are vital, but his ability to draw on other specialists at critical times greatly increases his effectiveness.

It is absolutely essential that the economist in business recognizes his responsibility to build a reputation as a successful forecaster. This means that he must be willing to make considered and positive statements about impending economic developments, based upon his best information and analysis, and stake his reputation upon his judgment. Nothing will build management confidence in an economist more quickly and thoroughly than a record of successful forecasts, well documented in advance and modestly evaluated when the actual results become available.

The economist-forecaster also has the responsibility to alert management the moment he detects an error in his forecast. By promptly calling attention to changes in forecast conditions, he will not only assist management in making appropriate adjustments in policies, but strengthen his own credibility and position as a member of the management team.

The economist-forecaster should recognize that his forecasts will often compete with highly accurate executive intuition forecasts as well as external professional forecasts. It is not unusual for an economist-forecaster to find himself continually defending his forecasts when they diverge from many competing forecasts, including those of directors and other executive officers. When the economist has a strong conviction, and makes a convincing contrary or "way out" forecast which proves to be correct, he obviously helps in building a favorable reputation. Consultant economists often believe they must do this with some frequency to survive.

Admittedly, because of the enormous sophistication among growing numbers of professional forecasters, it is getting more and more difficult to be markedly "different" and correct in making general business forecasts. Nevertheless, consistent "me too" forecasting has little value to a sophisticated management. In other words, neither acceptance of the "safe" standard or consensus forecast nor widely different forecasting is wise strategy, but being correct obviously must always be the number one goal of the economist-forecaster.

Within any management organization there is a wealth of knowledge, training, and experience which enables the company to progress. It follows, therefore, that the economist-forecaster will be most helpful if he can *supplement* existing management know-how rather than engage in intellectual competition with other members of management. Moreover, in pointing out the policy implications of any forecast, the economist must recognize that he may at times seem to be preempting a line officer's responsibilities. This does not mean that he should avoid challenging what he believes to be erroneous information or interpertation by his colleagues; rather it suggests that he should endeavor principally to bring new data and ideas into management's discussions and decision making. He must continually demonstrate a desire to contribute to profitable line operating results through staff helpfulness.

The economist can best serve management if he never loses sight of the principal objective of his company, namely, to make a profit on invested capital. Without adequate profits, there can be no enduring enterprise and no job for the economist-forecaster.

Academic training, as well as anti-profit comments by critics outside the field of business, may cause some economic analysts to adopt a semiapologetic or defensive attitude toward profits. Once this is detected by management, the effectiveness of the economist is almost certain to be lost. Consequently, no economist can expect to succeed in serving management unless he has a strong personal conviction that profits are essential and that his chief obligation is to help increase the ability of the company to make profits. Along with this strong profit orientation, the economist can and should also use his training and talents to assist management in the development of programs to improve the social performance of the firm and the social cost budgeting to accompany it. In this area the role of the business economist is certain to grow.

The economist who contributes most to management, in my judgment, is the one who does an outstanding job of research and analysis, and of preparing and delivering reports. But he goes still further. His purpose becomes dynamic as he seeks to be a fully recognized contributor to profits and to the social performance of the firm. Otherwise he tends to be merely someone who fills an obscure static position in the management hierarchy, with the eventual danger of having his role terminated.

HOW SHOULD FORECASTS BE REPORTED?

Once a forecast has been carefully prepared, what does the economist-forecaster (and his management) do with it? A quick answer is that ideally the forecasting process should be so continual and management so well informed of changing important economic conditions that the newest forecast will fit smoothly into the organization's regular planning, budgeting, and decision-making activities.

In practice, however, a new formalized forecast deserves special attention and if warranted can lead to some changes in management goals and policies. Thus, the economist will find it necessary from time to time to schedule special meetings for a formal presentation of his economic forecasts to management—usually at several levels. These meetings are scheduled most appropriately prior to budget preparation for the coming quarter or year. Regular written reports are popular with economists and can be useful, but receive serious management readership only if they are timely, contain fresh information and significant analysis, and are directed toward specific areas of management interest.

When the economist-forecaster has earned a position as a full-fledged member of the management team, the reporting of forecasts—except for occasional major presentations—tends to become a less formal and preferably a "suitable for the occasion" part of the decision process. A low-key running interpretation of exceptional economic developments is quite acceptable to the majority of senior managements. In fact, most economist-forecasters soon realize that they must always be ready to make a constructive statement on the economic outlook, frequently without warning.

Because the economist-forecaster has analytical ability, a wide range of knowledge, and communication skills, he will be asked from time to time to prepare a forecast and other statements which management in turn will use in whole or in part as reports, testimony, or speeches to its various publics. These will include stockholders, employees, business associations, and government bodies at all levels, as well as citizens at large.

This type of assignment can pose some challenging and occasionally difficult problems for the economist-forecaster. Two guiding principles, however, usually prove useful. The economist-forecaster must see his role as (1) providing authoritative data and forecasts which he must be prepared to defend publicly and (2) a contributor and not the person with the final responsibility.

To violate either of these principles is to invite a serious undermining of acceptability by senior management. Moreover, there will be some inevitable differences over content and semantics, especially with public relations writers. The economist-forecaster must learn how to negotiate these differences skillfully without permanently damaging his relations with other strong-minded executives.

In a final sense, the economist-forecaster always has the option of resigning his position if he cannot accept management's use of his efforts, but this seldom occurs because responsible managements never ask an economist or any other officer to make statements which they do not believe. Honest differences of opinion are healthy, and the economist-forecaster can never forget that his forecasts and views are not infallible and that the chief executive officer makes the final decision and accepts full responsibility for it.

MANAGEMENT'S RESPONSIBILITY IN USING THE ECONOMIST-FORECASTER

In order for an economist-forecaster to report successfully to management and for the latter to make effective use of his forecasts and advice, there necessarily has to be a satisfactory atmosphere and understanding between the economist and his management colleagues. Therefore, it behooves the economist, especially before accepting his position initially, to make some effort to see that management recognizes its responsibilities.

A major responsibility of management is to set forth as clearly as possible what it expects the economist to do, and sometimes what not to do. Merely exposing a new economist to a management organization invites trouble. Someone within the organization no doubt has previously performed the general functions of the economist, formally or informally. (Sometimes these functions may not always have been fully recognized as economist-type activities.) Accordingly, early general agreement as to areas of specific responsibility will help avoid friction and conflicts between the economist and other members of management. All too often executives tend to resent an economist if they feel he is trying to tell them how to run their business. Instead, his role should be seen consistently as trying to help the same executives reduce the probability of errors in their policy decisions.

The economist-forecaster should be held accountable at least in some general way for a contribution to profits. While this is never easily measured, general guidelines of performance can be linked to forecasting accuracy, as well as to the profit significance of his new ideas, interpretations, and recommendations. Sharing to some recognizable degree senior management's overall profit responsibility will usually give the economist-forecaster a still greater incentive to do a better job, and also strengthen his position among his management colleagues.

Along with accountability, there must be adequate competitive compensation and sufficient stature within the company to enable the economist to perform his function. If the economist is to make an important contribution to management, he must be encouraged to meet directly with the principal members of management. Preferably he should report to a senior officer, if not the chief executive officer. Unless he has this rank, many of his reports and observations will never reach top management, where they should be most effectively used.

The economist needs fairly complete knowledge of management's thinking on particular problems which he is asked to help solve. Never should he be placed in the impossible position of being asked to make a contribution without having the internal corporate information he requires. Unless management has sufficient confidence in the economist to discuss problems quite frankly with him, it should anticipate only limited help from him.

In short, management has an important responsibility to work closely with the economist-forecaster, especially during the early period of his tenure. Some important adjustments by the economist, as well as by management, are inevitable whenever a new economist is employed to become a member of the executive organization. Above all, management must be willing to evaluate the economist's contribution regularly so that he knows clearly where he stands and how he can improve his efforts on behalf of the company's profitable growth. Executives must give the economist some reaction to his reports and recommendations—nothing is more frustrating than to submit findings and recommendations without ever receiving comments.

When management recognizes that one of the principal functions of the economist is to bring new and important external information into company deliberation, it follows that it must encourage the economist to travel outside as well as throughout the company. Outside travel is essential, not only to get information of the moment, but also to establish contacts to provide further data and analysis promptly in the future. There is simply no substitute for personal acquaintance and conversation in developing information. Obviously, the utmost discretion must be used in establishing contacts, limited to those which are legally appropriate and in accordance with the principles of his management.

In short, the corporate economist must strive to be continuously in a position to know what other professional economists are thinking and to stay abreast of economic research developments pertaining to his company's fields of interest. To accomplish this end requires an adequate travel and expense budget, as well as management recognition that these outside activities are an essential part of his job. Unless this point is thoroughly understood, there is danger that some members of the management organization will misconstrue the economist's absences as wasteful and unproductive. Needless to say, the economist must prove that this is not the case.

Finally, management has a responsibility to treat the economist as it would any other member of the organization by giving him an opportunity to advance in the company to the extent that his particular abilities and qualifications warrant. In numerous organizations individuals who have been employed as economists have made a contribution in this capacity and have used their talents to serve in still higher positions of responsibility. Therefore, it is important that any economist be evaluated on the grounds of how well he may serve as an economist, and also on whether he has the potential to climb still higher on the management ladder.

OUTLOOK FOR THE ECONOMIST-FORECASTER'S CONTRIBUTION TO MANAGEMENT DECISION MAKING

The demand for the skills of the economist-forecaster remains firm and promising. This is because more managements are recognizing the need for more economic guidance; because business economist incumbents are making tangible contributions to management decisions; and because increasing numbers of business economist-forecasters are moving up in management, thus creating vacancies that must be filled.

The continuing problem will be to find enough interested, qualified applicants to fill the demand. There is no shortage of

technically qualified economists, but many do not meet the requirements for the successful corporate economist-forecaster as set forth here. As more academic economists realize the opportunities for their graduate students in business, and as more practicing business economist-forecasters convey their specific needs to university faculties, the supply of well-rounded economists to serve managements is certain to increase.

In any event, the job of the economist in management must and will be performed. The key uncertainty is how *well* it will be performed.

As scientific and technical advances multiply, managements will become more technically oriented and surround themselves with more technically trained personnel. The economist-forecaster himself is becoming better equipped technically, and progress is being made in refining many management techniques through management science developments. There is some danger, however, that overemphasis upon the technical aspects will lead to a false sense of security among economists and managements. In my opinion, forecasting and all its uncertainties will always remain an integral part of the management decision-making process. Hence, there can be no substitute for individual judgment. The objective of economic analysis is to limit the range of uncertainty within which such judgment is exercised.

Whatever the future rate of scientific progress—and it will accelerate—major economic problems will persist. Managements will have to pay more attention to their economic environment and to the political, social, and psychological changes which constantly disrupt plans and expectations. By focusing attention on fundamental economic trends, especially with the help of the economist-forecaster, it will be possible to minimize potential dislocations in company operations and thus enhance profits.

The allowable margin of error for management decision making seems likely to become even smaller as national and international competition increases. International investments and payments problems will endure over the years ahead. Financial liquidity and credit problems at the national, international, and company level will not disappear soon. Market conditions are shifting dramatically all over the world as incomes and living standards rise and as consumerism and nationalism become more pronounced. The life cycle of products and technological processes is changing noticeably. What business managements can safely ignore these prospects or rely upon superficial knowledge about them as a basis for their key decisions?

Perhaps the most challenging note for business executives is that the major problems to be faced by our nation will require far more concerted efforts by business and government in economic and related fields than at any previous time. Yet, the ground rules to effectively blend such efforts are either vague or nonexistent. Government economic influence and control are increasing at a marked rate. Simultaneously, business managements are being charged with the responsibility for solving more of our social and environmental as well as economic problems. In addition, managements will more effectively assert their leadership in complex national and international economic affairs to the extent that they have an early and constructive appreciation of economic problems—including an understanding of the economic forces at work and the consequences of expedient economic policies.

The professional economist-forecaster may not be the man of the hour or of destiny, but he can offer significant help to management in meeting whatever lies ahead. Given adequate management support, he can make a major and continuing contribution to profitable economic growth as well as human welfare. He will not be able to offer panaceas or foolproof answers to management's increasingly complex decision-making problems, but in my judgment, solutions will be much sounder with his help than without it.

HAROLD C. PASSER & EDGAR R. FIEDLER

Economic Forecasting in Government

Just as business firms and financial institutions require economic forecasts for their planning and operating functions, so the federal government requires economic forecasts as a vital input to its many operations. Economic analysis and forecasting have been a part of the work of government for many decades—going back in the Department of Agriculture to the time of the Civil War. However, it was not until the mid-1940s—after the government had increased in size relative to the private sector so that its activities had a major impact on the economy at large and after its revenues had become highly dependent on income-sensitive taxes—that the federal establishment engaged in economic analysis and forecasting on an intensive and systematic basis. A milestone in this process was the Employment Act of 1946, which created the Council of Economic Advisers and assigned to it, among other responsibilities, the task of preparing general economic forecasts.

Economic forecasting is carried on in many government agencies, but most importantly in the Council of Economic Advisers working with the Treasury Department and the Office of Management and Budget (formerly the Bureau of the Budget). Through the 1950s, these three agencies kept each other informed about their forecasting activities, and in the process conducted regular meetings, usually weekly, of their staff personnel. This collaboration became much more extensive and formalized in the early years of the Kennedy administration. It was then that the label "Troika" was adopted, following the Russian word for a three-horse vehicle that Soviet Premier Khrushchev had used to describe his plan for reorganizing the United Nations.

PRESENT STRUCTURE OF FORECASTING IN THE FEDERAL GOVERNMENT

Historically and presently, the Troika operation is carried on at three levels (commonly referred to as T1, T2, and T3). The top level (T1) is the policy level of the Troika, and its members are referred to as the principals: the chairman of the Council of Economic Advisers, the secretary of the Treasury, and the director of the Office of Management and Budget. Because of the broad and extensive responsibilities associated with their cabinet rank, the principals of the Troika tend to be concerned more with the implications of forecasts for policy —Does the forecast call for a change in policy?—than with the forecasting process itself.

The chairman of the Council has always been a professional economist, but not always a specialist in economic forecasting. The other two members of the T1 level of the Troika may or may not be economists.

Officials, at the second level of the Troika are also concerned with policy matters, but generally are directly involved in the forecasting process as well. The T2 level consists of a member of the Council of Economic Advisers, the assistant secretary of the Treasury for economic policy, and the economist of the Office of Management and Budget. The persons who fill these slots, which are at the subcabinet level, are political appointees, but they are professionally trained economists, generally of high standing within the economics fraternity.

The third level of the Troika is made up of career civil service employees of the government and persons on leave for a year or two from universities and research institutions, all of whom are trained economists. As such, they are less concerned with policy and political matters, and concentrate on the detailed work of forecasting.

In the past, several of the participants in the Troika operation have served at more than one level: Charles Schultze and Charles Zwick moved from the intermediate to the policy level and Arthur Okun served, at various times, at all three levels.

The second major locus of forecasting activity within the federal government is the Board of Governors of the Federal Reserve System. In fact, major economic policy discussions within the government usually include the chairman of the Federal Reserve Board, at which point the Troika becomes the "Quadriad." The Board of Governors, which has a large staff of professional economists, has been involved in the analysis of current business conditions for many decades, although forecasting as a regularized, full-scale, systematic procedure has been in operation for only the last ten years or so. As would be expected, the Federal Reserve forecasts extend to more of the detailed monetary and banking indicators than do the forecasting efforts of the Troika.[1]

Forecasting in the federal government is, of course, not limited to the Quadriad. Because of their general responsibilities, many other departments are vitally interested in the business outlook. Furthermore, many departments and agencies have special responsibilities that require specific economic forecasting. The Treasury has its own specific needs for projections of government receipts, assessment of the impact of proposed tax changes, financial market analysis, and forecasts of the balance of payments. The Department of Commerce, in addition to its interest in the general economic outlook, has special interests in several areas of both domestic and international economic conditions. The Department of Labor has particular interests in the manpower field and in prices. Other agencies with special interests in economic forecasting include the Department of Housing and Urban Development, the Department of Agriculture, the Office of Emergency Preparedness, and the Department of State. The newest agency with important responsibilities in economic matters is the Council on International Economic Policy, which was recently established in the White House.

The legislative branch of government also gets involved in forecasting through the Joint Economic Committee of the Congress. Generally speaking, the Joint Economic Committee does not issue forecasts of its own, but once each year it does a complete —and often critical—review of the forecast contained in the President's Economic Report. Throughout the year, moreover, members of the Joint Economic Committee make forecasts of their own, often based on the work of the staff of the Joint Economic Committee.

For the most part, the other departments and agencies of the executive branch that are involved in economic forecasting follow the lead of the Troika. Coordination

---

[1] For a full description of the Federal Reserve operation see Joseph Zeisel, "Forecasting at the Federal Reserve," *Business Economics* (September 1971), pp. 182–187.

among these agencies is achieved by regular (usually monthly) meetings of responsible officials and their staffs. The meetings are usually chaired by a member of the Council of Economic Advisers. In addition, inter-agency groups are frequently formed to study important special topics and this, too, serves as a primary means of coordination among economists in the executive branch. Perhaps most important, however, is the extensive informal network of contacts that has been built up over the years by long-time members of the staffs. Many employees of the statistical agencies, for example, move into positions of higher responsibility in the area of economic forecasting and analysis, and the many contacts they have from their previous positions represent an invaluable means of coordination throughout the federal government. It should be noted that these employees, who come from extraordinarily diverse backgrounds, are almost invariably highly competent and hardworking public servants.

FORECASTING TECHNIQUES USED IN GOVERNMENT

The methods used within the federal government for short-term forecasting of the gross national product and related economic variables include almost all approaches commonly used by economists everywhere. Because no single forecasting technique has proved superior in performance, and because economic forecasting is of such crucial importance in government, every avenue that shows any sign of providing useful insight into the future course of the economy is explored in depth.

Forecasting in government tends to focus on the short-term outlook. Most forecasts are made for a time horizon of four to six quarters ahead. As a result, the forecasting process tends to be cumulative, i.e., every forecast builds on the one before. Minor revisions are incorporated into the forecast frequently, at least monthly. Major review and restructuring is done three or four times a year.

A fundamental prerequisite of all forecasting systems is the availability of up-to-the-minute empirical economic information. The problem is a familiar one. The state of the art is one of such uncertainty that forecasts are often of a very fragile nature. On occasion, in fact, some parts of the forecast will hinge on the availability or interpretation of just a few statistics. There are few in the forecasting business who have escaped the frustration and pain of seeing the rug pulled out from under their latest forecast by the appearance of new data—data that turn out to have been available before the forecast was made.

To minimize this possibility and to insure·that all key officials with major responsibilities for economic analysis and forecasting have the latest economic information at their fingertips, a daily economic intelligence system has been set up in the federal government. This system—the brainchild of Julius Shiskin—is operated by the Bureau of the Census and based on the publication *Business Conditions Digest*. The updated information is kept in a loose-leaf notebook containing the latest issue of *BCD*. Each morning, Census Bureau employees update (by hand) a master copy of the tables in *BCD* (Part II) with all data that became available on the previous day. The necessary pages are then reproduced and the copies are distributed by special messenger to a half-dozen key agencies. Thus, at all times each economic forecasting official has at his disposal, at a minimum (since he will have additional information from a variety of other sources) an up-to-date copy of *Business Conditions Digest*. Census also produces and distributes each day copies of various analytical tables and charts—diffusion indexes, for example, or charts comparing the current position of the economy with similar periods in the past.

Of the myriad forecasting techniques used in government, the multidimensional, eclectic, sector-by-sector, ad hoc approach generally know as "judgmental forecasting" is the method most often employed. In this process, all of the usual inputs and cross-checks are brought to bear: assumed fiscal and monetary policies, income-expenditure and investment-savings relationships, the inflation-unemployment tradeoff, the price-wage-productivity-profit nexus, expected effects of various financial impingements and stimulants, etc. In short, the judgmental approach is used in government in essentially the same way and with essentially the same inputs that are used elsewhere.[2]

Although the judgmental approach is dominant, it would be a serious mistake to assume that other techniques are minimized. The judgmental approach, by its nature, accommodates itself readily to every other technique. Econometrics, leading indicators, anticipation surveys, trend extension, cyclical patterns, multipliers—all these are employed extensively as inputs to judgmental forecasting in government.

By far the most important of these is econometrics, which plays a large and growing role in the forecasting efforts of government. In some cases, this is in the form of a full-scale, detailed, income-expenditure model of the economy, of the kind developed at the Office of Business Economics and the Federal Reserve Board. Econometric models from outside the federal government are used extensively, as well.

Another approach is the smaller model in which forecasts of major economic magni-tudes are obtained directly from a limited number of key exogenous variables. The six-equation model of the Federal Reserve Bank of St. Louis, which is based primarily on the money supply, is perhaps the best know example of this variety. On other occasions, the econometric technique employed is a single equation for a single sector of the economy.

It should be noted that, just as econometric techniques are widely used by judgmental forecasters, so does judgment play a crucial role in the process of forecasting with econometric models. Sometimes, in fact, the judgmental input into even a large formal model becomes so extensive that the only major sector that is forecast econometrically is consumption; everything else has been entered as an exogenous variable.

The leading indicator approach is also widely used within the government, especially at the Bureau of Labor Statistics, the Office of Management and Budget, and the Department of Commerce. The publication, *Business Conditions Digest* is, in effect, built around the indicator approach as developed at the National Bureau of Economic Research.[3]

Other forecasting techniques are regularly employed for special sectors of the economy and for special purposes. The Federal Reserve forecasts the financial structure of the economy through its flow-of-funds accounts and also uses a special model to forecast short-term changes in the money markets. The Treasury Department has its own methods of forecasting the balance of payments, the impact of proposed tax changes (for which Treasury and the Troika have special econometric models), and various aspects of its debt management function. Anticipation surveys are taken by the Office of Business Economics for plant and equipment expenditures and inventory invest-

[2] For a thorough description of the forecasting methods utilized by the Troika in the early 1960s, see chapter 7, "The United States: Short-Term Forecasting by the President's Council of Economic Advisers," in *Techniques of Economic Forecasting* (Paris: Organization for Economic Cooperation and Development, 1965). Dr. Arthur Okun, who later became chairman of the Council of Economic Advisers, was the principal author of this chapter.

[3] For a description of the indicator approach see chapter 2 by Julius Shiskin and Leonard H. Lempert.

ment and by the Bureau of the Census for consumer purchases of homes and big-ticket durables. The Office of Business Economics also does regional analysis and forecasting.

Although fewer resources are devoted to it, long-term forecasting is also a major activity in the government, particularly at the Federal Interagency Growth Project in the Department of Labor, the Council of Economic Advisers, and the Department of Commerce. Frequently, this is a judgmental forecast, with the total gross national product built up from the supply side, but in some instances an econometric approach is used. Long-term forecasts of the industry mix of output are made with the use of OBE's input-output matrix.

A major additional source of forecasting help to the federal government is obtained from outside the government. Groups of business and university forecasters meet regularly with all of the agencies that have primary economic responsibilities. Individual consultants are frequently employed for special projects. In addition, commercial economic forecasting services are utilized in several agencies.

TRENDS IN GOVERNMENT FORECASTING

One aspect of the forecasting scene in Washington that the foregoing sections do not give an adequate sense of are the many changes that have taken and are taking place. One such change—and it is probably the most pervasive trend in forecasting in recent years—is the growing awareness of the importance of business forecasting and the increasing attention paid to it. This is true within the executive branch, in the Congress, and among the public at large. More and more, policy decisions are based on economic judgments and economic forecasts.

Only a few years ago, whenever tax leg-

islation or a change in the debt ceiling was under consideration, congressional testimony focused almost exclusively on budget expenditures, receipts, and deficits. Today, however, testimony on these matters is dominated by the economics of the situation, especially the impact on employment and prices.

Along with this increased awareness of the importance of forecasting has come an enlargement of the resources devoted to it and an increasing coordination of forecasts within the government. The formation of the Troika in 1961 is probably the most concrete example. Another is the greater coordination between the executive branch and the Federal Reserve, especially since 1965. Formation of the Cabinet Committee on Economic Policy in 1969 represents a continuation of the trend.

Another developing trend is the lessening secrecy of economic analysis and forecasting. In the 1950s, the President's Economic Report generally projected only the direction that the economy was expected to take. Forecasts of personal income and corporate profits were explicit in the budget, but no other detail was published by the administration. However, through its annual hearings on the Economic Report, the Joint Economic Commitee of the Congress, under the leadership of Senators Joseph O'Mahoney and Paul Douglas, developed and published forecasts of the gross national product and its major components that tended to be consistent with the Economic Report.

Forecasts became a more explicit part of the Economic Report during the early sixties when Walter Heller was chairman of the Council of Economic Advisers. Total gross national product for the year ahead was specified, within a range, and the major components were usually indicated.

The forecasts of the Federal Reserve Board have also become more available. For many years, the minutes of the meetings of the Open Market Committee were published only once a year. More recently, these minutes, which contain implicitly or explicitly the forecast of the Federal Reserve staff, are published 90 days after the meeting.

Two other important trends in forecasting within the government are the increased use of more formal techniques, especially econometrics, and the greater use of the monetary aggregates in forecasting. Both of these developments follow trends that have been evident in business and academic forecasting for some time.

COMPARISON TO BUSINESS FORECASTING

It is apparent from the foregoing sections that almost every aspect of economic forecasting within the government has its counterpart in the business world. The increasing importance of forecasting, the trends toward more formal techniques and toward the use of monetary aggregates, the emphasis on short-term forecasts, the use of a great variety of methods, the frequent reviews—all of these are very similar to developments in forecasting among business economists in recent years.

Another similarity is the way that economic analysis and forecasting are used to advise management. Government economists advise their "management"—the President, departmental secretaries, governors of the Federal Reserve System, etc.—in very much the same way that business economists advise the presidents and other officers of their companies.

Just as business economists are always talking to one another—"intellectual incest" as the practice is sometimes called—so do government economists consult constantly with one another and with outside forecasters. In some instances, this will create pressure not to take too extreme a position in forecasting, i.e., not to deviate too far from

the standard forecast. Such pressure is reinforced by the fact that in government large errors in economic forecasting can be extremely costly, while there is only a very small payoff for a forecast that manages to achieve an extra marginal degree of precision. Thus, both sides of the equation push the forecaster toward the common expectation—where the risk of a sizable miss is probably minimized. Perhaps the best known example of the cost of a large error is the experience of 1968, when the expectation of most economists, within and outside the government, was that the tax surcharge had created a serious danger of economic overkill. Unfortunately, this led to excessive easing in monetary policy and to a worsening of inflation.

The similarity between government forecasters and business forecasters extends to their accuracy. The forecasts published by the Council of Economic Advisers in the 1960s proved to be very similar in accuracy to the forecasts of several groups of business forecasters, as shown by Geoffrey H. Moore.[4] Similarly, the record of the Federal Reserve Open Market Committee in recognizing business cycle turning points, as reported by Fels and Hinshaw, is generally similar to the average performance of eight regularly published forecasts, although it may have been superior in the avoidance of false alarms.[5]

Although the similarities between forecasting in government and forecasting in business dominate this comparison, there are also some very important differences. The organizational structure of the Troika,

[4] Geoffrey H. Moore, "Forecasting Short-Term Economic Change," *Journal of the American Statistical Association,* Vol. 64 (March 1969), pp. 1–22. See also, Victor Zarnowitz, *Forecasting Economic Conditions: The Record and the Prospect* (New York: National Bureau of Economic Research, forthcoming).
[5] Rendigs Fels and C. Elton Hinshaw, *Forecasting and Recognizing Business Cycle Turning Points* (New York: National Bureau of Economic Research, 1968).

with its three distinctly defined levels of personnel and activity, is one such difference.

Perhaps the major difference is the importance of the forecast. A particularly good or particularly bad forecast can have a considerable impact on a business operation, but a bad forecast by the government, as in 1968, affects the entire nation, sometimes seriously. It is precisely for this reason that such great effort is devoted to forecasting within the government and that no technique that shows any promise is overlooked. The expertise in every area of economic analysis and the total resources that are available to the forecaster in the federal government far exceed what the typical business or academic analyst can command.

Business and government forecasts often differ in the assumptions on which they are made. All federal forecasts are "conditional" in that they start with the premise that the administration's economic programs will be adopted by Congress. They assume, for example, that the aggregate expenditure levels in the budget will not be changed materially, that tax changes will be enacted substantially as proposed, etc. Economists outside government will sometimes choose to make different assumptions than those used by the administration, a choice that can lead to wide differences in forecasts.

Another important difference arises from the fact that in government the chief forecasters, who are also policymakers, have considerable ability to make their forecasts come true, because they "manage" the economy. In these instances, the "forecast" is really a "target." If under current policies the economy appears to be falling short of the target, or overshooting it, policy changes may be made to alter the economy's path in the desired direction. To make such changes is not a simple matter, for many reasons. But pushing the economy in the direction of the forecast is an option that is sometimes open to government forecasters, while business economists only have the option of pushing their forecasts in the direction of

the economy. Consequently, in evaluating a government forecast, it is useful to know not only what assumptions lie behind it but also whether it is a target as well as a forecast.

Although policymakers have open to them the option of changing policy when the economy seems to be going off course, it generally takes a rather large deviation—i.e., a large change in the forecast—to bring about a change in policy. The decisions of economic policymakers (the President, the Federal Reserve Board, and the Congress) are based on many economic, social, and political factors. Even though the economic outlook may change, that is only one of many inputs, and it will not always be enough to tip the balance toward a new economic policy. Furthermore, the fact that the government expends great energy in explaining and defending its policies—another distinction between forecasters in government and their colleagues in business—tends to make the process of changing the policies a difficult one. Under these conditions, a large change in the economic forecast is necessary to bring about a change in economic policy.

This problem of promptly effecting changes in economic policy is made more difficult by the fact that economic forecasting is an uncertain art. To change a policy decision with an economic forecast requires a large change in the forecast *and* a high degree of certainty. This is usually not possible, which is why it is difficult for a government economist to effect a change in policy solely on the basis of a change in his economic forecast.

A final difference that should be noted is the much greater public attention devoted to government forecasters and policymakers —both those in office at the moment and those who, although not in office currently, are identified with a particular administration or political party. The demand by the news media for comment and interpretation by these economists is incessant. At the same time, because of their known political commitment, they have a problem of credibility. Herbert Stein has drawn an interesting parallel between this situation and the Heisenberg principle of uncertainty.

> The Heisenberg principle says that certain physical phenomena can never be accurately observed because the process of observing them distorts them. The parallel is that the public never gets to hear any opinions about economics that it is likely to believe. If a person is sufficiently detached, especially politically, so that his views can be considered to be objective, the press is unlikely to report his views. On the other hand, if a person has connections and commitments that make his opinions newsworthy, the public is unlikely to regard him as honest, whether justly or unjustly.[6]

[6] Herbert Stein. A speech delivered to the Business Economists Conference, Chicago, Illinois, April 26, 1971.

CONCLUSION

A comparison of the preparation and uses of economic forecasts in government and in business reveals a great many similarities and only a few important differences. The processes and the people in both camps are very much alike in all their fundamental characteristics.

Any experienced and competent economic forecaster in business would feel at home in the forecasting activities of government. He would be favorably impressed by the professional expertise of his colleagues. He would also find that the importance of the work, the ready availability of up-to-date information, and his participation in the formation and defense of economic policies would significantly enhance the excitement of his job and the satisfaction he derives from it.

ALAN GREENSPAN & M. KATHRYN EICKHOFF

Economic Consulting

Economic consulting, far from being a narrow specialty, has become an industry in its own right. It does not yet have its own four-digit SIC classification,[1] but it is a clearly definable industrial entity. Moreover, it is one of the newest growth industries in the country. This should not be surprising. Since growth in an industrial society implies an ever-increasing proportion of output coming from intellectual rather than physical components, intellectual services are among the most rapidly growing areas of the economy. Economic consultation is one of these services.

Firms in the economic consulting industry vary in size from five to fifty employees. These firms differ significantly from the older, and generally larger, management consulting firms with which they are often confused. (Few management consultants do very much in the area of business economics.) In addition, there are many individuals, associated primarily with the universities, who also serve as part-time economic consultants.

The major reason for the existence of this industry derives from the economics of sale implicit in the type of work performed. In almost all cases the initial cost of the economic product or service being offered is quite high, while the incremental costs asso-

ciated with servicing additional clients with the same information are low. As a result, whenever the costs of forecasts or research projects can be spread over two or more clients, there is an advantage to having the job performed by an economic consulting firm. Even when a company already has an internal staff of economists, it may be less costly to subcontract particular projects to a consulting firm than to hire additional permanent staff to handle the project internally.

The work of the economic consultant varies from the most macro analyses of the economy (both domestic and international), to the most micro of technical problems. As a result, both the generalist and the specialist fill important roles in economic consulting. Almost every economic consultant offers some system of general business forecasts. The demand for these services is quite large and growing very rapidly. Less universally, consulting firms supply highly technical information on relatively narrow specialties to both business and government, e.g. the economics of rate regulations affecting the public utilities industry. The specialist represents the older, more established part of the economic consulting business. Although in total dollar terms it is still significant, it is certainly the slowest growing sector of the business. Not unexpectedly, many firms perform both functions. The economic consultant offers his services not only to nonecono-

[1] It is combined with "business and management consulting services" under SIC 7392.

629

mist clients but often accepts subcontracts from the economic departments of major corporations as well.

The work performed by economic consultants can be cross-classified by the major client groups whom they serve. The larger and more important part of the work is done for private nonfinancial businesses. However, while the work performed differs, financial institutions are only slightly less important to the economic consulting field. Sporadically, work is also contracted from government agencies.

Only a small number of economic consultants working in the government area are concerned with overall economic policy. The work done by them is essentially the same as that seen in the academic community. However, there is surprisingly a real role for the nonpolicy economic consultant in advising government departments and agencies.

Most economists who have not worked for government agencies usually significantly overrate the latter's technical economic capabilities. There is an increasing interest among the government agencies in having outside consultants come in, process their internal data, and provide them with an objective analysis of what is happening. Because these analyses are usually used as back-up material to the agency's request for funding of the program, the range of what the economist can provide is limited. As a result, it is doubtful whether this type of government work will become a significant growth area for the consulting industry.

There is another type of analysis, quasi-governmental in nature, where the specialist most often appears. Particularly in regard to the regulated industries, there is a great deal of work done preparing testimony to be presented at the various commission hearings in rate cases or in preparing material and giving testimony before congressional hearings on special problems. For want of a better term, this area could be called polemic economics. The economic consultant performs essentially the same function as a legal advocate: marshalling all the data supporting his client's position. This was perhaps the earliest role played by economic consultants. Its growth has been steady but not spectacular.

Although many economic consulting firms had industrial clients in years past, everyone seemed to be doing something special. Hence, no generalizations could be made about the nature of the work. Sufficient time has now elapsed for one to begin to see certain broad patterns emerging which are pretty much characteristic of the work engaged in by all economic consultants. Excluding for the moment consultants working only in specialized areas, almost every economic consulting firm provides some system of general business forecasts. These forecasts are often related in some manner to the business of the particular client.

The demand for aggregate forecasts has become surprisingly large in recent years. A decade ago there simply was not that much interest in aggregate information. This points up how important business forecasting has become as a decision-making tool. As an increasing number of economists have devoted their energies to developing better methods of analyzing the economy, the quantity and quality of forecasts being offered has grown rapidly.

The amount of detail offered in the general business forecasts varies among the firms in the industry. However, in recent years the extent of the detail published has grown at an incredible rate. As recently as the mid-1960s, forecasts often included only an eight- or ten-item breakdown of GNP plus a total industrial production forecast. If the system provided for deflated GNP estimates, it was considered quite advanced. Breaking the industrial production index into a half dozen of the market groupings was the sign of a truly sophisticated system. Today, of course, almost any consultant can supply twenty pages of computer print-out on a moment's notice.

This proliferation, both in the detail offered and the frequency with which the forecasts are updated, ties directly to the widespread switch to formal econometric models and the use of computers. However, this technological advance has been a mixed blessing. Unfortunately, much of the information being generated by fixed-structure models spews forth without being critically evaluated.

Examination of the initial full printouts from any of the standard published econometric models will too often show as much as 10 to 15 percent of the observations to be unreasonable. In an unrealistic attempt to change the art of forecasting to a science, the system has become overmechanized. This is not to say that econometric models are inappropriate vehicles for aggregative forecasting. Rather, the time has come to understand what the proper uses for these models are and how they relate to reality.

The basic premise of the typical model is that there is an underlying structure to the economy which engenders economic movement in accordance with certain principles. If the interrelationships among the key variables of an economy have remained relatively stable for a period of time, it is presumed to be possible, by applying standard econometric techniques, to obtain unbiased estimates of the true relationships among the variables from historical observation.

Unfortunately, even the most elaborate models are gross oversimplifications of reality; neither the world in general, nor an economy in particular, is definable in terms of a simple fixed structure. Moreover, it is by no means certain that accuracy is improved by building ever more elaborate models. Essentially, the Keynesian type structured models are very elaborate accounting systems. It is only necessary for someone (in the interests of sanity, preferably a computer) to make all the necessary computations to produce twenty or more

pages containing values for all possible variables, relevant and otherwise. That is, given any set of inputs, the output is mathematically predetermined by the equations of the model. Assuming, however, that the inputs are controlled, these models can be an indispensable aid in checking the internal consistency of a forecast. They cannot be used without very heavy editing to generate the forecast itself.

What does it mean to "edit" the output of an econometric model? As a first step, it means to ask of each interrelationship within the model whether the average experience of the earlier years from which the model was fitted will be relevant in determining economic activity over the next six, twelve, or eighteen months, or for five or ten years out. Clearly, the answer in all cases will be "not exactly." The majority of the interrelationships will be "more or less" correct since the economy, and particularly its cause and effect structure, does not change radically except over prolonged periods of time. But it does change. Thus, the business economist must continuously question whether the form of the equations being used is still appropriate, whether the various parameters have changed, and whether new variables should be introduced into the system.

For example, the business economist might say to himself, "While I know that price elasticity for automobiles has been running about x in recent years, such and such an event, which will not be captured by my system, has occurred and will now change this relationship. How do I adjust my model to account for this difference?"

He may further wonder, "If I make a change at this point, are there other changes which must be made in other equations to keep my system consistent?" Thus, he must know exactly how the model works, and the real world economic meaning of all of the equations.

Given a reasonable set of inputs, the typical econometric model will produce a good first approximation of a forecast. This brings the business economist to the second stage—the heart of the editing process. Each of the variables must now be examined in turn and the question asked, "Is this the way I would expect the economy to behave granted my 'institutional' knowledge of the business system?" If not, "Why not?" The inputs must then be reevaluated, some changed, and the system rerun. Often the parameters of the system may even have to be altered. At this point and for this reason, there is no mathematical substitute for the experienced economist's knowledge and judgmental ability. The human mind can make far finer gradations of judgment than any set of equations can reflect. The econometric model simply provides a framework within which to check the internal consistency of the economist's judgments.

Perhaps the role of editing the output of an econometric model can best be summarized as follows. The experienced business economist has a vast amount of economic knowledge, both theoretical and empirical, acquired over a long period of time. Some of it is specific knowledge (1) of how the economy changes in the real world and (2) of how the whole socio-politico-economic structure is integrated, which cannot readily be embodied in an econometric model. In editing the output of a model, the economist strives to bring this part of his total experience to bear on the particular forecast under consideration.

Anyone looking at the present extremely detailed forecast probably recognizes, at least implicitly, that the same degree of thought and consideration cannot have been expended on each forecast number. But the user is rarely able to make a judgment on the degree of accuracy which should be ascribed to the various details of a forecast print-out. As this problem becomes more widely recognized, it is to be hoped that where appropriate, we will see fewer pages of print-out, but more meaningful sets of numbers.

In addition to the standard GNP (product and income) models, there are other types of general business forecasting models that economic consulting firms create. For example, flow-of-funds models can be very helpful as an adjunct to a GNP model. The flow of funds model, of course, forecasts the sources and uses of funds implicit in a GNP forecast. In addition to its immediate usefulness, it serves as a further check on the reasonableness of the GNP forecast. Detailed industrial production models can also be very useful. For consistency and reliability, it is most desirable that as many of the so-called subsidiary systems as possible be integrated into the GNP forecast system.

To the extent that it is not possible to integrate all potential types of forecasts into a single system, there must be a finite limit on the amount of editing that can be done on any given forecasts. Thus, the initial editing will usually stop when an individual system, however complex it may be, looks "right." Each additional system's results, however, lead to a modification of the view the economist holds of the reliability of his primary (i.e., product and income) forecast. Unless a major change in the outlook has occurred, no attempt would ordinarily be made to change the primary forecast until the time for the next regularly scheduled review or update. Ideally, a consulting firm's forecasts represent a continuous flow process. But it is the business economist himself, not the econometric model, that is the real-time part of the system. This is the reason why a business economist, a week after the publication of a forecast, will invariably say, "If I were doing the forecast today I would do thus and so. However, the major conclusions are still correct." While this is necessarily the case, if care is not taken it can lead to communication problems and a credibility gap with all but the most knowledgeable of clients.

Despite the avowed interest in aggregate forecasts, except when dealing with sophisticated internal corporate economists who already know how to use the forecasts in their work, a great deal of education must accompany any forecast. Business forecasts are not ends in themselves. Unless they can be utilized in formulating corporate policy, they are no more than costly numerical exercises. To be used effectively, not only must the forecast reach the appropriate people in the client organization; the tremendous pool of company information which exists must also be tapped and related to the economist's aggregate forecasts. One of the most valuable services a business economist can provide an industrial client is to make both these sources of information (and the knowledge necessary to relate them) available to each other. Otherwise, from the time the aggregative economic output begins to filter through the corporate structure until the time it is actually utilized at the company action level, the information loss becomes tremendous.

Here is where business economics has its farthest distance to travel but its greatest contribution to make: the transformation of aggregate economic forecasts into individual product level forecasts in a consistent manner. The way this is accomplished varies among the several economic consulting firms. More importantly, the techniques used will differ depending upon the industry whose product flows are to be forecast. We usually attempt to build a fairly detailed structure of sources and uses of materials (i.e., a partial input-output system) for the industry we are studying.

One of the earliest models of this type which we built was for the steel industry. We were interested in determining in significant detail not only the level, but also the type, of steel mill product shipments implicit in a specific aggregate forecast of economic activity.

As a first step, we historically analyzed the types of steel products used by each of the steel-consuming industries. We then attempted to interrelate these detailed product data with other available data on the steel-using industries. For example, we utilized data on footage of oil wells drilled, machinery component production, etc. For some industries, very great detail was available. In the automotive industry, not only the total production of motor vehicles but also the number and size of each of the various models assembled was factored in for each given year. Once we had created consumption data for the steel-using industries, it was possible historically to relate these data to the shipments of steel received by these industries and to determine the pattern of inventory change. From knowledge of consistent historical patterns of inventory change for each of the industries, it was possible to forecast these patterns in the future.

Thus, we arrived at the point where given a GNP forecast which implied production forecasts for the various steel-consuming industries, we were able, by analyzing the trends in unit utilization factors, to forecast steel consumption by industries. By then projecting the pattern of inventory change over the forecast period for each industry, we reached a total shipments forecast by end use. Disaggregating these shipments and recombining them by product yields a forecast of shipments equivalent to the official shipment figures reported by the American Iron and Steel Institute. Since each steel company reports to the AISI on a comparable basis, it is possible with this system to link up with internal company data and begin market share analyses, profit maximization studies, plant and equipment expenditure requirements studies, etc., at a level where the communication with management can be translated directly into the corporation decision-making process.

There are several advantages to this modified input-output analysis. The most important of these is also the reason why we favor its use, where feasible, over regression techniques. Regression analysis can be very valuable so long as the calculated values from the regression yield reliable forecasts. However, when the actual and calculated values diverge, two alternate hypotheses are possible. First, the actual value is abnormal and will be followed by a return to trend. Alternatively, the divergence signals a fundamental change in the system and future observations will be astride a new trend for which this is the first observation. The dilemma is that these two explanations imply diametrically opposed corporate policies. This is not to say that with input-output analyses the forecasts are always right. They are not. However, when they are wrong, you can evaluate why they are wrong and make the necessary adjustments. For example, the basic GNP forecast may have been wide of the mark; or automotive assembly plans may have changed; or the steel use per car was off; or the inventory or market share analyses were wrong. Any or all of these things can result in a poor industry forecast. But when they do, the problem is an understandable one; it can be explained in meaningful terms to the people trying to use the forecast and it can be corrected in the next forecast.

The other definite advantage to the input-output type of system is that it has a built-in feedback mechanism from company product managers to the economist. Invariably, comments will come back on the order of, "This is crazy" or "How can you say we are only going to ship x next quarter when I've got orders on the books for more than that amount already?" This may be a very valuable piece of information or it may be worthless. The important thing is that the business economist probably did not know it when he started out. It can now be evaluated and merged with the other information in the system. The important thing is not whether the manager's forecasts are accurate or not but that scattered throughout the company are many bits and pieces of data and market insight. The individuals possessing them may not even know they are relevant until someone tries to have a forecast implemented which contradicts their firsthand knowledge. It is important for a company to have a sort of central clearinghouse mechanism where all of the bits and pieces can coalesce and be merged with the consultant's knowledge and then fed back through the model to generate an improved forecast. If the total forecast is being continuously reexamined, company insiders who have knowledge of specific pieces can see that information fitted into the system and watch the implications develop themselves throughout the whole corporate model. Thus, the model itself serves as a wonderful communications mechanism for the entire corporate structure.

Moreover, implicit in this kind of a model is a wealth of detail that can be siphoned off to use in other models covering the whole gamut of corporate decision making. You can, for example, create price elasticity relationships from this type of model. You can examine the relationship between a company's market share and its pricing policies, or analyze the company's prices vis-a-vis estimates of total industry prices. Useful internal company inventory models can be developed.

It can even form the base from which a financial optimization model can be structured. By obtaining detailed costs and prices, an income statement and balance sheet equivalent to the product forecast can be created. Granted a general theory of finance and a given industry outlook, appropriate corporate policy can be determined not only with respect to production rates on individual product lines, but also with respect to such issues as short-term versus long-term debt financing, equity versus debt financing, inventory accumulation policies, facilities planning, and rates of return from new capital expenditures versus the cost of acquisitions. In short, the whole structure of corporate planning, both short-term and long-term, can be significantly facilitated by this type of model building. In fact, it is only when an economist can simulate a company at all its critical decision-making points and can understand how changes in the overall economy affect the company at these points, that aggregative business forecasts reach their real potential. With the channels of causation from the economy to the industry to the company clearly defined and continuously audited, it can mean something to the top management whether real GNP is going to rise by five percent or only three percent in any given year.

Obviously, such a system of interrelated models, developed to its full potential, becomes incredibly elaborate. Thus, one of the consultant's jobs is to define an internal information system within the client company to make the forecasting system function. Who should audit the incoming new orders data for the various products, what are to be the rules for triggering a review when the company is off plan, etc.? Wherever possible, information should be transmitted between the client and the consultant in machine readable form. Otherwise, the client and the consultant often find themselves confronted with an indigestible bulk of detailed information. The ideal arrangement, of course, is a real-time connection between the consulting firm's computer and the client firm's computer.

The end product of models for industrial clients naturally involves a good deal of oral presentation by the consultant. Oral presentations buttressed by brief written summations of the key items are usually more effective than detailed written reports. Too often the client becomes lost in the wealth of material presented in a full written report. And when only the conclusions are given, he may be left with the sense that the economist has not proved his case. Oral presentations have the further advantage of enabling management to clear up immediately any questions they may have on specific points. Areas not currently of interest can be quickly bypassed without fear of omitting any issue of concern to management. Hard-copy of more obscure questions can always be supplied to any executive requiring the information without feeding the "paper bog" (which lurks in every company) in the meantime.

Although the type of model described is primarily used for industrial clients, less elaborate but conceptually similar models fill the needs of financial institutions. Financial institutions are rarely interested in the detailed product line stage of such systems. They are usually more interested in the third stage, namely, the profit forecasting mechanism. Moreover, the profits forecasts in this case are for industries as a whole rather than the individual firms within an industry. Aggregative economic models generally are more widely understood and better utilized by the financial institutions than by industrial clients, since their businesses are tied more directly to the aggregate economy. Thus, models for projecting interest rates, stock prices, and the development of portfolio investment strategy are of particular interest to this type of client.

In terms of the number of consultants actively devoting time to an area, financial institutions probably represent the fastest growing client segment for the economic consulting industry. Still, the potential for consulting to this group is virtually untapped. Most of the work being done is directed toward portfolio investment strategy. As investment portfolio management gets ever larger (and this is almost certainly the trend of the future), there is going to be greater and greater demand for aggregative economic analysis, particularly at the industry level. It is no longer the case that one or two stocks make or break investment performance. The available funds of financial institutions are becoming so huge that large institutions can no longer take a position in only one stock in an industry. To do so would mean acquiring the company, not investing in the stock. Even then the position could be too small for a few of the monoliths of the industry. Thus, funds must be distributed across the whole spectrum of an industry. As this trend continues, industry analyses—where a large number of economic consultants are working—should increasingly replace individual company analyses in importance.